T0184291

Lecture Notes in Computer Science 12477

More information about this series at http://www.springer.com/series/7407

Tiziana Margaria · Bernhard Steffen (Eds.)

Leveraging Applications of Formal Methods, Verification and Validation

Engineering Principles

9th International Symposium
on Leveraging Applications of Formal Methods, ISoLA 2020
Rhodes, Greece, October 20–30, 2020
Proceedings, Part II

 Springer

Editors
Tiziana Margaria ⓘ
University of Limerick and Lero
Limerick, Ireland

Bernhard Steffen ⓘ
TU Dortmund
Dortmund, Germany

ISSN 0302-9743   ISSN 1611-3349   (electronic)
Lecture Notes in Computer Science
ISBN 978-3-030-61469-0   ISBN 978-3-030-61470-6   (eBook)
https://doi.org/10.1007/978-3-030-61470-6

LNCS Sublibrary: SL1 – Theoretical Computer Science and General Issues

This Springer imprint is published by the registered company Springer Nature Switzerland AG
The registered company address is: Gewerbestrasse 11, 6330 Cham, Switzerland

Introduction

It is our responsibility, as general and program chairs, to welcome the participants to the 9th International Symposium on Leveraging Applications of Formal Methods, Verification and Validation (ISoLA), planned to take place in Rhodes, Greece, during October 20–30, 2020, endorsed by the European Association of Software Science and Technology (EASST).

This year's event follows the tradition of its symposia forerunners held in Paphos, Cyprus (2004 and 2006), Chalkidiki, Greece (2008), Crete, Greece (2010 and 2012), Corfu, Greece (2014 and 2016), and most recently in Limassol, Cyprus (2018), and the series of ISoLA workshops in Greenbelt, USA (2005), Poitiers, France (2007), Potsdam, Germany (2009), Vienna, Austria (2011), and Palo Alto, USA (2013).

Considering that this year's situation is unique and unlike any previous one due to the ongoing COVID-19 pandemic, and that ISoLA's symposium touch and feel is much unlike most conventional, paper-based conferences, after much soul searching we are faced with a true dilemma. "Virtualizing" the event, as many conferences have done, violates the true spirit of the symposium, which is rooted in the gathering of communities and the discussions within and across the various communities materialized in the special tracks and satellite events. Keeping with the physical meeting and holding it in a reduced form (as many may not be able to or feel comfortable with travel) under strict social distancing rules may also end up not being feasible. At the time of writing there is a resurgence of cases in several countries, many nations are compiling "green lists" of countries with which they entertain free travel relations, and these lists are updated – most frequently shortened – at short notice, with severe consequence for the travelers. Many governments and universities are again strengthening the travel restrictions for their employees, and many of us would anyway apply caution due to our own specific individual situation.

To be able to react as flexibly as possible to this situation, we decided to split ISoLA 2020 into two parts, one this year and one in October 2021, with the track organizers deciding when their track will take place. So far both dates have promoters, but it may still happen that, in the end, the entire event needs to move. All accepted papers are published in time, but some tracks will present their papers at the 2021 event.

As in the previous editions, ISoLA 2020 provides a forum for developers, users, and researchers to discuss issues related to the adoption and use of rigorous tools and methods for the specification, analysis, verification, certification, construction, test, and maintenance of systems from the point of view of their different application domains. Thus, since 2004, the ISoLA series of events serves the purpose of bridging the gap between designers and developers of rigorous tools on one side, and users in engineering and in other disciplines on the other side. It fosters and exploits synergetic relationships among scientists, engineers, software developers, decision makers, and other critical thinkers in companies and organizations. By providing a specific, dialogue-oriented venue for the discussion of common problems, requirements, algorithms, methodologies, and practices, ISoLA aims in particular at supporting researchers in their quest to improve the usefulness, reliability, flexibility, and efficiency of tools for building systems, and users in their search for adequate solutions to their problems.

The program of the symposium consists of a collection of special tracks devoted to the following hot and emerging topics:

- Reliable Smart Contracts: State-of-the-art, Applications, Challenges and Future Directions
  (Organizers: Gordon Pace, César Sànchez, Gerardo Schneider)
- Engineering of Digital Twins for Cyber-Physical Systems
  (Organizers: John Fitzgerald, Pieter Gorm Larsen, Tiziana Margaria, Jim Woodcock)
- Verification and Validation of Concurrent and Distributed Systems
  (Organizers: Cristina Seceleanu, Marieke Huisman)
- Modularity and (De-)composition in Verification
  (Organizers: Reiner Hähnle, Eduard Kamburjan, Dilian Gurov)
- Software Verification Tools
  (Organizers: Markus Schordan, Dirk Beyer, Irena Boyanova)
- X-by-Construction: Correctness meets Probability
  (Organizers: Maurice H. ter Beek, Loek Cleophas, Axel Legay, Ina Schaefer, Bruce W. Watson)
- Rigorous Engineering of Collective Adaptive Systems
  (Organizers: Rocco De Nicola, Stefan Jähnichen, Martin Wirsing)
- Automated Verification of Embedded Control Software
  (Organizers: Dilian Gurov, Paula Herber, Ina Schaefer)
- Automating Software Re-Engineering
  (Organizers: Serge Demeyer, Reiner Hähnle, Heiko Mantel)
- 30 years of Statistical Model Checking!
  (Organizers: Kim G. Larsen, Axel Legay)
- From Verification to Explanation
  (Organizers: Holger Herrmanns, Christel Baier)
- Formal methods for DIStributed COmputing in future RAILway systems (DisCo-Rail 2020)
  (Organizers: Alessandro Fantechi, Stefania Gnesi, Anne Haxthausen)
- Programming: What is Next?
  (Organizers: Klaus Havelund, Bernhard Steffen)

With the embedded events:

- RERS: Challenge on Rigorous Examination of Reactive Systems (Falk Howar, Markus Schordan, Bernhard Steffen)
- Doctoral Symposium and Poster Session (A. L. Lamprecht)
- Industrial Day (Falk Howar, Johannes Neubauer, Andreas Rausch)

Colocated with the ISoLA symposium is:

- STRESS 2020 – 5th International School on Tool-based Rigorous Engineering of Software Systems (J. Hatcliff, T. Margaria, Robby, B. Steffen)

Altogether the ISoLA 2020 proceedings comprises four volumes, Part 1: Verification Principles, Part 2: Engineering Principles, Part 3: Applications, and Part 4: Tools, Trends, and Tutorials, which also covers the associated events.

We thank the track organizers, the members of the Program Committee and their referees for their effort in selecting the papers to be presented, the local organization chair, Petros Stratis, and the EasyConferences team for their continuous and precious support during the entire two-year period preceding the events, and Springer for being, as usual, a very reliable partner for the proceedings production. Finally, we are grateful to Kyriakos Georgiades for his continuous support for the website and the program, and to Markus Frohme and Julia Rehder for their help with the editorial system Equinocs.

Special thanks are due to the following organization for their endorsement: EASST (European Association of Software Science and Technology) and Lero – The Irish Software Research Centre, and our own institutions – TU Dortmund University and the University of Limerick.

We wish you, as an ISoLA participant, a wonderful experience at this edition, and for you, reading the proceedings at a later occasion, valuable new insights that hopefully contribute to your research and its uptake.

August 2020   Tiziana Margaria
                                                               Bernhard Steffen

Organization

Symposium Chair

Tiziana Margaria   University of Limerick and Lero, Ireland

PC Chair

Bernhard Steffen   TU Dortmund University, Germany

PC Members

Christel Baier	Technische Universität Dresden, Germany
Maurice ter Beek	ISTI-CNR, Italy
Dirk Beyer	LMU Munich, Germany
Irena Bojanova	NIST, USA
Loek Cleophas	Eindhoven University of Technology, The Netherlands
Rocco De Nicola	IMT Lucca, Italy
Serge Demeyer	Universiteit Antwerpen, Belgium
Alessandro Fantechi	University of Florence, Italy
John Fitzgerald	Newcastle University, UK
Stefania Gnesi	CNR, Italy
Kim Guldstrand Larsen	Aalborg University, Denmark
Dilian Gurov	KTH Royal Institute of Technology, Sweden
John Hatcliff	Kansas State University, USA
Klaus Havelund	Jet Propulsion Laboratory, USA
Anne E. Haxthausen	Technical University of Denmark, Denmark
Paula Herber	University of Münster, Germany
Holger Hermanns	Saarland University, Germany
Falk Howar	Dortmund University of Technology and Fraunhofer ISST, Germany
Marieke Huisman	University of Twente, The Netherlands
Reiner Hähnle	Technische Universität Darmstadt, Germany
Stefan Jähnichen	TU Berlin, Germany
Eduard Kamburjan	Technische Universität Darmstadt, Germany
Anna-Lena Lamprecht	Utrecht University, The Netherlands
Peter Gorm Larsen	Aarhus University, Denmark
Axel Legay	Université Catholique de Louvain, Belgium
Heiko Mantel	Technische Universität Darmstadt, Germany
Tiziana Margaria	University of Limerick and Lero, Ireland
Johannes Neubauer	Materna, Germany
Gordon Pace	University of Malta, Malta
Cesar Sanchez	IMDEA Software Institute, Madrid, Spain

Ina Schaefer	TU Braunschweig, Germany
Gerardo Schneider	University of Gothenburg, Sweden
Markus Schordan	Lawrence Livermore National Laboratory, USA
Cristina Seceleanu	Mälardalen University, Sweden
Bernhard Steffen	TU Dortmund University, Germany
Bruce Watson	Stellenbosch University, South Africa
Martin Wirsing	Ludwig-Maximilians-Universität München, Germany
James Woodcock	University of York, UK

Reviewers

Aho, Pekka
Aichernig, Bernhard
Backeman, Peter
Baranov, Eduard
Basile, Davide
Beckert, Bernhard
Bensalem, Saddek
Bettini, Lorenzo
Beyer, Dirk
Bourr, Khalid
Bubel, Richard
Bures, Tomas
Casadei, Roberto
Castiglioni, Valentina
Ciatto, Giovanni
Cimatti, Alessandro
Damiani, Ferruccio
Di Marzo Serugendo, Giovanna
Duong, Tan
Filliâtre, Jean-Christophe
Fränzle, Martin
Gabor, Thomas
Gadducci, Fabio
Galletta, Letterio
Geisler, Signe
Gerostathopoulos, Ilias
Guanciale, Roberto
Heinrich, Robert
Hillston, Jane
Hnetynka, Petr
Hoffmann, Alwin

Hungar, Hardi
Inverso, Omar
Iosti, Simon
Jacobs, Bart
Jaeger, Manfred
Jensen, Peter
Johnsen, Einar Broch
Jongmans, Sung-Shik
Jähnichen, Stefan
Kanav, Sudeep
Konnov, Igor
Kosak, Oliver
Kosmatov, Nikolai
Kretinsky, Jan
Könighofer, Bettina
Lanese, Ivan
Lecomte, Thierry
Lluch Lafuente, Alberto
Loreti, Michele
Maggi, Alessandro
Mariani, Stefano
Mazzanti, Franco
Morichetta, Andrea
Nyberg, Mattias
Omicini, Andrea
Orlov, Dmitry
Pacovsky, Jan
Parsai, Ali
Peled, Doron
Piho, Paul
Pugliese, Rosario

Pun, Violet Ka I
Reisig, Wolfgang
Schlingloff, Holger
Seifermann, Stephan
Soulat, Romain
Steinhöfel, Dominic
Stolz, Volker
Sürmeli, Jan
Tiezzi, Francesco
Tini, Simone
Tognazzi, Stefano
Tribastone, Mirco

Trubiani, Catia
Tuosto, Emilio
Ulbrich, Mattias
Vandin, Andrea
Vercammen, Sten
Viroli, Mirko
Wadler, Philip
Wanninger, Constantin
Weidenbach, Christoph
Wirsing, Martin
Zambonelli, Franco

Contents – Part II

Automating Software Re-Engineering

Automating Software Re-engineering: Introduction to the ISoLA
2020 Track. 3
    Serge Demeyer, Reiner Hähnle, and Heiko Mantel

Formal Verification of Developer Tests: A Research Agenda Inspired
by Mutation Testing 9
    Serge Demeyer, Ali Parsai, Sten Vercammen, Brent van Bladel,
    and Mehrdad Abdi

Modular Regression Verification for Reactive Systems 25
    Alexander Weigl, Mattias Ulbrich, and Daniel Lentzsch

Finding Idioms in Source Code Using Subtree Counting Techniques 44
    Dmitry Orlov

Parametric Timed Bisimulation 55
    Malte Lochau, Lars Luthmann, Hendrik Göttmann, and Isabelle Bacher

A Unifying Framework for Dynamic Monitoring and a Taxonomy
of Optimizations 72
    Marie-Christine Jakobs and Heiko Mantel

Thirty-Seven Years of Relational Hoare Logic: Remarks on Its Principles
and History 93
    David A. Naumann

Safer Parallelization. 117
    Reiner Hähnle, Asmae Heydari Tabar, Arya Mazaheri,
    Mohammad Norouzi, Dominic Steinhöfel, and Felix Wolf

Refactoring and Active Object Languages 138
    Volker Stolz, Violet Ka I Pun, and Rohit Gheyi

Rigorous Engineering of Collective Adaptive Systems

Rigorous Engineering of Collective Adaptive Systems Introduction
to the 3rd Track Edition. 161
    Martin Wirsing, Rocco De Nicola, and Stefan Jähnichen

Composition of Component Models - A Key to Construct Big Systems 171
    Wolfgang Reisig

Degrees of Autonomy in Coordinating Collectives
of Self-Driving Vehicles   189
    Stefano Mariani and Franco Zambonelli

Engineering Semantic Self-composition of Services Through Tuple-Based
Coordination.   205
    Ashley Caselli, Giovanni Ciatto, Giovanna Di Marzo Serugendo,
    and Andrea Omicini

A Dynamic Logic for Systems with Predicate-Based Communication   224
    Rolf Hennicker and Martin Wirsing

Abstractions for Collective Adaptive Systems.   243
    Omar Inverso, Catia Trubiani, and Emilio Tuosto

Verifying AbC Specifications via Emulation.   261
    Rocco De Nicola, Tan Duong, and Omar Inverso

Adaptive Security Policies   280
    Flemming Nielson, René Rydhof Hansen, and Hanne Riis Nielson

Capturing Dynamicity and Uncertainty in Security and Trust
via Situational Patterns   295
    Tomas Bures, Petr Hnetynka, Robert Heinrich, Stephan Seifermann,
    and Maximilian Walter

Guaranteeing Type Consistency in Collective Adaptive Systems   311
    Jonas Schürmann, Tim Tegeler, and Bernhard Steffen

Epistemic Logic in Ensemble Specification.   329
    Jan Sürmeli

FScaFi : A Core Calculus for Collective Adaptive Systems Programming . . .   344
    Roberto Casadei, Mirko Viroli, Giorgio Audrito, and Ferruccio Damiani

Writing Robotics Applications with X-Klaim   361
    Lorenzo Bettini, Khalid Bourr, Rosario Pugliese, and Francesco Tiezzi

Measuring Adaptability and Reliability of Large Scale Systems   380
    Valentina Castiglioni, Michele Loreti, and Simone Tini

Centrality-Preserving Exact Reductions of Multi-Layer Networks   397
    Tatjana Petrov and Stefano Tognazzi

Towards Dynamic Dependable Systems Through Evidence-Based
Continuous Certification   416
    Rasha Faqeh, Christof Fetzer, Holger Hermanns, Jörg Hoffmann,
    Michaela Klauck, Maximilian A. Köhl, Marcel Steinmetz,
    and Christoph Weidenbach

Forming Ensembles at Runtime: A Machine Learning Approach.   440
  Tomáš Bureš, Ilias Gerostathopoulos, Petr Hnětynka, and Jan Pacovský

Synthesizing Control for a System with Black Box Environment, Based
on Deep Learning.   457
  *Simon Iosti, Doron Peled, Khen Aharon, Saddek Bensalem,
  and Yoav Goldberg*

A Formal Model for Reasoning About the Ideal Fitness in Evolutionary
Processes.   473
  Thomas Gabor and Claudia Linnhoff-Popien

A Case Study of Policy Synthesis for Swarm Robotics   491
  Paul Piho and Jane Hillston

Maple-Swarm: Programming Collective Behavior for Ensembles
by Extending HTN-Planning.   507
  *Oliver Kosak, Lukas Huhn, Felix Bohn, Constantin Wanninger,
  Alwin Hoffmann, and Wolfgang Reif*

Swarm and Collective Capabilities for Multipotent Robot Ensembles.   525
  *Oliver Kosak, Felix Bohn, Lennart Eing, Dennis Rall,
  Constantin Wanninger, Alwin Hoffmann, and Wolfgang Reif*

Author Index   541

Automating Software Re-Engineering

Automating Software Re-engineering

Introduction to the ISoLA 2020 Track

Serge Demeyer[1(✉)], Reiner Hähnle[2(✉)], and Heiko Mantel[2(✉)]

[1] University of Antwerp, Antwerp, Belgium
`serge.demeyer@uantwerpen.be`
[2] Technical University Darmstadt, Darmstadt, Germany
{`reiner.haehnle,eduard.kamburjan`}`@tu-darmstadt.de`

Abstract. Software Engineering as a discipline and, in particular, as a research field within Computer Science, is still mainly focused on methods, techniques, processes, and tools to develop software from scratch. In reality, however, greenfield scenarios are not the most common ones. It is important to realize that dynamic evolution of software became a much more common and relevant issue in recent times, and its importance keeps growing. Software refactoring, parallelization, adaptation, therefore, become central activities in the value chain: automating them can realize huge gains. Formal approaches to software modeling and analysis are poised to make a substantial contribution to software re-engineering, because they are fundamentally concerned with automation and correctness. This potential, however, is far from being realized. Formal methods tend to aim at software development ab ovo or look at some piece of given software as a static object. This state of affairs motivated a track on Automating Software Re-Engineering, where we invited a group of leading researchers with an active interest in the automation of software re-engineering to discuss the state of the art.

1 Introduction

Software Engineering as a discipline and, in particular, as a research field within Computer Science, is still mainly focused on methods, techniques, processes, and tools to develop software from scratch. In reality, however, greenfield scenarios are not the most common ones [7]. This has not only to do with the usual reasons: protection of possibly huge investments made, as well as preservation of the knowledge embodied in existing software. It is important to realize that dynamic evolution of software became a much more common and relevant issue in recent times, and its importance keeps growing, because of these technological key drivers:

- the advent of massively parallel hardware and the desire to optimally exploit it by software,
- the need to diversify and customize, particularly, in Internet-of-Things and Industry 4.0, and

T. Margaria and B. Steffen (Eds.): ISoLA 2020, LNCS 12477, pp. 3–8, 2020.
https://doi.org/10.1007/978-3-030-61470-6_1

– novel application scenarios for existing software, fueled by digitalization of everything.

Software refactoring [4], parallelization [1], adaptation [2], therefore, become central activities in the value chain: automating them can realize huge gains.

Formal approaches to software modeling and analysis are poised to make a substantial contribution to software re-engineering, because they are fundamentally concerned with automation and correctness. This potential, however, is far from being realized. The reason is that there is something inherently wrong with the current focus of formal approaches to software analysis and development. They tend to aim at software development *ab ovo* or look at some piece of given software as a static object [6]. In other words, automated software re-engineering is usually not on the radar.

2   Track Organization

The situation sketched above was the motivation to submit a track on Automating Software Re-Engineering to the 9th edition of the International Symposium On Leveraging Applications of Formal Methods, Verification and Validation (ISoLA 2020). We invited a group of leading researchers with an active interest in the automation of software re-engineering. People working on formal foundations, on tools, as well as practitioners of re-engineering, for example, from the High-Performance Computing or the Industry 4.0 domains. We also broadcasted an open invitation on several channels with the intent of reaching out to a wider audience of interested researchers.

In our call for papers, we solicited either research, survey, experience or tool papers. We did not necessarily seek for new contributions, but also allowed individuals to shed new insights on results that have been published earlier. The corona pandemic caused a few organisational issues. But in the end we decided to proceed with the submission and review process, hoping that we will be able to have an actual physical meeting.

We received eight submissions. Each paper was reviewed by at least two experts in the field. We encouraged the reviewers to be inclusive and write constructive reviews and we explicitly aimed for non-competitive reviewing. In the end, we accepted eight submissions that can be classified into research, systematization, and tool paper as follows (where some papers fall into more than one category), see Table 1.

3   Track Contributions

We classified the eight accepted papers into three thematic sessions: the first group, *Verification for Program Analysis* encompasses contributions suggesting verification approaches that, ultimately, will be used to analyse different versions of a program. The second group is about formal foundations with the eponymous label. The third group focuses on correct refactoring of concurrent programs.

Table 1. Overview and classification of the papers in the ISoLA ASRE track

Authors	Title	Classification
Serge Demeyer, Ali Parsai, Sten Vercammen, Brent van Bladel, Merdhad Abdi	Formal Verification of Developer Tests: A Research Agenda Inspired by Mutation Testing	Systematization
Malte Lochau, Lars Luthmann, Hendrik Göttmann, Isabelle Bacher	Parametric Timed Bisimulation	Research
Dmitry Orlov	Finding Idioms in Source Code using Subtree Counting Techniques	Research + Tool
Reiner Hähnle, Asmae Heydari Tabar, Arya Mazaheri, Mohammad Norouzi, Dominic Steinhöfel, Felix Wolf	Safer Parallelization	Research + Tool
Alexander Weigl, Mattias Ulbrich, Daniel Lentzsch	Modular Regression Verification for Reactive Systems	Research + Tool
Marie-Christine Jacobs, Heiko Mantel	A Unifying Framework for Dynamic Monitoring and a Taxonomy of Optimizations	Systematization + Research
David Naumann	37 years of Relational Hoare Logic: Remarks on its Principles and History	Systematization + Research
Violet Ka I Pun, Volker Stolz, Rohit Gheyi	ReAct: Refactoring and Active Object Languages	Research

It is worth observing that many of the papers indeed are motivated by the "key drivers" of software re-engineering identified in Sect. 1, for example, [5, 9] are concerned with parallel programs, [10, 12] have an Industrie 4.0 context, etc.

Below we provide a short summary of each paper. We refer interested readers to the actual paper later in this volume for more information.

3.1 Verification for Program Analysis

In the paper *Formal Verification of Developer Tests: a Research Agenda Inspired by Mutation Testing* [3], five authors from the University of Antwerp present a research agenda on how formal verification may contribute to verifying test code. The paper briefly describes five problems from the perspective of mutation testing, which is a technique to evaluate the fault detection capability of a test suite, and discusses, for each of these five problems, how formal verification can be helpful to alleviate the issue.

In the paper *Modular Regression Verification for Reactive Systems* [12], three authors from the Karlsruhe Institute of Technology present an extension on regression verification proofs specifically geared towards Programmable Logic Controllers. The approach is incorporated into a tool which chains a series of conformance checkers (from lightweight to heavyweight) to model check the subgoals.

In the paper *Finding Idioms in Source Code using Subtree Counting Techniques* [11], a single author from National Research University in Moscow proposes an algorithm to find idioms in source code. The algorithm first builds an abstract syntax tree and then enumerates all subtrees above a certain size. If the same subtree is found, it is replaced so after the algorithm processed the whole abstract syntax tree, it results in a large trie structure where common subtrees are all on the same nodes. The algorithm is implemented in Python 3 and validated on three small open source systems also written in Python.

3.2   Formal Foundations

The paper *Parametric Timed Bisimulation* [10] by one author from the University of Siegen and three from Technical University of Darmstadt consider parametric timed automata: a variant of timed automata supporting parametric time constraints. They lift the definition of timed bisimulation from timed automata to parametric timed automata. The authors propose an approximation of this bisimulation that treats parameters as symbols, and they show that this is a sufficient approximation of the parametric bisimulation. They also propose a necessary condition that substitutes parameters by values at the end of the time spectrum.

The paper *A Unifying Framework for Dynamic Monitoring and a Taxonomy of Optimizations* [8] by two researchers from Technical University of Darmstadt provides a framework for runtime monitoring that makes it possible to give fully formal definitions of soundness for optimizations. In particular, the authors identify various preconditions to preservation theorems that can be used as sufficient conditions on soundness. The paper closes with a suggested taxonomy of run time monitoring optimizations that partly is derived from the formal framework. Several representative optimization approaches from the literature are classified with respect to the taxonomy.

In the paper *Thirty-seven years of relational Hoare logic: remarks on its principles and history* one author from Stevens Institute of Technology revisits several decades of Relational Hoare Logic, and reminds the community about highly relevant work that has not received due attention so far. The author revisits product constructions for programs that enable one to use traditional Hoare Logic for relational reasoning, and he points out differences between variants of such product constructions. The author systematizes proof rules for Relational Hoare Logic and augments them by a novel rule. Finally, the paper clarifies better on how Relational Hoare Logic relates to the use of product programs in combination with traditional Hoare Logic.

3.3   Formal Verification for Concurrency

In the paper *Safer Parallelization* [5], six authors from Technical University of Darmstadt describe a semi-automatic approach to formally prove a suite of program transformations that prepare a sequential program for subsequent parallelisation. The approach is supported by a tool (REFINITY) which supports the Java programming language and is implemented as a front-end to the program prover KeY.

In the paper *ReAct: Refactoring and Active Object Languages* [9], two authors from the Western Norway University of Applied Sciences and one from the Federal University of Campina Grande, Brazil investigate the impact of well-known refactorings for sequential OO languages in the context of concurrency. It focuses on the cooperative scheduling paradigm, because of its formal and well-understood semantics. This allows to give a formal definition of equivalence and to argue about correctness of refactorings at least semi-formally. The paper contains valuable insights about what can (and what can't) happen when refactoring Active Object programs. It is an important step towards providing better assistance to developers for refactoring concurrent programs. The authors also argue convincingly that such assistance is necessary.

4   Conclusion

While we were highly satisfied with the breadth, depth, and quality of the contributions, we do realize that this track can only be a (first) snapshot of what promises to be an exciting, dynamic, and, most of all, practically relevant, new direction of research: Automating Software Re-Engineering will certainly shape our research agenda for years to come. We express the hope that it gets due attention also in the Software Engineering research community at large.

References

1. Atre, R., Jannesari, A., Wolf, F.: Brief announcement: meeting the challenges of parallelizing sequential programs. In: Scheideler, C., Hajiaghayi, M.T. (eds.) Proceedings of the 29th ACM Symposium on Parallelism in Algorithms and Architectures, SPAA, Washington DC, USA, pp. 363–365. ACM (2017)
2. Barbier, F., Cariou, E., Goaer, O.L., Pierre, S.: Software adaptation: classification and a case study with state chart XML. IEEE Softw. **32**(5), 68–76 (2015)
3. Demeyer, S., Parsai, A., Vercammen, S., van Bladel, B., Abdi, M.: Formal verification of developer tests: a research agenda inspired by mutation testing. In: Margaria, T., Steffen, B. (eds.) ISoLA 2020. LNCS, vol. 12477, pp. 9–24. Springer, Cham (2020)
4. Fowler, M.: Refactoring: Improving the Design of Existing Code. Object Technology Series. Addison-Wesley, Boston (1999)
5. Hähnle, R., Heydari Tabar, A., Mazaheri, A., Norouzi, M., Steinhöfel, D., Wolf, F.: Safer parallelization. In: Margaria, T., Steffen, B. (eds.) ISoLA 2020. LNCS, vol. 12477, pp. 117–137. Springer, Cham (2020)

6. Hähnle, R., Huisman, M.: Deductive software verification: from pen-and-paper proofs to industrial tools. In: Steffen, B., Woeginger, G. (eds.) Computing and Software Science. LNCS, vol. 10000, pp. 345–373. Springer, Cham (2019). https://doi.org/10.1007/978-3-319-91908-9_18

7. Hopkins, R., Jenkins, K.: Eating the IT Elephant: Moving from Greenfield Development to Brownfield. IBM Press, Upper Saddle River (2011)

8. Jacobs, M.-C., Mantel, H.: A unifying framework for dynamic monitoring and a taxonomy of optimizations. In: Margaria, T., Steffen, B. (eds.) ISoLA 2020. LNCS, vol. 12477, pp. 72–92. Springer, Cham (2020)

9. Ka I Pun, V., Stolz, V., Gheyi R.: ReAct: refactoring and active object languages. In: Margaria, T., Steffen, B. (eds.) ISoLA 2020. LNCS, vol. 12477, pp. 138–158. Springer, Cham (2020)

10. Lochau, M., Luthmann, L., Göttmann, H., Bacher, I.: Parametric timed bisimulation. In: Margaria, T., Steffen, B. (eds.) ISoLA 2020. LNCS, vol. 12477, pp. 55–71. Springer, Cham (2020)

11. Orlov, D.: Finding idioms in source code using subtree counting techniques. In: Margaria, T., Steffen, B. (eds.) ISoLA 2020. LNCS, vol. 12477, pp. 44–54. Springer, Cham (2020)

12. Weigl, A., Ulbrich, M., Lentzsch, D.: Modular regression verification for reactive systems. In: Margaria, T., Steffen, B. (eds.) ISoLA 2020. LNCS, vol. 12477, pp. 25–43. Springer, Cham (2020)

Formal Verification of Developer Tests: A Research Agenda Inspired by Mutation Testing

Serge Demeyer[1,2](✉) iD, Ali Parsai[1](✉) iD, Sten Vercammen[1](✉),
Brent van Bladel[1], and Mehrdad Abdi[1]

[1] Universiteit Antwerpen, Antwerp, Belgium
{serge.demeyer,ali.parsai,sten.vercammen}@uantwerpen.be
[2] Flanders Make vzw, Kortrijk, Belgium

Abstract. With the current emphasis on DevOps, automated software tests become a necessary ingredient for continuously evolving, high-quality software systems. This implies that the test code takes a significant portion of the complete code base—test to code ratios ranging from 3:1 to 2:1 are quite common.

We argue that "testware" provides interesting opportunities for formal verification, especially because the system under test may serve as an oracle to focus the analysis. As an example we describe five common problems (mainly from the subfield of mutation testing) and how formal verification may contribute. We deduce a research agenda as an open invitation for fellow researchers to investigate the peculiarities of formally verifying testware.

Keywords: Testware · Formal verification · Mutation testing

1 Introduction

DevOps is defined by Bass *et al.* as "*a set of practices intended to reduce the time between committing a change to a system and the change being placed into normal production, while ensuring high quality*" [6]. The combination of these practices enables a continuous flow, where the development and operations of software systems are combined in one seamless (automated) process. This allows for frequent releases to rapidly respond to customer needs. Tesla, for example, uploads new software in its cars once every month [30]. Amazon pushes new updates to production on average every 11.6 s [22].

The key to the DevOps approach is a series of increasingly powerful automated tests that scrutinise the commits. As a consequence, test code takes a significant portion of the complete codebase. Several researchers reported that test code is sometimes larger than the production code under test [13,43,48]. More recently, during a large scale attempt to assess the quality of test code, Athanasiou *et al.* reported six systems where test code takes more than 50% of the complete codebase [5]. Moreover, Stackoverflow posts mention that test to code ratios between 3:1 and 2:1 are quite common [3].

© Springer Nature Switzerland AG 2020
T. Margaria and B. Steffen (Eds.): ISoLA 2020, LNCS 12477, pp. 9–24, 2020.
https://doi.org/10.1007/978-3-030-61470-6_2

Knowing about the popularity of automated tests and the sheer size of resulting test suites, software engineers need tools and techniques to identify lurking faults in the test code. The "testware", as it is called, should be treated as a regular software system involving requirements, architecture, design, implementation, quality assurance, and—last but not least—maintenance [15]. Indeed, we have witnessed first-hand that not all software projects uphold graceful co-evolution between production code and test code [48]. This effectively means that the software is vulnerable for extended periods of time whenever the production code evolves but the test code does not follow (immediately).

> ⟹ *Just like all software, testware would benefit from formal verification.*

Test code (unit-test code in particular) is written in standard programming languages, thus amenable to formal verification. It is therefore possible to augment test code with annotations (invariants, pre-conditions) and verify that certain properties hold: loop termination, post-conditions, … [17,21]. Moreover, most test code follows a quite consistent structure: the *setup-stimulate-verify-teardown* (S-S-V-T) cycle [45]. The purpose of statements within the test code is therefore rather easy to deduce, making it possible to focus the verification process on the relevant test slices.

> ⟹ *Test code is quite amenable to formal verification.*

The Reach–Infect–Propagate–Reveal criterion (a.k.a. the RIPR model) provides a fine-grained framework to assess effective tests, or, conversely, weaknesses in a test suite [27]. It states that an effective test should first of all *Reach* the fault, then *Infect* the program state, after which it should *Propagate* as an observable difference, and eventually *Reveal* the presence of a fault (probably via an assert statement).

> ⟹ *The system under test provides an oracle for effective tests.*

In this position paper we argue that "testware" provides interesting opportunities for formal verification, especially because the system under test may serve as an oracle to focus the analysis. As an example we describe five common problems (mainly from the subfield of mutation testing) and how formal verification may contribute. We deduce a research agenda as an open invitation for fellow researchers to investigate the peculiarities of formally verifying testware.

The remainder of this paper is organised as follows. Section 2, provides the necessary background information on formal verification and mutation testing. Section 3 goes over the five items in the research agenda explaining the problem and how formal verification of the test code could alleviate the problem. Section 4 list a few papers which investigated how formal verification could help in analysing test programs. We conclude with an open invitation to the community in Sect. 5.

2   Background

2.1   Formal Specification and Verification

Formal verification and formal specification are two complementary steps, used when adopting formal methods in software engineering [18]. During formal specification one rigorously specifies what a software system ought to do, and afterwards, during formal verification, one uses mathematical proofs to show that the system indeed does so. It should come as no surprise that the two steps go hand in hand, as illustrated by the discovery of a bug in the JDK linked list [20]. In this paper we restrict ourselves to a particular kind of formal verification—the ones based on a tool tightly integrated with a normal programming language— exemplified by KeY [17] and VeriFast [21]. These tools insert special program statements (pragmas, annotations) into the code to express properties by means of invariants, pre-conditions, and post-conditions. A series of mathematical theorem provers are then used to show that these properties indeed hold.

2.2   Mutation Testing

Mutation testing (also called mutation analysis—within this text the terms are used interchangeably) is the state-of-the-art technique for evaluating the fault-detection capability of a test suite [23]. The technique deliberately injects faults into the code and counts how many of them are caught by the test suite. Within academic circles, mutation testing is acknowledged as the most effective technique for a fully automated assessment of the strength of a test suite. The most recent systematic literature survey by Papadakis *et al.* revealed more than 400 scientific articles between 2007 and 2016 investigating mutation testing from various angles [35]. Despite this impressive body of academic work, the technique is seldom adopted in an industrial setting because it comes with a tremendous performance overhead: each mutant must be compiled and tested separately [37]. During one of our experiments with an industrial codebase, we witnessed 48 h of mutation testing time on a test suite comprising 272 unit tests and 5,258 lines of test code for a system under test comprising 48,873 lines of production code [46].

Example. Throughout this paper, we will use the C++ code in Fig. 1 as a running example. It scans a vector from back to front, looking for an element. Upon finding the element, it returns its index (base zero) and −1 if the element is not found.

Now consider the test suite in Fig. 2. The first test (`emptyVector`, lines 1–3) checks for the exceptional case of an empty vector. The second test (`doubleOccurrence`, lines 5–7), verifies the happy-day scenario: we look for an element in the vector and it should be found on position 3. This is a very relevant test because it actually looks for an element which appears two times in the vector and it correctly asserts that it should return the position of the last occurrence. The third test (`noOccurrence`, lines 9–11), checks what happens when we look for an element that is not in the vector, in which case it should

```
1 int findLast(std::vector<int> x, int y) {
2     if (x.size() == 0) return -1;
3     for (int i = x.size() - 1; i >= 0; i--)
4         if (x[i] == y)
5             return i;
6     return -1;
7 }
```

Fig. 1. C++ code searching for an element in a vector starting at the end

return −1. Executing the test suite shows that all 3 tests pass. When calculating the code coverage, we even obtain a 100% statement, line and branch coverage.

```
1 TEST(FindLastTests, emptyVector) {
2   EXPECT_EQ(-1, findLast({}, 3));
3 }
4
5 TEST(FindLastTests, doubleOccurrence) {
6   EXPECT_EQ(3, findLast({1, 2, 42, 42, 63}, 42));
7 }
8
9 TEST(FindLastTests, noOccurrence) {
10   EXPECT_EQ(-1, findLast({1, 2, 42, 42, 63}, 99));
11 }

[==========] 3 tests from 1 test suite ran. (0 ms total)
[  PASSED  ] 3 tests.
```

Fig. 2. Test suite for the findLast in Fig. 1

Terminology. As with every field of active research, the terminology is extensive. Below we list the most important terms readers should be familiar with.

Mutation Operators. Mutation testing mutates the program under test by artificially injecting a fault based on one of the known mutation operators. A mutation operator is a source code transformation which introduces a change into the program under test. Typical examples are replacing a conditional operator (>= into <) or an arithmetic operator (+ into −). The first set of mutation operators were reported in King et al. [24]. Afterwards, special purpose mutation operators have been proposed to exercise novel language constructs, such as Java null-type errors [36] or C++11/14 lambda expressions and move semantics [38].

Killed and Survived (Live) Mutants. After generating the defective version of the software, the mutant is passed onto the test suite. If a test fails, the mutant is marked as killed (Killed Mutant). If all tests pass, the mutant is marked as survived or live (Survived Mutant).

Consider the mutated example in Fig. 3, where we apply a mutation operator named "Relational Operator Replacement" (ROR). On line 3, >= is replaced by < and the complete test suite is executed. One test fails so the mutant is considered killed; the test suite was strong enough to detect this mutant.

```
1 int findLast(std::vector<int> x, int y) {
2     if (x.size() == 0) return -1;
3     for (int i = x.size() - 1; i < 0; i--)
4         if (x[i] == y)
5             return i;
6     return -1;
7 }
```

```
[ PASSED ] 2 tests.
[ FAILED ] 1 test, listed below:
[ FAILED ] FindLastTests.doubleOccurrence
```

Relational Operator Replacement (ROR): On line 3, i >= 0 is replaced by i < 0. At least one test fails, so the mutant is killed.

Fig. 3. Killed mutant in findLast from Fig. 1

We again apply a "Relational Operator Replacement" (ROR), this time replacing >= by > and arriving at the situation in Fig. 4. If we execute the complete test suite, all tests pass so the test suite needs to be strengthened to detect this mutant.

Examining, why this mutant is not detected shows that the test suite fails to check for an important boundary condition: looking for an element which appears on the first position in the vector. If we add an extra test (see Fig. 5) the test suite now detects the mutant (1 test fails, occurrenceOnBoundary). Now it is now capable of killing the mutant.

Mutation Coverage. The whole mutation analysis ultimately results in a score known as the mutation coverage: the number of mutants killed divided by the total number of non-equivalent mutants injected. A test suite is said to achieve full mutation test adequacy whenever it can kill all mutants, thus reaching a mutation coverage of 100%. Such test suite is called a mutation-adequate test suite.

Reach–Infect–Propagate–Reveal (RIPR). The Reach–Infect–Propagate–Reveal criterion (a.k.a. the RIPR model) provides a fine-grained framework to assess weaknesses in a test suite which are conveniently revealed by mutation testing [27]. It states that an effective test should first of all *Reach* the fault, then *Infect* the program state, after which it should *Propagate* as an observable difference, and eventually *Reveal* the presence of a fault (probably via an assert statement but this depends on the test infrastructure).

```
1 int findLast(std::vector<int> x, int y) {
2     if (x.size() == 0) return -1;
3     for (int i = x.size() - 1; i > 0; i--)
4         if (x[i] == y)
5             return i;
6     return -1;
7 }
```

```
[==========] 3 tests from 1 test suite ran. (0 ms total)
[  PASSED  ] 3 tests.
```

Relational Operator Replacement (ROR): On line 3, i >= 0 is replaced by i > 0. No test fails, so the mutant is live.

Fig. 4. Survived mutant in `findLast` in Fig. 1

```
13 TEST(FindLastTests, occurrenceOnBoundary) {
14    EXPECT_EQ(0, findLast({1, 2, 42, 42, 63}, 1));
15 }
```

```
[==========] 4 tests from 1 test suite ran. (0 ms total)
[  PASSED  ] 3 tests.
[  FAILED  ] 1 test, listed below:
[  FAILED  ] FindLastTests.occurrenceOnBoundary
```

We add an extra test to the test suite in Figure 2 which tests for the boundary condition, an element to be found on the first position.

Fig. 5. Strengtened test suite for `findLast`

Consider the test suite in Fig. 2 and Fig. 5 together with the mutant that exposed the weakness in the test suite in Fig. 4. The first test (`emptyVector`, lines 1–3) does not even reach the fault injected on line 2. The second test (`doubleOccurrence`, lines 5–7), *reaches* the fault because it executes the faulty i > 0 condition, but does not infect the program state; so it cannot propagate nor reveal. The third test (`noOccurrence`, lines 9–11), infects the program state because it actually creates a state where the loop counter should have become 0, yet this is never propagated hence not revealed. It is only the fourth test (`occurrenceOnBoundary`, lines 13–15) which effectively infects the program state (i does not become 0), propagates to the output (returns −1) where it is revealed by the assert statement (expected 0).

Invalid Mutants. Mutation operators introduce syntactic changes, hence may cause compilation errors in the process. A typical example is the arithmetic mutation operator which changes a '+' into a '−'. This works for numbers but does not make sense when applied to the C++ string concatenation operator. If the compiler cannot compile the mutant for any reason, the mutant is considered invalid and is not incorporated into the mutation coverage.

Redundant ("Subsumed") Mutants. Sometimes there is an overlap in which tests kill which mutants, hence some mutants may be considered redundant. Redundant mutants are undesirable, since they waste resources and add no value to the process. In addition, they inflate the mutation score because often it is easy to kill many redundant mutants just by adding a single test case. To express this redundancy more precisely, the mutation testing community defined the concept of *subsuming* mutants.

Take for instance the mutant in Fig. 6, which replaces `x[i] == y` with `x[i] != y` on line 4. It is an easy to kill mutant as it is killed by three tests (doubleOccurrence, noOccurrence and occurrenceOnBoundary). The mutant in Fig. 6 is therefore said to be *subsumed by* the mutant in Fig. 3. Any test in our test suite which kills the latter mutant (difficult) one will also kill the former (easy) one.

```
1 int findLast (std::vector<int> x, int y) {
2       if (x.size() == 0) return -1;
3       for (int i = x.size() - 1; i >= 0; i--)
4           if (x[i] != y)
5               return i;
6       return -1;
7 }
```

```
[ PASSED ] 1 test.
[ FAILED ] 3 tests, listed below:
[ FAILED ] FindLastTests.doubleOccurrence
[ FAILED ] FindLastTests.noOccurrence
[ FAILED ] FindLastTests.occurrenceOnBoundary
```

Relational Operator Replacement (ROR): On line 4, x[i] == y is replaced by x[i] != y. This is a redundant mutant which is subsumed by the mutant in Figure 3 and Figure 4. Any test in our test suite which kills the mutant on line 2 will also kill the one on line 4.

Fig. 6. Redundant mutant for `findLast`

Equivalent Mutants. Some mutants do not change the semantics of the program, i.e. the output of the mutant is the same as the original program for any possible input. Therefore, no test case can differentiate between a so-called "equivalent mutant" and the original program. Equivalent mutants are not incorporated into the mutation coverage. Unfortunately, the detection of equivalent mutants is undecidable due to the halting problem. Therefore, it is left to the software engineer to manually weed out equivalent mutants.

Consider again the running example, now in Fig. 7. This time we apply the Relational Operator Replacement (ROR) on line 2, replacing the `== 0` with `<= 0`. Executing the test suite shows that all test pass so at first glance we have a live mutant. However, a deeper analysis shows that since the size of a vector is always positive, the value of `== 0` will always be the same as `<= 0`. So there is no input we can provide to the program under test to kill this mutant. Thus, this is an equivalent mutant.

```
1 int findLast(std::vector<int> x, int y) {
2       if (x.size() <= 0) return -1;
3       for (int i = x.size() - 1; i >= 0; i--)
4           if (x[i] == y)
5               return i;
6       return -1;
7 }


[==========] 4 tests from 1 test suite ran. (0 ms total)
[ PASSED ] 4 tests.
```

Relational Operator Replacement (ROR): On line 2, == 0 is replaced by <= 0. Not a single test fails, so the mutant is live. But since the size of a vector is always positive, the value of x.size() == 0 will always be the same as x.size() <= 0, regardless of the vector x. This mutant is therefore equivalent.

Fig. 7. Equivalent mutant of findLast from Fig. 1

3 Research Agenda

3.1 Equivalent Mutants

Equivalent mutants have been heavily studied in the literature as they may induce heavy overhead on test engineers aiming for 100% mutation coverage [31]. The most pragmatic approach so far has been to compare the generated (byte) code of the mutated program against the original [34]. Due to compiler optimizations the syntactic differences between the original and mutated program may disappear and then they are considered *trivially* equivalent. This allows to identify the easy cases, however, for the difficult ones, further analysis is required.

A paper by Offutt *et al.* illustrates how program analysis can help to identify equivalent mutants by demonstrating that they belong to an *infeasible path* [33]. The authors argue that a mutant is equivalent if the injected mutant lies on an *infeasible path*, thus (according to the RIPR model) the injected mutant can never propagate to the assert statements that reveals it.

Research Agenda. We would even go one step further and use program verification to prove that a mutant is equivalent to the original. And if not, the counter example should provide us with an extra test that illustrate where they may differ, hence would strengthen the test suite even further.

```
 1 int findLast(std::vector<int> x, int y) {
 2       if (x.size() == 0) return -1;

...

 9 int findLastEquivalentCandidate(std::vector<int> x, int y) {
10       if (x.size() <= 0) return -1;

...

11 TEST(FindLastTests, emptyVector) {
12       int res1, res2;
13       EXPECT_EQ(-1, res1 = findLast({}, 3));
14       EXPECT_EQ(-1, res2 = findLastEquivalent({}, 3));
15              //@ ensures res1 == res2;
16 }
```

Fig. 8. Inserting post-conditions to prove equivalence of mutant of `findLast` in Fig. 1

To formally verify that a mutant is indeed equivalent we create a copy of the mutated function. Lines 1–3 and lines 9–10 in Fig. 8 show two version of findLast that can thus be tested by the same test suite. Then we rely on code coverage (which is easy to obtain) or program slicing to identify the assert statement in the unit tests that are affected. Inserting a post-condition on the assert expressions would allow to show that the mutant can never be revealed, thus is equivalent. Line 15 in Fig. 8 added such a post-condition to an adapted version of the emptyVector test. It compares the result of the original method under test (`findLast`) with the mutated one (`findLastEquivalent`). If the program verifier shows that this post-condition actually holds, then we have shown that this is indeed an equivalent mutant. If not, the program verifier should give us a counter example which corresponds to a different execution path enforced by the mutant. This then provides a concrete execution path to create an additional test that highlights the difference.

> ⟹ *Formal verification may be helpful in confirming that a live mutant can never change the output of the system under test, thus is an equivalent mutant.*

3.2   Infinite Loops

Some mutants induce an infinite loop into the program under test. Therefore, most mutation tools abort the program under test when it runs an order of magnitude longer than expected and mark the corresponding mutant as "killed". Note that this assumption is not always correct, as in rare occasions the mutant can take much longer to be analysed due to other circumstances. In such cases, the mutant should be counted as "survived", but automatic detection of these scenarios is undecidable due to the halting problem.

Research Agenda. To formally verify that a mutant is indeed causing an infinite loop, we would first do the mutation analysis as normal, thus aborting the program when it runs an order of magnitude longer than expected. However, we do not yet mark the mutant as *"killed"* but instead put it in a special category *"further analysis required"*. Next we would insert a trivial post-condition right after the injected mutant and use program verification to show that the loop before never terminates.

⟹ *Formal verification may confirm that a mutant created an infinite loop, thus should be marked as "killed".*

3.3 Flaky Tests

Mutation testing assumes tests to be completely deterministic: every test run should produce the exact same output. However, there is the phenomenon of flaky tests: tests whose outcome can non-deterministically differ even when run on the same code under test [29]. When a test suite contains flaky tests, the mutation analysis is unpredictable, as some mutants might be killed when in fact the tests are failing due to flakiness and not the injected fault itself.

Shi *et al.* reported the first technique to tackle flaky tests during a mutation analysis [41]. When running each mutant-test pair, they keep track of whether the mutant is covered or not. When a mutant is not covered by a test, they mark the status as "unknown" and perform further analysis. Essentially they rerun the test suite multiple times to see whether the test coverage indeed changes.

Research Agenda. To formally verify that a mutant is suffering from flaky tests, we would extend the process described by Shi *et al.* with an extra step [41]. Once a potentially flaky test is identified, we would insert a trivial post-condition at the end of the test case and use program verification to show that the post-condition is not necessarily satisfied. Ideally, the verification would also provide a counter example, highlighting the program statements that cause the flaky behaviour.

⟹ *Formal verification may identify the root cause of a mutant suffering from flaky tests.*

3.4 Test Clones

When two fragments of code are either exactly the same or similar to each other, we call them a code clone. A code clone is also synonymous with a software clone or duplicated code, and these terms can be used interchangeably. Code clones can be differentiated based on their degree of similarity. First, code clones can be divided into syntactic clones and semantic clones. Syntactic clones are code clones that are syntactically similar, and are further divided in three types: Type I, Type II, and Type III clones. Type I clones are exactly the same, only allowing differences in comments, whitespaces, and indentation. Type II clones are a little less strict than Type I clones as they also allow differences in variable names and literal values. Finally, Type III clones are even less strict than Type II clones. They also allow for lines of code to be added or removed in the clone fragment. Note that it is not required for these types of clones to be functionally similar. Semantic clones on the other hand are code clones that are semantically similar without necessarily being syntactically similar. They are often called Type IV clones and are the most challenging clones to detect.

A lot of research has already been performed on software clones. In 2007, Koschke performed a survey of the literature on software clones [26]. This was followed in 2009 by him and his colleagues (Roy *et al.*) with an extensive comparison and evaluation of all code clone detection techniques and tools [40]. Svajlenko *et al.* manually curated a data set containing six million inter-project clones (Type I, II, III, and IV), including various strengths of Type III similarity (strong, moderate, weak) [42]. Over the years, a lot of research has been performed to further investigate the prevalence, characteristics, impact, and detection methods of software clones. However, most of this research focuses on production code; test code is rarely ever considered separately [26, 39, 40].

In 2018, Hasanain *et al.* performed an industrial case study to better understand code clones (i.e. duplicated code) in test code. They used NiCad to detect clones on a large test suite provided by Ericsson and discovered that 49% (in terms of LOC) of the entire test code are clones [19]. In a follow-up study our lab confirmed the prevalence of clones in test code [8]. We observed between 23% and 29% test code duplication in three well-tested open source systems, which is significantly more than the average amount of clones found in production code (between 10% and 15%). Worse, we discovered that most of the clone detection tools suffer from false negatives (NiCad [10] = 83%, CPD–PMD [1] = 84%, iClones [16] = 21%, TCORE [7] = 65%), which leaves ample room for improvement.

Research Agenda. Mutation analysis can give an indication on duplicated test logic. By carefully analysing subsumption relationships between mutants, we can infer which tests are likely to target the same program logic, thus being so-called *semantic clones*, also known as *Type IV* clones. We would consider them candidate clones, likely to be part of the aforementioned false negatives. By inserting invariants at relevant locations, formal verification may give indications on why certain test clones go undetected.

> $\implies$ *Formal verification might indicate why certain test clones appear as false negatives.*

3.5   Test Amplification

Test amplification is the act of automatically transforming a manually written unit-test to exercise boundary conditions [11]. In that sense, test amplification is a special kind of test generation: it relies on test cases previously written by developers which it tries to improve.

DSpot is an example of a test amplification tool for Java projects [12] which has been replicated for Pharo/Smalltalk within our lab under the name of SmallAmp [2]. These tools combine two techniques: (i) evolutionary test case generation or *Input Amplification* [44], and (ii) regression oracle generation or *Assert Amplification* [47]. They iteratively create extra test cases by changing the setup and the assertions, resulting in a new and larger set of test cases. The tools rely on genetic algorithms to select tests which increase the mutation coverage, discarding others. This process is performed for a fixed number of steps which eventually results in a new test suite, with a better mutation coverage than the initial one, thus covering more corner cases. In that sense, test amplification is a brute force approach which relies on machine learning techniques to select an optimal solution.

Research Agenda. Formal verification may be able to complement brute force test amplification. In a recent proof-of-concept we demonstrated that it is possible to amplify test cases with extra asserts for the *easy-to-kill* mutants [28]. The idea is inspired by dynamic program analysis and the RIPR model. We build a complete program trace of both the normal test execution and the mutated one. We then associate *easy-to-kill* mutants with test cases that reach, infect, propagate, yet do not reveal the fault. These are cases of missing assert statements and the tool prototype is capable of suggesting an assert statement to be added, even providing concrete values for the assert expressions. The *difficult-to-kill* mutants however require an in-depth investigation to understand why the fault does not infect the program state or why it does not propagate to the output. That is where formal verification may help. By adding a post-condition right after the infected statement the formal verification tool should be able to tell us whether the program state gets infected and whether the fault gets propagated. Inspecting the counter-examples generated by the theorem prover, we should be able to come up with extra statements in the test which would stimulate the unit under test to infect and propagate the fault.

> $\Longrightarrow$ *Formal verification may help in generating stimuli on the unit under test for the difficult-to-kill mutants.*

4   Related Work

The relationship between mutation testing and formal verification has been explored before. Aichernig *et al.* [4] argue that tests can be generated from formally verified requirements, using mutation testing to supervise where to generate additional test cases. To avoid difficult to maintain test suites (such as cloned test code discussed in Sect. 3.4), they introduce the concept of abstract test cases which are refined into concrete ones and regenerated when appropriate. In a similar vein, Brillout *et al.* [9] generate test cases from Simulink models achieving a high mutation coverage. Nevertheless, all these approaches take the perspective of the system under test specified using some kind of formal model of its behaviour and using mutation testing to create a strong test suite.

We argue that the opposite angle is equally relevant: that one should apply formal verification on the test code itself. This angle remains largely unexplored, except for the problem of equivalent mutants (see Sect. 3.1). There, several authors already confirmed that formal verification indeed may help to detect equivalent mutants. Kintis *et al.* [25] exploited patterns of data flow to identify mutants that are equivalent to the original program for a specific subset of paths. Devroey *et al.* [14] assert that for finite behavioural models, the equivalent mutant problem can be transformed to the language equivalence problem of non-deterministic finite automata. Marcozzi *et al.* [32] attempt to prove the validity of logical assertions in the code under test. The technique is implemented in a tool that relies on weakest-precondition calculus and SMT solving for proving the assertions.

5   Conclusion

In this position paper we argue that "testware" provides interesting opportunities for formal verification, especially because the system-under-test may serve as an oracle to focus the analysis and reduce the search space. We described five common problems: (1) Equivalent Mutants; (2) Infinite Loops; (3) Flaky tests; (4) Test Clones; (5) Test Amplification; and explained how formal verification of the test-code could partially alleviate them. This results in a research agenda which serves as on open invitation for fellow researchers to investigate the peculiarities of formally analysing testware.

References

1. Finding duplicated code with CPD (2020). https://pmd.github.io/latest/pmd_userdocs_cpd.html. Accessed July 2020
2. Abdi, M., Rocha, H., Demeyer, S.: Test amplification in the pharo smalltalk ecosystem. In: Proceedings IWST 2019 International Workshop on Smalltalk Technologies. ESUG (2019)
3. Agibalov, A.: What is a normal "functional lines of code" to "test lines of code" ratio? (2015). https://softwareengineering.stackexchange.com/questions/156883/. Accessed Aug 2020
4. Aichernig, B.K., Lorber, F., Tiran, S.: Formal test-driven development with verified test cases. In: Proceedings MODELSWARD 2014 2nd International Conference on Model-Driven Engineering and Software Development, pp. 626–635 (2014)
5. Athanasiou, D., Nugroho, A., Visser, J., Zaidman, A.: Test code quality and its relation to issue handling performance. IEEE Trans. Softw. Eng. **40**(11), 1100–1125 (2014). https://doi.org/10.1109/TSE.2014.2342227
6. Bass, L., Weber, I., Zhu, L.: DevOps: A Software Architect's Perspective. Addison-Wesley Longman Publishing Co. Inc., Boston (2015)
7. van Bladel, B., Demeyer, S.: A novel approach for detecting Type-IV clones in test code. In: Proceedings IWSC 2019 IEEE 13th International Workshop on Software Clones, pp. 102–118. IEEE (2019). https://doi.org/10.1109/IWSC.2019.8665855

8. van Bladel, B., Demeyer, S.: Clone detection in test code: an empirical evaluation. In: Proceedings SANER 2020 International Conference on Software Analysis, Evolution and Reengineering (SANER), pp. 492–500. IEEE (2020). https://doi.org/ 10.1109/SANER48275.2020.9054798

9. Brillout, A., et al.: Mutation-based test case generation for simulink models. In: de Boer, F.S., Bonsangue, M.M., Hallerstede, S., Leuschel, M. (eds.) FMCO 2009. LNCS, vol. 6286, pp. 208–227. Springer, Heidelberg (2010). https://doi.org/10. 1007/978-3-642-17071-3_11

10. Cordy, J.R., Roy, C.K.: The NiCad clone detector. In: 2011 IEEE 19th International Conference on Program Comprehension, pp. 219–220. IEEE (2011)

11. Danglot, B., Vera-Perez, O., Yu, Z., Zaidman, A., Monperrus, M., Baudry, B.: A snowballing literature study on test amplification. J. Syst. Softw. **157**, 110398 (2019)

12. Danglot, B., Vera-Pérez, O.L., Baudry, B., Monperrus, M.: Automatic test improvement with dspot: a study with ten mature open-source projects. Empirical Softw. Eng. **24**, 2603–2635 (2019)

13. Daniel, B., Jagannath, V., Dig, D., Marinov, D.: Reassert: Suggesting repairs for broken unit tests. In: Proceedings ASE 2009 International Conference on Automated Software Engineering, pp. 433–444. IEEE CS (2009). https://doi.org/10. 1109/ASE.2009.17

14. Devroey, X., Perrouin, G., Papadakis, M., Legay, A., Schobbens, P.Y., Heymans, P.: Model-based mutant equivalence detection using automata language equivalence and simulations. J. Syst. Softw. **141**, 1–15 (2018). https://doi.org/10.1016/j.jss. 2018.03.010

15. Fewster, M., Graham, D.: Software Test Automation: Effective Use of Test Execution Tools. ACM Press Series. Addison-Wesley (1999)

16. Göde, N., Koschke, R.: Incremental clone detection. In: 2009 13th European Conference on Software Maintenance and Reengineering, pp. 219–228. IEEE (2009)

17. Hähnle, R.: Quo vadis formal verification? In: Ahrendt, W., Beckert, B., Bubel, R., Hähnle, R., Schmitt, P.H., Ulbrich, M. (eds.) Deductive Software Verification - The KeY Book: From Theory to Practice, pp. 1–19. Springer, Cham (2016). https:// doi.org/10.1007/978-3-319-49812-6_1

18. Hall, A.: Seven myths of formal methods. IEEE Softw. **7**(5), 11–19 (1990). https:// doi.org/10.1109/52.57887

19. Hasanain, W., Labiche, Y., Eldh, S.: An analysis of complex industrial test code using clone analysis. In: Proceedings QRS 2018 IEEE International Conference on Software Quality, Reliability and Security, pp. 482–489. IEEE (2018). https://doi. org/10.1109/QRS.2018.00061

20. Hiep, H.D.A., Maathuis, O., Bian, J., de Boer, F.S., van Eekelen, M., de Gouw, S.: Verifying openjdk's linkedlist using key. In: Biere, A., Parker, D. (eds.) Tools and Algorithms for the Construction and Analysis of Systems, pp. 217–234. Springer, Cham (2020). https://doi.org/10.1007/978-3-030-45237-7_13

21. Jacobs, B., Smans, J., Philippaerts, P., Vogels, F., Penninckx, W., Piessens, F.: VeriFast: a powerful, sound, predictable, fast verifier for C and Java. In: Bobaru, M., Havelund, K., Holzmann, G.J., Joshi, R. (eds.) NFM 2011. LNCS, vol. 6617, pp. 41–55. Springer, Heidelberg (2011). https://doi.org/10.1007/978-3-642-20398-5_4

22. Jenkins, J.: Velocity culture. In: Keynote Address at the Velocity 2011 Conference (2011)

23. Jia, Y., Harman, M.: An analysis and survey of the development of mutation testing. IEEE Trans. Softw. Eng. **37**(5), 649–678 (2011). https://doi.org/10.1109/TSE.2010.62

24. King, K.N., Offutt, A.J.: A fortran language system for mutation-based software testing. Softw. Pract. Exp. **21**(7), 685–718 (1991). https://doi.org/10.1002/spe.4380210704

25. Kintis, M., Malevris, N.: MEDIC: a static analysis framework for equivalent mutant identification. Inf. Softw. Technol. **68**, 1–17 (2015). https://doi.org/10.1016/j.infsof.2015.07.009

26. Koschke, R.: Survey of research on software clones. In: Dagstuhl Seminar Proceedings. Schloss Dagstuhl-Leibniz-Zentrum für Informatik (2007)

27. Li, N., Offutt, J.: Test oracle strategies for model-based testing. IEEE Trans. Softw. Eng. **43**(4), 372–395 (2016). https://doi.org/10.1109/TSE.2016.2597136

28. Lu, Z.X., Vercammen, S., Demeyer, S.: Semi-automatic test case expansion for mutation testing. In: Proceedings VST 2020 IEEE Workshop on Validation, Analysis and Evolution of Software Tests, pp. 1–7 (2020). https://doi.org/10.1109/VST50071.2020.9051637

29. Luo, Q., Hariri, F., Eloussi, L., Marinov, D.: An empirical analysis of flaky tests. In: Proceedings FSE 2014 22nd ACM SIGSOFT International Symposium on Foundations of Software Engineering, pp. 643–453. Association for Computing Machinery, New York (2014). https://doi.org/10.1145/2635868.2635920

30. Rob, M.: Everything you need to know about tesla software updates (2014). https://www.teslarati.com/everything-need-to-know-tesla-software-updates/. Accessed May 2020

31. Madeyski, L., Orzeszyna, W., Torkar, R., Jozala, M.: Overcoming the equivalent mutant problem: a systematic literature review and a comparative experiment of second order mutation. IEEE Trans. Softw. Eng. **40**(1), 23–42 (2014). https://doi.org/10.1109/TSE.2013.44

32. Marcozzi, M., Bardin, S., Kosmatov, N., Papadakis, M., Prevosto, V., Correnson, L.: Time to clean your test objectives. In: Proceedings ICSE 2018 40th International Conference on Software Engineering, pp. 456–467. Association for Computing Machinery, New York (2018). https://doi.org/10.1145/3180155.3180191

33. Offutt, A.J., Pan, J.: Automatically detecting equivalent mutants and infeasible paths. Softw. Test. Verification Reliab. **7**(3), 165–192 (1997). https://doi.org/10.1002/(SICI)1099-1689(199709)7:3⟨165::AID-STVR143⟩3.0.CO;2-U

34. Papadakis, M., Jia, Y., Harman, M., Le Traon, Y.: Trivial compiler equivalence: a large scale empirical study of a simple, fast and effective equivalent mutant detection technique. In: Proceedings of the 37th International Conference on Software Engineering, Piscataway, NJ, USA, vol. 1, pp. 936–946. IEEE Press (2015). https://doi.org/10.1109/ICSE.2015.103

35. Papadakis, M., Kintis, M., Zhang, J., Jia, Y., Traon, Y.L., Harman, M.: Mutation testing advances: an analysis and survey. Adv. Comput. **112**, 275–378 (2019). https://doi.org/10.1016/bs.adcom.2018.03.015

36. Parsai, A., Demeyer, S.: Do null-type mutation operators help prevent null-type faults? In: Catania, B., Královič, R., Nawrocki, J., Pighizzini, G. (eds.) SOFSEM 2019. LNCS, vol. 11376, pp. 419–434. Springer, Cham (2019). https://doi.org/10.1007/978-3-030-10801-4_33

37. Parsai, A., Demeyer, S.: Comparing mutation coverage against branch coverage in an industrial setting. Int. J. Softw. Tools Technol. Transfer (2020). https://doi.org/10.1007/s10009-020-00567-y

38. Parsai, A., Demeyer, S., De Busser, S.: C++11/14 mutation operators based on common fault patterns. In: Medina-Bulo, I., Merayo, M.G., Hierons, R. (eds.) ICTSS 2018. LNCS, vol. 11146, pp. 102–118. Springer, Cham (2018). https://doi.org/10.1007/978-3-319-99927-2_9

39. Roy, C.K., Cordy, J.R.: Benchmarks for software clone detection: a ten-year retrospective. In: 2018 IEEE 25th International Conference on Software Analysis, Evolution and Reengineering (JSS), pp. 26–37. IEEE (2018)

40. Roy, C.K., Cordy, J.R., Koschke, R.: Comparison and evaluation of code clone detection techniques and tools: a qualitative approach. Sci. Comput. Program. **74**(7), 470–495 (2009)

41. Shi, A., Bell, J., Marinov, D.: Mitigating the effects of flaky tests on mutation testing. In: Proceedings ISSTA 2019 the 28th ACM SIGSOFT International Symposium on Software Testing and Analysis, pp. 112–122. Association for Computing Machinery, New York (2019). https://doi.org/10.1145/3293882.3330568

42. Svajlenko, J., Islam, J.F., Keivanloo, I., Roy, C.K., Mia, M.M.: Towards a big data curated benchmark of inter-project code clones. In: 2014 IEEE International Conference on Software Maintenance and Evolution, pp. 476–480 (2014)

43. Tillmann, N., Schulte, W.: Unit tests reloaded: parameterized unit testing with symbolic execution. IEEE Softw. 23(4) (2006). https://doi.org/10.1109/MS.2006.117

44. Tonella, P.: Evolutionary testing of classes. In: Proceedings ISSTA 2004 ACM SIGSOFT International Symposium on Software Testing and Analysis, pp. 119–128. Association for Computing Machinery, New York (2004). https://doi.org/10.1145/1007512.1007528

45. Van Rompaey, B., Du Bois, B., Demeyer, S., Rieger, M.: On the detection of test smells: a metrics-based approach for general fixture and eager test. IEEE Trans. Softw. Eng. **33**(12), 800–817 (2007). https://doi.org/10.1109/TSE.2007.70745

46. Vercammen, S., Demeyer, S., Borg, M., Eldh, S.: Speeding up mutation testing via the cloud: lessons learned for further optimisations. In: Proceedings ESEM 2018 12th ACM/IEEE International Symposium on Empirical Software Engineering and Measurement, pp. 26:1–26:9. ACM, New York (2018). https://doi.org/10.1145/3239235.3240506

47. Xie, T.: Augmenting automatically generated unit-test suites with regression oracle checking. In: Thomas, D. (ed.) ECOOP 2006. LNCS, vol. 4067, pp. 380–403. Springer, Heidelberg (2006). https://doi.org/10.1007/11785477_23

48. Zaidman, A., Rompaey, B.V., van Deursen, A., Demeyer, S.: Studying the co-evolution of production and test code in open source and industrial developer test processes through repository mining. Int. J. Empirical Softw. Eng. **16**(3), 325–364 (2011). https://doi.org/10.1007/s10664-010-9143-7

Modular Regression Verification for Reactive Systems

Alexander Weigl[✉], Mattias Ulbrich, and Daniel Lentzsch

Karlsruhe Institute of Technology, Karlsruhe, Germany
weigl@kit.edu

Abstract. Reactive software is often deployed in long-running systems with high dependability requirements. Despite their safety- and mission-critical use, their functionalities must occasionally be adapted, for example to support new features or regulations. But software evolution bears the risk of introducing new malfunctions. Regression verification helps preventing the introduction of unintended, faulty behaviour.

In this paper we present a novel approach for modular regression verification proofs for reactive systems based on the idea of relational regression verification contracts. The approach allows the decomposition of a larger regression verification proof into smaller proofs on its subcomponents. We embedded the decomposition rule in a new algorithm for regression verification, which orchestrates several light- and heavyweight techniques. We implemented our approach for software used by Programmable Logic Controllers (PLC) written in Structured Text (IEC 611131-3) and show the potential of the approach with selected scenarios of a Pick-and-Place-Unit case study.

1 Introduction

Reactive software driving technical systems is often in operation for long periods of time, sometimes for many years or even decades. Guarantees regarding its correctness must be ensured over the entire system lifetime, and the software must go along and maintain quality through all hardware and software evolution steps. To avert malfunctions which may cause harm to humans or substantial financial losses, such reactive software is typically very thoroughly tested before deployment. In long-living systems, the confidence that the system's control software behaves correctly increases also with its successful operation time, as experience of its behaviour are gathered in various configurations and situations.

When software changes during an evolution step, thorough testing helps to identify software flaws and to increase confidence in the correctness of the system. While this is the standard in the industry, it has drawbacks: A test suite can never cover all possible scenarios, and confidence gained by experience with an old software revision cannot be transferred to a new revision.

Research supported by the DFG in Priority Programme SPP1593: Design for Future – Managed Software Evolution (BE 2334/7-2, and UL 433/1-2).

T. Margaria and B. Steffen (Eds.): ISoLA 2020, LNCS 12477, pp. 25–43, 2020.
https://doi.org/10.1007/978-3-030-61470-6_3

A solution to this problem is *regression verification*: Instead of using two separate specifications for two revisions, the two revisions are compared directly to each other, where the old revision serves as a functional specification for the new one. The goal is then to prove equivalence, or a different specified relation, between both revisions. To this end, both software revisions are transformed into a logical representation, and then the combination is passed to a model checker for verification [1]. In previous work, we have shown that the resulting proof obligations can be discharged in some cases, but that the size of the system may make the verification approach suffer from the potential problem of state space explosion. Even for a simple case study with less complexity than real-world scenarios, proving equivalence with the approach described above took up to a day of computing time.

As a response to this challenge, this paper presents a technique to modularise regression verification by decomposing the verification condition into smaller subgoals which can be regression-verified individually. The novelty in comparison to existing model checking modularisation approaches is not that individual programs are decomposed into manageable fragments, but that the programs are split into pairwise blocks combined to be verified relationally.

The modular verification approach is embedded into a new regression verification algorithm which combines different lightweight (syntactical) and more heavyweight regression verification analyses.

Modularising the verification has multiple gains: Firstly, it reduces the state space of proof obligations, allowing them to be more feasible for model checking. Moreover, it introduces a locality principle: Parts of a program not touched at all by a refactoring can be factored out and equivalence be proven by simpler, syntactical techniques. For modules that occur more often, the verification effort can also be reduced since they only need to be analysed once.

A characteristic of reactive systems is that their code is executed periodically to react to changes in their application environment. Software for reactive systems is usually limited in the used (or allowed) programmatic constructs because they have to ensure real-time guarantees with deterministic runtimes. In many cases this means that there are no unbounded loops (or unconstrained recursion) in reactive systems software which allows us to unroll the code fully (thus eliminating the need for loop invariants or bounded analyses).

Contribution. In this paper, we present a sound modularisation technique for the regression verification of reactive system software; it requires that relational specifications of subroutines are given (by the user). Moreover, we present a new algorithm for regression verification which orchestrates a collection of diverse heavy- and lightweight verification techniques making the new modular analysis more powerful in practice. We implemented the algorithm for PLC software, and demonstrate the feasibility of our approach on the Pick-and-Place-Unit (PPU) [12] – a community demonstrator for showing the evolution of manufacturing systems.

Outline. In Sect. 2 we present the foundations of regression verification for reactive systems which is the basis for the modularisation approach. The approach itself is presented in Sect. 3 along with a formal definition on a basic program structure and specification. The approach is embedded into a new verification algorithm which we present in Sect. 4. The evaluation on the PPU and its results are discussed in Sect. 5.

2   Foundations

2.1   Regression Verification

Throughout their lifetime, systems have to adapt to new situations (bug fixes, hardware replacements, new function requirements, etc.) and many system changes will also incorporate changes in the software. Each software modification potentially introduces incorrect behaviour as a side-effect. To avoid the effect, *regression tests* are widely used in the industry as they yield good results and can easily be extended to new functionality of the software. However, software testing cannot guarantee correct behaviour since there will always be scenarios which are not covered by the test suite. Functional verification can help overcoming this problem: A formal specification describes the expected behaviour of the software and a verification system analyses whether the specification holds in all possible scenarios. But, the specification must be user-provided and is, in most cases, not trivial to find, especially when developers are less experienced with formal specification. For the verification in an evolutionary environment, two specifications are required: one for the existing software revision, and one for the new revision.

In regression verification, instead of using two specifications for two revisions, both revisions are compared directly to each other, and the old software revision serves as a functional specification for the new one. However, the old revision can only *partially* specify the new one since only those scenarios (input sequences) where the behaviour should not change can be checked for equivalence. The input sequences, for which the behaviour has been intentionally changed, need to be verified separately using functional verification or testing. Regression verification does not necessarily imply the software behaves correctly for all inputs, it rather says that the software has the same behaviour as the previous revision – including all potentially undiscovered errors. The confidence and trust gained by experience in the earlier revision is thus transferred to the new revision, as has been elaborated in [4].

2.2   Programmable Logic Controllers

The techniques in this paper are applicable to all kinds of reactive software systems. However, we put a special focus on Programmable Logic Controllers (PLC) as an example application area for the approach.

PLCs are computing units which are used to drive and control automated production systems. They are thus reactive real-time systems, and are usually in operation for a long time. In a PLC, the code is repeatedly executed once every few milliseconds. The constant time between two runs is called the *cycle time*.[1]

A family of programming languages for PLCs has been defined in the standard IEC 61131-3 [8]. While the languages are Turing-complete, PLC programs hardly ever contain general while-loops. If they contain loops, they have a known fixed upper bound on the number of iterations since PLC code has to meet strict real-time conditions. Dynamic memory allocation is not possible in the programming languages which makes them more predictable. This makes the state space for the software bounded, and the correctness problem theoretically decidable.

IEC 61131-3 has a concept of *modules* for structuring programs, similar to those used in common imperative programming languages. They allow one to encapsulate functionality into so-called *function blocks*. A function block consists of a variable signature (input, state and output variables) and an operation defined on this signature. It can be instantiated multiple times in other function blocks, and the invocation of an operation evaluates against the state of a particular instance.

In each execution cycle, the PLC obtains the current sensor values, executes the program, and emits newly computed actuator commands. Thus a PLC program is in continuous interaction with its environment. Besides the sensor and actuator values, PLC programs maintain an internal state. To work with deterministic and causal PLC programs formally, we hence model a PLC software as a function $P : I \times \Sigma \to O \times \Sigma$ which takes sensor readings (a value in I) and its current state from Σ and produces actuator values (in O) and the modified state. We lift P to $\overline{P} : I^* \to O^*$ with $\overline{P}(i_0, \ldots, i_n) = (o_0, \ldots, o_n)$, which takes a sequence of input values and returns the sequence of output values. $\overline{P}$ captures the iterated sequential execution of the effects of P. Formally, $\overline{P}$ is defined by the execution of $P(i_k, \sigma_k) = (o_k, \sigma_{k+1})$ for $0 \leq k \leq n$, and a sequence of memory states $(\sigma_0, \ldots, \sigma_n) \in \Sigma^*$ with a fixed initial memory state σ_0.

2.3   Formal Equivalence Relations

We briefly repeat the regression verification notions from [1], as these notion form the base of the modularisation our approach.

When we consider regression verification formally, we need to set two program behaviours into relation. The first notion that comes to mind is *perfect equivalence*, which requires that the behaviours of two PLCs programs P and Q are identical, i.e., that they produce the same output when presented with the same input trace. Formally, this means that they – interpreted as the two functions $\overline{P}$ and $\overline{Q}$ – are equal:

$$\text{for all } \bar{i}, \bar{i}' \in I^* : \ i = i' \implies \overline{P}(\bar{i}) = \overline{Q}(\bar{i}') \ . \tag{1}$$

However, they may very well differ on the chain of memory states reached in their traces, i.e., P and Q need not be identical. Perfect equivalence is a very strict

---

[1] There are also different execution modes for PLCs (event-driven, continuous, ...) that we do not consider here.

notion for evolution scenarios, as it does not allow any behavioural difference between the old and new revision. Still it is useful to prove that a *software refactoring* maintains the system behaviour.

In many evolution cases, behavioural differences must be taken into consideration to capture intended changes, like bug fixes or performance optimisations. The differences can be handled with the more flexible notions of *conditional and relational equivalence*. They extend perfect equivalence in two ways: Firstly, conditional equivalence allows us to filter scenarios that should not be included in the equivalence analysis using a predicate τ on the input values. Secondly, in relational equivalence one can replace the equalities in (1) by different relations that express the equivalence between input ($\approx_{in}$) and output ($\approx_{out}$) values:

$$\text{for all } \bar{i}, \bar{i}' \in I^* : \ \tau(\bar{i}, \bar{i}') \wedge \bar{i} \approx_{in} \bar{i}' \implies \overline{P}(\bar{i}) \approx_{out} \overline{Q}(\bar{i}') \ . \tag{2}$$

The triple $C = (\tau, \approx_{in}, \approx_{out})$ that parameterises (2) is called a *semantical regression verification contract* for P and Q. Perfect equivalence EQ is a special case of a regression verification contract with $EQ = (true, =, =)$. This generalises the ideas of design-by-contract [10] for single program properties to multi-program analyses. The condition (2), which we denote as $RV(C, P, Q)$, defines when the contract C is satisfied by the programs P and Q.

3   Modularisation

Modularisation is a technique to split up the program code into individual separate modules with defined interfaces. The effects of a module are limited to a specific scope, allowing a separate analysis. Wherever one module calls another module, the effects of the call can be abstracted rather than to include the full module implementation. Thus the complexity introduced by the control flow and internal state of the submodule are invisible in the caller module.

We present a decomposition rule which allows us to exploit the modularisation of reactive software to break down the regression proof obligation $RV(C, P, Q)$ into simpler proof obligations.

3.1   Motivational Example

Consider the plant in Fig. 1a representing an assembly line with a conveyor belt B and two processing stations s_1 and s_2 (e.g., a drill and a stamp). A detector d at the beginning of the conveyor belt recognises the arrival of a work piece W. Once a work piece has arrived, the automatic process starts, and W is moved from left to right, passing both processing stations, and eventually falling into the basket at the end of the belt.

In the original software revision, every work piece is unconditionally processed by both processing stations. While a piece is being processed, the conveyor belt halts for a defined amount of time. Let us assume that experience has shown that the process at s_1 may occasionally fail. The software has hereupon been

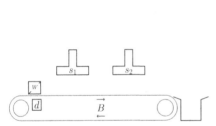

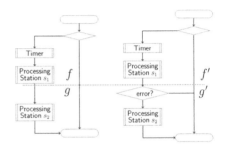

(a) Schematic of the plant consisting of a conveyor belt B with two processing stations s_1 and s_2.

(b) Sketch of the program flow: the original revision on the left and the adapted revision on the right.

Fig. 1. Motivating example

adapted, and, after the revision, the plant can recognise work pieces for which s_1 has failed. If a faulty work piece leaves s_1, the second processing station should be skipped and the piece should be sent to the output basket directly.

Software Structure. Figure 1b shows a sketch of the program flow of the main program for both revisions. The difference is that a branching statement has been introduced after s_1. The modules "Timer" and the code for the processing stations remain unchanged.

Regression Verification and Modularisation. Obviously, both software revisions behave differently when a faulty work piece occurs. To apply regression verification, a regression verification contract is required that specifies when both revisions should behave equally. In this example, the two revisions behave equally if no faulty work piece occurs. The contract for this example would therefore encode in the filter predicate that no faulty work piece is ever detected.

The non-modular approach for regression verification in [1] does not exploit the fact that the subroutines for controlling the hardware components remain unchanged. The full code of both programs is encoded for the translation against the regression contract with a model checker. The evaluation [1] (revisited in Sect. 5) shows that some evolution scenarios cannot be solved in a reasonable amount of time.

With the approach that we introduce here, we are able to replace the implementation of the modules in the encoding by their contracts, and can hence lower the verification effort by this abstraction which can thus become an enabler for the regression verification for larger programs.

This abstraction does not come for free. For a successful abstraction, sufficiently strong contracts that imply the necessary properties must be found. Finding them automatically may be as difficult as the whole program analysis itself. In the presented approach the user has to come up with suitable contracts.

3.2 Formalisation

The goal of this section is to look at composed programs and to introduce an inference rule that allows one to modularise regression verification proofs for such programs. Let therefore the two programs P, Q be implemented as a composition of two subprograms, say $P = f; g$ and $Q = f'; g'$. We have introduced programs as functions and the semicolon operator is the forward composition of functions (i.e. $(f; g)(x) = g(f(x))$).

For the modular analysis, it must be possible to identify the similar subprograms in P and Q that then become the corresponding parts between the two revisions. In the example from Sect. 3.1, for instance, the two programs can be split into two subprograms along the dotted line.

If one pair of corresponding subprograms can be verified in isolation (in this example g and g') for a contract C_g, this result can be used for the verification of the relation of the remainder programs where g and g' can be abstracted by (uninterpreted) placeholder function symbols x and x' which stand in for the programs g and g'. As a precondition in this proof obligation, we may assume the regression verification contract C_g for x, x' without knowing the exact functionality of g and g'.

The inference rule for the verification of $RV(C, \ f; g, \ f'; g')$ for a regression verification contract C has two premises which encode (1) that C_g is a valid regression verification contract for g and g' and (2) that the two programs satisfy contract C under the modular assumption that g and g' satisfy C_g.

$$\frac{RV(C_g, g, g') \qquad \forall x, x'. \ RV(C_g, x, x') \rightarrow RV(C, \ f; x, \ f'; x')}{RV(C, \ f; g, \ f'; g')} \tag{3}$$

3.3 Modularisation for Conditional and Relational Equivalence

In this section we present how the modularisation rule (3), formulated over functions, can be concretely used for the regression verification of programs. We start with the definition of a very general concept of a reactive programming language with frame structures, then introduce the decomposition rule, and close this section with remarks on properties of the rule.

Programs. We consider simple loop-free programs, containing assignment- and if-statements. Additionally, we introduce a **frame**-construct for marking program parts which should be modularised. Programs are constructed by the grammar

$$\langle Prg \rangle \rightarrow \langle name \rangle := \langle expr \rangle \mid \langle Prg \rangle \ ; \ \langle Prg \rangle$$
$$\mid \texttt{if} \ (\langle expr \rangle) \ \{ \ \langle Prg \rangle \ \} \mid \texttt{frame}(\langle name \rangle) \ \{ \ \langle Prg \rangle \ \} \tag{4}$$

in which the $\langle name \rangle$ denotes identifiers and $\langle expr \rangle$ side-effect-free expressions.

The set for programs produced by *Prg* is rather abstract and limited. However, it is expressive enough to encode reactive programs without (unbounded) loops. Programs in the low-level language (4) can, e.g., be constructed from more complex program languages like STRUCTURED TEXT or C by unwinding (bounded) loops and arrays, unfolding record data types and inlining procedure calls.

Frames and the Scope of Variables. Frames structure the otherwise unstructured programs into modules. During the translation from input programs into the low-level language (4), structuring elements from the source language, like function-blocks or method invocations, are translated into frames. Frames can also be manually added by a user – to be able to handle complex code refactorings which took place across the boundaries of the structural elements in the source code, e.g., when a computation from inside a method is pulled out to the method caller.

For a sound abstraction and modularisation, the scopes of variables must be restricted, and the `frame` constructs mark these scopes. With every frame identifier N we associate three disjoint sets of variables: input (in_N), state $(state_N)$ and output (out_N) variables. Every variable v occurring inside a frame named N must belong to one of them. The variables in these categories are constrained as follows: Input variables are only read within the frame, but may be written from outside the frame. For state variables read and written access inside the frame is allowed, but any access outside the frame is forbidden. Output variables are write-only within the frame, and read-only outside the frame. Global variables do not fit into this scheme, but can be encoded into it by an automatic program transformation.[2] Therefore, such a variable categorisation can always be established.

In a modularisation step, frames will be replaced by an abstraction using their contracts. The variables play an important role then: They manifest the interface at which the frame is abstracted for modular treatment. The input variables must adhere to a precondition on entry of the frame, the state variables can be removed from the program when the frame is abstracted, and the output variables assume values which adhere to a postcondition for the frame.

It is important to note that frame identifiers can occur on several frames within the same program. This models the case that multiple operations are invoked on the same module within a program. This happens, e.g., if the same function-block is invoked twice in an IEC-61131 context, or if a (stateful) procedure is called multiple times from the original program.

Frames that modify the same variables must have the same identifier, and all frames with the same identifier must have the same code and the same variable signature. This is not a restriction: If different functionalities access the same variables (e.g., different methods of an object in an object-oriented setting), programs can be refactored such that all frames contain the same integrated code that implements all functionalities. An additional parameter together with a case distinction is used to decide the concrete functionality in each frame.

Specification and Verification. For both modular functional and modular regression verification, one needs contracts for the abstraction. In Sect. 2.3 we have

---

[2] The program transformation introduces a new input and output variable for each global variable, which occurs in the frame. The global variable is assigned to the input variable at the beginning of the frame. The effect of the frame on a global variable is captured in the output variable, which is assigned to global variable after the frame.

already encountered the concept of regression verification contracts on the semantic level. We will refine this notion now to program entities. Let two loop-free programs P and Q be given. A *regression verification contract* is a triple (ϕ, α, ω) of three formulas: the functional precondition ϕ, the relational precondition α and the relational postcondition ω. The semantics of these regression verification contracts are semantical contracts (Sect. 2.3). The formula ϕ evaluates to the filter predicate τ, and the interpretation of α and ω are the input and output equivalence relations.

The programs P and Q operate on disjoint sets of variables such that their statements programs cannot interfere with each other's state spaces, and are only connected in formulas within contracts. We can therefore use the sequential composition $P \,;Q$ to obtain the effects of their independent executions. The proof obligation which needs to be verified reads – written as a Hoare triple [7] –

$$\{\phi \wedge \alpha\}\ P \,;Q\ \{\omega\}\ . \tag{5}$$

In Sect. 4 we will describe efficient techniques to encode such proof obligations for decision procedures.

Modularisation Rule. Let in the scenario introduced above, f and g be frame identifiers such that a frame for f occurs in P and a frame for g occurs in Q. For modular treatment, we need to look at the programs that abstract from the code of inner frames within their enclosing programs (as a parallel to the replacement of x for g in (2)):

Definition 1 (Factor program). *Let P be a program according to (4) and f be an identifier. The frames for f in P all have a unique occurrence number i. The factor program $P\big/f$ is then derived from P by replacing each frame i for identifier f with the following sequence of statements:*

1. $\mathtt{in}_i := \mathtt{in}$ *for every input variable* $\mathtt{in}$
2. $\mathtt{count}_f := \mathtt{count}_f + 1$
3. $\mathtt{out} := \mathtt{out}_i$ *for every output variable* $\mathtt{out}$

The freshly introduced variable $\mathtt{count}_f$ for the factored frame f is used to keep book about the number of invocations of f during a run of the program, and is needed to make the upcoming modularisation rule sound.

In non-regression program verification, modularised subprograms are often replaced by an obligation to show the precondition of the block and an assumption of the postcondition afterwards. Since in regression verification, we deal with two programs at a time, all we can do in the local context is to *remember* the values of all invocations for a global, program-spanning argument to take them into account. The following inference rule does precisely that. Instead of proving (5), one can show the two formulas that together imply it: (a) f and g together satisfy a regression verification contract $(\phi^{fg}, \alpha^{fg}, \omega^{fg})$, and (b) the factored programs satisfy the original regression contract. The intermediate variables in_i

and out_i introduced by the factor program allow us to specialise a formula and set it into the context of one concrete call-site of the frame identifier. For a formula γ over the variables of P and Q, the instantiated formula $[\gamma]_{i,j}$ denotes the formula in which all occurring variables from P have been replaced by the counterpart of the i-th invocation and all variables in Q with the variables of the j-th invocation. For perfect equivalence $\varepsilon = (in^f = in^g \rightarrow out^f = out^g)$, the instantiated formula $[\varepsilon]_{1,2}$ would read $in_1^f = in_2^g \rightarrow out_1^f = out_2^g$.

Definition 2 (Modular regression verification). *For two programs P and Q (with disjoint variables) and frame identifiers f and g, let π_f and π_g denote the programs which are inside the corresponding frames f and g and let n (m) be the number of occurrences of f (g) in P (Q). For a regression verification contract $(\phi^{fg}, \alpha^{fg}, \omega^{fg})$ for π_f and π_g the inference rule*

$$\frac{\{\phi^{fg} \wedge \alpha^{fg}\} \; \pi_f \, ; \pi_g \; \{\omega^{fg}\} \qquad \{\phi \wedge \alpha \wedge \kappa \wedge \Gamma\} \; {P}/{f} \, ; {Q}/{g} \; \{\omega \wedge \kappa\}}{\{\phi \wedge \alpha\} \; P \, ; Q \; \{\omega\}}$$

with $\Gamma = \bigwedge_{i=1}^{n} \bigwedge_{j=1}^{m} \left[\phi^{fg} \wedge \kappa \wedge \alpha^{fg} \rightarrow \omega^{fg} \right]_{i,j}$ and $\kappa = (\text{count}_f = \text{count}_g)$ is called the modularity rule.

The assumption Γ of the second premise couples the variables modelling the invocations of f and g. Whenever the input values for invocation occurrences i and j satisfy the precondition $\left[\phi^{fg} \wedge \alpha^{fg}\right]_{i,j}$ of the regression verification contract, the relational postcondition $\left[\omega^{fg}\right]_{i,j}$ is known to hold on the output values.

This rule is quite similar to the differential assertion checking approach using mutual function summaries by Lahiri et al. [9], but is applied here to frames with potentially more than one invocation and in the context of reactive systems in which the programs are called repeatedly. To allow for that, additional checks (encoded using the counting variables count_f and count_g in κ) have to be included that ensure that the number of invocations of the two abstracted frames is the same in both programs.

Properties. This modularisation rule is sound. Although we do not elaborate on this here, an induction proof on the number of coupled invocations (captured in the program variables count_f and count_g introduced for this reason) can be conducted. The approach is not complete since we require that both systems invoke their frames equally often. There are systems which fulfil a regression contract, but do not have this property. Then this approach can currently not be applied. The rule is compositional, in the sense that it can applied recursively on the resulting proof obligations.

4   An Algorithm for Modular Regression Verification

In this section we construct a new regression verification algorithm for reactive software that combines a number of different modular and non-modular verification techniques. The algorithm takes two programs and a regression verification

---

function $Reve(f, f')$:
   Input: Two frames f, f'
   Data: A regression verification contract (ϕ, α, ω) for f and f'.
   Output: true iff f and f' together satisfy the contract
   if *check cache for* $(f, f', \phi, \alpha, \omega)$ **then**
      // earlier results are cached
      return cached result;
   end
   if $(\phi, \alpha, \omega) = (true, =, =)$ **then**
      // only applicable for perfect equivalence
      return if true $EqualSource(f, f')$;
      return if true $EqualSE(f, f')$;
   end
   return if true $EqualSmt(f, f', \phi, \alpha, \omega)$;
   return if true $EqualAbstraction(f, f', \phi, \alpha, \omega)$;
   return $EqualityMC(f, f', \phi, \alpha, \omega)$;

Algorithm 1: Algorithm to check the equivalence of two frames

---

contract as input and checks if the programs satisfy the relational specification. We assume both programs have a top-level frame with the identifier `main` that contains all program statements. The algorithm works recursively – comparing first the outermost frames, trying to establish equality from going top to bottom in the program structures, recursively verifying the equality of enclosed subframes.

The algorithm orchestrates several different checkers and runs them in sequence returning on the first positive result. In the orchestration, we call the more syntactical, faster, but imprecise checkers first before falling back to more powerful, and more precise, but slower checkers. All checkers are sound: If they report that frames conform to their contract, then this is the case. They are not necessarily complete, and some checkers are only applicable on a restricted set of cases, for example perfect equivalence. The full algorithm – shown in Algorithm 1 – *is* complete as the last checker *EqualityMC* uses heavyweight model checking without abstractions and is complete.

The following sections briefly introduce the involved checkers.

4.1   Conformance by Syntactical Congruence

In case a contract specifies perfect equivalence, the checker *EqualSource* checks equivalence via a comparison of the syntax trees of the two source code artefacts. Prior to the comparison, we normalise the code (remove comments, unify capitalisation, . . .). Identical normalised source code implies equal software behaviour. Despite its severe restrictions, this method is a fast and useful checker, especially for frames resulting from often reused standard library procedures.

4.2   Conformance by Symbolic Execution

Checking equality by comparing the source code is very restricted, and fails, e.g., if two independent lines are swapped, or an irrelevant new variable is introduced. The next checker in the orchestration is *EqualSE*, which can handle such cases. It is still a syntactical checker; hence, it is also only able to handle perfect equivalence. This checker is based on symbolic execution to compute the symbolic results of a frame.

The result of the symbolic execution of a frame f is a function $F: Var \rightarrow Expr$ which maps every state and output variable to an expression which is the aggregation of all assignments to the variable in f. The term $F(v)$ computes to the value of v at the end of the frame and may depend on the input and state variables of f.

One possibility to show perfect equivalence between two frames f and f' is to establish syntactical equality between the symbolic execution results for all output variables. The equality must also be checked for those state variables which occur in the aggregated expressions of output variables to guarantee that the following cycles will produce equal output.

Thus far, we described the case where all input, output and state variables have the same name in both frames. To make this analysis more flexible, we allow arbitrary one-to-one mappings of variables between frames where the correspondence of input and output variables is given by a conjunction of equalities between variables in α and ω in the regression verification contract. For state variables, the mapping can be inferred. Furthermore, the mapping can be lifted from equalities over variables to equalities over expressions. The equality between output expressions given in the relational post-condition ω can be checked modulo the equalities in the relational precondition α.

The checker *EqualSE* is able to show the equality of $o = 2 * i + s$ and $o' = 2 * i' + t'$, where s, t' are state and i, i' are input variable. A matching needs to include the equality $s = t'$, and $i = i'$. Moreover, the equality of $i = i'$ (input variables) must be justified by the given regression contract ($\alpha \models i = i'$).

Due to its syntactical nature, this checker is incomplete, e.g., the equality between $o = 1 + 1$ vs. $o' = 2$, cannot be handled.

4.3   Conformance by Reduction to SMT

If these last syntactical checkers fail or are not applicable, the first semantical checker is triggered. This checker is backed up by a reduction to a Satisfiability Modulo Theories (SMT) problem using the previously computed symbolic execution results $F(v)$ and $F'(v')$ of the given frames. This checker is not limited to perfect equivalence, but can be used for arbitrary regression verification contracts.

The checker *EqualSMT* verifies an inductive relational invariant χ over the state variables of the two frames. In the simplest form we show that any state variables s and s' in f and f' evolve identically (i.e. $s = s'$). The formula to be checked for satisfiability is then

$$\left(\bigwedge_{v \in V} v^+ = F(v)\right) \wedge \left(\bigwedge_{v \in V'} v^+ = F'(v)\right) \wedge \phi \wedge \alpha \wedge \chi \wedge \neg(\omega^+ \wedge \chi^+) \quad (6)$$

where the sets of variables V and V' contain all output and state variables of f and f'. Variable v^+ holds the result of the symbolic execution for v (via the function F or F'). It differs from v to distinguish variables before the execution from after it. A predicate χ^+ results from χ by replacing v with v^+. If this formula is not satisfiable, χ is an invariant for the frames and, additionally, they conform to the regression verification contract (ϕ, α, ω).

As an example, consider the following contract $(true, i = i', o = o')$ for $o = 2 * i + s$ and $o' = t' + 2 * i'$. The instantiated SMT formula (6) for this example is

$$\underbrace{(o^+ = 2 * i + s \wedge s = s^+)}_{v^+ = F(v)} \wedge \underbrace{(o'^+ = t' + 2 * i' \wedge t' = t'^+)}_{v'^+ = F'(v)}$$
$$\wedge \underbrace{i = i'}_{\alpha} \wedge \underbrace{s = t'}_{\phi} \wedge \underbrace{o = o'}_{\omega} \wedge \neg (\underbrace{o^+ = o'^+}_{\omega^+} \wedge \underbrace{s = t'}_{\chi^+}) ,$$

where o and o' are the output variables, s and t' state variables, and i and i' input variables, respectively. The relational invariant χ has been chosen as $s = t'$ in the example. It is a parameter of the checker, and in general non-trivial to infer. In our implementation we use the equality of equally named state variables for χ. In a further SMT verification condition (not shown here), it has to be shown that the initial memory states (cf. Section 2.2) of f and f' initially satisfy the coupling invariant χ.

4.4   Conformance by Modular Abstraction

The checker *EqualAbstraction* is the checker that exploits the modularisation rule introduced in Definition 2. Therefore, given two frames f, f', this checker starts with abstracting the top-level frames inside f and f', and uses Algorithm 1 for checking contract conformance of inner subframe pairs.

We assume that the subframes in f and f' are collected in pairs and that each frame pair is specified with a regression verification contract. Let g be a subframe in f, and g' in f', respectively. After the body of all subframes have been abstracted, we obtain the two factor programs f/g and f'/g' of both original frames together with a regression verification contract that has additional assumptions and postconditions. The regression verification algorithm is called recursively for $Reve(g, g')$ of each subframe pair and for $Reve(f/g, f'/g')$.

The modularisation rule may be applicable to several different subframes. In our implementation we eagerly apply it to all possible subframe combinations. The recursive procedure is applied recursively and exhaustively, but will eventually terminate since the frames are always finitely nested in a program.

If the modular abstraction step fails, it produces a counterexample (a finite trace, see Sect. 4.5) which may describe a genuine flaw in the system or it may be spurious if a regression verification contract does not hold or is not strong enough to serve as a suitable abstraction in the proof.

4.5 Conformance by Model Checking

The final checker is the most precise and most powerful one and encodes the verification condition into a model checking problem. This checker makes use of the non-modular regression verification approach by Beckert et al. [1] and verifies a regression verification contract specification between two complete frames f, f' without using abstraction. More precisely, the target is a problem in which an invariant (derived from the regression verification contract) for the system consisting of the two compared frames must be verified. Experience has shown that invariant-inferring techniques like the IC3 [2] approach (in particular the implementation within the model checker nuXmv [3]) work quite well for this type of regression verification problems.

Since the state space is finite, this checker is theoretically complete, i.e., returns within finite time for any input. However, experience shows that it can take hours or even days until the model checker comes back with a result. The modularisation technique and the combination with simpler techniques in *Reve* have been devised to reduce the time needed for regression verification challenges.

The model checker returns either that the inductive invariant has been proved (implying correctness of the contract), or it produces a counterexample, which is a concrete trace, i.e., finite sequence of assignments of input, state and output variables for both frames exemplifying the violation of the contract. We currently do not provide tool support, but these values can be used as inputs for a simulation of the reactive system like it is present in many modern IDEs for reactive software.

5 Evaluation

In this section, we show the applicability of our new regression verification algorithm on selected scenarios of the Pick-and-Place Unit (PPU) community demonstrator [1,12]. The PPU is a down-scaled model of a manufacturing plant employing industry-level hardware components that has been designed for researching

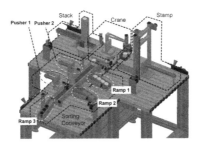

Fig. 2. Community demonstrator: the Pick-and-Place Unit

the management of the evolution (hardware and software) of automated manufacturing systems. Therefore, there are multiple evolution scenarios – with software and/or hardware changes – of this plant. We selected representative evolution scenarios to cover different situations.

Figure 2 gives an impression of the PPU in a medium expansion stage, as hardware configuration depends on the scenarios. Briefly described, the PPU consists of a magazine for providing new work pieces, a stamp for imprinting, a conveyor belt for sorting, and a crane for transportation of work pieces. All of these components and their actuators are controlled by the software in a PLC written in Structured Text (ST) and Sequential Function Chart (SFC), which we translated into ST code automatically (cf. [8]).

5.1   Selected Evolution Scenarios

We briefly explain the three selected evolution scenarios. The software revisions correspond to the different scenarios of the PPU in [12, Fig. 48].

Revision 1 vs. Revision 2. A new sensor is introduced for detecting metallic work pieces as a preparation for the next evolution. The software mainly changes the Crane module, but changes on the top-level module are needed to route the sensors to this submodule. An influence to the system behaviour is not expected: Both revisions are perfectly equivalent.

Revision 3 vs. Revision 5. Revision 5 introduces an optimisation which allows using the waiting time during stamping to transport work pieces which do not need to be stamped to the conveyor belt. The optimisation is only triggered if work pieces of different types are present (metallic and non-metallic). If only metallic work pieces are present, the two revisions behave perfectly equivalently. The work piece type can be determined by the program using the input variable *CapacitiveSensor*. We obtain a regression contract ($CapacitiveSensor = true, =, =$) which intuitively formalises that the old and new revisions behave equivalently (equal inputs give equal outputs) under the condition that the sensor variable *CapacitiveSensor* is *true* in every cycle.

Revision 12 vs. Revision 13 In the old revision, the position of the crane is measured with three switches (with Boolean sensor values *OnConveyor*, *OnMagazin* and *OnStamp*). These are replaced by a single angular sensor. We need to define a relation R between the three boolean sensor values and the angle position

$$(16160 < AnalogPosition \land AnalogPosition < 16260) = OnConveyor \land$$
$$(24290 < AnalogPosition \land AnalogPosition < 24390) = OnMagazin \land$$
$$(8160 < AnalogPosition \land AnalogPosition < 8260) = OnStamp$$

which serves the relational precondition in the regression verification contract ($true, R, =$).

Table 1. Results

| Rev./Module | Runtime | | | | | | | Code size | |
| | Non-Mod | Modular | Checkers [ms] | | | | | | |
	Total [s]	Total [s]	Src	SE	SMT	Modul	Classic	LoC	#Vars
1 vs. 2	8.96	1.51						744	136
Main			0	48	65	545	–	744	136
– Main/*			0	10	0	–	–	174	203
Crane			0	21	35	441	–	415	51
– Crane/*			0	19	28	–	386	403	207
Magazine			0	13	–	–	–	234	38
3 vs. 5	750.0	7.05						1,605	256
Main			–	–	90	5,213	–	1,605	256
– Main/*			–	–	43	–	2,846	294	364
Crane			–	–	101	2,130	–	810	74
– Crane/*			–	–	101	–	1,987	768	376
Stamp			0	–	–	–	–	402	56
Magazine			0	–	–	–	–	240	44
12 vs. 13 −SE	t/o	34.76						4,808	520
Main			0	–	512	24,544	–	4,808	520
– Main/*			0	–	79	–	6,727	453	1,250
Conveyor			0	–	–	–	–	468	50
Crane			0	–	227	14,408	–	1,326	77
– Crane/*			0	–	238	–	14,168	1,284	631
Pusher			3	–	–	–	–	2,144	154
Stamp			0	–	78	4,801	–	403	57
Stamp/*			0	–	–	–	4,680	375	639
Magazine			0	–	61	–	2,795	241	45
12 vs. 13 +SE	t/o	34.76						4,808	520
Main			0	440	–	-	–	4,808	520

5.2 Results

Table 1 summarises the performance of the verification. The runtimes are shown for each checker on a frame. The first column describes the compared revisions and modules, where *Main* or *Crane* denotes the regression verification between the corresponding frames of both revisions. *Main/*∗ denotes the frame with all subframes factored out. For convenience, Table 1 only shows the first and second level of nested frames. In particular, the frequently used timer module is hidden.

"Non-Modular Total" is the comparison reference value of applying the non-modular approach as in [1] with our pipeline. In comparison, "Modular Total" gives the overall runtime of the modular pipeline. Both total columns state the runtime measured from the command line. Hence they include the work needed to prepare the programs (parsing, symbolic execution, etc.). In contrast, the checker runtimes are given in milliseconds and are measured internally. A checker is skipped (marked with a dash (–) in the table) if either it was not capable of proving the regression contract, or a checker invoked earlier was able to solve this case. Note, for the comparison of Rev 12. vs. Rev 13 ("12 vs.13 −SE"), we have disabled *EqualSE* to evaluate the modularisation rule, because we want to demonstrate the capabilities of the decomposition rule. *EqualSE* can solve this comparison directly in half a second (cf. "12 vs.13 +SE" in Table 1). The lines of code do not include empty lines or comments and cover both code modules. Also the number of variables (#Vars) give the sum of input, state and output variables of both frames.

The runtimes (wall clock) are the median of three samples, computed on an Intel Core i7-8565U, 16 GB RAM, using the model checker nuXmv 1.1.1 [3] with IC3 for invariant checking, and z3 4.8.8 for solving the SMT instances. The time-out was set to 1 hour. Our algorithm implementation is single-threaded. All of the verification artefacts and a link to the source code are available online[3].

5.3   Discussion

The evaluation shows a huge speed-up against the previous non-modular app-roach from [1]. It shows the potential of modularisation to enable the handling of large reactive systems. For fair comparison, we repeated the experiments of [1], but we use the default bit-width for integers on PLC languages, and also we did not reduce the blocking time of the used timers. Rev. 12 against Rev. 13 ran into a time-out, [1] gives a clue that the verification can take more than 22 hours. Most of the performance should result from abstracting these timer, which are used to wait a particular amount of time. During this time span, the system stutters partially, resulting in long phases of forward searches in IC3.

6   Related Work

Beckert et al. [1] applies regression verification to PLC software and is the first base for this work. Subroutines in PLC software is handled by inlining the sub-routines in its caller context. We reuse their notion of regression verification (Sect. 2.3). Also we use their pipeline to simplify PLC programs and prepare them for model checker.

Modularisation for regression verification is covered in [5] which serves as a second basis to our work. Godlin and Strichman [5], who also coined the term "regression verification" exploit both regression verification and decomposition to prove equivalence between similar programs. They are able to handle programs with recursive function calls and unbounded loops, both are paradigms are not common in software for reactive systems. Nevertheless, their work does not cover

---

[3] http://formal.iti.kit.edu/isola20.

our topic completely: They only consider functions that do not have an internal state and require them to be perfectly equivalent. Moreover, the decomposition in [5] works bottom-up if possible. Our approach work from top to bottom.

The work on differential assertion checking [9] modularises relational proofs in a similar fashion to the one presented in this paper. They employ *mutual function summaries* to abstract two related functions blocks, which is essentially the same concept as our regression verification contracts. They do not target reactive systems but individual single function invocations, and use the intermediate verification language Boogie to encode their conditions rather than a model checking verification backend.

The goal of Guthmann et al. [6] is similar to ours: Modularising the equivalence proof. For matched procedures two partial sets are computed. One contains input states where the procedures behave equivalent and one where they differ. Both sets are approximated. The approximation are made stronger the longer the algorithm runs. They extended their approach work with demand-based refinement of the approximated sets in [11].

7   Conclusion

In this paper, we have motivated and presented a new verification rule for the modular decomposition of regression verification proof obligations for reactive system software. Moreover, we have integrated the rule into a novel regression verification algorithm which orchestrates five different regression verification approaches into one proof technique. Thanks to the modularisation, simpler equality checkers allow one to show properties more easily on subproblems.

The evaluation indicates a tremendous performance improvement: Modularisation can allow regression verification proofs to run orders of magnitudes faster.

Future Work. A drawback of the decomposition technique is the need for (user-specified) regression contracts. In most cases, these specification seem to be automatically inferable, e.g., by using heuristics, symbolic execution or Horn solvers. In our implementation, we have not used any sophisticated strategy to decide whether a frame should rather be kept inlined or be abstracted. The implementation tries to abstract all allowed frames at once, which seems to be a good strategy. A more restrictive selection could bring further advantage.

References

1. Beckert, B., Ulbrich, M., Vogel-Heuser, B., Weigl, A.: Regression verification for programmable logic controller software. In: Butler, M., Conchon, S., Zaïdi, F. (eds.) ICFEM 2015. LNCS, vol. 9407, pp. 234–251. Springer, Cham (2015). https://doi.org/10.1007/978-3-319-25423-4_15
2. Bradley, A.R.: SAT-based model checking without unrolling. In: Jhala, R., Schmidt, D. (eds.) VMCAI 2011. LNCS, vol. 6538, pp. 70–87. Springer, Heidelberg (2011). https://doi.org/10.1007/978-3-642-18275-4_7

3. Cavada, R., et al.: The NUXMV symbolic model checker. In: Biere, A., Bloem, R. (eds.) CAV 2014. LNCS, vol. 8559, pp. 334–342. Springer, Cham (2014). https://doi.org/10.1007/978-3-319-08867-9_22

4. Cha, S., Ulbrich, M., Weigl, A., Beckert, B., Land, K., Vogel-Heuser, B.: On the preservation of the trust by regression verification of PLC software for cyber-physical systems of systems. In: INDIN 2019, pp. 413–418. IEEE (2019). https://doi.org/10.1109/INDIN41052.2019.8972210

5. Godlin, B., Strichman, O.: Regression verification: proving the equivalence of similar programs. Softw. Test. Verification Reliab. **23**(3), 241–258 (2013)

6. Guthmann, O., Strichman, O., Trostanetski, A.: Minimal unsatisfiable core extraction for SMT. In: Piskac, R., Talupur, M. (eds.) FMCAD 2016, pp. 57–64. IEEE (2016). https://doi.org/10.1109/FMCAD.2016.7886661

7. Hoare, C.A.R.: An axiomatic basis for computer programming. Commun. ACM **12**(10), 576–580 (1969). https://doi.org/10.1145/363235.363259

8. International Electrotechnical Commission: IEC 61131: Programmable controllers - Part 3: Programming languages, February 2002

9. Lahiri, S.K., McMillan, K.L., Sharma, R., Hawblitzel, C.: Differential assertion checking. In: ESEC/FSE 2013, pp. 345–355. ACM (2013). https://doi.org/10.1145/2491411.2491452

10. Meyer, B.: Applying "design by contract". IEEE Comput. **25**(10), 40–51 (1992)

11. Trostanetski, A., Grumberg, O., Kroening, D.: Modular demand-driven analysis of semantic difference for program versions. In: Ranzato, F. (ed.) SAS 2017. LNCS, vol. 10422, pp. 405–427. Springer, Cham (2017). https://doi.org/10.1007/978-3-319-66706-5_20

12. Vogel-Heuser, B., Legat, C., Folmer, J., Feldmann, S.: Researching evolution in industrial plant automation: scenarios and documentation of the pick and place unit. Tech. rep. Institute of Automation and Information Systems, Technische Universität München (2014). https://mediatum.ub.tum.de/node?id=1208973

Finding Idioms in Source Code Using Subtree Counting Techniques

Dmitry Orlov[(✉)]

National Research University "MPEI",
14, Krasnokazarmennaya str., 11250 Moscow, Russia
orlovdma1@mpei.ru

Abstract. This paper is dedicated to extracting idioms from source code written in Python language. Programming language idiom is the fragment of code which often occur in different programs. In this research and idiom is represented as the part of program abstract syntax tree (AST). For idiom extracting the subtree computing techniques are used. Idiom extracting process is similar to numeric function optimization: starting with root node, on each step we add one node to the subtree and compute subtree efficiency metric. When metric stops to grow, we consider subtree obtained the idiom. As subtree efficiency metric different functions can be used. These functions can have subtree length or subtree frequency as an arguments.

Keywords: Source code analysis · Static analysis · Programming language idioms · Frequent subtree counting · Python · Data mining

1 Introduction

Learning programming languages doesn't finish with learning syntax and semantics. Practice for typical tasks solving is also needed. Programming idioms are code fragments which occur in different software projects, and which solve one typical task. So the term "idiomatic code" is the code that is written in a manner that other experienced developers find natural [1]. Programming idioms can give us knowledge about the best practices used in programming language being studied. Nevertheless, there isn't formal definition of programming idiom. The informal definition "small fragment of code which common and informative" need to be clarified.

In this paper we propose an idiom extraction algorithm, based on subtree counting and information metrics. Though the algorithm proposed is language-independent, we apply it to the source code written in Python3 language, since Python3 has large codebase, widely used idiomatic code style (so called "pythonic" code [2]), and convenient AST tools.

© Springer Nature Switzerland AG 2020
T. Margaria and B. Steffen (Eds.): ISoLA 2020, LNCS 12477, pp. 44–54, 2020.
https://doi.org/10.1007/978-3-030-61470-6_4

2   Idiom Formalization

Consider idiom as a subtree of program abstract syntax tree (AST). In that case all idiom occurrences in code do not have to be exact code clones. In clone analysis, four clone types are considered [3]:

- type-1: syntactically identical code snippets;
- type-2: syntactically identical code snippets, except for differences in identifier names, literal values, etc.;
- type-3: syntactically similar code snippets, which have statements added, modified and/or removed with respect to each other;
- type-4: syntactically dissimilar code snippets, which implement the same functionality.

There is difference between code clone and programming idiom. To become a clone, a snippet of code should appear in the program (in sense of clone types described above) at least twice. The idiom, on the other hand, should appear more frequently and in different projects. Therefore, to distinct between code clone and programming idiom one should build idiom value metric.

Considering an idiom as a part of AST frequently occurring in code, we cover type-1, type-2, and, partially, type-3 clones. Type-4 clones analysis is out of the scope of the current research. Also in the current research the quality of code snippet is not considered. Therefore, during analysis, patterns and anti-patterns will be found.

The idiom extraction should use different technique than frequent tree counting used for clone analysis [4]. As mentioned in [1, 5], frequent subtree extraction can be used for idiom extraction, but results will have poor quality, because short subtrees will occur more frequently. So, on one hand, short subtrees don't give us additional information, on the other hand, long but rare subtrees are useless, as well. Therefore, we need metric to estimate subtree value.

Let's use information theory to build such metric. Consider the following: if an idiom in AST of the program source code is replaced by special node, then the source code compresses. Denote T – the subtree, $N(T)$ – number of T occurrences in the source code, $I(T)$ – quantity of information in T. Therefore, $N(T)I(T)$ – effective length of all idiom occurrences. Let's estimate $I(T)$. Let T_1 is T extended with one node. Then:

$$I(T_1) = I(T) - log(N(T_1)/N(T)) \tag{1}$$

Consider R is the root node of T. Define $I_1(T) = I(T) - I(R)$. If we replace all occurrences of T with special tree node V, we reduce information containing in AST at least by:

$$E(T) = N(T)(I(T) - I(V)) = N(T)(I(R) + I_1(T) - I(V))$$

Assume $I(R) = I(V)$, because number of root nodes of the idiom is the same as number of new nodes, i.e. $I(V)$. Then:

$$E(T) = N(T) I_1(T) \tag{2}$$

Let's call $E(T)$ subtree efficiency. Then T is an idiom, if and only if $E(T) \geq E(T_1)$ and $E(T_2) \geq E(T)$, where T_1 is a subtree of T, and T is a subtree of T_2. Thus, the idiom is the subtree with maximal efficiency. We omit logarithm base here, since changing it leads only to $E(T)$ scaling, and keeps subtree for which $E(T)$ maximal.

Thus we need to find all subtrees with maximal efficiency against their preceders and successors. Enumerating all subtrees has an exponential complexity, so it is important to reduce number of subtrees inspected. Let's build subtree iteratively, at each step adding one node, which leads to maximal increase of $E(T)$. We stop the process when $E(T)$ stops to grow, therefore, steepest descent method will be used. Thus we obtain local maximum of $E(T)$.

3 Data Structures for Subtree Representation

The data structure for representation of the tree is straightforward. Let

$$TreeNode = \{name, \ children\},$$

where *name* is the node name (corresponds to non-terminal symbol in programming language grammar), and *children* is an array of either *TreeNode* or *TreeLeaf*. The *TreeLeaf* structure is used for terminal symbols representation. It contains only terminal symbol name.

The data structure for tree database representation should be able to provide $N(T)$ quickly, and keep large amount of trees which can have common parts. The most convenient structure for that case is trie [6]. The trie in consideration is an oriented acyclic graph, consisting of two types of nodes: "or"-nodes and "and"-nodes. The root of the trie is the "or"-node. "Or"-nodes are used to group different subtrees. The other type of node is "and"-node. Such nodes are used to represent subtrees having common operation. On Fig. 1 the example of trie is represented. "Or"-nodes are denoted with circles, while "and"-nodes are denoted with rectangles. The example trie stores syntax trees built for the following expression set:

$$\{b * d, a + (b + c), a + d, b + (b + c)\}$$

AST of each expression has its own id. Expressions are enumerated from 0. Outputs of "or"-nodes are marked with sets of numbers, which correspond to ids of trees having the certain child node. At Fig. 1(a)–(d) the trees for the expressions are shown. At Fig. 1(e) the trie built is represented.

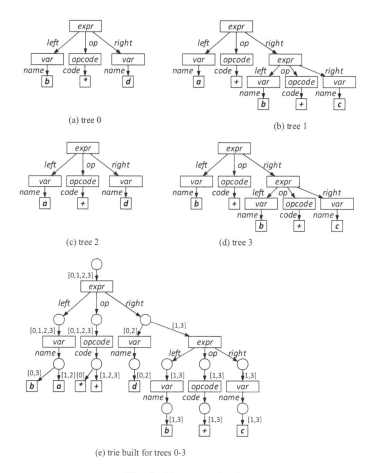

(a) tree 0

(b) tree 1

(c) tree 2

(d) tree 3

(e) trie built for trees 0-3

Fig. 1. The example trie.

When working with dataset containing lots of equal trees, it is convenient to store number of occurrences for each distinct tree added to the trie. This technique reduces sets of tree ids stored for each "or"-node. Therefore tree database can be defined as

$$B = \{root, freq\},$$

where *root* is the root of the trie and *freq* is an array which stores $N(T)$ for each tree id. Tree T receives id when it is inserted in B. Tree id grows serially with number of unique trees inserted in B.

"Or"-node of the trie is represented with

$$OrNode = \{nodes, nameToIds\},$$

where *nodes* maps node id to the next "and"-node, and *nameToIds* maps node name to the set of unique tree ids contains the node with certain name. The "and"-node structure is similar one of treeNode, but its children are "or"-nodes of the trie:

$$AndNode = \{name, \ children\},$$

Also there is special structure for terminal symbol variants representation:

$$TrieLeaf = \{valToIds, \ idToVal\},$$

where *valToIds* maps the terminal symbol value (e.g., variable name or number) to the set of unique tree ids contains the value, *idToVal*, in its turn, maps tree id to value occurs in leaf of the tree with certain id.

Let's describe the following algorithms:

- finding if the tree database contains the tree T (Contains);
- number of trees having T as a subtree, in case T contains tree root (TreeCount);
- adding tree T in tree database B (Insert).

The algorithms developed are represented at Fig. 2, Fig. 3 and Fig. 4. At these figures the set of all tree ids in database is denoted as U.

```
Algorithm Contains(T, B):
begin
      return FindIDs(T.root, B.root, U)≠ ∅
end

Algorithm FindIDs (treeNode, dbNode, foundIDs):
begin
      if isinstance(treeNode, TreeNode) and
          isinstance(dbNode, OrNode):
      begin
          ids = dbNode.nameToIds[treeNode.name]
          foundIDs = foundIDs ∩ ids
          if foundIDs == ∅
              return ∅
          nextdbNode=dbNode.nodes[treeNode.name]
          for i:=1 to len(treeNode.children):
              foundIDs=FindIDs(
                  treeNode.children[i],
                  nextdbNode.children[i],
                  foundIDs)
          return foundIDs
      end
      if isinstance(treeNode, TreeLeaf) and
          isinstance(dbNode, TrieLeaf):
      begin
          ids = dbNode.valToIds[treeNode.name]
          foundIDs = foundIDs ∩ ids
          if foundIDs == ∅
              return ∅
          return foundIDs
      end
      return ∅
end
```

Fig. 2. Algorithm Contains.

To obtain number of subtrees (containing tree root), one should sum B.freq[id], for all ids returned by FindIDs.

```
Algorithm TreeCount(T, B):
begin
    count:=0
    for id in FindIDs(T.root, B.root, U):
        count+=B.freq[id]
    return count
end
```

Fig. 3. Algorithm TreeCount.

```
Algorithm Insert(T, B):
begin
    ids= FindIDs(T.root, B.root, U)
    if ids≠∅:
    begin
        ++B.freq[inf(ids)]
        return
    end
    newId=|B.freq|
    B.freq[newId]=1
    InsertRecursive(T.root, B.root, newId)
end

Algorithm InsertRecursive(treeNode, dbNode, id):
Begin
    if isinstance(treeNode, TreeNode):
    begin
        if dbNode.nameToIds[treeNode.name] == ∅
            dbNode.addNode(treeNode)

        dbNode.nameToIds[treeNode.name] =
            dbNode.nameToIds [treeNode.name] ∪ {id}

        nextdbNode=dbNode.node[treeNode.name]
        for i:=1 to len(treeNode.children):
            InsertRecursive(
                treeNode.children[i],
                nextdbNode.children[i],
                id)
    end
    else:
        dbNode.add(id, treeNode.nodeName)
end
```

Fig. 4. Algorithm Insert.

4 Function Optimization on Subtree Space

As mentioned earlier, for finding subtree efficiency maximum, steepest descent method will be used. At each step, the node which provides maximal increase to the subtree efficiency is chosen.

For the subtree being optimized (denote is as T), we store edgeNodes – the list of "or"-nodes and trie leaves stored in B. Each node in edgeNodes can be expanded. When it is expanded: one node is added at the end of the subtree, and the "or"-node in consideration is replaced by its children. At each step, one needs to probe expansion of each node in edgeNodes and choose the node which provides maximal efficiency.

Let T_1 is the subtree obtained from T by expanding one of the edge nodes. Then $N(T)$ can be obtained as TreeCount(T, B), and $N(T_1)$ = TreeCount(T′, B), respectively. So, we have enough data to compute $E(T)$.

To get all possible idioms, we try to perform optimization process for each tree in B. Thus we obtain straightforward idiom finding algorithm (Fig. 5).

```
Algorithm FindIdioms(B):
begin
    for i in B.freq:
    begin
        edgeNodes={B.root}
        efficiency=0
        information=0
        T={}
        while true:
        begin
            expandNode={}
            potentialEfficiency=efficiency
            for node in edgeNodes:
            begin
                T'=T or node
                newInformation=information-log2(N(T')/N(T))
                newEfficiency=newInformation*N(T')
                if newEfficiency>=potentialEfficiency:
                begin
                    newEfficiency =potentialEfficiency
                    expandNode=node
                end
                if expandNode=={}
                    produceIdiom()
                else
                begin
                    edgeNodes.remove(expandNode)
                    edgeNodes.add(expandNode.children(i))
                    efficiency=potentialEfficiency
                    T'=T or expandNode
                    information-log2(N(T')/N(T))
                    T=T'
                end
            end
        end
    end
end
```

Fig. 5. Idiom finding algorithm

The algorithm represented is slow, because each idiom will be computed several times, since it is found in different trees. Reusing optimization results can speed up this algorithm. There are two ideas. First, if optimization process for tree T with id stopped at some subtree S, which occurs in trees having different ids, we can continue optimization for each tree in ids, because optimizing it from scratch will lead us to the same point. Second, if optimization process for each tree in ids is finished, we can return one step back and optimize data for ids, excluded at previous step. To do this, we need to save the search state (edge nodes, current values of information and efficiency and current ids) every time we add a new node to the subtree. Thus, search states are saved in search state stack. When at some step optimization process for all ids is finished, we need to pop search state from the search state stack and continue optimization process.

5 Using Developed Algorithm for Source Code Analysis

For the experiment, Python3 programming language is chosen. The language is chosen because Python is developing rapidly, has large codebase, widely used idiomatic code style, and Python has convenient built-in tools for building abstract syntax trees for Python programs.

Python uses built-in module ast to parse source code into AST, modify AST and execute it. The grammar for Python3 and Python AST data structure are represented in [7]. The structure almost ready for analysis, expect the fact that some of the nodes have variable number of children. All nodes which represent language fragments containing operator body (class, function definitions, loops, conditions, exception handling etc.) represent it with list. The same is true for nodes representing lists, tuples, sets and dictionaries. And last, but not least, compare operators (since Python supports expressions like a < b < c < d). However, the algorithm described before, requires all tree nodes with the same names have the same number of children. Therefore, lists in Python AST should be transformed into subtrees. Moreover, for Dict and Compare nodes information is stored in two different lists.

Let's introduce special kind of node (denote it as LIST), which has two children. Left child represents the first element in list, and the right child represents the rest of the list. Thus, list of nodes can be easily converted to subtrees. AST conversion for $a \leq b < c < d$ expression is shown at Fig. 6. On that figure, the upper tree is AST produced by Python ast module, the lower tree is the result of tree transform procedure.

After this transformation, we obtain AST for the entire module loaded. Since algorithm proposed is able to find only subtrees containing root, we need to generate subtrees of AST and add them to the database. To get all meaningful idioms and achieve good performance, we need to carefully choose subtrees. Let's restrict idioms type we are looking for.

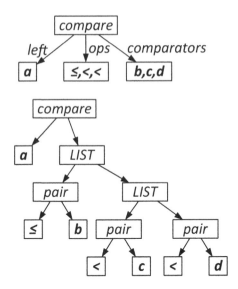

Fig. 6. Example of Python AST transformation.

Restrictions of idiom type considered are used often. E.g., in [8] the authors consider only loop idioms. Let the idiom can be represented with one operator (i.e., class definition, function definition, loop, condition, try/except block or expression). We are not interested in expression parts, since this subtrees are very small and non-informative. Also we do not consider sequences of operators. This restriction seriously speeds up the loading process, because in this case we don't need to load subtrees of LIST sequences. This restriction eliminates idioms consisting of operator sequence, but they can be found as part of parent operator body. Another useful restriction is to limit minimal subtree length. This prevents us from adding small but non-informative subtrees.

6   Idiom Extraction Experiment

The proposed algorithm is implemented in Python3 language. The properties of datasets used – size and number of lines of code (LOC) are shown in Table 1. Html5lib is codebase of html5lib-python project[1], the html parser, django is codebase of django project[2], top8 is codebase of top 8 projects hosted on github and tagged with "python" tag[3]. To remove small idioms from output, we introduce minimal idiom length. For the experiment value 7 is used. Minimal tree length for the experiment is also 7. Experiment results are also represented in Table 1.

---

[1] html5lib-python, https://github.com/html5lib/html5lib-python.

[2] django, https://github.com/django/django.

[3] https://github.com/topics/python?o=desc&s=stars.

Table 1. Results of the experiment.

Test set	LOC	Size, KB	Processing time, s
html5lib	11822	436	7
django	111028	3910	51
top8	185674	6481	122

Unfortunately, the significant part of results consists of trivial idioms. It means that metric should be improved. But on datasets consists of one project, the algorithm produces idioms specific for the project considered.

Consider idioms for html5lib test set at Fig. 7. Terms beginning with "$" denote content of not expanded tree nodes. The name after "$" is the name of child node, as described in [7].

```
def $name($args,$defaults):
    return $value
$decorator_list


def $name($args,$vararg,$kwarg,$defaults):
    if $test:
        $body
    else:
        $orelse


self.$attr[$value]+=$value


$value[(- 1)][$n]+=$value


while $value.name $op $expr:
    $body
```

Fig. 7. Examples of found idioms.

7   Conclusion

In this paper, the algorithm of source code idiom extraction is proposed. The algorithm implemented in Python3 language. The algorithm test shown that efficiency metric proposed should be improved for extracting idioms from datasets consists of different projects. But the efficiency metric can be used for extracting idioms for datasets consisting of one project.

References

1. Allamanis, M., Sutton, C.: Mining idioms from source code. In: FSE 2014 Proceedings of the 22nd ACM SIGSOFT International Symposium on Foundations of Software Engineering, Hong Kong, China, 16–21 November 2014, pp. 472–483 (2014)
2. Merchante, J., Robles, G.: From Python to Pythonic: Searching for Python idioms in GitHub (2017)
3. Svajlenko, J., Roy, C.K.: A Survey on the Evaluation of Clone Detection Performance and Benchmarking (2020)
4. Jiménez, A., Berzal, F., Cubero, J.-C.: Frequent tree pattern mining: a survey. Intell. Data Anal. **14**(6), 603–622 (2010)
5. A Language-Parametric Modular Framework for Mining Idiomatic Code Patterns
6. Ésik, Z. (ed.): FCT 1993. LNCS, vol. 710. Springer, Heidelberg (1993). https://doi.org/10.1007/3-540-57163-9
7. Abstract Syntax Trees. https://docs.python.org/3/library/ast.html. Accessed 30 May 2020
8. Allamanis, M., Barr, E., Bird, C., Devanbu, P., Marron, M., Sutton, C.: Mining semantic loop idioms. IEEE Trans. Softw. Eng., 651–668 (2018). https://doi.org/10.1109/tse.2018.2832048

Parametric Timed Bisimulation

Malte Lochau[1(✉)] , Lars Luthmann[2(✉)] , Hendrik Göttmann[2(✉)] ,
and Isabelle Bacher[2(✉)]

[1] Model-Based Engineering Group, University of Siegen, Siegen, Germany
malte.lochau@uni-siegen.de
[2] Real-Time Systems Lab, Technical University of Darmstadt, Darmstadt, Germany
{lars.luthmann,hendrik.goettmann}@es.tu-darmstadt.de,
isabelle.bacher@es.tu-darmstadt.de

Abstract. Timed automata (TA) constitute a mature formalism for
discrete-state/continuous-time behavior of time-critical cyber-physical
systems. Concerning the fundamental analysis problem of comparing a
candidate implementation against a specification both given as TA, it
has been shown that timed trace equivalence is undecidable, whereas
timed bisimulation is decidable. However, the limited expressiveness of
TA is a serious obstacle in practice such that many TA extensions have
been proposed. For instance, parametric timed automata (PTA) incorporate parametric clock constraints with freely-adjustable time intervals
thus generalizing the constant time bounds of TA. In this way, PTA
constitute a promising theoretical foundation for re-engineering static
real-time specifications, originally given as TA, in a generic and customizable way. In this paper, we provide, to the best of our knowledge,
the first proposal for lifting the notion of timed bisimulation from TA
to PTA. Unfortunately, as PTA are Turing-complete, most interesting
semantic properties being decidable for TA (including timed bisimulation), become undecidable for PTA. To tackle this issue, we propose an
over-approximation of PTA semantics in terms of plain TA semantics
and investigate decidability properties of a promising sub-class of PTA,
called L/U-PTA.

Keywords: Software re-engineering · Timed automata ·
Bisimulation · Parametric timed automata

1 Introduction

Background. In the context of the ever-progressing digitization of nearly every
application domain as, for instance, propagated by the Industry 4.0 initiative
for the automation-engineering domain, so-called *cyber-physical systems* become

---

L. Luthmann—This work was funded by the Hessian LOEWE initiative within the
Software-Factory 4.0 project.
H. Göttmann—This work has been funded by the German Research Foundation (DFG)
as part of project A4 within the Collaborative Research Center (CRC) 1053 MAKI.

© Springer Nature Switzerland AG 2020
T. Margaria and B. Steffen (Eds.): ISoLA 2020, LNCS 12477, pp. 55–71, 2020.
https://doi.org/10.1007/978-3-030-61470-6_5

more and more ubiquitous in recent days. *Timed automata (TA)* [1,6] constitute a theoretically-founded, yet practically applicable modeling formalism for
specifying and automatically analyzing discrete-state/continuous-time behavior
of time-critical reactive software systems which lie at the core of modern cyber-
physical systems. Timed automata, therefore, extend labeled state-transition
graphs of classical automata models by a set of *clocks* constituting constantly
and synchronously increasing, yet independently resettable numerical read-only
variables. The current values of clocks, quantifying the time elapsed since its last
reset, can be referenced within *clock constraints* in order to specify boundaries
for time intervals to be satisfied for safe occurrences of actions in valid *timed
runs* of the system.

A fundamental analysis problem arises from the comparison of a candidate
implementation against a specification both specified as TA (e.g., using reverse-
engineering techniques for model extraction from existing code [15]). It has been
shown that *timed trace inclusion* is undecidable, whereas *timed (bi-)simulation* is
decidable thus making timed bisimilarity a particularly useful equivalence notion
for verifying time-critical behaviors [8,19].

Problem Statement. Nevertheless, the limited expressive power of TA in their
most basic form constitutes a serious obstacle in practice. One of the most problematic restrictions in TA models is the need to specify *static* real-time constraints requiring precise constant (i.e., a-priori bounded) minimum/maximum
values for timing intervals for action occurrences. To overcome this limitation,
parametric timed automata (PTA) have been proposed as a promising generalization of TA [2]. To this end, PTA generalize the clock-constraint language of
TA to *parametric clock constraints* permitting *dynamically* and *freely* adjustable
boundaries of timing intervals. In this way, a PTA model virtually comprises a
(potentially infinite) number of structurally similar, yet behaviorally adaptable
TA models. Thus, PTA constitute a promising theoretical foundation for re-
engineering static real-time specifications, originally given as TA, in generic and
customizable way (e.g., enabling parameter-fine-tuning to fit to platform-specific
requirements). Unfortunately, the increased expressiveness make PTA Turing-
complete such that most interesting semantic properties, being decidable for TA
(including timed bisimulation), are undecidable for PTA [3,5]. More specifically,
even a conclusive adaptation of the definition of timed bisimilarity from TA to
PTA models is an open issue. This limitation of automated analysis capabilities
may obstruct the applicability of PTA as a practical (re-)engineering tool.

Contributions. In this paper, we propose, to the best of our knowledge, the
first characterization of *parametric timed bisimulation* for PTA models by lifting
the notion of timed bisimilarity from TA to PTA. Intuitively, a PTA simulates
another PTA if the behavior of any possible parametrization of the second PTA
is timed simulated by a parametrization of the first PTA.

However, iterating over a generally infinite set of TA models derivable from
a PTA model for parametric bisimilarity-checking is not a reasonable approach
in practice. Hence, we provide an alternative, yet slightly weaker and inherently

incomplete characterization of parametric timed bisimulation. This characterization is based on a single (yet still generally infinite) representation of PTA semantics, called *parametric timed labeled transition system* (PTLTS), which (semi-)symbolically comprises the semantics of all TA models derivable from a PTA model.

Finally, we consider an over-approximation of PTA semantics in terms of plain TA semantics in order to apply bisimilarity-checking for TA models also for parametric bisimilarity-checking of PTA models. To conclude, we investigate decidability properties of this technique for a restricted sub-class of PTA called *lower-bound/upper-bound PTA (L/U-PTA)* [14].

2 Preliminaries

In this section, we first recall basic notions of *timed automata*, *timed bisimulation* as well as the generalization of timed automata to *parametric timed automata*.

2.1 Timed Automata

Syntax. A *timed automaton (TA)* can be represented as a finite state-transition graph. States of a TA are called *locations* (including a distinguished *initial location*) and edges of a TA, denoting transitions between locations, are called *switches* [1]. Each switch is labeled by a name from a finite alphabet Σ of *visible actions*. Alternatively, a switch performing a silent move is labeled by a distinguished symbol $\tau \notin \Sigma$ comprising all kinds of *internal action*. We will range over Σ by σ and over $\Sigma_\tau = \Sigma \cup \{\tau\}$ by μ.

A TA further consists of a finite set C of *clocks* defined over a numerical *clock domain* $\mathbb{T}_C$. For instance, $\mathbb{T}_C = \mathbb{N}_0$ may be used to model *discrete-time* behavior, whereas $\mathbb{T}_C = \mathbb{R}_+$ represents *dense-time* behavior. Clocks can be seen as constantly and synchronously increasing, yet independently resettable variables over $\mathbb{T}_C$. In this way, clocks allow for measuring and restricting time intervals for the durations—or *delays* between occurrences—of actions within *runs* (i.e., sequences of locations and switches) of a TA model. Those restrictions are expressed by *clock constraints* φ, by denoting *guards* of switches and *invariants* of locations. In particular, guards specify those time intervals in which the corresponding switch is enabled in a run, whereas invariants restrict time intervals in which runs are permitted to reside in a particular location. In addition, each switch is labeled with a subset of clocks $R \subseteq C$ denoting those clocks which will be *reset* whenever that switch is taken in a run.

Definition 1 (Timed Automaton). *A TA is a tuple* $(L, \ell_0, \Sigma, C, I, E)$, *where*

- *L is a finite set of* locations *with* initial location $\ell_0 \in L$,
- *Σ is a finite set of* actions *such that* $\tau \notin \Sigma$,
- *C is a finite set of* clocks *such that* $C \cap \Sigma_\tau = \emptyset$,
- *$I : L \to \mathcal{B}(C)$ is a function assigning* invariants *to locations, and*
- *$E \subseteq L \times \mathcal{B}(C) \times \Sigma_\tau \times 2^C \times L$ is a relation defining* switches.

The set $\mathcal{B}(C)$ of clock constraints φ *over C is inductively defined as*

$$\varphi := \mathsf{true} \mid c \sim n \mid c - c' \sim n \mid \varphi \wedge \varphi, \text{ where } \sim \in \{<, \leq, \geq, >\}, c, c' \in C, n \in \mathbb{T}_C.$$

We range over TA by $\mathcal{A}$ where we may omit an explicit mentioning of the sets C and/or Σ if not relevant. Furthermore, we denote switches $(\ell, g, \mu, R, \ell') \in E$ by $\ell \xrightarrow{g, \mu, R} \ell'$ for convenience. Please note that clock constraints φ as defined above neither contain operators for equality nor disjunction as both are expressible by the given grammar (e.g., $x = 2$ may be expressed by $x \leq 2 \wedge x \geq 2$, and $x < 2 \vee x > 2$ may be expressed by two different switches labeled $x < 2$ and $x > 2$). We further consider *diagonal-free* TA in which clock constraints φ only consist of atomic constraints of the form $c \sim n$. This is, in fact, only a syntactic restriction as for every TA, an equivalent diagonal-free TA can be constructed [7]. However, we will (implicitly) permit *difference constraints* $c - c' \sim n$ in $\mathcal{B}(C)$ only for the sake of a concise representation of our subsequent constructions, but not as part of the visible syntax. Similarly, we may assume all location invariants being unequal to true to be *downward-closed* (i.e., only having clauses of the form $c \leq n$ or $c < n$), as upward-closed invariants clock constraints can be moved to the guards of all incoming switches of that location.

However, as two actual restrictions, we limit our considerations to (1) clock constraints over rational constants $n \in \mathbb{Q}_0$ as clock constraints with real-valued bounds would obstruct fundamental decidability properties of TA, as well as to (2) so-called timed *safety* automata. Concerning (2), our definition of TA does not include distinguished *acceptance locations* used for employing Büchi acceptance semantics for infinite TA runs [1,13].

Semantics. The operational semantics of TA defining its *valid runs* may be defined in terms of *Timed Labeled Transition Systems (TLTS)* [12]. *States* of TLTS are pairs $\langle \ell, u \rangle$ consisting of the currently *active location* $\ell \in L$ and *clock valuation* $u \in C \to \mathbb{T}_C$. The clock valuation assigns to each clock $c \in C$ the amount of time $u(c)$ elapsed since its last reset. Thereupon, two kinds of *transitions* can be distinguished in TLTS: (1) passage of time of duration $d \in \mathbb{T}_C$ while (inactively) residing in location ℓ, leading to an updated clock valuation u', and (2) instantaneous execution of switches $\ell \xrightarrow{g, \mu, R} \ell'$, triggered by an occurrence of action $\mu \in \Sigma_\tau$ and leading from source location ℓ to target location ℓ'.

Given a clock valuation u, we denote by $u + d$, with $d \in \mathbb{T}_C$, the *updated clock valuation* mapping each clock $c \in C$ to the new value $u(c) + d$ resulting from the passage of a duration d. By $[R \mapsto 0]u$, with $R \subseteq C$, we further denote the updated clock valuation mapping each clock $c \in R$ to value 0 (due to a *clock reset*) while preserving the values $u(c')$ of all other clocks $c' \in C \setminus R$ not being reset. By $u \in \varphi$, we denote that clock valuation u *satisfies* clock constraint $\varphi \in \mathcal{B}(C)$. Finally, in case of τ-labeled transitions, we distinguish between *strong* and *weak* TLTS transitions, where internal transitions are visible in the former, but omitted in the latter.

Definition 2 (Timed Labeled Transition System). *The TLTS of TA $\mathcal{A}$ over Σ is a tuple $(S, s_0, \hat{\Sigma}, \to)$, where*

- $S = L \times (\mathcal{C} \to \mathbb{T}_{\mathbb{C}})$ *is a set of* states *with* initial state $s_0 = \langle \ell_0, [C \mapsto 0] \rangle \in S$,
- $\hat{\Sigma} = \Sigma \cup \Delta$ *is a set of* transition labels, *where* $\Delta \to \mathbb{T}_{\mathbb{C}}$ *is bijective such that* $(\Sigma \cup \{\tau\}) \cap \Delta = \emptyset$, *and*
- $\to \,\subseteq S \times (\hat{\Sigma} \cup \{\tau\}) \times S$ *is a set of* strong transitions *being the least relation satisfying the rules:*
  - $\langle \ell, u \rangle \xrightarrow{d} \langle \ell, u + d \rangle$ *if* $(u + d) \in I(\ell)$ *for* $d \in \mathbb{T}_{\mathbb{C}}$, *and*
  - $\langle \ell, u \rangle \xrightarrow{\mu} \langle \ell', u' \rangle$ *if* $\ell \xrightarrow{g, \mu, R} \ell'$, $u \in g$, $u' = [R \mapsto 0]u$, $u' \in I(\ell')$ *and* $\mu \in (\Sigma \cup \{\tau\})$.

By $\twoheadrightarrow \,\subseteq S \times \hat{\Sigma} \times S$, *we denote a set of* weak transitions *being the least relation satisfying the rules:*

- $s \stackrel{a}{\Rrightarrow} s'$ *if* $s \xrightarrow{\tau^n} s_1 \xrightarrow{a} s_2 \xrightarrow{\tau^m} s'$ *with* $n, m \in \mathbb{N}_0$,
- $s \stackrel{d}{\Rrightarrow} s'$ *if* $s \xrightarrow{d} s'$,
- $s \stackrel{0}{\Rrightarrow} s'$ *if* $s \xrightarrow{\tau^n} s'$ *with* $n \in \mathbb{N}_0$, *and*
- $s \stackrel{d+d'}{\Longrightarrow} s'$ *if* $s \stackrel{d}{\Rrightarrow} s''$ *and* $s'' \stackrel{d'}{\Rrightarrow} s'$.

We refer to the TLTS semantics of TA $\mathcal{A}$ as $\mathcal{S}_{\mathcal{A}}$ or simply as $\mathcal{S}$ if clear from the context. We only consider *strongly convergent* TA $\mathcal{A}$ (i.e., with $\mathcal{S}_{\mathcal{A}}$ having no infinite τ-sequences). In addition, if not further stated, we apply strong TLTS semantics, where the weak version can by obtained by replacing $\to$ by $\twoheadrightarrow$ in all definitions. Obviously, a TLTS representation of TA semantics is, in general, not finite and therefore only of theoretical interest. In practical tools, a finite representation of TA semantics (e.g., zone graphs [13]) is used instead, where it has been proven that such a finite representation exists for every TA model according to Definition 1.

Example 1. Figure 1 shows sample TA specifying two different variants of the real-time behavior of (simplified) coffee machines. Extracts from the corresponding TLTS semantics are shown in Figs. 1c and 1d. In both cases, in state $\langle \text{Warm Up}, x = 0 \rangle$, we can only let further time pass whereas in $\langle \text{Warm Up}, x = 1 \rangle$, we have to choose *coffee* due to the invariant. In contrast, as neither location *Idle* nor *Fill Cup* has an invariant, we may wait for an unlimited amount of time thus resulting in infinitely many consecutive TLTS states (which we indicate by the delay transitions at the bottom of the TLTS). Further note that the TLTS in Fig. 1d contains a τ-transition thus leading to different *strong* TLTS semantics than the TLTS in Fig. 1c. In contrast, the additional clock reset performed by the *coffee*-switch of the TA in Fig. 1b in combination with the differing switch guard $y \geq 1$ (as compared to $x \geq 2$ in Fig. 1a) lead to exactly the same (weak) TLTS semantics for both TA.

As illustrated by the previous example, semantic equivalence of two given TA variants is not obvious. We next recall the notion of *timed bisimulation*, providing a well-founded notion of behavioral equivalence for TA models.

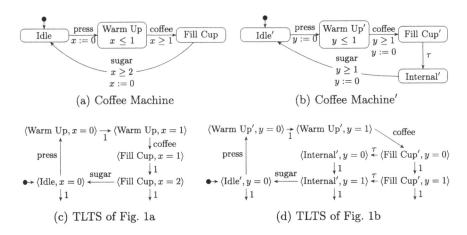

Fig. 1. TA of Two Similar Coffee Machines (Figs. 1a, 1b) and TLTS (Figs. 1c, 1d)

2.2 Timed Bisimulation

A timed (bi-)simulation relation may be defined by adapting the classical notion of (bi-)simulation from LTS to TLTS. A state s' of TLTS $\mathcal{S}'$ *timed simulates* state s of TLTS $\mathcal{S}$ if every transition enabled in s, either labeled with action $\mu \in \Sigma_\tau$ or with delay $d \in \Delta$, is also enabled in s' and the target state in $\mathcal{S}'$, again, simulates the target state in $\mathcal{S}$. Hence, TA $\mathcal{A}'$ *timed simulates* $\mathcal{A}$ if initial state s'_0 *simulates* initial state s_0. In addition, $\mathcal{A}'$ and $\mathcal{A}$ are *bisimilar* if the simulation relation is symmetric.

Definition 3 (Timed Bisimulation [20]). *Let $\mathcal{A}$, $\mathcal{A}'$ be TA over Σ with $C \cap C' = \emptyset$ and $\mathcal{R} \subseteq S \times S'$ such that for all $(s_1, s'_1) \in \mathcal{R}$ it holds that*

- *if $s_1 \xrightarrow{\mu} s_2$ with $\mu \in \Sigma_\tau$, then $s'_1 \xrightarrow{\mu} s'_2$ and $(s_2, s'_2) \in \mathcal{R}$ and*
- *if $s_1 \xrightarrow{d} s_2$ with $d \in \Delta$, then $s'_1 \xrightarrow{d} s'_2$ with $(s_2, s'_2) \in \mathcal{R}$.*

$\mathcal{A}'$ (strongly) timed simulates $\mathcal{A}$, denoted $\mathcal{A} \sqsubseteq \mathcal{A}'$, iff $(s_0, s'_0) \in \mathcal{R}$. In addition, $\mathcal{A}'$ and $\mathcal{A}$ are (strongly) timed bisimilar, denoted $\mathcal{A} \simeq \mathcal{A}'$, iff $\mathcal{R}$ is symmetric.

Weak timed (bi-)simulation (ignoring τ-steps) can be obtained by replacing $\rightarrow$ with $\Rightarrow$ in definitions (which we will omit whenever not relevant).

Lemma 1. *If $\mathcal{A}'$ strongly timed simulates $\mathcal{A}$, then $\mathcal{A}'$ weakly timed simulates $\mathcal{A}$.*

Proof. We prove Lemma 1 by contradiction. Assume TA $\mathcal{A}$ and $\mathcal{A}'$ with $\mathcal{A}'$ strongly timed simulating $\mathcal{A}$ and $\mathcal{A}'$ *not* weakly timed simulating $\mathcal{A}$. In this case, we require TLTS states $\langle \ell_1, u_1 \rangle \in S$ and $\langle \ell'_1, u'_1 \rangle \in S'$ being reachable by a τ-step such that for each $\langle \ell_1, u_1 \rangle \xrightarrow{\eta} \langle \ell_2, u_2 \rangle \in \rightarrow$ with $\eta \in \hat{\Sigma}$ there exists a $\langle \ell'_1, u'_1 \rangle \xrightarrow{\eta} \langle \ell'_2, u'_2 \rangle \in \rightarrow'$. Due to the definition of weak transitions (cf. Definition 2), we also require a transition $\langle \ell'_1, u'_1 \rangle \xrightarrow{\eta} \langle \ell'_2, u'_2 \rangle \in \rightarrow'$ not being enabled in $\langle \ell_1, u_1 \rangle$ to prove that $\mathcal{A}'$ strongly timed simulates $\mathcal{A}$ and $\mathcal{A}'$ weakly timed

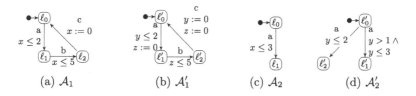

Fig. 2. Examples for Timed Bisimilarity Checking

simulates $\mathcal{A}$. However, as these two assumptions are contradicting, it holds that $\mathcal{A}'$ weakly timed simulates $\mathcal{A}$ if $\mathcal{A}'$ strongly timed simulates $\mathcal{A}$.   □

Example 2. Consider TA $\mathcal{A}$ and $\mathcal{A}'$ in Figs. 1a and 1b. In this case, strong timed (bi-)simulation does not hold due to the τ-step in $\mathcal{A}'$. In contrast, for the weak case, we have $\mathcal{A} \sqsubseteq \mathcal{A}'$ as every action and delay of $\mathcal{A}$ is also permitted by $\mathcal{A}'$ (cf. TLTS in Figs. 1c and 1d in Example 1). Similarly, $\mathcal{A}' \sqsubseteq \mathcal{A}$ also holds such that $\mathcal{A}$ and $\mathcal{A}'$ are weakly timed bisimilar.

Figure 2 provides further examples to demonstrate particularly tricky cases of timed bisimilarity. In $\mathcal{A}_1$, we may wait for at most 5 time units in location ℓ_1 before performing action b only if we have performed action a before with delay 0. In contrast, in $\mathcal{A}'_1$, the delay of at most 5 time units before performing b in location ℓ_1 is independent of the previous delay of action a due to the reset of clock z. Hence, $\mathcal{A}_1 \simeq \mathcal{A}'_1$ does not hold. Finally, we have $\mathcal{A}_2 \simeq \mathcal{A}'_2$ as both TA permit action a to be performed within time interval $[0, 3]$.

The notion of (strong) timed bisimulation goes back to Moller and Tofts [17] as well as Yi [21], both initially defined on real-time extensions of the process algebra CCS. Again, the characterization of timed bisimulation using the (infinite) TLTS representation of real-time behavior is only of theoretical interest. The pioneering work of Čerāns [8] includes the first decidability proof of timed bisimulation on TA, by providing a finite characterization of bisimilarity-checking utilizing a region-graph representation of real-time processes. Amongst others, the improved (i.e., less space-consuming) approach of Weise and Lenzkes [20] employs a variation of zone graphs, called FBS graphs.

In the next section, we consider a generalization of TA, called parametric timed automata (PTA), incorporating parametric clock constraints with freely-adjustable time intervals instead of constant time bounds as enforced in TA.

3   Parametric Timed Automata

In this section, we consider a generalized definition of TA, called Parametric Timed Automata (PTA) [2]. PTA improve expressiveness of TA by incorporating dynamically and freely adjustable time intervals within clock constraints instead of statically fixed time bounds as required in TA. In this way, PTA facilitate re-engineering of existing real-time specifications into more generic models

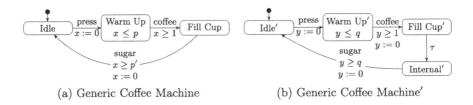

(a) Generic Coffee Machine   (b) Generic Coffee Machine$'$

Fig. 3. Parametric Timed Automata of Two Re-egineered Coffee Machines

being flexibly customizable to a-priori unknown and/or dynamically changing environmental requirements (e.g., enabling fine-tuning of parameter values to optimize performance for a specific hardware platform). We further consider an interesting sub-class of PTA called L/U-PTA.

3.1 Illustrating Examples

Parametric Timed Automata (PTA) generalize TA such that lower and upper bounds of clock constraints occurring as switch guards and location invariants may, instead of predefined constants, be represented as *parameters* denoting a-priori unknown constants of dynamically adjustable time intervals [2].

Example 3. For instance, assume that the two coffee machines specified by the TA models in Fig. 1 shall be used to (re-)engineer further machines having similar control software. The real-time behavior of these new machines may, however, slightly differ from the original ones, depending on the hardware used. For instance, the duration of *warm-up* may differ depending on the performance of the heating device used. Hence, the maximum value of the timing interval of the invariant of the locations *Warm Up* and *Warm Up$'$* respectively which has been originally fixed to constant value 1 should become a dynamically adjustable parameter after (re-)engineering.

Figure 3 shows the resulting PTA models of the (re-)engineered coffee machines. As before, the PTA in Fig. 3a waits in initial location *Idle* until a button is *pressed*, then resets clock x and switches to location *Warm up*. From here, the guard of the outgoing switch and the location invariant enforces the PTA to proceed by choosing *coffee* within a time interval between 1 to p time units. Then, sugar is poured until x elapsed at least to the value of parameter p'.

The PTA in Fig. 3b, again, defines very similar, yet slightly differing behavior: Clock y is additionally reset after choosing *coffee* and a silent τ-step follows the choice of *coffee*. In addition, in contrast to the first PTA, this PTA employs only one parameter q for restricting both time intervals. Hence, the TLTS extracts initially shown in Figs. 1c and 1d result from the parameter valuations $p = q = 1$ and $p' = 2$, respectively.

We now proceed by providing a formal definition of the syntax and semantics of PTA as well as a sub-class of PTA, called L/U-PTA.

3.2   Defining Parametric Timed Automata

Given a finite set P of *parameters* over *parameter domain* $\mathbb{T}_P$, PTA extend the definition of clock constraints to *parametric clock constraints* for guards and invariants by comparing clock values with *parametric linear terms (plt)* $(\sum_{1\leq i\leq |P|} \alpha_i p_i) + n$, where $\alpha_i \in \mathbb{Z}$, $p_i \in P$ and $n \in \mathbb{T}_C$. Here, the sum is a shorthand notation for $\alpha_1 p_1 + \ldots + \alpha_m p_m + n$, where we use $\alpha_i = 0$ to denote that parameter p_i is not part of a given parametric linear term.

Definition 4 (Parametric Timed Automaton). *A* PTA *is a tuple* $(L, \ell_0, \Sigma,$ $C, P, I, E)$, *where*

- *L is a finite set of* locations *with* initial location $\ell_0 \in L$,
- *Σ is a finite set of* actions *such that* $\tau \notin \Sigma$,
- *C is a finite set of* clocks *such that* $C \cap \Sigma_\tau = \emptyset$,
- *P is a finite set of* parameters *such that* $P \cap (C \cup \Sigma_\tau) = \emptyset$,
- *$I : L \to \mathcal{B}(C, P)$ assigns* parametric invariants *to locations, and*
- *$E \subseteq L \times \mathcal{B}(C, P) \times \Sigma_\tau \times 2^C \times L$ is a relation defining* switches.

The set $\mathcal{B}(C, P)$ of parametric clock constraints ϕ *over C and P is defined as*

$$\phi := \mathsf{true} \mid c \sim plt \mid c - c' \sim plt \mid \phi \wedge \phi, \text{ where } plt := \left(\sum_{1\leq i\leq |P|} \alpha_i p_i\right) + n$$

and $\sim \in \{<, \leq, \geq, >\}$, $c, c' \in C$, $\alpha_i \in \mathbb{Z}$, $p_i \in P$ and $n \in \mathbb{T}_C$.

Again, we include difference constraints in $\mathcal{B}(C, P)$ for technical reasons. We range over PTA by $\mathcal{P}$ and use the same notational conventions as for TA.

Semantics. The operational semantics of a PTA is defined in terms of the semantics of the set of TA resulting from all possible parameter valuations. Hence, given a PTA $\mathcal{P}$ defined over parameter set P and a *parameter valuation* $\nu : P \to \mathbb{T}_P$ (i.e., replacing all parameters by constants from $\mathbb{T}_P$), by $\nu(\mathcal{P})$ we denote the TA resulting from replacing all occurrences of all parameters $p \in P$ within invariants and guards by the constant value $\nu(p)$. For the resulting TA $\nu(\mathcal{P})$, the corresponding (strong and weak) TLTS semantics $\mathcal{S}_{\nu(\mathcal{P})}$ can be derived as described above.

Example 4. The TA models in Figs. 1a and 1b result from applying the parameter valuations $\nu = \{p \mapsto 1, p' \mapsto 2\}$ and $\nu' = \{q \mapsto 1\}$ to the PTA models in Figs. 3a and 3b, respectively.

As PTA are Turing-complete, almost all non-trivial properties, being decidable for TA (including timed bisimulation), become undecidable in case of PTA [5]. Hence, we conclude this section by considering an interesting sub-class of PTA, called *lower-bound/upper-bound PTA (L/U-PTA)* [14].

3.3   L/U-PTA

A PTA model is a L/U-PTA model if each parameter is exclusively used either as lower bound or upper bound throughout all parametric clock constraints in which the parameter occurs. This restriction limits the influence of those parameters on the reachability of locations. As a result, L/U-PTA are more expressive than TA while some essential semantic properties (e.g., reachability), being undecidable for PTA, remain decidable [5].

More formally, parameter $p_i \in P$ is *lower-bounded* in a parametric clock constraint ϕ if it occurs in at least one clause $c \geq plt$ or $c > plt$ with $\alpha_i \neq 0$, and it is *upper-bounded* if it occurs in at least one clause $c < plt$ or $c \leq plt$ with $\alpha_i \neq 0$ (where α_i is the factor for multiplication with parameter p_i, see Definition 4). By $P_L \subseteq P$, we denote the subset of all lower-bounded parameters, and by $P_U \subseteq P$ the subset of all upper-bounded parameters of a given PTA model $\mathcal{P}$.

Definition 5 (L/U-PTA). *PTA $\mathcal{P}$ is a L/U-PTA if $P_L \cap P_U = \emptyset$ holds.*

Example 5. The PTA in Fig. 3a is a L/U-PTA as parameter p only occurs upper-bounded and parameter p' only occurs lower-bounded. In contrast, the PTA in Fig. 3b is not a L/U-PTA as parameter q occurs both upper-bounded and lower-bounded.

In the next section, we elaborate on the notion of timed bisimulation for PTA models.

4   Parametric Timed Bisimulation

In this section, we discuss how to lift the notion of timed bisimulation from TA models to define *parametric timed bisimulation* on PTA models. To gain an intuitive understanding of parametric timed bisimulation, we first provide a collection of illustrating examples.

4.1   Illustrating Examples

Intuitively, one may define that PTA $\mathcal{P}'$ *parametric-timed-simulates* PTA $\mathcal{P}$, denoted $\mathcal{P} \sqsubseteq \mathcal{P}'$, if for each parameter valuation ν of $\mathcal{P}$ there exists a corresponding valuation ν' of $\mathcal{P}'$ such that $\nu(\mathcal{P}) \sqsubseteq \nu'(\mathcal{P}')$ holds (i.e., every TA derivable from $\mathcal{P}$ can be simulated by a TA derivable from $\mathcal{P}'$).

Figure 4 shows a collection of six sample PTA, $\mathcal{P}_0, \mathcal{P}_1, \ldots, \mathcal{P}_5$, over $\Sigma = \{a, b\}$, where the pairs $\mathcal{P}_0 - \mathcal{P}_1$, $\mathcal{P}_2 - \mathcal{P}_3$ as well as $\mathcal{P}_4 - \mathcal{P}_5$ are each structurally similar and mostly slightly differ in the usage of parameters.

- Both $\mathcal{P}_1 \sqsubseteq \mathcal{P}_0$ and $\mathcal{P}_0 \sqsubseteq \mathcal{P}_1$ hold. In particular, $\mathcal{P}_1 \sqsubseteq \mathcal{P}_0$ holds as for every derivable TA $\nu_1(\mathcal{P}_1)$ an identical TA $\nu_0(\mathcal{P}_0)$ exists with $p = p' = q$. Conversely, it is not possible to find an identical TA $\nu_1(\mathcal{P}_1)$ for every derivable TA of $\mathcal{P}_0$ as $\mathcal{P}_0$ allows for two independent parameters p and p' in the guards. However, by setting q in ν_1 to the maximum value of p and p' in ν_0, it is

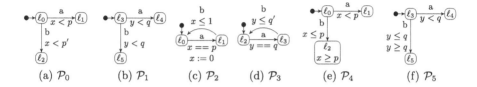

Fig. 4. Sample PTA models

in fact possible to derive $\nu_1(\mathcal{P}_1)$ simulating $\nu_0(\mathcal{P}_0)$. For instance, consider the parameter valuations $\nu_0 = \{p \mapsto 1, p' \mapsto 2\}$ and $\nu_1 = \{q \mapsto 2\}$ where $\nu_0(\mathcal{P}_0) \sqsubseteq \nu_1(\mathcal{P}_1)$ holds.

- $\mathcal{P}_2 \sqsubseteq \mathcal{P}_3$ and $\mathcal{P}_3 \sqsubseteq \mathcal{P}_2$ do not hold. Both $\mathcal{P}_2$ and $\mathcal{P}_3$ must perform the switches labeled with action a exactly after either p or q time units, respectively. Afterwards, the clock reset permits $\mathcal{P}_2$ to wait for at most 1 time unit before performing the switch labeled with action b. However, in order for the switch labeled with action a to become enabled in the next round, exactly p time units must elapse after the last clock reset. In contrast, in $\mathcal{P}_3$, each parameter valuation with $q' < q$ would cause the resulting TA to get stuck after performing the switch labeled with action a. In case of $q' \geq q$, however, the next round is only possible if no further time elapses due to the absence of any clock reset (thus enforcing zeno behavior).
- $\mathcal{P}_4 \sqsubseteq \mathcal{P}_5$ and $\mathcal{P}_5 \sqsubseteq \mathcal{P}_4$ hold such that both models are parametric timed bisimilar as the semantic difference between the parametric switch guard and the parametric location invariant is not observable.

Furthermore, note that, for instance, $\mathcal{P}_3$, is not a L/U-PTA as parameter q occurs lower-bounded as well as upper-bounded (as $x == p$ is actually a shorthand for $x \geq p$ and $x \leq p$). As a result, the parameter valuation may influence reachability of locations in non-obvious ways as described above.

4.2   Defining Parametric Timed Bisimulation

Timed (bi-)simulation may be lifted to PTA by simply considering pairs of parameter valuations independently one-by-one. However, as illustrated above, this definition would result in a mutual simulation relation between $\mathcal{P}_0$ and $\mathcal{P}_1$. This would be a rather unintuitive result as $\mathcal{P}_0$ contains an additional degree of parametric freedom due to the two independent parameters p and p' as compared to the one single parameter q in $\mathcal{P}_1$. Furthermore, this definition would yield an inconsistent notion of timed bisimilarity. For instance, it is possible to derive a TA $\nu_0(\mathcal{P}_0)$ with $\nu_0 = \{p \mapsto 1, p' \mapsto 2\}$ for which in fact no bisimilar TA $\nu_1(\mathcal{P}_1)$ exists.

In order to obtain a feasible notion of parametric timed bisimulation, we propose to incorporate in our definition an explicit relation $\Re$ on parameter valuations. Given a relation $R \subseteq A \times B$, $\Pi_1(R) \subseteq A$ denotes the *projection* of elements from A related under R to elements in B.

Definition 6 (Parametric Timed Bisimulation). *Let* $\mathcal{P}, \mathcal{P}'$ *be PTA over* Σ*, where* $C \cap C' = \emptyset$*,* $P \cap P' = \emptyset$ *and* $\mathfrak{R} \subseteq (P \to \mathbb{T}_P) \times (P' \to \mathbb{T}_{P'})$ *such that* $(\nu, \nu') \in \mathfrak{R} \Leftrightarrow \nu(\mathcal{P}) \sqsubseteq \nu'(\mathcal{P}')$ *holds. We may consider the following cases:*

- $\mathcal{P}'$ *$\exists$-simulates* $\mathcal{P}$ *iff* $\Pi_1(\mathfrak{R}) \neq \emptyset$*,*
- $\mathcal{P}'$ *$\forall$-simulates* $\mathcal{P}$ *iff* $\Pi_1(\mathfrak{R}) = (P \to \mathbb{T}_P)$*,*
- $\mathcal{P}'$ *and* $\mathcal{P}$ *are bisimilar iff* $\mathfrak{R}$ *is symmetric and* $\sqsubseteq$ *is replaced by* $\simeq$*.*

By $\mathcal{P} \sqsubseteq \mathcal{P}'$, we denote that $\mathcal{P}'$ simulates $\mathcal{P}$, where we again may omit further details if not relevant. Relation $\forall$-simulates is a preorder, whereas relation $\exists$-simulates is not. Please note, that we mention $\exists$-similarity only for the sake of completeness, but we will limit our considerations to $\forall$-(bi-)similarity.

In order to characterize parametric timed (bi-)similarity for PTA in a more concise way, we next present a (partially) symbolic PTA semantics comprising all parameter valuations in one *parametric timed labeled transition system (PTLTS)*. A PTLTS consists of *parametric states* $\langle \ell, u, \xi \rangle$ containing *parameter constraints* ξ denoting sets of parameter valuations $\nu \in \xi$ for which the state is reachable. Thus, we decompose parametric clock constraints $\phi = \phi_c \wedge \phi_p$ into a *non-parametric* (constant) part ϕ_c and a *parametric* part ϕ_p. Hence, ϕ_c conjuncts all those parametric linear terms in ϕ with $\alpha_i = 0$, $1 \leq i \leq |P|$, whereas ϕ_p conjuncts all remaining terms with at least one parameter occurrence. We refer to the non-parametric and parametric parts of invariants and guards of a PTA by I_c, I_p, g_c and g_p, respectively. By $[C/u]\varphi$ we denote that every occurrence of any clock $c \in C$ in clock constraint φ is replaced by clock value $u(c)$ thus resulting in a parameter constraint.

We define PTLTS semantics by (1) constructing TLTS semantics from the non-parametric parts of clock constraints as usual, and by (2) aggregating parametric parts of clock constraints in parameter constraints ξ of states $\langle \ell, u, \xi \rangle$ by replacing clocks c within constraints by their current values $u(c)$.

Definition 7 (Parametric TLTS). *The PTLTS of PTA $\mathcal{P}$ over Σ is a tuple* $(\overline{S}, \overline{s}_0, \hat{\Sigma}, \twoheadrightarrow)$*, where*

- $\overline{S} = L \times (\mathcal{C} \to \mathbb{T}_C) \times \mathcal{B}(P)$ *is a set of* parametric states *with initial state* $\overline{s}_0 = \langle \ell_0, [C \mapsto 0], \text{true} \rangle \in S$*,*
- $\hat{\Sigma} = \Sigma \cup \Delta$ *is a set of transition labels, where* $\Delta \to \mathbb{T}_C$ *is bijective such that* $(\Sigma \cup \{\tau\}) \cap \Delta = \emptyset$*,*
- $\twoheadrightarrow \subseteq \overline{S} \times (\hat{\Sigma} \cup \{\tau\}) \times \overline{S}$ *is a set of* strong parametric transitions *being the least relation satisfying the rules:*
  - $\langle \ell, u, \xi \rangle \xrightarrow{d} \langle \ell, u+d, \xi \wedge [C/(u+d)]I_p(\ell) \rangle$ *for each* $d \in \mathbb{T}_C$ *with* $(u+d) \in I_c(\ell)$*, and*
  - $\langle \ell, u, \xi \rangle \xrightarrow{\mu} \langle \ell', [R \mapsto 0]u, \xi \wedge [C/u]g_p \wedge [C/[R \mapsto 0]u]I_p(\ell') \rangle$ *for each* $\ell \xrightarrow{g, \mu, R} \ell'$ *with* $u \in g_c \wedge [R \mapsto 0]u \in I_c(\ell')$*.*

The set $\mathcal{B}(P)$ of parameter constraints *ξ over P is inductively defined as*

$$\xi := \text{true} \mid n \sim plt \mid \xi \wedge \xi, \text{ where } \sim \in \{<, \leq, \geq, >\} \text{ and } n \in \mathbb{T}_P.$$

$$\begin{array}{cc}
\xleftarrow[1]{} \langle \ell_0, x = 0, \text{true} \rangle \xrightarrow[a]{} \langle \ell_1, x = 0, p > 0 \rangle \\
\downarrow b \qquad\qquad \downarrow 1 \\
\langle \ell_2, x = 0, p' > 0 \rangle \quad \langle \ell_1, x = 1, p > 1 \rangle \\
\downarrow 1 \qquad\qquad \downarrow 1 \\
\langle \ell_2, x = 1, p' > 1 \rangle \quad \langle \ell_1, x = 2, p > 2 \rangle \\
\downarrow 1 \qquad\qquad \downarrow 1
\end{array}$$

(a) PTLTS of $\mathcal{P}_0$

$$\begin{array}{cc}
\xleftarrow[1]{} \langle \ell_3, y = 0, \text{true} \rangle \xrightarrow[a]{} \langle \ell_4, y = 0, q > 0 \rangle \\
\downarrow b \qquad\qquad \downarrow 1 \\
\langle \ell_5, y = 0, q > 0 \rangle \quad \langle \ell_4, y = 1, q > 1 \rangle \\
\downarrow 1 \qquad\qquad \downarrow 1 \\
\langle \ell_5, y = 1, q > 1 \rangle \quad \langle \ell_4, y = 2, q > 2 \rangle \\
\downarrow 1 \qquad\qquad \downarrow 1
\end{array}$$

(b) PTLTS of $\mathcal{P}_1$

Fig. 5. Example for PTA Bisimulation of $\mathcal{P}_0$ and $\mathcal{P}_1$ (cf. Figs. 4a and 4b)

PTLTS enable an alternative definition of parametric timed (bi-)simulation. Intuitively, $\mathcal{P}'$ parametric-timed-simulates $\mathcal{P}$ if any occurrence of parameters $p' \in P'$ in parametric clock constraints of $\mathcal{P}'$ can be substituted by either some parameter $p \in P$ from $\mathcal{P}$ or by a constant $d \in \mathbb{T}_P$ such that the resulting PTLTS of $\mathcal{P}'$ timed-simulates the PTLTS of $\mathcal{P}$. By $[\Psi]\xi \in \mathcal{B}(P)$ we denote the parameter constraint resulting from applying *parameter substitution* $\Psi : P' \to P \cup \mathbb{T}_P$ to parameter constraint $\xi \in \mathcal{B}(P')$.

Definition 8 (PTLTS Bisimulation). *Let* $\mathcal{P}, \mathcal{P}'$ *be PTA over* Σ, *where* $C \cap C' = \emptyset$ *and* $P \cap P' = \emptyset$, $\overline{\mathcal{R}} \subseteq \overline{S} \times \overline{S}'$, *and* $\Psi : P' \to P \cup \mathbb{T}_P$ *such that for all* $(\overline{s}_1, \overline{s}_1') \in \overline{\mathcal{R}}$

- *if* $\overline{s}_1 \xrightarrow{\mu} \overline{s}_2$ *with* $\mu \in \Sigma_\tau$, *then* $\overline{s}_1' \xrightarrow{\mu} \overline{s}_2'$ *and* $(\overline{s}_2, \overline{s}_2') \in \overline{\mathcal{R}}$ *and* $\xi_2 \Rightarrow [\Psi]\xi_2'$, *and*
- *if* $\overline{s}_1 \xrightarrow{d} \overline{s}_2$ *with* $d \in \Delta$, *then* $\overline{s}_1' \xrightarrow{d'} \overline{s}_2'$ *with* $d' \in \Delta$ *and* $(\overline{s}_2, \overline{s}_2') \in \overline{\mathcal{R}}$ *and* $\xi_2 \Rightarrow [\Psi]\xi_2'$.

$\mathcal{P}'$ *(strongly) timed-simulates* $\mathcal{P}$ *iff* $(\overline{s}_0, \overline{s}_0') \in \overline{\mathcal{R}}$. $\mathcal{P}$ *and* $\mathcal{P}'$ *are (strongly) timed bisimilar if there further exists* $\Psi' : P \to P' \cup \mathbb{T}_P$ *such that* $\overline{\mathcal{R}}$ *is symmetric.*

By $\mathcal{P} \sqsubseteq_\Psi \mathcal{P}'$ we denote that the PTLTS of $\mathcal{P}'$ parametric-timed-simulates the PTLTS of $\mathcal{P}$. Hence, Definition 8 requires a correspondence Ψ between *parameters* of $\mathcal{P}$ and $\mathcal{P}'$ rather than a correspondence $\mathfrak{R}$ between *parameter valuations* as in Definition 6.

Example 6. Figures 5a and 5b show PLTS extracts of the PTA shown in Figs. 4a and 4b. Action a in $\mathcal{P}_0$ leads to a state with parameter constraint $p > 0$ due to the parametric clock constraint $x < p$ and clock valuation $x = 0$. Hence, $\mathcal{P}_1 \sqsubseteq_\Psi \mathcal{P}_0$ holds for $\Psi(q) = p$ or $\Psi(q) = p'$.

Theorem 1. *Let* $\mathcal{P}, \mathcal{P}'$ *be PTA over* Σ. *If* $\mathcal{P} \sqsubseteq_\Psi \mathcal{P}'$, *then* $\mathcal{P} \sqsubseteq \mathcal{P}'$.

Proof. We prove Theorem 1 by using Ψ to derive $\mathfrak{R}$. Here, Ψ provides a correspondence between parameters in $\mathcal{P}$ and $\mathcal{P}'$ such that if there exists such a Ψ, this Ψ directly provides a canonical correspondence between equivalent parameter valuations ν, ν'. Hence, it holds that $\mathcal{P} \sqsubseteq_\Psi \mathcal{P}' \Rightarrow \mathcal{P} \sqsubseteq \mathcal{P}'$.

In contrast, $\mathcal{P} \sqsubseteq \mathcal{P}' \Rightarrow \mathcal{P} \sqsubseteq_\Psi \mathcal{P}'$ does not hold. Consider as a counter-example two PTA $\mathcal{P}$ and $\mathcal{P}'$ with $L = \{\ell_0, \ell_1\}$ and $L = \{\ell_0', \ell_1'\}$, respectively, having switches $\ell_0 \xrightarrow{x > p \wedge x > 42, a, \emptyset} \ell_1$ and $\ell_0' \xrightarrow{x > q, a, \emptyset} \ell_1'$. $\mathcal{P} \sqsubseteq \mathcal{P}'$ holds by defining $\mathfrak{R}$ such that the constant value 42 is assigned to q if $p \leq 42$ and by assigning the value of p, else. However, $\mathcal{P} \not\sqsubseteq_\Psi \mathcal{P}'$ as we have to decide whether we substitute q by 42 or by p in Ψ. $\qquad\qquad\qquad\qquad\qquad\square$

Similar to TLTS, PTLTS are, in general, infinite-state and infinitely-branching state-transition graphs thus not providing a practical basis for effectively checking parametric-timed bisimilarity.

As a future work, we plan to employ a fully symbolic semantics of PTA, called *parametric zone graphs*, to facilitate an effective (yet still incomplete) parametric-timed bisimilarity checking [5].

Concluding this section, we investigate an over-approximation of PTA semantics by means of plain TA semantics which allows us to apply imprecise, yet decidable TA bisimilarity-checking to PTA models.

4.3   Parameter-Abstracted Timed Bisimulation

We consider *parameter-abstracted PTA (PA-PTA)*, an over-approximation of PTA semantics by means of TA semantics. In PA-PTA, every occurrence of a lower-bounded parameter within a parametric clock constraint is replaced by the smallest possible value (i.e., constant 0). Correspondingly, every occurrence of upper-bounded parameter within a parametric clock constraint is replaced by the greatest possible values which is, however, not representable as a proper numeric constant. Instead, we replace the entire clause in which the upper-bounded parameter occurs by constant *true*. The resulting model is a proper TA model which comprises the union of all behavior of every TA model derivable from the respective PTA.

Definition 9 (PA-PTA). *The PA-PTA of a PTA $\mathcal{P}$, denoted $[\mathcal{P}]$, is derived from $\mathcal{P}$ by*

– *replacing each occurrence of lower-bounded parameters p_i by constant 0, and*
– *replacing each clause with upper-bounded parameter p_i by constant* true.

Obviously, PA-PTA $[\mathcal{P}]$ of PTA $\mathcal{P}$ is a TA according to Definition 1. Hence, given two PTA models, $\mathcal{P}$ and $\mathcal{P}'$, we can apply a (decidable) timed-bisimilarity check to the corresponding PA-PTA models, $[\mathcal{P}]$ and $[\mathcal{P}']$. Unfortunately, $[\mathcal{P}] \sqsubseteq [\mathcal{P}']$ does not imply that $\mathcal{P} \sqsubseteq \mathcal{P}'$ holds. For instance, considering Figs. 4a and 4f, we have $[\mathcal{P}_0] \sqsubseteq [\mathcal{P}_5]$, but $\mathcal{P}_0 \sqsubseteq \mathcal{P}_5$ does not hold.

However, considering the sub-class of *L/U-PTA* models (cf. Definition 5), timed (bi-)similarity of the corresponding PA-PTA models at least constitutes a *necessary* precondition for parametric (bi-)similarity of the respective PTA models.

Theorem 2. *Let* $\mathcal{P}$, $\mathcal{P}'$ *be L/U-PTA over* Σ. *If* $[\mathcal{P}] \not\sqsubseteq [\mathcal{P}']$, *then* $\mathcal{P} \not\sqsubseteq \mathcal{P}'$.

Proof. Let $\mathcal{P}$, $\mathcal{P}'$ be L/U-PTA over Σ. We prove Theorem 2 by contradiction. In particular, $[\mathcal{P}]$ and $[\mathcal{P}']$ constitutes the most permissive parameter valuation by means of the union of all behavior of all other valuations. Hence, we need an example with $[\mathcal{P}] \not\sqsubseteq [\mathcal{P}']$ such that when stepping back from PA-PTA to PTA, re-introduced parameters constraints of $\mathcal{P}$ are more restrictive than those of $\mathcal{P}'$ thus resulting in $\mathcal{P} \sqsubseteq \mathcal{P}'$. This would require combinations of parametric clock constraints making states, being reachable in $[\mathcal{P}]$, unreachable in $\mathcal{P}$. However, in case of L/U-PTA, additional parametric clock constraints can never affect reachability [14]. □

Hence, the restrictions of PTA as imposed by the sub-class of L/U-PTA models enables us to practically *falsify* parametric timed bisimularity. On the other hand, it remains an open questions whether also *verifying* parametric timed bisimilarity becomes decidable for L/U-PTA. In addition, to gain a deeper understanding of the practical relevance of the restricted usage parametric clock constraints as imposed in L/U-PTA requires further real-world case studies in a future work.

5   Related Work

The notion of timed bisimulation goes back to Moller and Tofts [17] as well as Yi [21], both defined on real-time extensions of the process algebra CCS. Similarly, Nicollin and Sifakis [18] define timed bisimulation on ATP (Algebra of Timed Processes). However, none of these works initially incorporated a technique for effectively checking bisimilarity. The pioneering work of Čerāns [8] includes the first decidability proof of timed bisimulation on TA, by providing a finite characterization of bisimilarity-checking on region graphs. The improved (i.e., less space-consuming) approach of Weise and Lenzkes [20] employs a variation of zone graphs, called FBS graphs, which also builds the basis for our zone-history graphs. Guha et al. [10,11] also follow a zone-based approach for bisimilarity-checking on TA as well as the weaker notion of timed prebisimilarity, by employing so-called zone valuation graphs and the notion of spans as also used in our approach.

Nevertheless, concerning PTA, almost all analysis problems investigated so far are concerned with properties of *one* PTA, whereas no equivalence notions such as timed bisimulation have been proposed so far [4,5].

In the context of software product line engineering, dynamically configurable extensions of timed automata have been proposed. For instance, featured timed automata (FTA) incorporate a finite set of Boolean feature parameters to define *presence conditions* to (de-)activate clock constraints as well as entire switches depending on the feature selection [9]. The resulting formalism is used to facilitate symbolic model-checking of all derivable TA models in a single run which is called family-based analysis. However, FTA only comprise a finite set of derivable TA models thus being strictly less expressive than PTA. In contrast,

Luthmann et al. propose configurable parametric timed automata combining PTA und FTA into one model [16] and describe a family-based, yet incomplete approach for generating test suites achieving location coverage on every derivable TA model. To summarize, neither for FTA nor for CoPTA models, a corresponding notion of timed bisimilarity has been proposed as done in this paper.

6 Conclusion

In this paper, we elaborated on the notion of parametric timed (bi-)simulation for semantically comparing PTA models which is inherently undecidable due to the Turing-completeness of PTA. We provided different characterizations of parametric timed bisimulation and investigated a sub-class of PTA called L/U-PTA with respect to decidability properties. As a future work, we explore further decidability properties of interesting sub-classes of PTA similar to L/U-PTA and to evaluate the practical impact of the respective modeling restrictions imposed by those sub-classes as compared to fully-fledged PTA models. In addition, we plan to characterize parametric timed bisimulation on a fully symbolic PTA semantics called parametric zone graphs which are based on zone-graph semantics of TA. This allows us to develop an effective, yet still incomplete, tool for parametric-timed-bisimilarity checking utilizing an SMT-solver for evaluating parameter constraints. Finally, we are also interested in compositionality properties of (parametric) timed bisimulation in order to further tackle scalability in the formal analysis of real-time critical systems.

References

1. Alur, R., Dill, D.: Automata for modeling real-time systems. In: Paterson, M.S. (ed.) ICALP 1990. LNCS, vol. 443, pp. 322–335. Springer, Heidelberg (1990). https://doi.org/10.1007/BFb0032042
2. Alur, R., Henzinger, T.A., Vardi, M.Y.: Parametric real-time reasoning. In: STOC 1993, pp. 592–601. ACM (1993). https://doi.org/10.1145/167088.167242
3. Alur, R., Madhusudan, P.: Decision problems for timed automata: a survey. In: Bernardo, M., Corradini, F. (eds.) SFM-RT 2004. LNCS, vol. 3185, pp. 1–24. Springer, Heidelberg (2004). https://doi.org/10.1007/978-3-540-30080-9_1
4. André, É.: What's decidable about parametric timed automata? In: Artho, C., Ölveczky, P.C. (eds.) FTSCS 2015. CCIS, vol. 596, pp. 52–68. Springer, Cham (2016). https://doi.org/10.1007/978-3-319-29510-7_3
5. André, É.: What's decidable about parametric timed automata? Int. J. Softw. Tools Technol. Transf. **21**(2), 203–219 (2017). https://doi.org/10.1007/s10009-017-0467-0
6. Bengtsson, J., Yi, W.: Timed automata: semantics, algorithms and tools. In: Desel, J., Reisig, W., Rozenberg, G. (eds.) ACPN 2003. LNCS, vol. 3098, pp. 87–124. Springer, Heidelberg (2004). https://doi.org/10.1007/978-3-540-27755-2_3
7. Bérard, B., Petit, A., Diekert, V., Gastin, P.: Characterization of the expressive power of silent transitions in timed automata. Fundamenta Informaticae **36**(2,3), 145–182 (1998). https://doi.org/10.3233/FI-1998-36233

8. Čerāns, K.: Decidability of bisimulation equivalences for parallel timer processes. In: von Bochmann, G., Probst, D.K. (eds.) CAV 1992. LNCS, vol. 663, pp. 302–315. Springer, Heidelberg (1993). https://doi.org/10.1007/3-540-56496-9_24

9. Cordy, M., Schobbens, P.Y., Heymans, P., Legay, A.: Behavioural modelling and verification of real-time software product lines. In: Proceedings of the 16th International Software Product Line Conference, vol. 1, pp. 66–75. ACM (2012)

10. Guha, S., Krishna, S.N., Narayan, C., Arun-Kumar, S.: A unifying approach to decide relations for timed automata and their game characterization. In: EXPRESS/SOS'13. EPTCS, vol. 120 (2013). https://doi.org/10.4204/EPTCS.120.5

11. Guha, S., Narayan, C., Arun-Kumar, S.: On decidability of prebisimulation for timed automata. In: Madhusudan, P., Seshia, S.A. (eds.) CAV 2012. LNCS, vol. 7358, pp. 444–461. Springer, Heidelberg (2012). https://doi.org/10.1007/978-3-642-31424-7_33

12. Henzinger, T.A., Manna, Z., Pnueli, A.: Timed transition systems. In: de Bakker, J.W., Huizing, C., de Roever, W.P., Rozenberg, G. (eds.) REX 1991. LNCS, vol. 600, pp. 226–251. Springer, Heidelberg (1992). https://doi.org/10.1007/BFb0031995

13. Henzinger, T.A., Nicollin, X., Sifakis, J., Yovine, S.: Symbolic model checking for real-time systems. Inf. Comput. **111**(2), 193–244 (1994). https://doi.org/10.1006/inco.1994.1045

14. Hune, T., Romijn, J., Stoelinga, M., Vaandrager, F.: Linear parametric model checking of timed automata. J. Logic Algebraic Program. **52–53**, 183–220 (2002). https://doi.org/10.1016/S1567-8326(02)00037-1

15. Liva, G., Khan, M.T., Pinzger, M.: Extracting timed automata from java methods. In: 2017 IEEE 17th International Working Conference on Source Code Analysis and Manipulation (SCAM), pp. 91–100. IEEE (2017)

16. Luthmann, L., Stephan, A., Bürdek, J., Lochau, M.: Modeling and testing product lines with unbounded parametric real-time constraints. In: Proceedings of the 21st International Systems and Software Product Line Conference - Volume A, SPLC 2017, pp. 104–103. ACM, New York (2017). https://doi.org/10.1145/3106195.3106204

17. Moller, F., Tofts, C.: A temporal calculus of communicating systems. In: Baeten, J.C.M., Klop, J.W. (eds.) CONCUR 1990. LNCS, vol. 458, pp. 401–415. Springer, Heidelberg (1990). https://doi.org/10.1007/BFb0039073

18. Nicollin, X., Sifakis, J.: The algebra of timed processes, ATP: theory and application. Inf. Comput. **114**(1), 131–178 (1994). https://doi.org/10.1006/inco.1994.1083

19. Waez, M.T.B., Dingel, J., Rudie, K.: A survey of timed automata for the development of real-time systems. Comput. Sci. Rev. **9**, 1–26 (2013). https://doi.org/10.1016/j.cosrev.2013.05.001

20. Weise, C., Lenzkes, D.: Efficient scaling-invariant checking of timed bisimulation. In: Reischuk, R., Morvan, M. (eds.) STACS 1997. LNCS, vol. 1200, pp. 177–188. Springer, Heidelberg (1997). https://doi.org/10.1007/BFb0023458

21. Wang, Y.: Real-time behaviour of asynchronous agents. In: Baeten, J.C.M., Klop, J.W. (eds.) CONCUR 1990. LNCS, vol. 458, pp. 502–520. Springer, Heidelberg (1990). https://doi.org/10.1007/BFb0039080

A Unifying Framework for Dynamic Monitoring and a Taxonomy of Optimizations

Marie-Christine Jakobs$^{(\boxtimes)}$ and Heiko Mantel$^{(\boxtimes)}$

Department of Computer Science, TU Darmstadt, Darmstadt, Germany
{jakobs,mantel}@cs.tu-darmstadt.de

Abstract. Reducing the performance overhead of run-time monitoring is crucial for making it affordable to enforce more complex requirements than simple security or safety properties. Optimizations for reducing the overhead are becoming increasingly sophisticated themselves, which makes it mandatory to verify that they preserve what shall be enforced. In this article, we propose a taxonomy for such optimizations and use it to develop a classification of existing optimization techniques. Moreover, we propose a semantic framework for modeling run-time monitors that provides a suitable basis both, for verifying that optimizations preserve reliable enforcement and for analytically assessing the performance gain.

1 Introduction

Run-time verification is a popular technique for ensuring that a program satisfies given requirements. Conceptually, a monitor observes runs of a target program and interferes, when a violation of some requirement is about to occur. In contrast to static analysis and formal verification, run-time verification does not analyze all possible runs of the target program, but only the ones that actually occur. This simplifies the analysis. In addition, a dynamic analysis has knowledge of actual values in a run and can thereby achieve better precision.

The down-side of run-time monitoring (short: RTM) is that the monitor induces a performance overhead each time the target program is run. This overhead can become unacceptably high, and it is a common reason for abstaining from using run-time monitoring in practice [7]. When complex requirements are enforced by RTM and complex target programs are monitored, then the performance overhead becomes an even bigger problem. This is, for instance, relevant when using RTM in software reengineering for adding properties to existing software.

The goal of optimizing RTM is to reduce this performance overhead. To achieve acceptable performance, complex optimizations for RTM [34, 18] are suggested. However, they are lacking full formal correctness proofs. When applying such optimizations, one currently gives up formal guarantees of RTM [33, 29]. Thus, we need better foundations to prove complex optimizations for RTM.

As a first step, we provide the foundations to prove RTM optimizations from two simple classes of optimizations. Along the way, we developed a semantic framework for characterizing the behavior of run-time monitors. Our framework allows

© Springer Nature Switzerland AG 2020
T. Margaria and B. Steffen (Eds.): ISoLA 2020, LNCS 12477, pp. 72–92, 2020.
https://doi.org/10.1007/978-3-030-61470-6_6

us to carry the distinction of observable and controllable events [8] over to optimizations. Moreover, we distinguish the affirmative treatment of requirements from a preventive treatment, which both occur in prior work. We clarify where they differ technically and how they can be used interchangeably. We aim at using our semantic framework in the future to verify further classes of optimizations.

Several heterogeneous optimizations for RTM are proposed in the literature [11, 10, 34, 30, 18, 5, 35, 22, 3]. Since we aim at using run-time monitoring to enforce specifications, we focus on optimizations that aim for soundness, i.e., to not miss any requirement violations. To identify (interesting) classes of optimizations proposed in the literature, we compare the existing approaches on a conceptual level. Previously proposed taxonomies for RTM [14, 27, 32, 20] do not cover optimizations. We introduce a 3-dimensional taxonomy for RTM optimizations, which considers how requirements are specified, how the necessary information for the optimization is obtained, and how the optimization is performed. We use our taxonomy to classify prior work on optimization of RTM.

In summary, we conduct first steps in a larger research effort to formally prove optimizations for RTM. We show how to formally prove optimizations for RTM and what needs to be done. As an unexpected bonus, our semantic framework helped us to come up with new, more sophisticated optimizations.

2   Preliminaries

Basic Notions and Notation. We use $\langle\rangle$ to denote the empty sequence, $\langle a\rangle$ to denote the sequence consisting of a single symbol a, and $a.w$ to denote the sequence starting with the symbol a, followed by the sequence w.

We define the concatenation of two sequences w_1 and w_2 (denoted by $w_1 \cdot w_2$) recursively by $\langle\rangle \cdot w_2 = w_2$ and $(a.w_1) \cdot w_2 = a.(w_1 \cdot w_2)$. Overloading notation, we use $w.a$ as an abbreviation for $w \cdot \langle a\rangle$. A sequence w_1 is a prefix (w_2 is a suffix) of a sequence w if there exists a sequence w_2 (a sequence w_1) such that $w = w_1 \cdot w_2$ holds. A set of sequences L is prefix-closed (is suffix-closed) if $w \in L$ implies that $w_1 \in L$ holds for each prefix (for each suffix) w_1 of w. The suffix-closure of L (denoted $\mathcal{SUF}(L)$) is the smallest suffix-closed super-set of L.

We define the projection of a sequence w to a set A (denoted by $w|_A$) recursively by $\langle\rangle|_A = \langle\rangle$, $(a.w)|_A = w|_A$ if $a \notin A$, and $(a.w)|_A = a.(w|_A)$ if $a \in A$.

We lift concatenation and projection from sequences to sets of sequences by $L_1 \cdot L_2 = \bigcup_{w_1 \in L_1, w_2 \in L_2}\{w_1 \cdot w_2\}$ and by $L|_A = \bigcup_{w \in L}\{w|_A\}$. We define the *-operator as the smallest fixed-point of $L^* = \{\langle\rangle\} \cup \{a.w \mid a \in L \wedge w \in L^*\}$.

Projection preserves the $\in$- and the $\subseteq$-relationship, i.e., $w \in L$ implies $w|_A \in L|_A$, and $L_1 \subseteq L_2$ implies $L_1|_A \subseteq L|_{A_2}$. By contraposition, $w|_A \notin L|_A$ implies $w \notin L$, and $L_1|_A \not\subseteq L_2|_A$ implies $L_1 \not\subseteq L_2$. We will exploit these facts in proofs.

We denote the space of total functions and the space of partial functions from A to B by $A \to B$ and $A \hookrightarrow B$, respectively. For $f : A \hookrightarrow B$, we write $f(a)\downarrow$ if f is defined at $a \in A$, i.e. $\exists b \in B. f(a) = b$, and $f(a)\uparrow$ if f is undefined at a.

2.1 Labeled Transition Systems and Properties

We use labeled transition systems to formally characterize the behavior of programs in a uniform fashion. Given a program in some programming, byte-code or machine language, it is straightforward to construct from the language's small-step operational semantics a corresponding labeled transition system where events correspond to executing individual instructions. Our use of labeled transition systems is also compatible with coarser-grained or finer-grained events.

Definition 1. *A* labeled transition system *(brief: LTS) is a tuple* (S, S_0, E, Δ), *where S is a set of states, $S_0 \subseteq S$ is a set of initial states, E is a set of events, and $\Delta \subseteq (S \times E \times S)$ is a transition relation.*

The relation $\Delta^* \subseteq (S \times E^* \times S)$ is defined inductively by $(s, \langle\rangle, s) \in \Delta^*$ and by $(s, a.w, s'') \in \Delta^*$ if $\exists s' \in S. ((s, a, s') \in \Delta \land (s', w, s'') \in \Delta^*)$.

As usual, we use traces to model program runs. The *set of traces induced by an* LTS $lts = (S, S_0, E, \Delta)$ *starting in* $s \in S$ is the smallest set $Traces(lts, s) \subseteq E^*$ such that $Traces(lts, s) = \{w \in E^* \mid \exists s' \in S. (s, w, s') \in \Delta^*\}$. The *set of traces induced by* lts *is* $Traces(lts) = \bigcup_{s_0 \in S_0} Traces(lts, s_0)$. Note that both sets, $Traces(lts)$ and $Traces(lts, s)$ are prefix-closed.

We focus on properties in the sense of Alpern and Schneider [4].

Definition 2. *A* property *over a set E is a function $prop : E^* \to Bool$.*

A labeled transition system $lts = (S, S_0, E, \Delta)$ satisfies a property $prop : E^* \to Bool$ iff $\forall tr \in Traces(lts). prop(tr) = \top$ holds.

2.2 Finite Automata and Formal Languages

We use automata to formally characterize the behavior of run-time monitors.

Definition 3. *A* finite automaton *(brief: FA) is a tuple (S, S_0, S_F, A, δ), where S and A are finite sets, $S_0 \subseteq S$ and $S_F \subseteq S$ are nonempty, and $\delta : (S \times A) \hookrightarrow S$.*

The function $\delta^* : (S \times A^*) \hookrightarrow S$ is defined inductively by $\delta^*(s, \langle\rangle) = s$ and by $\delta^*(s, a.w) = s''$ if $\exists s' \in S. (\delta(s, a) = s' \land \delta^*(s', w) = s'')$.

Given a finite automaton $fa = (S, S_0, S_F, A, \delta)$, S is *the set of states*, S_0 is *the set of initial states*, S_F is *the set of final states*, A is *the alphabet*, and δ is *the transition function of fa*. An FA $fa = (S, S_0, S_F, A, \delta)$, is *total in* $a \in A$ iff $\forall s \in S. \exists s' \in S. \delta(s, a) = s'$, and fa is *total in* $A' \subseteq A$ iff fa is total in each $a \in A'$.

A *word over an alphabet A* is a finite sequence over A. A *language over an alphabet A* is a set of words over A. We call a language L over A *simple* iff $L = \{\}$, $L = \{\langle\rangle\}$, or $L = \{\langle a\rangle\}$ holds for some $a \in A$. A language L is *regular* iff L can be composed from simple languages using the operators $\cup$, $\cdot$, and *.

Definition 4. *A word $w \in A^*$ is* accepted *in $s \in S$ by a finite automaton $fa = (S, S_0, S_F, A, \delta)$ iff $\delta^*(s, w) \in S_F$. The* language accepted by fa in $s \in S$ *is the set of all such words, i.e., $Lang(fa, s) = \{w \in A^* \mid \delta^*(s, w) \in S_F\}$.*

A word $w \in A^*$ is accepted by fa *iff fa accepts w in some initial state $s_0 \in S_0$. The* language accepted by fa *is $Lang(fa) = \bigcup_{s_0 \in S_0} Lang(fa, s_0)$.*

A word $w \in A^*$ is rejected by fa *iff w is not accepted by fa.*

The expressiveness of finite automata is given by Kleene's theorem [26]. The language $Lang(fa)$ is regular for each finite automaton fa, and, for each regular language L, there exists a finite automaton fa with $Lang(fa) = L$.

Finite automata where every state is final, have a prominent role in this article. The languages accepted by this class of finite automata coincide with the languages that are regular and prefix closed [25].

We introduce three operations for adapting transition functions: The lifting of a transition function $\delta: (S \times A) \hookrightarrow S$ to an alphabet B augments the domain of δ by adding stuttering steps for all pairs in $(S \times (B \setminus A))$. The restriction of δ to B restricts the domain of δ to events in $(A \cap B)$. The completion of δ to B adds a stuttering step for each $b \in B$ and $s \in S$, wherever $\delta(s, b)$ is undefined.

Definition 5. *Let* $\delta : (S \times A) \hookrightarrow S$ *be a transition function and* B *be an alphabet. The* lifting *of* δ *to* B *is* $\delta \uparrow^{B} \colon (S \times (A \cup B)) \hookrightarrow S$, *the* restriction *of* δ *to* B *is* $\delta|_{B} \colon (S \times (A \cap B)) \hookrightarrow S$, *and the* completion *of* δ *to* B *is* $\delta \circlearrowleft^{B} \colon (S \times A) \hookrightarrow S$ *with*

$$\delta\uparrow^{B}(s,a) = \delta(s,a) \quad if\ a \in A \qquad\qquad \delta\uparrow^{B}(s,a) = s \quad if\ a \in (B \setminus A)$$
$$\delta|_{B}(s,a) = \delta(s,a) \quad if\ a \in (A \cap B)$$
$$\delta\circlearrowleft^{B}(s,a) = \delta(s,a) \quad if\ \delta(s,a)\downarrow \qquad \delta\circlearrowleft^{B}(s,a) = s \quad if\ a \in (A \cap B) \wedge \delta(s,a)\uparrow$$

Definition 6. *The* lifting *of a finite automaton* $fa = (S, S_0, S_F, A, \delta)$ *to an alphabet* B *is the finite automaton* $fa^{\uparrow B} = (S, S_0, S_F, (A \cup B), \delta\uparrow^{B})$.

3 A Framework for Monitoring and Enforcement

A run-time monitor checks whether actions of a target program are permissible before they occur. If the monitor classifies an action as affirmative, then the action may occur, and, otherwise, the monitor takes appropriate countermeasures.

Historically, the field of run-time monitoring has close ties to automata theory. This connection is beneficial since constructions and insights from automata theory can be exploited in the development and analysis of RTM solutions.

The use of automata for run-time monitoring, however, is not uniform. For using finite automata, e.g., one can observe two approaches:

1. Each word accepted by an FA corresponds to an *affirmative* behavior.
2. Each word accepted by an FA corresponds to a *preventive* behavior.

At the level of formal languages, the approaches are duals of each other, and switching from the one to the other is straightforward: Given a regular language L specifying the affirmative behaviors, one can use an FA that recognizes L for monitoring (following the first approach). Alternatively, one can use an FA that recognizes the complement of L (following the second approach to monitoring).

Due to this duality at the level of formal languages, the two approaches are sometimes treated as if they were fully interchangeable. However, when implementing run-time monitoring, one needs to commit to one of these approaches. This choice might impact performance overhead, and this is not merely an implementation-level issue, as we will clarify in Sect. 4.

In the development of our semantic framework, we carefully distinguish

- between finite automata and the requirements that shall be enforced and
- between two approaches of using finite automata for RTM.

As usual, we use formal languages to specify the requirements to be enforced. However, to clearly distinguish between the two approaches to run-time monitoring, we refer to such languages as *policies*, if they specify affirmative runs, and as *anti-policies*, if they specify preventive runs. We deliberately do not identify policies/anti-policies with accepting automata, because this would limit the use of our framework for verifying soundness of optimizations.

We formally introduce a notion of monitors on top of finite automata. This allows us to explicitly distinguish between events of the target that can be fully controlled from events that can be observed but not controlled. This distinction is relevant for the enforceability of properties [8], as well as for the performance overhead (see Sect. 4). We use the term *monitor* when following the first approach to RTM and the term *watch-dog* when following the second approach.

The interplay between target programs, monitors/watch-dogs, properties, and policies/anti-policies is visualized on the left-hand side of Fig. 1.

3.1 Policies and Anti-policies

We use policies and anti-policies to specify restrictions that shall be enforced when a target program is running. A policy specifies which behaviors are affirmed, while an anti-policy specifies which behaviors are prevented.

Definition 7. *A* policy *is a pair* $pol = (A, Tr)$, *where A is an alphabet, and $Tr \subseteq A^*$ is a non-empty and prefix-closed language over A, the* affirmative traces.

An anti-policy *is a pair* $apol = (A', Tr')$, *where A' is an alphabet and $Tr' \subseteq A'^*$ is a language over A' with $\langle\rangle \notin Tr'$, the* preventive traces.

We define the meaning of policies/anti-policies for labeled transition systems:

Definition 8. *The properties specified by* $pol = (A, Tr)$ *and* $apol = (A', Tr')$, *respectively, for a set E are* $prop^E_{pol}, \overline{prop}^E_{apol} : E^* \to Bool$ *defined by:*

$$prop^E_{pol}(w) = \begin{cases} \top & \text{if } w|_A \in Tr \\ \bot & \text{otherwise.} \end{cases}$$

$$\overline{prop}^E_{apol}(w) = \begin{cases} \bot & \text{if } \exists w_1, w_2 \in E^*. (w = w_1 \cdot w_2 \wedge w_1|_{A'} \in Tr') \\ \top & \text{otherwise.} \end{cases}$$

Intuitively, policies and anti-policies are dual concepts. The following theorem substantiates this conceptual duality more precisely based on our definitions.

Theorem 1. *Let* $pol = (A, Tr)$ *be a policy and* $apol = (A, Tr')$ *be an anti-policy. If* $Tr' = A^* \setminus Tr$ *then* $prop^E_{pol}(w) = \overline{prop}^E_{apol}(w)$ *holds for all* $w \in E^*$.

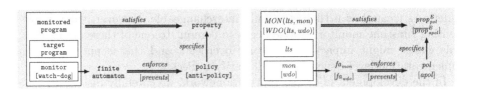

Fig. 1. Run-time monitoring and enforcement conceptually (lhs) and formally (rhs)

Theorem 1 can be used to construct from a policy an anti-policy that specifies the same property. This construction is universal in the set of events. In the other direction, constructing a policy from an anti-policy $apol = (A, Tr')$ is only possible if Tr' is suffix-closed, as, otherwise, $(A, (A^* \setminus Tr'))$ is not a policy.

3.2   Monitors and Enforcement of Policies

For monitors, we use transition functions as follows to specify which actions are affirmed in which states: If the transition function is defined for a given state and action, then this action is affirmed in this state and, otherwise, not. This reflects, e.g., the behavior of security automata [33] or truncation automata [29].

A monitor might only supervise a subset of a target program's actions. Among those actions, we distinguish between actions whose occurrences the monitor can prevent and actions whose occurrences the monitor cannot prevent. This allows us to faithfully capture actions whose occurrences simply cannot be prevented (e.g., the progress of time). This distinction will also be relevant for our performance model (see Sect. 4) and optimizations (see Sect. 5).

The distinction of observable and controllable events has been exploited before in other contexts. For instance, Basin et al. [8] use it to analyze enforceability.

As a notational convention, we use Γ_o to denote the set of events whose occurrences a monitor can observe but not control, and we use Γ_c to denote the set of events whose occurrences a monitor can observe and also control.

Definition 9. *A* monitor *is a tuple* $mon = (MS, ms_0, \Gamma_o, \Gamma_c, \delta)$, *where*

- *MS is a finite set of monitor states with initial state $ms_0 \in MS$,*
- *Γ_o is a finite set of observed events,*
- *Γ_c is a finite set of controlled events with $\Gamma_o \cap \Gamma_c = \emptyset$, and*
- *$\delta : (MS \times (\Gamma_o \cup \Gamma_c)) \hookrightarrow MS)$ is a transition function that is total in $(MS \times \Gamma_o)$.*

For the rest of this subsection, let $mon = (MS, ms_0, \Gamma_o, \Gamma_c, \delta)$ be a monitor, let $\Gamma = \Gamma_o \cup \Gamma_c$, and let $lts = (S, S_0, E, \Delta)$ be a labeled transition system.

We model the effects of supervising a target program by a monitor.

Definition 10. Monitoring *the labeled transition system lts with monitor mon results in the labeled transition system* $MON(lts, mon) = (S', S'_0, E, \Delta')$, *where*

$$
\begin{aligned}
S' &= S \times MS \ , \\
S'_0 &= S_0 \times \{ms_0\} \ , \ and
\end{aligned}
$$

$$
((s,ms), e, (s',ms')) \in \Delta' \quad iff \quad \begin{pmatrix} (s, e, s') \in \Delta \\ \wedge \ (e \in \Gamma \Rightarrow ms' = \delta(ms, e)) \\ \wedge \ (e \notin \Gamma \Rightarrow ms' = ms) \end{pmatrix} \ .
$$

Definition 10 captures the intended operational behavior of monitors: A monitor updates its state whenever events occur that the monitor can observe (i.e., events in $\Gamma_o \cup \Gamma_c$). When non-observable events occur, the monitor does not modify its state. Moreover, a monitored program can perform an event in Γ_c only if the target program and the monitor can make a transition for this event. If the event is in $E \setminus \Gamma_c$, then it suffices that the target can make a transition for this event.[1]

---

[1] Recall from Definition 9 that a monitor is total in Γ_o.

Before characterizing the effects of monitoring denotationally, let us make the conceptual similarity between monitors and finite automata precise.

Definition 11. $fa_{mon} = (MS, \{ms_0\}, MS, \Gamma, \delta)$ *is the FA induced by mon.*

Note that all monitor states are final states of the finite automaton fa_{mon}. This reflects that the acceptance of an event by a monitor solely depends on whether the transition relation is defined for the current monitor state and this event.

Recall from Sect. 2 that the expressiveness of finite automata where all states are final is the class of regular languages that are prefix-closed [25].

The denotational effects of monitoring a target by a monitor now can be captured concisely by using the lifting of fa_{mon} to the events of the target:

Theorem 2. $Traces(MON(lts, mon)) = Traces(lts) \cap Lang(fa_{mon}^{\uparrow E})$ *holds.*

Given $pol = (A, Tr)$, one can construct a monitor that soundly enforces this policy via the construction of an FA that accepts a sub-language of Tr.

Theorem 3. *Let* $fa = (MS, \{ms_0\}, MS, \Gamma, \delta)$ *and* $mon = (MS, ms_0, \emptyset, \Gamma, \delta)$. *Then, for every policy* $pol = (A, Tr)$, *the following implication holds:*
$$Lang(fa) \subseteq Tr \text{ implies that } MON(lts, mon) \text{ satisfies } prop_{pol}^E.$$

Therefore, we say that fa *enforces* pol if $Lang(fa) \subseteq Tr$ holds. In the theorem, the set Γ_o of the monitor is empty. We will clarify in Sect. 4 what the benefits are of moving events from Γ_c to Γ_o and in Sect. 5 when it is safe to do so.

The right-hand side of Fig. 1 visualizes the interplay between the formal representations of target programs, monitors, properties, and policies.

3.3   Watch-Dogs and Prevention of Anti-policies

As explained, we use the terms watch-dog and anti-policy instead of monitor and policy, respectively, when the specification focuses on preventive behavior. We observed that in this case, finite automata are usually used in a slightly different way than described in Sect. 3.2, including prior work on optimizations of run-time monitoring. As such technical details matter when verifying optimizations, we extend our semantic framework to watch-dogs and clarify the technical differences to monitors. We also present a construction suitable for moving from watch-dogs to monitors while preserving the behavior of a monitored target.

If a watch-dog reaches a final state, then a preventive behavior has occurred. Therefore, a watch-dog must take countermeasures *before* it reaches a final state.

The main differences to the definition of monitors (see Definition 9) are the existence of a set of final states and that the transition function is total.

Definition 12. *A* watch-dog *is a tuple* $wdo = (WS, ws_0, WS_F, \Gamma_o, \Gamma_c, \delta)$ *where*

- WS *is a finite set of watch-dog states* *with initial state* $ws_0 \in WS$,
- $WS_F \subseteq WS$ *is a set of final watch-dog states* *with* $ws_0 \notin WS_F$,
- Γ_o *is a finite set of observed events,*
- Γ_c *is a finite set of controlled events with* $\Gamma_o \cap \Gamma_c = \emptyset$, *and*
- $\delta : (WS \times (\Gamma_o \cup \Gamma_c)) \to WS)$ *is a transition function that is total and for which* $\delta(ws, \gamma) \in (WS \setminus WS_F)$ *holds for all* $\gamma \in \Gamma_o$ *and* $ws \in WS$.

For the rest of this subsection, let $wdo = (WS, ws_0, WS_F, \Gamma_o, \Gamma_c, \delta)$ be a watch-dog, let $\Gamma = \Gamma_o \cup \Gamma_c$, and let $lts = (S, S_0, E, \Delta)$ be an LTS.

We model the effects of supervising a target program by a watch-dog.

Definition 13. *Monitoring lts with the watch-dog wdo results in the labeled transition system* $WDO(lts, wdo) = (S', S'_0, E, \Delta')$, *where*

$$S' = S \times WS ,$$
$$S'_0 = S_0 \times \{ws_0\} , \text{ and}$$
$$((s,ws), e, (s',ws')) \in \Delta' \text{ iff } \begin{pmatrix} (s,e,s') \in \Delta \\ \wedge\ (e \in \Gamma \Rightarrow (ws' = \delta(ws, e) \wedge ws' \notin WS_F)) \\ \wedge\ (e \notin \Gamma \Rightarrow ws' = ws) \} \end{pmatrix} .$$

Note that Definition 13 faithfully captures the intended operational behavior of watch-dogs: A monitored target can perform an event in Γ_c only if the non-monitored target is able to make a transition for this event and if the occurrence of this event would not result in a final watch-dog state. If the event is in $E \setminus \Gamma_c$, then it suffices that the target is able to make a transition for this event.[2]

We identify which finite automaton corresponds to a given watch-dog:

Definition 14. $fa_{wdo} = (WS, \{ws_0\}, WS_F, \Gamma, \delta)$ *is the FA induced by wdo.*

Analogously to Sect. 3.2, we capture the denotational effects of monitoring a target by a watch-dog using the liftings of fa_{wdo} to the events of the target:

Theorem 4. $Traces(WDO(lts, wdo)) = Traces(lts) \setminus \mathcal{SUF}(Lang(fa_{wdo}^{\uparrow E}))$ *holds.*

Note that, in Theorem 4, the suffix closure of the automaton's language occurs on the right-hand side of the equation. This is a difference to the analogous theorem for monitors (i.e., Theorem 2). Operationally, this is due to the fact that an action of a target program is prevented by a watch-dog if the action would result in the watch-dog reaching a final state. That is, a watch-dog not only prevents all words that it accepts but also all suffixes of such words.

Remark 1. Note that for the finite automaton corresponding to a monitor, every state is final and the transition function may be partial. In contrast, for a finite automaton corresponding to a watch-dog, at least the initial state must not be final, and the transition function must be total. Despite these differences in the underlying classes of automata, one can construct a monitor from a watch-dog while preserving the behavior of all monitored target systems. To this end, one changes the transition function of fa_{wdo} to be undefined for all arguments that would lead to a final state, afterwards one removes all final states from the set of states, and finally, one applies the usual complement constructions on finite automata by making all final states non-final and vice versa.

4   A Performance Model for Monitors

Run-time monitoring and enforcement inherently comes at the cost of some performance overhead. A monitor needs to learn about the action that the target

---

[2] Recall that a watch-dog cannot reach a final state when events in Γ_o occur.

program is about to perform. The monitor then needs to decide whether to affirm or prevent an action. If an action is affirmed, the target needs to be enabled to perform the action and, otherwise, countermeasures must be taken.

Usually the individual actions of a monitor are rather fast, but such delays accumulate during a run. This is why it has become good practice to accompany the development of tools for run-time monitoring and enforcement with experimental performance evaluations, e.g., at a benchmark like DaCapo [9].

The overhead caused by monitoring depends on how the monitor itself is implemented and also on how the combination with the target program is technically realized. The *inlining-technique* [19] is a popular technique that incorporates the monitor code sequentially into the target's code. *Outlining* places the monitor into a separate process [27] that runs in parallel to the target. The *crosslining technique* [23] combines the two by sequentially inlining parts of the monitor code while outlining other parts to run in parallel.

While experimental performance evaluations of tools for run-time monitoring and enforcement have become common practice, there is little work on analytical performance evaluations. A notable exception is an article by Drábik et al. [15]. They propose a framework for analyzing the costs of enforcement.

In this section, we propose a novel performance model for run-time monitoring and enforcement. Our model is similar in spirit to the one in [15], but we take a broader set of events and context-dependence of costs into account.

We introduce performance vectors to model the time needed by a monitor to observe an action, to check whether it is permissible, to permit an action to happen, and to terminate a run. In addition, a performance vector models any base overhead that is induced by the mere existence of a monitor.

Definition 15. *A performance vector for a set of events E is a tuple $\mu = (\mu_o, \mu_c, \mu_p, \mu_t, \mu_\emptyset)$, where $\mu_o, \mu_c, \mu_p, \mu_t, \mu_\emptyset : ((E \times E^*) \to Time)$.*
A performance vector $\mu = (\mu_o, \mu_c, \mu_p, \mu_t, \mu_\emptyset)$ is context independent iff $\mu_\alpha(e, w) = \mu_\alpha(e, w')$ holds for all $\alpha \in \{o, c, p, t, \emptyset\}$, $e \in E$, and $w, w' \in E^*$.

Intuitively, $\mu_o(e, tr)$ models the time a monitor needs to learn that the target is about to perform the event $e \in E$. The second parameter, i.e. tr, models the context in which e occurs by the trace of events that have happened before.

Similarly, $\mu_c(e, tr)$ models the time needed to check whether e is permissible in context tr. The functions μ_p and μ_t model the time needed for enabling the target to perform e and for preventing e by terminating the run, respectively. The values of μ_p and μ_t shall include time needed to update the monitor's internal state. The function $\mu_\emptyset$ models the base overhead of monitoring for events that the monitor can neither observe nor control.

We parametrized the functions in a performance vector by both, an event and a context. This design choice allows one to specify the performance overhead very precisely. If determining such a precise performance vector, in practice, is infeasible or too expensive, one can coarsen the model, e.g., by defining a context-independent performance vector that approximates the actual performance costs.

We are now ready to introduce a novel performance model for monitors.

Definition 16. *The overhead caused by a monitor mon* $= (MS, ms_0, \Gamma_o, \Gamma_c, \delta)$ *under a performance vector* $\mu = (\mu_o, \mu_c, \mu_p, \mu_t, \mu_\emptyset)$ *for* $e \in E$ *and* $tr \in E^*$ *is*

$$\mu_{mon}(e, tr) = \begin{cases} \mu_\emptyset(e, tr) & , \text{ if } e \in (E \setminus (\Gamma_o \cup \Gamma_c)) \\ \mu_o(e, tr) & , \text{ if } e \in \Gamma_o \\ \mu_o(e, tr) + \mu_c(e, tr) + \mu_p(e, tr) & , \text{ if } e \in \Gamma_c \text{ and } \delta(ms_{tr}, e) \downarrow \\ \mu_o(e, tr) + \mu_c(e, tr) + \mu_t(e, tr) & , \text{ if } e \in \Gamma_c \text{ and } \delta(ms_{tr}, e) \uparrow \end{cases}$$

where $ms_{tr} = \delta^*(ms_0, tr|_{\Gamma_o \cup \Gamma_c})$. *The* overhead *of mon for a trace is defined recursively by* $\mu^*_{mon}(\langle\rangle) = 0$ *and* $\mu^*_{mon}(tr.e) = \mu^*_{mon}(tr) + \mu_{mon}(e, tr)$.

In Sect. 5, we use this model to characterize the performance gain by selected optimizations, while using the terms in Definition 16 purely symbolically.

Remark 2. The definition of an analogous performance model for watch-dogs is straightforward based on our semantic framework. When instantiating the resulting performance models, however, be aware that differences between monitors and watch-dogs should be taken into account when defining performance vectors. In particular, supervising events in Γ_c might have higher performance costs for watch-dogs than for monitors: While a watch-dog needs to compute the resulting watch-dog state and check that it is not final before allowing the target to continue, a monitor only needs to check whether a transition for the event exists and may update its state in parallel to the target's execution.

5 Towards a More Formal Treatment of Optimizations

Optimizations are crucial for lowering the performance overhead of run-time monitoring and enforcement. However, such optimizations need to be applied with care, because optimizing a monitor could endanger its effectiveness.

In our study of prior work on optimizing run-time monitoring and enforcement, we observed that the arguments for the preservation of properties mostly remain at an informal level. Given the growing importance of optimizations and their increasing level of sophistication, we think the time is ready for more scrutiny. After all, what is the value of formal verifications of run-time monitors, if afterward optimizations are applied that have only been informally analyzed?

The advantages of a more formal treatment of optimizations are twofold:

– precise, formal definitions of preconditions clarify better what one needs to check for before applying a given optimization and
– formally verified preservation results provide reliable guarantees for the preservation of properties under an optimization if the preconditions are met.

One possibility for decreasing performance overhead, is to limit the events tracked in run-time monitoring and enforcement. This optimization technique is popular, and it also appeared as an integral part of more complex optimizations (see Sect. 6). This is the optimization on which we focus in this section.

Based on our semantic framework, we clarify which preconditions guarantee the preservation of which properties under this optimization. Formally, the optimization corresponds to removing events from the alphabet of the automaton underlying a monitor or watch-dog while restricting the transition function accordingly. However, our framework provides a more fine-grained distinction, namely between events under the control of a monitor/watch-dog (i.e., Γ_c) and events whose occurrences the monitor/watch-dog can observe but not control (i.e., Γ_o). This allows us to split the optimization into two more primitive ones:

- removal of events from the control while keeping track of them and
- removal of events from the set of events that are tracked.

In our formal model, *reduction of control* (brief: *ROC*) corresponds to moving events from Γ_c to Γ_o, and *reduction of tracking* (brief: *ROT*) corresponds to removing events from Γ_o. Each of these transformations reduces the performance overhead already if applied in isolation. If applied in combination, *ROC* and *ROT* result in the *removal of events from the supervision* (brief: *ROS*). Our split is increasing the application spectrum of such optimizations as there are cases, where *ROC* may be applied, while applying *ROS* would be problematic.

Like in the previous section, we limit our technical exposition to monitors. For the rest of this section, let $mon = (MS, ms_0, \Gamma_o, \Gamma_c, \delta)$ be a monitor.

5.1   Formal Definitions of Optimizations and Performance Gain

We define reduction of control, reduction of tracking, and reduction of supervision as operators that transform monitors. Each of these operators takes an event as second argument. This is the event whose supervision is altered.

Definition 17. *Let* $\gamma_c \in \Gamma_c$, $\gamma_o \in \Gamma_o$, *and* $\gamma \in \Gamma_o \cup \Gamma_c$.

$$ROC(mon, \gamma_c) = (MS, ms_0, (\Gamma_o \cup \{\gamma_c\}), (\Gamma_c \setminus \{\gamma_c\}), \delta Q^{\{\gamma_c\}})$$
$$ROT(mon, \gamma_o) = (MS, ms_0, (\Gamma_o \setminus \{\gamma_o\}), \Gamma_c, \delta|_{(\Gamma_o \cup \Gamma_c) \setminus \{\gamma_o\}})$$
$$ROS(mon, \gamma) = ROT(ROC(mon, \gamma), \gamma)$$

Note that, if $mon = (MS, ms_0, \Gamma_o, \Gamma_c, \delta)$ is a monitor then $\delta Q^{\{\gamma_c\}}$ is total in $(\Gamma_o \cup \{\gamma_c\})$ and $\delta|_{(\Gamma_o \cup \Gamma_c) \setminus \{\gamma_o\}}$ is total in $(\Gamma_o \setminus \{\gamma_o\})$. Therefore, if *mon* is a monitor then ROC(mon, γ_c) and ROT(mon, γ_o), indeed, are monitors.

In the definition of *ROC*, $\delta Q^{\{\gamma_c\}}$ is a transition function that is total in $\{\gamma_c\}$. The addition of stuttering steps to δ by this completion makes a monitor more affirmative. The removal of Γ_o from the alphabet of a monitor in the definition of *ROT* also makes monitoring more affirmative (cf. Definition 10).

We characterize the effects of the transformations on the monitoring overhead based on our performance model. For simplicity, we assume the monitoring overhead for any given action of the target to depend only on this action.

Theorem 5. *Let* $\mu = (\mu_o, \mu_c, \mu_p, \mu_t, \mu_\emptyset)$ *be a context-independent performance vector, and let E be a set of events. The following conditions hold for all $tr \in E^*$, $\gamma_c \in \Gamma_c$, roc $= ROC(mon, \gamma_c)$, $\gamma_o \in \Gamma_o$, and rot $= ROT(mon, \gamma_o)$:*

$$\mu_o(\gamma_c) \leq \mu_c(\gamma_c) \implies \mu^*_{roc}(tr) \leq \mu^*_{mon}(tr)$$
$$\mu_\emptyset(\gamma_o) \leq \mu_o(\gamma_o) \implies \mu^*_{rot}(tr) \leq \mu^*_{mon}(tr)$$

On the implementation level, moving γ_c from Γ_c to Γ_o corresponds to reducing the monitor code that runs at each program point where γ_c might occur. The monitor still needs to be informed about such occurrences, but no run-time check is needed, as it is clear a priori that the decision will be positive. Applying ROT corresponds to reducing the number of program points at which monitor code runs. That is, $\mu_o(\gamma_c) \leq \mu_c(\gamma_c)$ and $\mu_\emptyset(\gamma_o) \leq \mu_o(\gamma_o)$ should hold for most monitor implementations, and, hence, ROC and ROT, indeed, are optimizations.

5.2   Application Scenarios for the Optimizations

We point out and informally discuss multiple possibilities for applying the optimizations ROC, ROT, and ROS. The informal presentation in this subsection, will be substantiated by formalizations of conditions and theorems in Sect. 5.3.

Assume a policy $pol = (A, Tr)$ that specifies the requirements to be enforced, and a monitor constructed by firstly, determining a sublanguage of Tr that is regular and prefix-closed, then synthesizing $fa = (MS, \{ms_0\}, MS, \Gamma, \delta)$ that accepts this sublanguage, and defining the monitor to be $mon = (MS, ms_0, \emptyset, \Gamma, \delta)$. According to Theorem 3, the monitor mon soundly enforces the property induced by pol (i.e., $prop_{pol}^E$) for every labeled transition system $lts = (S, S_0, E, \Delta)$.

At the level of program code, one could check whether the policy's alphabet contains events that cannot be generated by the target program. This check can be realized, e.g., by a syntactic search in the program code for patterns that correspond to these events, or, more sophisticated, by a reachability analysis.

At the level of labeled transition systems, the syntactic check corresponds to checking whether the set $A \setminus E$ is non-empty, and the reachability analysis corresponds to checking, based on Δ, whether any events in A are never enabled. Intuitively, monitoring such events is unnecessary. Hence, one could exempt them from the monitor's supervision by applying ROS for all such events.   [A]

A reachability analysis using the monitor's transition function could be used to detect events that are always permitted. For such events the monitor's check is unnecessary, and, hence, one can optimize the monitor by ROC.[3]   [B1]

A more sophisticated variant is to detect events the monitor permits in all states that the monitor reaches by observing possible traces of the target. [B2]

Note that optimizations might make other optimizations applicable. For instance, removing an event from a monitor's control by ROS [A] might make, for some other event, all monitor states unreachable in which this event is prevented by the monitor and, hence, ROC could become applicable due to [B1] or [B2].

5.3   Preservation Theorems

The following theorem justifies our uses of ROC in Sect. 5.2. The three preconditions in the theorem, respectively, correspond to [A], [B1], and [B2].

---

[3] In such a situation, one might be tempted to instead apply the more powerful optimization ROS, but this, in general, does not guarantee the preservation of $prop_{pol}^E$.

Theorem 6. *Let* $\gamma_c \in \Gamma_c$, $\Gamma = \Gamma_o \cup \Gamma_c$, *and* $roc = ROC(mon, \gamma_c)$. *The equation*

$$Traces(lts) \cap Lang(fa_{roc}^{\uparrow E}) = Traces(lts) \cap Lang(fa_{mon}^{\uparrow E})$$

holds if at least one of the following conditions is satisfied:

1. $\Delta \cap (S \times \{\gamma_c\} \times S) = \emptyset$,
2. $\forall w \in \Gamma^*. \ (\delta^*(ms_0, w)) \downarrow \implies (\delta^*(ms_0, w.\gamma_c)) \downarrow$, *or*
3. $\forall (tr.\gamma_c) \in Traces(lts). \ (\delta^*(ms_0, tr|_\Gamma)) \downarrow \implies (\delta^*(ms_0, (tr|_\Gamma).\gamma_c)) \downarrow$.

The following theorem justifies our uses of ROT in Sect. 5.2. The precondition in the theorem corresponds to [A].

Theorem 7. *Let* $\gamma_o \in \Gamma_o$, $\Gamma = \Gamma_o \cup \Gamma_c$, *and* $rot = ROT(mon, \gamma_o)$. *The equation*

$$Traces(lts) \cap Lang(fa_{rot}^{\uparrow E}) = Traces(lts) \cap Lang(fa_{mon}^{\uparrow E})$$

holds if $\Delta \cap (S \times \{\gamma_o\} \times S) = \emptyset$.

If the respective preconditions are fulfilled, Theorems 6 and 7 guarantee that ROC and ROT do not alter the intersection of the sets of traces of the non-monitored target with the language of the lifted automaton. In combination with Theorem 2, this guarantees the set of traces of a monitored target to remain unchanged. Thus, *all* properties are preserved if the preconditions are met.

Remark 3. The application spectrum of optimizations could be broadened by taking the policy into account to relax the preconditions of optimizations. Here, we see substantial room for improving optimizations, as it suffices to preserve one property, namely $prop_{pol}^E$. This could be a valuable direction for future work.

6   Optimizations for Run-Time Monitoring

We focus on optimizations [11, 10, 34, 30, 18, 5, 35, 22, 3] that aim at sound enforcement. For such optimizations, we develop a taxonomy for RTM optimizations and then classify the existing approaches in our taxonomy.

Most publications on optimizations for run-time monitoring use a more technical and a less formal description than Sects. 3 and 5. Although we encountered ambiguities in descriptions of optimizations or monitors and the different representations made it difficult to identify similarities, we follow the optimizing approaches and describe our taxonomy on an informal level, too.

Optimization approaches for RTM get as input a program and a specification. We use the general term specification for the technical input(s) that describe the objective of RTM, e.g., which execution traces are allowed and how to deal with forbidden traces. The shape of the specification differs among the RTM approaches. For example, one can use a finite state automaton to describe the forbidden execution traces and specify that forbidden traces are truncated.

The first step of all optimization approaches for RTM is to gather information about the program with respect to the specification. This information is then used for optimization, which tackles the program's structure, its instrumentation, or the specification. Although the general workflow is the same, approaches for optimizing RTM differ a lot, as we have seen for ROC and ROT.

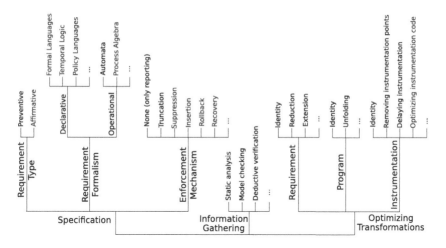

Fig. 2. A taxonomy for optimizing run-time monitoring

6.1   A Taxonomy of Optimizations for RTM

Figure 2 shows the taxonomy we propose to classify optimizations for RTM. Elements shown in blue do not occur in any of the reviewed optimizations, but we think they are natural extensions. Our taxonomy uses three main dimensions to characterize optimizations: the specification, information gathering, and optimizing transformations. The latter two specify the two steps in the workflow. A specification in run-time monitoring defines which enforcement is applied to which execution trace. Next, we discuss the dimensions in more detail.

Specification. The requirement type and formalism describe the requirement. The requirement type determines whether the requirement specifies the allowed behavior (affirmative) or the forbidden behavior (preventive). This corresponds to the two approaches distinguished in Sect. 3. The formalism fixes the requirement language. We distinguish between declarative and operational formalisms. Commonly, RTM uses both [33, 29]: a declarative requirement to describe the intended behavior and an operational requirement to implement the monitoring. Optimizations rarely consider both, but focus on operational requirements.

Formal languages [7], temporal logic [28] or dedicated policy languages like policy and anti-policy are possible declarative formalisms for requirements. Process algebras [37] and automata [33] are options for operational formalisms. All optimizations we know optimize RTM approaches that (1) are preventive and (2) express requirements in automata formalisms, which range from simple finite state automaton to more advanced automata in DATE [13] and ppDATE [3]. This motivated us to include watch-dogs into our semantic framework. The third element of a specification is the enforcement mechanism. Some optimizations [35, 22] specify that they optimize an RTM approach that uses truncation[4].

---

[4] Recall that we also focused on truncation in Sects. 3–5.

However, for most of the approaches it remains unclear what enforcement mechanism is used by the underling RTM approach. Countermeasures suggested by StaRVOOS [3] and Clara [11] are for example error reporting and error recovery. Further enforcement mechanisms [7] used in RTM are rollback and suppression or insertion of events. Since the information gathering phase of all reviewed optimizations does not consider enforcement, it is likely that enforcement beyond truncation is not fully compatible with those optimizations.

Information Gathering. All approaches we reviewed statically inspect the program to gather information. StaRVOOS [3] uses deductive verification. Often, reachability analyses like model checking [35, 22] or more efficient dataflow analyses [10] are applied. Also, syntactic, flow-insensitive analyses are run [11].

Optimizing Transformations. Reviewing approaches that optimize RTM, we identified three basic concepts for optimizations: transformations of the operational requirement description, the program, or the instrumentation of the program. Since some optimizing approaches apply more than one concept, we describe an optimizing transformation by a triple of the three concepts and use the identity transformation for concepts that are not applied. Thus, unoptimized RTM is identical to only using identity transformations. The three transformations presented in Sect. 5.1 reduce the operational requirement, i.e., they (re)move events. Requirement reduction can remove transitions and conditions, too. In addition, operational requirements can be extended, e.g., by adding transitions and events. Both, reduction and extension, occur standalone [11, 3, 5] like in Sect. 5 or in combination with the removal of instrumentation points [6], a transformation of the instrumentation code. The program transformation unfolding is typically combined with the removal of instrumentation points [35, 30]. However, the removal of instrumentation points can also be used stand-alone [10, 22]. In contrast, delayed instrumentation [18] is currently only used in combination with requirement extension because it replaces sets of instrumentation points by a later instrumentation that aggregates their effect. We are not aware of any approach that optimizes the instrumentation code, e.g., specializes the instrumentation code at instrumentation points using partial evaluation [24], which we think is an interesting direction.

Our taxonomy excludes optimizations for multiple policies [31], online optimizations [17, 36], and unsound optimizations [12, 21, 16] that may miss violations.

6.2   Classifying Optimizations into Optimizing Transformations

In the following, we present six classes for the taxonomy dimension optimizing transformation. All classes occur in the literature and are future candidates for formalizing and proving optimizations for RTM. We start with three classes that only take one of the optimization concepts into account. Thereafter, we discuss three classes that combine different optimizing transformations.

Fig. 3. Workflow of removal of instrumentation points

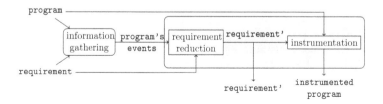

Fig. 4. Workflow of stand-alone requirement reduction

Stand-alone Removal of Instrumentation Points. This class of optimizations keeps the requirement and program as they are and decreases the number of instrumentation points. The left-hand side of Fig. 3 shows the workflow. It first determines the required instrumentation points. The instrumentation includes the optimization and leaves out instrumentation points that are not required.

Nop-shadow analysis [10] and its optimization [34] employ forward and backward, flow-sensitive analyses to detect the instrumentation points (called shadows) that are irrelevant. JAM [22] uses model checking and counterexample-guided abstraction refinement with a limited number of refinement steps. The model checker outputs all traces that violate the requirement and are either real or could not be ruled out. The instrumentation step adds monitoring code for the reported traces and stops the program just before a violation would occur.

Stand-alone Requirement Reduction. Stand-alone requirement reduction describes optimizations that neither change the program nor the instrumentation procedure, which is unaware of the optimization and uses the reduced requirement. Based on the gathered information, these optimizations (re)move elements from automata (the operational requirement formalism).

The most inexpensive reduction (see right-hand side of Fig. 4) in the literature applies the ROS transformation in scenario A (Sect. 5.2). It is used in Clara's QuickCheck [11] to reduce finite state automata and in absent event pruning [5] to reduce requirements written in DATE. Additionally, QuickCheck removes transitions that cannot reach one of the automaton's final states.

Clara's orphan-shadow analysis [11[and object-specific absent event pruning [5] extend this reduction idea with object sensitivity. Since type state requirements track the automaton state per object of interest, used events are detected per object and a requirement reduction (an ROS transformation) is performed for each object. Afterward, the reduced requirements are combined again.

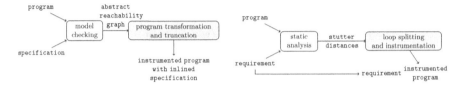

Fig. 5. Zero overhead RTM (lhs) and stutter-equivalent loop optimization (rhs)

Unusable transition pruning [5] integrates flow-sensitive information to the reduction. It takes the control-flow into account and removes automaton transitions that are not activated by any (syntactic) trace of the program.

In its first optimization step, StarVOORS [2] deletes all pre- and postcondition pairs from its ppDATE requirement that are proven by the verifier KeY [1].

Stand-alone Requirement Extension. Stand-alone requirement extension is similar to stand-alone requirement reduction. The only difference is that the gathered information is used to adapt the automaton (operational requirement) by generalizing existing or adding new elements. The only approach in this class we are aware of is the second step of the StaRVOORS [3, 2] approach. To reduce the overhead caused by checking the pre- and postconditions in the ppDATE requirement, StaRVOORS tries to discharge the pre- and postcondition pairs with the deductive verifier KeY [1]. While complete proofs are used for reduction, open proof goals are used to split the precondition into a proven and non-proven part and the pre-/postcondition pair is replaced by a refined pair consisting of the non-proven precondition and the unmodified postcondition.

Combining Unfolding with Removal of Instrumentation Points. Optimizations in this class do not modify the requirement, but unfold the program to enable the removal of instrumentation points.

Zero overhead run-time monitoring [35], shown on the left-hand side of Fig. 5, starts to model check the program with respect to the requirement. The model checking algorithm parallely executes the requirement and a predicate abstraction (with a limited number of refinements). The result of model checking is an abstract reachability graph (ARG) that represents the explored abstract state space. Due to the combination of the requirement and predicate abstraction, the ARG unfolds the program such that all paths leading to a final state of the requirement automaton are syntactic error traces. For optimization, the ARG is translated back into a program and statements leading to a final state in the ARG, i.e., causing a requirement violation, are replaced by HALT statements. The result is a transformed program with inlined enforcement, in which all instrumentation code except for the enforcement itself is delete.

Stutter-equivalent loop optimization [30], shown on the right-hand side of Fig. 5, splits loops into two loops. The first loop runs as long as RTM may change the requirement state. The second loop is not instrumented and executes the remaining loop iterations, for which the requirement state remains stable. A

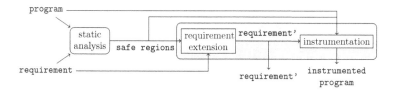

Fig. 6. Workflow of safe regions approach

static analysis is used to determine for each loop the maximal number of loop iterations, the stutter distance, required to reach a stable requirement state. The stutter distance is used to restrict the execution of the first loop.

Delayed Instrumentation with Requirement Extension. In this class, optimizations do not transform the program, but extend the operational requirement and replace groups of instrumentation points by a summary instrumentation point. The only approach in this category we are aware of is the safe regions approach [18]. Its workflow is shown in Fig. 6. The safe regions approach starts with a static analysis to detect safe regions, i.e., code blocks that cannot reach a requirement violation and all paths through the code block that start in the same requirement state end in the same requirement state. Instrumentation does not insert instrumentation code into safe regions, but adds instrumentation code after a safe region, which triggers a special region event. The requirement is extended with transitions for the region events, which summarize the regions' behavior with respect to the requirement.

Combining Requirement Reduction with the Removal of Instrumentation Points. Optimization approaches in this class reduce the operational requirement and remove unnecessary instrumentation points, but do not change the program. Clara [11], which combines QuickCheck, the orphan and nop-shadows analysis, and CLARVA [6], which combines the DATE requirement reductions [5] with the removal of instrumentation points, fall into this category.

On Correctness of Optimizations. Full correctness of an optimization is rarely shown. Exceptions are zero overhead RTM [35] and the DATE reductions [5]. For Clara's nop shadow [10, 11], the stutter-equivalent loop optimization [30], and the safe regions approach [18] only the underlying idea for the optimization is proven. The correctness of Clara's QuickCheck and orphan-shadow analysis [11] is discussed rather informally. The StarVOORS approach [2] provides the foundations and proves the soundness of the ppDate translation, but lacks to prove the correctness of the ppDate optimization. At worst, for the JAM approach [22] and the improvement of the nop shadow approach [34] correctness of the optimization is hardly discussed at all.

7   Conclusion

We presented a semantic framework for formalizing different approaches to RTM in a uniform fashion and a novel performance model. Their intended application domain is the analysis of optimizations of RTM. We showed at selected optimizations that both are suitable for this purpose. In fact, the formalization of optimizations alone already inspired ideas for broadening the application spectrum of known optimizations and for the development of novel optimizations.

Our taxonomy and classification provide a broader conceptual clarification about previously proposed optimizations. Since the taxonomy also covers possibilities not yet explored, it could serve as a road map for future directions.

Naturally, this article can only be one step towards making a more rigorous treatment of optimizations common practice in the field of RTM. Broadening the application spectrum of optimizations, improving their effects, and clarifying which optimizations can be safely applied under which conditions is an exciting research area that deserves and will require substantial future research.

Acknowledgments. We thank Barbara Sprick for helpful discussions. This work was funded by the Hessian LOEWE initiative within the Software-Factory 4.0 project and by the German Federal Ministry of Education and Research and the Hessen State Ministry for Higher Education, Research and the Arts within their joint support of the National Research Center for Applied Cybersecurity ATHENE.

References

1. Ahrendt, W., Beckert, B., Bubel, R., Hähnle, R., Schmitt, P.H., Ulbrich, M. (eds.): Deductive Software Verification - The KeY Book - From Theory to Practice. LNCS, vol. 10001. Springer, Cham (2016). https://doi.org/10.1007/978-3-319-49812-6
2. Ahrendt, W., Chimento, J.M., Pace, G.J., Schneider, G.: Verifying data- and control-oriented properties combining static and runtime verification: theory and tools. Formal Methods Syst. Des. **51**(1), 200–265 (2017)
3. Ahrendt, W., Pace, G.J., Schneider, G.: A unified approach for static and runtime verification: framework and applications. In: Margaria, T., Steffen, B. (eds.) ISoLA 2012. LNCS, vol. 7609, pp. 312–326. Springer, Heidelberg (2012). https://doi.org/10.1007/978-3-642-34026-0_24
4. Alpern, B., Schneider, F.B.: Defining liveness. Inf. Process. Lett. **21**, 181–185 (1985)
5. Azzopardi, S., Colombo, C., Pace, G.J.: Control-flow residual analysis for symbolic automata. In: Pre- and Post-Deployment Verification Techniques. EPTCS, vol. 254, pp. 29–43 (2017)
6. Azzopardi, S., Colombo, C., Pace, G.J.: CLARVA: model-based residual verification of Java programs. In: Model-Driven Engineering and Software Development, pp. 352–359 (2020)
7. Bartocci, E., Falcone, Y. (eds.): Lectures on Runtime Verification Introductory and Advanced Topics. LNCS, vol. 10457. Springer, Cham (2018). https://doi.org/10.1007/978-3-319-75632-5
8. Basin, D.A., Jugé, V., Klaedtke, F., Zalinescu, E.: Enforceable security policies revisited. Trans. Inf. Syst. Secur. **16**(1), 3:1–3:26 (2013)

9. Blackburn, S.M., Garner, R., Hoffmann, C., Khan, A.M., McKinley, K.S., Bentzur, R., Diwan, A., Feinberg, D., Frampton, D., Guyer, S.Z., Hirzel, M., Hosking, A.L., Jump, M., Lee, H.B., Moss, J.E.B., Phansalkar, A., Stefanovic, D., VanDrunen, T., von Dincklage, D., Wiedermann, B.: The DaCapo benchmarks: Java benchmarking development and analysis. In: Object-Oriented Programming, Systems, Languages, and Applications, pp. 169–190 (2006)
10. Bodden, E.: Efficient hybrid typestate analysis by determining continuation-equivalent states. In: International Conference on Software Engineering, pp. 5–14 (2010)
11. Bodden, E., Hendren, L.J.: The Clara framework for hybrid typestate analysis. J. Softw. Tools Technol. Transf. **14**(3), 307–326 (2012)
12. Bodden, E., Hendren, L., Lam, P., Lhoták, O., Naeem, N.A.: Collaborative runtime verification with tracematches. In: Sokolsky, O., Taşıran, S. (eds.) RV 2007. LNCS, vol. 4839, pp. 22–37. Springer, Heidelberg (2007). https://doi.org/10.1007/978-3-540-77395-5_3
13. Colombo, C., Pace, G.J., Schneider, G.: Dynamic event-based runtime monitoring of real-time and contextual properties. In: Cofer, D., Fantechi, A. (eds.) FMICS 2008. LNCS, vol. 5596, pp. 135–149. Springer, Heidelberg (2009). https://doi.org/10.1007/978-3-642-03240-0_13
14. Delgado, N., Gates, A.Q., Roach, S.: A taxonomy and catalog of runtime software-fault monitoring tools. Trans. Softw. Eng. **30**(12), 859–872 (2004)
15. Drábik, P., Martinelli, F., Morisset, C.: Cost-aware runtime enforcement of security policies. In: Jøsang, A., Samarati, P., Petrocchi, M. (eds.) STM 2012. LNCS, vol. 7783, pp. 1–16. Springer, Heidelberg (2013). https://doi.org/10.1007/978-3-642-38004-4_1
16. Dwyer, M.B., Diep, M., Elbaum, S.G.: Reducing the cost of path property monitoring through sampling. In: Automated Software Engineering, pp. 228–237 (2008)
17. Dwyer, M.B., Kinneer, A., Elbaum, S.G.: Adaptive online program analysis. In: International Conference on Software Engineering, pp. 220–229 (2007)
18. Dwyer, M.B., Purandare, R.: Residual dynamic typestate analysis exploiting static analysis: results to reformulate and reduce the cost of dynamic analysis. In: Automated Software Engineering, pp. 124–133 (2007)
19. Erlingsson, U., Schneider, F.B.: SASI enforcement of security policies: a retrospective. In: New Security Paradigms, pp. 87–95 (1999)
20. Falcone, Y., Krstić, S., Reger, G., Traytel, D.: A taxonomy for classifying runtime verification tools. In: Colombo, C., Leucker, M. (eds.) RV 2018. LNCS, vol. 11237, pp. 241–262. Springer, Cham (2018). https://doi.org/10.1007/978-3-030-03769-7_14
21. Fei, L., Midkiff, S.P.: Artemis: practical runtime monitoring of applications for execution anomalies. In: Programming Language Design and Implementation, pp. 84–95 (2006)
22. Fredrikson, M., et al.: Efficient runtime policy enforcement using counterexample-guided abstraction refinement. In: Madhusudan, P., Seshia, S.A. (eds.) CAV 2012. LNCS, vol. 7358, pp. 548–563. Springer, Heidelberg (2012). https://doi.org/10.1007/978-3-642-31424-7_39
23. Gay, R., Hu, J., Mantel, H.: CliSeAu: securing distributed Java programs by cooperative dynamic enforcement. In: Prakash, A., Shyamasundar, R. (eds.) ICISS 2014. LNCS, vol. 8880, pp. 378–398. Springer, Cham (2014). https://doi.org/10.1007/978-3-319-13841-1_21
24. Jones, N.D.: An introduction to partial evaluation. ACM Comput. Surv. **28**(3), 480–503 (1996)

25. Kao, J., Rampersad, N., Shallit, J.O.: On NFAs where all states are final, initial, or both. Theoret. Comput. Sci. **410**(47–49), 5010–5021 (2009)
26. Kleene, S.C.: Representation of events in nerve nets and finite automata. In: Automata Studies, pp. 3–41 (1956)
27. Leucker, M.: Teaching runtime verification. In: Khurshid, S., Sen, K. (eds.) RV 2011. LNCS, vol. 7186, pp. 34–48. Springer, Heidelberg (2012). https://doi.org/10.1007/978-3-642-29860-8_4
28. Leucker, M., Schallhart, C.: A brief account of runtime verification. J. Logic Algebraic Program. **78**(5), 293–303 (2009)
29. Ligatti, J., Bauer, L., Walker, D.: Edit automata: enforcement mechanisms for run-time security policies. J. Inf. Secur. **4**(1–2), 2–16 (2005)
30. Purandare, R., Dwyer, M.B., Elbaum, S.G.: Monitor optimization via stutter-equivalent loop transformation. In: Object-Oriented Programming, Systems, Languages, and Applications, pp. 270–285 (2010)
31. Purandare, R., Dwyer, M.B., Elbaum, S.G.: Optimizing monitoring of finite state properties through monitor compaction. In: Software Testing and Analysis, pp. 280–290 (2013)
32. Rabiser, R., Guinea, S., Vierhauser, M., Baresi, L., Grünbacher, P.: A comparison framework for runtime monitoring approaches. J. Syst. Softw. **125**, 309–321 (2017)
33. Schneider, F.B.: Enforceable security policies. Trans. Inf. Syst. Secur. **3**(1), 30–50 (2000)
34. Wang, C., Chen, Z., Mao, X.: Optimizing nop-shadows typestate analysis by filtering interferential configurations. In: Legay, A., Bensalem, S. (eds.) RV 2013. LNCS, vol. 8174, pp. 269–284. Springer, Heidelberg (2013). https://doi.org/10.1007/978-3-642-40787-1_16
35. Wonisch, D., Schremmer, A., Wehrheim, H.: Zero overhead runtime monitoring. In: Hierons, R.M., Merayo, M.G., Bravetti, M. (eds.) SEFM 2013. LNCS, vol. 8137, pp. 244–258. Springer, Heidelberg (2013). https://doi.org/10.1007/978-3-642-40561-7_17
36. Wu, C.W.W., Kumar, D., Bonakdarpour, B., Fischmeister, S.: Reducing monitoring overhead by integrating event- and time-triggered techniques. In: Legay, A., Bensalem, S. (eds.) RV 2013. LNCS, vol. 8174, pp. 304–321. Springer, Heidelberg (2013). https://doi.org/10.1007/978-3-642-40787-1_18
37. Yamagata, Y., et al.: Runtime monitoring for concurrent systems. In: Falcone, Y., Sánchez, C. (eds.) RV 2016. LNCS, vol. 10012, pp. 386–403. Springer, Cham (2016). https://doi.org/10.1007/978-3-319-46982-9_24

Thirty-Seven Years of Relational Hoare Logic: Remarks on Its Principles and History

David A. Naumann[✉]

Stevens Institute of Technology, Hoboken, USA
naumann@cs.stevens.edu

Abstract. Relational Hoare logics extend the applicability of modular, deductive verification to encompass important 2-run properties including dependency requirements such as confidentiality and program relations such as equivalence or similarity between program versions. A considerable number of recent works introduce different relational Hoare logics without yet converging on a core set of proof rules. This paper looks backwards to little known early work. This brings to light some principles that clarify and organize the rules as well as suggesting a new rule and a new notion of completeness.

1 Introduction

Even in the archivally published part of the scientific literature, there are some gems known to few but deserving the attention of many. Such a gem is a paper by Nissim Francez published in 1983, around the time of Apt's two-part paper "Ten Years of Hoare Logic" [2,3]. Relational Hoare Logic (RHL) formalizes reasoning about two programs. The term, and a version of the logic, are introduced in a well known gem by Nick Benton published in 2004 [19]. Relating two programs is far from new, and is important: it encompasses equivalence (as in compilation), refinement and conditional similarity (as in software development, evolution, and re-engineering), and properties of a single program (like determinacy of output) for which one must consider two executions. Reasoning about two executions inevitably leads to reasoning about two different programs—that is one of the principles already articulated in the paper by Francez titled "Product Properties and Their Direct Verification" [31] which introduces many rules of RHL.

The fundamental safety property is *partial correctness*: for each of the program's runs, if the initial state satisfies the designated precondition, and the run terminates, then the final state satisfies the designated postcondition. The fundamental liveness property is *termination*: for each of the program's runs, if the initial state satisfies the precondition then the run is finite. Many interesting or desirable behavioral properties of a program are such *trace properties*, that is, a condition on runs is required to hold for all runs. Relations between programs involve two runs at a time, for example one notion of equivalence is that from

T. Margaria and B. Steffen (Eds.): ISoLA 2020, LNCS 12477, pp. 93–116, 2020.
https://doi.org/10.1007/978-3-030-61470-6_7

the same initial state, runs of the two programs reach the same final state. One cannot expect this property if the programs are nondeterministic. What then is determinacy? It is the property of a program that from any initial state, its runs all diverge or all terminate in the same state. This can be defined more parsimoniously: from any initial state, any two runs either both diverge or both terminate in the same state. Behavioral program properties involving multiple runs have been dubbed *hyperproperties* and an important subclass are the *k-safety* properties which, for some fixed $k \geq 1$ can be defined by requiring all k-tuples of runs satisfy a condition on k-tuples [23,62]. Francez uses the term *power property* for what is now called k-safety, and *product property* for relations between programs.

The k-safety properties are an attractive object of study because they are amenable to reasoning techniques that are natural generalizations of those for safety properties. As is likely to occur to anyone familiar with programming or automata theory, to prove a 2-safety property one may construct a *product program* whose runs represent pairs of runs of the original. Francez points out that product programs can be expressed as ordinary programs, so that Hoare logic (HL) can be used to prove 2-safety: If C is a sequential program acting on variables, we can choose fresh names and obtain a renamed copy C', and then $C; C'$ serves as a product. This particular product construction is often called *self-composition*, a term from Barthe et al. [14,15] who rediscover the idea (and also consider other forms of product) for proving information flow security.

By now, scientific interest together with practical importance has led to exciting achievements. Related challenges are under active study by a number of research groups, often making use of some form of RHL. Quite a few papers have appeared with RHLs, some emphasizing frameworks meant to provide unifying principles [1,13,19,44], but there is considerable variety in the proof rules included or omitted. By contrast, the core rules of HL for imperative programs appear in many places with relatively little variation. There is a scientific explanation for this situation: the recipe for boiling a logic down to its essentials is to state and prove a completeness theorem that says true properties are provable. But, through product programs, relational reasoning is reduced to HL—so completeness in this sense is a trivial consequence of completeness for *unary* (i.e., 1-safety) properties, as Francez observes. His paper concludes with a problem that is still open: "It would be interesting to obtain a formal characterization of the situation in which the proposed method achieves actual proof simplification over the indirect proofs using Hoare's (unary) logic."

In this paper I describe, in as plain terms as I can, various reasoning principles and their embodiment in proof rules. One contribution is to systematize knowledge and in particular to emphasize the importance of program equivalences to reduce the number of core rules. I also introduce a new rule to fill a gap that becomes evident when one considers one of the key motivations for relational reasoning. Finally, I introduce a new notion: alignment completeness. It appears naturally when one recapitulates, as Francez does and I do with slightly more generality, the development from Floyd to Hoare.

Scientists thrive on getting credit and good scientists take care in giving credit. But it is not always easy to determine the origin of ideas, in part because good ideas may be independently rediscovered several times before becoming firmly ensconced in the edifice of the known. My primary aim in this paper is to explain some principles as I have understood them, not to give a survey of prior work. I do point out ideas found in the paper by Francez, and cite some other work in passing. Other early works that may have been overlooked can be found in the first paragraph of Sect. 5.

Outline. Following background on the inductive assertion method and HL (Sect. 2), the method is extended to aligned pairs of runs in Sect. 3, as background for RHL which comprises Sect. 4. Sect. 5 discusses related work and Sect. 6 concludes. An extended version of the paper is at http://arxiv.org/abs/1910.14560.

2 Preliminaries

2.1 The Inductive Assertion Method

We focus on the simple imperative or "while" language with assignments and possibly other primitive commands like nondeterministic assignment. The reader is expected to be familiar with transition semantics, in which the program acts on stores, where a store is a total mapping from variables to values. The following abstraction of a program's semantics is convenient.

An **automaton** is a tuple $(Ctrl, Sto, init, fin, \mapsto)$ where Sto is a set (the data stores), $Ctrl$ is a finite set that contains distinct elements $init$ and fin, and $\mapsto \subseteq (Ctrl \times Sto) \times (Ctrl \times Sto)$ is the transition relation. We require $(c, s) \mapsto (d, t)$ to imply $c \neq fin$ and $c \neq d$ and call these the **finality** and **non-stuttering** conditions respectively. A pair (c, s) is called a **state**. Let β and γ range over states. A **trace** of an automaton is a non-empty sequence τ of states, consecutive under the transition relation, with $ctrl(\tau_0) = init$. It is **terminated** provided τ is finite and $ctrl(\tau_{-1}) = fin$, where τ_{-1} denotes the last state of τ.

In structural operational semantics, transitions act on configurations of the form (c, s) where c is a command, and skip by itself indicates termination. This fits our model: take $init$ to be the program of interest, $Ctrl$ to be all commands, and fin to be skip. Another instantiation treats $Ctrl$ as the points in the program's control flow graph (CFG).

A partial correctness property is given by a pair of store predicates, P, Q, for which we write $P \rightsquigarrow Q$. In a formal logic, P and Q range over formulas in some assertion language, usually first order logic for a designated signature that includes types and operations used in the program. We write $s \models P$ to say s satisfies predicate P, and define $(c, s) \models P$ iff $s \models P$. As a means to specify requirements, the notation is inadequate. The postcondition $y = x + 1$ can be achieved by changing x or by changing y. This problem is best solved by including a **frame condition** which for simple imperative programs is just a list $\overline{x}$ of variables permitted to change, which we write as $P \rightsquigarrow Q[\overline{x}]$. Its meaning can be reduced to the simpler form provided we distinguish between program variables and spec-only variables not allowed to occur in programs. That being so, we focus on the form $P \rightsquigarrow Q$ and use for it the succinct term **spec**.

Let us spell out two semantics for specs in terms of an automaton A. The **basic semantics** is as follows. For a finite trace τ to satisfy $P \rightsquigarrow Q$ means that $\tau_0 \models P$ and $ctrl(\tau_{-1}) = fin$ imply $\tau_{-1} \models Q$, in which case we write $\tau \models P \rightsquigarrow Q$. Then A satisfies $P \rightsquigarrow Q$ just if all its finite traces do. The **non-stuck semantics** adds a second condition for τ to satisfy the spec: $ctrl(\tau_{-1}) \neq fin$ implies $\tau_{-1} \mapsto -$, where $\tau_{-1} \mapsto -$ means there is at least one successor state. Stuck states are often used to model runtime faults.

The inductive assertion method (IAM) of Floyd [30], is a way to establish that command C satisfies spec $P \rightsquigarrow Q$. The first idea is to generalize the problem: in addition to establishing that Q must hold in a final state, we establish additional conditions at intermediate steps, with the aim to reason by induction on steps of execution. The second idea is to designate which intermediate steps in terms of C's CFG. An **assertion** is thus a formula R associated with a particular point in the CFG, designating the claim that in any run, R holds whenever control is at that point. This beautiful idea, called **annotation**, has a simple representation in syntax which has become commonplace: the assert statement. The third idea ensures that the claim is strong enough to be inductive hypothesis to prove the spec: (i) The entry point is annotated as P and the exit point is annotated as Q. (ii) Every cycle in the CFG is annotated with at least one assertion. The annotated points are said to form a **cutpoint set**. Such an annotation determines a finite set of acyclic paths through the CFG, each starting and ending with an annotation and having no intervening one—we call these **segments**.

Floyd shows, by induction on execution steps, that C satisfies $P \rightsquigarrow Q$ provided that the **verification conditions** (VCs) all hold [30]. Each segment determines the following VC: for any state that satisfies the initial assertion, and any execution along the segment, such that the branch conditions hold, the final assertion holds in the last state. In effect, the VCs are cases of the induction step in a proof that the assertions hold in any run from a state satisfying P.

Given a program and cutpoint set for its CFG, there is an automaton with $Ctrl$ the cutpoint set; the transitions $(c, s) \mapsto (d, t)$ are given by the semantics of the segment from c to d. An annotation assigns a store predicate $anno(c)$ to each cutpoint c. Define the state set $S \subseteq (Ctrl \times Sto)$ by $(c, s) \in S$ iff $s \models anno(c)$. Then the VCs amount to the condition that S is closed under $\mapsto$.

The IAM requires us to reason about the semantics of straight-line program fragments, which is amenable to automation in a number of different ways, including the direct use of operational semantics [45]. What makes program verification difficult is finding inductive intermediate assertions.

2.2 Hoare Logic

Hoare showed that the IAM can be presented as a deductive system, in which inference rules capture the semantics of the constructs of the programming language and verification conditions are, to some degree, compositional in terms of

$$x := e : P_e^x \rightsquigarrow P$$

$$\frac{C : P \rightsquigarrow R \qquad D : R \rightsquigarrow Q}{C; D : P \rightsquigarrow Q}$$

$$\frac{C : P \wedge e \rightsquigarrow Q \qquad D : P \wedge \neg e \rightsquigarrow Q}{\text{if } e \text{ then } C \text{ else } D : P \rightsquigarrow Q}$$

$$\frac{C : P \rightsquigarrow Q \qquad D : P \rightsquigarrow R}{C + D : P \rightsquigarrow Q \vee R}$$

$$\frac{C : P \wedge b \rightsquigarrow P}{\text{while } b \text{ do } C \text{ od} : P \rightsquigarrow P \wedge \neg b}$$

Fig. 1. Syntax-directed rules of HL for simple imperative programs.

$$\frac{P \Rightarrow R \qquad C : R \rightsquigarrow S \qquad S \Rightarrow Q}{C : P \rightsquigarrow Q} \text{ (Conseq)}$$

$$\frac{C : P \rightsquigarrow Q \qquad C : P \rightsquigarrow R}{C : P \rightsquigarrow Q \wedge R} \text{ (Conj)} \qquad \frac{C : P \rightsquigarrow R \qquad C : Q \rightsquigarrow R}{C : P \vee Q \rightsquigarrow R} \text{ (Disj)}$$

$$\frac{C : P \rightsquigarrow Q \qquad FV(R) \cap Vars(C) = \emptyset}{C : P \wedge R \rightsquigarrow Q \wedge R} \text{ (Frame)}$$

Fig. 2. Rules to manipulate specs in HL.

program syntax. The system derives what are known variously as *partial correctness assertions*, Hoare triples, etc., and which ascribe a spec to a program. Hoare wrote $P\{C\}Q$ but it has become standard to write $\{P\}C\{Q\}$. We write $C : P \rightsquigarrow Q$ and call it a **correctness judgment**.

There are many Hoare logics, because a deductive system is defined for a particular language, i.e., set of program constructs. The textbook by Apt et al. [5] has logics encompassing procedures, concurrency, etc. In this paper we focus on sequential programs but the principles apply broadly.

Rules for some program constructs can be found in Fig. 1. The axiom for assignment involves capture-avoiding substitution of an expression for a variable, written P_e^x, wherein we see that the system treats program expressions and variables as mathematical ones, a slightly delicate topic that does not obtrude in the sequel. These rules transparently embody the reasoning that underlies the IAM. The sequence rule adds an intermediate assertion, changing one verification condition into two (typically simpler) ones. The rule for conditional alternatives has two premises, corresponding to the two paths through the CFG. Nondeterministic choice (notation $+$) again gives rise to two paths. The rules in Fig. 1 provide for deductive proof following the program structure but are incomplete; e.g., they give no way to prove the judgment $x := x + 1 : (x = y) \rightsquigarrow (x > y)$. Such gaps are bridged by rules like those in Fig. 2. For HL to be a self-contained deductive system it needs to include means to infer valid formulas, such as the first and third premises of rule Conseq.

For while programs, the syntax-directed rules together with CONSEQ are complete in the sense that any true judgment can be proved. The other rules embody useful reasoning principles. DISJ provides proof by cases, which is useful when a program's behavior has two quite different cases. In terms of IAM, one might apply the method twice, to prove $C : P \rightsquigarrow R$ and $C : Q \rightsquigarrow R$ with entirely different annotations, and then conclude $C : P \vee Q \rightsquigarrow R$ by some argument about the meaning of specs. This principle is expressed directly in Hoare logic, as is the oft-used principle of establishing conjuncts of a postcondition separately.

Modular Reasoning. HL easily admits procedure-modular reasoning, sometimes formalized by judgments of the form $H \vdash C : P \rightsquigarrow Q$ where hypothesis H comprises procedure signatures and their specs [8,54]. With the addition of procedures, CONSEQ is not sufficient for completeness. Other rules are needed to manipulate specs, such as substitution rules to adapt procedure specs to their calling contexts [5,36,55]. We use the name FRAME for a rule Hoare called Invariance [36], with a nod towards a similar rule in separation logic [53] where disjointness of heap locations is expressed by using the separating conjunction in place of $\wedge$. With explicit frame conditions the rule can be phrased like this: From $C : P \rightsquigarrow Q[\overline{x}]$ and $FV(R) \cap \overline{x} = \emptyset$ infer $C : P \wedge R \rightsquigarrow Q \wedge R[\overline{x}]$. The principle here is to reason "locally" with assertions P, Q pertinent to the effect of C, and then infer a spec $P \wedge R \rightsquigarrow Q \wedge R$ needed to reason about a larger program of which C is a part. Locality is important for effective reasoning about programs involving the heap. (Explicit frame conditions for the heap can be found, for example in the Dafny language [43] and in the variation of HL dubbed region logic [8].) The notion of *adaptation completeness* characterizes the extent to which a HL has sufficient rules for reasoning about specs [6,39,50,55].

Refinement. Validity of assertions is a separate concern from program correctness and CONSEQ brings the two together in a simple way—but it has nothing to do with a specific command. It connects two specs, in a way that can be made precise by defining the ***intrinsic refinement order*** ($\sqsubseteq$, "refined by") on specs. Fixing a class of programs, we define $P \rightsquigarrow Q \sqsubseteq R \rightsquigarrow S$ iff $C : R \rightsquigarrow S$ implies $C : P \rightsquigarrow Q$ for all C. This relation can itself be given a deductive system, with rules including that $P \rightsquigarrow Q \sqsubseteq R \rightsquigarrow S$ can be inferred from $P \Rightarrow R$ and $S \Rightarrow Q$. The program correctness rule infers $C : spec_1$ from $C : spec_0$ and $spec_1 \sqsubseteq spec_0$. Using frame conditions, the FRAME rule can also be phrased as a spec refinement: $P \wedge R \rightsquigarrow Q \wedge R[\overline{x}] \sqsubseteq P \rightsquigarrow Q[\overline{x}]$ provided $FV(R) \cap \overline{x} = \emptyset$.

Disentangling spec reasoning from reasoning about the correctness judgment helps clarify that adaptation completeness is about spec refinement [50]. But it does come at a cost: To account for the CONJ and DISJ rules one needs not only the relation $\sqsubseteq$ on specs but also meet/join operators. Explicit formalization of spec refinement could be useful for relational specs, owing to the additional manipulations that exist owing to the additional dimension. But I do not develop the topic further in this paper.

Program Transformation. Verification tools employ semantics-preserving transformations as part of the process of generating VCs. Less commonly, transformations are an ingredient in a Hoare logic. An instance of this is the logic for distributed programs of Apt et al. [4,5], where the main rule for a distributed program has as premise the correctness of a derived sequential program. Another instance is rules to justify the use of auxiliary or **ghost** state in reasoning [56]. One such rule uses variable blocks var $\bar{x}$ in C. The variables $\bar{x}$ are called **auxiliary in** C provided their only occurrences are in assignments to variables in $\bar{x}$. Writing $C \setminus \bar{x}$ for the command obtained by replacing all such assignments with skip, the rule is

$$\frac{\bar{x} \notin FV(P,Q) \quad \bar{x} \text{ auxiliary in } C \quad \text{var } \bar{x} \text{ in } C : P \rightsquigarrow Q}{C \setminus \bar{x} : P \rightsquigarrow Q} \text{ (AuxVar)}$$

It is sound because the auxiliary variables cannot influence values or branch conditions, and thus have no effect on the variables in P or Q, nor on termination. As relational correctness judgments can express both dependency and program equivalences, we should be able to bring both the condition "auxiliary in" and the transformation $C \setminus \bar{x}$ into the logic, making the above rule admissible.

3 Relational Properties, Alignment, and Program Products

Here are some example relational properties of a single program.

(determinacy) For all terminated traces τ, υ from the same initial state, the final states are the same: $\tau_0 = \upsilon_0$ implies $\tau_{-1} = \upsilon_{-1}$.

(monotonicity) For all terminated traces τ, υ, if $\tau_0(x) \leq \upsilon_0(x)$ then $\tau_{-1}(z) \leq \upsilon_{-1}(z)$. Here x, z are integer variables.

(dependence, non-interference) ("z depends on nothing except possibly x") For all terminated traces τ, υ, if $\tau_0(x) = \upsilon_0(x)$ then $\tau_{-1}(z) = \upsilon_{-1}(z)$.

Here are some example relations between programs C and D.

(equivalence) For all terminated traces τ of C and υ of D, if $\tau_0 = \upsilon_0$ then $\tau_{-1} = \upsilon_{-1}$. Determinacy is self-equivalence in this sense.

(majorization) For all terminated traces τ of C and υ of D, if $\tau_0(x) = \upsilon_0(x)$ then $\tau_{-1}(z) > \upsilon_{-1}(z)$

(refinement) For all terminated traces τ of C, there is a terminated trace υ of D with $\tau_0 = \upsilon_0$ and $\tau_{-1} = \upsilon_{-1}$.

(relative termination) (For a given relation $\mathcal{R}$.) For all initial states β, γ that satisfy $\mathcal{R}$, if C has a terminated trace from β then D has a terminated trace from γ [35].

(mutual termination) For all initial β, γ that satisfy $\mathcal{R}$, C can diverge from β iff D can diverge from γ [33].

P0: (∗ z := x! ∗) *y:= x; z:= 1;* **while** *y ≠ 0* **do** *z:= z∗y; y:= y−1* **od**

P1: (∗ z := 2^x ∗) *y:= x; z:= 1;* **while** *y ≠ 0* **do** *z:= z∗2; y:= y−1* **od**

P2: (∗ z := x!, half as fast ∗)
y:= x; z:= 1; w:= 0;
while *y ≠ 0* **do** **if** *w* mod *2 = 0* **then** *z:= z∗y; y:= y−1* **fi**; *w:= w+1* **od**

P3: (∗ z := 2^x , a third as fast ∗)
y:= x; z:= 1; w:= 0;
while *y ≠ 0* **do** **if** *w* mod *3 = 0* **then** *z:= z∗2; y:= y−1* **fi**; *w:= w+1* **od**

Fig. 3. Example programs. $P0$ and $P1$ are from [31].

Refinement and relative termination involve existential quantification over traces, as do generalizations of refinement such as simulation and also dependence for nondeterministic programs (if τ is terminated and $\tau_0(x) = \gamma(x)$ then there is terminated υ with $\upsilon_0 = \gamma$ and $\upsilon_{-1}(z) = \tau_{-1}(z)$). We refer to these as ∀∃ properties, by contrast with the preceding items which universally quantify traces (denoted ∀∀). The ∀∀ properties above are also **termination-insensitive** in the sense that they only constrain terminating traces. In this paper we focus on termination-insensitive ∀∀ properties while discussing some ∀∃ properties (which are hyperliveness [23], not 2-safety) in passing. Mutual termination also involves existentials, unless programs are deterministic as they are in Benton [19] where mutual termination is used.

Let $A' = (Ctrl', Sto', init', fin', \mapsto')$ be an automaton. A relational spec $\mathcal{R} \approx> \mathcal{S}$ is comprised of relations $\mathcal{R}$ and $\mathcal{S}$ from Sto to Sto'. We write $(c, s), (c', s') \models \mathcal{R}$ to mean $s, s' \models \mathcal{R}$. Finite traces τ of A and τ' of A' satisfy $\mathcal{R} \approx> \mathcal{S}$, written $\tau, \tau' \models \mathcal{R} \approx> \mathcal{S}$, just if $\tau_0, \tau_0' \models \mathcal{R}$, $ctrl(\tau_{-1}) = fin$, and $ctrl(\tau_{-1}') = fin'$ imply $\tau_{-1}, \tau_{-1}' \models \mathcal{S}$. The non-stuck semantics of relational specs requires, in addition, that $ctrl(\tau_{-1}) \neq fin$ implies $\tau_{-1} \mapsto -$ and $ctrl(\tau_{-1}') \neq fin'$ implies $\tau_{-1}' \mapsto' -$. Finally, the pair A, A' satisfies $\mathcal{R} \approx> \mathcal{S}$ just if all pairs of finite traces do, and we write $A|A' : \mathcal{R} \approx> \mathcal{S}$ for satisfaction. (Where I write $A|A'$, as in [9,47], Francez writes $A \times A'$, and Benton's $A \sim A'$ is popular.)

A key idea (in [31] and elsewhere) is to form a single automaton, runs of which encode pairs of runs of the considered programs, and to which IAM can be applied. For a single program there is not much flexibility in how it is represented as an automaton or CFG but there are many product automata for a given pair of programs—these represent different ways of aligning the steps of the two programs. This flexibility is crucial for the effectiveness of the IAM, specifically on the simplicity of annotations and thus the ease of finding them and proving the VCs. To discuss this we consider the four examples in Fig. 3.

Consider proving monotonicity of $P0$. To express relations we use dashed ($'$) identifiers for the second run, so the spec can be written $x \leq x' \approx\!\!> z \leq z'$. One can prove the functional property that $P0$ computes factorial $(x!)$ and then prove monotonicity for the recursive definition of !. But, as pointed out in [31], one can also consider two runs from initial values x, x' with $x \leq x'$, aligning their iterations in lockstep with invariant $y \leq y' \wedge z \leq z'$ and no use of !.

Consider proving that $P2$ is equivalent to $P0$, which we again specify just using the relevant variables: $P0|P2 : x = x' \approx\!\!> z = z'$. Lockstep alignment of their iterations is not helpful; we would like to align each iteration of $P0$ with two iterations of $P2$ in order to use simple annotations like $y = y' \wedge z = z'$.

3.1   Product Automata Represent Alignments

Let $\otimes$ denote the cartesian product of relations, so $\mapsto \otimes \mapsto'$ is a relation on $(Ctrl \times Sto) \times (Ctrl' \times Sto')$, i.e., on state pairs. Let id_A be the identity relation on states of A. A **pre-product** of A and A' is an automaton $P_{A,A'}$ of the form $((Ctrl \times Ctrl'), (Sto \times Sto'), (init, init'), (fin, fin'), \Mapsto)$ such that we have $\Mapsto \subseteq (\mapsto \otimes \mapsto') \cup (\mapsto \otimes id_{A'}) \cup (id_A \otimes \mapsto')$. The union is disjoint, owing to non-stuttering of A and A'. Each transition of $P_{A,A'}$ corresponds to one of both A and A', or else one of A or A' leaving the other side unchanged. Such $\Mapsto$ satisfies the requirements of finality and non-stuttering.

Let T be a trace of a pre-product of A, A'. Mapping the first projection (fst) over T does not necessarily yield a trace of A, as it may include stuttering steps (related by id_A). So we define $left(T)$ to be $destutter(map(fst, T))$ where $destutter$ removes stuttering transitions. Observe that $left(T)$ is a trace of A, and we obtain *mutatis mutandis* a trace, $right(T)$, of A'. A **pre-product** is **adequate** if it covers all finite traces: For all finite traces τ of A and τ' of A' there is a trace T of $P_{A,A'}$ with $\tau\,left(T)$ and $\tau'\,right(T)$, where means prefix. It is **weakly adequate** if it covers all finite prefixes τ, τ' of terminated traces. (To see that equality $\tau = left(T)$ and $\tau' = right(T)$ would be too restrictive, consider lockstep alignment with τ strictly shorter or longer than τ'.)

Owing to the definition of states of a pre-product, a relational spec $\mathcal{R} \approx\!\!> \mathcal{S}$ for A, A' can be seen as a unary spec $\mathcal{R} \leadsto \mathcal{S}$ for $P_{A,A'}$. For a trace T of $P_{A,A'}$ we have $T \models \mathcal{R} \leadsto \mathcal{S}$ iff $left(T), right(T) \models \mathcal{R} \approx\!\!> \mathcal{S}$ by definitions. We obtain the following by definition of adequacy.

Theorem 1. *For the basic semantics of specs, if $P_{A,A'}$ is a weakly adequate preproduct of A, A' then $P_{A,A'}$ satisfies $\mathcal{R} \leadsto \mathcal{S}$ iff the pair A, A' satisfies $\mathcal{R} \approx\!\!> \mathcal{S}$. For the non-stuck semantics, if $P_{A,A'}$ is an adequate pre-product and satisfies $\mathcal{R} \leadsto \mathcal{S}$ then A, A' satisfies $\mathcal{R} \approx\!\!> \mathcal{S}$.*

This confirms that a relational spec can be proved using the IAM with a product, i.e., a suitably adequate pre-product. The challenge is to construct one that admits a simple annotation.

For the non-stuck semantics an adequate pre-product may have stuck states that do not correspond to stuck states of A or A'; it is this possibility that makes it possible for a pre-product to be helpful by rendering unreachable states such as those where the guards of a conditional are not in agreement. The number of cutpoints needed for a product may be on the order of the product of the number for the underlying automata, but a good alignment makes many unreachable; those can be annotated as false so the corresponding VCs are vacuous.

Here are some pre-products defined for arbitrary A, A'.

only-lockstep. $(\gamma, \gamma') \Mapsto_{olck} (\beta, \beta')$ iff $\gamma \mapsto \beta$ and $\gamma' \mapsto' \beta'$.

eager-lockstep. $(\gamma, \gamma') \Mapsto_{elck} (\beta, \beta')$ iff $(\gamma, \gamma') \Mapsto_{olck} (\beta, \beta')$, or $ctrl(\gamma) = fin$ and $\gamma' \mapsto' \beta'$ and $\gamma = \beta$, or $ctrl(\gamma') = fin'$ and $\gamma \mapsto \beta$ and $\gamma' = \beta'$.

interleaved. $(\gamma, \gamma') \Mapsto_{int} (\beta, \beta')$ iff $\gamma \mapsto \beta$ and $\gamma' = \beta'$ or $\gamma' \mapsto' \beta'$ and $\gamma = \beta$.

maximal. The union $\Mapsto_{olck} \cup \Mapsto_{int}$.

sequenced. $(\gamma, \gamma') \Mapsto_{seq} (\beta, \beta')$ iff $\gamma \mapsto \beta$ and $ctrl(\gamma') = init'$ and $\gamma' = \beta'$ or $ctrl(\gamma) = fin$ and $\gamma = \beta$ and $\gamma' \mapsto' \beta'$.

simple-condition. Given "alignment condition" $ac \subseteq (Ctrl \times Sto) \times (Ctrl' \times Sto')$, define $\Mapsto_{scnd}$ by $(\gamma, \gamma') \Mapsto_{scnd} (\beta, \beta')$ iff either $(\gamma, \gamma') \in ac$ and $(\gamma, \gamma') \Mapsto_{olck} (\beta, \beta')$ or $(\gamma, \gamma') \notin ac$ and $(\gamma, \gamma') \Mapsto_{int} (\beta, \beta')$.

As Francez observes, interleaved has a relatively large reachable state space, making it more difficult to find inductive invariants.

The only-lockstep form is not adequate, in general, because a terminated state or stuck state can be reached on one side before it is on the other. The eager-lockstep, interleaved, and maximal pre-products are all adequate. The sequenced form is not adequate in general: a stuck or divergent state on the left prevents coverage on the right. Sequenced is weakly adequate if A, A' have no stuck states.

The simple-condition product can also fail to be adequate: if ac holds, both sides are required to take a step, which may be impossible if one side is stuck or terminated. It is also insufficiently general: as we show later, it may be most convenient to designate that steps should be taken on one side or the other. This suggests the following, which subsumes the preceding constructions.

3-condition. Given state conditions l, r, b, define $(\gamma, \gamma') \Mapsto_{3cnd} (\beta, \beta')$ iff either $(\gamma, \gamma') \in l$ and $\gamma \mapsto \beta$ and $\gamma' = \beta'$, or $(\gamma, \gamma') \in b$ and $(\gamma, \gamma') \Mapsto_{olck} (\beta, \beta')$, or $(\gamma, \gamma') \in r$ and $\gamma' \mapsto' \beta'$ and $\gamma = \beta$.

3.2   Examples

Consider proving that $P0$ majorizes $P1$, for inputs $x > 3$, that is, $P0|P1 : x = x' \wedge x > 3 \approx\!\!> z > z'$. Francez observes that using sequenced product would require reasoning about $z = x!$ and $z' = 2^{x'}$, and suggests aligning the iterations in lockstep and using this relational invariant: $y = y' \wedge (z = z' = 1 \vee z > z')$. This condition is not preserved by the loop bodies under guard condition $y > 0$, for example in the state $y = 2, z = 6, z' = 4$ reached when $x = x' = 3$, but here we are concerned with the case $x > 3$. If we add $x > 3$ as a conjunct we get a condition that is indeed invariant for lockstep executions, but it is not inductive— that is, the verification condition for the loop body is not valid. But there is a simple invariant with which the relation can be proved:

$$y = y' \wedge ((y > 4 \wedge z = z' = 1) \vee (y > 0 \wedge z > 2 * z') \vee (y = 0 \wedge z > z')) \quad (1)$$

This is not established by the initialization, in case $x = 4$. Instead we use this invariant to prove correctness under precondition $x > 4$ and separately prove correctness under the very specific precondition $x = 4$ which can be proved, for example, by unrolling the loops. In short, we do case analysis, as in rule DISJ.

Program $P2$ is equivalent to $P0$, and $P3$ to $P1$, but neither fact is easily proved using lockstep alignment. For the simplest invariants in proving $P0$ equivalent to $P2$ we should let $P2$ take two iterations for each one of $P0$. The question is how to formulate that nicely.

As another example, $P2$ majorizes $P3$, for $x > 4$, but again this is not easily proved by reasoning about lockstep alignment of the loops. Both programs have gratuitous iterations in which y and z are not changed. We would like to align the computations so that when $w = w' = 0$ we can assert (1). Indeed, when $w \neq 0$ (respectively $w' \neq 0$), an iteration on the left (resp. right) has no effect on the other variables and thus maintains (1). For this proof we may try a simple-condition product so joint steps are taken when *(w* mod *2) = 0 = (w'* mod *3)*. But this is insufficient: it allows one side to run ahead in states where the condition does not require both sides to step together, precluding a simple invariant. What we need is a 3-condition product. The left may advance independently when *w* mod *2 ≠ 0* and *w/2=w'/3*; the right when *w'* mod *3 ≠ 0* and *w/2=w'/3*. Then (1) is invariant.

The examples only scratch the surface. Compilation, refactoring, and program revision need less obvious alignments, but often do admit alignments for which simple and even inferrable invariants suffice.

In examples like equivalence of $P0$ and $P2$ there is a fixed correspondence between loops of one versus the other program, a pattern that arises in some loop transformations used in compilers (e.g., to introduce vector operations). For majorization of $P3$ by $P2$ our alignment is more data-dependent, although it is not surprising that it can be described succinctly since the iterations have a regular pattern. Here is a less regular example (from [9]): the program uses a loop to sum the integers in a list, where list elements have a boolean flag that indicates an element should be ignored. The property is that two runs yield the same sum, provided the two lists have the same non-deleted elements in the same order. This can be handled nicely using a 3-condition product.

One can imagine more elaborate product automata using ghost state to track alignment conditions, but it seems that in any case what is needed is to designate when to advance on one side, the other side, or both.

4   Rules of Relational Program Logic

As has been rediscovered and noted several times, it is not difficult to use program syntax to make a program that behaves as a product of programs. A simple case, mentioned earlier, is the sequence $C; C'$ where C' has no variables in common with C, and which corresponds to the sequenced product automaton. But it is also natural to interleave code from such disjoint programs, so as to align intermediate points in control flow. For a deductive system one also needs to account for the connection between such a product and the original program (or programs), the primary objects of interest. It is also desirable to disentangle reasoning principles, such as various alignments, from details of encoding. Furthermore, although disjoint variables suffice to reduce relational reasoning to standard HL for simple imperative programs, this is no longer the case for languages with more elaborate notions of state. For example, many languages feature a single heap and it is not trivial to use it to encode two disjoint heaps (see [20,51]). Another example is assembly language for a conventional architecture with a fixed set of registers. In such situations it may be preferable to work more directly with the relational correctness judgment, suitably interpreted, rather than depending entirely on products encoded as single programs.

We have reached the main topic of this paper, deductive systems for the relational judgment $C|C' : \mathcal{R} \approx\!\!> \mathcal{S}$, in which various principles of reasoning are manifest in proof rules. With HL in mind we may expect syntax-directed rules that embody program semantics, rules for manipulation of specs, and rules for program transformation. In addition, relational reasoning benefits from judicious alignment of program fragments. For lockstep automata, the corresponding rules are dubbed "diagonal" [31] and relate programs with the same control structure. The sequenced and interleaved automata involve one-sided steps, corresponding to proof rules syntax-directed on one side. The 3-condition product is manifest in a three-premise rule for relating two loops. There are also rules that involve both relational and unary judgments.

Good alignment not only enables use of simple assertions, it is also essential to enable the use of relational specs for procedure calls. For lack of space we do not delve into this topic.

We refrain from formalizing relational formulas but we do assume they are closed under the propositional connectives with classical semantics. Usual formulations of HL rely on the use of program variables and expressions both as part of programs and as terms in formulas; in relational formulas we need to designate whether they refer to the left or right execution. As an alternative to the dashed/undashed convention used in Sect. 3, we use the notation $\langle\!|e|\!\rangle$ (resp. $\langle\!\rangle e|\!\rangle$) for the value of expression e on the left (resp. right) side. As naming convention we tend to use dashed names for commands on the right side, but this does not imply renaming of variables or anything of the sort. In the logic, the programs are considered to act on distinct states which may or may not have the same variables. For example, we can write $\langle\!|x|\!\rangle \leq \langle\!\rangle x|\!\rangle$ rather than $x \leq x'$.

4.1 Diagonal and One-Side Rules

The rules in Fig. 4 relate programs with the same control structure. Such rules are found in [19,31,64] and many other papers. In the assignment rule, the notation $\mathcal{R}_{e|e'}^{x|x'}$ is meant to be the formula $\mathcal{R}$ in which left-side occurrences of x are replaced by e and right-side occurrences of x' by e'. For example, $(\langle\!|x|\!\rangle = \langle\!\rangle x|\!\rangle)_{x+1|y}^{x|x}$ is $\langle\!|x+1|\!\rangle = \langle\!\rangle y|\!\rangle$. The first rule for if/else is general, covering the possible control

$$x := e \mid x' := e' : \mathcal{R}^{x \mid x'}_{e \mid e'} \approx\!\!> \mathcal{R} \qquad \frac{C \mid C' : \mathcal{R} \approx\!\!> \mathcal{Q} \qquad D \mid D' : \mathcal{Q} \approx\!\!> \mathcal{S}}{C ; D \mid C' ; D' : \mathcal{R} \approx\!\!> \mathcal{S}}$$

$$\frac{C \mid C' : \mathcal{R} \wedge \{e\} \wedge \{e'\} \approx\!\!> \mathcal{S} \qquad D \mid D' : \mathcal{R} \wedge \{\neg e\} \wedge \{\neg e'\} \approx\!\!> \mathcal{S}}{C \mid D' : \mathcal{R} \wedge \{e\} \wedge \{\neg e'\} \approx\!\!> \mathcal{S} \qquad D \mid C' : \mathcal{R} \wedge \{\neg e\} \wedge \{e'\} \approx\!\!> \mathcal{S}}{\text{if } e \text{ then } C \text{ else } D \mid \text{if } e' \text{ then } C' \text{ else } D' : \mathcal{R} \approx\!\!> \mathcal{S}}$$

$$\frac{\mathcal{R} \Rightarrow \{e\} = \{e'\}}{C \mid C' : \mathcal{R} \wedge \{e\} \wedge \{e'\} \approx\!\!> \mathcal{S} \qquad D \mid D' : \mathcal{R} \wedge \{\neg e\} \wedge \{\neg e'\} \approx\!\!> \mathcal{S}}{\text{if } e \text{ then } C \text{ else } D \mid \text{if } e' \text{ then } C' \text{ else } D' : \mathcal{R} \approx\!\!> \mathcal{S}} \ (\textsc{AltAgree})$$

$$\frac{\mathcal{Q} \Rightarrow \{e\} = \{e'\} \qquad C \mid C' : \mathcal{Q} \wedge \{e\} \wedge \{e'\} \approx\!\!> \mathcal{Q}}{\text{while } e \text{ do } C \text{ od} \mid \text{while } e' \text{ do } C' \text{ od} : \mathcal{Q} \approx\!\!> \mathcal{Q} \wedge \{\neg e\} \wedge \{\neg e\}} \ (\textsc{IterAgree})$$

$$\frac{\mathcal{Q} \Rightarrow \{e\} = \{e'\} \vee \mathcal{L} \vee \mathcal{R}}{C \mid C' : \mathcal{Q} \wedge \{e\} \wedge \{e'\} \approx\!\!> \mathcal{Q} \qquad C \mid \text{skip} : \mathcal{L} \wedge \{e\} \approx\!\!> \mathcal{Q} \qquad \text{skip} \mid C' : \mathcal{R} \wedge \{e\} \approx\!\!> \mathcal{Q}}{\text{while } e \text{ do } C \text{ od} \mid \text{while } e' \text{ do } C' \text{ od} : \mathcal{Q} \approx\!\!> \mathcal{Q} \wedge \{\neg e\} \wedge \{\neg e\}}$$

Fig. 4. Diagonal syntax-directed rules.

flows, whereas AltAgree is applicable when the guard conditions are in agreement (and can be understood in terms of simple-condition pre-product with a condition to ensure adequacy). AltAgree can be derived from the first rule, using that $C \mid C' : \text{false} \approx\!\!> \mathcal{S}$ and RelConseq (Fig. 6).

The IterAgree rule (e.g., [19,64]) is applicable when the loop conditions remain in agreement under lockstep alignment; it uses a single invariant relation $\mathcal{Q}$ much like the unary loop rule. The rule can be use to prove example $P0$ majorizes $P1$, for $x > 4$, using (1) as invariant. Francez gives a loop rule that corresponds to the eager-lockstep product: with a single invariant like in IterAgree but with additional premises $C \mid \text{skip} : \mathcal{Q} \wedge \{e\} \wedge \{\neg e'\} \approx\!\!> \mathcal{Q}$ and $\text{skip} \mid C' : \mathcal{Q} \wedge \{\neg e\} \wedge \{e'\} \approx\!\!> \mathcal{Q}$ to handle the situation that one loop continues while the other has terminated; it is seldom helpful. Our second loop rule, from Beringer [20], corresponds to the 3-condition product: It augments the invariant $\mathcal{Q}$ with two other relations: $\mathcal{L}$ is precondition for an iteration on the left while the right side remains stationary; *mutatis mutandis* for $\mathcal{R}$. The side condition $\mathcal{Q} \Rightarrow ((\{b\} = \{b'\}) \vee \mathcal{L} \vee \mathcal{R})$ ensures adequacy, i.e., covering all pairs of unary traces.

To relate differing programs, a natural idea is one-side rules, some of which we give in Fig. 5. The assignment rule is from Francez, where several one-side rules are given with skip on the other side, corresponding to interleaved product. The alternation rule is given in the more general form found in Barthe et al [11,13] and in Beringer [20] which also gives LeftSeq. If we identify D' with skip; D' (see Sect. 4.5), rule LeftSeq can be derived from sequence rule in Fig. 4 by replacing $C ; D \mid D'$ with $C ; D \mid \text{skip} ; D'$. Right-side rules can be derived using rule Swap (Sect. 4.4).

$$x := e \,|\, \text{skip} : \mathcal{R}_{e|}^{x|} \approx\!\!> \mathcal{R}$$

$$\frac{C \,|\, \text{skip} : \mathcal{R} \approx\!\!> \mathcal{Q} \qquad D \,|\, D' : \mathcal{Q} \approx\!\!> \mathcal{S}}{C; D \,|\, D' : \mathcal{R} \approx\!\!> \mathcal{S}} \text{ (LeftSeq)}$$

$$\frac{B \,|\, C : \mathcal{R} \wedge (\!| e |\!) \approx\!\!> \mathcal{S} \qquad D \,|\, C : \mathcal{R} \wedge (\!| \neg e |\!) \approx\!\!> \mathcal{S}}{\text{if } e \text{ then } B \text{ else } D \,\mid\, C : \mathcal{R} \approx\!\!> \mathcal{S}}$$

$$\frac{\text{while } e \wedge b \text{ do } B \text{ od} \,|\, C : \mathcal{P} \approx\!\!> \mathcal{Q}}{\text{while } e \text{ do } B \text{ od} \,|\, D : \mathcal{Q} \approx\!\!> \mathcal{R} \qquad \mathcal{Q} \wedge (\!| \neg e |\!) \Rightarrow \mathcal{R}}{\text{while } e \text{ do } B \text{ od} \,\mid\, C; D : \mathcal{P} \approx\!\!> \mathcal{R}} \text{ (WhSeq)}$$

Fig. 5. Some left side and mixed structure rules.

In addition to one-side rules that relate a structured program with an arbitary one, Francez considers rules for relating different program structures, for example WhSeq. The rule is unusual in that the premises are not judgments for subprograms of the one in the conclusion. The rule is derivable provided there are rules to rewrite programs to equivalent ones (see Sect. 4.5). Since while e do B od is unconditionally equivalent to the sequence (while $e \wedge b$ do B od); while e do B od, rewriting the conclusion results in a relation between two sequences.

4.2 From Unary Correctness to Relational

If the variables of C' are disjoint from those of C then the semantics of command $C; C'$ amounts to the sequenced product of the corresponding automata, suggesting:

$$\frac{C \text{ and } C' \text{ have disjoint variables} \qquad C; C' : \mathcal{R} \rightsquigarrow \mathcal{S}}{C | C' : \mathcal{R} \approx\!\!> \mathcal{S}} \text{ (SeqProd)}$$

For programs that cannot get stuck, it is sound in basic semantics according to Theorem 1 and the weak adequacy of sequenced product. Stuckness can be addressed using additional unary premises.

SeqProd is useful as means to obtain relational judgments for small subprograms such as assignments and basic blocks where a functional spec is not difficult to prove. An alternative way to get relational correctness from unary is by this rule, essentially introduced by Yang [64].

$$\frac{C : P \rightsquigarrow Q \qquad D : R \rightsquigarrow S}{C | D : (\!| P |\!) \wedge \langle\!| R |\!\rangle \approx\!\!> (\!| Q |\!) \wedge \langle\!| S |\!\rangle} \text{ (Embed)}$$

It is sound in both basic and non-stuck semantics.

Typically, the relational assertion language does not express equality of entire states, but rather of specific variables and sometimes of partial heaps [9,64]. Equivalence of two programs can be specified as $C | C' : \mathcal{E} \approx\!\!> \mathcal{F}$ where $\mathcal{E}$ (resp. $\mathcal{F}$) expresses agreement on whatever parts of the state are read (resp. written) by C or C'. In a unary logic with frame conditions, suitable $\mathcal{E}, \mathcal{F}$ can be derived from the frame condition [52] but I leave this informal in the following rule which yields a relational judgment from a unary one.

$$\frac{C : P \rightsquigarrow Q}{C|C : \mathcal{E} \wedge \mathbb{B}P \approx\!\!> \mathcal{F}} \ (\text{EREFL})$$

Here $\mathbb{B}P$ abbreviates $\langle\!\langle P \rangle\!\rangle \wedge \langle\!\langle P \rangle\!\rangle$. One can add postcondition $\mathbb{B}Q$ by means of EMBED and RELCONSEQ. Further agreements can be added using RELFRAME (Fig. 6).

4.3   From Relational Correctness to Unary

Preservation of unary correctness by equivalence transformation can be expressed as follows, where $\mathcal{E}, \mathcal{F}$ are suitable agreements as in EREFL.

$$\frac{C : P \rightsquigarrow Q \qquad C|D : \mathcal{E} \wedge \mathbb{B}P \approx\!\!> \mathcal{F}}{D : P \rightsquigarrow Q} \ (\text{ECORR})$$

whereas using unary judgments to infer relational ones allows for a deductive system in which the unary judgment stands on its own, this rule makes a dependency in reverse. We now take a further step which entangles assertion reasoning with correctness judgments.

Francez [31] motivates interest in the property of monotonicity by considering that it could be a requirement on a procedure passed to a routine for numeric integration. Similarly, a sorting routine requires that the comparator passed to it computes a transitive relation, and collections libraries require that the *equals* method compute a symmetric relation (at least) [61]. Evidently the functional correctness of such routines relies on these k-safety properties, but the cited papers do not even sketch such reasoning. Let us do so, glossing over details about parameter passing.

Consider a sorting routine that uses comparator *comp* with inputs x, y and output z. Suppose in the proof of $sort(a, comp) : \text{true} \rightsquigarrow sorted(a)$ we rely on symmetry. That is, some use of CONSEQ is for an entailment that is valid owing to symmetry of comparison. Symmetry can be expressed as the relational judgment $comp|comp : x = y' \wedge y = x' \approx\!\!> z = z'$. But we need to connect this with reasoning about unary assertions, within the confines of a logic of relational and unary correctness judgments.

Such a connection is made in tools and theories that allow "pure methods" to be used in assertions while avoiding illogical nonsense using arbitrary program functions as mathematical ones [10, 25]. Let C be some command meant to compute a function of input variables $\overline{x}$ as output z. Let f be an uninterpreted (and fresh) name which we will use to represent that function. We have already seen how to express that z depends only on $\overline{x}$, deterministically: $C|C : \overline{x} = \overline{x}' \approx\!\!> z = z'$. A property such as symmetry or monotonicity has the form $C|C : \mathcal{R}(\overline{x}, \overline{x}') \approx\!\!> \mathcal{S}(z, z')$. To express that f is the function computed in z

we use a unary spec, thus $C : \text{true} \rightsquigarrow z = f(\overline{x})$. Finally, we express the relational property of f as a first order (unary) formula: $\forall \overline{x}, \overline{x}'.\, \mathcal{R}(\overline{x}, \overline{x}') \Rightarrow \mathcal{S}(f(\overline{x}), f(\overline{x}'))$. With these ingredients we can state a rule.

$$\frac{C|C : \overline{x} = \overline{x}' \approx z = z' \quad C|C : \mathcal{R}(\overline{x}, \overline{x}') \approx \mathcal{S}(z, z') \quad f \text{ fresh}}{C : \text{true} \rightsquigarrow z = f(\overline{x})\,;\, (\forall \overline{x}, \overline{x}'.\, \mathcal{R}(\overline{x}, \overline{x}') \Rightarrow \mathcal{S}(f(\overline{x}), f(\overline{x}'))) \vdash D : P \rightsquigarrow Q} \text{(CMDFUN)}$$
$$\text{``link } D \text{ with } C\text{''} : P \rightsquigarrow Q$$

$$\frac{\mathcal{P} \Rightarrow \mathcal{R} \quad C|D : \mathcal{R} \approx \mathcal{S} \quad \mathcal{S} \Rightarrow \mathcal{Q}}{C|D : \mathcal{P} \approx \mathcal{Q}} \text{(RELCONSEQ)}$$

$$\frac{C|C' : \mathcal{P} \approx \mathcal{Q} \quad FV(\mathcal{R}) \text{ disjoint from } Vars(C, C')}{C|C' : \mathcal{P} \wedge \mathcal{R} \approx \mathcal{Q} \wedge \mathcal{R}} \text{(RELFRAME)}$$

$$\frac{C|C' : \mathcal{P} \approx \mathcal{Q}}{C'|C : \mathcal{P}^{\sim} \approx \mathcal{Q}^{\sim}} \text{(SWAP)} \qquad \frac{C_0|C_1 : \mathcal{P} \approx \mathcal{Q} \quad C_1|C_2 : \mathcal{R} \approx \mathcal{S}}{C_0|C_2 : \mathcal{P}; \mathcal{R} \approx \mathcal{Q}; \mathcal{S}} \text{(COMP)}$$

Fig. 6. Some rules that manipulate specs.

We are glossing over procedures and parameter passing, and termination of C. The last premise, for D, is meant to indicate reasoning under a hypothesis. The hypothesis includes a unary judgment, as in formalizations of HL with procedures. It also includes the axiom about f for reasoning about assertions. The rule does not require C to be entirely deterministic and have no effects on other variables besides z, but we should disallow writes to $\overline{x}$, so $z = f(\overline{x})$ means what we want.

From $C : \text{true} \rightsquigarrow z = f(\overline{x})$ one can derive $C|C : \overline{x} = \overline{x}' \approx z = z'$ by EMBED and RELCONSEQ. But CMDFUN does not require proof of $C : \text{true} \rightsquigarrow z = f(\overline{x})$. Instead, that spec is used to define f in terms of C, in reasoning about D.

4.4 Reasoning About Specs

The reasoning embodied by CONSEQ and other spec rules in HL is also needed in RHL, e.g., in Sect. 3.2 we suggested an appeal to the relational disjunction rule. Some of these rules are in Fig. 6. In addition to logical connectives, it is natural to consider formulas with converse and relational composition, for which I write $\mathcal{R}^{\sim}$ and $\mathcal{R}; \mathcal{S}$ respectively. Rule SWAP is sound in basic and non-stuck semantics (but not for relative termination). Rule COMP is not sound in basic or non-stuck semantics, owing to possible divergences of C_1; these are precluded under relative termination and mutual termination semantics. Soundness of COMP can also be achieved using an additional premise for termination.

Let us abbreviate the agreement $\langle x \rangle = \langle x \rangle$ by $\mathbb{A}x$. We have focused on local agreements like $\mathbb{A}x$, but one may wish to include a global identity relation, for which we write $\mathcal{I}$. As Benton shows, partial equivalences (symmetric and transitive relations, **per** for short) are particularly important, and relation operations let us express such properties as valid implications: $\mathcal{R}^\sim \Rightarrow \mathcal{R}$ (symmetry) and $\mathcal{R};\mathcal{R} \Rightarrow \mathcal{R}$ (transitivity). Several works use relational specs to express partial declassification of secrets (e.g., [49]). To declassify the value of expression e, a typical precondition has the form $\mathbb{A}e \wedge \mathbb{B}P$ which is a per but not reflexive. Apropos rule COMP instantiated in the form $C_0|C_2 : \mathcal{R};\mathcal{R} \approx> S;S$, if S is transitive we obtain $C_0|C_2 : \mathcal{R};\mathcal{R} \approx> S$ using RELCONSEQ. Then if $\mathcal{R}$ is reflexive ($\mathcal{I} \Rightarrow \mathcal{R}$) we obtain $C_0|C_2 : \mathcal{R} \approx> S$, as $\mathcal{I};\mathcal{R}$ is equivalent to $\mathcal{R}$.

By analogy with rule ECORR we would like to reason about preservation of a relational property by equivalence transformation. Consider the relation $C|C' : \mathcal{R} \approx> S$ together with equivalences $D|C : \mathcal{E} \approx> \mathcal{F}$ and $C'|D' : \mathcal{E} \approx> \mathcal{F}$ where $\mathcal{E}, \mathcal{F}$ are suitable agreements. By COMP we get $D|D' : \mathcal{E};\mathcal{R};\mathcal{E} \approx> \mathcal{F};S;\mathcal{F}$. If $\mathcal{E}$ is a conjunction of agreements including variables of $\mathcal{R}$, then $\mathcal{R}$ is equivalent to $\mathcal{E};\mathcal{R};\mathcal{E}$ and likewise for S so by RELCONSEQ we obtain $D|D' : \mathcal{R} \approx> S$. Besides enabling derivation of right-side rules from left-side rules, rule SWAP facilitates instantiating the preceding reasoning in case $C = C'$ and $D = D'$, to show a security property of C is preserved by the equivalence. (Take $\mathcal{R}, S$ to be agreement on non-secret variables.)

Benton [19] makes the beautiful observation that just as the relational spec $\mathbb{A}x \approx> \mathbb{A}z$ characterizes a dependency property of a single program, it also captures that two programs are equivalent with respect to their effect on z, e.g. $z := x; y := z \,|\, z := x : \mathbb{A}x \approx> \mathbb{A}z$ captures a dead-code elimination transform, for a context where the subsequent code does not use y and therefore requires no agreement on it.

With this in mind, consider programs in which atomic actions happen in different orders, for example $z := x + 1; w := y$ versus $w := y; z := w + 1$, the equivalence of which can be expressed by the spec $\mathbb{A}x \wedge \mathbb{A}y \approx> \mathbb{A}z \wedge \mathbb{A}w$. A general rule for commuting assignments can be formulated requiring disjointness of the variables read in the assignments. Moreover, one can express such a rule for assignments involving heap locations, given means to express agreements thereof.

Heap agreements are often needed up to bijective renaming of pointers [7, 20], which can be encoded in ghost state. Such specs can be localized to the locations read and written by a given command, since preservation of additional agreements can be derived by RELFRAME. Yang's logic [64] features a frame rule taking advantage of separating conjunction of relations. It is also possible to formulate a frame rule based on relational specs with frame conditions, as in the work of Banerjee et al [52] which features local equivalence specs derived from frame conditions.

4.5   Transformations

The diagonal and one-side rules enable reasoning in terms of convenient alignments but apply only to specific control structure patterns. Programs that do not exactly match the patterns can be rewritten by equivalences such as $\mathsf{skip}; C \cong C$, $C; \mathsf{skip} \cong C$, and the following:

while e do C od $\cong$ while e do C; while $e \wedge e0$ do C od od
while e do C od $\cong$ if e do C fi; while e do C od

Commands C, C' are **unconditionally equivalent**, written $C \cong C'$, if they have exactly the same store traces. The relation can be formalized using laws like these together with congruence rules. Such equivalences can be used to desugar fancy control structures, as done in some verification tools; the justification is that $C : P \rightsquigarrow Q$ and $C \cong D$ implies $D : P \rightsquigarrow Q$ (cf. rule ECORR in Sect. 4.4). The relational logic of Banerjee et al. [9] features a rule like this: from $C|C' : \mathcal{R} \approx\!\!> \mathcal{S}$, $D \cong C$, and $C' \cong D'$, infer $D|D' : \mathcal{R} \approx\!\!> \mathcal{S}$. The rule is applied in proving a loop tiling transformation, using the above rewrites to enable application of diagonal rules. Transformations are used similarly in [16,38]. To enable use of sequenced product one may use the equivalence var x in $C \cong$ var x' in $C^x_{x'}$, for fresh x'.

It seems unparsimonious to rely on an additional program relation ($\cong$) for which axioms and rules must be provided and proved sound, in a setting where we already consider a form of program relation. On the other hand, we have seen in Sect. 4.4 that there are limitations on the use of equivalence judgments for reasons of termination. Having a separate judgment of unconditional equivalence is one way to address termination in connection with the basic or non-stuck semantics of relational judgments.

4.6 Alignment Completeness

The usual notion of completeness is that true judgments are provable. Suppose the relational judgment $C|C' : \mathcal{R} \approx\!\!> \mathcal{S}$ is true. In a setting where $\mathcal{R}, \mathcal{S}$ can be expressed as, or considered to be, unary formulas, one can prove it by application of SEQPROD. In turn, the sequence can be reduced to true judgments $C : \mathcal{R} \rightsquigarrow \mathcal{Q}$ and $C' : \mathcal{Q} \rightsquigarrow \mathcal{S}$. What matters is not that an explicit product $C; C'$ can be formed but rather that store relations can be expressed as store predicates [14, 20,21,31]. If so, the judgment is provable provided the unary HL is complete. Then a single rule for relational judgments (SEQPROD or EMBED) is complete on its own! A different notion is needed.

Suppose $C : P \rightsquigarrow Q$ can be proved using IAM with a particular annotation. Then there is a HL proof using that annotation, in the sense that at least the loop rule is instantiated according to the annotation (assuming that loops are cut at loop headers). Why? Because the VCs will be provable, by completeness of HL, and the syntax-directed rules suffice to compose the VCs. In this sense, HL is complete with respect to IAM for unary correctness.

A natural measure of completeness for RHL is whether any proof of $C|C' : \mathcal{R} \approx\!\!> \mathcal{S}$ using IAM with a product automaton can be represented by an RHL proof *using the same annotation and alignment*. Turning this into a precise definition requires, first, a convincing general definition of product automaton; our 3-condition form is relatively general but does not encompass the use of ghost state for alignment conditions or store relations. Second, the correspondence between proof rules and aligned products, discussed informally throughout Sects. 4.1–4.5, needs to be made precise. To this end it may help to limit attention to annotations in which all branch points are cutpoints. We leave this to future work but note that formal proof outlines [5] may be a convenient intermediary.

It is straightforward to add ghost state to our notions of pre-product and adequacy, to express store relations and alignments. But some program transformations used in optimizing compilers reorder an unbounded number of atomic actions. These do not have an obvious representation by pre-product and they have not been formalized using RHL rules [48].

5   Selected Additional Related Work

The idea of relating C to C' by unary reasoning about a program that represents their product goes back at least to the 1970s. In Reynolds' book [58] we find stepwise refinement from an algorithm C using local variables of abstract mathematical types to C' acting on concrete data structures, expressed by augmenting C with parts of C' interwoven in such a way that assertions can express the coupling relation between abstract and concrete data. DeRoever and Engelhardt call this Reynolds' method and devote a chapter to it, citing work by Susan Geary as precursor [59]. Morgan [46] formalizes the idea in terms of auxiliary variables, cf. rule AuxVar. The idea of encoding two runs as a sequence of disjoint copies, and specifying determinacy as a Hoare triple, appears (in passing) in a 1986 paper by Csirmaz and Hart [27].

The influential papers by Benton [19] and Barthe et al. [14] have been followed by many works. The rest of this section gives selected highlights.

Barthe, Crespo and Kunz [13] give several ways of formulating deductive reasoning about relational properties, including deductive systems for product programs in conjunction with unary HL. They formalize a judgment that connects two commands with a command that represents their product. Products include assertions which must be verified to ensure what we call adequacy.

Beringer [20] considers partial correctness specs in "VDM style" i.e., as relations from pre- to post-state, so partial correctness means the relational semantics of the program is a subset of the spec. He defines relational decompositions, essentially the relations that hold at the semicolon of a product $C; C'$ (as in rule SeqProd), and observes that given such an "interpolant" one can derive VCs for C and C' as quotients in the sense of relational calculus (also known as weakest prespecification [37]). This is used to derive a collection of RHL rules including diagonal and one-side rules as well as relational Disj/Conj, for imperative commands including the heap.

Beckert and Ulbrich [18] survey some of the main ideas in relational verification and describe a range of applications and works on verification. Maillard et al. [44] introduce a general framework for relational logics, applicable to a range of computational effects such as exceptions. Aguirre et al. [1] develop a logic based on relational refinement types, for terminating higher order functional programs, and provide an extensive discussion of work on relational logics. Recent proceedings of CAV include quite a few papers on relational verification, and further perspectives can be found in the report from a recent Dagstuhl Seminar on program equivalence [42].

Numerous works develop variations and extensions of the ideas in this paper. Terauchi and Aiken [62] observe that sequenced product necessitates use of strong intermediate assertions, and use a dependency type system to guide the construction of more effective products. They also coin the term 2-safety. Several works focus on modular reasoning and product constructions that enable use of relational specs for procedures [9,29,33,35,40,41,63,65]. Sousa and Dillig [61] formulate a logic for k-safety, with notation that stands for "any product" and may be understood as providing for lazy product construction. Eilers et al. [29] give a k-product encoding that lessens code duplication. Whereas many works handle only lockstep alignment of loops, some cover the 3-condition automata [16,20]; Shemer et al. [60] provide for more general alignment and infer state-dependent alignment conditions. Other works on inferring or expressing effective alignments include [22,32,57]. Product constructions for $\forall\exists$ properties appear in [12,24].

Richer formalisms like Dynamic Logic [17,28] and embedding in higher order logic [1,34,44] have their advantages and can address reasoning like rule CMD-FUN and the linking of procedures to their implementations which is often left semi-formal. But such embeddings, in particular, are far from providing the level of automation (and teachability!) that more direct implementations of HL/RHL can provide. Completeness results show how HL/RHL suffice for proving correctness judgments.

6   Conclusion

I spelled out a number of patterns of reasoning for program relations and relational properties of programs, in terms of product automata that model pairs of executions, and also as rules of relational program logic. Almost all the rules can be found in at least one prior publication but some "obvious" and useful rules are missing in several papers. Spelling out the inductive assertion method for relational properties, as Francez [31] does, makes explicit the alignment principles that should be embodied in deductive rules, guiding the design of such rules. On this basis I introduced the notion of alignment completeness, leaving its formalization to future work; it should be done for a more general form of product than the one I chose for expository purposes.

To streamline notation I focused on 2-run properties but there is strong motivation for some 3-run (e.g., transitivity). I am not aware of fundamentally different techniques or principles for k-run that are not at hand for 2-run.

Although several papers have described the need for k-safety properties in order to reason about unary correctness, to my knowledge this pattern of reasoning has not been provided by relational logics (aside from those embedded in expressive higher order logics). I present a new rule for this (CMDFUN) that stays within the limited resources of RHL, i.e., assertions, unary correctness, and relational correctness judgments.

A couple of years ago I moved to a smaller office. While winnowing paper files I came across the paper by Francez, which I had acquired but not fully appreciated when working full time at IBM as a programmer in the '80s. The dearth of citations shows I am not alone in not finding it when I searched online for relevant work. My copy is a publisher's reprint, affixed with stickers that indicate IBM paid a fee. Such stickers became obsolete but the flow of scientific knowledge is still too tangled with commerce.

Acknowledgments. The paper was improved thanks to comments from Krzysztof Apt, Anindya Banerjee, Gilles Barthe, Ramana Nagasamudram, and anonymous reviewers. The research was partially supported by NSF CNS 1718713 and ONR N00014-17-1-2787.

References

1. Aguirre, A., Barthe, G., Gaboardi, M., Garg, D., Strub, P.: A relational logic for higher-order programs. J. Funct. Program. **29**, e16 (2019). https://doi.org/10.1017/S0956796819000145
2. Apt, K.: Ten years of Hoare's logic, a survey, part I. ACM Trans. Program. Lang. Syst. **3**(4), 431–483 (1981)
3. Apt, K.: Ten years of Hoare's logic, a survey, part II: nondeterminism. Theor. Comput. Sci. **28**, 83–109 (1984)
4. Apt, K.R.: Correctness proofs of distributed termination algorithms. ACM Trans. Program. Lang. Syst. **8**, 388–405 (1986)
5. Apt, K.R., de Boer, F.S., Olderog, E.R.: Verification of Sequential and Concurrent Programs, 3rd edn. Springer, Heidelberg (2009). https://doi.org/10.1007/978-1-84882-745-5
6. Apt, K.R., Olderog, E.: Fifty years of Hoare's logic. Formal Asp. Comput. **31**(6), 751–807 (2019)
7. Banerjee, A., Naumann, D.A.: Ownership confinement ensures representation independence for object-oriented programs. J. ACM **52**(6), 894–960 (2005)
8. Banerjee, A., Naumann, D.A.: Local reasoning for global invariants, part II: dynamic boundaries. J. ACM **60**(3), 19:1–19:73 (2013)
9. Banerjee, A., Naumann, D.A., Nikouei, M.: Relational logic with framing and hypotheses. In: Foundations of Software Technology and Theoretical Computer Science, pp. 11:1–11:16 (2016). Technical report at http://arxiv.org/abs/1611.08992
10. Banerjee, A., Naumann, D.A., Nikouei, M.: A logical analysis of framing for specifications with pure method calls. ACM Trans. Program. Lang. Syst. **40**(2), 6:1–6:90 (2018)
11. Barthe, G., Crespo, J.M., Kunz, C.: Relational verification using product programs. In: Butler, M., Schulte, W. (eds.) FM 2011. LNCS, vol. 6664, pp. 200–214. Springer, Heidelberg (2011). https://doi.org/10.1007/978-3-642-21437-0_17
12. Barthe, G., Crespo, J.M., Kunz, C.: Beyond 2-safety: asymmetric product programs for relational program verification. In: Artemov, S., Nerode, A. (eds.) LFCS 2013. LNCS, vol. 7734, pp. 29–43. Springer, Heidelberg (2013). https://doi.org/10.1007/978-3-642-35722-0_3
13. Barthe, G., Crespo, J.M., Kunz, C.: Product programs and relational program logics. J. Logical Algebraic Methods Program. **85**(5), 847–859 (2016)
14. Barthe, G., D'Argenio, P.R., Rezk, T.: Secure information flow by self-composition. In: IEEE CSFW, pp. 100–114 (2004). See extended version [15]

15. Barthe, G., D'Argenio, P.R., Rezk, T.: Secure information flow by self-composition. Math. Struct. Comput. Sci. **21**(6), 1207–1252 (2011)
16. Barthe, G., Grégoire, B., Hsu, J., Strub, P.: Coupling proofs are probabilistic product programs. In: POPL, pp. 161–174 (2017)
17. Beckert, B., Hähnle, R., Schmitt, P.H. (eds.): Verification of Object-Oriented Software. The KeY Approach. LNCS (LNAI), vol. 4334. Springer, Heidelberg (2007). https://doi.org/10.1007/978-3-540-69061-0
18. Beckert, B., Ulbrich, M.: Trends in relational program verification. In: Müller, P., Schaefer, I. (eds.) Principled Software Development, pp. 41–58. Springer, Cham (2018). https://doi.org/10.1007/978-3-319-98047-8_3
19. Benton, N.: Simple relational correctness proofs for static analyses and program transformations. In: POPL, pp. 14–25 (2004)
20. Beringer, L.: Relational decomposition. In: van Eekelen, M., Geuvers, H., Schmaltz, J., Wiedijk, F. (eds.) ITP 2011. LNCS, vol. 6898, pp. 39–54. Springer, Heidelberg (2011). https://doi.org/10.1007/978-3-642-22863-6_6
21. Beringer, L., Hofmann, M.: Secure information flow and program logics. In: IEEE CSF, pp. 233–248 (2007)
22. Churchill, B.R., Padon, O., Sharma, R., Aiken, A.: Semantic program alignment for equivalence checking. In: PLDI, pp. 1027–1040 (2019)
23. Clarkson, M.R., Schneider, F.B.: Hyperproperties. J. Comput. Secur. **18**(6), 1157–1210 (2010)
24. Clochard, M., Marché, C., Paskevich, A.: Deductive verification with ghost monitors. Proc. ACM Program. Lang. **4**(POPL), 2:1–2:26 (2020)
25. Cok, D.R.: Reasoning with specifications containing method calls and model fields. J. Object Technol. **4**(8), 77–103 (2005)
26. Csirmaz, L.: Program correctness on finite fields. Periodica Mathematica Hungarica **33**(1), 23–33 (1996)
27. Csirmaz, L., Hart, B.: Program correctness on finite fields. In: IEEE Symposium on Logic in Computer Science (LICS), pp. 4–10 (1986). See also [26]
28. Darvas, Á., Hähnle, R., Sands, D.: A theorem proving approach to analysis of secure information flow. In: Hutter, D., Ullmann, M. (eds.) SPC 2005. LNCS, vol. 3450, pp. 193–209. Springer, Heidelberg (2005). https://doi.org/10.1007/978-3-540-32004-3_20
29. Eilers, M., Müller, P., Hitz, S.: Modular product programs. ACM Trans. Program. Lang. Syst. **42**(1), 3:1–3:37 (2020)
30. Floyd, R.: Assigning meaning to programs. In: Symposium on Applied Mathematics, Mathematical Aspects of Computer Science, vol. 19, pp. 19–32. American Mathematical Society (1967)
31. Francez, N.: Product properties and their direct verification. Acta Inf. **20**, 329–344 (1983)
32. Girka, T., Mentré, D., Régis-Gianas, Y.: Verifiable semantic difference languages. In: Principles and Practice of Declarative Programming (PPDP) (2017)
33. Godlin, B., Strichman, O.: Inference rules for proving the equivalence of recursive procedures. Acta Inf. **45**(6), 403–439 (2008)
34. Grimm, N., et al.: A monadic framework for relational verification: applied to information security, program equivalence, and optimizations. In: CPP (2018)
35. Hawblitzel, C., Kawaguchi, M., Lahiri, S.K., Rebêlo, H.: Towards modularly comparing programs using automated theorem provers. In: Bonacina, M.P. (ed.) CADE 2013. LNCS (LNAI), vol. 7898, pp. 282–299. Springer, Heidelberg (2013). https://doi.org/10.1007/978-3-642-38574-2_20

36. Hoare, C.A.R.: Procedures and parameters: an axiomatic approach. In: Engeler, E. (ed.) Symposium on Semantics of Algorithmic Languages. LNM, vol. 188, pp. 102–116. Springer, Heidelberg (1971). https://doi.org/10.1007/BFb0059696

37. Hoare, C.A.R., He, J.: The weakest prespecification. Inf. Process. Lett. **24**(2), 127–132 (1987)

38. Kiefer, M., Klebanov, V., Ulbrich, M.: Relational program reasoning using compiler IR: combining static verification and dynamic analysis. J. Autom. Reason. **60**, 337–363 (2018)

39. Kleymann, T.: Hoare logic and auxiliary variables. Formal Aspects Comput. **11**, 541–566 (1999)

40. Lahiri, S.K., Hawblitzel, C., Kawaguchi, M., Rebêlo, H.: SYMDIFF: a language-agnostic semantic diff tool for imperative programs. In: Madhusudan, P., Seshia, S.A. (eds.) CAV 2012. LNCS, vol. 7358, pp. 712–717. Springer, Heidelberg (2012). https://doi.org/10.1007/978-3-642-31424-7_54

41. Lahiri, S.K., McMillan, K.L., Sharma, R., Hawblitzel, C.: Differential assertion checking. In: Joint Meeting of the European Software Engineering Conference and the ACM Symposium on the Foundations of Software Engineering (2013)

42. Lahiri, S.K., Murawski, A.S., Strichman, O., Ulbrich, M.: Program equivalence (Dagstuhl Seminar 18151). Dagstuhl Rep. **8**(4), 1–19 (2018)

43. Leino, K.R.M.: Dafny: an automatic program verifier for functional correctness. In: Clarke, E.M., Voronkov, A. (eds.) LPAR 2010. LNCS (LNAI), vol. 6355, pp. 348–370. Springer, Heidelberg (2010). https://doi.org/10.1007/978-3-642-17511-4_20

44. Maillard, K., Hriţcu, C., Rivas, E., Muylder, A.V.: The next 700 relational program logics. Proc. ACM Program. Lang. **4**(POPL), 4:1–4:33 (2020)

45. Moore, J.S.: Inductive assertions and operational semantics. Int. J. Softw. Tools Technol. Transf. **8**(4–5), 359–371 (2006)

46. Morgan, C.: Auxiliary variables in data refinement. Inf. Process. Lett. **29**(6), 293–296 (1988)

47. Müller, C., Kovács, M., Seidl, H.: An analysis of universal information flow based on self-composition. In: IEEE CSF (2015)

48. Namjoshi, K.S., Singhania, N.: Loopy: programmable and formally verified loop transformations. In: Rival, X. (ed.) SAS 2016. LNCS, vol. 9837, pp. 383–402. Springer, Heidelberg (2016). https://doi.org/10.1007/978-3-662-53413-7_19

49. Nanevski, A., Banerjee, A., Garg, D.: Verification of information flow and access control policies with dependent types. In: IEEE Symposium on Security and Privacy (2011)

50. Naumann, D.A.: Calculating sharp adaptation rules. Inf. Process. Lett. **77**, 201–208 (2001)

51. Naumann, D.A.: From coupling relations to mated invariants for secure information flow. In: ESORICS. LNCS, vol. 4189, pp. 279–296 (2006)

52. Nikouei, M., Banerjee, A., Naumann, D.A.: Data abstraction and relational program logic. CoRR abs/1910.14560 (2019). http://arxiv.org/abs/1910.14560

53. O'Hearn, P., Reynolds, J., Yang, H.: Local reasoning about programs that alter data structures. In: Fribourg, L. (ed.) CSL 2001. LNCS, vol. 2142, pp. 1–19. Springer, Heidelberg (2001). https://doi.org/10.1007/3-540-44802-0_1

54. O'Hearn, P.W., Yang, H., Reynolds, J.C.: Separation and information hiding. ACM Trans. Program. Lang. Syst. **31**(3), 1–50 (2009)

55. Olderog, E.R.: On the notion of expressiveness and the rule of adaptation. Theor. Comput. Sci. **30**, 337–347 (1983)

56. Owicki, S., Gries, D.: An axiomatic proof technique for parallel programs I. Acta Inf. **6**, 319–340 (1976)
57. Pick, L., Fedyukovich, G., Gupta, A.: Exploiting synchrony and symmetry in relational verification. In: Chockler, H., Weissenbacher, G. (eds.) CAV 2018. LNCS, vol. 10981, pp. 164–182. Springer, Cham (2018). https://doi.org/10.1007/978-3-319-96145-3_9
58. Reynolds, J.C.: The Craft of Programming. Prentice-Hall, Upper Saddle River (1981)
59. de Roever, W.P., Engelhardt, K.: Data Refinement: Model-Oriented Proof Methods and their Comparison. Cambridge University Press, Cambridge (1998)
60. Shemer, R., Gurfinkel, A., Shoham, S., Vizel, Y.: Property directed self composition. In: Dillig, I., Tasiran, S. (eds.) CAV 2019. LNCS, vol. 11561, pp. 161–179. Springer, Cham (2019). https://doi.org/10.1007/978-3-030-25540-4_9
61. Sousa, M., Dillig, I.: Cartesian Hoare Logic for verifying k-safety properties. In: PLDI, pp. 57–69 (2016)
62. Terauchi, T., Aiken, A.: Secure information flow as a safety problem. In: Hankin, C., Siveroni, I. (eds.) SAS 2005. LNCS, vol. 3672, pp. 352–367. Springer, Heidelberg (2005). https://doi.org/10.1007/11547662_24
63. Wood, T., Drossopolou, S., Lahiri, S.K., Eisenbach, S.: Modular verification of procedure equivalence in the presence of memory allocation. In: Yang, H. (ed.) ESOP 2017. LNCS, vol. 10201, pp. 937–963. Springer, Heidelberg (2017). https://doi.org/10.1007/978-3-662-54434-1_35
64. Yang, H.: Relational separation logic. Theor. Comput. Sci. **375**, 308–334 (2007)
65. Zaks, A., Pnueli, A.: CoVaC: compiler validation by program analysis of the cross-product. In: Cuellar, J., Maibaum, T., Sere, K. (eds.) FM 2008. LNCS, vol. 5014, pp. 35–51. Springer, Heidelberg (2008). https://doi.org/10.1007/978-3-540-68237-0_5

Safer Parallelization

Reiner Hähnle$^{(\boxtimes)}$ [iD], Asmae Heydari Tabar$^{(\boxtimes)}$, Arya Mazaheri$^{(\boxtimes)}$,
Mohammad Norouzi$^{(\boxtimes)}$, Dominic Steinhöfel$^{(\boxtimes)}$ [iD], and Felix Wolf$^{(\boxtimes)}$ [iD]

Department of Computer Science, TU Darmstadt, Darmstadt, Germany
{haehnle,heydaritabar,mazaheri,norouzi,
steinhoefel,wolf}@cs.tu-darmstadt.de

Abstract. Adapting sequential legacy software to parallel environments
can not only save time and money, but additionally avoids the loss of
valuable domain knowledge hidden in existing code. A common parallelization approach is the use of standardized *parallel design patterns*,
which allow making best use of parallel programming interfaces such as
OpenMP. When such patterns cannot be implemented directly, it can
be necessary to apply code transformations beforehand to suitably reshape the input program. In this paper, we describe how we used *Abstract
Execution*, a semi-automatic program proving technique for second-order
program properties, to formally prove the conditional correctness of the
restructuring techniques *CU Repositioning*, *Loop Splitting* and *Geometric Decomposition*—for all input programs. The latter two techniques
require an advanced modeling technique based on families of abstract
location sets.

1 Introduction

Using design patterns to parallelize programs [18,30] is a powerful method: first,
since it starts from *sequential* programs that already serve their intended purpose, one avoids the loss of domain knowledge, documentation, or the investments into existing software. Second, patterns embody best practices and correct
and efficient usage of parallelization interfaces—knowledge that many programmers lack. Therefore, such a pattern-based approach to parallelization constitutes a safe, efficient and even semi-automatic [34] migration path from sequential to parallel code.

Unfortunately, pattern-based parallelization suffers from a severe practical
limitation: sequential legacy code often does not quite have the form that would
allow the immediate application of a pattern. Assume, for example, the for-loop
in Listing 1, where $stmt_2$ depends on the result of $stmt_1$ and $stmt_1$ depends
on the result of $stmt_3$. At first sight, the code might seem not parallelizable
because of a forward-dependency among loop iterations. However, an astute
programmer might find a case where it is possible to successfully parallelize the
code by just reordering the statements, placing $stmt_3$ before $stmt_1$, as depicted
in Listing 2. Such a transformation preserves the semantics of the original code

This work was funded by the Hessian LOEWE initiative within the Software-Factory
4.0 project.

T. Margaria and B. Steffen (Eds.): ISoLA 2020, LNCS 12477, pp. 117–137, 2020.
https://doi.org/10.1007/978-3-030-61470-6_8

and makes it parallelizable using the pipeline pattern. The execution of different loop iterations can now overlap as long as $stmt_3$ is completed in iteration i before $stmt_1$ and $stmt_2$ start in iteration $i + 1$. This was not possible before because $stmt_3$ came last.

Listing 1: Original code	Listing 2: After restructuring
```for (i=0; i<n-1; i++) { a[i] = b[i]; // → stmt₁ c[i] = a[i]; // → stmt₂ b[i+1] = b[i]; // → stmt₃ }```	```for (i=0; i<n-1; i++) { b[i+1] = b[i]; // → stmt₃ a[i] = b[i]; // → stmt₁ c[i] = a[i]; // → stmt₂ }```

Fig. 1. A rudimentary sample code parallelizable using the pipeline pattern

We observed that a certain amount of *code restructuring* is unavoidable in most cases before pattern-based parallelization is applicable. With in the framework of DiscoPoP [34], we developed a small number of code transformation schemata that are in many cases sufficient to bring sequential code into the form required for pattern-based parallelization to succeed. We stress that, while these restructuring schemata *prepare* code for parallelization, they still work on *sequential* code. Finally, we call the combined application of a sequential transformation schema and, subsequently, a parallel design pattern *schema-based* parallelization.

The main problem when restructuring code is that it is easy to inadvertently change its behavior or to introduce errors. Therefore, it is essential to ensure the correctness of restructuring schemata with suitable applicability conditions and to *prove* that under these conditions they preserve the behavior of the restructured code. In the present paper, we identify syntactic conditions and prove that they suffice to guarantee the preservation of behavior for three representative restructuring schemata.

The (relative) correctness of a program transformation is a *second-order, relational* property: for *any* instance of a schematic program, one needs to show that the code *before* and *after* the transformation behaves in the same manner—provided the preconditions are met. Recently, the technique of *abstract execution* (AE) has been shown to be suitable for this problem class [35,37]. Our main contribution is to demonstrate that AE can be extended to formalize and prove the correctness of typical restructuring schemata needed for schema-based parallelization. This is possible, even though AE so far is limited to sequential programs, because the restructuring schemata work on sequential code.

The paper is organized as follows: In Sect. 2, we provide background about schema-based parallelization and present three typical restructuring schemata. In Sect. 3, we rehash the essentials of AE from [37]. Restructuring schemata that benefit parallelization need to be able to specify programs with loops. To show their correctness, so-called *abstract strongest loop invariants* [35] are used and explained in Sect. 4. The core of the paper is Sect. 5, where we extract sufficient preconditions for restructuring schemata and mechanically prove their correctness with the deductive verification system KeY [2]. To achieve this we had to extend the existing AE framework. We close the paper with Sect. 6 on related work and Sect. 7 containing future work and concluding remarks.

2   Restructuring for Parallelization

Design patterns [13] are a well-known technique that help designers and programmers to create reusable and maintainable (sequential) programs. Specifically, design patterns for parallel programs [30] support the development of software for parallel computers. Parallel design patterns help to avoid concurrency-related errors in the code such as deadlocks and data races. These are, when present, difficult to locate [18]. Mattson et al. [31] provide a catalogue of well-known parallel design patterns, organized on different abstraction levels—from decomposing a problem into parallel tasks down to a specific parallel implementation.

Jahr et al. [20] suggest using parallel design patterns to convert an existing sequential program to a parallel one. They aim at parallel software that can be mapped onto different many-core target architectures, providing high performance with low development effort. The central idea is to admit parallelism *only* as a result of applying parallel design patterns from a catalog. In the first phase, one exposes the maximum degree of parallelism expressible with a pattern through the *activity and pattern diagram*. In the second phase, this degree of parallelism is reduced to the level that provides the best performance and the optimal mapping of the program onto different cores of the target platform. The activity and pattern diagram is an extension of UML activity diagrams. Here, activity nodes can encapsulate not merely single, but multiple functionalities modeled as separate diagrams. The **fork** and **join** bars used in sequential activity diagrams to model creation and join of threads is forbidden [20]. This approach is unsuitable for automatic parallelization because deciding on the applicability of a parallel design pattern to a given sequential program requires intimate familiarity with the target code as well as comprehensive knowledge of parallel constructs and patterns [18].

To decide automatically whether a given parallel design pattern can be applied, Huda et al. [18] suggest *template matching*. This idea is derived from a matching technique that identifies suitable sequential design patterns [11]. It works by mapping the UML diagram of the design pattern to the UML diagram of the target program. When template matching is used to infer parallel design patterns, data dependence graphs replace the role of UML diagrams. Nodes in a dependence graph represent pieces of code, and its edges represent data dependences. The latter determine whether two nodes can be executed concurrently.

The dependence graph is generated approximately and automatically based on the output of the dependence profiler *DiscoPoP* [28]. The tool treats a program as a collection of *Computational Unit (CUs)* connected via data dependences. A CU is a piece of code with little to no internal parallelism that follows the read-compute-write pattern. A data dependence graph over CUs is a CU graph. Template and target program are represented as vectors and their cross-correlation determines their similarity, which indicates whether a successful template match is likely.

Often a match is not possible, even though the given sequential program has the potential for parallelization. In this case, the program has to be *restructured* before it becomes eligible for a parallel design pattern. Depending on the target pattern, there are different restructuring schemata. In the following, we discuss three representative schemata, previously developed within the DiscoPoP framework [34].

CU Repositioning. This is the restructuring schema before applying the *pipeline* pattern. A pipeline achieves functional parallelism, similar to an assembly line. The pipeline consists of stages, which process data concurrently as it passes through the pipeline. A pipeline can also be used to parallelize the body of a loop if the loop cannot be parallelized in the conventional way by dividing the iteration space using the do-all pattern. The pipeline pattern assigns each CU to a unit of execution and provides a mechanism whereby each CU of the pipeline can send data elements to the next CU [31]. Then it runs the CUs in parallel. In the pipeline pattern, each CU can depend on a CU running in the loop iteration or pipeline stage prior to it, but *not* on the CU after. Therefore, no CU depends on the result of the final CU. If this final CU also does not depend on other CUs, then it can be merged with the first CU. Moving the final CU from its assigned execution unit and merging it into the first CU, is called a *CU Repositioning* restructuring step. We refer to our explanations in the introduction (Fig. 1) for an example of *CU Repositioning*.

Loop Splitting. This is the restructuring step before applying the *Do-All* pattern. Do-all divides the iteration space into disjoint subsets and assigns each of them to an execution unit, then runs them in parallel. A loop is parallelizable with the do-all pattern when there are no data dependences among different loop iterations [18]. Such cross-iteration dependences are called *loop-carried* dependences. But, even when an initial or final segment of loop iterations has external dependences, these iterations can be outsourced to a separate loop and the remaining iterations still can be parallelized. Then, before (or after) the new loop runs, the do-all pattern is applied to the remaining loop. This is called a *Loop Splitting* restructuring step.

For example, in Fig. 2, Listing 3, assume *body* of the loop has external dependences (dependences to locations outside of the loop) at the first D iterations, but from iteration D+1 onward there is no dependence among different iterations. By splitting up the first D iterations in a separate Loop, like in Listing 4, the second loop now matches the do-all pattern.

Geometric Decomposition. This is a parallel design pattern that already includes the restructuring step. For programs that are understood as a sequence of operations on a main data structure, often the best way of parallelization is to decompose this data structure. For example, arrays and other linear data structures can be decomposed into substructures in a similar manner as dividing

Listing 3: Input Code	Listing 4: Output Code

```int i = 0;```	```int i = 0;```
	```while (i <= D) {```
	    ```body```
	    ```i++;```
	```}```

```while (i < t) {```
    ```body```
    ```i++;```
```}```
	```while (i < t) {```
	    ```body```
	    ```i++;```
	```}```

Fig. 2. *Loop Splitting*

Listing 5: Input Code	Listing 6: Output Code
	```int j = 0;``` ```while (j < N) {```

```int i = 0;```
```while (i < t) {```
    ```body```
    ```i++;```
```}```
	``` int i = j * (t / N);```
	``` while (i < (j + 1) * (t / N)) {```
	        ```body```
	        ```i++;```
	``` }```

	``` j++;``` ```}```

Fig. 3. *Geometric Decomposition*

a geometric region into sub-regions—hence the name *Geometric Decomposition* [31]. The resulting substructures can be processed in parallel.

For example, in Fig. 3 the **while** loop in Listing 5 is decomposed into N loops of the size t / N and gathered in the outer loop of size N in Listing 6. The N iterations of the outer loop can run in parallel.

3   Abstract Execution and Dynamic Frames

Abstract Execution (AE) [35,37] extends Symbolic Execution (SE) [9,23] by permitting abstract statements to occur in executed programs. Thus, AE reasons about an infinite sets of concrete programs. An abstract program contains at least one Abstract Statement (AS). The semantics of an AS is given by the set of concrete programs it represents, its set of *legal instances*. To keep the presentation succinct, here we only consider normally completing JAVA code as instances: an instance may not throw an exception, break from a loop, etc.

Each AS has an *identifier* and a specification consisting of its frame and its footprint. Semantically, AS instances with identifier P may write at most to memory locations specified in P's frame and may only read the values of locations in its footprint. All occurrences of an AS with the *same identifier* symbol have the same legal instances (possibly modulo renaming of variables if variable names in frame and footprint specifications differ). For example, by writing P(x, y :≈ y, z), we declare an AS with identifier "P". The left-hand side of ":≈" is the frame, the right-hand side the footprint; P can thus be instantiated by programs writing at most to variables x and y, while only depending on variables y and z. The program "x=y; y=17;" is a legal instantiation of this AS, but not "x=y; y=w;", which accesses the value of variable w not contained in the footprint.

Abstract programs allow the expression of second order properties like "all programs assigning at most x, y while reading at most y, z leave the value of i unchanged". As a *Hoare triple* [17] (where i_0 is a fresh constant relative to P):

$$\{i \doteq i_0\}\, P(x, y :\approx y, z)\, \{i \doteq i_0\}$$

It is desirable to express such properties more generally without referring to the concrete variable names occurring in P: "all programs not assigning i leave the value of i unchanged". To achieve this, we allow *abstract* location sets in frame and footprint specifications, inspired by the theory of *dynamic frames* [21]. We can generalize the above example to

$$\{i \doteq i_0 \wedge i \notin \mathit{frame}\}\, P(\mathit{frame} :\approx \mathit{footprint})\, \{i \doteq i_0\} \qquad (*)$$

where *frame* and *footprint* are set-valued variables representing arbitrary locations. We use standard set notation ($i \notin \mathit{frame}$, etc.) to express constraints on these sets. We define the abstract syntax and semantics of abstract programs.

Definition 1 (Abstract Program). *An* abstract program *is a tuple* $\mathcal{P} = (\mathit{locSymbs}, \mathit{predSymbs}, \mathit{constr}, \mathit{abstrStmts}, p_{\mathit{abstr}})$ *of a set of location set symbols* locSymbs, *a set of abstract predicate symbols* predSymbs, *constraints* constr *on location set and predicate symbols, ASs* abstrStmts $\neq \emptyset$ *and a program fragment* p_{abstr} *such that* abstrStmts *contains exactly the ASs in* p_{abstr}, *and* locSymbs *contains exactly the location symbols used in the specification of those ASs.*

Definition 2 (Legal Instance). *A concrete program* p *is a* legal instance *of* $\mathcal{P}$ *if it arises from substituting in* p_{abstr} *concrete location sets, boolean expressions, and statements for* locSymbs, predSymbs, *and* abstrStmts, *respectively, where (i) instances of location set and predicate symbols satisfy the constraints* constr, *(ii) all ASs are instantiated legally, i.e., by statements respecting the constraints on frames and footprints, and (iii) all ASs with the same identifier are instantiated with the same concrete program (modulo renaming in the presence of differently named frame and footprint locations). The semantics* $[\![\mathcal{P}]\!]$ *of* $\mathcal{P}$ *consists of all its legal instances.*

The abstract program consisting of AS P in (∗) above is formally defined as:

$$(\{\mathit{fr}, \mathit{fp}\}, \emptyset, \{i \notin \mathit{fr}\}, \{P(\mathit{fr} :\approx \mathit{fp})\}, P(\mathit{fr} :\approx \mathit{fp});)$$

The program "$P^0 \equiv$ x=y; y=2∗i;" is a legal instance: it obviously respects the constraints on the frame (i is not assigned).

4   Correctness of Transformation Schemata with Loops

The problem of proving the correctness of program transformations can be understood as a *relational verification* problem of *abstract* programs. The term "relational verification" [4,5] describes a problem class where a *program*, and not a more abstract, declarative description, serves as specification for another program. For example, to prove that the restructuring schema *CU Repositioning* (Sect. 2) is safely applicable, one can prove that the abstract programs "P; Q;" and "Q; P;" behave equivalently, i.e., have identical effects on the state. Obviously, this equivalence is only valid under suitable assumptions. Therefore, we prove *conditional* correctness, or in other words, equivalence of *constrained* abstract programs.

To symbolically execute programs with loops, deductive verification normally uses *loop invariants* to obtain a finite abstraction of unbounded loop behavior [16]. Loop invariants embody an inductive argument: If the invariant holds before entering loop *and* at each loop exit point, we can continue proving the program after the loop assuming the invariant. If a loop invariant is strong enough to imply the weakest precondition of the remaining program (or directly the postcondition if there is no remaining program), it is called *inductive*.

In functional verification, there is usually a choice between several inductive loop invariants, ranging from abstract descriptions that are merely sufficient to prove the postcondition to precise ones capturing the whole semantics of a loop. To prove equivalence of two programs using loop invariants in *relational* verification, it turns out that there is *no choice*: One has to come up with the *strongest* inductive loop invariant (up to logical equivalence) [5], which is generally hard to find. For this reason, state-of-art relational verification tools for concrete programs use different concepts, such as *coupling invariants* [5], to decrease specification effort and increase automation. The advantage of traditional loop invariants, on the other hand, is the "black box" encapsulation achieved by abstraction from loop behavior. Moreover, coupling is non-trivial for structurally different programs, as in the loop transformation schemata in Figs. 2 and 3.

Fortunately, while strongest loop invariants for relational verification of concrete programs are hard to find, this is not the case in the abstract setting: Instead of having to come up with a concrete invariant, one uses an abstract predicate and adds as a constraint the requirement that its instances are strongest invariants.[1] We formalize this intuition.

Definition 3 (Strongest Loop Invariant). *Let Pre be a precondition and $L \equiv$ "while (guard) body" a loop, where $l_1, \ldots, l_n$ are the locations assigned in L. A formula φ is a* strongest loop invariant *for L if it is a loop invariant for L and there is exactly one assignment of the l_i satisfying Pre, $\neg guard$ and φ, i.e., $\exists l'_1; \cdots \exists l'_n; \forall l_1; \cdots \forall l_n; (Pre \wedge \neg guard \wedge \varphi \rightarrow (l'_1 \doteq l_1 \cdots l'_n \doteq l_n))$.*

---

[1] Note that a strongest loop invariant is not necessarily *inductive*. Indeed, if there are runs of the analyzed programs not satisfying the postcondition, there is no inductive invariant, although there is always a strongest one.

The concept of an *abstract strongest loop invariant* [35] adds an abstract predicate *Inv* to the set *predSymbs* of an abstract program, and to *constr* a constraint restricting instances of *Inv* to formulas satisfied by exactly one assignment. One then designates *Inv* as the loop invariant of the specified loop, as demonstrated by the following example.

Example 1 (Abstract Strongest Loop Invariant). We aim to equip the program "i=0; **while**(i<t) {P(*frame* :≈ *footprint*); i++; }" with an abstract strongest invariant for the contained loop, assuming i, t ∉ *frame*. To that end, we create a new abstract predicate *Inv*(i, *frame*) and use it to specify the loop as in Listing 7. The highlighted parts in Lines 2 and 4 of the listing restrict instances of *Inv* to expressions that are valid when entering the loop the first time, and are satisfied by further iterations. We specified the bounds of the loop counter i separately: Since instantiations of P must not assign i, they cannot establish that part of the invariant. Let *p* be the whole abstract program fragment in Listing 7. We define the abstract program $\mathcal{P}$ as

$$\mathcal{P} := (\{frame, footprint\}, \{Inv\}, \{\text{i} \notin frame, \text{t} \notin frame, invConstr\},$$
$$\{\text{P}(frame :\approx footprint)\}, p), \text{ where}$$
$$invConstr := \exists \text{i}'; \exists frame'; \forall \text{i}; \forall frame; \left(Inv(0, frame) \wedge \right.$$
$$0 \leq \text{i} \wedge \text{i} \leq \text{t} \wedge Inv(\text{i}, frame) \wedge \text{i} \geq \text{t} \rightarrow (\text{i}' \doteq \text{i} \wedge frame' \doteq frame))$$

Observe that the partial invariant i ≤ t, together with the negated guard i ≥ t, determines i ≐ t as the final value of i after loop termination.

Consider an instantiation of AS P to "x += i;" for an integer variable x with initial value 0. Hence, the resulting concrete program fragment p^0 computes in x the sum of the numbers between 0 and t. Clearly, p^0 respects the constraints on *frame*, since it assigns neither i nor t. The formula "true" is a loop invariant for p^0. However, it is not an admissible instantiation for *Inv*, since *invConstr* is not satisfied: There are multiple assignments of i and x (the latter being the concrete instance of *frame*) satisfying this weak invariant. The other extreme, "false", does also not satisfy *invConstr*: it has no satisfying assignments, although one is required, and violates the specification in the code *p* (it is neither initially valid nor preserved by loop iterations). Another insufficient invariant is "i ≤ x", which is a non-trivial, but not the *strongest* invariant. Finally, the expression "$x \doteq \sum_{j \geq 0}^{j < i} j$" is the strongest (modulo logical equivalence) instance of *Inv* for p^0: It allows to deduce, together with i ≐ t, the final value of x after loop termination, which is $\sum_{j \geq 0}^{j < t} j$.   ◇

5   Preconditions for Safe Transformation Schemata

We modeled the transformation schemata from Sect. 2 in REFINITY [35,37], a workbench for proving relational properties of abstract JAVA programs, implemented as a frontend of the program prover KeY [2]. Figure 4 shows a screenshot

Listing 7: Specified abstract program fragment for Example 1

```
1  i = 0;
2  //@ constraint Inv(i, frame);
3
4  //@ loop_invariant 0 ≤ i ∧ i ≤ t ∧ Inv(i, frame);
5  while (i < t) {
6    P(frame :≈ footprint);
7    i++;
8  }
```

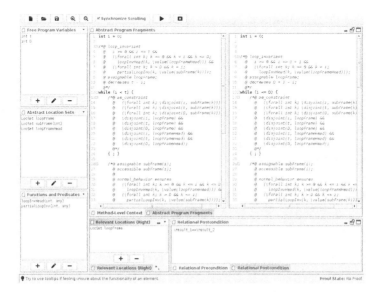

Fig. 4. The REFINITY window

of the REFINITY GUI. Starting from simple initial abstract program models, we specialize the intended legal instances by adding constraints until conditional correctness of the transformation is provable. Feedback needed for this stepwise refinement loop is drawn from interpreting failed proof attempts in KeY; we refer to the AE literature [35, 37] for a detailed description.

In the following, we describe the abstract program models we created, which yield preconditions for safe application of the considered transformation schemata. The section is concluded by considerations of the practical applicability of our findings and concise descriptions of the discovered preconditions. All REFINITY models, proofs, and the tool itself can be downloaded at the companion webpage https://www.key-project.org/papers/safer-parallelization/.

5.1   CU Repositioning

CU Repositioning prepares a program for parallelization based on the pipeline pattern by swapping CUs. Usually, statements occurring after a loop or method

Listing 8: Input model	Listing 9: Output model
/*@ constraint	/*@ constraint
@ $frameA \cap frameB \doteq \emptyset$ &&	@ $frameA \cap frameB \doteq \emptyset$ &&
@ $frameA \cap footprintB \doteq \emptyset$ &&	@ $frameA \cap footprintB \doteq \emptyset$ &&
@ $frameB \cap footprintA \doteq \emptyset$;	@ $frameB \cap footprintA \doteq \emptyset$;
@*/	@*/
A($frameA :\approx footprintA$);	B($frameB :\approx footprintB$);
B($frameB :\approx footprintB$);	A($frameA :\approx footprintA$);

Fig. 5. Abstract program model for *CU Repositioning*

call are moved in front of the loop or call. This transformation is an instance of the more general *Slide Statements* refactoring technique [12], where the first statement in the sequence "A; B;" to be swapped is required to be a loop or method call. Consequently, the preconditions for a safe application of the *CU Repositioning* transformation are the same as reported in [35] for *Slide Statements*. The abstract program model is shown in Fig. 5. The included constraints specify that ASs A and B have to be *independent*, i.e., their frames and footprints have to be disjoint. Specifically, this means that neither statement depends on the output of the other one, and cannot overwrite state changes of the other.

The fully automatic proof for this simple transformation technique consists of ca. 1,000 nodes and takes less than 7 s.

5.2 Loop Splitting

Loop Splitting or "fission" [1] is an optimization splitting one into several loops to prepare a subsequent parallelization step. We assume a loop from 0 to (exclusively) a strictly positive threshold t, from which we aim to pull the first $D + 1$ iterations, i.e., we split the loop after index "D". The abstract program model for *Loop Splitting* is in Fig. 8, global constraints in Fig. 10.

We define disjoint (Eq. (2) in Fig. 10) abstract location sets *loopFrameS* and *loopFrame* which the input and split loop may write to. The split loop portion works on *loopFrameS*, the remaining iterations on *loopFrame*. Further, we assign to each iteration its own part of the memory using an indexed family of abstract location sets *subFrame(i)*, such that the first D+1 elements cover *loopFrameS* and the remaining elements *loopFrame* (Eqs. (3) and (5)). The location sets from D+1 onwards must be disjoint from each other (Eq. (4)). This final requirement is not necessary for the correctness of the transformation itself, but for running the iterations of the second loop in parallel. Figure 6 visualizes these constraints (the concrete memory layout may be different, as we use *abstract* location sets).

Remark 1 (Location Set Families). The concept of indexed *families* of abstract location sets is an original contribution of this paper. It looks straightforward at the first glance, but it required several generalizations of the abstract store

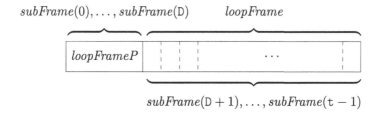

Fig. 6. Visualization of memory constraints for *Loop Splitting*

simplification rules implemented in KeY's AE framework. Without the extension, transformations such as *Loop Splitting* can be modeled [35], but assigning separate memory areas to *different* iterations of a loop is impossible. It turns out that constraints quantifying over indices of location set families are detrimental to automation, a problem whose full solution we defer to future work. ◇

The memory constraints alone are insufficient to prove the equivalence of the input and output model. For this, we need the *abstract strongest loop invariants* of Sect. 4. They allow to infer the exact final value of *loopFrameS* and *loopFrame*, thus show conditional equivalence of the input and output model. The abstract invariants are defined as abstract predicates $invSplit(i, loopFrameS)$, representing the invariant for the iterations until index D, and $inv(i, loopFrame)$, representing the invariant for the remaining iterations. During the first D+1 iterations, instances of the loop body AS Body have to ensure *invSplit*. Afterward, they have to ensure *inv*. Equation (6) is the constraint restricting instances of the abstract predicates to *strongest* loop invariants. To facilitate running the iterations of the second loop part in parallel, we specify in Listings 12 and 13 "partial" invariants $pInv(i, subFrame(i))$ on the disjoint subframes. Equivalence of those with the invariant *inv* on *loopFrame* is ensured by the **constraint**s in Lines 37 to 42.

The proof of *Loop Splitting* has 15,600 nodes. It requires 7 simple and 16 non-trivial interactive rule applications (8 quantifier instantiations, 8 cuts). KeY needed ca. 5 min for the automatic part of the proof search. Cuts were used to assert lemmas about set inclusion such as $subFrame(i) \subseteq loopFrame$, where $i > D$, which are needed to simplify abstract stores, but cannot be inferred automatically. Quantifier instantiations were necessary to prove the quantified parts of the loop invariants as well as to suitably instantiate the strongest loop invariant constraint. The remaining, trivial interactive applications consisted in hiding assumptions distracting the prover, which lead to superfluous case distinctions and instantiations. In total, 99.9% of all rule applications are performed automatically, while less than 0.1% are *non-trivial* user interactions.

Despite the necessity of human interactions with the proofs and the comparatively long time required for proof search, our results are practically applicable to real projects: We proved equivalence for *all instances* of our models at once. When using the correctness result of, e.g., *Loop Splitting*, to transform a real program, one only needs to show that this program is represented by the model. The proof of the transformation itself does not have to be redone. Even if formal instance checking is not considered for the moment, the insights obtained from our models can help tool designers to construct sound transformation systems.

5.3 Geometric Decomposition

Geometric Decomposition can be seen as a generalization of *Loop Splitting*: Instead of dividing a loop into *two* parts, it is split into $N > 1$ parts which are executed inside a newly introduced outer loop. Afterward, the do-all pattern can be applied to the outer loop, such that all N parts are run in parallel. We assume a loop from 0 to (exclusively) a threshold t which is strictly greater than N. The latter restriction excludes parts consisting of only one iteration of the original loop, which would contradict the intention of the pattern. Furthermore, t should be divisible by N. The abstract program model for *Geometric Decomposition* is shown in Fig. 9, global constraints in Fig. 11.

The abstract memory setup is similar as in our model of *Loop Splitting*: The loop works on an abstract set of memory locations *loopFrame*; each of the N portions resulting from the split is assigned its own subset *subFrame(i)* of *loopFrame* which is disjoint from the frame of all other loop portions (Eq. (9)).

Again, we use "partial" loop invariants $pInv(k, subFrame(l))$. Assuming, e.g., a loop with $t = 12$ which we split into $N = 3$ portions, the first loop portion ensures the partial invariants from $pInv(0, subFrame(0))$ to $pInv$ $(3, subFrame(0))$, the second from $pInv(4, subFrame(1))$ to $pInv(7, subFrame(1))$, etc. The final **constraint** in Fig. 9 ensures that all partial invariants from $pInv(0, subFrame(0))$ to $pInv(t-1, subFrame(N))$ together imply a loop invariant $inv(k, loopFrame)$ on the whole loop frame. Instances of this abstract predicate are, similar to *Loop Splitting*, constrained to be strongest invariants (Eq. (11)).

The proof of *Geometric Decomposition* consists of ca. 84,000 rule applications of which 215 are manual (0.26%—conversely, more than 99.7% are automatic), including 23 cuts, 26 quantifier instantiations, 29 case distinctions and one inductive side proof. There are three main reasons for the relative difficulty of this proof. (1) It involves assertions on relations between different abstract location sets (as in Sect. 5.2, but more complex). (2) The proof requires deep insight into the model. E.g., to prove the invariant of the outer loop in Listing 15, the partial invariants defined on *subFrame(j)* are retrieved by instantiating the invariant for the inner loop, while for prior iterations, the induction hypothesis, i.e., the invariant of the outer loop for the previous iterations, has to be used. This argument depends on the subframes being disjoint. (3) The model uses integer division, which is difficult for first-order solvers in general, and KeY in particular. Most cuts (and the inductive sub proof) are due to nonlinear arithmetic problems.

We briefly discuss one particular arithmetic problem linked to the example mentioned in item (2). To prove the outer invariant, we proceed via case distinction based on the value of j. Among the resulting proof cases, there is an "impossible" one assuming $j \neq k/(t/N)$, but also $k \geq j * (t/N)$ and $k < (j+1) * (t/N)$. To rule this case out, we prove the following lemma, for natural numbers a, b, c:

$$\forall a; \forall b; \forall c; (c > 0 \land a \geq b * c \land a < (b+1) * c \to a/c = b)$$

KeY could prove this fact automatically (using a strategy called "Model Search"), needing 18,800 steps and over two mins. However, it turns out that the prover was "distracted" by the large number of irrelevant assumptions collected at this point in the proof. Starting from a proof goal without any additional assumptions, KeY produced a short proof of 291 nodes in less than a second. It is interesting to observe that attempts to prove the lemma with the SMT solver Z3 [32] and the first-order prover Vampire [24] (in "portfolio" mode) failed with time outs.

5.4   Practical Application of Abstract Program Models

A thorough understanding of code transformations is always helpful to apply them safely. Ideally, the constraints embodied in our abstract program models should then automatically be checked by (semi-)automatic code parallelization approaches [27] to ensure correctness of transformations and parallelization directives such as OpenMP "pragmas".

Applying an abstract program model involves three steps: (1) Instantiation of the abstract input model (i.e., abstract program, location sets and predicates) for a given transformation schema and a given program; (2) transformation of the program instance in conforming to the abstract output model; (3) verification of the conformance of instances of abstract location sets, predicates, ASs with the requirements of Definition 2.

This process requires addressing two difficult problems:

(1) Checking validity of first-order constraints is undecidable in general, and the corresponding proofs can be time consuming.
(2) For loop transformations, instantiating the input model requires finding strongest loop invariants, which is in general impossible to automate.

Fortunately, a problem that is *in general* undecidable does not exclude the existence of practically occurring instances which are relatively easy, or even trivial, to solve. The main constraints in our abstract models concern memory access. Consider, for example, the program in Listing 10, which replaces each element in an integer array by its square. It can be transformed using *Geometric Decomposition* to the program in Listing 11. The location written and read in each loop iteration is arr[i]. It is easy to prove that the program satisfies an even stronger requirement than imposed by the constraints of *Geometric Decomposition* in Fig. 11, which require that the locations for each block of size N, not necessarily for all iterations, are disjoint.

What about item (2)—the invariants? The strongest loop invariant for the example in Listing 10 is

$$\forall k; k \geq 0 \wedge k < \texttt{arr.length} \rightarrow$$
$$\big((k < \texttt{i} \rightarrow \texttt{arr}[k] \doteq \texttt{arr}'[k] * \texttt{arr}'[k]) \wedge (k \geq \texttt{i} \rightarrow \texttt{arr}[k] \doteq \texttt{arr}'[k]) \big).$$

where arr' is the initial value of the array. Finding this invariant, for such a simple problem, is already difficult. Yet, inspecting the constraints for *Geometric Decomposition* in Fig. 11 and Listing 14 lets us observe that the *only*

Listing 10: Input program	Listing 11: Output program

```
                                 int j = 0;
                                 while (j < N) {
  int i = 0;                       int i = j * (arr.length/N);
  while (i < arr.length) {         while (i < (j+1) * (arr.length/N)) {
      arr[i] = arr[i] * arr[i];        arr[i] = arr[i] * arr[i];
      i++;                             i++;
  }                                }
                                   j++;
                                 }
```

Fig. 7. Simple instantiation of *Geometric Decomposition*

constraint on the abstract predicate $inv(k, loopFrame)$ is the requirement that it represents the strongest loop invariant. Moreover, the partial invariants ("$arr[i] \doteq (arr'[i])^2$" in the example) only need to imply the strongest loop invariant (Fig. 9, lines 38–43).

The proof depends on the *existence* of strongest invariants to deduce the exact symbolic memory state after loop termination. Due to the absence of additional constraints on these invariants, and since *any* loop has *some* strongest loop invariant, it is *not* necessary to actually supply a concrete strongest invariant during instantiation. The only "real" restriction results from the parameters supplied to the predicates, which represent the locations from which invariant expressions may be built. The parameters, in turn, conform to the memory constraints. Consequently, it is already sufficient to check whether an instantiation candidate satisfies all memory restrictions. The relevant constraints encoded in our abstract transformation models can thus be rephrased as follows:

CU Repositioning: The frames and footprints of the swapped statements have to be disjoint.

Loop Splitting: $D + 1$ is strictly smaller than the loop threshold t. All loop iterations from index $D + 1$ have to operate on memory regions disjoint from each other as well as disjoint from those of the iterations until index D.

Geometric Decomposition: N is strictly positive and strictly smaller than t; t is divisible by N. When dividing all iterations in blocks of size t/N, each such block has to operate on a memory region that is disjoint from all others.

6   Related Work

We formally specify and prove conditional correctness of program transformation schemata for sequential code, aiming to prepare input programs for subsequent parallelization. Such transformations, especially *Loop Splitting*, are also discussed in the classic compiler literature (e.g., [1]), where Program-Dependence Graphs (PDGs) are used to expose splitting opportunities. Formal, let alone *mechanized*, proofs of the transformations are absent. The same holds for work on design patterns for parallel programming [31].

Listing 12: Input model	Listing 13: Output model

```
1  int i = 0;
2
3  /*@ constraint
4  @      {i,D,t} ∩ loopFrame ≐ ∅
5  @   && {i,D,t} ∩ loopFrameS ≐ ∅;
6  @*/
7
8
9
10
11
12
13
14
15
16
17
18
19
20
21  /*@ loop_invariant
22  @    i ≥ 0 ∧ i ≤ t ∧
23  @    (∀k; k ≥ 0 ∧ k < i →
24  @        invSplit(k, loopFrameS))∧
25  @    (∀k; k > D ∧ k < i →
26  @        pInv(k, subFrame(k)));
27  @ assignable loopFrameS,
28  @                loopFrame;
29  @ decreases t - i;
30  @*/
31  while (i < t) {
32      Body(subFrame(i) :≈ subFrame(i));
33
34      i++;
35  }
36
37  /*@ constraint
38  @    (∀k; k > D ∧ k < t →
39  @        pInv(k, subFrame(k))) ↔
40  @    (∀k; k > D ∧ k < t →
41  @        inv(k, loopFrame));
42  @*/
```

```
int i = 0;

/*@ constraint
@      {i,D,t} ∩ loopFrame ≐ ∅
@   && {i,D,t} ∩ loopFrameS ≐ ∅;
@*/

/*@ loop_invariant
@    i ≥ 0 ∧ i ≤ D + 1 ∧
@    (∀k; k ≥ 0 ∧ k < i →
@        invSplit(k, loopFrameS));
@ assignable loopFrameS;
@ decreases D + 1 - i;
@*/
while (i <= D) {
    Body(subFrame(i) :≈ subFrame(i));

    i++;
}

/*@ loop_invariant
@    i ≥ D + 1 && i ≤ t &&
@
@
@    (∀k; k > D ∧ k < i →
@        pInv(k, subFrame(k)));
@ assignable loopFrame;
@
@ decreases t - i;
@*/
while (i < t) {
    Body(subFrame(i) :≈ subFrame(i));

    i++;
}

/*@ constraint
@    (∀k; k > D ∧ k < t →
@        pInv(k, subFrame(k))) ↔
@    (∀k; k > D ∧ k < t →
@        inv(k, loopFrame));
@*/
```

Fig. 8. Abstract program model for *Loop Splitting*

Listing 14: Input model	Listing 15: Output model

```
 1                                              int j = 0;
 2
 3                                              /*@ constraint
 4                                              @      {j, t, N} ∩ loopFrame ≐ ∅;  @*/
 5
 6                                              /*@ loop_invariant
 7                                              @    j ≥ 0 ∧ j ≤ N ∧
 8                                              @    ∀k; (k ≥ 0 ∧ k < j * (t/N) →
 9                                              @        pInv(k, subFrame(k/(t/N))));
10                                              @ assignable loopFrame;
11                                              @ decreases N - j;
12                                              @*/
13                                              while (j < N) {
14 int i = 0;                                       int i = j * (t / N);
15 /*@ constraint                                   /*@ constraint
16 @      {i, t, N} ∩ loopFrame ≐ ∅;  @*/           @      {i} ∩ loopFrame ≐ ∅;  @*/
17
18 /*@ loop_invariant                               /*@ loop_invariant
19 @    i ≥ 0 ∧                                      @    i ≥ j * (t/N) ∧
20 @    i ≤ t ∧                                      @    i ≤ (j + 1) * (t/N) ∧
21 @    ∀k; (k ≥ 0 ∧ k < i →                         @    ∀k; (k ≥ j * (t/N) ∧ k < i →
22 @        pInv(k, subFrame(k/(t/N))));             @        pInv(k, subFrame(j)));
23 @ assignable loopFrame;                           @ assignable subFrame(j);
24 @ decreases t - i;                                @ decreases t - i;
25 @*/                                               @*/
26 while (i < t) {                                   while (i < (j + 1) * (t / N) {
27     //@ ghost int j = i/(t/N);
28     /*@ constraint
29     @      {j} ∩ loopFrame ≐ ∅;  @*/
30     Body(subFrame(j) :≈                               Body(subFrame(j) :≈
31         subFrame(j));                                     subFrame(j));
32     i++;                                              i++;
33 }                                                 }
34
35                                                  j++;
36                                              }
37
38 /*@ constraint                                  /*@ constraint
39 @    ∀k; (k ≥ 0 ∧ k < t →                        @    ∀k; (k ≥ 0 ∧ k < t →
40 @        pInv(k, subFrame(k/(t/N))))) ↔         @        pInv(k, subFrame(k/(t/N))))) ↔
41 @    ∀k; (k ≥ 0 ∧ k < t →                        @    ∀k; (k ≥ 0 ∧ k < t →
42 @        inv(k, loopFrame));                     @        inv(k, loopFrame));
43 @*/                                             @*/
```

Fig. 9. Abstract program model for *Geometric Decomposition*

$$t \geq 0 \wedge D \geq 0 \wedge D+1 < t \tag{1}$$

$$\wedge\ loopFrameS \cap loopFrame \doteq \emptyset \tag{2}$$

$$\wedge\ \forall int\ i; (i \geq 0 \wedge i \leq D \rightarrow subFrame(i) \subseteq loopFrameS) \tag{3}$$

$$\wedge\ \forall int\ i; (i > t \wedge i < t \rightarrow subFrame(i) \subseteq loopFrame)$$

$$\wedge\ \forall int\ i; (i > D \wedge i < t \rightarrow \forall int\ j; (j > D \wedge j < t \wedge i \neq j \rightarrow \tag{4}$$

$$subFrame(i) \cap subFrame(j) \doteq \emptyset))$$

$$\wedge\ \forall Object\ o,\ Field\ f; ((o, f) \notin loopFrameS\ \vee \tag{5}$$

$$\exists int\ i; (i \geq 0 \wedge i \leq D \rightarrow (o, f) \in subFrame(i)))$$

$$\wedge\ \forall ProgVar\ pv; (pv \notin loopFrameS\ \vee$$

$$\exists int\ i; (i \geq 0 \wedge i \leq D; pv \in subFrame(i)))$$

$$\wedge\ \forall Object\ o,\ Field\ f; ((o, f) \notin loopFrame\ \vee$$

$$\exists int\ i; (i > D \wedge i < t \rightarrow (o, f) \in subFrame(i)))$$

$$\wedge\ \forall ProgVar\ pv; (pv \notin loopFrame\ \vee$$

$$\exists int\ i; (i > D \wedge i < t; pv \in subFrame(i)))$$

$$\wedge\ \exists\ any\ frP',\ any\ fr',\ int\ i'; \forall any\ frP,\ any\ fr,\ int\ i; \big((i \geq 0 \wedge i \doteq t \wedge \tag{6}$$

$$\forall int\ k; (k \geq 0 \wedge k < i \wedge k \leq D; invSplit(k, frP)) \wedge$$

$$\forall int\ k; (k > D \wedge k < i; inv(k, fr)))\ \leftrightarrow$$

$$fr' \doteq fr \wedge i' \doteq i)$$

Fig. 10. Global constraints for Loop Splitting

$$t \geq 0 \wedge N > 1 \wedge N < t \wedge \exists int\ k; (k \geq 0; k * N \doteq t) \tag{7}$$

$$\wedge\ \forall int\ i; (i \geq 0 \wedge i < N \rightarrow subFrame(i) \subseteq loopFrame) \tag{8}$$

$$\wedge\ \forall int\ i; (i \geq 0 \wedge i < N \rightarrow \forall int\ j; (j \geq 0 \wedge j < N \wedge i \neq j \rightarrow \tag{9}$$

$$subFrame(i) \cap subFrame(j) \doteq \emptyset))$$

$$\wedge\ \forall Object\ o,\ Field\ f; ((o, f) \notin loopFrame\ \vee \tag{10}$$

$$\exists int\ i; (i \geq 0 \wedge i < N \rightarrow (o, f) \in subFrame(i)))$$

$$\wedge\ \forall ProgVar\ pv; (pv \notin loopFrame\ \vee$$

$$\exists int\ i; (i \geq 0 \wedge i < N; pv \in subFrame(i)))$$

$$\wedge\ \exists\ any\ fr',\ int\ i'; \forall any\ fr,\ int\ i; (i \geq 0 \wedge i \doteq t \wedge \tag{11}$$

$$(\forall int\ k; (k \geq 0 \wedge k < i; inv(k, fr)))\ \leftrightarrow$$

$$(fr' \doteq fr \wedge i' \doteq i))$$

Fig. 11. Global constraints for Geometric Decomposition

The work of Khatchadourian et al. [22] considers safe, automated refactoring of sequential to parallel Java 8 streams. They define preconditions determining when it is safe and (possibly) advantageous to execute streams in parallel. Compared to our work, this approach is limited to a very specific problem (parallel streams), but verifies equivalence of the sequential input and parallel output programs, which is not within the scope of this paper.

There is a range of general-purpose deductive software verification [16] tools for sequential programs, including WHY [8], DAFNY [26], KIV [3], and KeY [2]. KeY is the only one of those supporting properties with universal quantification over *programs* (thanks to the AE framework). *Interactive* proof assistants such as Isabelle [33] or Coq [6] also support more or less expressive abstract program fragments, but lack automation. A few tools for proving functional correctness of *parallel* programs in industrial programming languages exist; prominent representatives are VerCors [7] and VeriFast [19]. Unlike KeY/AE, they natively support the verification concurrent programs, but can only prove the correctness of transformations of *concrete* programs and not of a transformation *schema*.

There are dedicated approaches involving schematic programs for proving the correctness of transformations in *specific* contexts, like regression verification [15], compilation [25,29,36] or derived symbolic execution rules [10]. Abstract Execution [35,37] comes closest to a general-purpose framework for the deductive verification of transformation rules with a high degree of automation.

The most prominent prior application of AE (also discussed in [35, 37]) focuses on the conditional correctness of *refactoring* techniques. Code refactoring [12] aims to improve the readability and, more generally, the maintainability of code, while preserving its behavior. There is a close relation between refactoring and the transformation techniques discussed here, even though the intentions differ fundamentally. We noted before that *CU Repositioning* can be seen as a special case of the refactoring *Slide Statements* (the first of the statements to be swapped is usually a method call or loop). *Loop Splitting* is a special case of the *Split Loop* refactoring, where all iterations of the second loop portion have to be independent. *Geometric Decomposition*, on the other hand, is a *generalization* of *Split Loop*, splitting a loop into $N > 1$ independent parts. For the mechanized proofs of *Loop Splitting* and *Geometric Decomposition*, we extended the existing AE framework to support indexed *families* of abstract location sets.

There is only one other work statically proving the semantic correctness of refactorings [14], where the correctness of two techniques (*Push Down Method*, *Pull Up Field*) is proved using a program semantics encoded in Maude. The proof is, however, not fully mechanized and complemented by pen-and-paper arguments. Statement-level transformations as discussed here are not considered.

7   Conclusion and Future Work

We presented formal models of three program transformation schemata, including two with loops, which are used by code parallelization tools to exploit parallelization opportunities in sequential programs. We defined sufficiently strong preconditions to prove the *conditional correctness* of the transformations *for any input program* satisfying the preconditions. To specify and verify our models, we used *Abstract Execution (AE)*, a framework allowing for a very high degree of proof automation. We extended the existing AE framework with the possibility to specify and reason about families of abstract location sets. This extension allows for versatile specifications, but is a challenge for the prover. Still, we reached a degree of automation of 99.7% even for the most complicated loop transformation; the loop-free problem was proven fully automatically.

Our models not only cover criteria necessary for proving the correctness of (sequential) program transformations, but additionally stronger constraints for the subsequent addition of parallelization directives. Crucial preconditions on memory access should be automatically checkable by parallelization tools, or can at least be closely approximated. By precisely stating these requirements explicitly, we hope that we cleared the way to safer parallelization.

One obvious future work direction connecting to these results is the generalization of AE to parallel programs. This would allow us to go one step further: To mechanically prove that the constraints in our models are sufficiently strong to ensure the preservation of the sequential program semantics *after* parallelization. Furthermore, we aim to improve the performance of the KeY prover in the presence of abstract location set families to get even closer to 100% automation.

References

1. Aho, A.V., Sethi, R., Ullman, J.D.: Compilers: Principles, Techniques, and Tools. Addison-Wesley, Boston (1986)
2. Ahrendt, W., Beckert, B., Bubel, R., Hähnle, R., Schmitt, P.H., Ulbrich, M. (eds.): Deductive Software Verification - The KeY Book. LNCS, vol. 10001. Springer, Cham (2016). https://doi.org/10.1007/978-3-319-49812-6
3. Balser, M., Reif, W., Schellhorn, G., Stenzel, K., Thums, A.: Formal system development with KIV. In: Maibaum, T. (ed.) FASE 2000. LNCS, vol. 1783, pp. 363–366. Springer, Heidelberg (2000). https://doi.org/10.1007/3-540-46428-X_25
4. Barthe, G., Crespo, J.M., Kunz, C.: Relational verification using product programs. In: Butler, M., Schulte, W. (eds.) FM 2011. LNCS, vol. 6664, pp. 200–214. Springer, Heidelberg (2011). https://doi.org/10.1007/978-3-642-21437-0_17
5. Beckert, B., Ulbrich, M.: Trends in relational program verification. In: Müller, P., Schaefer, T. (eds.) Principled Software Development, pp. 41–58. Springer, Cham (2018). https://doi.org/10.1007/978-3-319-98047-8_3
6. Bertot, Y., Castéran, P.: Interactive Theorem Proving and Program Development - Coq'Art: The Calculus of Inductive Constructions. TTCS. Springer, Heidelberg (2004). https://doi.org/10.1007/978-3-662-07964-5
7. Blom, S., Huisman, M.: The VerCors tool for verification of concurrent programs. In: Jones, C., Pihlajasaari, P., Sun, J. (eds.) FM 2014. LNCS, vol. 8442, pp. 127–131. Springer, Cham (2014). https://doi.org/10.1007/978-3-319-06410-9_9
8. Bobot, F., Filliâtre, J.C., Marché, C., Paskevich, A.: Why3: shepherd your herd of provers. In: Boogie 2011: First International Workshop on Intermediate Verification Languages, pp. 53–64 (2011)

9. Boyer, R.S., Elspas, B., Levitt, K.N.: SELECT–a formal system for testing and debugging programs by symbolic execution. ACM SIGPLAN Not. **10**(6), 234–245 (1975)
10. Bubel, R., Roth, A., Rümmer, P.: Ensuring the correctness of lightweight tactics for JavaCard dynamic logic. Electr. Notes Theor. Comput. Sci. **199**, 107–128 (2008). https://doi.org/10.1016/j.entcs.2007.11.015
11. Dong, J., Sun, Y., Zhao, Y.: Design pattern detection by template matching. In: Wainwright, R.L., Haddad, H. (eds.) Proceedings of the 2008 ACM Symposium on Applied Computing (SAC), pp. 765–769. ACM (2008)
12. Fowler, M.: Refactoring: Improving the Design of Existing Code. Addison-Wesley Signature Series, 2nd edn. Addison-Wesley Professional, Boston (2018)
13. Gamma, E., Helm, R., Johnson, R., Vlissides, J.: Design Patterns: Elements of Reusable Object-Oriented Software. Addison-Wesley, Boston (1995)
14. Garrido, A., Meseguer, J.: Formal specification and verification of Java refactorings. In: Proceedings of the 6th IEEE International Workshop on Source Code Analysis and Manipulation, SCAM 2006, pp. 165–174. IEEE Computer Society, Washington, D.C. (2006). https://doi.org/10.1109/SCAM.2006.16
15. Godlin, B., Strichman, O.: Regression verification: proving the equivalence of similar programs. Softw. Test. Verif. Reliab. **23**(3), 241–258 (2013). https://doi.org/10.1002/stvr.1472
16. Hähnle, R., Huisman, M.: Deductive software verification: from pen-and-paper proofs to industrial tools. In: Steffen, B., Woeginger, G. (eds.) Computing and Software Science. LNCS, vol. 10000, pp. 345–373. Springer, Cham (2019). https://doi.org/10.1007/978-3-319-91908-9_18
17. Hoare, C.A.R.: An axiomatic basis for computer programming. Commun. ACM **12**(10), 576–580 (1969)
18. Huda, Z.U., Jannesari, A., Wolf, F.: Using template matching to infer parallel design patterns. TACO **11**(4), 64:1–64:21 (2015). https://doi.org/10.1145/2688905
19. Jacobs, B., Smans, J., Philippaerts, P., Vogels, F., Penninckx, W., Piessens, F.: VeriFast: a powerful, sound, predictable, fast verifier for C and Java. In: Bobaru, M., Havelund, K., Holzmann, G.J., Joshi, R. (eds.) NFM 2011. LNCS, vol. 6617, pp. 41–55. Springer, Heidelberg (2011). https://doi.org/10.1007/978-3-642-20398-5_4
20. Jahr, R., Gerdes, M., Ungerer, T.: A pattern-supported parallelization approach. In: Balaji, P., Guo, M., Huang, Z. (eds.) Proceedings of the 2013 PPOPP International Workshop on Programming Models and Applications for Multicores and Manycores (PMAM), pp. 53–62. ACM (2013). https://doi.org/10.1145/2442992.2442998
21. Kassios, I.T.: The Dynamic Frames Theory. Formal Asp. Comput. **23**(3), 267–288 (2011). https://doi.org/10.1007/s00165-010-0152-5
22. Khatchadourian, R., Tang, Y., Bagherzadeh, M., Ahmed, S.: Safe automated refactoring for intelligent parallelization of Java 8 streams. In: Atlee, J.M., Bultan, T., Whittle, J. (eds.) Proceedings of the 41st International Conference on Software Engineering (ICSE), pp. 619–630. IEEE/ACM (2019). https://doi.org/10.1109/ICSE.2019.00072
23. King, J.C.: Symbolic execution and program testing. Commun. ACM **19**(7), 385–394 (1976)
24. Kovács, L., Voronkov, A.: First-order theorem proving and VAMPIRE. In: Sharygina, N., Veith, H. (eds.) CAV 2013. LNCS, vol. 8044, pp. 1–35. Springer, Heidelberg (2013). https://doi.org/10.1007/978-3-642-39799-8_1

25. Kundu, S., Tatlock, Z., Lerner, S.: Proving optimizations correct using parameter-ized program equivalence. In: Proceedings of the PLDI 2009, pp. 327–337 (2009)
26. Leino, K.R.M.: Dafny: an automatic program verifier for functional correctness. In: Clarke, E.M., Voronkov, A. (eds.) LPAR 2010. LNCS (LNAI), vol. 6355, pp. 348–370. Springer, Heidelberg (2010). https://doi.org/10.1007/978-3-642-17511-4_20
27. Li, Z., Jannesari, A., Wolf, F.: Discovery of potential parallelism in sequential programs. In: 42nd International Conference on Parallel Processing, ICPP, pp. 1004–1013. IEEE Computer Society (2013)
28. Li, Z., Jannesari, A., Wolf, F.: An efficient data-dependence profiler for sequential and parallel programs. In: Proceedings of the 29th IEEE International Parallel and Distributed Processing Symposium (IPDPS), Hyderabad, India, pp. 484–493. IEEE Computer Society, May 2015. https://doi.org/10.1109/IPDPS.2015.41
29. Lopes, N.P., Menendez, D., Nagarakatte, S., Regehr, J.: Practical verification of peephole optimizations with alive. Commun. ACM **61**(2), 84–91 (2018)
30. Massingill, B.L., Mattson, T.G., Sanders, B.A.: Parallel programming with a pattern language. Int. J. Softw. Tools Technol. Transf. **3**(2), 217–234 (2001). https://doi.org/10.1007/s100090100045
31. Mattson, T.G., Sanders, B., Massingill, B.: Patterns for Parallel Programming. Pearson Education, London (2004)
32. de Moura, L., Bjørner, N.: Z3: an efficient SMT solver. In: Ramakrishnan, C.R., Rehof, J. (eds.) TACAS 2008. LNCS, vol. 4963, pp. 337–340. Springer, Heidelberg (2008). https://doi.org/10.1007/978-3-540-78800-3_24
33. Nipkow, T., Wenzel, M., Paulson, L.C. (eds.): Isabelle/HOL. LNCS, vol. 2283. Springer, Heidelberg (2002). https://doi.org/10.1007/3-540-45949-9
34. Norouzi, M., Wolf, F., Jannesari, A.: Automatic construct selection and variable classification in OpenMP. In: Proceedings of the International Conference on Supercomputing (ICS), Phoenix, AZ, USA, pp. 330–341. ACM, Jun 2019. https://doi.org/10.1145/3330345.3330375
35. Steinhöfel, D.: Abstract Execution: automatically proving infinitely many programs. Ph.D. thesis, Technical University of Darmstadt, Department of Computer Science, Darmstadt, Germany (2020). https://doi.org/10.25534/tuprints-00008540
36. Steinhöfel, D., Hähnle, R.: Modular, correct compilation with automatic soundness proofs. In: Margaria, T., Steffen, B. (eds.) ISoLA 2018. LNCS, vol. 11244, pp. 424–447. Springer, Cham (2018). https://doi.org/10.1007/978-3-030-03418-4_25
37. Steinhöfel, D., Hähnle, R.: Abstract Execution. In: Proceedings of the Third World Congress on Formal Methods - The Next 30 Years (FM), pp. 319–336 (2019). https://doi.org/10.1007/978-3-030-30942-8_20

Refactoring and Active Object Languages

Volker Stolz[1(✉)], Violet Ka I Pun[1(✉)], and Rohit Gheyi[2]

[1] Western Norway University of Applied Sciences, Bergen, Norway
{vsto,vpu}@hvl.no
[2] Federal University of Campina Grande, Campina Grande, Brazil
rohit@dsc.ufcg.edu.br

Abstract. Refactorings are important for object-oriented (OO) programs. Actor- and active object programs place an emphasis on concurrency. In this article, we show how well-known OO refactorings such as Hide Delegate, Move Method, and Extract Class interact with a concurrency model that distinguishes between local and remote objects. Refactorings that are straightforward in Java suddenly force the developers to reflect on the underlying assumptions of their actor system. We show that this reflection is primarily necessary for refactorings that add or remove method calls, as well as constructor invocations. We present a general notion of correctness of refactorings in a concurrent setting, and indicate which refactorings are correct under this notion. Finally, we discuss how development tools can assist the developer with refactorings in languages with rich semantics.

1 Introduction

During its life cycle, software may change due to the introduction of new features and enhancements that improve its internal structure, or make its processing more efficient. Systems continue to evolve over time and become more complex as they grow. Developers can take some actions to avoid that, such as code refactoring, a kind of perfective maintenance [1]. The term *Refactoring* was originally coined by Opdyke [2], and popularized in practice by Fowler [3], as the process of changing the internal structure of a program to improve its internal quality while preserving its external behavior.

Over the years refactoring has become a central part of the software development processes, such as eXtreme Programming [4]. Refactorings can be manually applied, which may be time consuming and error prone, or automatically by using implementations of refactoring engines available in IDEs, such as Eclipse, NetBeans, IntelliJ, and JastAdd Refactoring Tools (JRRT) [5]. Refactoring engines may contain a number of refactoring implementations, such as Rename Class, Pull Up Method, and Encapsulate Field. For correctly applying a refactoring, and thus ensuring behavior preservation, the refactoring implementations usually need to consider preconditions, such as checking for naming

Partially supported by DIKU/CAPES project "Modern Refactoring" and CNPq.

T. Margaria and B. Steffen (Eds.): ISoLA 2020, LNCS 12477, pp. 138–158, 2020.
https://doi.org/10.1007/978-3-030-61470-6_9

conflicts. However, defining and implementing refactorings is a nontrivial task since it is difficult to define all preconditions to guarantee that the transformation preserves the program behavior. In fact, proving refactoring correctness for entire languages, such as Java and C, constitutes a challenge [5]. For instance, previous approaches found bugs in refactoring implementations for sequential Java [6, 7].

Fowler advocates that the correctness of refactorings is specified through the unit tests of the software being refactored. This elegantly avoids the discussion of the correctness in all situations of a particular refactoring, which is not given especially in object-oriented programs anyway: even though the required preconditions can be captured statically (see, e.g., [5]), checking them at refactoring-time may yield "don't-know" due to over-approximation and hence limit their applicability [8], or a required notion of equivalence between original and refactored program is impossible to formulate in general due to the different structure of states in both runs [9].

Active object languages [10] for concurrent programs go beyond traditional object oriented method calls. Developers have to actively choose between synchronous and asynchronous method calls. In asynchronous calls, an explicit additional instruction is required to synchronize again with the result. This makes it very obvious to the developers that they are in charge of proper synchronization, and semantic consistency (i.e., to make sure that concurrency within the same object is handled correctly).

The ABS language [11] goes even beyond that distinction: in its component model, objects within the same component, called *concurrent object group* (cog), share the same processor and hence cannot run concurrently. Within the same component, primarily *asynchronous* calls are affected: the caller has to relinquish control to give the component the opportunity to eventually process a pending asynchronous call. In the case of *synchronous* calls *between* components, the calling object does not release control, which hence introduces the potential for deadlocks if the callee directly or indirectly requires a callback into the caller. As the distinction between remote or local is purely semantical, and not visible in the source code, any method call requires careful consideration. This has been addressed, e.g., in [12] through an inference and annotation mechanism, which helps the developer in tracking which objects may be local or remote, and through whole-program static analyses in [13,14]. In general however, as other static analyses for object-oriented programs, this inference has to default to "don't know" in case the location of an object cannot statically be determined.

This has direct effects on well-known refactorings in object-oriented programs. Fowler's refactorings [3] often either remove or introduce additional method calls. His refactorings are exclusively on sequential code and in general preserve the behaviour of the application. After our discussion above on the behaviour of actor languages, we can now easily see that these refactorings can have adverse effects when ported to active object languages.

In this article, we are going to investigate those effects in detail for some of Fowler's refactorings. We derive a notion of correctness of a refactoring and show

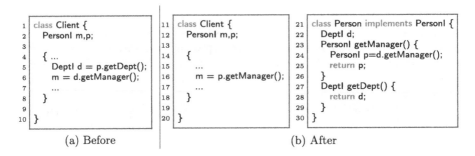

Fig. 1. Before/after Hide Delegate

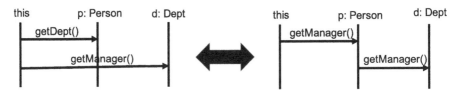

Fig. 2. Sequence diagrams for both scenarios (before/after *Hide Delegate*)

that the refactorings are not correct in general, and identify which refactorings are correct under this notion.

A Motivating Example

Consider Fowler's *Hide Delegate* refactoring and its inverse *Remove Middle Man*. Figure 1 illustrates a common application of a Java refactoring: assuming that a Client has a reference to a Person, in a good OO design the developer may change person.getDept().getManager() (above broken up into two statements) into a call to a new proxy person.getManager(). While both solutions are considered equivalent in, e.g., Java, the refactoring may introduce a deadlock in the actor setting!

The sequence diagram in Fig. 2 illustrates the difference between the two scenarios: in the *before*-scenario, the client is first communicating with Person, then with Dept. This will never be a problem regardless of how many components are actually involved. In the *after*-scenario however, due to the delegation from the client to Person, the behaviour now depends on the component that provides Dept. If Dept is either in a separate component or shares a component with Person, the programs are equivalent. But in one particular case we have just introduced a new deadlock into the program: if the caller and Dept are in the same component, yet Person is not, then the call-back from Person to Dept will deadlock,

Table 1. Allocation of objects to components A,B,C

			Effect	
:Client	:Person	:Dept	Before	After
A	A	A	ok	ok
A	A	B	ok	ok
A	B	A	ok	deadlock!
A	B	B	ok	ok
A	B	C	ok	ok

since the component hosting the caller and Dept cannot process any request before the synchronous call to Person returns.

Table 1 shows the different possible allocations of objects to components. This information is derived from the ABS operational semantics for (synchronous) method calls. In the remainder of this paper, we investigate this and similar effects in more detail.

The remainder of the paper is structured as follows: Sect. 2 gives a brief introduction to the ABS language and its component model. Afterwards, we discuss in detail the implications of some prominent Fowler's refactorings on the behaviour of synchronous and asynchronous calls, and outline proofs to show correctness or derive correctness conditions for particular scenarios in Sect. 3. We then survey Fowler's refactorings as to whether they suggest changes that would result in equivalent Java code, but may change the behaviour in ABS. Finally, in Sect. 4 we put our work into the context of existing research, and conclude with recommendations for refactoring tool developers.

2   The ABS Language

In this section, we will briefly introduce the ABS language, with active objects and Java-like syntax. We will first discuss the concurrency model of the language, then present the runtime syntax and finally we show the part of the semantics that we used to illustrate the effect of selected refactorings. The complete details of the language can be found in [11].

The concurrency model. ABS is a modeling language for designing, verifying, and executing concurrent software. The language has a Java-like syntax, features with actor-based concurrency model [15], which uses *cooperative scheduling* of method activations to explicitly control the internal interleaving of activities inside a concurrent object group (*cog*). A cog can be conceptually considered as a processor, which can contain a set of objects. An object may have a set of processes, triggered by method invocations, to be executed. Inside a cog, at most one process is *active* while the others are *suspended* in the process pool of the corresponding objects. Process scheduling is non-deterministic, but is explicitly controlled by the *processor release points* in the language. Such a cooperative scheduling ensures data-race freedom inside a cog. In addition, objects are hidden behind interfaces. As any fields are private, any non-local read or write to fields must be performed explicitly through method invocations. Different cogs can only communicate through asynchronous method calls.

```
class C(Mutexl m) {...
  { ...
    await m!enter();
    /* critical section */
    await m!leave();
  ...} }
class Mutex implements Mutexl {
  Bool avail = True;
  Unit enter() {await avail; avail = False;}
  Unit leave() {avail = True;} }
```

To provide an intuition, we discuss about the concurrency model with the simple ABS code to the right, which shows the implementation of a class C that acquires exclusive access to a critical section by using a block-structured binary lock that is modelled by the class Mutex implementing

$$cn ::= \epsilon \mid fut \mid object \mid invoc \mid cog \mid cn\ cn$$
$$fut ::= fut(f, val)$$
$$object ::= ob(o, a, p, q)$$
$$q ::= \epsilon \mid process \mid q\ q$$
$$invoc ::= invoc(o, f, m, \overline{v})$$
$$s ::= s; s \mid x = rhs \mid \textbf{suspend} \mid \textbf{await}\ g \mid \textbf{skip}$$
$$\mid \textbf{if}\ b\ \{s\}\ [\ \textbf{else}\ \{s\}\ ]\ \mid \textbf{while}\ b\ \{s\} \mid \textbf{return}\ e \mid \textbf{cont}(f)$$
$$rhs ::= e \mid \textbf{new}\ [\textbf{cog}]\ C[(\overline{e})] \mid e!m(\overline{e}) \mid e.m(\overline{e}) \mid x.\textbf{get}$$

$$cog ::= cog(c, act)$$
$$val ::= v \mid \bot$$
$$a ::= T\ x\ v \mid a, a$$
$$p ::= process \mid idle$$
$$v ::= o \mid f \mid b \mid t$$
$$act ::= o \mid \varepsilon$$

Fig. 3. Runtime syntax of ABS [11]; o, f, c are identifiers of object, future, and cog

the straightforward interface MutexI (not shown). The execution of statement **await** m!enter() invokes enter *asynchronously* on object m by putting the method in the process pool of m. The **await** statement suspends the calling method and *releases the control* of the caller object, which can then proceed with the execution of other methods in the process pool. If the statement **await** m!enter() is replaced by a synchronous call m.enter(), the caller object will be *blocked* (does not release control) until the method returns. The enter method on the callee object m will return when the boolean variable avail becomes true. Similar to awaiting an asynchronous method, awaiting a boolean condition will put the currently executing method in the process pool and suspend until the condition becomes true.

Runtime syntax. The runtime syntax is given in Fig. 3. A configuration cn can be empty ϵ or consists of futures, objects, invocation messages and concurrent object groups. The associative and commutative union operator on configurations is denoted by whitespace. A *future* $fut(f, v)$ has an identifier f and a value v (which is $\bot$ when the associated method call has not returned). An object is a term $ob(o, a, p, q)$, where o is the object's identifier, a a substitution representing the object's fields, p an active process, and q a pool of suspended processes. A substitution is a mapping from variable names to values. A process p is idle or consists of a substitution l of local variable bindings and a list s of statements, denoted as $\{l|s\}$. Most of the statements are standard. The statement **suspend** unconditionally releases the processor, suspending the active process. The statement **await** g releases the processor depending on the guard g, which is either Boolean conditions b or return tests x?, which evaluates to true if x is a future variable and its value can be retrieved; otherwise false. The statement **cont**(f) controls scheduling when local synchronous calls complete their execution, returning control to the caller.

Right-hand side expressions rhs for assignments include object creation within the same cog, denoted as **new** $C(e)$, and in a fresh cog, denoted as **new cog** $C(e)$, asynchronous and synchronous method calls, and (pure) expressions e.[1] An invocation message $invoc(o, f, m, \overline{v})$ consists of the callee o, the

---

[1] We refer to the semantics in [11], although the ABS surface language has evolved and among other small changes now uses **new local** and **new** instead of **new/new cog**.

$$\frac{(\textsc{Await-True})}{[\![g]\!]_{aol}^{cn}} \qquad \frac{(\textsc{Await-False})}{\neg[\![g]\!]_{aol}^{cn}}$$

$$\frac{[\![g]\!]_{aol}^{cn}}{ob(o, a, \{l|\mathbf{await}\ g; s\}, q)\ cn} \qquad \frac{\neg[\![g]\!]_{aol}^{cn}}{ob(o, a, \{l|\mathbf{await}\ g; s\}, q)\ cn}$$
$$\to ob(o, a, \{l|s\}, q)\ cn \qquad \to ob(o, a, \{l|\mathbf{suspend}; \mathbf{await}\ g; s\}, q)\ cn$$

$$\text{(Suspend)} \qquad\qquad \frac{(\textsc{Release-Cog})}{c = a(cog)}$$
$$\frac{ob(o, a, \{l|\mathbf{suspend}; s\}, q)}{\to ob(o, a, \mathrm{idle}, q \cup \{l|s\})} \qquad \frac{c = a(cog)}{ob(o, a, \mathrm{idle}, q)\ cog(c, o)}$$
$$\to ob(o, a, \mathrm{idle}, q)\ cog(c, \epsilon)$$

$$\frac{(\textsc{Activate})}{p = \mathrm{select}(q, a, cn)\ \ c = a(cog)}$$
$$\frac{ob(o, a, \mathrm{idle}, q)\ cog(c, \epsilon)\ cn}{\to ob(o, a, p, q\backslash p)\ cog(c, o)\ cn}$$

$$\frac{(\textsc{Async-Call})}{o' = [\![e]\!]_{aol}\ \ \bar{v} = [\![\bar{e}]\!]_{aol}\ \ \mathrm{fresh}(f)}{ob(o, a, \{l|x = e!m(\bar{e}); s\}, q)}$$
$$\to ob(o, a, \{l|x = f; s\}, q)\ invoc(o', f, m, \bar{v})\ fut(f, \bot)$$

$$\frac{(\textsc{Bind-Mtd})}{p' = \mathrm{bind}(o, f, m, \bar{v}, class(o))}{ob(o, a, p, q)\ invoc(o, f, m, \bar{v})}$$
$$\to ob(o, a, p, q \cup p')$$

$$\frac{(\textsc{Return})}{v = [\![e]\!]_{aol}\ \ f = l(\text{destiny})}{ob(o, a, \{l|\mathbf{return}\ e; s\}, q)\ fut(f, \bot)}$$
$$\to ob(o, a, \{l|s\}, q)\ fut(f, v)$$

$$\frac{(\textsc{Read-Fut})}{v \neq \bot\ \ f = [\![e]\!]_{aol}}{ob(o, a, \{l|x = e.\mathbf{get}; s\}, q)\ fut(f, v)}$$
$$\to ob(o, a, \{l|x = v; s\}, q)\ fut(f, v)$$

$$\frac{(\textsc{Cog-Sync-Call})}{o' = [\![e]\!]_{aol}\ \ \bar{v} = [\![\bar{e}]\!]_{aol}\ \ \mathrm{fresh}(f)}$$
$$c = a'(cog)\ \ f' = l(\text{destiny})$$
$$\{l'|s'\} = \mathrm{bind}(o', f, m, \bar{v}, class(o'))$$
$$ob(o, a, \{l|x = e.m(\bar{e}); s\}, q)$$
$$ob(o', a', \mathrm{idle}, q')\ cog(c, o)$$
$$\to ob(o, a, \mathrm{idle}, q \cup \{l|x = f.\mathbf{get}; s\})\ fut(f, \bot)$$
$$ob(o', a', \{l'|s'; \mathbf{cont}(f')\}, q')\ cog(c, o')$$

$$\frac{(\textsc{Cog-Sync-Return-Sched})}{c = a'(cog)\ \ f = l'(\text{destiny})}$$
$$ob(o, a, \{l|\mathbf{cont}(f)\}, q)\ cog(c, o)$$
$$ob(o', a', \mathrm{idle}, q' \cup \{l'|s'\})$$
$$\to ob(o, a, \mathrm{idle}, q)\ cog(c, o')$$
$$ob(o', a', \{l'|s'\}, q')$$

$$\frac{(\textsc{Self-Sync-Call})}{o = [\![e]\!]_{aol}\ \ \bar{v} = [\![\bar{e}]\!]_{aol}\ \ f' = l(\text{destiny})}$$
$$\mathrm{fresh}(f)\ \ \{l'|s'\} = \mathrm{bind}(o, f, m, \bar{v}, class(o'))$$
$$ob(o, a, \{l|x = e.m(\bar{e}); s\}, q)$$
$$\to ob(o, a, \{l'|s'; \mathbf{cont}(f')\}, q \cup \{l|x = f.\mathbf{get}; s\})\ fut(f, \bot)$$

$$\frac{(\textsc{Self-Sync-Return-Sched})}{f = l'(\text{destiny})}{ob(o, a, \{l|\mathbf{cont}(f)\}, q \cup \{l'|s\})}$$
$$\to ob(o, a, \{l'|s\}, q)$$

$$\frac{(\textsc{Rem-Sync-Call})}{o' = [\![e]\!]_{aol}\ \ \mathrm{fresh}(f)\ \ a(cog) \neq a'(cog)}{ob(o, a, \{l|x = e.m(\bar{e}); s\}, q)\ ob(o', a', p', q')}$$
$$\to ob(o, a, \{l|f = e!m(\bar{e}); x = f.\mathbf{get}; s\}, q)\ ob(o', a', p', q')$$

Fig. 4. Part of Semantics of Core ABS [11]

future f to which the call returns its result, the method name m, and the actual parameter values $\bar{v}$ of the call. Values are object and future identifiers, Boolean values, and ground terms from the functional subset of the language. For simplicity, classes are not represented explicitly in the semantics, as they may be seen as static tables.

Semantics. Here, we discuss some of the transition rules, given in Fig. 4, of the ABS semantics that we used in evaluation of the refactored ABS programs. Full semantics can be found in [11]. Assignment of an object's fields and a process' local variables is standard and therefore is not shown here. The **await** statements are handled as follows: if the guard g evaluates to *true* in the object's current state, Await-True consumes the statement; otherwise, Await-False appends a **suspend** statement to the process. Rule Suspend puts the active process to the process pool, leaving the processor *idle*, and if a cog's active object is idle, rule Release-Cog releases the cog from the object. When a cog is idle, rule Activate selects a process p from the process pool of an object residing in the cog for execution. Note that the function *select(q, a, cn)* selects a *ready* process from q; if q is empty or no process is ready, the function returns an idle process [16]. A process is *ready* if it will not directly be resumed or block the processor.

Rule ASYNC-CALL controls the asynchronous communications between objects by sending an invocation message to the callee o' with a new, unique future f (guaranteed by *fresh(f)*), the method name m and actual parameters $\overline{v}$. The value of f is initialised to $\perp$. Rule BIND-MTD puts the process corresponding to a method invocation in the process pool of the callee. A reserved variable *destiny* local in the method is used to store the identity of the future associated with the call. Rule RETURN puts the return value of the call into the associated future. Rule READ-FUT retrieves the value from the future f if $v \neq \perp$; otherwise, the reduction on this object is blocked.

The remaining rules in Fig. 4 handle synchronous communication among objects. Rules COG-SYNC-CALL and COG-SYNC-RETURN-SCHED are responsible for synchronous calls between two objects residing in the same cog, in which case the possession of the cog is directly transferred between the caller and callee by appending a special **cont** statement at the end of the invoked method. Synchronous self-calls are implemented similarly by rules SELF-SYNC-CALL and SELF-SYNC-RETURN-SCHED. Rule REM-SYNC-CALL handles synchronous calls to an object in a different cog, which is in fact syntactic sugar for an asynchronous call immediately followed by a blocking **get** operation.

3 Refactorings and Their Effects on Concurrency

In this section, we discuss different cases of refactorings that can affect program behaviour in a concurrent setting. First, we define a notion of equivalence of configurations that is suitable for our purpose, as we deal with concurrent systems, and some refactorings may affect the allocation of objects to components (cogs).

Definition 1 (Equivalence of configurations). *Two configurations cn_1 and cn_2 are equivalent, denoted as $cn_1 \equiv_\mathcal{R} cn_2$, if and only if for any object o such that $ob(o, a_1, \{l_1|s_1\}, q_1) \in cn_1$ and $ob(o, a_2, \{l_2|s_2\}, q_2) \in cn_2$,*

1. $\forall x \in dom(a_1) \cap dom(a_2) \cdot (x \neq this \wedge x \neq cog) \Rightarrow a_1(x) = a_2(x)$; and
2. $\forall x \in dom(l_1) \cap dom(l_2) \cdot l_1(x) = l_2(x)$

Note that this definition specifically mandates that all attributes, local variables and activation state coincide, and the assignment of objects to cogs can be different in the refactored program.

Definition 2 (Notion of refactoring correctness). *Given two equivalent configurations cn_o and cn_r where $cn_o = cn_1 \; ob(o, a_1, \{l_1|s_1; s_1'\}, q_1)$, $cn_r = cn_2 \; ob(o, a_2, \{l_2|s_2; s_2'\}, q_2)$ and a refactoring $\mathcal{R}f$ such that $s_2 = \mathcal{R}f(s_1)$. We say $\mathcal{R}f$ is correct if and only if for all $cn_r \rightarrow^* cn_r'$ where $cn_r' = cn_2' \; ob(o, a_2', \{l_2'|s_2'\}, q_2')$, there exists $cn_o' \rightarrow^* cn_r'$ such that $cn_o' \equiv_\mathcal{R} cn_r'$ and $cn_o' = cn_1' \; ob(o, a_1', \{l_1'|s_1'\}, q_1')$.*

We will see that usually we will not achieve unconditional correctness for all refactorings. Most crucially, changes to method calls can result in addition or removal of deadlocks which hence do not result in equivalent configurations. We will capture these side-conditions accordingly.

3.1 *Hide Delegate*

In the following, we revisit the source code before and after applying the *Hide Delegate* refactoring from Fig. 1, in which we elide the obvious, necessary ABS interface declarations **PersonI** and **DeptI**. We then discuss the different possible executions (modulo interleaving in the environment) of the original program in Fig. 1(a), and show that while all non-deterministic executions of the refactored program in Fig. 1(b) are contained in the original, there exists a situation that will deadlock after refactoring for a given object-to-component mapping.

Let us first consider the two synchronous method calls in Fig. 1(a). For illustration, we assume object p lives in a cog *different* from the calling object o, while object d lives in the *same* cog. The first call on Line 5 is handled by one of the three rules for synchronous calls, determined by the component-relationship between the calling object and p. If both are in the same component (or even the same object), we first use COG-SYNC-CALL (or SELF-SYNC-CALL). In the case where they are in different cogs, we thus proceed with REM-SYNC-CALL.

The execution is illustrated in Fig. 5. The rule creates an intermediate *asynchronous* call immediately followed by a **get**, which begins execution through a ASYNC-CALL and the ASSIGNMENT for the intermediate future. Now the current object cannot proceed, and must wait for the environment to BIND-MTD and ACTIVATE the called object, which then immediately RETURNS, giving the scheduler the opportunity to complete the READ-FUT and ASSIGN to variable d in the caller o. Note that we elided any possible interleavings with cogs in the environment; as the current cog is never released, its state cannot change in between. Next, we continue with the second synchronous method call on Line 6. Since object d resides in the *same cog* as the caller o, we continue with COG-SYNC-CALL, which introduces an intermediate future and immediately passes control to d, which after the trivial RETURN statement in turn COG-SYNC-RETURN-SCHEDS and then resumes execution in the caller o with READ-FUT, ASSIGN.

Recall that our correctness criterion is that a *refactored* execution should exist within the original executions. We now study the corresponding scenario after the refactoring, and illustrate in detail how the refactoring introduces a deadlock. Figure 6 presents the transition steps of the refactored code in Fig. 1(b). Object o executes the single refactored synchronous call on Line 16 to getManager into the cog hosting object p using REM-SYNC-CALL, with the corresponding follow-up through ASYNC-CALL, ASSIGN, BIND-MTD, ACTIVATE as before. Now, in object p, we see the difference in execution: the proxy getManager now has to make its own REM-SYNC-CALL since we assume that d lives in the same cog as o but different from o. However, after the necessary intermediate ASYNC-CALL, ASSIGN, BIND-MTD, it is now *not* possible to execute ACTIVATE to continue execution: since object o is blocked on the synchronous call to object p, it does not release control of the cog it is residing, and consequently object d will never be scheduled. Thus, the three objects in the two cogs are now locked forever in a deadly embrace, as shown in the last configuration in Fig. 6.

Analysing all possible execution scenarios in detail will give us Table 1. We can see that the dynamic behaviour of the source code has to be carefully

$$cn \; cog(c_1, o) \; cog(c_2, \epsilon) \; ob(o, a, \{l | d = p.gD(); m = d.gM(); s\}, q)$$
$$ob(o_p, a_p, \text{idle}, q_p) \; ob(o_d, a_d, \text{idle}, q_d)$$

REM-
SYNC-CALL $\rightarrow$
$$cn \; cog(c_1, o) \; cog(c_2, \epsilon) \; ob(o, a, \{l | f_1 = p!gD(); d = f_1.\textbf{get}; m = d.gM(); s\}, q)$$
$$ob(o_p, a_p, \text{idle}, q_p) \; ob(o_d, a_d, \text{idle}, q_d)$$

ASYNC-
CALL $\rightarrow$
$$cn \; cog(c_1, o) \; cog(c_2, \epsilon) \; ob(o, a, \{l | f_1 = f_p; d = f_1.\textbf{get}; m = d.gM(); s\}, q)$$
$$ob(o_p, a_p, \text{idle}, q_p) \; ob(o_d, a_d, \text{idle}, q_d) \; invoc(o_p, f_p, gD, \emptyset) \; fut(f_p, \perp)$$

ASSIGN $\rightarrow$
$$cn \; cog(c_1, o) \; cog(c_2, \epsilon) \; ob(o, a, \{l[f_1 \mapsto f_p] | d = f_1.\textbf{get}; m = d.gM(); s\}, q)$$
$$ob(o_p, a_p, \text{idle}, q_p) \; ob(o_d, a_d, \text{idle}, q_d) \; invoc(o_p, f_p, gD, \emptyset) \; fut(f_p, \perp)$$

BIND-MTD $\rightarrow$
$$cn \; cog(c_1, o) \; cog(c_2, \epsilon) \; ob(o, a, \{l[f_1 \mapsto f_p] | d = f_1.\textbf{get}; m = d.gM(); s\}, q)$$
$$ob(o_p, a_p, \text{idle}, q_p \cup \{l_p | s_p; \textbf{return } e_p\}) \; ob(o_d, a_d, \text{idle}, q_d) \; fut(f_p, \perp)$$
$$\{l_p | s_p; \textbf{return } e_p\} = bind(o_p, f_p, gD, \emptyset, class(o_p))$$

ACTIVATE $\rightarrow$
$$cn \; cog(c_1, o) \; cog(c_2, o_p) \; ob(o, a, \{l[f_1 \mapsto f_p] | d = f_1.\textbf{get}; m = d.gM(); s\}, q)$$
$$ob(o_p, a_p, \{l_p | s_p; \textbf{return } e_p\}, q_p) \; ob(o_d, a_d, \text{idle}, q_d) \; fut(f_p, \perp)$$

$\vdots$ $\qquad\qquad\qquad$ $\vdots$

$\rightarrow$
$$cn \; cog(c_1, o) \; cog(c_2, o_p) \; ob(o, a, \{l[f_1 \mapsto f_p] | d = f_1.\textbf{get}; m = d.gM(); s\}, q)$$
$$ob(o_p, a'_p, \{l'_p | \textbf{return } e_p\}, q'_p) \; ob(o_d, a_d, \text{idle}, q_d) \; fut(f_p, \perp)$$

RETURN $\rightarrow$
$$cn \; cog(c_1, o) \; cog(c_2, o_p) \; ob(o, a, \{l[f_1 \mapsto f_p] | d = f_1.\textbf{get}; m = d.gM(); s\}, q)$$
$$ob(o_p, a'_p, \text{idle}, q'_p) \; ob(o_d, a_d, \text{idle}, q_d) \; fut(f_p, v_p) \qquad v_p = [\![e_p]\!]_{a'_p \circ l'_p}$$

READ-FUT $\rightarrow$
$$cn \; cog(c_1, o) \; cog(c_2, o_p) \; ob(o, a, \{l[f_1 \mapsto f_p] | d = v_p; m = d.gM(); s\}, q)$$
$$ob(o_p, a'_p, \text{idle}, q'_p) \; ob(o_d, a_d, \text{idle}, q_d) \; fut(f_p, v_p)$$

ASSIGN $\rightarrow$
$$cn \; cog(c_1, o) \; cog(c_2, o_p) \; ob(o, a, \{l'' | m = d.gM(); s\}, q) \; ob(o_p, a'_p, \text{idle}, q'_p)$$
$$ob(o_d, a_d, \text{idle}, q_d) \; fut(f_p, v_p) \qquad\qquad l'' = l[f_1 \mapsto f_p, d \mapsto v_p]$$

COG-
SYNC-CALL $\rightarrow$
$$cn \; cog(c_1, o_d) \; cog(c_2, o_p) \; ob(o, a, \text{idle}, q \cup \{l'' | m = f_d.\textbf{get}; s\})$$
$$ob(o_p, a'_p, \text{idle}, q'_p) \; ob(o_d, a_d, \{l_d | s_d; \textbf{return } e_d; \textbf{cont}(f)\}, q_d) \; fut(f_p, v_p)$$
$$fut(f_d, \perp) \qquad \{l_d | s_d; \textbf{return } e_d\} = bind(o_d, f_d, gM, \emptyset, class(o_d)) \; f = l(\text{destiny})$$

$\vdots$ $\qquad\qquad\qquad$ $\vdots$

$\rightarrow$
$$cn \; cog(c_1, o_d) \; cog(c_2, o_p) \; ob(o, a, \text{idle}, q \cup \{l'' | m = f_d.\textbf{get}; s\})$$
$$ob(o_p, a'_p, \text{idle}, q'_p) \; ob(o_d, a'_d, \{l'_d | \textbf{return } e_d; \textbf{cont}(f)\}, q'_d) \; fut(f_p, v_p) \; fut(f_d, \perp)$$

RETURN $\rightarrow$
$$cn \; cog(c_1, o_d) \; cog(c_2, o_p) \; ob(o, a, \text{idle}, q \cup \{l'' | m = f_d.\textbf{get}; s\}) \qquad v_d = [\![e_d]\!]_{a'_d \circ l'_d}$$
$$ob(o_p, a'_p, \text{idle}, q'_p) \; ob(o_d, a'_d, \{l'_d | \textbf{cont}(f)\}, q'_d) \; fut(f_p, v_p) \; fut(f_d, v_d)$$

COG-SYNC-
RETURN-
SCHED $\rightarrow$
$$cn \; cog(c_1, o) \; cog(c_2, o_p) \; ob(o, a, \{l'' | m = f_d.\textbf{get}; s\}, q) \; ob(o_p, a'_p, \text{idle}, q'_p)$$
$$ob(o_d, a'_d, \text{idle}, q'_d) \; fut(f_p, v_p) \; fut(f_d, v_d)$$

READ-FUT $\rightarrow$
$$cn \; cog(c_1, o) \; cog(c_2, o_p) \; ob(o, a, \{l'' | m = v_d; s\}, q) \; ob(o_p, a'_p, \text{idle}, q'_p)$$
$$ob(o_d, a'_d, \text{idle}, q'_d) \; fut(f_p, v_p) \; fut(f_d, v_d)$$

ASSIGN $\rightarrow$
$$cn \; cog(c_1, o) \; cog(c_2, o_p) \; ob(o, a, \{l''[m \mapsto v_d] | s\}, q) \; ob(o_p, a'_p, \text{idle}, q'_p)$$
$$ob(o_d, a'_d, \text{idle}, q'_d) \; fut(f_p, v_p) \; fut(f_d, v_d)$$

Fig. 5. Execution of the code before *Hide Delegate* (Fig. 1(a)). We abbreviate *getDept* to *gD*, and *getManager* to *gM*. We let o be the object executing Lines 5–6, o_p executing *getDept* and o_d executing *getManager*, and assume $a(cog) = a_d(cog)$, $a(cog) \neq a_p(cog)$.

analysed. Many refactorings are bi-directional; here the application from right to left is Fowler's *Remove Middle Man* refactoring. This example here also illustrates how this refactoring could accidentally *remove* an existing deadlock from a program, and hence cannot immediately fulfil our notion of correctness either.

$$cn \; cog(c_1, o) \; cog(c_2, \epsilon) \; ob(o, a, \{l|m = p.gM(); s\}, q) \; ob(o_p, a_p, \text{idle}, q_p)$$
$$ob(o_d, a_d, \text{idle}, q_d)$$

REM-
SYNC-CALL $\to$
$$cn \; cog(c_1, o) \; cog(c_2, \epsilon) \; ob(o, a, \{l|f_2 = p!gM(); m = f_2.\text{get}; s\}, q)$$
$$ob(o_p, a_p, \text{idle}, q_p) \; ob(o_d, a_d, \text{idle}, q_d)$$

ASYNC-
CALL $\to$
$$cn \; cog(c_1, o) \; cog(c_2, \epsilon) \; ob(o, a, \{l|f_2 = f_p'; d = f_2.\text{get}; s\}, q) \; ob(o_p, a_p, \text{idle}, q_p)$$
$$ob(o_d, a_d, \text{idle}, q_d) \; invoc(o_p, f_p', gM, \emptyset) \; fut(f_p', \bot)$$

ASSIGN $\to$
$$cn \; cog(c_1, o) \; cog(c_2, \epsilon) \; ob(o, a, \{l[f_2 \mapsto f_p']|d = f_2.\text{get}; s\}, q) \; ob(o_p, a_p, \text{idle}, q_p)$$
$$ob(o_d, a_d, \text{idle}, q_d) \; invoc(o_p, f_p', gM, \emptyset) \; fut(f_p', \bot)$$

BIND-MTD $\to$
$$cn \; cog(c_1, o) \; cog(c_2, \epsilon) \; ob(o, a, \{l[f_2 \mapsto f_p']|d = f_2.\text{get}; s\}, q)$$
$$ob(o_p, a_p, \text{idle}, q_p \cup \{l_p|p = d.gM(); \text{return } e_p'\}) \; ob(o_d, a_d, \text{idle}, q_d) \; fut(f_p', \bot)$$
$$\{l_p|p = d.gM(); \text{return } e_p\} = \text{bind}(o_p, f_p', gM, \emptyset, class(o_p))$$

ACTIVATE $\to$
$$cn \; cog(c_1, o) \; cog(c_2, o_p) \; ob(o, a, \{l[f_2 \mapsto f_p']|d = f_2.\text{get}; s\}, q)$$
$$ob(o_p, a_p, \{l_p|p = d.gM(); \text{return } e_p'\}, q_p) \; ob(o_d, a_d, \text{idle}, q_d) \; fut(f_p', \bot)$$

REM-
SYNC-CALL $\to$
$$cn \; cog(c_1, o) \; cog(c_2, o_p) \; ob(o, a, \{l[f_2 \mapsto f_p']|d = f_2.\text{get}; s\}, q)$$
$$ob(o_p, a_p, \{l_p|f_3 = d!gM(); p = f_3.\text{get}; \text{return } e_p'\}, q_p) \; ob(o_d, a_d, \text{idle}, q_d)$$
$$fut(f_p', \bot)$$

ASYNC-
CALL $\to$
$$cn \; cog(c_1, o) \; cog(c_2, o_p) \; ob(o, a, \{l[f_2 \mapsto f_p']|d = f_2.\text{get}; s\}, q)$$
$$ob(o_p, a_p, \{l_p|f_3 = f_d'; p = f_3.\text{get}; \text{return } e_p'\}, q_p) \; ob(o_d, a_d, \text{idle}, q_d) \; fut(f_p', \bot)$$
$$invoc(o_d, f_d', gM, \emptyset) \; fut(f_d', \bot)$$

ASSIGN $\to$
$$cn \; cog(c_1, o) \; cog(c_2, o_p) \; ob(o, a, \{l[f_2 \mapsto f_p']|d = f_2.\text{get}; s\}, q)$$
$$ob(o_p, a_p, \{l_p[f_3 \mapsto f_d']|p = f_3.\text{get}; \text{return } e_p'\}, q_p) \; ob(o_d, a_d, \text{idle}, q_d) \; fut(f_p', \bot)$$
$$invoc(o_d, f_d', gM, \emptyset) \; fut(f_d', \bot)$$

BIND-MTD $\to$
$$cn \; cog(c_1, o) \; cog(c_2, o_p) \; ob(o, a, \{l[f_2 \mapsto f_p']|d = f_2.\text{get}; s\}, q)$$
$$ob(o_p, a_p, \{l_p[f_3 \mapsto f_d']|p = f_3.\text{get}; \text{return } e_p'\}, q_p) \; ob(o_d, a_d, \text{idle}, q_d \cup gM)$$
$$fut(f_p', \bot) \; fut(f_d', \bot) \qquad \textbf{Deadlocked}$$

Fig. 6. Execution of the code after *Hide Delegate* (Fig. 1(b)). We abbreviate *getManager* to *gM*. We let o be the object executing Line 16, o_p executing Line 24 and o_d executing *getManager*, and assume $a(cog) = a_d(cog)$, $a(cog) \neq a_p(cog)$.

3.2 *Async-to-Sync* Refactoring

In some situations it may be useful to reduce the amount of concurrency in a program. Figure 7(a) shows a common idiom in ABS, where we release control while waiting for the asynchronous call to return. This permits **this** object to process other calls in the meantime, though of course this may affect the state of the object. An obvious attempt to reduce such ensuing (mental) complexity would be to use a synchronous call instead. However, whether this is actually safe or not, depends very much on the body of m. Again, a callback into the current component across component boundaries will result in a deadlock. This is compounded by the fact the O o' is only typed by an interface, and additional effort will be required to statically identify the underlying object and then its cog.

We first show the general correctness of this refactoring if both caller and callee are in the *same* cog, and then discuss a similar scenario as in *Hide Delegate*, which leads to a deadlock in the refactored version that does not exist in the original. However, we will see that the latter is not unconditional as in *Hide Delegate*, but rather (also) depends on the body of m.

We consider the two code fragments in Fig. 7, where Fig. 7(b) is the refactored version of Fig. 7(a), and let o be the calling object and o' be the called object. Let us investigate whether this refactoring is correct wrt. Definition 2, i.e., given

```
1    class C {
2      O o';
3      { ...
4        fut = o'!m();
5        await fut;
6        x = fut.get;
7        ...
8      } }
```

```
9    class C {
10     O o';
11     { ...
12
13       x = o'.m();
14
15       ...
16     } }
```

(a) Asynchronous   (b) Synchronous

Fig. 7. Asynchronous to synchronous

$$
\text{Cog-Sync-Call} \rightarrow
\begin{array}{l}
cn \ cog(c,o) \ ob(o,a,\{l|x = o.m(\overline{e}); s\}, q) \ ob(o', a', \text{idle}, q') \\
\hline
cn \ cog(c,o') \ ob(o,a,\text{idle}, q \cup \{l|x = f.\mathbf{get}; s\}) \\
ob(o', a', \{l'|s'; \mathbf{return}\ e_m; \mathbf{cont}(f')\}, q') \ fut(f, \bot) \\
\quad \{l'|s'; \mathbf{return}\ e_m\} = \text{bind}(o', f', m, \emptyset, class(o')) \quad f' = l(\text{destiny})
\end{array}
$$

$\vdots$ $\vdots$

$$
\text{Return} \rightarrow
\begin{array}{l}
cn \ cog(c,o') \ ob(o,a,\text{idle}, q \cup \{l|x = f.\mathbf{get}; s\}) \\
ob(o', a'', \{l''|\mathbf{return}\ e_m; \mathbf{cont}(f')\}, q'') \ fut(f, \bot) \\
\hline
cn \ cog(c,o') \ ob(o,a,\text{idle}, q \cup \{l|x = f.\mathbf{get}; s\}) \ ob(o', a'', \{l''|\mathbf{cont}(f')\}, q'') \\
fut(f, v_m) \qquad\qquad\qquad\qquad\qquad\qquad\qquad\qquad v_m = [\![e_m]\!]_{a''o l''}
\end{array}
$$

$$
\text{Cog-Sync-Return-Sched} \rightarrow cn \ cog(c,o) \ ob(o,a,\{l|x = f.\mathbf{get}; s\}, q) \ ob(o', a'', \text{idle}, q'') \ fut(f, v_m)
$$

$$
\text{Read-Fut} \rightarrow cn \ cog(c,o) \ ob(o,a,\{l|x = v_m; s\}, q) \ ob(o', a'', \text{idle}, q'') \ fut(f, v_m)
$$

$$
\text{Assign} \rightarrow cn \ cog(c,o) \ ob(o,a,\{l[x \mapsto v_m]|s\}, q) \ ob(o', a'', \text{idle}, q'') \ fut(f, v_m)
$$

Fig. 8. Execution of the synchronous call after refactoring (Fig. 7(b)). We let o be the object executing Line 13, o' executing m, and assume $o \neq o'$, $a(cog) = a'(cog)$

equivalent configurations cn_1 and cn_2 before executing Lines 4–6 respectively Line 13, there exists at least one execution in the original program such that the configurations cn_1' and cn_2' after executing Line 6 respectively Line 13 are also equivalent.

For the sake of brevity, as there are many different cases to consider, we look at only one particular case in detail and derive the condition under which the refactoring results in an equivalent program. We essentially distinguish the initial set of different cases by whether we have to invoke SELF-SYNC-CALL (if $o = o'$), COG-SYNC-CALL (if $o \neq o'$ but live in the same cog) or REM-SYNC-CALL (if o and o' live in different cogs). We only present COG-SYNC-CALL in detail, and provide an additional observation on the REM-SYNC-CALL case afterwards.

We first consider the refactored program in Fig. 7(b) and assume that $o \neq o'$ but live in the same cog. Figure 8 shows the detailed execution of this scenario. We start the execution with a COG-SYNC-CALL, which introduces an intermediate future and yields control to o'. At this point, although there can be interleavings with the environment, wlog. we ignore those, as they cannot interfere with the current cog, except by posting additional tasks into queues. Furthermore, any such interleaving can be simulated in the original program as well. The current cog will proceed evaluating method m through some rule applications $r_0, \ldots, r_m$

$$
\begin{array}{rl}
 & cn\ cog(c,o)\ ob(o,a,\{l\,|\,fut = o!m(\overline{e});\textbf{await}\ fut;x = fut\textbf{.get};s\},q) \\
 & ob(o',a',\text{idle},q') \\
\text{ASYNC-} \rightarrow & cn\ cog(c,o)\ ob(o,a,\{l\,|\,fut = f;\textbf{await}\ fut;x = fut\textbf{.get};s\},q)\ ob(o',a',\text{idle},q') \\
\text{CALL} & invoc(o',f,m,\emptyset)\ fut(f,\bot) \\
\text{ASSIGN} \rightarrow & cn\ cog(c,o)\ ob(o,a,\{l[fut \mapsto f]\,|\,\textbf{await}\ fut;x = fut\textbf{.get};s\},q)\ ob(o',a',\text{idle},q') \\
 & invoc(o',f,m,\emptyset)\ fut(f,\bot) \\
\text{AWAIT-} \rightarrow & cn\ cog(c,o)\ ob(o,a,\{l[fut \mapsto f]\,|\,\textbf{suspend};\textbf{await}\ fut;x = fut\textbf{.get};s\},q) \\
\text{FALSE} & ob(o',a',\text{idle},q')\ invoc(o',f,m,\overline{v})\ fut(f,\bot) \\
\text{SUSPEND} \rightarrow & cn\ cog(c,o)\ ob(o,a,\text{idle},q \cup \{l[fut \mapsto f]\,|\,\textbf{await}\ fut;x = fut\textbf{.get};s\}) \\
 & ob(o',a',\text{idle},q')\ invoc(o',f,m,\emptyset)\ fut(f,\bot) \\
\text{RELEASE-} \rightarrow & cn\ cog(c,\epsilon)\ ob(o,a,\text{idle},q \cup \{l[fut \mapsto f]\,|\,\textbf{await}\ fut;x = fut\textbf{.get};s\}) \\
\text{COG} & ob(o',a',\text{idle},q')\ invoc(o',f,m,\emptyset)\ fut(f,\bot) \\
 & cn\ cog(c,\epsilon)\ ob(o,a,\text{idle},q \cup \{l[fut \mapsto f]\,|\,\textbf{await}\ fut;x = fut\textbf{.get};s\}) \\
\text{BIND-MTD} \rightarrow & ob(o',a',\text{idle},q' \cup \{l'\,|\,s';\textbf{return}\ e_m\})\ fut(f,\bot) \\
 & \qquad\qquad\qquad\qquad\qquad\qquad \{l'\,|\,s';\textbf{return}\ e_m\} = \text{bind}(o',f',m,\emptyset,\text{class}(o')) \\
\text{ACTIVATE} \rightarrow & cn\ cog(c,o')\ ob(o,a,\text{idle},q \cup \{l[fut \mapsto f]\,|\,\textbf{await}\ fut;x = fut\textbf{.get};s\}) \\
 & ob(o',a',\{l'\,|\,s';\textbf{return}\ e_m\},q')\ fut(f,\bot) \\
 & \quad\vdots \qquad\qquad\qquad\qquad\qquad \vdots \\
\rightarrow & cn\ cog(c,o')\ ob(o,a,\text{idle},q \cup \{l[fut \mapsto f]\,|\,\textbf{await}\ fut;x = fut\textbf{.get};s\}) \\
 & ob(o',a'',\textbf{return}\ e_m,q'')\ fut(f,\bot) \\
\text{RETURN} \rightarrow & cn\ cog(c,o')\ ob(o,a,\text{idle},q \cup \{l[fut \mapsto f]\,|\,\textbf{await}\ fut;x = fut\textbf{.get};s\}) \\
 & ob(o',a'',\text{idle},q'')\ fut(f,v_m) \qquad\qquad\qquad\qquad v_m = [\![e_m]\!]_{a''\circ l''} \\
\text{RELEASE-} \rightarrow & cn\ cog(c,\epsilon)\ ob(o,a,\text{idle},q \cup \{l[fut \mapsto f]\,|\,\textbf{await}\ fut;x = fut\textbf{.get};s\}) \\
\text{COG} & ob(o',a'',\text{idle},q'')\ fut(f,v_m) \\
\text{ACTIVATE} \rightarrow & cn\ cog(c,o)\ ob(o,a,\{l[fut \mapsto f]\,|\,\textbf{await}\ fut;x = fut\textbf{.get};s\},q)\ ob(o',a'',\text{idle},q'') \\
 & fut(f,v_m) \\
\text{AWAIT-} \rightarrow & cn\ cog(c,o)\ ob(o,a,\{l[fut \mapsto f]\,|\,x = fut\textbf{.get};s\},q)\ ob(o',a'',\text{idle},q'') \\
\text{TRUE} & fut(f,v_m) \\
\text{READ-FUT} \rightarrow & cn\ cog(c,o)\ ob(o,a,\{l[fut \mapsto f]\,|\,x = v_m;s\},q)\ ob(o',a'',\text{idle},q'')\ fut(f,v_m) \\
\text{ASSIGN} \rightarrow & cn\ cog(c,o)\ ob(o,a,\{l[fut \mapsto f,x \mapsto v_m]\,|\,s\},q)\ ob(o',a'',\text{idle},q'')\ fut(f,v_m)
\end{array}
$$

Fig. 9. Execution of the asynchronous call before refactoring (Fig. 7(a)). We let o be the object executing Lines 4–6, o' executing m, and assume $o \neq o'$, $a(cog) = a'(cog)$

and may eventually RETURN. Note that the refactoring will preserve any potential deadlocks resulting from method m in the original program. We continue the case to completion in the non-deadlocked scenario: the final configuration is easily derived (only) through rules COG-SYNC-RETURN-SCHED, READ-FUT, ASSIGN. Note that in the calling object, the computed value v_m is uniquely determined by the sequence $r_0, \ldots, r_m$ above, as there are no changes in other objects.

We now turn our attention over to the original program in Fig. 7(a) and show in Fig. 9 that we can derive an equivalent state which only differs in the presence of an explicit, now unused future. Executing Lines 4–6 in the original program can replicate the behaviour of the refactored program in the following way: after the ASYNC-CALL and storing the associated future via ASSIGN, execution SUSPENDS until completion of the call. Wlog., we can RELEASE-COG control and immediately BIND-MTD and ACTIVATE the pending call in o. At this point, we are now entering the execution of m which can proceed exactly with rule sequence

$r_0, \ldots, r_m$ as above, which eventually terminates with a RETURN. The cog hence becomes available through RELEASE-COG. As the scheduler is not guaranteed to provide any particular behaviour, there exists the behaviour where we ACTIVATE the calling object, which now completes with AWAIT-TRUE, READ-FUT, ASSIGN.

Although this is of course not a detailed proof-case, it is easy to see that the resulting configurations are equivalent: the computation of the value of x coincide, and any other state changes can only come from the r-sequence which is identical in both cases. Nonetheless, we would like to motivate the underlying reason for the deadlock in the *Hide Delegate* refactoring, which is only indirectly visible here: assume a program where o and o' are in distinct cogs (which means proceeding with REM-SYNC-CALL in the refactored case). Assume further that within $r_0, \ldots, r_m$ there exists a synchronous callback back into the cog of o. In the original program, since o suspends and releases the cog it resides in, by AWAIT-FALSE, this callback can be processed. This execution in the refactored program will however deadlock as the object o blocks on the **get** statement. To summarize, there is again an underlying dynamic condition on the remainder of the code that needs to be checked to ensure correctness.

Since the scheduling is non-deterministic, our conversion to a synchronous call *removes* behaviour from the application. There is now only a single scheduling which directly continues into the body of the method.

As for the directionality of this refactoring, while a right-to-left application seemingly enables some degree of concurrency, it is only concurrency on the objects of class C, which as explained initially opens up the caller for possible state changes that may or may not violate assumed invariants by the developer.

3.3 Inline Method

The *Inline Method* refactoring is straightforward: within a class, we replace a method call with its body. In the ABS setting, we have two points to consider: as Fowler already points out, this can only be done when the code is not polymorphic. This applies doubly so in ABS, where any variables are only typed by interfaces in the first place. However, it also becomes quickly clear that we only need to consider calls to methods within the same class anyway: a method generally makes use of attributes, and these are private in ABS; so a method from another class cannot easily be inlined but needs to be moved into the current class first (see *Move Method* in Sect. 3.5 below). Consequently, here we only consider calls for inlining the target **this**.

In the case of a synchronous call, inlining is straightforward and does not affect the behaviour. In fact, from looking at rule SELF-CALL, it is immediately clear that inlining *is* the semantics of a synchronous self-call.

3.4 Move Field

The *Move Field* refactoring is not as easily applicable in ABS as it is in Java. Declaring the field in a new class is straightforward, however, since all fields are private, as a follow-up we either require the introduction of a getter, relocation

```
 1 │ class C {              12 │ class C {              23 │ class Tgt implements TgtI {
 2 │    O x;                13 │    O getX() {          24 │    O x;
 3 │                        14 │      getTgt().getX();  25 │
 4 │    O getX() {          15 │    }                   26 │    O getX() {
 5 │      return x;         16 │    Unit setX(O o) {    27 │      return x;
 6 │    }                   17 │      getTgt().setX();  28 │    }
 7 │                        18 │    }                   29 │    Unit setX(O o) {
 8 │    Unit setX(O o) {    19 │    TgtI getTgt() {     30 │      x:=o;
 9 │      x:=o;             20 │      return ...expr...; 31 │    }
10 │    }                   21 │    }                   32 │    ...
11 │ }                      22 │ }                      33 │ }
```

(a) Before   (b) After

Fig. 10. Move Field

of affected methods, or both. We decompose this refactoring into an application of *Self Encapsulate Field*, which first introduces a (synchronous) getter in the current class.

As per the ABS semantics, this introduction results in an equivalent configuration. After that, we can proceed with moving the attribute, introducing a getter, and turning the previous getter into proxy to the getter in the new class. This requires identifying how to reference the target object from the source.

Here, again the ABS language specification makes this easy: as the field was private, the code locations that set this value are immediately identified and we assume for simplicity that we only have to deal with a single setter. After identifying a target, setter and getter now become proxies.

As we have seen before, we now have new (synchronous) calls to objects that may or may not be in the same component as the current object. If the target object is referenced through an attribute in the current class, this is always unproblematic. If the target is derived through a chain of calls, e.g., getTgt().getX() (assuming we move attribute x), we may have accidentally introduced a deadlock: if getTgt() either directly or indirectly calls back (either synchronously or asynchronously) into our object, we will produce a deadlock that did not exist in the original program. Note that if the original program already contained expression getTgt(), it already contains the same deadlock, albeit in a different method. The general situation is illustrated in Fig. 10.

3.5 Move Method

This refactoring moves a method into a different class, leaving behind a proxy if necessary. Fowler proposes as first step an analysis whether any other features of the class should also be moved. Of the several strategies to handle references to original features, we here focus on passing the source object as a parameter. We illustrate a relatively simple case, and will focus our attention on constructor invocations this time, not just method calls.

Figure 11 shows the initial situation and the refactoring which also leaves behind the proxy. Assuming that the target has been suitably identified as object

```
 1 │ class C {                    9 │ class C {                   17 │ class O implements OI {
 2 │   T moveMe(...) {           10 │                             18 │   U m(..) { /* unchanged */ }
 3 │     /* Create object in     11 │   /* proxy */               19 │
 4 │         current cog */      12 │   T moveMe(...) {           20 │   T moved(CI that,...) {
 5 │     this.setS(new S());     13 │     ...o.moved(this,..)...  21 │     that.setS(new S());
 6 │     ...o.m(..)...           14 │   }                         22 │     ...this.m(..)...
 7 │   }                         15 │                             23 │   }
 8 │ }                           16 │ }                           24 │ }
```

| (a) Before | (b) After |

Fig. 11. Move Method

O o, e.g., if o is a parameter of moveMe, without going through the detailed evaluation by semantic rules, we immediately spot two problematic issues: any reference back to the source object in the refactored code through parameter that has the potential to be a cross-component callback with the associated risk of deadlock, e.g., through the setter, as discussed earlier.

The second issue, which is the novel observation that we can make here is about constructor invocations: in the original in Fig. 11(a), the new object of class S is created in the same cog as the calling object as we use **new**, not **new cog** (the former creates an object in the *same* cog while the latter in a *new* cog). In the refactored code, however, it is now created in a potentially different cog. Note that this is always uncritical when the code uses **new cog**. A similar effect has been observed in Java, where moving a method annotated with @Synchronized can change its synchronization context [17].

As one of the last steps in this refactoring, Fowler suggests to consider removing the remaining proxy and updating call-sites to refer to the new location. This again would have either no effect on deadlocks, or even remove an existing deadlock, as it removes an intermediate call into a potentially different component, but does not otherwise change the sequence of interactions.

3.6 Extract Class

The *Extract Class* refactoring is a well-known refactoring simplifying complexity in a class by dividing it into two. Attributes and methods are partitioned between the original program and the new class. It is easy to see that this refactoring primarily relies on *Move Field* and *Move Method*, and hence inherits their properties. Fowler [3] here explicitly suggests that this refactoring in particular *"[improves] the liveness of a concurrent program because it allows you to have separate locks on the two resulting classes"* and points out the potential concurrency issues. In ABS, this issue is made explicit: the split-off class needs to be instantiated through a constructor invocation, at which point the developer has to decide allocating the new object either in a new component, which may increase concurrency in the future through the introduction of further asynchronous calls, or in the current component. However, as we have now seen, calls across components can lead to deadlocks, if we end up calling back into the current component. Hence the allocation within the same component is always safe, whereas a new component can *only* be used when the split-off class does not have any dependency back into the source class.

3.7 Discussion

We have seen in the above refactorings that the root cause of differences in behaviour in the refactored program are method calls that now cross component boundaries. This may happen either because an invocation is changed (call on a different object, or new call), or because we have moved a constructor invocation into a different class, and hence possibly into a different cog. There is no syntactic criterion to judge changes safe. Even though moving a (local) constructor invocation into a different class through, e.g., the *Move Method* refactoring may be more visible, there is little difference between this and a moved call.

Our *Async-to-Sync* refactoring is an ABS-specific refactoring. From left to right, it may reduce (mental) complexity, at the cost of understanding the safety of the refactored code, first. Applied from right to left, it can be an easy starting point to introduce additional concurrency in the long run. It does not necessarily add concurrency, but enables it by making the code yield, e.g., before a long-running transaction. Also here the effect of yielding needs some up-front analysis and understanding whether any subsequent code after the call may be affected by side-effects while being suspended here. As we have seen in the detailed examples above, there are two main concerns for concurrency: changing method calls can introduce or remove deadlocks, as can moving constructor invocations into a different cog.

In Table 2, we survey a range of refactorings from Fowler [3] for their effect on concurrency. The columns indicate whether a refactoring effects any particular change that we now know to have implications on behaviour. The first six we have studied above, the remainder we classify informally. "Yes/No" indicate whether this change occurs as part of the refactoring, and hence whether careful consideration of effects is required. "Safe" indicates that the change is present in the refactoring, yet will always result in a call to the same object, or in the case of *Replace Method with Method Object* can be kept safe with a local constructor invocation.

While plenty of these refactorings have either no effect or are safe (as calls will still be on the same object), almost any of the major refactorings is affected in some way. Most of the refactoring are innocuous in the Java-world, yet can have surprising effects in ABS, indicating that ABS developers could most likely benefit from dedicated refactoring support.

Suggestions to Tool Developers. It is clear from our discussion that an IDE or tooling for a language like ABS with its rich semantics should assist developers better. Mere syntactical transformations checking structural properties, e.g., on the level of interfaces and classes are of course still essential to guarantee syntactically correct code, but cannot give strong guarantees as to dynamic behaviour. We think that it is important that any further correctness properties also come

Table 2. Classification of common refactorings whether they affect concurrency

Refactoring	Change Target of Call?	New Method Call?	Removed Method Call?	New/Moved Constructor?
Inline Method	No	No	Safe	No
Move Method	Yes	No	No	Yes
Move Field	Yes	No	No	Safe
Hide Delegate	Yes	Yes	Yes	Yes
Remove Middle Man	Yes	Yes	Yes	Yes
Extract Class	Yes	Yes	Yes	Yes
Extract Method	No	Safe	No	No
Inline Temp	No	No	No	No
Replace Temp with Query	No	Safe	No	No
Introduce Explaining Variable	No	No	No	No
Split Temporary Variable	No	No	No	No
Replace Method...	No	Safe	No	Safe
Inline Class	Yes	No	Yes	Yes
(Self) Encapsulate Field	No	Safe	No	No

with a reasonable cost, but do not put undue burden on developers. For example, we feel that any further analysis and checking should be automated, and even though it might be costly in terms of computational power, should avoid requiring any additional input from the developer, e.g., in the form of partial proofs, though light-weight annotations may be acceptable.

We have only focused on program-independent correctness properties here, that we have been able to discharge by showing that mostly identical sequences of evaluation rules can be applied, possibly interleaved with small distinct segments using other semantic rules, that nonetheless do not affect the state that we capture in our notion of correctness. As one would expect for a language with a focus on concurrency, many of the refactorings can introduce potential deadlocks, that fortunately can in principle be tackled through inference of object-to-component allocation. Such inference exists either stand-alone [12], or as part of static deadlock checkers like DF4ABS and DECO [13,14], and could ideally be re-used to only partially analyse changed code. Currently, the developers' best hope is applying those tools at intermediate stages, though due to their high complexity this may hardly be feasible frequently.

4   Related Work and Conclusion

Related Work. Our work focusses on a dynamic language-feature (object-to-component mapping) that does not exist as such in plain object-oriented languages. The closest related work we are aware of is a precise analysis of the effect of refactorings on concurrent Java code [17], where most notably moving members between classes will change their synchronization context. Agha and Palmskog [18] infer annotations from execution traces that can be used to transform programs from threads to actors, eliding explicit concurrency primitives. How refactorings affect object lifetime in Rust programs is analysed by Ringdal [19].

Garrido and Meseguer reason about the correctness of refactorings for Java by capturing an executable Java formal semantics in the Maude rewriting logic [20]. As they are concerned with structural refactorings and focus on Pull Up/Push Down and the Rename refactoring, they avoid some of the complexities as to comparing states where refactorings change the bound variables, or produce intermediate states. Schäfer et al. [21] aim for control and data flow preservation, and focus on the *Extract Method* refactoring and decompose it into smaller so-called *micro-refactorings*, for which it is easier to derive or prove properties.

Steinhöfel and Hähnle [22,23] propose Abstract Execution, which generalises Symbolic Execution to partially unspecified programs. They have formalised several of Fowler's refactorings in the KeY framework to prove preservation of a form of behavioural equivalence of Java programs. Careful derivation of preconditions for refactorings is required to prove suitable equivalence of refactored code.

Gheyi et al. [9] use a user-defined equivalence notion between states conforming to different meta-models, e.g., after a refactoring changed the structure of a class. They require an explicit alphabet and a mapping function between added/removed attributes in Alloy models and then check mutual refinement. We conjecture that this could augment our approach, and both alphabet and mapping could be derived from a refactoring and the code that it is applied on.

Eilertsen et al. [8] use assertions to provide runtime warnings in the refactored code in cases where a combination of *Extract* and *Move Method* results in unexpected changes to the object graph. We could easily introduce a similar check on component assignment to provide some protection in those cases where a static safety analysis would have to give up due to imprecision.

Soares et al. [7] propose a technique to automatically identify behavioral changes in a number of refactoring implementations of Eclipse, NetBeans, and JRRT. It uses an automatic program generator (called JDOLLY [24]) and a tool to automatically detect behavioral changes (called SAFEREFACTOR [25]) to identify a number of bugs in these tools for sequential Java programs. We believe that we may find more behavioral changes when considering concurrent programs, e.g. by following an approach by Pradel et al. [26]. They combine (incomplete) test case generation with (complete) exploration of interleavings through JPF to discover output-diverging substitutes (replacing super-classes with sub-classes). Corresponding necessary generation of test cases for actor systems has been studied e.g. by Li et al. [27].

Rachatasumrit and Kim [28] conduct an empirical study and found that a number of test suites do not test the entities impacted by a refactoring. Test suites do not have a good change coverage. For instance, only 22% of refactored methods and fields are tested by existing regression tests. Mongiovi et al. [29]

implement a change impact analyzer tool called SAFIRA, and included it in SAFEREFACTOR. It automatically generates test cases for the entities impacted by the transformation. The tool could find some behavioral changes that could not be found without SAFIRA. Alves et al. [30] concluded that combining change impact analysis with branch coverage could be highly effective in detecting faults introduced by refactoring edits. A change impact analyzer may be also useful when refactoring concurrent programs. As future work, we intend to evolve SAFIRA to consider transformations applied to concurrent programs.

Conclusion. In this article, we have given an overview of how well-known refactorings from object-oriented programming languages like Java have non-obvious behaviour in actor languages. Here, we have focused on some selected refactorings from Fowler's book [3]. On the example of the ABS active object language, we illustrate the concurrency effects that have to be taken into account.

As the ABS language has a formal semantics [11], we can use it to derive proofs for a suitable notion equivalence of the refactored program. Here, we specify correctness as the refactored behaviour being contained within the original behaviour, in the form of a limited comparison of objects and their attributes/local variables. In the absence of a formal correctness specification of the program being refactored, we find that this gives reasonable expectations as to the effect of the refactoring. Furthermore, from our formal derivations we obtain side conditions that can be checked effectively with existing tools, e.g., related to deadlocks, and can be used to produce counter examples.

Future Work. We have not surveyed refactoring support for other languages such as the Akka library for Scala yet. As a general strategy for identifying high-value targets for closer investigation, it would be useful to first categorize existing static analyses and runtime checks that codify the correctness (usually program-independent properties such as "no crash", "no deadlock"), and then check –as we have done here– to what degree refactorings can affect this. The biggest rewards could be achieved in cases where an expensive analysis or runtime check could be replaced with a modular analysis reasoning only about the performed change in the context of analysis information from the original program.

ABS currently has no refactoring support at all and is in the process of moving towards an Xtext-based compiler infrastructure. This enables deriving a Language Server[2] which should allow us to prototype some of the refactorings with a convenient interface to the outside. This will give us the opportunity to try and integrate some of the inferences as pre-condition checks. A possible feasible approach could be to first transfer the results from the Abstract Execution framework to an active-object language, and then extending it with concurrency.

Another interesting venue of research would be looking into the built-in support for specifying software product lines in ABS through so-called Deltas, which have also already been studied as a subject of refactorings [31]. Deltas specify among other things replacement of methods, but are primarily concerned with evolution, and not refactoring. They could be a convenient vehicle to express

---

[2] https://microsoft.github.io/language-server-protocol/.

and implement refactorings in: an inference and check of the correctness conditions could also be applied to the change specified via a Delta, and hence not only benefit refactorings, but another branch of the ABS language altogether. Developers could then receive warnings if the behaviour of one product diverges from another one, although of course that could be intentional, and is most likely more useful with a proper specification of the program.

References

1. Swanson, E.B.: The dimensions of maintenance. In: Proceedings of the International Conference on Software Engineering, ICSE. IEEE (1976)
2. Opdyke, W.: Refactoring object-oriented frameworks. Ph.D. thesis, University of Illinois at Urbana-Champaign (1992)
3. Fowler, M.: Refactoring - Improving the Design of Existing Code. Addison Wesley Object Technology Series. Addison-Wesley, Boston (1999)
4. Beck, K.: Extreme Programming Explained: Embrace Change. Addison-Wesley Longman Publishing Company, Inc. (2000)
5. Schäfer, M., de Moor, O.: Specifying and implementing refactorings. In: Object-Oriented Programming, Systems, Languages, and Applications (2010)
6. Daniel, B., Dig, D., Garcia, K., Marinov, D.: Automated testing of refactoring engines. In: Proceedings of the Foundations of Software Engineering. ACM (2007)
7. Soares, G., Gheyi, R., Massoni, T.: Automated behavioral testing of refactoring engines. IEEE Trans. Softw. Eng. **39**(2), 147–162 (2013)
8. Eilertsen, A.M., Bagge, A.H., Stolz, V.: Safer refactorings. In: Margaria, T., Steffen, B. (eds.) ISoLA 2016. LNCS, vol. 9952, pp. 517–531. Springer, Cham (2016). https://doi.org/10.1007/978-3-319-47166-2_36
9. Gheyi, R., Massoni, T., Borba, P.: An abstract equivalence notion for object models. Electron. Notes Theor. Comput. Sci. **130**, 3–21 (2005)
10. Boer, F.D., et al.: A survey of active object languages. ACM Comput. Surv. **50**(5), 76:1–76:39 (2017)
11. Johnsen, E.B., Hähnle, R., Schäfer, J., Schlatte, R., Steffen, M.: ABS: a core language for abstract behavioral specification. In: Aichernig, B.K., de Boer, F.S., Bonsangue, M.M. (eds.) FMCO 2010. LNCS, vol. 6957, pp. 142–164. Springer, Heidelberg (2011). https://doi.org/10.1007/978-3-642-25271-6_8
12. Welsch, Y., Schäfer, J., Poetzsch-Heffter, A.: Location types for safe programming with near and far references. In: Clarke, D., Noble, J., Wrigstad, T. (eds.) Aliasing in Object-Oriented Programming. Types, Analysis and Verification. LNCS, vol. 7850, pp. 471–500. Springer, Heidelberg (2013). https://doi.org/10.1007/978-3-642-36946-9_16
13. Giachino, E., Laneve, C., Lienhardt, M.: A framework for deadlock detection in core ABS. Softw. Syst. Model. **15**(4), 1013–1048 (2016)
14. Flores-Montoya, A.E., Albert, E., Genaim, S.: May-happen-in-parallel based deadlock analysis for concurrent objects. In: Beyer, D., Boreale, M. (eds.) FMOODS/-FORTE -2013. LNCS, vol. 7892, pp. 273–288. Springer, Heidelberg (2013). https://doi.org/10.1007/978-3-642-38592-6_19
15. Hewitt, C., Bishop, P., Steiger, R.: A universal modular ACTOR formalism for artificial intelligence. In: Proceedings of the International Joint Conference on Artificial Intelligence. Morgan Kaufmann Publishers Inc. (1973)

16. Johnsen, E.B., Owe, O.: An asynchronous communication model for distributed concurrent objects. In: Software Engineering and Formal Methods. IEEE Computer Society (2004)
17. Schäfer, M., Dolby, J., Sridharan, M., Torlak, E., Tip, F.: Correct refactoring of concurrent Java code. In: D'Hondt, T. (ed.) ECOOP 2010. LNCS, vol. 6183, pp. 225–249. Springer, Heidelberg (2010). https://doi.org/10.1007/978-3-642-14107-2_11
18. Agha, G., Palmskog, K.: Transforming threads into actors: learning concurrency structure from execution traces. In: Lohstroh, M., Derler, P., Sirjani, M. (eds.) Principles of Modeling. LNCS, vol. 10760, pp. 16–37. Springer, Cham (2018). https://doi.org/10.1007/978-3-319-95246-8_2
19. Ringdal, P.O.: Automated refactorings of Rust programs. Master's thesis, Institute for Informatics, University of Oslo, Norway, June 2020
20. Garrido, A., Meseguer, J.: Formal specification and verification of Java refactorings. In: International Workshop on Source Code Analysis and Manipulation. IEEE (2006)
21. Schäfer, M., Verbaere, M., Ekman, T., de Moor, O.: Stepping stones over the refactoring Rubicon. In: Drossopoulou, S. (ed.) ECOOP 2009. LNCS, vol. 5653, pp. 369–393. Springer, Heidelberg (2009). https://doi.org/10.1007/978-3-642-03013-0_17
22. Steinhöfel, D., Hähnle, R.: Abstract execution. In: ter Beek, M.H., McIver, A., Oliveira, J.N. (eds.) FM 2019. LNCS, vol. 11800, pp. 319–336. Springer, Cham (2019). https://doi.org/10.1007/978-3-030-30942-8_20
23. Steinhöfel, D.: Abstract execution: automatically proving infinitely many programs. Ph.D. thesis, TU Darmstadt, Department of Computer Science, May 2020
24. Mongiovi, M., Mendes, G., Gheyi, R., Soares, G., Ribeiro, M.: Scaling testing of refactoring engines. In: Software Maintenance and Evolution. ICSME (2014)
25. Soares, G., Gheyi, R., Serey, D., Massoni, T.: Making program refactoring safer. IEEE Softw. **27**(4), 52–57 (2010)
26. Pradel, M., Gross, T.R.: Automatic testing of sequential and concurrent substitutability. In: International Conference on Software Engineering, ICSE. IEEE (2013)
27. Li, S., Hariri, F., Agha, G.: Targeted test generation for actor systems. In: Proceedings European Conference on Object-Oriented Programming, LIPIcs, vol. 109. Schloss Dagstuhl - Leibniz-Zentrum für Informatik (2018)
28. Rachatasumrit, N., Kim, M.: An empirical investigation into the impact of refactoring on regression testing. In: International Conference on Software Maintenance. ICSM (2012)
29. Mongiovi, M., Gheyi, R., Soares, G., Teixeira, L., Borba, P.: Making refactoring safer through impact analysis. Sci. Comput. Program. **93**, 39–64 (2014)
30. Alves, E.L.G., Massoni, T., de Lima Machado, P.D.: Test coverage of impacted code elements for detecting refactoring faults: an exploratory study. J. Syst. Softw. **123**, 223–238 (2017)
31. Schulze, S., Richers, O., Schaefer, I.: Refactoring delta-oriented software product lines. In: Aspect-Oriented Software Development. ACM (2013)

Rigorous Engineering of Collective Adaptive Systems

Rigorous Engineering of Collective Adaptive Systems Introduction to the 3rd Track Edition

Martin Wirsing[1]([✉]), Rocco De Nicola[2], and Stefan Jähnichen[3]

[1] Ludwig-Maximilians-Universität München, Munich, Germany
wirsing@lmu.de
[2] IMT School for Advanced Studies Lucca, Lucca, Italy
rocco.denicola@imtlucca.it
[3] TU Berlin and FZI Forschungszentrum Informatik Berlin, Berlin, Germany
stefan.jaehnichen@tu-berlin.de

Abstract. A collective adaptive system consists of collaborating entities that are able to adapt at runtime to dynamically changing, open-ended environments and to evolving requirements. Rigorous engineering requires appropriate methods and tools that help guarantee that a collective adaptive system lives up to its intended purpose. This note gives an introduction to the track "Rigorous Engineering of Collective Adaptive Systems" and its 21 scientific contributions.

Keywords: Adaptive system · Collective system · Ensemble · Software engineering · Formal method · Rigorous method

Modern IT systems are increasingly distributed and consist of collaborating entities that are able to adapt at runtime to dynamically changing, open-ended environments and to new requirements. Such systems are called collective adaptive system or also ensembles [29,33]. Examples are cyber-physical systems, the internet of things, socio-technical systems as well as smart systems and robot swarms.

Rigorous engineering of collective adaptive systems requires devising appropriate methods and tools to guarantee that such systems behave as expected. To achieve this goal, we need to develop theories for modelling and analysing collective adaptive systems, techniques for programming and running such systems, and specific methods for adaptation, validation and verification while ensuring security, trust and performance.

The track "Rigorous Engineering of Collective Adaptive Systems" is a follow-up of three other successful tracks [16,32,53] at ISOLA 2014 [38], ISOLA 2016 [39], and ISOLA 2018 [40]. The first track [53] was entitled "Rigorous Engineering of Autonomic Ensembles" and was organised within the activities of the EU-funded research project ASCENS [54]. The latter two tracks [16,32] addressed the same theme as this year's edition and included research results from several research approaches and projects. Recently, also a Special Section of

© Springer Nature Switzerland AG 2020
T. Margaria and B. Steffen (Eds.): ISoLA 2020, LNCS 12477, pp. 161–170, 2020.
https://doi.org/10.1007/978-3-030-61470-6_10

the International Journal on Software Tools for Technology Transfer was devoted to the rigorous engineering of collective adaptive systems [15].

The present edition of the track comprises 21 research papers; each of which has gone through a rigorous check by three reviewers. In the following, these papers are briefly introduced in the order of their presentations and grouped according to seven thematic sessions, namely: Coordination and Composition, Attribute-based Coordination, Security and Trust, Specifying Ensembles and Computing with them, Validating and Analysing Collective Adaptive Systems, Machine Learning and Evolutionary Computing for Collective Adaptive Systems, and Programming and Analysing Swarm Robotics.

Coordination and Composition. For building high quality collective adaptive systems, it is important to choose the right mechanisms for coordinating the autonomous entities of the ensemble and to seek for engineering methods supporting the compositional analysis and construction of collective adaptive systems. In this session coordination and composition techniques are discussed.

In the paper "Composition of Component Models - a Key to Construct Big Systems" [46], Wolfgang Reisig discusses the importance of the associative law for component systems and points out that for well-known modelling formalisms such as Petri nets, BPMN, and UML, the "naive" choice of gluing composition does not satisfy this law. As an alternative, he proposes an abstract graph-based notion of component together with a composition operator which can be shown to be associative.

The second paper "Degrees of Autonomy in Coordinating Collectives of Self-Driving Vehicles" [56] by Franco Zambonelli and Stefano Mariani addresses the problem of coordinating self-driving vehicles. The authors propose four different coordination approaches - called centralised, negotiation-based, agreement-based, and emergent - which provide the autonomous entities with different degrees of freedom in their decision making.

The final paper of this session "Engineering Semantic Self-composition of Services through Tuple-based Coordination" [13] by Ashley Caselli, Giovanni Ciatto, Giovanna Di Marzo Serugendo and Andrea Omicini defines a model for spontaneous service composition based on tuple spaces à la Linda [23] that supports semantic reasoning leveraging logic-tuples and unification. Usability of the proposed technology is vindicated by introducing a Java-based software architecture that implements it.

Attribute-Based Coordination. In contrast to message passing, attribute-based coordination abstracts from the names of senders and receivers and provides a kind of selective broadcast communication. Senders and receivers are determined by properties such as role, status, and position that can be modified at runtime. Several recent languages including SCEL [17], CARMA [8] and AbC [1,2] use attribute-based communication for modelling interactions in collective adaptive systems. The three papers of this session study logics, verification, and behavioural abstractions for collective systems interacting by means of attribute-based communication.

Typically, languages with attribute-based coordination mechanisms model systems as parallel compositions of components, each component being equipped with a local process description. In the paper "A Dynamic Logic for Systems with Predicate-based Communication" [26], Rolf Hennicker and Martin Wirsing complement such local descriptions with a global requirements specification format that is well-suited to specify abstract properties, like safety and liveness, as well as allowed and forbidden interaction scenarios. Specifications are written in a dynamic logic [25] according to a style similar to the approach in [27]. Atomic interactions are expressed by predicates involving one sender and a set of receivers. An appropriate notion of correctness is defined relating such global specifications with local systems specifications written in a variant of the AbC calculus.

Also the paper "Abstractions for Collective Adaptive Systems" [30] by Omar Inverso, Catia Trubiani and Emilio Tuosto provides a global view on attribute-based coordination. The so-called "AbC-inspired behavioural types" are based on atomic interactions similar to those in [26] but feature separate predicates for senders and receivers and explicit matching requirements. Like [26], this approach abstracts away from asynchrony and from the number of the autonomous entities and their local behaviour.

The paper "Verifying AbC Calculus via Emulation" [19] by Rocco De Nicola, Tan Duong and Omar Inverso addresses the issue of verifying AbC programs. The proposed approach consists in translating AbC into the C language and to annotate C programs with assertions encoding temporal logic state formulas. State-of-the-art bounded model checkers can then be used to verifying properties of AbC systems. A number of interesting case studies are considered and properties of interest are checked.

Security and Type Safety. The three papers of this session address methods for controlling non-interference, for dealing with situations unanticipated by the access control policies, and for ensuring type safety.

In the paper "Adaptive Security Policies" [42] Flemming Nielson, René Rydhof Hansen, and Hanne Riis Nielson propose an approach aiming at guaranteeing that the local security policies of agents are respected while avoiding to imposing a global security policy on all agents. Individual agents can define their own security policy and the framework ensures that agents cannot observe any violation of such policy in an environment where the other agents do change. It is shown that security is preserved under evaluation by taking advantage of operational semantics and type systems.

The paper "Capturing Dynamicity and Uncertainty in Security and Trust via Situational Patterns" [11] by Tomáš Bureš, Petr Hnětynka, Robert Heinrich, Stephan Seifermann, and Maximilian Walter studies solutions for access-control in modern smart systems when unanticipated situations are encountered and extends previous work on security ensembles [3]. Some typical examples for uncertainty of access control are considered and a classification of uncertainty of access control in Industry 4.0 systems, inspired by [43] is proposed. It is suggested that such classification can be used as a guide to dynamically adapt the security access rules by providing situational patterns for each type of uncertainty.

Many of today's socio-technical systems are realised over distributed web-based architectures. Communication relies on plain text HTTP-protocol data transfer which is untyped and therefore prone to errors. The recent data query and manipulation language GraphQL [20] for mobile web applications addresses this problem by strongly typing expressions at the server side, but at the client side data remain untyped. In the paper "Guaranteeing Type Consistency in Collective Adaptive Systems" [48] Jonas Schürmann, Tim Tegeler and Bernhard Steffen propose an approach to automatically generate type-safe communication interfaces for both, clients and servers. The main achievement is a novel type-safe, functional domain specific language called "Type-safe Functional GraphQL" (TFG). This language ensures type safety in three ways: at generation time by verifying queries against the GraphQL schema, at compile time by leveraging the type system of TypeScript [41], and at runtime by using decoders to validate payloads. A collaborative development scenario based on the GraphQL API of Github illustrates the approach.

Specifying Ensembles and Computing with Them. With epistemic logic, aggregate computing, and distributed tuple space coordination, this session addresses applications of different foundational approaches for specifying and computing in collective adaptive systems.

Epistemic logic [52] is a classical formal tool for studying the notion of knowledge. It has been used for reasoning about knowledge and belief in many application areas including strategic games and distributed computing. In the paper "Epistemic Logic in Ensemble Specification" [49] Jan Sürmeli focusses on the knowledge of the members of an ensemble and on the inherent information asymmetry between them. He introduces a new knowledge operator for ensemble knowledge and formalises ensemble-specific axioms for peer relationship, collaboration, and the ensemble life cycle.

The key idea of aggregate computing is to program a large ensemble of interacting devices as a whole. Coordination and composition are hidden to programmers [5]. A modern aggregate programming language is ScaFi which integrates declarative aggregate programming techniques into Scala. In the paper "FSCAFI: a Core Calculus for Collective Adaptive Systems Programming" [12] Roberto Casadei, Mirko Viroli, Giorgio Audrito and Ferruccio Damiani present a minimal core calculus, called FScaFi, that models the aggregate computing aspects of ScaFi. In particular, FScaFi provides the novel notion of "computation against a neighbour" where expressions are evaluated against the values computed by neighbour devices.

The third paper of this session "Writing Robotics Applications with X-Klaim" [6] by Lorenzo Bettini, Khalid Bourr, Rosario Pugliese and Francesco Tiezzi presents a framework for programming distributed robotics applications. X-KLAIM [7] is a programming language specifically devised to design distributed applications consisting of software components interacting through multiple distributed tuple spaces. The framework integrates X-KLAIM with the popular framework ROS [45] for writing robot software, and with a simulator providing a 3D visualization of scenarios and robot movements. Feasibility and effectiveness of the proposed approach is vindicated by implementing a scenario with robots looking for victims in a disaster area.

Validating and Analysing Collective Adaptive Systems. In this session new methods are presented for analysing collective adaptive systems and for certifying their quality.

Metric approaches have a long tradition in semantics for analysing relationships between programs as well as between processes, see e.g. [4, 18, 55]. The paper "Measuring Adaptability and Reliability of Large Scaled Systems" [14] by Valentina Castiglioni, Michele Loreti and Simone Tini proposes a metric approach for analysing large self-organising collective systems. A main contribution is the so-called population metric for comparing the behaviour of self-organising systems. Based on this metric, the notions of adaptability and reliability are used to determine whether a system is able to adjust its behaviour to perturbations in the initial conditions. A randomised algorithm for computing the distance between two systems is defined and used for verifying systems' adaptability and reliability. It is also shown that the proposed approach scales to large systems by resorting to mean-field approximation.

Network centrality is a key notion in network analysis and helps to identify the most important nodes of a network by assigning an importance measure to each node (see e.g. [51]). The paper "Centrality-preserving Exact Reductions of Multi-Layer Networks" [50] by Stefano Tognazzi and Tatjana Petrov studies centrality of multi-layer networks. A novel technique for exact model reduction of multiplex multi-layer networks is defined and implemented. It is not only shown that the technique preserves *eigenvector* centrality but also that for many real-world networks it achieves considerable reductions of the network size and speed-ups in the computation of the centrality measure.

In the third paper of this session "Towards Dynamic Dependable Systems through Evidence-Based Continuous Certification" [21] Rasha Faqeh, Christof Fetzer, Holger Hermanns, Jörg Hoffmann, Michaela Klauck, Maximilian A. Köhl, Marcel Steinmetz and Christoph Weidenbach address the quality control of frequently updated/changing cyber-physical systems and outline their vision of "evidence-based continuous supervision and certification of software variants". They imagine to run both old and new variants of component software inside the same system, together with a supervising instance for monitoring the behaviour of the components. Certification of updated components is based on evidence from automated component analysis and micro-experiments. To show feasibility of the approach, a first formalisation including a logic for efficient certification is presented.

Machine Learning and Evolutionary Computing for Collective Adaptive Systems. This session addresses sub-symbolic AI techniques in two complementary ways: AI techniques are used for supporting decisions in collective adaptation applications and formal methods are used for reasoning about AI techniques.

In many smart systems, the set of members of an ensemble may change dynamically. Membership is determined by a set of soft and hard constraints but - as constraint solvers may require exponential time - it may be problematic to use them at runtime. In the paper "Forming Ensembles at Runtime: A Machine Learning Approach" [9] Tomáš Bureš, Ilias Gerastathopoulos, Petr Hnětynka and Jan Pacovský extend their work on autonomous ensembles [10] and study a new approach to runtime ensembles formation in which they consider the association of autonomic entities to ensembles as a classification problem and use machine learning methods, namely decision trees and neural networks, to solve it. These methods need a considerable amount of data and runs for training but have a linear behaviour at runtime. The experiments show that in comparison with a state-of-the-art constraint solver, well-trained decision trees and neural networks have a similar performance and in some cases achieve marginally better solutions than the constraint solver.

The automated construction of controllers is another excellent application for AI methods. The paper "Synthesizing Control for a System with Black Box Environment, based on Deep Learning" [31] by Simon Iosti, Doron Peled, Khen Aharon, Saddek Bensalem and Yoav Goldberg proposes a methodology to use recurrent neural networks to synthesise controllers. A key to the success of the controller is that the training uses a set of small, well designed examples, which is exposed to various potential challenges. The proposed method works for unknown "blackbox" environments and various types of systems. It is adaptive in the sense that in case of changes in the environment, the training can be resumed after the system has been deployed.

In the third paper "A Formal Model For Reasoning About The Ideal Fitness In Evolutionary Processes" [22] Thomas Gabor and Claudia Linnhoff-Popien consider evolutionary computing as a process that looks for solutions to complex problems via the application of comparatively simple local operators and uses the knowledge gained through trial and error to guide systems towards reaching an externally given target. They provide a formal abstract account of evolutionary computing and discuss different fitness functions such as effective, reproductive, and productive fitness. As a main result they show that the notion of productive fitness represents the ideal fitness function for evolutionary processes.

Programming and Analysing Ensembles of Robots. Multi-robot systems and swarm robotics are active research areas with many promising applications; the reader is referred to [47] for an overview of current applications in research, education, and industry. The last session of the track presents new approaches for programming and analysing ensembles of robots.

The language CARMA-C [44] is an extension of CARMA [8] for modelling the nondeterministic stochastic behaviour of collective adaptive systems in terms of Continuous Time Markov Decision Processes [24]. In the paper "A Case-Study of Policy Synthesis for Swarm Robotics" [28] Jane Hillston and Paul Piho show how CARMA-C can be used to specify and resolve a policy synthesis problem from swarm robotics by taking advantage of the processes algebraic constructions in CARMA which lend themselves well to stochastic policy or parameter synthesis problems.

The last two papers of the track address so-called multipotent robot systems [37] where both hardware and software capabilities of robots can be reconfigured at runtime.

In the paper "Swarm and Collective Capabilities for Multipotent Robot Ensembles" [34] Oliver Kosak, Felix Bohn, Lennart Eing, Dennis Rall, Constantin Wanninger, Alwin Hoffmann and Wolfgang Reif propose a new pattern for expressing collective swarm behaviour. The so-called "Movement-Vector Based Swarm Capability" pattern extracts the common behaviour of several swarm algorithms such as particle swarm optimization, flocking, and triangle formation. The pattern is integrated into the reference architecture [37] for multipotent robot systems and an interface to the aggregate programming language Protelis is provided.

The paper "Maple-Swarm: Programming Collective Behavior for Ensembles by Extending HTN-Planning" [35] by Oliver Kosak, Lukas Huhn, Felix Bohn, Constantin Wanninger, Alwin Hofmann and Wolfgang Reif extends the Maple approach [36] (Multi-Agent script Programming Language for multipotent Ensembles) to deal with collective swarm behaviour. In particular, the concepts of agent groups and virtual swarm capabilities are introduced and it is shown how hierarchical task networks can be used to allocate tasks for agent groups. As proof of concepts they consider a real-life scenario where robots have to coordinate to fight fires.

Acknowledgements. As organisers of the track, we would like to thank all authors for their valuable contributions, all reviewers for their careful evaluations and constructive comments. We are also grateful to the ISOLA chairs Tiziana Margaria and Bernhard Steffen for giving us the opportunity to organise this track and to them and Springer–Verlag for providing us with the very helpful Equinocs conference system.

References

1. Abd Alrahman, Y., De Nicola, R., Loreti, M.: A calculus for collective-adaptive systems and its behavioural theory. Inf. Comput. **268**, 104457 (2019)
2. Abd Alrahman, Y., De Nicola, R., Loreti, M.: Programming interactions in collective adaptive systems by relying on attribute-based communication. Sci. Comput. Program. **192**, 102428 (2020)
3. Al Ali, R., Bures, T., Hnetynka, P., Matejek, J., Plasil, F., Vinarek, J.: Toward autonomically composable and context-dependent access control specification through ensembles. Int. J. Softw. Tools Technol. Transf. **22**(4), 511–522 (2020). https://doi.org/10.1007/s10009-020-00556-1
4. Arnold, A., Nivat, M.: Metric interpretations of infinite trees and semantics of non deterministic recursive programs. Theor. Comput. Sci. **11**, 181–205 (1980)
5. Beal, J., Viroli, M.: Aggregate programming: from foundations to applications. In: Bernardo, M., De Nicola, R., Hillston, J. (eds.) SFM 2016. LNCS, vol. 9700, pp. 233–260. Springer, Cham (2016). https://doi.org/10.1007/978-3-319-34096-8_8
6. Bettini, L., Bourr, K., Pugliese, R., Tiezzi, F.: Writing robotics applications with X-KLAIM. In: Margaria, T., Steffen, B. (eds.) ISoLA 2020. LNCS, vol. 12477, pp. 361–379. Springer, Cham (2020)

7. Bettini, L., Merelli, E., Tiezzi, F.: X-KLAIM is back. In: Boreale, M., Corradini, F., Loreti, M., Pugliese, R. (eds.) Models, Languages, and Tools for Concurrent and Distributed Programming. LNCS, vol. 11665, pp. 115–135. Springer, Cham (2019). https://doi.org/10.1007/978-3-030-21485-2_8

8. Bortolussi, L., et al.: CARMA: collective adaptive resource-sharing Markovian agents. In: QAPL 2015, EPTCS, vol. 194, pp. 16–31 (2015)

9. Bureš, T., Gerastathopoulos, I., Hnětynka, P., Pacovský, J.: Forming ensembles at runtime: a machine learning approach. In: Margaria, T., Steffen, B. (eds.) ISoLA 2020. LNCS, vol. 12477, pp. 440–456. Springer, Cham (2020)

10. Bureš, T., et al.: A language and framework for dynamic component ensembles in smart systems. Int. J. Softw. Tools Technol. Transf. **22**(4), 497–509 (2020). https://doi.org/10.1007/s10009-020-00558-z

11. Bureš, T., Hnětynka, P., Heinrich, R., Seifermann, S., Walter, M.: Capturing dynamicity and uncertainty in security and trust via situational patterns. In: Margaria, T., Steffen, B. (eds.) ISoLA 2020. LNCS, vol. 12477, pp. 295–310. Springer, Cham (2020

12. Casadei, R., Viroli, M., Audrito, G., Damiani, F.: FSCAFI: a core calculus for collective adaptive systems programming. In: Margaria, T., Steffen, B. (eds.) ISoLA 2020. LNCS, vol. 12477, pp. 344–360. Springer, Cham (2020)

13. Caselli, A., Ciatto, G., Di Marzo Serugendo, G., Omicini, A. Engineering semantic self-composition of services through tuple-based coordination. In: Margaria, T., Steffen, B. (eds.) ISoLA 2020. LNCS, vol. 12477, pp. 205–223. Springer, Cham (2020)

14. Castiglioni, V., Loreti, M., Tini, S.: Measuring adaptability and reliability of large scaled systems. In: Margaria, T., Steffen, B. (eds.) ISoLA 2020. LNCS, vol. 12477, pp. 380–396. Springer, Cham (2020)

15. De Nicola, R., Jähnichen, S., Wirsing, M.: Rigorous engineering of collective adaptive systems: special section. Int. J. Softw. Tools Technol. Transf. **22**(4), 389–397 (2020). https://doi.org/10.1007/s10009-020-00565-0

16. De Nicola, R., Jähnichen, S., Wirsing, M.: Rigorous engineering of collective adaptive systems introduction to the 2nd track edition. In: Margaria, T., Steffen, B. (eds.) ISoLA 2018. LNCS, vol. 11246, pp. 3–12. Springer, Cham (2018). https://doi.org/10.1007/978-3-030-03424-5_1

17. De Nicola, R., Loreti, M., Pugliese, R., Tiezzi, F.: A formal approach to autonomic systems programming: the SCEL language. ACM Trans. Auton. Adapt. **9**(2), 7:1–7:29 (2014)

18. Desharnais, J., Gupta, V., Jagadeesan, R., Panangaden, P.: Metrics for labelled Markov processes. Theor. Comput. Sci. **318**(3), 323–354 (2004)

19. De Nicola, R., Duong, T., Inverso, O.: Verifying AbC specifications via emulation. In: Margaria, T., Steffen, B. (eds.) ISoLA 2020. LNCS, vol. 12477, pp. 261–279. Springer, Cham (2020)

20. Facebook, Inc.: GraphQL specification, June 2018 Edition (2018). http://spec.graphql.org/June2018/. Accessed 12 Aug 2020

21. Faqeh, R., et al.: Towards dynamic dependable systems through evidence-based continuous certification. In: Margaria, T., Steffen, B. (eds.) ISoLA 2020. LNCS, vol. 12477, pp. 261–279. Springer, Cham (2020)

22. Gabor, T., Linnhoff-Popien, C.: A formal model for reasoning about the ideal fitness in evolutionary processes. In: Margaria, T., Steffen, B. (eds.) ISoLA 2020. LNCS, vol. 12477, pp. 473–490. Springer, Cham (2020)

23. Gelernter, D.: Generative communication in Linda. ACM Trans. Program. Lang. Syst. **7**(1), 80–112 (1985)

24. Guo, X., Hernández-Lerma, O.: Continuous-Time Markov Decision Processes: Theory and Applications. Springer, Heidelberg (2009). https://doi.org/10.1007/978-3-642-02547-1
25. Harel, D., Kozen, D., Tiuryn, J. (eds.): Dynamic Logic. MIT Press, Cambridge (2000)
26. Hennicker, R., Wirsing, M.: A dynamic logic for systems with predicate-based communication. In: Margaria, T., Steffen, B. (eds.) ISoLA 2020. LNCS, vol. 12477, pp. 473–490. Springer, Cham (2020)
27. Hennicker, R., Wirsing, M.: Dynamic logic for ensembles. In: [40], pp. 32–47 (2018)
28. Hillston, J., Piho, P.: A case study of policy synthesis for swarm robotics. In: Margaria, T., Steffen, B. (eds.) ISoLA 2020. LNCS, vol. 12477, pp. 491–501. Springer, Cham (2020)
29. Hölzl, M., Rauschmayer, A., Wirsing, M.: Engineering of software-intensive systems: state of the art and research challenges. In: Wirsing, M., Banâtre, J.-P., Hölzl, M., Rauschmayer, A. (eds.) Software-Intensive Systems and New Computing Paradigms. LNCS, vol. 5380, pp. 1–44. Springer, Heidelberg (2008). https://doi.org/10.1007/978-3-540-89437-7_1
30. Inverso, O., Trubiani, C., Tuosto. ,E.: Abstractions for collective adaptive systems. In: Margaria, T., Steffen, B. (eds.) ISoLA 2020. LNCS, vol. 12477, pp. 243–260. Springer, Cham (2020)
31. Iosti, S., Peled, D., Aharon, K., Bensalem, S., Goldberg, Y.: Synthesizing control for a system with black box environment, based on deep learning. In: Margaria, T., Steffen, B. (eds.) ISoLA 2020. LNCS, vol. 12477, pp. 457–472. Springer, Cham (2020)
32. Jähnichen, S., Wirsing, M.: Rigorous engineering of collective adaptive systems track introduction. In: Margaria, T., Steffen, B. (eds.) ISoLA 2016. LNCS, vol. 9952, pp. 535–538. Springer, Cham (2016). https://doi.org/10.1007/978-3-319-47166-2_37
33. Kernbach, S., Schmickl, T., Timmis, J.: Collective adaptive systems: challenges beyond evolvability. CoRR abs/1108.5643 (2011)
34. Kosak, O., et al.: Swarm and collective capabilities for multipotent robot ensembles. In: Margaria, T., Steffen, B. (eds.) ISoLA 2020. LNCS, vol. 12477, pp. 525–540. Springer, Cham (2020)
35. Kosak, O., Huhn, L., Bohn, F., Wanninger, C., Hofmann, A., Reif, W.: Maple-Swarm: programming collective behavior for ensembles by extending HTN-planning. In: Margaria, T., Steffen, B. (eds.) ISoLA 2020. LNCS, vol. 12477, pp. 507–524. Springer, Cham (2020)
36. Kosak, O., Wanninger, C., Angerer, A., Hoffmann, A., Schiendorfer, A., Seebach, H.: Towards self-organizing swarms of reconfigurable self-aware robots. In: Elnikety, S., Lewis, P.R., Müller-Schloer, C. (eds.) 2016 IEEE 1st International Workshops on Foundations and Applications of Self* Systems (FAS*W), Augsburg, Germany, 12–16 September 2016, pp. 204–209. IEEE (2016)
37. Kosak, O., Wanninger, C., Hoffmann, A., Ponsar, H., Reif, W.: Multipotent systems: combining planning, self-organization, and reconfiguration in modular robot ensembles. Sensors **19**(1), 17 (2019)
38. Margaria, T., Steffen, B. (eds.): ISoLA 2014. LNCS, vol. 8802. Springer, Heidelberg (2014). https://doi.org/10.1007/978-3-662-45234-9
39. Margaria, T., Steffen, B. (eds.): ISoLA 2016. LNCS, vol. 9952. Springer, Cham (2016). https://doi.org/10.1007/978-3-319-47166-2
40. Margaria, T., Steffen, B. (eds.): ISoLA 2018. LNCS, vol. 11246. Springer, Cham (2018). https://doi.org/10.1007/978-3-030-03424-5

41. Microsoft Corporation: TypeScript: Typed JavaScript at any scale (2020). https://www.typescriptlang.org/. Accessed 8 Aug 2020
42. Nielson, F., Hansen, R.R., Nielson, H.R.: Adaptive security policies. In: Margaria, T., Steffen, B. (eds.) ISoLA 2020. LNCS, vol. 12477, pp. 507–524. Springer, Cham (2020)
43. Pérez-Palacín, D., Mirandola, R.: Dealing with uncertainties in the performance modelling of software systems. In: Seinturier, L., Bureš, T., McGregor, J.D. (eds.) Proceedings of the 10th International ACM SIGSOFT Conference on Quality of Software Architectures (part of CompArch 2014), QoSA 2014, Marcq-en-Baroeul, Lille, France, 30 June–04 July 2014, pp. 33–42. ACM (2014)
44. Piho, P., Hillston, J.: Policy synthesis for collective dynamics. In: McIver, A., Horvath, A. (eds.) QEST 2018. LNCS, vol. 11024, pp. 356–372. Springer, Cham (2018). https://doi.org/10.1007/978-3-319-99154-2_22
45. Quigley, M., et al.: ROS: an open-source robot operating system. In: ICRA Workshop on Open Source Software (2009)
46. Reisig, W.: Composition of component models - a key to construct big systems. In: Margaria, T., Steffen, B. (eds.) ISoLA 2020. LNCS, vol. 12477, pp. 507–524. Springer, Cham (2020)
47. Schranz, M., Umlauft, M., Sende, M., Elmenreich, W.: Swarm robotic behaviors and current applications. Front. Rob. AI **7**, 36 (2020)
48. Schürmann, J., Tegeler, T., Steffen, B.: Guaranteeing type consistency in collective adaptive systems. In: Margaria, T., Steffen, B. (eds.) ISoLA 2020. LNCS, vol. 12477, pp. 311–328. Springer, Cham (2020)
49. Sürmeli, J.: Epistemic logic in ensemble specification. In: Margaria, T., Steffen, B. (eds.) ISoLA 2020. LNCS, vol. 12477, pp. 329–343. Springer, Cham (2020)
50. Tognazzi, S., Petrov, T.: Centrality-preserving exact reductions of Multi-Layer Networks. In: Margaria, T., Steffen, B. (eds.) ISoLA 2020. LNCS, vol. 12477, pp. 397–415. Springer, Cham (2020)
51. Tognazzi, S., Tribastone, M., Tschaikowski, M., Vandin, A.: Differential equivalence yields network centrality. In: [40], pp. 186–201 (2018)
52. van Ditmarsch, H., Halpern, J.Y., van der Hoek, W., Kooi, B.P.: Handbook of Epistemic Logic. College Publications, London (2015)
53. Wirsing, M., De Nicola, R., Hölzl, M.: Introduction to "rigorous engineering of autonomic ensembles"– track introduction. In: [38], pp. 96–98 (2014)
54. Wirsing, M., Hölzl, M., Koch, N., Mayer, P. (eds.): Software Engineering for Collective Autonomic Systems. LNCS, vol. 8998. Springer, Cham (2015). https://doi.org/10.1007/978-3-319-16310-9
55. Ying, M., Wirsing, M.: Approximate bisimilarity. In: Rus, T. (ed.) AMAST 2000. LNCS, vol. 1816, pp. 309–322. Springer, Heidelberg (2000). https://doi.org/10.1007/3-540-45499-3_23
56. Zambonelli, F., Mariani, S.: Degrees of autonomy in coordinating collectives of self-driving vehicles. In: Margaria, T., Steffen, B. (eds.) ISoLA 2020. LNCS, vol. 12477, pp. 189–204. Springer, Cham (2020)

Composition of Component Models - A Key to Construct Big Systems

Wolfgang Reisig$^{(\boxtimes)}$

Humboldt-Universität zu Berlin, 10099 Berlin, Germany
`reisig@informatik.hu-berlin.de`

Abstract. Modern informatics based systems are mostly composed from self-contained components. To be useful for really big systems, composed of many components, proper abstraction mechanisms for components are necessary. Furthermore, when composing many components, composition must be associative, i.e. for components **A, B, C** must hold: $(\mathbf{A} \bullet \mathbf{B}) \bullet \mathbf{C} = \mathbf{A} \bullet (\mathbf{B} \bullet \mathbf{C})$. This paper suggests a general framework for such components and their composition. With examples of systems represented in different formalisms such as Petri nets, BPMN, and UML, we show the high degree of independence of the formal framework from concrete modeling techniques.

Keywords: Modeling techniques · Components · Composition

Introduction

Modern informatics based systems are frequently large. Examples include embedded systems; business information systems; information infrastructures; the internet of people, things and services; as well as cyber-physical systems; digital eco-systems; health and mobility supporting systems; industry 4.0; etc. There is a rich body of literature on such systems, including e.g. [2,5]. To understand, build, and use such systems, we need specific concepts, methods, and paradigms. In particular, *modeling techniques* are required to represent and to analyze such systems, before parts of them will be implemented.

It is understood that large systems exhibit some kind of a *structure*. There are two main systematic structuring principles: *refinement* and *composition* of components. Refinement is supported by a number of universal principles. In particular, one starts out with an abstract specification and refines it systematically, i.e. one adds more and more details, but in such a way that the refined description implies the more abstract specification. Refinement is supported by encapsulation techniques, class hierarchies, refinement calculi such as [7], etc.

When it comes to the *composition* of components, matters are quite different: Many modeling techniques come with their own, specific composition operators. A general framework of principles, supporting the composition of any kind of components, based on a minimum of assumptions about components, is merely missing. This observation is the starting point of this contribution: We contribute a framework of such principles, to be applicable to merely any kind of components.

T. Margaria and B. Steffen (Eds.): ISoLA 2020, LNCS 12477, pp. 171–188, 2020.
https://doi.org/10.1007/978-3-030-61470-6_11

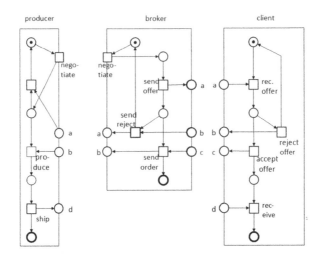

Fig. 1. Three components: **producer**, **broker**, and **client**

The core idea of this framework is a generally applicable, intuitively and technically simple concept of *composition*, combined with the idea of *adapters*. Instead of composing two components A and B by help of specific interfaces and a specific composition operator, we suggest to design a 3rd component, an adapter C; and to compose A with C, and C with B. This way, the interfaces of A and B still may remain large, but can be kept structurally simple. And among other advantages, it may be much easier to compose adapters, than to re-design interfaces.

This approach may help reduce the increasing complexity of many architecture description languages (ADLs), without reducing their expressive power. In particular, specific interface connection architectures, as implemented by most ADLs, become obsolete. As a restriction, the framework sticks to models that are graph based, such as Petri nets, BPMN, some versions of UML diagrams, and others. Networks of components are assumed to be static.

In Sect. 1 we start with a number of motivating examples, with components formulated in different modeling techniques, including Petri nets, BPMN, and UML. In Sect. 2, we discuss a general problem of the idea to compose components by gluing interface elements. The rest of the paper is dedicated to a framework that overcomes this problem and provides a number of concepts for the systematic modeling of big systems by means of composing systems.

1   Motivating Examples

1.1   Example: a *producer*, a *broker*, and a *client*

Figure 1 models the behavior of three components: a *producer*, a *broker*, and a *client*. The behavior of each component is represented as a Petri net inside a

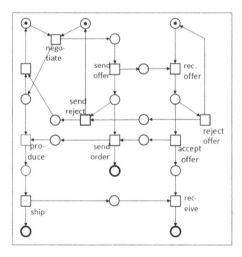

Fig. 2. Composed component **producer** • **broker** • **client**

box; some elements are drawn on the box surface, thus serving as an *interface* to other components. The three components can be composed; the graphical layout intuitively suggests the result of composing all three components, as in Fig. 2 the broker has a left interface towards the producer, and a right interface towards the client. In Fig. 2, each element of the producer's interface is "glued" with the likewise labeled element of the broker's left interface. And each element of the client's interface is "glued" with the likewise labeled element of the broker's right interface. The "d" labeled elements of the producer has no counterpart in the left interface of the broker; so it is glued with the "d" labelled element of the clients interface. An interface element may be a transition (such as "negotiate" in Fig. 1) as well as a place (such as all other interface elements in Fig. 1). The forthcoming formal framework will allow to write Fig. 2 just as **producer** • **broker** • **client**.

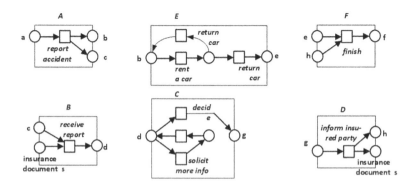

Fig. 3. Components **A**, . . . , **F** of the business process of a car insurer

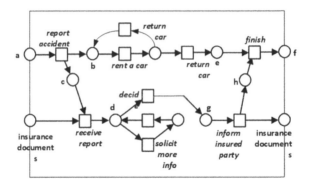

Fig. 4. The business process $\mathbf{A} \bullet \ldots \bullet \mathbf{F}$ of a car insurer

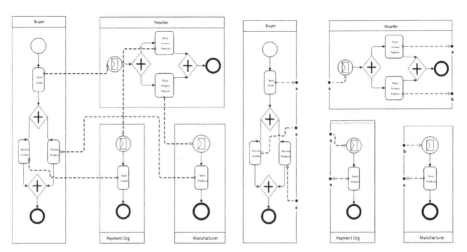

Fig. 5. BPMN model [12]

Fig. 6. Four components, with Buyer •
Reseller • Payment Org • Manufactorer,
yielding Fig. 5

1.2   Example: The Business Process of a Car Insurer

Figure 3 shows six components of the business process of a car insurer, again as
Petri nets. We can write their composition, shown in Fig. 4, as $\mathbf{A} \bullet \mathbf{B} \bullet \mathbf{C} \bullet \mathbf{D} \bullet \mathbf{E} \bullet \mathbf{F}$,
but also as $\mathbf{A} \bullet \mathbf{B} \bullet \mathbf{C} \bullet \mathbf{E} \bullet \mathbf{D} \bullet \mathbf{F}$, and in two more ways.

1.3   Example: A BPMN Model

This example shows that the forthcoming composition operator is applicable
not only to Petri net models, but is applicable to any modelling technique with
interface elements. Figure 5 shows a BPMN model of a business process as of
[12], consisting of four pools and five message flows. Each message flow connects

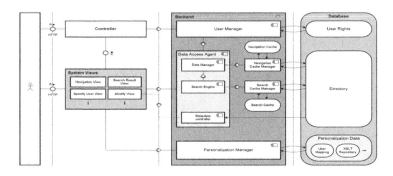

Fig. 7. UML diagram [11]

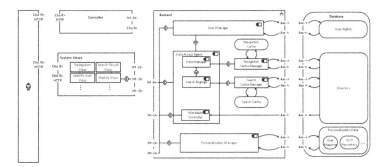

Fig. 8. Components of the UML diagram of Fig. 7

elements of two different pools. In the forthcoming framework one would capture each pool as a component. A message flow, connecting an element a in a component A with an element b in a component B would be represented by additional elements a' of A and b' of B on the surface of A and B, respectively, and connecting a with a' and b with b'. Figure 6 shows this (with the new elements labeled **a** and **b**). In fact, Fig. 6 represents uniquely the BPMN model of Fig. 5., i.e., Fig. 5 can be re-gained from Fig. 6. We deliberately chose equal labels for different interface elements (pairwise different labels for each interface were of course also viable, and might even be more intuitive). The connections of the components of Fig. 6 are specified by the labels of the interface elements, together with the forthcoming composition operator.

1.4 UML Diagram

As a final example, Fig. 7 shows an UML diagram (taken from [11]), consisting of five components and 16 arcs of three types of arcs. Figure 8 shows the detached components, with labeled interface elements to describe Fig. 7 as the composition of the five components. Figure 7 includes arcs starting at a component's surface, and ending at an element inside another component. This is represented by arcs starting at an isolated node on the surface of components.

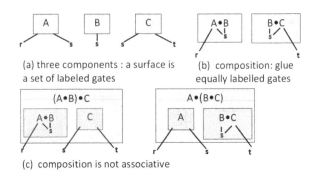

(a) three components : a surface is
a set of labeled gates

(b) composition: glue
equally labelled gates

(c) composition is not associative

Fig. 9. Composition: gluing equally labelled gates

2   A Fundamental Problem

Though the above examples employ diverse modeling techniques, they share similar features: each model consist of *components*, and each component includes a *surface*, consisting of labelled elements (we will denote them as *gates*). Composition $A \bullet B$ of two components A and B is gained by "gluing" pairs of equally labeled gates of A and of B. Glued gates then turn into inner elements of $A \bullet B$. Figure 9 outlines this conception. Numerous modeling techniques suggest this most intuitive kind of composition operator.

However, this kind of composition is fundamentally flawed: Upon composing three (or more) components, the order of composition matters, i.e. $(A \bullet B) \bullet C$ may differ from $A \bullet (B \bullet C)$, as exemplified in Fig. 9(c). In technical terms: This kind of composition is not associative! But associativity is a most wanted property whenever more than two components are composed. And really large systems are composed of many components!

This brings us to the fundamental problem addressed in this paper: We search for a general framework of components and their composition, where each component

– has some kind of an inner structure, and
– has a surface, consisting of labeled elements (gates).

Composition of components then

– results again in a component,
– means technically to glue equally labeled gates,
– is associative.

As the above showed, this is not a simple enterprise.

3   Components

3.1   The Notion of *Component*

As a technicality, we start with notions and notations of labeled and ordered sets:

Definition 1. *(i) Assuming a set Σ of labels, a labeling of a set A assigns each element of A a label, i.e. an element of Σ.*
(ii) A set A is (totally, strictly) ordered by a relation "$<$" iff $<$ is transitive, irreflexive and total.

To capture the most general case of components, we abstract a component as a *graph*:

Definition 2. *Let V be a set and let $E \subseteq V \times V$. Then $G = (V, E)$ is a graph.*

V and E are the *vertices* and the *edges* of G, written V_G and E_G, resp.

A *component* consists of an inner structure and a surface. As the examples in Sect. 1 show, a component's surface can in many cases intuitively be partitioned into two groups of elements, such as *suppliers* and *customers*, *providers* and *requesters*, *producers* and *consumers*, *buy side* and *sell side*, *predecessors* and *successors*, *inputs* and *outputs*, *assumptions* and *guarantees*, etc. This motivates the following definition:

Definition 3. *Let $G = (V, E)$ be a graph and let $^*G, G^* \subseteq V$ be two finite, labeled and ordered sets of nodes. Then G together with $^*G$ and G^* is a component.*

Notations. (i)$^*G$ and G^* are the *left* and *right interface* of G, respectively.
(ii) $V \setminus (^*G \cup G^*)$ is the inner of G, written inner$_G$.

Graphically, a component G is represented as usual for graphs: each vertex and each edge is depicted as a node and an arrow, respectively. Undirected vertices are as usual represented as arcs without arrow heads. Nodes and arcs are placed inside a rectangle, with the elements of $^*G$ and G^* on its left and right margin, respectively. We are frequently not interested in the individuality of nodes. In this case, an inner node is represented as a dot, and an interface node by its label. With the convention of representing the order of the interfaces $^*G$ and G^* increasingly top-down, Figs. 1 to 4, 13 to 17 and 20 are typical graphical representations of components.

3.2   Elementary Components and Abstractions

A component is *elementary* if its inner consists of just one node (usually labeled with the component's name):

Definition 4. *A component $A = (V, E)$ is elementary iff $V = {}^*A \cup A^* \cup \{\text{"}A\text{"}\}$ and $E = ({}^*A \times \{\text{"}A\text{"}\}) \cup (\{\text{"}A\text{"}\} \times A^*)$.*

Notations. An elementary component A is usually written $(^*A, \text{"}A\text{"}, A^*)$.

Figure 10 shows an example. Elementary components can be used to abstract given components: each component A can be assigned its unique abstraction $ab(A)$:

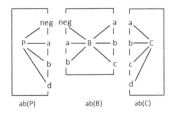

Fig. 10. An elementary component, A

Fig. 11. The abstractions of producer, P, broker, B, and client, C, of Fig. 1

Definition 5. *Let A be a component. Then $ab(A) =_{def} (^*A, "A", A^*)$ is the abstract version of A.*

Figure 11 show abstract versions of the components of Fig. 1.

The following Lemma is obvious:

Lemma 1. *Let A be a component. Then $ab(ab(A)) = ab(A)$.*

4   Composition of Components

4.1   The Composition Operator

The composition $A \bullet B$ of two components A and B is a component again. Composition is governed by the "matching" elements of A^* and $^*B$. An element a of A^* *matches* with an element b of $^*B$ iff a and b are equally labelled, and their position in the order of A and of B corresponds.

The inner of $A \bullet B$ consists of the inner of A, the inner of B, and the elements (a, b) that are "glued" from an element $a \in A^*$ that matches with an element $b \in {}^*B$. Each edge adjacent to a to-be-glued element turns into an edge of the glued element, as obvious. Finally, $^*A$ goes to $^*(A \bullet B)$, and B^* goes to $(A \bullet B)^*$. An element of A^* without a matching element in $^*B$ goes to $(A \bullet B)^*$. In forthcoming Fig. 13, the "d" labeled element of A^* has this property. Likewise, an element of $^*B$ without a matching element in A^* goes to $^*(A \bullet B)$. In the forthcoming Fig. 13, the "c" labeled element of $^*B$ has this property.

The definition of composing components is based on operations on interfaces, i.e. on labeled and ordered sets of nodes:

Definition 6. *Let A be a finite, labelled and ordered set, let l be a label, let $a \in A$ be l-labeled and assume there are n l-labeled elements of A that are smaller than a. Then n is the index of a in A.*

Figure 12(a) shows a technical example.

Observation 1. Let A be a finite, labelled and ordered set, and let $B \subseteq A$.

(i) The labeling and the order of A canonically yield a labeling and an order on B.

| Let M = {α,β,γ,δ}.
With labeling λ, let λ.(α) = a,
λ(β) = b, λ.(γ) = a, and λ.(δ) = a.
Let α<β<γ<δ. | graphical
represen-
tation: | a
b
a
a | Then, in M,
index(α) = 1, index(β) = 1,
index(γ) = 2, index(δ) = 3. |

(a) a labeled and ordered set, M, its graphical representation, and the indices of its elements

| Let N = {β,δ} ⊆ M.
Then M induces the labeling
λ.(β) = b and λ.(δ) = a,
as well as the order β<δ. | graphical
represen-
tation: | b
a | Then, in N,
index(β) = 1, index(δ) = 1. |

(b) labeling and order as induced on a subset N of M

| Let L = {ε,ζ,η},
with λ.(ε) =b, λ.(ζ) = a , λ.(η) = b,
and order ε<ζ<η. | graphical
represen-
tation: | b
a
b | Then, in L,
index(ε) = index(ζ) = 1,
index(η) =2. |

matching pairs of M and L: (α,ζ) and (β,ε)

(c) labeled and ordered set L, and matching pairs of M and L

| Then N ^L = {β,δ,ε,ζ,η},
with λ.(β) = b, λ.(δ) = a, λ.(ε) =
b, and λ.(ζ) = a and λ.(η) = b.
Let α<β<γ<δ. | graphical
represen-
tation: | b
a
b
a
b | Then, in N^L,
index(β) = 1 index(δ) = 1
index(ε) = 2, index(ζ) = 2,
index(η) = 3. |

(d) extension of N by L

Fig. 12. Examples for operations on labeled and ordered sets

(ii) For $b \in B$, the index of b in A is equal or larger than the index of b in B.

Figure 12(b) shows a technical example.

Definition 7. *Let A and B be disjoint, finite, labelled and ordered sets. With $a \in A$ and $b \in B$, the pair (a, b) is a matching pair of A and B iff a and b are labeled alike, and the index of a in A is equal to the index of b in B.*

Figure 12(c) shows a technical example.

Definition 8. *Let A and B be disjoint, finite, labeled and ordered sets. Then the extension of A by B, written $A\,\hat{}\,B$, is the labeled and ordered set $A \cup B$; with its labeling inherited by the labeling of A and of B, and its order extending the orders of A and of B, such that additionally, in $A\,\hat{}\,B$, each element of A is smaller than each element of B.*

Figure 12(d) shows a technical example.

Observation 2. Let A and B be disjoint, finite, labeled and ordered sets, let $a \in A$ and $b \in B$. The index of a in $A\,\hat{}\,B$ equals the index of a in A; the index of b in $A\,\hat{}\,B$ is equal or larger than the index of b in B.

We are now prepared to define the composition of components:

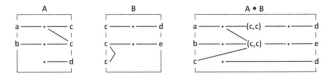

Fig. 13. Technical example for the composition of components

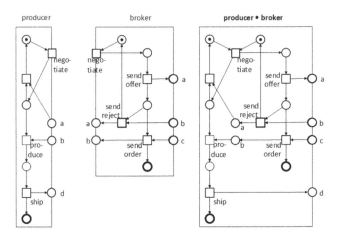

Fig. 14. Composed component **producer • broker**

Definition 9. *Let A and B be components. Let W be the set of matching pairs of A^* and $^*B$; let $A^+ \subseteq A^*$ contain the elements a of A^* that don't belong to a matching pair (a, b) of W and let $^+B \subseteq {}^*B$ contain the elements b of $^*B$ that don't belong to a matching pair (a, b) in W.*

Then $A \bullet B$ is a component, defined as follows:

(i) $V_{A \bullet B} =_{def} V_A \cup V_B \cup W$;
(ii) $(x, y) \in E_{A \bullet B}$ *iff*
  – $x, y \in V_A \cup V_B$ and $(x, y) \in E_A \cup E_B$, or
  – $y = (a, b) \in W$, and $(x, a) \in E_A$ or $(x, b) \in E_B$, or
  – $x = (a, b) \in W$, and $(a, y) \in E_A$ or $(b, y) \in E_B$.
(iii) $^*(A \bullet B) =_{def} (^*A) \char94 (^+B)$, *and* $(A \bullet B)^* =_{def} (B^*) \char94 (A^+)$.

Figure 13 shows a technical example. Figure 14 shows the composition of two components of Fig. 1. All Figures in this paper, except Fig. 9, in fact show examples of this version of composition. It is most important and not at all trivial that composition is associative:

Theorem 1. *Let A and B be components. Then $(A \bullet B) \bullet C = A \bullet (B \bullet C)$.*

This Theorem has been proven in [10].
This Theorem justifies writing **producer • broker • client** in Fig. 2, skipping any brackets.

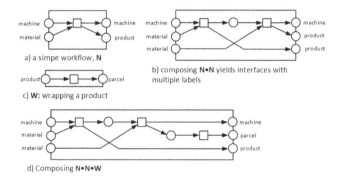

Fig. 15. Composition may yield interfaces with multiple labels

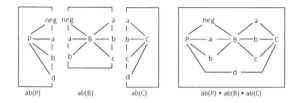

Fig. 16. The abstractions of producer, P, broker, B, and client, C, of Fig. 1, as well as their composition

4.2   Some Aspects of Composition

A special case is perfect match of A^* and $^*B$:

Lemma 2. *Let A and B be components.*

(i) If each element of A^* matches with an element of $^*B$, then $(A \bullet B)^* = B^*$.
(ii) If each element of $^*B$ matches with an element of A^*, then $^*(A \bullet B) = {}^*A$.

To keep matters simple, one may be tempted to just "forbid" equally labeled elements in the interfaces $^*A$ and A^* of components A. This, however, would disallow many components to be composed, as Fig. 15 shows.

A system $A_1 \bullet \ldots \bullet A_n$ consisting of n components A_i can be abstracted to $ab(A_1) \bullet \ldots \bullet ab(A_n)$, with the abstraction operation ab as defined in Sect. 3.2 As an example, Fig. 16 shows the abstractions of the components of Fig. 1, as well as their composition. Notice that the abstraction $ab(A_1 \bullet \ldots \bullet A_n)$ of a composed system $A_1 \bullet \ldots \bullet A_n$ is elementary, whereas the composition $ab(A_1) \bullet \ldots \bullet ab(A_n)$ of the abstractions $ab(A_i)$ of the components A_i shows the structure of the composition and is not elementary.

Composition and abstraction are related as follows:

Lemma 3. *Let A and B be components. Then $ab(A \bullet B) = ab(ab(A) \bullet ab(B))$.*

In Sect. 6 we will discuss further properties like this in greater detail.

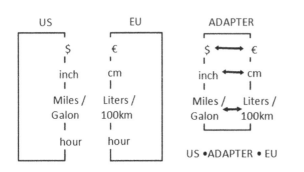

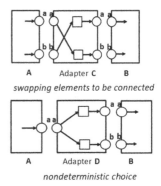

A   Adapter C   B

swapping elements to be connected

A   Adapter D   B

nondeterministic choice

Fig. 17. Adapting measurement standards between US American and European car industries

Fig. 18. Behavior adaptation

5 Adapters

Many formal modeling techniques come with specific composition operators, defining composition with additional composability criteria or some kind of interoperability. Composition is sometimes intended to be nondeterministic, i.e. composition of two components may result in a set of alternative outcomes. So, it may sound surprising that we suggest one and only one composition operator, claiming to fit all purposes and to possess the potential to express an kind of composition. To tackle this issue, we suggest *adapters*: any particular assumption or property π of the composition $A \bullet B$ of two components A and B should not be gathered into the definition of a composition operator. Instead, π should be formulated by means of an additional component, C. Composition $A \bullet C \bullet B$ then would express the property π of the composed system, while the components A, C, and B are composed by means of the standard operator, $\bullet$. This has a number of advantages. Firstly, the interfaces of the components A and B are not affected at all. Secondly, two properties π and π' can be composed by composing corresponding adaptors $[\pi]$ and $[\pi']$ as in $A \bullet [\pi] \bullet [\pi'] \bullet B$, whereas combining π and π' into a composition operator would be much less simple. Thirdly, a software tool would implement composition just once.

As an example for a data adapter, Fig. 17 shows the problem of adapting data standards between US American and European measurement differences of the motor car industry. Figure 18 shows examples of behavior adaption in terms of Petri nets. In Fig. 1, the broker may be conceived as a behavior adapter for the producer and the consumer.

6 An Algebraic Calculus

The above definitions give rise to an algebraic calculus of components and their composition, in analogy to - and as a generalization of - functions and their composition. We start with the observation that a given set Σ of labels defines the class

$$K_\Sigma$$

of all components with labels in Σ. Fundamental, and non-trivial is the

Theorem 2. *Composition* $\bullet: K_\Sigma \times K_\Sigma \to K_\Sigma$ *is total and associative on* K_Σ.

As mentioned above already, this property has been proven in [10]. Furthermore, composition with the empty graph leaves components untouched:

Lemma 4. *Let N be the graph with $V_E = \emptyset$. Then for each $A \in K_\Sigma$ holds:* $A \bullet N = N \bullet A = A$.

Corollary 1. $(K_\Sigma, \bullet, N)$ *is a monoid.*
This monoid has a number of important submonoids, including

- *Petri nets with places and transitions in their interfaces (with each symbol in the alphabet serving to label either places or transitions),*
- *BPMN diagrams, with interfaces including nodes as in Fig. 6,*
- *Particular UML diagrams such as in Fig. 8,*
- *The set $[A \to A]$ of functions over a set A (with 1-elementary interfaces, all labelled alike).*

7   Derived Components

A component gives rise to derive abstractions, mirrored, and half closed versions.

7.1   The Mirror of a Component

The mirror of a component A swaps the right and left interface of A:

Definition 10. *Let $A = (V, E)$ be a component. As usual, let $^*A$ and A^* be the left and the right interface of A. Then the component $\underline{A} = (V, E)$ with left interface A^* and right interface $^*A$ is the* mirror *of A.*

The following observations are obvious:

Lemma 5. *Let A and B be components.*

(i) $\underline{A \bullet B} = \underline{B} \bullet \underline{A}$,
(ii) $\underline{\underline{A}} = A$,
(iii) $^*(A \bullet \underline{A}) = (A \bullet \underline{A})^* = {}^*A$,
(iv) $^*(\underline{A} \bullet A) = (\underline{A} \bullet A)^* = A^*$,
(v) $\underline{N} = N$.

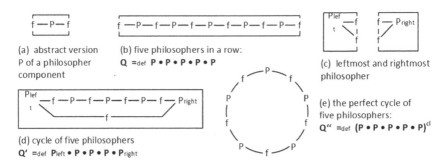

(a) abstract version
P of a philosopher
component

(b) five philosophers in a row:
$Q =_{def} P \bullet P \bullet P \bullet P \bullet P$

(c) leftmost and rightmost
philosopher

(d) cycle of five philosophers
$Q' =_{def} P_{left} \bullet P \bullet P \bullet P \bullet P_{right}$

(e) the perfect cycle of
five philosophers:
$Q'' =_{def} (P \bullet P \bullet P \bullet P \bullet P)^{cl}$

Fig. 19. Abstraction of philosophers

7.2   Semi Closed Components

Sometimes, in particular in the context of verification, it is useful to cut off one of the interfaces:

Definition 11. *Let* $A = (V, E)$ *be a component with left and right interfaces* $^*A$ *and* A^*, *as usual. Then*

(i) $[A$ *is the component* (V, E) *with* $^*[A = \emptyset$ *and* $[A^* = A^*$, *called the* left closure *of* A.
(ii) $A]$ *is the component* (V, E) *with* $^*A] = {}^*A$ *and* $A]^* = \emptyset$, *called the* right closure *of* A.

Lemma 6. *Let* A *and* B *be components. Then*

(i) $([A]) = [(A]) = E$,
(ii) $[A = \underline{A}]$,
(iii) $\overline{A]} = [\underline{A}$,
(iv) $\overline{[A} \bullet [B = [(A \bullet B)$,
(v) $A] \bullet B] = (A \bullet B)]$.

8   The Closure Operator

In addition to the binary composition operator $\bullet$, a unary "closure" operator, $(\_^{cl})$, is useful. For example, Fig. 19(a) shows the abstract version of the behavior of a "philosopher" according to Dijkstra's well known paradigm, with its left and right fork in its left and right interface. Figure 19(b) shows five philosophers in a row; however, what we want is the left fork of the leftmost philosopher to be "glued" with the right fork of the rightmost philosopher. A solution were distinguished leftmost and rightmost philosophers P_{left} and P_{right}, with both forks in its right and in its left interface, respectively, as in Fig. 19(c) and 19(d). This corresponds e.g. to indexing the forks of the ith philosopher by $i - 1$ and i, and identifying the forks f_0 and f_5. More elegant, however, is the closure operator $(\_^{cl})$, which, for a component A, glues elements of A^* with likewise labelled elements of $^*A$. As an example, Fig. 19(e) shows a perfect cycle of five philosophers.

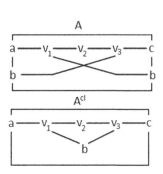

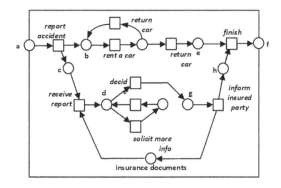

Fig. 20. Technical example for the closure A^{cl} of a component A.

Fig. 21. Closure of Fig. 4: The business process $(A \dots F)^{cl}$ of a car insurer, clients' view

Definition 12. *Let A be a component. Let W be the set of matching pairs of A^* and $^*A$; let $A^+ \subseteq A^*$ contain the elements a of A^* that don't belong to a matching pair (a, b) of W and let $^+A \subseteq {}^*A$ contain the elements b of $^*A$ that don't belong to a matching pair (a, b) in W.*

Then A^{cl} is a component (V, E), defined as follows:

(i) $V =_{def} V_A \cup W;$
(ii) $(x, y) \in E$ iff
    – $(x, y) \in E_A$, or
    – $y = (a, b) \in W$, and $(x, a) \in E_A$ or $(x, b) \in E_A$, or
    – $x = (a, b) \in W$, and $(a, y) \in E_A$ or $(b, y) \in E_A$.
(iii) $^*(A^{cl}) =_{def} {}^+A$, and
    $(A^{cl})^* =_{def} A^+$.

Figure 20 shows a technical example.
Observations:

Lemma 7. *Let A be a component.*

(i) *The labels occurring in $^*A^{cl}$ and in A^{cl*} are disjoint.*
(ii) $(A^{cl})^{cl} = A^{cl}$
(iii) $A = A^{cl}$ *iff the labels of $^*A$ and A^* are disjoint.*

A typical application of the closure operator is a variant of Fig. 4, as shown in Fig. 21: From the client's perspective, insurance documents belong to the inner of the insurer.

9   Related Work

The quest for general principles of composition of components has frequently been addressed, usually in the light of implementability. Our approach is more abstract, as it describes composition on the *modeling* level.

Our approach differs from many architectural languages in two aspects: firstly, we suggest to describe different semantical aspects of coordination of components not by means of many different variants of connectors, but instead by means of *additional components*, called *adapters*. This includes aspects such as basic synchronization, mutual exclusion and hiding (as considered, e.g. in [3]), but also much more involved coordination aspects. In particular, "glue code", i.e. code that serves to connect separate parts of a program for compatibility or interoperability, is an obvious candidate for an adapter. This in turn leads to the second aspect of our approach: composition of components can be defined, once and for all, in a very simple way that fits all kind of special requirements. To remain independent of concrete implementations, we define this kind of composition on a symbolic, schematic, level, whereas approaches such as [3], but also languages such as REO [4], describe coordination on the level of software.

Formulated differently, while we agree with [6] that "computing has grown into informatics and Turing's logical computing machines are matched by a logic of interaction", we suggest to formulate the "logic of interaction" by just one fundamental composition operator, and to represent all required variants in terms of conventional components. Both, the composition operator as well as the required semantical variants of interaction, may then be formulated in any language as preferred by the respective programmer.

The symbolic, schematic level of composition assumes components that essentially are structured as node labelled graphs. Such graphs may be concrete programs, Petri nets, BPM diagrams, etc. but also abstractly represent classes of systems in the style of algebraic specifications [13], including well known concepts such as parametrization and refinement, but also the new composition operator as introduced here.

So far, we don't cover dynamic reconfigurabiliy, as discussed e.g. in [8].

Conclusion

The notion of components and their composition, as introduced above, is not intended as yet another formalism to cope with components. We rather claim to provide fundamentals and universal principles of a comprehensive theory for components with interfaces and their composition, as they typically occur in many computer integrated systems.

Those principles are in particular liberal w.r.t. internal behavior, but strict w.r.t. interfaces and composition. This implies a number of advantages. Most important is the possibility to manage composition of components, while abstracting from their internal details. This is in particular useful in case of legacy software, components based on business secrets, not yet fully specified components, etc. In a more technical framework, the most important aspect is associativity of the composition operator. As mentioned above, this nontrivial property has been proven, once and for all, in [10]. This decisive property, together with technical simplicity of the composition operator is based on two ideas: to distinguish a left and a right interface, and to express more involved properties and aspects of specific composition operators in terms of adapters. Further aspects are presented in [9].

Components with interfaces strictly generalize functions over the word over an alphabet. We relate this observation to the conventional framework of the basics of theoretical informatics: there, for a given alphabet Σ, we canonically derive the set Σ^* of all words over Σ, the set $[\Sigma^* \to \Sigma^*]$ of all functions over Σ^*, and finally the composition operator $\bullet$ that is total and associative on $[\Sigma^* \to \Sigma^*]$. This, in turn, leads to the theory of computable functions, and is often considered the starting point of theoretical informatics.

We suggest to start with an alphabet Σ as well, canonically deriving the set K_Σ of all components with interface elements labelled over Σ, with the composition operator $\bullet$ that is total and associative on K_Σ. Functions over Σ are a very special case then. This framework should provide the starting point of a theory of component based systems. Such systems emerge as the new computing paradigm for informatics based systems. The need for a general theory of components and their composition has been stressed for decades; as an early contribution on this subject we refer to [1].

References

1. Allen, R., Garlan, D.: A formal basis for architectural connection. ACM Trans. Softw. Eng. Methodol. **6**(3), 213–249 (1997). https://doi.org/10.1145/258077. 258078
2. Bennaceur, A., et al.: Modelling and analysing resilient cyber-physical systems. In: Litoiu, M., Clarke, S., Tei, K. (eds.) Proceedings of the 14th International Symposium on Software Engineering for Adaptive and Self-Managing Systems, SEAMS@ICSE 2019, Montreal, QC, Canada, 25–31 May 2019, pp. 70–76. ACM (2019). https://doi.org/10.1109/SEAMS.2019.00018
3. Bruni, R., Lanese, I., Montanari, U.: A basic algebra of stateless connectors. Theor. Comput. Sci. **366**(1–2), 98–120 (2006). https://doi.org/10.1016/j.tcs.2006.07.005
4. Dokter, K., Jongmans, S., Arbab, F., Bliudze, S.: Combine and conquer: relating BIP and Reo. J. Log. Algebraic Methods Program. **86**(1), 134–156 (2017). https://doi.org/10.1016/j.jlamp.2016.09.008
5. Dustdar, S., Nastic, S., Scekic, O.: Smart Cities - The Internet of Things People and Systems. Springer, Cham (2017). https://doi.org/10.1007/978-3-319-60030-7
6. Milner, R.: Turing, computing and communication. In: Goldin, D., Smolka, S.A., Wegner, P. (eds.) Interactive Computation, pp. 1–8. Springer, Heidelberg (2006). https://doi.org/10.1007/3-540-34874-3_1
7. Morgan, C.: Programming from Specifications, 2nd edn. Prentice Hall International series in computer science. Prentice Hall, Upper Saddle River (1994)
8. Nicola, R.D., Maggi, A., Sifakis, J.: The dream framework for dynamic reconfigurable architecture modelling: theory and applications. Int. J. Softw. Tools Technol. Transf. **22**(4), 437–455 (2020). https://doi.org/10.1007/s10009-020-00555-2
9. Reisig, W.: Composition: a fresh look at an old topic. In: Margaria, T., Graf, S., Larsen, K.G. (eds.) Models, Mindsets, Meta: The What, the How, and the Why Not? - Essays Dedicated to Bernhard Steffen on the Occasion of His 60th Birthday. LNCS, vol. 11200, pp. 372–389. Springer, Cham (2019). https://doi.org/10.1007/978-3-030-22348-9_22

10. Reisig, W.: Associative composition of components with double-sided interfaces. Acta Inf. **56**(3), 229–253 (2019). https://doi.org/10.1007/s00236-018-0328-7
11. SAP: Standardized technical architecture modeling: conceptual and design level (2007)
12. Weske, M.: Business Process Management - Concepts, Languages, Architectures, 2nd edn. Springer, Heidelberg (2012). https://doi.org/10.1007/978-3-642-28616-2
13. Wirsing, M.: Algebraic specification: Semantics, parameterization and refinement. In: Formal Description of Programming Concepts, pp. 259–318 (1989)

Degrees of Autonomy in Coordinating Collectives of Self-Driving Vehicles

Stefano Mariani and Franco Zambonelli[✉]

Department of Sciences and Methods of Engineering,
University of Modena and Reggio Emilia, Via Amendola 2, 42122 Reggio Emilia, Italy
{stefano.mariani,franco.zambonelli}@unimore.it

Abstract. Our streets will be soon populated by multitudes of self-driving vehicles, calling for appropriate solutions to coordinate their collective movements in order to ensure safety and efficiency. In this paper, after introducing the general issues associated to coordination of self-driving vehicles, we show that a key engineering issue is identifying the most suitable degree of autonomy in decision making that should be left to vehicles during the coordination process. This issue also includes the possibility, depending on factors such as traffic conditions or the need to enact specific mobility policies, to dynamically adjust such degree of autonomy and thus the adopted coordination scheme. This introduces many theoretical and practical challenges in modelling self-driving vehicles coordination schemes and in their rigorous engineering, as in the case of intersection crossing, analysed in the paper.

Keywords: Self-driving vehicles · Coordination · Autonomy · Intersection crossing

1 Introduction

Autonomous self-driving vehicles will soon populate our streets [8]. Besides the advantage of relieving us from the duty of driving and paying attention, thus making it possible to exploit travel time in other activities, self-driving vehicles will bring further important benefits. They will reduce crashes, now mostly due to bad human behaviours and human errors, most likely saving millions of injuries and lives. They will notably reduce the number of circulating vehicles and, also thanks to route optimisation, will definitely reduce traffic and pollution [22]. Moreover, they will pave the way for a number of innovative solutions in the provisioning of mobility services [30], to serve our needs with much greater levels of quality and efficiency than today: car sharing, where fleets of autonomous vehicles (whether provided by public actors or by private companies) will be available to serve our urban mobility needs; personalised public transport and ride sharing, where autonomous vehicles and buses can dynamically gather people based on their actual required routes; smart and more effective parking approaches, in that autonomous vehicles can search for parking

T. Margaria and B. Steffen (Eds.): ISoLA 2020, LNCS 12477, pp. 189–204, 2020.
https://doi.org/10.1007/978-3-030-61470-6_12

slots based on criteria different from the "very soon and very close" one that we human usually adopt, and exploiting additional information that they might have.

The current focus of industrial and applied research in the area is on the methods and tools to enable *individual* vehicles to hit the road safely, there including rigorous engineering approaches based on formal specification and verification languages and models [34]. However, to get full advantage of self-driving vehicles, a number of situations will compulsory require *coordinating* the relative activities and movements of vehicles [1,31]. Examples of very diverse situations that require a proper and careful coordination amongst collectives of vehicles include: crossing intersections, entering a motorway, platooning, organising urban deployment and rides for fleets of ride/car-sharing vehicles, trying to improve parking occupancies and reduce parking times. Effectively supporting such coordination implies devising effective mechanisms and strategies to support coordination activities.

In this paper, we overview the key issues associated to the coordination of autonomous self-driving vehicles, and the possible approaches to attack the problem, with a specific focus on the problem of intersection crossing. We show that the different approaches to the problem are characterised by different *degree of autonomy in decision making* that is left to individual vehicles during the coordination process (not to be confused with the "level of autonomy" in driving as defined in [14]). Following, we argue that a single approach can hardly suit all possible situations. On this base, we also introduce the concept of *adjustable autonomy* in coordination, and discuss the many issues associated with the rigorous engineering of the behaviour of self-driving collectives based on adjustable autonomy. Finally, we also discuss additional general research challenges in the engineering of collectives of self-driving vehicles.

The paper is organised as follows. Section 2 characterises the problem of coordinating collectives of self-driving vehicles according to a taxonomy of coordination problems and analyses the spectrum of possible solutions; Sect. 3 focusses on the specific case of intersection crossing; Sect. 4 introduces and analyses the concept of adjustable autonomy in coordination; Sect. 5 introduces additional research challenges and Sect. 6 concludes the paper.

2   Coordinating Collectives of Self-Driving Vehicles

The problem of coordinating a collective of self-driving vehicles can be modelled as a *decision making process*, involving vehicles themselves and possibly some infrastructural entities, aimed at orchestrating vehicles' actions so as to achieve a *goal* which cannot be achieved, or not optimally, by each vehicle in isolation.

Depending on the specific nature of the coordination problem, the goal may be: *(i)* shared among a collective of vehicles, such as allocating parking slots to the vehicles of a company fleet, making the coordination problem *collaborative*, or *(ii)* individual, and possibly contrasting with the ones of the other vehicles of the collective, such as finding a parking slot in the presence of multiple private cars looking for a slot in the same zone, making the coordination problem *competitive*.

Independently of the specific problem, the issues to be faced by vehicles in coordinating are associated to the fact that in order to achieve the coordination goal, whether individual or shared, vehicles may have to: *(i)* acquire access to a shared limited resource, such as a shared intersection, calling for the coordination process to safely regulate such access according to specific strategies and rules; *(ii)* completing a specific task, such as bring a group of persons home, calling for the coordination process to properly allocate to vehicles the responsibilities and actions required to achieve such task.

The above characterisation of the problem of coordinating collectives of self-driving vehicles fits well the general characterisation of coordination problems in the areas of distributed systems [10] and multiagent systems [25]. Likewise, coordination has to satisfy the following general properties, often subject to formal verification: *safety*, expressing that "something bad never happens" during the coordination process, such as that two cars never crash while crossing an intersection; *liveness*, expressing that "something good eventually happens", such as that all cars will eventually manage to cross an intersection; *quality*, that is it should solve the coordination problem in a way to optimise some specific quality measure, such as the average or cumulative delay at which cars manage to cross an intersection.

2.1   Overview of Coordination Problems

Intersection crossing is the most representative coordination problem in urban areas, definitely the most studied in the literature, and the one we adopt as case study in this article. Intersection crossing concerns the need of coordinating vehicles while concurrently crossing intersections [29]. As such, it is a *competitive* problem in which vehicles are self-interested agents willing to obtain the right-of-way as soon as possible across the shared *resource* represented by the intersection. A proper solution to intersection crossing should enable vehicles to *safely* cross an intersection by avoiding collisions, eventually giving each vehicle the right-of-way (*liveness*), while possibly minimising the average *delay* experienced by vehicles in waiting the right-of-way (*quality measure*).

Smart parking is the problem of coordinating vehicles to have access to parking resources [27]. It assumes a competitive form in the case of private vehicles and a *collaborative* form in the case of "fleets" of vehicles made available by private companies or municipalities. A solution to this problem requires safely avoiding overbooking and starvation, whereas quality concerns the timeliness and the distance at which parking is found.

Ride sharing is the problem of coordinating vehicles to collectively satisfy "mobility tasks", such as carrying people around [4]. As in the case of parking, it has a *competitive* form for privately owned vehicles and a *collaborative* one for fleets of vehicles belonging to the same owner. Here, safety concerns assigning mobility requests only once whereas liveness amounts to guaranteeing that no user is excluded. Quality may concern maximizing car usage and monetary gains, or minimise waiting time and limit the walking distance, depending on the perspective (users or owners).

Ramp merging deals with the task of entering and leaving highway ramps [29], and requires a *cooperative* solution, as if the vehicles on the main lane are selfish, those in the merging lane will starve (hence the system as a whole would fail to achieve its goal), and if the selfish vehicles are those on the merging lane, they could cause crashes for those on the main lane, or congestion by making them slow down or change lane abruptly. Avoiding collisions and starvation while minimising the time required to perform the task are the non-functional properties to care about. Lane changing is an equivalent problem.

Platooning deals with the task of coordinating manoeuvres of vehicles so that they travel altogether as a single entity, for instance by keeping the same speed and relative positions [15]. As in ramp merging, vehicles in the platoon have incentives to cooperate with each other. Safety again concerns avoiding collisions, whereas liveness and quality mostly deal with preserving the platoon while optimising measures such as fuel consumption or speed.

Traffic flow optimisation is the large-scale coordination problem subsuming all the other ones, as it is meant to achieve a balanced exploitation of road resources so as to limit traffic congestion [33]. The problem requires *cooperative* solutions, as the routing plans that vehicles elaborate together can facilitate all individual goals. Safety amounts to avoiding congestion and traffic jams, while liveness amounts at routing vehicles so as to avoid loops and never-ending trips. A quality metric could instead be the degree of balance in the exploitation of the road network (measured by a density map) and the overall fluidity of the traffic flow (measured by the throughput of selected roads).

2.2   Coordination Solutions and Decision Making Autonomy

Independently of the specific coordination problem addressed, approaches to tackle it can be classified in terms of the *degree of autonomy in decision making* left to vehicles during the coordination process.

By "degree of autonomy in decision making" we refer to the extent to which vehicles can decide their own course of actions by themselves while coordinating. Such decision of course can be based on information acquired by vehicles about the current state of the affairs, information that can be obtained by the vehicles' own sensors, by road-side infrastructural elements, or from the other vehicles participating in the coordination process.

By definition, in any coordination process, the entities to be coordinated cannot act completely freely, and must undertake actions that account for the actions of the other entities involved in the process [10]. Thus, there is never full autonomy and freedom. However, different approaches to coordination may leave to entities different degrees of freedom in their decision making, i.e., in selecting the actions to perform during the process. Hence, the degree of autonomy may range from fully externally imposed actions (lowest autonomy) to fully self-determined action (highest autonomy), with a direct impact on the difficulty

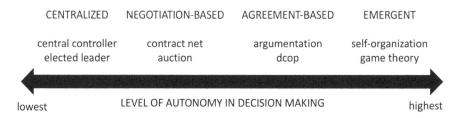

Fig. 1. Coordination approaches and level of autonomy in decision making.

of applying rigorous engineering techniques such as formal specification and verification. In particular, as depicted in Fig. 1, we can identify four main classes of coordination approaches centred around the concept of degree of autonomy: centralised, negotiation-based, agreement-based, and emergent.

In *Centralised* approaches the burden of coordination, that is, the decision making determining the outcome of the coordination process, is entirely charged upon an individual computational entity, i.e., a *coordinator*, whose decisions on how everyone should act are undebatable, and to whom vehicles must abide by design without any autonomous decision making left to them. A traditional traffic light exemplifies the role of such centralised coordinator. We emphasise that the term "centralised" here refers to the decision making process, not to the actual computing infrastructure supporting it, which can include for instance distributed processing of information by multiple sensors/cameras and/or services to perform reasoning in the Cloud.

In *Negotiation-based* approaches the burden of coordination is distributed amongst the ensemble of coordinating vehicles, who participate in a specific *negotiation protocol*, typically inspired by economic mechanisms. In a negotiation protocol, the vehicles involved can "propose" solutions and actions, each according to its own internal strategy and its own situation and goals, amongst a set of admissible moves dictated by the protocol at each step. If properly designed, the protocol will eventually guarantee the convergence towards an equilibrium solution, determining *who* (i.e., which vehicle) should do *what*, and *when*, to solve the coordination problem. Most representative negotiation protocols are: *Contract Net*, for collaborative problems, and *auctions*, for competitive ones [18].

In *Agreement-based* approaches vehicles participate in a *dynamic protocol* defined by themselves in a collective way, in a sort of dynamic meta-coordination process whose outcome is both the set of admissible moves, now jointly defined, and possibly even a re-determination of the goals to be achieved during the coordination process. The distinguishing feature here is the ability of agents to collectively define the protocol itself, that is, the goal to pursue and their strategy to make moves. Examples of these dynamic protocols include those based on *argumentation* [28], where involved entities discuss and argue together to reach a common perspective on situations, goals, and solutions, and *distributed constraint optimisation* [19], where agents try to collectively find a solution to an optimisation problem.

In *Emergent* approaches vehicles do not explicitly engage in any coordination protocol, thus do not even share the goal of reaching a common agreement. Rather, every vehicle behaves in a selfish way according to its goals and to maximise utility of actions w.r.t. the goals, and according to the perceptions it collects about other participants to the coordination process. It is worth emphasising that this does not contrast with the achievement of a systemic, shared goal: for instance, in ant colonies, individual ants pursue their own goal of travelling between the nest and the food source as quickly as possible, but depositing pheromone while doing so (an innate behaviour, not a coordination act) delivers the systemic goal of finding the shortest path despite disruption (e.g. due to adverse weather). Examples include: *game theoretic* approaches [24], where explicit communication is lacking, each vehicle merely assumes rationality of others, and computes its own course of actions based on informed guesses about others' expected behaviour; and *self-organising algorithms* [20], typically nature-inspired, where vehicles act in a purely reactive way, based on the implicitly perceived presence and state of other vehicles, typically expressed via "traces" in the environment, such as virtual pheromones or virtual computational fields.

3   The Case of Intersection Crossing

Today, intersection crossing is managed either by a central controller, the traffic light, or by imposing to vehicles (i.e., to their drivers) pre-defined coordination rules to be obeyed, such as stop at sign or give right-of-way to vehicles coming from the right.

In the future, thanks to self-driving vehicles, it will be possible to conceive a variety of innovative solutions, safer and more efficient, eventually making traffic lights and stop signs obsolete. Based on the classification of coordination solutions along the level of autonomy in decision making, let us now overview the variety of such solutions.

3.1   Centralised

Centralised approaches to intersection crossing assume the existence of a computational central authority, the intersection manager, bearing alone the burden of decision making. It is typically in charge of: *(i)* receiving information from vehicles approaching the intersection (i.e., origin, destination, speed); *(ii)* elaborating a set of collision free trajectories enabling vehicles to safely cross the intersection, which may require some vehicles to slow down or change lane; and *(iii)* instructing, or directly commanding, the vehicles about what to do, or informing them about what constraints they must abide to while crossing the intersection. Centralised approaches are usually the easiest to rigorously engineer, as the whole coordination algorithm is executed by a single component amenable of formal verification, without vehicles autonomy to hinder the process.

Examples of centralised proposals to intersection crossing include [40], which attack the problem in terms of a traditional mutual exclusion approach, and [16], in which the authors propose a control algorithm implementing a nonlinear constrained optimisation in charge of computing the best moves for every vehicle and then directly manipulating vehicles' driving parameters. A similar stance is taken in [41], where cooperative adaptive cruise control is exploited for intersection crossing by assuming that a smart controller device placed in the intersection can communicate with incoming vehicles to instruct them about the actions to perform.

Other approaches are a little more permissive and let the inbound vehicles decide how to fulfil a set of constraints set by the intersection manager, which may regard the time slot assigned for crossing, as in the work by Dresner and Stone [7]: the authors propose a *reservation-based approach* in which incoming vehicles request assignment of a time slot for crossing to the intersection manager, who computes decisions based on a local control policy.

In general terms, all the above approaches ensure safety and avoid starvation by giving every vehicles the possibility to cross the intersection. Most importantly, simulations show that such approaches dramatically reduce the waiting time for vehicles with respect to traditional approaches based on stop signs or traffic lights [7], because: *(i)* the occupancy of the intersection is maximised and *(ii)* vehicles from different directions can cross the intersection without waiting, provided they are not in direct collision—i.e., they occupy different portions of the intersection, or occupy the same portion at different times.

A problem of centralised approaches is requiring the presence of a dedicated infrastructural element (the intersection manager) and the capability of vehicles to interact with it at all times. Thus, they can hardly be applicable in the wild. Also, such a central authority is an obvious bottleneck for both performance and tolerance to failures. A recent proposal [36] suggests the possibility for vehicles to be engaged in a leader election algorithm, to elect a transient leader vehicle in charge to act as intersection manager for a predefined amount of time.

3.2 Negotiation-Based

In negotiation-based approaches, vehicles are required to actively participate in a protocol aimed at establishing in which order vehicles will gain access to the intersection. Such protocol, given the competitive nature of the problem, can take the form of an *auction*. In approaching the intersection, vehicles may contact an intersection manager or a broker temporarily elected amongst themselves, by placing a "bid", that is, by making an offer to "buy" the portions of the intersection they require for crossing, for the time required to cross. The value of the bid expresses the urgency of the vehicle in crossing, it is autonomously set by each individual vehicle according to its own strategy, and can correspond to some real-world currency or some sort of "road credits" assigned to vehicles. The broker collects the bids, gives the right-of-way to the set of vehicles that are in a collision free trajectory and, amongst those that are in collision, to the ones having placed the highest bid.

Examples of auction-based protocols for intersection crossing are described in [38], [6], and [5]. There, different policies to resolve the auction are analysed, based on different strategies put in place by the bidding vehicles, as well as different strategies by the broker in establishing the winners. Such strategies can also attempt at incentivising fair bidding while discouraging malicious behaviours.

Auction-based mechanisms, with slight variations depending on the adopted strategies, generally exhibit performances comparable and at times superior to that of centralised ones: the waiting time of vehicles is dramatically lower than that of traditional traffic lights. Safety is ensured provided that vehicles respect the "rules of the game", and accept waiting when losing the auction. A problem intrinsic to any auction mechanism concerns liveness, that is, the property of having every vehicle achieve its goal without starvation, in that the strategy of bidding vehicles can sometimes make others to experience indefinitely long waiting times. Also, if implemented through a dedicated intersection manager acting as broker, they inherit the "bottleneck" drawbacks of centralised approaches.

3.3   Agreement-Based

Intersection crossing with agreement techniques essentially amounts to give vehicles approaching an intersection the possibility to interact so as to affect each others' original goals (e.g., directions) and priorities.

An example proposal, specifically conceived in the context of bimodal traffic (vehicular plus public transport), is discussed in [3]. There, agreement between vehicles happens through a repeated communication protocol running between approaching vehicles and buses, with the assistance of an heterogeneous pool of agents representing conflicting goals, such as the need to minimise private vehicles travel time while prioritising public transportation. Depending on both macro and micro scale criteria, in fact, the agents participating in the protocol may decide to prioritise, hence, ultimately, giving right-of-way to, either private traffic or public transportation, as a result of a conflict resolution protocol.

Another interesting approach models intersection crossing as a *Distributed Constrained Optimisation Problem* (DCOP) [39], that is, interpreting vehicles as a multi-agent system in which agents have to find an agreement about the best solution possible to a dynamic set of shared constraints. This kind of modelling lends itself to a distributed implementation, where each vehicle interacts in a peer-to-peer way with the neighbouring ones to solve a local problem, that is, DCOP limited to those vehicles actually approaching the intersection. For doing so, the involved agents actually resort to a messaging protocol to exchange their current solutions as they try to adjust their individual values to converge to a feasible (hopefully, optimal) solution.

Finally, let us mention the approach we envisioned in [17], which proposes to adopt *argumentation technologies*. In particular, we suggest vehicles can engage in open dialogues while approaching the intersection, discussing their beliefs about the best way to approach the intersection, and in case of conflicting needs, arguing with each other about possible ways to avoid that conflict. During the dialogue, vehicles can change the argumentation strategy, and may evaluate assertions differently based on the dynamic contingencies arising in the meantime. For instance, a vehicle A approaching the intersection in the north-to-south direction can express arguments about its urgency to cross, and can argue that another vehicle B in the east-to-west direction (and thus conflicting with A) could/should decide to cross right, as that move would make B reach destination anyways, but would avoid the conflict with A. Persuaded by solidity of A's argument, B could eventually decide to turn right. Although still at the conceptual level, an argumentation-based approach to intersection crossing shows potential for greater flexibility and adaptivity in facing unforeseen situations. In addition, the power of argumentation approaches in the area of autonomous driving is advocated also by other conceptual proposals as a way to solve conflicts and increase trustworthiness and safety of decisions [9].

3.4   Emergent

Handling intersection crossing with coordination by emergence implies giving absolute freedom to vehicles in choosing how to cross intersections, with the only constraints of acting in a safe way and avoiding starvation. To this end, one can let vehicles either: *(a)* play a selfish game where each agent attempts to maximise its expected utility in crossing despite other agents' needs and goals [24]; or *(b)* be engaged in an implicit, self-organising coordination scheme, where each vehicle responds in a reactive way to the actions of the other agents, according to some sort of "natural laws" enforced in the intersection "ecosystem" [26]. In both cases, coordination does not consider an explicit agreement about what to do.

In [21], the authors interpret the intersection crossing problem using *game theory*, that is, modelling each vehicle as the player of a game involving other approaching vehicles, each playing its own game, thus each having different payoffs and utility models—that is, essentially, each player is unaware of the formalisation of the game others are playing. The proposed approach investigates how to build decision matrices in such a way that minimal information can be assumed by agents while still being able to find a solution for their own game—that is, a safe way to cross the intersection in the lowest possible time. Alternatively, it is possible to model the collective behaviour of vehicles at intersections in terms of a self-organised collective movement, similar to that of flocking birds [35].

Actually deploying autonomous vehicles that cross intersections by relying on such approaches seems hardly feasible, as delivering guarantees about safety and liveness may be prohibitively difficult or impractical in the general case of emergent approaches to coordination, because these approaches often exploit stochastic decision making and partial, local information. Possibly, however, in mixed scenarios with the presence (as discussed in Subsect. 5.3) of non connected human-driven vehicles, emergent approaches can be the only solutions for individual vehicles to coordinate with each other.

4   Adjustable Autonomy

In previous section, for the specific coordination problem of intersection crossing, we have presented different approaches based on a different degree of autonomy left to vehicles. The selection of the best strategy, though, may depend on the specific current traffic situation at an intersection, and a single solution can hardly handle all possible situations optimally. For instance, in the case of intersection crossing:

- A solution based on distributed negotiation or argumentation between vehicles can be very effective in rather low traffic situations, when the number of vehicles involved in such negotiations is quite low, thus a collective outcome can be reached quickly because the number of messages to exchange even in the case of completely connected topology would remain low.
- In the case of congested traffic situations, with a large number of vehicles involved, reaching a shared agreement can be harder and induce notable overhead and delay in communications. Also, in the case of auctions, it can induce inflationary effects on the bids. In these situations, thus, on the one hand it could be more appealing to rely on centralised solutions so as to reduce the complexity of communications (e.g. bandwidth consumption), on the other hand emergent ones may further help avoiding the bottleneck of having a single point of failure while still keeping communication costs low.
- Emergent approaches can possibly work both in very low-traffic situations and in highly congested ones, as mentioned above, for their capacity to scale seemingly with the scale of the problem (e.g. as regards communication costs and computational complexity of the protocol), but further experiments are needed to confirm this opportunity.
- Likely, as discussed in [13], it can be necessary for different intersections to adopt different coordination schemes at different times in order to support traffic flow optimisation.

Similar issues can apply also to other classes of coordination problems. For example, consider the need to coordinate vehicles in order to optimise the usage of parking slots. In general, a centralised parking scheme that works well to let the city governance control the distribution of parked vehicles, may fall short in the presence of a high number of vehicles by inducing notable delays in parking. In this case it is better to switch to an approach that lets individual vehicles negotiate for parking slots according to their own preferences.

All the above considerations suggest the possibility, for coordinating vehicles to properly enforce safety, liveness, and to maximise quality in coordination, to dynamically switch from one coordination scheme to another upon changing conditions. Indeed, many municipalities already often adopt a similar dynamic adaptation of the scheme to regulate intersection crossing: the traffic lights that regulate access to an intersection during the day (i.e., in situations of expected intense traffic) are switched off at night (expected low traffic) to let vehicles directly coordinate with each other.

In the area of robotics and multiagent systems the theme of "coordination with adjustable autonomy" [23] (sometimes referred to as "flexible autonomy", also [11]) has been extensively discussed, either referring to the fact that, at times, a human actor may wish to reclaim autonomy in decisions from agents or robots [32], or to the fact that (as in our scenario) specific conditions may require to dynamically switch the coordination scheme [37].

In the real world, and in the context of safety-critical situations such as those involving the coordination of autonomous vehicles, though, designing and realising such dynamic switch in a rigorous and reliable way can be conceptually and technically very hard, and requires facing several challenges. In particular:

- For evaluating the switch to a different coordination scheme, there is the need of well-defined metrics and background knowledge to evaluate which situation fits which coordination scheme. This requires extensive simulations and real-world experiences to compare the effectiveness of different schemes in different situations. For instance, based on the description of the different autonomy classes and their representative protocols, it is likely that factors to consider while deciding which scheme to adopt include *(i) raw performance* aspects, such as the number of messages exchanged and the number of iterations the protocol needs to converge (both tend to increase with decentralisation), as well as *(ii)* accounting for the *amount of information* needed for the protocol to work, such as whether it needs global information (for which a centralised approach may be the only reliable option) or not, and finally *(iii) liability* issues, to establish individual responsibilities in case something bad happens (the more autonomy vehicles have, the less an individual responsible is likely to be found). Whether for performance we might already have the right tools to rigorously measure it, the same does not hold for the information and liability aspects, which remain open issues.
- Identifying the situation for a switch requires continuous detailed monitoring of the traffic situation and of the effectiveness of the coordination process. Also, predictive monitoring techniques should be adopted, to let the switch take place before a degradation of quality in coordination occurs. This obviously implies having means to precisely measure coordination effectiveness, which as far as we know are not widely established, yet.
- Deciding the actual process by which the switch should be decided and enacted. In other words, the vehicles and/or the centralised manager involved in coordination should agree on the switch and on the actions by which to actually perform it. That is, there must be a meta-coordination protocol taking place for the switch to a different coordination scheme. This could again rely on a centralised controller to decide and enact it, or on vehicles negotiating/agreeing with each other on how and when to switch, as it may be required in the absence of infrastructures supporting the existence of a centralised controller. Hence, the same considerations we made for the coordination protocols regarding performance and autonomy trade-offs, will apply to this meta-coordination layer, too, further complicating the open challenge of deciding when to switch.

All of the above, should lead to solutions with provable properties of stability and with provable convergence times. We do not have solutions ready to use to propose here, but certainly the vast amount of literature on adjustable autonomy can suggest useful research directions.

5   Additional Research Challenges

Let us now introduce a few additional general challenges, i.e., issues concerning vehicles coordination beside the specific case of intersection crossing. Autonomous vehicles can hardly be deployed in the real-world and start coordinating without also identifying rigorous solutions to these challenges.

5.1   Systemic Coordination

So far, we discussed the issue of coordination mostly at the level of individual, isolated systems, such as a single intersection. However, thinking at a more systemic level, such as at urban scale, coordination actions in one part of the system may indeed impact other parts of the system. For example, queues at an intersection can induce queues at nearby intersections, or a slow down in a motorway due to an intense flux of traffic in an entering lane can quickly propagate backwards to impact previous entering lanes.

The inter-related effects of individual coordination acts along with the need to respect global level policies imply that the solutions and the policies adopted to solve an individual coordination problem cannot be designed without accounting for the systemic impact of such solutions and policies. In other words, the level of individual coordination must be coupled with a co-coordination one, in which an agreement at the global level is reached on how to act, that is, according to which policies and constraints, at the local level. In the area of autonomous vehicles, a few works exist that handle such systemic problems. For instance, [38] analyses how global coordination of intersections can be achieved by trying to affect, at the local level, the choices of individual vehicles. A similar analysis is presented in [13]. In different fields such as logistics, energy management, robotics, and multi-agent systems, a variety of mechanisms have been proposed for coordination in large-scale systems of systems: hierarchical mechanisms, market-based, self-organising [25]. Such mechanisms can be a source of inspiration for the field of autonomous vehicles as well, but would also call for tools to enable accurate simulation and prediction of the global impacts of coordination solutions.

5.2   Intersection Markets

Today, while driving, we are already used to pay for the usage of infrastructures such as parking slots, bridges, motorways. However, these payments are based on static pricing schemes and offer a neutral service. If, as in negotiation-based solutions, vehicles can dynamically request access to intersections, or to other road infrastructures such as parkings and motorways, and pay them automatically, it may become possible for the manager of such infrastructures to impose dynamic pricing mechanisms, based on the current demand. Doing so implies that a vehicle, while starting its ride, may have no a priori idea about how much it will eventually cost. Also, this opens up the way for imposing fees on intersection crossing, imposing payments for crossing busy intersections with fees varying depending on traffic and time-to-wait.

The mechanisms of dynamic payments could also enable a model in which passengers can decide to pay more to get better services, e.g., crossing an intersection quickly, breaking the current neutrality of road infrastructures. In the future, such mechanisms could become based on a real auction with real money, with the consequence that vehicles whose owners/drivers/passengers have higher budget will always bid higher and buy priority in crossing the intersection, while vehicles whose owners/drivers/passengers have lower budget will risk starvation. The above issues, other than calling for proper algorithmic solutions to avoid unfairness or inflationary effects, also call for the definition of suitable regulations to avoid mobility becoming a privilege, and suitable means to integrate such regulation into a coordination scheme.

5.3   Mixed Scenarios

This article assumes that all the cars are fully autonomous, or at least that they act and interact autonomously with each other during the coordination act. This can match a not-so-near future when we can expect that human-driven cars will no longer exist or when, for safety and efficiency reasons, it will be forbidden for humans to drive but in specific controlled situations: the same as today, for instance, it is forbidden to ride a horse in motorways and high-speed roads. However, there will be a rather long transition phase in which our streets will be populated by a mixture of fully autonomous cars, partially autonomous ones, and traditional human-driven cars, other than bicycles and motorbikes. Such a scenario clearly challenges the possibility of relying on the surveyed coordination schemes, unless one devises dependable means to involve human-driven cars (that is, their human drivers) in the process of coordination, and suitable means to formalise and ensure properties in such mixed scenarios.

These scenarios have several characteristics in common with the issue of coordinating the movements of mixed teams of robots and humans, which has been extensively analysed in the context of robotics and autonomous systems [12], but assumes the existence of means for robots and humans to communicate with each other. Also, designing a coordination scheme according to the solutions discussed in this article would require accounting for the possible inaccuracy of actions by human-driven cars, and possibly for the presence of non-connected vehicles (e.g. bicycles) whose behaviour cannot be rigorously predicted. For this latter case, emergent approaches to coordination could provide solutions, though possibly much less effective.

6   Conclusions

For future autonomous vehicles to populate our streets, it will be necessary to identify rigorous solutions for coordinating their relative movements in order to let them circulate safely and without conflicts and crashes. In this article, we focussed on the problem of crossing intersections, and showed how a variety of solutions can be conceived, each characterised by a different level of autonomy in decision making left to vehicles during coordination.

Selection of the appropriate solution to handle intersection crossing will require proper modelling of the problem and of the domain, other than rigorous approaches to analyse and compare the different solutions, in order to select the most appropriate one depending on the context. Furthermore, it will require addressing a number of additional challenges that represent promising directions for future research.

Finally, but this problem would require a full analysis on its own, the safety-critical nature of autonomous vehicles will possibly require them to solve ethical dilemmas while coordinating with each other, e.g., multi-vehicle instantiations of the trolley problem [2], which raises the additional issue of somewhat engineering a sort of moral dimension for vehicles.

References

1. Abeywickrama, D.B., Mamei, M., Zambonelli, F.: Engineering collectives of self-driving vehicles: the SOTA approach. In: Margaria, T., Steffen, B. (eds.) ISoLA 2018. LNCS, vol. 11246, pp. 79–93. Springer, Cham (2018). https://doi.org/10.1007/978-3-030-03424-5_6
2. Awad, E., et al.: The moral machine experiment. Nature **563**(7729), 59 (2018)
3. Balbo, F., Bhouri, N., Pinson, S.: Bimodal traffic regulation system: a multi-agent approach. Web Intell. **14**(2), 139–151 (2016). https://doi.org/10.3233/WEB-160336
4. Bicocchi, N., Mamei, M., Sassi, A., Zambonelli, F.: On recommending opportunistic rides. IEEE Trans. Intell. Transp. Syst. **18**(12), 3328–3338 (2017). https://doi.org/10.1109/TITS.2017.2684625
5. Cabri, G., Gherardini, L., Montangero, M.: Auction-based crossings management. In: Proceedings of the 5th EAI International Conference on Smart Objects and Technologies for Social Good, GoodTechs 2019, pp. 183–188. ACM, New York (2019). https://doi.org/10.1145/3342428.3342689
6. Carlino, D., Boyles, S.D., Stone, P.: Auction-based autonomous intersection management. In: 2013 16th International IEEE Conference on Intelligent Transportation Systems-(ITSC), pp. 529–534. IEEE (2013)
7. Dresner, K., Stone, P.: A multiagent approach to autonomous intersection management. J. Artif. Intell. Res. **31**, 591–656 (2008)
8. Fagnant, D.J., Kockelman, K.: Preparing a nation for autonomous vehicles: opportunities, barriers and policy recommendations. Transp. Res. Part A Policy Pract. **77**, 167–181 (2015)
9. Fridman, L., Ding, L., Jenik, B., Reimer, B.: Arguing machines: human supervision of black box AI systems that make life-critical decisions (2017)

10. Gelernter, D., Carriero, N.: Coordination languages and their significance. Commun. ACM **35**(2), 96–107 (1992). https://doi.org/10.1145/129630.376083
11. Gerber, C., Siekmann, J., Vierke, G.: Flexible autonomy in holonic agent systems. In: Proceedings of the 1999 AAAI Spring Symposium on Agents with Adjustable Autonomy. AAAI (1999)
12. Goodrich, M.A., Schultz, A.C., et al.: Human-robot interaction: a survey. Found. Trends Hum. Comput. Interact. **1**(3), 203–275 (2008)
13. Hausknecht, M., Au, T.C., Stone, P.: Autonomous intersection management: multi-intersection optimization. In: 2011 IEEE/RSJ International Conference on Intelligent Robots and Systems, pp. 4581–4586. IEEE (2011)
14. International, S.: Taxonomy and definitions for terms related to driving automation systems for on-road motor vehicles, June 2018
15. Jia, D., Lu, K., Wang, J., Zhang, X., Shen, X.: A survey on platoon-based vehicular cyber-physical systems. IEEE Commun. Surv. Tutorials **18**(1), 263–284 (2016). (Firstquarter). https://doi.org/10.1109/COMST.2015.2410831
16. Lee, J., Park, B.: Development and evaluation of a cooperative vehicle intersection control algorithm under the connected vehicles environment. IEEE Trans. Intell. Transp. Syst. **13**(1), 81–90 (2012). https://doi.org/10.1109/TITS.2011.2178836
17. Lippi, M., Mamei, M., Mariani, S., Zambonelli, F.: An argumentation-based perspective over the social iot. IEEE Internet Things J. **5**(4), 2537–2547 (2018). https://doi.org/10.1109/JIOT.2017.2775047
18. Lopes, F., Wooldridge, M., Novais, A.Q.: Negotiation among autonomous computational agents: principles, analysis and challenges. Artif. Intell. Rev. **29**(1), 1–44 (2008)
19. Maheswaran, R.T., Tambe, M., Bowring, E., Pearce, J.P., Varakantham, P.: Taking DCOP to the real world: efficient complete solutions for distributed multi-event scheduling. In: Proceedings of the Third International Joint Conference on Autonomous Agents and Multiagent Systems-Volume 1, pp. 310–317. IEEE Computer Society (2004)
20. Mamei, M., Menezes, R., Tolksdorf, R., Zambonelli, F.: Case studies for self-organization in computer science. J. Syst. Architect. **52**(8–9), 443–460 (2006)
21. Mandiau, R., Champion, A., Auberlet, J.M., Espié, S., Kolski, C.: Behaviour based on decision matrices for a coordination between agents in a urban traffic simulation. Appl. Intell. **28**(2), 121–138 (2008). https://doi.org/10.1007/s10489-007-0045-3
22. Menon, N., Barbour, N., Zhang, Y., Pinjari, A.R., Mannering, F.: Shared autonomous vehicles and their potential impacts on household vehicle ownership: an exploratory empirical assessment. Int. J. Sustain. Transp. **13**, 1–12 (2018)
23. Mostafa, S.A., Ahmad, M.S., Mustapha, A.: Adjustable autonomy: a systematic literature review. Artif. Intell. Rev. **51**(2), 149–186 (2017). https://doi.org/10.1007/s10462-017-9560-8
24. Nisan, N., Roughgarden, T., Tardos, E., Vazirani, V.V.: Algorithmic Game Theory. Cambridge University Press, Cambridge (2007)
25. Omicini, A., Zambonelli, F.: Challenges of decentralized coordination in large-scale ubicomp systems. In: Proceedings of the 2016 ACM International Joint Conference on Pervasive and Ubiquitous Computing, UbiComp Adjunct 2016, Heidelberg, Germany, 12–16 September, 2016, pp. 1315–1320. ACM Press (2016)
26. Parunak, H.V.D., Brueckner, S., Sauter, J.: Digital pheromone mechanisms for coordination of unmanned vehicles. In: Castelfranchi, C., Johnson, W.L. (eds.) 1st International Joint Conference on Autonomous Agents and Multiagent systems, vol. 1, pp. 449–450. ACM, New York, 15–19 July 2002 (2012)

27. Polycarpou, E., Lambrinos, L., Protopapadakis, E.: Smart parking solutions for urban areas. In: 2013 IEEE 14th International Symposium on "A World of Wireless, Mobile and Multimedia Networks" (WoWMoM). IEEE (2013). https://doi.org/10.1109/WoWMoM.2013.6583499

28. Rahwan, I., Ramchurn, S.D., Jennings, N.R., Mcburney, P., Parsons, S., Sonenberg, L.: Argumentation-based negotiation. Knowl. Eng. Rev. **18**(4), 343–375 (2003)

29. Rios-Torres, J., Malikopoulos, A.: A survey on the coordination of connected and automated vehicles at intersections and merging at highway on-ramps. IEEE Trans. Intell. Transp. Syst. **18**(5), 1066–1077 (2017). https://doi.org/10.1109/TITS.2016.2600504

30. Röth, T., Pielen, M., Wolff, K., Lüdiger, T.: Urban vehicle concepts for the shared mobility. ATZ Worldwide **120**(1), 18–23 (2018). https://doi.org/10.1007/s38311-017-0163-4

31. Sassi, A., Zambonelli, F.: Coordination infrastructures for future smart social mobility services. IEEE Intell. Syst. **29**(5), 78–82 (2014). https://doi.org/10.1109/MIS.2014.81

32. Scerri, P., Pynadath, D., Tambe, M.: Adjustable autonomy in real-world multi-agent environments. In: Proceedings of the Fifth International Conference on Autonomous Agents, pp. 300–307. ACM Press (2001)

33. Seredynski, M., Bouvry, P.: A survey of vehicular-based cooperative traffic information systems. In: 2011 14th International IEEE Conference on Intelligent Transportation Systems (ITSC), pp. 163–168. IEEE, October 2011. https://doi.org/10.1109/ITSC.2011.6083055

34. Seshia, S.A., Sadigh, D., Sastry, S.S.: Formal methods for semi-autonomous driving. In: 2015 52nd ACM/EDAC/IEEE Design Automation Conference (DAC), pp. 1–5 (2015)

35. Toner, J., Tu, Y.: Flocks, herds, and schools: a quantitative theory of flocking. Phys. Rev. E **58**(4), 4828 (1998)

36. Tonguz, O.K.: Red light, green light–no light: Tomorrow's communicative cars could take turns at intersections. IEEE Spectr. **55**(10), 24–29 (2018). https://doi.org/10.1109/MSPEC.2018.8482420

37. van der Vecht, B., Dignum, F., Meyer, J.-J.C., Neef, M.: A dynamic coordination mechanism using adjustable autonomy. In: Sichman, J.S., Padget, J., Ossowski, S., Noriega, P. (eds.) COIN -2007. LNCS (LNAI), vol. 4870, pp. 83–96. Springer, Heidelberg (2008). https://doi.org/10.1007/978-3-540-79003-7_7

38. Vasirani, M., Ossowski, S.: A market-inspired approach for intersection management in urban road traffic networks. J. Artif. Int. Res. **43**(1), 621–659 (2012)

39. Vu, H., Aknine, S., Ramchurn, S.D.: A decentralised approach to intersection traffic management. In: IJCAI, pp. 527–533. AAAI Press (2018)

40. Wu, W., Zhang, J., Luo, A., Cao, J.: Distributed mutual exclusion algorithms for intersection traffic control. IEEE Trans. Parallel Distrib. Syst. **26**(1), 65–74 (2015). https://doi.org/10.1109/TPDS.2013.2297097

41. Zohdy, I.H., Kamalanathsharma, R.K., Rakha, H.: Intersection management for autonomous vehicles using iCACC. In: 2012 15th International IEEE Conference on Intelligent Transportation Systems, pp. 1109–1114. IEEE, September 2012. https://doi.org/10.1109/ITSC.2012.6338827

Engineering Semantic Self-composition of Services Through Tuple-Based Coordination

Ashley Caselli[1]([✉])[iD], Giovanni Ciatto[2]([✉])[iD],
Giovanna Di Marzo Serugendo[1]([✉])[iD], and Andrea Omicini[2]([✉])[iD]

[1] Centre Universitaire d'Informatique (CUI),
University of Geneva, Geneva, Switzerland
{ashley.caselli,giovanna.dimarzo}@unige.ch
[2] Department of Computer Science and Engineering (DISI),
Alma Mater Studiorum—Università di Bologna, Cesena, Italy
{giovanni.ciatto,andrea.omicini}@unibo.it

Abstract. Service self-composition is a well-understood research area focusing on service-based applications providing new services by automatically combining pre-existing ones. In this paper we focus on tuple-based coordination, and propose a solution leveraging logic tuples and tuple spaces to support semantic self-composition for services. A full-stack description of the solution is provided, ranging from a theoretical formalisation to a technologically valuable design and implementation.

Keywords: Service self-composition · Semantic reasoning ·
Tuple-based coordination

1 Introduction

Nowadays an ever increasing number of IT scenarios leverages a services-based architecture. These sorts of systems are modelled as a collection of heterogeneous and loosely-coupled fine-grained processes, namely *services*, that communicate among them. Arguably, the pervasive adoption of services-based architectures will lead to an explosion in the number of services populating the Internet. In other words, *scalability* issues are going to arise soon.

On the other hand, novel business opportunities are likely to become available as the amount of services increases. In fact, the public availability of disparate services is commonly a key enabler for the creation of secondary services built on top of the pre-existing ones. To this end, effective techniques – such as *service composition* – are required at the technical level, in order to reuse the available functionalities. However, service composition sets many challenges from a system administration perspective. The experience of developers, as well as their careful work, is a necessary prerequisite for composition of services to be effective. Unfortunately, the effectiveness of human experts in tackling an increasing number of services does not scale up linearly with the total amount of services.

© Springer Nature Switzerland AG 2020
T. Margaria and B. Steffen (Eds.): ISoLA 2020, LNCS 12477, pp. 205–223, 2020.
https://doi.org/10.1007/978-3-030-61470-6_13

To deal with these issues, a viable solution may be represented by automatically handling the composition. To this end, approaches focused on the composition of the existing services have been proposed. The mechanism that combines two or more basic services into a more complex one is known as *service composition* [17]. It aims at creating higher-level functionalities within the system by leveraging the available resources.

The static nature of traditional approaches has been challenged by dynamic service composition approaches [7], which range over syntax-based composition to semantic-based composition and AI planning techniques. The adoption of such approaches paved the way to the design of systems with innate autonomous computational properties, such as *self-adaptation* and *self-composition*.

Many research works focus on coping with *"challenging problem of composing services dynamically"* [2]. Nevertheless, most of them solve it only partially: to the best of our knowledge, most of the existing solutions to the dynamic service composition challenge present limitations—e.g., syntax-based composition. Other approaches, although well-designed and sound at a conceptual level, are either discontinued or based on obsolete technologies [5].

This paper aims at providing a comprehensive tuple-based technology for semantic self-composition of services. A self-composition model that promotes and supports spontaneous service composition based on LINDA [15] is proposed. The solution supports semantic reasoning leveraging on logic tuples and LINDA tuple spaces. Moreover, a Java-based implementation of such model is also proposed, relying on the recent TuSoW [6] technology for tuple-based coordination.

The remainder of this paper is organised as follows. Section 2 provides an overview of the current approaches for service composition. Section 3 shows a formal definition of the designed system in terms of its syntax and operational semantics. The Java-based software architecture that implements the proposed technology is shown in Sect. 4. Section 5 presents a case study in a formal way. Finally, Sect. 6 concludes the paper by summarising the proposed solution.

2 State of the Art

2.1 Service Composition

Service composition is broadly known as the mechanism that combines two or more basic services into a more complex one that provides higher-level functionalities [17]. It deals with the needs of users to search for appropriate compositions of services that meet the required processes [27].

Service composition approaches may be categorised in terms of many orthogonal properties. A possible grouping considers the composition policy: *(i)* syntax-based: the matching among services is computed as mere equality operation on the input/output parameters of the services; *(ii)* semantic-based: it requires a taxonomy of concepts on which the composition process relies on to compute the matches; and *(iii)* through AI-planning solutions: it concerns the task of finding a course of action to reach a goal. From a different point of view, a composition process may be defined as the outcome of two minor phases – i.e., *selection* and *binding* –, hence a different grouping may be provided. A service composition approach may then be defined as *(i)* static, when the binding occurs at design-time; or *(ii)* dynamic, when the binding occurs either at deployment- or run-time. Using a static approach, the compositions are built during the design of the system (design-time), by the system designer that creates them once for all. This approach leads to correct compositions but lacks of scalability and adaptability. On the other hand, a dynamic approach ensures scalability and adaptability by adding computational overhead to the system. Dynamic approaches differ in the stage the binding phase occurs, which may be at *(i)* deployment-time, where the service binding phase occurs each time a service shows up in the system; or at *(ii)* run-time, where the binding occurs when a request is published.

Among these categories, we can mention the following works. From the semantic web domain, Talib et al. [25] provide a semi-automatic method to generate static web service composition in BPEL4WS language. Talantikite et al. [24] present a model for automatic Web services discovery and composition that exploits semantically annotated web services through an upper ontology (i.e. OWL-S [20]). In the field of ambient intelligence, Vallee et al. [26] propose an approach that combines multi-agent techniques with semantic web services to enable dynamic, context-aware service composition. In the field of multi-agent systems (MAS) approaches to self-composition usually involve planification, where agents reason on their respective services and the user's needs [14]. In this area, works on self-composition of method fragments bring a more dynamic solution based on cooperative agents, each representing a fragment and participating to the design of the fragments composition [3]. Using similar cooperative principles, Degas [9] proposes a syntax-based composition approach with collaborative agents for dynamic composition of aerial plane trajectories. Other approaches specifically involving chemical reactions for self-composition, possibly include the followings. Frei et al. [13] propose the use of chemical reactions, in the field of industrial robotics, to build self-organising assembly systems that participate in their own design by spontaneously organising themselves. Di Napoli et al. [11] show how a specified workflow can be instantiated using chemical reactions. In the context of tuple spaces, Viroli [27] proposes a syntax-based approach inspired by chemical reactions combined with the notion of competition among services. De Angelis [7] proposes a chemical-inspired model that promotes syntax-based self-composition of services at run-time. To alleviate the lack of semantics in the composition in [7], Ben Mahfoudh et al. [1] extend the original tuple space model with learning-based capabilities, thus providing pertinent and reliable services to the user.

2.2 Linda and TuSoW

LINDA [15] is the archetypal tuple-based coordination model [22], inspiring and influencing a huge number of coordination models and technologies throughout the years [5]. The main elements of LINDA are *tuples*, *templates*, *tuple spaces*, and *communication primitives*. A tuple is a piece of information represented according to a well-defined *tuple language*, specifying the structure of admissible tuples. A template is a concise way of representing a set of tuples: it consists of a pattern, represented according to a particular *template language*, which may be matched by several tuples. A tuple space is a repository where tuples may be inserted, observed, or withdrawn by an arbitrary number of agents willing to synchronise while being uncoupled in reference, space, and time. On purpose, a communication primitive is an operation provided to interacting agents to *synchronise* themselves upon tuples' insertion, observation, and consumption.

LINDA is characterised by a few peculiar features: *(i) generative communication*, that is, tuples existing independently of the agents who produced them; *(ii) associative access*, namely, agents can access (i.e., observe or withdraw) the tuples stored in a tuple space by simply specifying a template, without the need of knowing the tuple "address" neither its "name"; and *(iii) suspensive semantics*, that is, agents' attempts of accessing a tuple matching a particular template are suspended until a tuple of such a sort actually exists.

LINDA provides three communication primitives: out to insert a tuple in a tuple space, in to withdraw one, rd to read one. Despite their simplicity, such primitives are expressive enough to cope with several common interaction patterns [15]. Suspensive semantics, in particular, is the cornerstone of the coordination mechanism proposed by LINDA, since it deals with synchronisation: whereas the out primitive always puts a tuple in the tuple space, in and rd *attempt* to get one based on a provided tuple template. If a tuple *matching* the template is found, it is returned to the caller agent that can continue execution; otherwise, the caller agent is *suspended* until a matching tuple becomes available.

Several variants of LINDA have been proposed throughout the years, either extending the set of communication primitives, adding features such as mobility or access control [8,21], enabling distribution of multiple tuple spaces on a network of interconnected computers [12,19], and much more [23]. Nevertheless, only a few have been developed as a *technology* [5]—and, among these, some have already been exploited for service composition, as already discussed in the related works section above.

TuSoW [6] is tuple-based technology for coordination for distributed agents via LINDA tuple spaces. It aims at providing a lightweight, modular, flexible, and highly interoperable implementation of LINDA. It is designed as a multi-platform technology, making it suitable to be used by a wide community of developers in a wide range of application domains. In particular, TuSoW coordination facilities are provided to agents *as-a-Service*, via the HTTP protocol. For this reason we chose it as reference technology in the remainder of this paper.

3   Formal Model

The proposed model formalises a system composed by a number of active entities – namely, *agents* – acting as either service requesters (a.k.a. clients, or users), or service providers (a.k.a. servers). Users and servers do not interact directly but rather they interact by means of a LINDA-like shared memory – that is, the *blackboard* –, acting as a coordination medium.

The interaction among users and servers is based on a simple protocol. On the one side, servers advertise their service descriptors by publishing them on the blackboard, upon startup. After that, they keep listening for incoming requests issued by users. As soon as a request is issued by some user, if a server exists which is capable of serving that request, then it is triggered. The invoked server must then execute its service, producing a result which is eventually output on the blackboard as well. On the other side, users are simple agents which may, from time to time, issue requests towards a particular service descriptor. When this happens, the user must then wait for a result to eventually appear on the blackboard, and finally consumes it before terminating.

Automatic semantic composition of services is provided by the blackboard using a dynamic deployment time approach [18]. In other words, whenever a novel service descriptor is published on the blackboard, the blackboard reacts by generating and automatically inserting a (possibly null) amount of *composite* service descriptors on it-self. In particular, the set of service descriptors to be generated is computed by combining the just-inserted one with *all* the service descriptors it may combine with, among the many already present on the blackboard.

Of course neither users nor clients are aware of the service composition performed by the blackboard. In other words, the service composition is transparent to both users and servers. To make this possible, the blackboard is in charge of *splitting* users' requests directed towards composite service descriptors into elementary request, which may then be served by servers. For the same reason, the blackboard is also in charge of handling the intermediary results possibly produced by servers when a composite service request is being served.

In the next sections we formalise such insights by means of process algebra. In particular, we first structurally define the most relevant notions of our model by means of an EBNF grammar, and then provide its semantics by means of a Labeled Transition System [16].

3.1   Syntax

Here we provide a syntax for the main concepts composing our model. To do so, we exploit EBNF grammars.

System. We define a system (Sys) as a parallel composition of one or more *agents* and a *blackboard* (B). In turn, each agent may be either a *user agent* (U) or *service agent* (S), according to their role in the system. Formally:

$$Sys ::= S_S \parallel U_S \parallel B \qquad \text{main system}$$
$$S_S ::= S \mid (S \parallel S_S) \qquad \text{list of services}$$
$$U_S ::= U \mid (U \parallel U_S) \qquad \text{list of users}$$

where $\parallel$ is the parallel composition operator—commutative and associative.

Blackboard. A blackboard is modelled as the space where the interaction among agents takes place. It is exploited as coordination medium by the agents, which may perform basic read/write operations on it. We define a blackboard (B) as a multiset that may either be empty or contain four sorts of data: *(i)* service descriptors, *(ii)* user requests, *(iii)* internal messages, or *(iv)* results. Formally:

$$B ::= \emptyset \mid SD \mid Req \mid \texttt{serve}(SD, C) \mid \texttt{serve\_comp}(SD, C) \mid Res \mid B \cup B$$

where $\cup$ is the union operator for multisets – associative and commutative –, whereas $\emptyset$ denotes the empty multiset.

Service. A service represents a *service agent*. It is capable of two operations embodied by *publish* and *accept*, which are grammar syntactic sugar. Intuitively, *publish* denotes the operation used by a service to advertise itself on the blackboard; *accept* says that the service is listening for incoming requests. Formally:

$$S ::= \texttt{publish}(SD) \mid \texttt{accept}(\texttt{service}(Q)) \mid S \cdot S$$

where $\cdot$ is the sequence operator—associative and not commutative.

User. A user represents a *user agent*. Similarly to a service agent, it is capable of two operations, represented through the *Req* and *Res* terms. They embody a request and a response message, respectively. At last, the `halt` term is used to represent the eventual termination event. Formally:

$$U ::= Req \cdot Res \cdot U \mid \texttt{halt}$$

where $\cdot$ operator is equivalent to the one defined above. By construction, well-formed users must wait for a response event after each request event.

Service Descriptor. A service descriptor (SD) provides the representation of a service. Thus, a service descriptor may either represent: *(i)* an *atomic service* – through its formal arguments: the (possibly empty) set of the *named input types* (I) it is able to accept and the *output type* (O) it produces as result –, or *(ii)* a *composed service*, as the concatenation of two services in such a way that the output of the first one is provided as input to the second one. Formally:

$$
\begin{aligned}
SD &::= \texttt{service}(Q) \mid SD \overset{N}{\texttt{argof}} SD & &\text{service descriptor} \\
Q &::= I,\, O & &\text{query} \\
I &::= \epsilon \mid N : T \mid I, I & &\text{input} \\
O &::= \epsilon \mid T & &\text{output} \\
N &::= n_1 \mid n_2 \mid n_3 \mid \dots & &\text{name} \\
T &::= t_1 \mid t_2 \mid t_3 \mid \dots & &\text{type}
\end{aligned}
$$

Request/Response. Agents may append *request* (*Req*) and *response* (*Res*) messages to the blackboard. A request message is defined as either *(i)* *query* (*Q*), or *(ii)* *call* (*C*). A query expresses an exploratory request, aimed at checking whether the system is capable of serving a particular signature or not, given the currently published services and their compositions. Conversely, a call represents an actual invocation of some service, which may involve the execution of one or more agents to serve the request. Requests are represented through their actual *input arguments* (*A*) – which are named as well – and the expected *output type* (*O*) they ask for. On the other side, response messages may instead contain a *(i)* *Const* term, which is a boolean value, or a *(ii)* *value* (*V*), that allows any kind of terminal value to be represented. Formally:

$$
\begin{array}{ll}
Req ::= \texttt{query}(Q) \mid \texttt{call}(C) & \text{request} \\
C ::= A, \ O & \text{call} \\
A ::= \epsilon \mid N : T(V) \mid A, A & \text{arguments} \\
V ::= v_1, v_2, \ldots, v_n & \text{terminal values} \\
Res ::= \texttt{res}(Const) \mid \texttt{res}(V) & \text{response} \\
Const ::= \top \mid \bot & \text{boolean value}
\end{array}
$$

3.2 Operational Semantics

A Labelled Transition System (LTS) is exploited to provide the operational semantics of our model. The transition relations model the effect of executing an action on the blackboard.

Labels. Labels are used in the LTS to formally capture events of interest for the operational semantics of our model. In order to ease their comprehension, all label names are suffixed by the name of the transition rules they are involved into. Only one exception is made for τ, denoting the silent transition.

$$
\begin{array}{l}
E ::= \textit{publish\_sd} \mid \textit{publish\_query} \mid \textit{publish\_call} \mid \textit{consume\_call} \mid \\
\quad \textit{consume\_comp\_call} \mid \textit{serve\_call} \mid \textit{comp\_call} \mid \textit{serve\_comp\_call} \mid \\
\quad \textit{last\_comp\_call} \mid \textit{prove} \mid \textit{compose} \mid \tau
\end{array}
$$

Operators. A definition of functions and operators exploited within the transition rules is following. For the sake of brevity we only provide an intuition of each. An exhaustive formal definition of their semantics can be found in [4]. Notice that, in what follows, we often leverage the notation $\mathcal{L}(X)$, where X is some non-terminal symbol among the many defined in the EBNF production rules above. There, we write $\mathcal{L}(X)$ meaning "the set of all possible strings produced by all possible production rules for X".

- The function $typeof : \mathcal{L}(C) \to \mathcal{L}(SD)$ retrieves the data type of a call request and encodes it under the form of a service descriptor.
- The *match* operator $\sim \subseteq \mathcal{L}(SD) \times \mathcal{L}(SD)$ evaluates the matching degree among two service descriptors through semantic reasoning.

The function $execute : \mathcal{L}(S) \times \mathcal{L}(Req) \to \mathcal{L}(V)$ triggers the service execution in order to fulfill the provided request and it subsequently provides the result.
- The function $prove : \mathcal{L}(Req) \times \mathcal{L}(SD) \to \mathcal{L}(Const)$ performs the evaluation of a query request.
- The function $fringe : \mathcal{L}(SD) \to \mathcal{L}(I)$ is in charge of retrieving a set containing the inputs of a compound service descriptor, namely its fringe.
- The function $compose : \mathcal{L}(SD) \times \mathcal{L}(SD) \to \mathcal{L}(SD)$ designs the binding among services, creating one or more new service descriptors which represent the composed service.
- Finally, the function $compositions : \mathcal{L}(B) \times \mathcal{L}(SD) \to \mathcal{L}(SD)$ aims to identify all the compositions in which a given service descriptor is involved.

Transition Rules. Transition rules define the admissible actions for a system compliant with our model. In a nutshell, admissible actions include: *(i)* publishing a service descriptor on the blackboard, *(ii)* composing two or more services, *(iii)* publishing a request message (call or query) on the blackboard, *(iv)* proving a query request, *(v)* serving a call request, and *(vi)* the decay of a service descriptor. The formal definition of the corresponding transition rules follows.

Service Descriptor Publication. The service descriptor publication is governed by the [PUBLISH-SD] transition rule. The rule may occur anytime during the system life-cycle. Its execution changes the blackboard state, enriching it with the published service descriptor. Formally:

$$\texttt{publish}(SD) \cdot S \parallel S_S \parallel U_S \parallel B \xrightarrow{publish\_sd} S \parallel S_S \parallel U_S \parallel B \cup SD \quad \text{[PUBLISH-SD]}$$

Composition. The composition is governed by the [COMPOSE] transition rule. It triggers each time a service is published and evaluates if there exists a service that matches with the published one. If it is the case, a composed service descriptor is generated and published on the blackboard.

$$\frac{SD = \texttt{service}(I, O) \wedge \exists\, (N : O) \in fringe(SD') \wedge SD'' = compose(SD,\ SD')}{S_S \parallel U_S \parallel B \cup SD \cup SD' \xrightarrow{compose} S_S \parallel U_S \parallel B \cup SD \cup SD' \cup SD''} \quad \text{[COMPOSE]}$$

Request Publication. The request publication is governed by the [PUBLISH-QUERY] and [PUBLISH-CALL] transition rules. Their execution publishes a query or call message, respectively, on the blackboard. They both may occur anytime during the system life-cycle.

$$\texttt{query}(Q) \cdot U \parallel S_S \parallel U_S \parallel B \xrightarrow{publish\_query} U \parallel S_S \parallel U_S \parallel B \cup \texttt{query}(Q) \qquad \texttt{[PUBLISH-QUERY]}$$

$$\texttt{call}(C) \cdot U \parallel S_S \parallel U_S \parallel B \xrightarrow{publish\_call} U \parallel S_S \parallel U_S \parallel B \cup \texttt{call}(C) \qquad \texttt{[PUBLISH-CALL]}$$

Proving. The result of a query request is generated by either the [POS-PROVE] or the [NEG-PROVE] transition rules. The former (resp. latter) is triggered when *(i)* there exists at least one service descriptor (either single or composed) on the blackboard that is able (resp. unable) to fulfill the current query, *(ii)* there exists a user waiting to consume the positive (resp. negative) result. Once triggered, each transition allows the waiting user to go on with its computation.

$$\frac{\texttt{service}(Q) \sim SD \land Const = prove(Q, SD)}{S_S \parallel \texttt{res}(\top) \cdot U \parallel U_S \parallel B \cup SD \cup \texttt{query}(Q) \xrightarrow{prove} S_S \parallel U \parallel U_S \parallel B \cup SD} \qquad \texttt{[POS-PROVE]}$$

$$\frac{\nexists \, SD \in B : \texttt{service}(Q) \sim SD}{S_S \parallel \texttt{res}(\bot) \cdot U \parallel U_S \parallel B \cup \texttt{query}(Q) \xrightarrow{prove} S_S \parallel U \parallel U_S \parallel B} \qquad \texttt{[NEG-PROVE]}$$

Serving. The management of a call request is governed by [CONSUME-CALL], [SERVE-CALL], [COMP-CALL], [CONSUME-COMP-CALL], [SERVE-COMP-CALL], and [LAST-COMP-CALL] transition rules.

The [CONSUME-CALL] rule is atomic: it is triggered each time a call request can be fulfilled by some simple service. The rule is triggered only if a simple service SD is listening for incoming requests. Once triggered, the rule consumes the call request and adds an internal call message **serve** to the blackboard.

$$\frac{SD = \texttt{service}(I, O) \land typeof(\texttt{call}(C)) \sim SD}{\texttt{accept}(SD) \cdot S \parallel S_S \parallel U_S \parallel B \cup SD \cup \texttt{call}(C) \xrightarrow{consume\_call} \texttt{accept}(SD) \cdot S \parallel S_S \parallel U_S \parallel B \cup SD \cup \texttt{serve}(SD, \texttt{call}(C))} \qquad \texttt{[CONSUME-CALL]}$$

The [SERVE-CALL] transition governs the serving of a call request. The rule is triggered only if *(i)* a simple service SD is listening for incoming requests, *(ii)* a user is waiting for a result, and *(iii)* an internal message **serve** generated from a call published by the same user is present on the blackboard. The transition allows both the waiting user and the service to go on with their computations, while the pending internal message **serve** is removed from the blackboard.

$$\frac{SD = \texttt{service}(I, O) \land typeof(\texttt{call}(C)) \sim SD \land V = execute(\texttt{accept}(SD), \texttt{call}(C))}{\texttt{accept}(SD) \cdot S \parallel S_S \parallel \texttt{res}(V) \cdot U \parallel U_S \parallel B \cup SD \cup \texttt{serve}(SD, \texttt{call}(C)) \xrightarrow{serve\_call} S \parallel S_S \parallel U \parallel U_S \parallel B \cup SD} \qquad \texttt{[SERVE-CALL]}$$

The [COMP-CALL] rule governs the serving of a call request by a composed service. The rule is triggered only if a composed service SD able to fulfil the published call request is present on the blackboard. During its execution, the blackboard state is modified and enriched with an internal call message `serve_comp` that contains the service descriptor SD of the composed service that is capable of serving the request, in addition to the original call request `call(C)`.

$$\frac{SD = SD' \stackrel{N}{argof} SD'' \wedge typeof(\text{call}(C)) \sim SD}{S_S \parallel U_S \parallel B \cup SD \cup \text{call}(C) \xrightarrow{comp\_call} S_S \parallel U_S \parallel B \cup SD \cup \text{serve\_comp}(SD, \text{call}(C))} \text{[COMP-CALL]}$$

The [CONSUME-COMP-CALL] rule is in charge of initiating the chain of services executions that leads to the fulfilment of a call request with a composed service. The rule is triggered whenever a message `serve_comp` is published on the blackboard. Once triggered, this transition modifies the blackboard state, adding an internal message `serve` containing (i) the first service descriptor SD of the composition, and (ii) the portion of the call request that is fulfillable by the service described via the service descriptor SD.

$$\frac{SD = SD' \stackrel{N}{argof} SD'' \wedge typeof(\text{call}(C')) \sim SD'}{S_S \parallel U_S \parallel B \cup SD \cup \text{serve\_comp}(SD, \text{call}(C)) \xrightarrow{consume\_comp\_call} S_S \parallel U_S \parallel B \cup SD \cup \text{serve}(SD', \text{call}(C'))} \text{[CONSUME-COMP-CALL]}$$

The [SERVE-COMP-CALL] rule is in charge of carrying on the execution of fulfilment of a call request using a composed service. It requires an internal message `serve` to be present. Once triggered, it generates a new internal message `serve` that contains (i) the service descriptor of the following service to be executed in the composition, and (ii) a new call with the result of the previous execution added as input parameter.

$$\frac{SD = SD' \stackrel{N}{argof} SD'' \wedge typeof(\text{call}(C')) \sim SD' \wedge V = execute(\text{accept}(SD'), \text{call}(C'))}{\text{accept}(SD') \cdot S \parallel S_S \parallel U_S \parallel B \cup SD' \cup \text{serve}(SD', \text{call}(C')) \xrightarrow{serve\_comp\_call} S \parallel S_S \parallel U_S \parallel B \cup SD' \cup \text{serve}(SD'', \text{call}(N : T(V), C'))} \text{[SERVE-COMP-CALL]}$$

The [LAST-COMP-CALL] rule concludes the computational chain. It handles the last service execution providing the final result. Therefore, the user that published the call may consume the result and go on with its computation.

$$\frac{SD = SD' \stackrel{N}{argof} SD'' \wedge typeof(\text{call}(C'')) \sim SD' \wedge V = execute(\text{accept}(SD''), \text{call}(C''))}{\text{accept}(SD'') \cdot S \parallel S_S \parallel U_S \parallel B \cup SD'' \cup \text{serve}(SD'', \text{call}(C'')) \xrightarrow{last\_comp\_call} S \parallel U \parallel S_S \parallel U_S \parallel B \cup SD''} \text{[LAST-COMP-CALL]}$$

Decay. The [DECAY] rule is defined with the purpose of keeping the *blackboard* (B) clean over the time.

$$\frac{B' = B - compositions(B, SD)}{S_S \parallel U_S \parallel B \cup SD \xrightarrow{\tau} S_S \parallel U_S \parallel B'} \text{[DECAY]}$$

This rule grants the system the capability of cleaning out the blackboard from obsolete services. The operation also requires to clean out the composed services in which the service targeted to be removed is involved. Label τ is used here to denote a time-related recurrent operation. No specific frequency or rate is defined by our formal specification. Yet, we assume [DECAY] executes frequently enough to clean up stale service descriptors, but not so much frequently to hinder the activity of services.

4   Architecture

This section discusses how a rigorously engineered solution for semantic self-composition of services based on our model can be attained. In particular, because of space limitations, our discussion is articulated in two parts, describing the design and implementation phases of our solution, respectively. More precisely, in the first part we show how a software architecture for our model can be constructed by leveraging the LINDA coordination model; whereas in the second part we show how such a software architecture can be reified into some actual JVM technology via the TuSoW framework.

4.1   Linda-Based Architecture

A LINDA system is composed by a number of agents interacting via tuple spaces. Our formal model as well can be briefly described in terms of agents interacting via blackboard, enacting a particular protocol. Thus, drawing a software architecture based on LINDA for our framework essentially requires *(i)* the blackboard behaviour to be mimicked via some tuple space, and *(ii)* users and service agents to be designed as agents performing LINDA operations on that tuple space.

We stick to a logic-based interpretation of LINDA, where both tuples and templates are first-order logic terms, and tuples are matched against templates via logic unification. Furthermore, we assume a wide spectrum of LINDA primitives are available for agents, including *(i)* LINDA's classic primitives – namely, out, in, rd –, with their ordinary generative and suspensive semantics; *(ii)* bulk primitives – such as out_all, in_all, rd_all –, letting agents insert, consume, or read multiple tuples at once; and *(iii)* predicative primitives – such as inp, rdp –, which differ from their classic counterparts because they are not suspensive.

Of course, given that the blackboard abstraction in our model is not a simple container of information – as it is in charge of automatically composing services as soon as they are deployed –, it cannot be simply reduced to a tuple space. To tackle this issue, at the architectural level, we introduce the notion of *helper agent*. An helper agent is a reactive entity which is in charge of implementing some transition rule from the model semantics described in Sect. 3.2. In other words, we translate each transition rule from Sect. 3.2 into an helper agent implementing it on the blackboard via LINDA operations. Thus, there exists a fixed number of helper agents, whose names and functions are described below. For the sake of readability, helper agents are named using the pattern

$$To\{EventName\}\{MessageName\}Agent$$

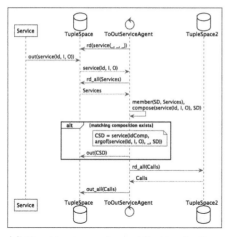

(a) Reaction to service publication in the tuple space

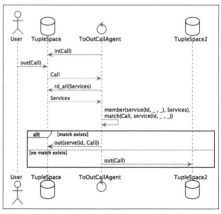

(b) Handling a call request that cannot be served

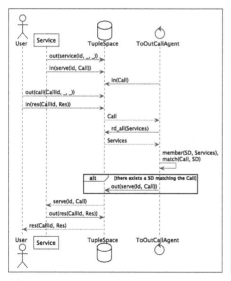

(c) Serving a call request with a single service

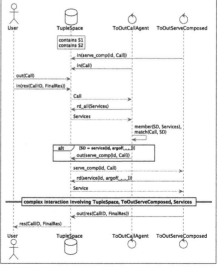

(d) Serving a call request with a composed service

Fig. 1. An overview of the most salient interactions among the system components during the publication, composition, and request serving phases

where {*EventName*} denotes the invocation of some LINDA operation on the blackboard tuple spaces – commonly, an out operation –, whereas {*MessageName*} is the tuple or template characterising that LINDA operation.

Accordingly, in the following we present a semi-formal definition of the LINDA-based architecture of our model via UML sequence diagrams. User agents publish the requests on the tuple space by means of the out primitive. Subsequently, they perform an in operation, waiting for a tuple to consume. Service agents, likewise, follow the same pattern of interactions. They publish their service descriptor and they consequently wait for tuples to be consumed.

Service Descriptor Publication and Service Composition. The transition rule [COMPOSE] has been implemented within the *ToOutServiceAgent* component. It reacts to the service publication action ([PUBLISH-SD]), evaluating all its viable compositions. If any, the composed service is generated and published on the *TupleSpace*. Figure 1a shows the full chain of interactions starting from the single service descriptor publication action to the subsequent composition evaluation and potential publication. Note that after a service descriptor is published, a list of unhandled call requests stored in a secondary tuple space is published on the primary tuple space. A more detailed description is provided in the following paragraphs.

Prove a Query Request. Operations [POS-PROVE] and [NEG-PROVE] are implemented by the *ToOutQueryAgent* component. It reacts to the publication action ([PUBLISH-QUERY]) of a query message, evaluating if there is an existing service configuration able to fulfil it: a positive result is returned *iff* any exists.

Serve a Call Request. Operations [CONSUME-CALL] and [SERVE-CALL] are implemented by the *ToOutCallAgent*. It reacts to the publication of a call request and evaluates if the current system configuration is capable of serving it—i.e. if there exists some service descriptor for the request at hand. Figure 1b shows the actions performed when a published call request cannot be fulfilled by any available service. Briefly, the matching among the call request and the available service is computed. If there exists no service that successfully matches the call, it is moved to another (secondary) tuple space, which is explicitly aimed at storing pending call requests which cannot be currently served. These calls are eventually moved back to the (primary) *TupleSpace* as soon as a service publication occurs—as the new service may make it possible to serve some of them. The involvement of two tuple spaces is an optimisation aimed at avoiding the waste of computational resources due to the processing of (currently) unsatisfiable calls.

Conversely, when the current system configuration allows the fulfillment of the call request, the request message is taken and processed. Figure 1c shows the serving of a call request in case it exists a single service that may wholly fulfil it. The opposite case is presented in Fig. 1d. In this case the rule [COMP-CALL], implemented by *ToOutCallAgent*, occurs; while operations

[CONSUME-COMP-CALL], [SERVE-COMP-CALL] and [LAST-COMP-CALL] are performed within the *ToOutServeComposedAgent* control flow.

4.2   Implementation Details

The aforementioned LINDA-based architecture is implemented upon TuSoW. Briefly, the elements composing the system are *(i)* the LINDA-like tuple space, i.e. blackboard, *(ii)* a number of agents, and *(iii)* a fixed number of helper agents.

TuSoW defines the LINDA-like tuple space as the so-called `LogicSpace` architectural entity, representing an abstract version of an actual tuple space that can be provided in several versions—e.g.. local, remote, inspectable. TuSoW agents are implemented as simple control flows—i.e. threads. We implement the user and service agent entities as threads that communicate among them through the shared `LogicSpace`. Helper agents, in turn, are implemented as threads augmented with a tuProlog engine [10]. In particular, they hold reasoning capabilities exploited within the system to evaluate *(i)* the viable service compositions, and *(ii)* the match degree between a request message and a service descriptor.

Adopting TuSoW makes handling the non-determinism of LINDA read and consume operations challenging. In order to cope with it, the inspectable version of the `LogicSpace` comes to our aid, since it presents an inspectable interface, allowing tuple space state to be observed. To clarify how the feature is exploited within our implementation, an example is provided. An helper agent constantly consumes tuples matching a tuple template. For instance, the *ToOutServiceAgent* consumes tuples unifying with a tuple template that resembles a service descriptor, in order to react to a service descriptor publication. However, when many service descriptors coexist in the tuple space, such operation consumes one of them in a non-deterministic manner. Therefore it might return any service that is currently published. To cope with it, the inspectable feature of the tuple space is exploited by filtering out the tuples that do not belong to the tuple space internal writing event. In other words, a routine is bound to the internal writing event of the tuple space, filtering out the tuples resulting from the writing event that do not comply with the provided tuple template.

5   Case Study

A real-world scenario is here provided. Due to space reasons, we only show its formal representation. The corresponding implementation leveraging a TuSoW-based system architecture is publicly available[1].

Let us assume that there exists a system holding a knowledge base composed of the taxonomy of concepts depicted in Fig. 2. Let us now consider the system as including two services willing to advertise themselves by publishing their service descriptors, respectively SD and SD', on the blackboard (B). We assume the formal parameters (input and output) of those services are defined using concepts

---

[1] https://gitlab.com/ashleycaselli/tusow-semantic-composition.

that belong to the knowledge base of the system. In particular, we define SD as the service that given a city name is able to provide its GPS coordinates. In turn, we define SD' as the service that provides the current temperature (in Kelvin degrees) at the location described by some GPS coordinates.

Formally, service descriptors are described as follows:

$$SD = \texttt{service}(name : City, \ GPS)$$
$$SD' = \texttt{service}(loc : GPS, \ Kelvin)$$

(for the sake of simplicity, we define GPS coordinates as a single value uniquely identifying a city), whereas the service initial configurations are as follows:

$$S_0 = \texttt{publish}(SD) \cdot \texttt{accept}(\texttt{service}(Q)) \cdot S_0$$
$$S_0' = \texttt{publish}(SD') \cdot \texttt{accept}(\texttt{service}(Q')) \cdot S_0'$$

We also assume the blackboard is initially empty ($B_0 = \emptyset$), and that the system includes a user willing to perform a service invocation:

$$U_0 = Req \cdot \texttt{res}(v) \cdot \texttt{halt}$$

where $Req = \texttt{call}(name : City(Geneva), \ Temperature)$ denotes an invocation to a service computing the current temperature for a city (namely, Geneva), and returning a temperature through any possible measurement unit. Under these hypotheses, the initial state of the system is $Sys_0 = S_0 \parallel S_0' \parallel U_0 \parallel B_0$.

The publication of the service descriptors (operation [PUBLISH-SD]) changes the state of the system as follows:

$$Sys_1 = \underbrace{\texttt{accept}(\texttt{service}(Q)) \cdot S_0}_{S_1} \parallel \overbrace{\texttt{accept}(\texttt{service}(Q')) \cdot S_0'}^{S_1'} \parallel U_0 \parallel \overbrace{SD \cup SD'}^{B_1}$$

Eventually, their publication triggers the component that computes the semantic matching among the two service descriptors, computing all the possible compositions (operation [COMPOSE]). In particular, in this case the compose operation detects that the services represented by SD and SD' are composable w.r.t the parameter named loc. We call $\widehat{SD} = SD \stackrel{loc}{\texttt{argof}} SD'$ the composed

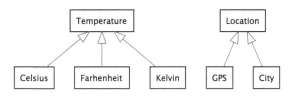

Fig. 2. An illustration of a taxonomy of concepts used in the presented case study

service attained by composing SD and SD'. The composed service $\widehat{SD}$ is then published on the blackboard, which can now be described as follows:

$$B_2 = SD \cup SD' \cup \widehat{SD}$$

The presence of $\widehat{SD}$ on the blackboard is what makes the user's invocation satisfiable. Suppose now that the user publishes (operation [PUBLISH-CALL]) its call request (Req). This would lead to a system state like the following:

$$Sys_3 = S_1 \parallel S_1' \parallel U_0 \parallel \underbrace{SD \cup SD' \cup \widehat{SD} \cup Req}_{B_3}$$

According to the current system configuration (Sys_3) there is no simple service capable of serving the request. However, the request may be fulfilled using the composed service $\widehat{SD}$. In more details, $\widehat{SD}$ and Req are compatible because *(i)* the input ($I_{\widehat{SD}}$) of the composed service $\widehat{SD}$ and the input of the request (I_{Req}) hold the *exact* match degree, and *(ii)* the output ($O_{\widehat{SD}}$) of the composed service $\widehat{SD}$ and the output of the request (O_{Req}) hold the *subsume* match degree according to the provided taxonomy. Formally:

$$I_{\widehat{SD}} \equiv I_{Req} \wedge O_{\widehat{SD}} \sqsubseteq O_{Req}$$

The call request publication triggers the helper agent that is in charge of handling the request message. Such component, leveraging a Prolog engine for reasoning purposes, computes the semantic matching among the request and the available services. In this case, the reasoning process leads to the solution proposed above, inferring that the request may only be served by the composed service $\widehat{SD}$. In order to manage the execution of all the services involved in the composition, another helper agent is triggered (operation [COMP-CALL] is executed). Formally:

$$B_4 = SD \cup SD' \cup \widehat{SD} \cup \texttt{serve\_comp}(\widehat{SD}, \texttt{call}(...))$$

The helping agent is also in charge of collecting the intermediary responses that each service provides, and of providing the final response. Each time a service is triggered to serve the call, it computes the result and publishes it as Res message on the blackboard (operation [SERVE-COMP-CALL]). For the sake of brevity we only show one round of the "service execution-response publication" loop:

$$B_5 = SD \cup SD' \cup \widehat{SD} \cup \texttt{serve}(SD_x, \texttt{call}_x(...))$$

where SD_x and $\texttt{call}_x$ represent respectively the service descriptor of the x-th service of the composition and the call request that is served by such service.

Finally, operation [LAST-COMP-CALL] is executed and the user agent gets the result.

$$B_6 = SD \cup SD' \cup \widehat{SD}$$
$$U_6 = \texttt{halt}$$

6 Conclusion

This paper proposes a solution for the semantic self-composition of services, exploiting tuple-based coordination. We provide an end-to-end description of the engineering challenges hidden in the production of such sorts of systems, and sketch the formalisation of a middleware supporting *(i)* the self-composition of services, at deploy time, and *(ii)* the transparent invocation of the composed services from the client-side. In particular, we rely on a central blackboard used by service providers to advertise their own service descriptors, and in charge of orchestrating the execution of composed services. In this way, clients may invoke both composed and simple service through a uniform API.

Accordingly, the design of our solution is deliberately minimal as our focus is on the engineering of an actual implementation. In particular, the actual design of our middleware leverages *(i)* LINDA-like tuple spaces exploiting logic terms as both clauses and templates, and *(ii)* logic programming to provide the system components with semantic reasoning. Finally, a prototype implementation is described exploiting the TuSoW coordination technology, and the tuProlog logic reasoner.

We consider this work as a starting point for a number of research directions. In fact, in the future, we plan to assess different strategies for implementing our model, from both the theoretical and technological perspectives. For instance, we are planning the exploitation of different matching mechanisms – possibly modelling semantic matching as a similarity function rather than a binary relation –, as well as different interaction protocols for the helper agents used in our prototype—possibly focusing on the scalability of service composition.

Acknowledgements. The authors would like to thanks the anonymous reviewers for their valuable remarks.

This work has been partially supported by the H2020 Project "AI4EU" (G.A. 825619).

References

1. Ben Mahfoudh, H., Di Marzo Serugendo, G., Naja, N., Abdennadher, N.: Learning-based coordination model for spontaneous self-composition of reliable services in a distributed system. Int. J. Softw. Tools Technol. Transfer **22**(4), 417–436 (2020). https://doi.org/10.1007/s10009-020-00557-0
2. Benatallah, B., Dumas, M., Fauvet, M.C., Rabhi, F.A.: Towards patterns of web services composition. In: Rabhi, F.A., Gorlatch, S. (eds.) Patterns and Skeletons for Parallel and Distributed Computing, pp. 265–296. Springer, London (2003). https://doi.org/10.1007/978-1-4471-0097-3_10
3. Bonjean, N., Gleizes, M.P., Maurel, C., Migeon, F.: SCoRe: a self-organizing multi-agent system for decision making in dynamic software development processes. In: International Conference on Agents and Artificial Intelligence (ICAART) (2013). (short paper)
4. Caselli, A.: Logic-based coordination: a semantic approach to self-composition of services. Master's thesis, Alma Mater Studiorum-Università di Bologna, School of Engineering (2019). http://amslaurea.unibo.it/17984

5. Ciatto, G., Di Marzo Serugendo, G., Louvel, M., Mariani, S., Omicini, A., Zambonelli, F.: Twenty years of coordination technologies: COORDINATION contribution to the state of art. J. Log. Algebraic Methods Program. **113**, 1–25 (2020). https://doi.org/10.1016/j.jlamp.2020.100531
6. Ciatto, G., Rizzato, L., Omicini, A., Mariani, S.: TuSoW: tuple spaces for edge computing. In: The 28th International Conference on Computer Communications and Networks (ICCCN 2019), Valencia, Spain, 29 July–1 August 2019. IEEE (2019). https://doi.org/10.1109/ICCCN.2019.8846916
7. De Angelis, F.L.: A logic-based coordination middleware for self-organising systems: distributed reasoning based on many-valued logics. Ph.D. thesis, University of Geneva, School of Social Sciences - Information Systems (2017)
8. De Nicola, R., Ferrari, G.L., Pugliese, R.: KLAIM: a kernel language for agents interaction and mobility. IEEE Trans. Softw. Eng. **24**(5), 315–330 (1998). https://doi.org/10.1109/32.685256
9. Degas, A.: Auto-structuration de trafic temps-réel multi-objectif et multi-critère dans un monde virtuel. Ph.D. thesis, Université de Toulouse III - Paul Sabatier, IRIT - UMR 5505, Toulouse, France (2020)
10. Denti, E., Omicini, A., Ricci, A.: tuProlog: a light-weight prolog for internet applications and infrastructures. In: Ramakrishnan, I.V. (ed.) PADL 2001. LNCS, vol. 1990, pp. 184–198. Springer, Heidelberg (2001). https://doi.org/10.1007/3-540-45241-9_13
11. Di Napoli, C., Giordano, M., Németh, Z., Tonellotto, N.: Using chemical reactions to model service composition. In: 2nd International Workshop on Self-organizing Architectures (SOAR 2010), pp. 43–50. ACM, New York (2010). https://doi.org/10.1145/1809036.1809047
12. Freeman, E., Arnold, K., Hupfer, S.: JavaSpaces Principles, Patterns, and Practice. Addison-Wesley Longman Ltd., Essex (1999)
13. Frei, R., Şerbănuţă, T.F., Di Marzo Serugendo, G.: Self-organising assembly systems formally specified in Maude. J. Ambient Intell. Humaniz. Comput. **5**(4), 491–510 (2012). https://doi.org/10.1007/s12652-012-0159-2
14. Gabillon, Y., Calvary, G., Fiorino, H.: Composing interactive systems by planning. In: 4th French-Speaking Conference on Mobility and Ubiquity Computing (UbiMob 2008), pp. 37–40. ACM, New York (2007). https://doi.org/10.1145/1376971.1376979
15. Gelernter, D.: Generative communication in Linda. ACM Trans. Program. Lang. Syst. **7**(1), 80–112 (1985). https://doi.org/10.1145/2363.2433
16. Gorrieri, R.: Labeled transition systems. Process Algebras for Petri Nets. MTCSAES, pp. 15–34. Springer, Cham (2017). https://doi.org/10.1007/978-3-319-55559-1_2
17. Kalasapur, S., Kumar, M., Shirazi, B.A.: Dynamic service composition in pervasive computing. IEEE Trans. Parallel Distrib. Syst. **18**(7), 907–918 (2007). https://doi.org/10.1109/TPDS.2007.1039
18. Lemos, A.L., Daniel, F., Benatallah, B.: Web service composition: a survey of techniques and tools. ACM Comput. Surv. **48**(3), 1–41 (2015). https://doi.org/10.1145/2831270
19. Louvel, M., Pacull, F.: LINC: a compact yet powerful coordination environment. In: Kühn, E., Pugliese, R. (eds.) COORDINATION 2014. LNCS, vol. 8459, pp. 83–98. Springer, Heidelberg (2014). https://doi.org/10.1007/978-3-662-43376-8_6
20. Martin, D., et al.: OWL-S: Semantic markup for web services. W3C Member Submission 22 (2004)

21. Murphy, A.L., Picco, G.P., Roman, G.C.: LIME: a coordination model and middleware supporting mobility of hosts and agents. ACM Trans. Softw. Eng. Methodol. (TOSEM) **15**(3), 279–328 (2006). https://doi.org/10.1145/1151695.1151698

22. Omicini, A.: On the semantics of tuple-based coordination models. In: 1999 ACM Symposium on Applied Computing (SAC 1999), 28 February–2 March 1999, pp. 175–182. ACM, New York (1999). https://doi.org/10.1145/298151.298229

23. Omicini, A., Zambonelli, F.: Coordination for Internet application development. Auton. Agent. Multi-Agent Syst. **2**(3), 251–269 (1999). https://doi.org/10.1023/A:1010060322135

24. Talantikite, H.N., Aissani, D., Boudjlida, N.: Semantic annotations for web services discovery and composition. Comput. Stand. Interfaces **31**(6), 1108–1117 (2009). https://doi.org/10.1016/j.csi.2008.09.041

25. Talib, M.A., Yang, Z.: Semi-automatic code generation of static web services composition. In: Student Conference on Engineering, Sciences and Technology, pp. 132–137. IEEE, January 2005. https://doi.org/10.1109/SCONES.2004.1564784

26. Vallée, M., Ramparany, F., Vercouter, L.: A multi-agent system for dynamic service composition in ambient intelligence environments. In: PERVASIVE 2005, Advances in Pervasive Computing, vol. 191, pp. 175–182. Austrian Comp. Soc. (OCG) (2005)

27. Viroli, M.: On competitive self-composition in pervasive services. Sci. Comput. Program. **78**(5), 556–568 (2013). https://doi.org/10.1016/j.scico.2012.10.002

A Dynamic Logic for Systems with Predicate-Based Communication

Rolf Hennicker$^{(\boxtimes)}$ and Martin Wirsing$^{(\boxtimes)}$

Ludwig-Maximilians-Universität München, München, Germany
hennicke@pst.ifi.lmu.de, wirsing@ifi.lmu.de

Abstract. Attribute-based broadcast communication is a novel paradigm for modelling interactions in collective systems. Used by several new languages (such as SCEL, CARMA, and AbC), it enables senders and groups of receivers to interact by considering predicates over their current attribute values. In these languages systems are modelled by the parallel composition of components, each component being equipped with a local process description. In this paper we complement this local view by a global requirements specification format that allows us to specify abstract properties, like safety and liveness, as well as allowed and forbidden interaction scenarios. We propose a first-order dynamic logic whose atomic actions are tailored to the needs of systems of collaborating components with multi-cast communication. As implementation language we consider (a variant of) the AbC calculus and show how our global ensemble specifications can be realised with local process declarations. Our correctness notion relates the semantics of global specifications to the labelled transition system semantics of AbC systems.

Keywords: Ensemble · Collective adaptive system · Component · Dynamic logic · Multi-cast communication · Global behaviour specification · Ensemble realisation · Ensemble transition system

1 Introduction

Collective systems - such as ensembles [22], organic computing systems [25], and collective adaptive systems [16] - consist of many dynamically interacting autonomic entities. For coordinating collective systems, the classical "single-entity-to-single-entity" communication of message-based and channel-based calculi is not adequate. Interaction has also to consider the environment of the system and more general properties of the system than explicit communication channels and the identities of system members.

Predicate-based communication is a novel paradigm which abstracts from the communication channels and the identities of the members of the collective system. It provides synchronous "one-to-many" multi-cast communication between a single sender and a group of receivers; communication partners are not determined at design time but are dynamically connected at run-time by considering

© Springer Nature Switzerland AG 2020
T. Margaria and B. Steffen (Eds.): ISoLA 2020, LNCS 12477, pp. 224–242, 2020.
https://doi.org/10.1007/978-3-030-61470-6_14

properties of the system and its environment. Properties are expressed by predicates and depend on the current attribute values of the members of the system and possibly on other parameters such as space and time. Therefore the term "attribute-based" communication is often used as well.

Several new languages use attribute-based communication for modelling interactions. The Service Component Ensemble Language (SCEL) [6,19] is a language for programming ensembles of autonomic computing components. Attribute-based communication is used by components to dynamically organise themselves into ensembles. SCEL was the first language to use this communication style. The CARMA [4] language aims at the specification and analysis of collective adaptive systems. It provides predicate-based broadcast communication as well as point-to-point unicast communication. The AbC [1,2] calculus focusses on a minimal set of primitives for defining attribute-based communication.

In all these languages, systems are modelled by the parallel composition of components, each component being equipped with a local process description. Often it is difficult to extract and understand the *global* effects of a collective system knowing only the *local* behaviours of their components. Therefore we are interested to complement these local views by a global view on collective systems based on the paradigm of predicate-based communication, i.e. we want to (1) deal with (synchronous) one-to-many broadcast communication and (2) formulate requirements for sender and receivers through logical predicates.

In this paper, we propose a novel logical framework for developing collective systems from a global perspective following the paradigm of predicate-based communication. The framework consists of ensemble specifications written in a dynamic logic [9] style, of ensemble realisations written in a variant of the AbC calculus, and of a notion of correctness relating an ensemble realisation with an ensemble specification.

A collective system or ensemble is given by a finite set of typed components. Specifications describe collaborations which are typical for the ensemble. They are expressed in a new instance of first-order dynamic logic suitable to specify global, predicate-based interaction behaviours. Two kinds of atomic actions - operation invocations and communication actions - are specifically tailored to the domain of collaborative systems. An operation invocation consists of an invocation predicate and an operation call; the latter can only be executed if all operation arguments fulfill the invocation predicate. A communication action expresses (synchronous) multi-cast message passing and by relying on the evaluation of predicates the establishment of communications is more flexible than direct binding of sender and receivers. Specifically, a communication action consists of a communication predicate and a message type binding a sender, a set of receivers and some arguments; communication can only happen if sender, receivers and parameters satisfy the predicate.

An ensemble specification consists of an ensemble signature and a set of first-order dynamic logic axioms. The semantics of an ensemble specification is defined over ensemble transition systems (ETS); it is given by the class of its models, i.e. by all ETS which satisfy the axioms of the specification. This allows us to define a refinement relation between ensemble specifications by model class inclusion.

Finally, we study ensemble realisations and a formal correctness notion. An ensemble realisation is written in a variant of the AbC calculus. For each single component type, we define the local behaviour of its components by an AbC expression. All instances of the type must respect the prescribed behaviour. The realisation is correct, if the ensemble transition system generated by the AbC implementation satisfies the (logical) sentences of the requirements specification.

This work can be seen as further step towards a semantic-based development methodology for ensemble-based systems. An early approach is the mathematically-based methodology of the ASCENS project [23,24] where requirements for autonomic ensembles are specified in two dedicated languages SOTA [3] and ARE [21] for autonomic systems. The HELENA development approach [12] for ensembles uses linear temporal logic formulas for expressing goal-oriented requirements [13,17]. The framework of multiparty session types [15] and the recently proposed Klaimographies [5] use process calculi to describe global and local behaviours. They are not aimed at a logic to specify requirements of collective systems which is our main concern.

Similarly to [11,14], we study a logic for ensemble specifications and a correctness notion. There the focus was on dynamically changing ensembles which interact through point-to-point message exchange. Here we consider synchronous multi-cast predicate-based communication where, for simplicity, the carriers of the ensembles do not change.

The paper is organised as follows: In Sect. 2 component systems are introduced as our underlying notion of ensemble. In Sects. 3 and 4 we define syntax and semantics of ensemble specifications. Then, in Sect. 5 we study correct ensemble realisations written in a variant of AbC. We conclude in Sect. 6.

2   Component Systems

In our approach a collective system consists of a finite set of typed interacting components. In this section we introduce the notions of type, signature, and state of a component system. Each state is formalised as a first-order structure with partial functions; its properties are specified by first-order logic formulas [7].

Component types. To classify components we use component types. A *component type* with name ct is a triple $(ct, attrs, opns)$ declaring a finite set of attributes *attrs* (for storing data) and a finite set of operations *opns* callable by the component instances of type ct. We write $attrs[ct]$ for *attrs* and $opns[ct]$ for *opns*.

An *attribute* is just a name a. An *operation* is of the form $op : n$ where $n \geq 0$ is the arity of op determining the number of arguments for which the operation can be called. For simplicity, we do not use specific types here, neither for the values of attributes nor for the arguments of operations.

Example 1. As a running example we consider a robot rescue ensemble. The ideas of the example stem from a case study [20] performed in the ASCENS-project [23,24]. In a robot rescue ensemble components of type Victim are supposed to be rescued by components of type Rescuer. The information where a victim can be found is transmitted by components of type Landmark. Each type of component has an attribute pos storing the current component position. Components of type Victim and Landmark have also an attribute bdist determining their broadcast distance. Components of type Landmark can walk around by their operation walk (with arity 0) while components of type Rescuer can perform a directed walk towards a given position by their operation move with arity 1. The three component types are graphically represented in Fig. 1.

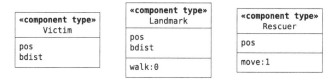

Fig. 1. Component types for the robot rescue ensemble

Component system signature. Let CT be a finite set of component types. A *component system signature* over CT is a first-order signature $C\Sigma(CT)$, simply denoted by $C\Sigma$ if CT is clear from the context, such that

1. the set of predicate symbols preds$[C\Sigma]$ contains
   - a unary predicate symbol ct for each $ct \in CT$,
   - two (predefined) unary predicate symbols cmp and cmps, and
   - a set of standard predicate symbols, for instance binary predicate symbols for expressing equality " $=$ " and membership " $\in$ ";
2. the set of functions symbols functs$[C\Sigma]$ contains
   - constant function symbols ct.allInst for each $ct \in CT$,
   - a set of standard function symbols, in particular for denoting functions on sets like union " $\cup$ ", intersection " $\cap$ ", etc., and
   - a unary function symbol a for each attribute $a \in \bigcup_{ct \in CT}$ attrs$[ct]$.

The predicate symbol cmp will be used to represent the (finite) set of all component instances of any component type while the predicate symbol cmps will be used to represent the powerset of sets of component instances (of any type). For an attribute a and term t we write $t.a$ for the term $a(t)$.

Component system states. For modelling (global) states of component systems we use first-order structures which give values to attributes. Let $C\Sigma(CT)$ be a component system signature. A *component system state* is a first-order $C\Sigma(CT)$-structure $c\sigma$ which satisfies the following constraints:

1. The carrier set $|c\sigma|$ contains, for each $ct \in CT$, a finite set $cinsts_{ct}$ of *component instance identifiers* (simply called component instances) of type ct such that the sets $cinsts_{ct}$ are pairwise disjoint. Moreover, we assume that $|c\sigma|$ contains all subsets of $\bigcup_{ct \in CT} cinsts_{ct}$ as elements.

2. Predicate symbols in $\mathsf{preds}[C\Sigma]$ are interpreted in $c\sigma$ as follows:
   - For each predicate symbol ct with $ct \in CT$, $ct^{c\sigma} = cinsts_{ct}$.
   - $\mathsf{cmp}^{c\sigma} = \bigcup\limits_{ct \in CT} cinsts_{ct}$ is the disjoint union of all sets of component instances.
   - $\mathsf{cmps}^{c\sigma} = \mathcal{P}(\mathsf{cmp}^{c\sigma}$ is the powerset of $\mathsf{cmp}^{c\sigma}$.
   - The equality symbol is interpreted as the identity of elements, the membership predicate as the usual membership test for elements $v \in \mathsf{cmp}^{c\sigma}$ and $vs \in \mathsf{cmps}^{c\sigma}$, and similarly all other standard predicate symbols.
3. Function symbols in $\mathsf{functs}[C\Sigma]$ are interpreted in $c\sigma$ as follows:
   - For each $ct \in CT$, $ct.\mathsf{allInst}^{c\sigma} = cinsts_{ct}$.
   - Standard function symbols are interpreted as expected. They are undefined if the arguments do not fit.
   - For each attribute a, $a^{c\sigma} : |c\sigma| \to |c\sigma|$ is a partial function such that $a^{c\sigma(v)}$ is defined if and only if there is a component type $ct \in CT$ such that $a \in \mathsf{attrs}[ct]$ and $v \in cinsts_{ct}$.

The set of component system states over $C\Sigma$ is denoted by $States(C\Sigma)$.

$C\Sigma$-formulas and satisfaction relation. Properties of states are specified in first-order predicate logic. In contrast to the classical calculus we use partial functions for the interpretation of function symbols and for variable environments.

Let X be a countable set of variables. For each $C\Sigma$-structure $c\sigma$, we denote the set of terms over $C\Sigma$ and X by $T(C\Sigma, X)$ and the set of first-order $C\Sigma$-formulas over X by $\mathrm{Fm}(C\Sigma, X)$. A *variable environment* is a partial function $\rho : X \to |c\sigma|$ and the set of such environments is denoted by $Env(X, c\sigma)$. We denote by $\rho_\perp$ the environment which is undefined for each $x \in X$. Updating a set of variables $\{x_i \mid i \in I\}$ with values v_i for each x_i is denoted by $\rho[x_i \mapsto v_i \mid i \in I]$ and by $\rho[x \mapsto v]$ if there is only one variable x to be updated. The *interpretation* of a term e in $c\sigma \in States(C\Sigma)$ w.r.t. $\rho \in Env(X, c\sigma)$ is denoted by $I_\rho^\sigma(e)$.

We write $c\sigma, \rho \models_{C\Sigma} \pi$ if a formula $\pi \in \mathrm{Fm}(C\Sigma, X)$ is satisfied by a component system state $c\sigma \in States(C\Sigma)$ w.r.t. a variable environment $\rho \in Env(X, c\sigma)$, i.e. $\rho : X \to |c\sigma|$.

Example 2. Let $C\Sigma_{\mathsf{Rescue}}$ be the component system signature built over the component types in Example 1. Let v be a variable whose current value in an environment ρ is a component instance of type Victim. We assume that there is a binary function symbol dist for computing the distance between two positions. Let $\mathsf{receivers}$ be a variable and π_{help} the following $C\Sigma_{\mathsf{Rescue}}$-formula:

$\forall \mathsf{x}.(\mathsf{x} \in \mathsf{receivers} \iff$
$(\mathsf{Landmark}(\mathsf{x}) \lor \mathsf{Rescuer}(\mathsf{x})) \land \mathsf{dist}(\mathsf{v.pos},\mathsf{x.pos}) \leq \mathsf{v.bdist})$

The formula is satisfied in a component system state $c\sigma \in States(C\Sigma_{\mathsf{Rescue}})$ if the value of variable $\mathsf{receivers}$ is the set of all landmarks and rescuers which are within the victim's broadcast distance. $\square$

3   Ensemble Specifications

The dynamics of ensemble-based systems relies on the execution of component operations and on the interaction between components via message exchange. We consider synchronous one-to-many communication where a single sender broad-casts messages that are simultaneously received by several (possibly none) receivers. From the global perspective the relevant point is to specify which messages are exchanged between which senders and receivers. Transferring the ideas of attribute-based communication of process calculi (SCEL [6], AbC [1,2], CARMA [4]) to the global system level our idea is to introduce a logic which allows us to describe admissible interactions by selecting sender and receivers through the evaluation of predicates. Such predicates will be first-order formulas over component system signatures; messages are classified by message types.

Ensemble Signature. A *message type* is of the form $mt : n$ where mt is a message type name and $n \geq 0$ is an arity determining the number of parameters that can be transmitted by a message of this type. In contrast to HELENA (see e.g. [12]), we do not restrict here the types of components that are allowed to exchange certain messages. So, in principle, any kind of message can be exchanged between any kind of component. An *ensemble signature* $E\Sigma = (mts, C\Sigma(CT))$ consists of a finite set mts of message types and a component system signature $C\Sigma$ over a finite set CT of component types.

Example 3. In a robot rescue ensemble we use two message types help:1 and rescue:0. Messages of type help have one parameter passing the position where a victim is located. Once a rescuer is arrived at a victim's position the victim is notified with a rescue message. The ensemble signature is then given by $E\Sigma_{\mathsf{Rescue}} = (mts_{\mathsf{Rescue}}, C\Sigma_{\mathsf{Rescue}})$ where $mts_{\mathsf{Rescue}} = \{\mathsf{help:1, rescue:0}\}$ and $C\Sigma_{\mathsf{Rescue}}$ is the component system signature in Example 2.   □

An ensemble specification describes, by means of a logical framework, properties of ensemble-based collective systems. It takes a global view focusing on the desired (and not desired) interactions between ensemble participants. To specify properties of such systems we use formulas in the style of first-order dynamic logic [9]. Such formulas allow us to specify abstract safety and liveness requirements as well as concrete scenarios. Like in first-order dynamic logic we use assignments as atomic programs but additionally we use two kinds of atomic actions expressing operation invocation and communication. In contrast to our previous approaches [11,14] communication actions express (synchronous) multicast message passing and the establishment of communications relies on the evaluation of predicates instead of explicit binding between sender and receiver.

In the following we assume that $E\Sigma = (mts, C\Sigma(CT))$ is an ensemble signature and that X is a countable set of variables. We refer with $\mathsf{opns}(C\Sigma)$ to the set $\bigcup_{ct \in CT} \mathsf{opns}[ct]$ of all operations occurring in component types of CT.

Actions. Three kinds of atomic actions are distinguished:

(a) A *communication action* has the form

$$\pi : (a_1 \rightarrow a_2).mt(a_3, \ldots, a_n)$$

where $\pi \in \mathrm{Fm}(C\varSigma, X)$ is a first-order formula, called *communication predicate*, $mt \in mts$ is a message type of arity n-2, and $a_1, \ldots, a_n$ are arguments. An argument is either a term $e \in T(C\varSigma, X)$ or it has the form $\mathbf{upd}\,x$ where $x \in X$ is a variable to be equipped with a new value. The idea is that a_1 represents a component instance, the sender of the message, and a_2 represents a (possibly empty) set of component instances, the receivers of the message, while $a_3, \ldots, a_n$ represent actual parameters. As described in the semantics later on (rule (comm) in Fig. 3), the communication can only happen if sender, receivers and parameters fulfill the communication predicate π. If an argument is a term then it must be evaluated in the current component system state and environment; if it is an update expression $\mathbf{upd}\,x$ then a value must be assigned to x such that the predicate π is satisfied. Since, in general, different values for x may be chosen to satisfy π the use of update expressions as arguments can express non-deterministic choice. In particular, a communication action of the form

$$\mathbf{true} : (\mathbf{upd}\,x_1 \rightarrow \mathbf{upd}\,x_2).mt(\mathbf{upd}\,x_3, \ldots, \mathbf{upd}\,x_n)$$

stands for any message of type mt with arbitrary sender, receivers, and parameter values. They are stored in the variables $x_1, \ldots, x_n$. This action can be abbreviated just by mt (assuming the variable names are irrelevant).

(b) An *operation invocation action* has the form

$$\pi : a_1.op(a_2, \ldots, a_n)$$

where $\pi \in \mathrm{Fm}(C\varSigma, X)$ is a first-order formula, called *operation invocation predicate*, $op \in \mathsf{opns}(C\varSigma)$ is an operation of arity n-1, and $a_1, \ldots, a_n$ are arguments. The idea is that a_1 represents a component instance for which the operation is invoked and $a_2, \ldots, a_n$ represent actual parameters. As described in the semantics later on (rule (op invoke) in Fig. 3), the operation invocation can only be executed if all arguments fulfill the invocation predicate π. Similarly as above, the use of update expressions in operation invocation actions allows to express non-deterministic choice. In particular, an action of the form $\mathbf{true} : \mathbf{upd}\,x_1.op(\mathbf{upd}\,x_2, \ldots, \mathbf{upd}\,x_n)$ can be abbreviated just by op (assuming the variable names are irrelevant).

(c) A variable assignment has the form $\mathbf{upd}\,x := e$ where $x \in X$ is a variable and $e \in T(C\varSigma, X)$ is a term. As described in the semantics later on (rule (assignment) in Fig. 3), an assignment has the usual effect.

The set $Act(E\varSigma)$ of (structured) actions over $E\varSigma$ is defined by the grammar

$$\alpha ::= a \mid \pi? \mid \alpha; \alpha \mid \alpha + \alpha \mid \alpha^*$$

where a is an atomic action and $\pi?$ is a *test* with $\pi \in \mathrm{Fm}(C\varSigma, X)$. Structured actions are composed by sequential composition "$;$", union "$+$" and iteration

"$*$" as in dynamic logic. Following dynamic logic we can express while-programs and conditional statements by

$$\textbf{while } \pi \textbf{ do } \alpha \textbf{ od} = (\pi?; \alpha)^*; \neg\pi? \qquad \textbf{if } \pi \textbf{ then } \alpha \textbf{ else } \beta \textbf{ fi} = (\pi?; \alpha) + \neg\pi?; \beta$$

Shorthand notations. Let $mts \cup \textsf{opns}(C\Sigma)$ be the set of all communication and operation invocation actions in the sense of the abbreviations explained in part (a) and (b) above. Note that this set is finite by assumption. We write $\textsf{allAct}$ for the composed action obtained by combining with "$+$" all elements of $mts \cup \textsf{opns}(C\Sigma)$. This captures the choice of all actions that are semantically possible in an ensemble transition system; see below. We write $-a$ for the composed action obtained by combining with "$+$" all elements of $(mts \cup \textsf{opns}(C\Sigma)) \backslash \{a\}$.

Ensemble formulas. Ensemble formulas are built like in first-order dynamic logic. They extend first-order formulas by the modal diamond operator (expressing possibility) and thus also by the derived box operator (expressing necessity). Test actions $\pi?$ are built on first-order formulas $\pi \in \text{Fm}(C\Sigma, X)$ (i.e. we do not use the "rich test" variant of dynamic logic [9]). The set $\text{Fm}(E\Sigma, X)$ of *ensemble formulas* over $E\Sigma$ with variables in X is defined by the grammar

$$\varphi ::= \textbf{true} \mid p(t_1, \ldots, t_n) \mid \neg\varphi \mid \varphi \vee \varphi \mid \exists x. \varphi \mid \langle \alpha \rangle \varphi$$

where p is a predicate symbol of arity n, $t_1, \ldots, t_n \in T(C\Sigma, X)$ are terms, $x \in X$, and $\alpha \in Act(E\Sigma)$ is a (structured) action. Formulas of the form $\textbf{true}$ or $p(t_1, \ldots, t_n)$ are *atomic formulas*. We use the usual abbreviations like $\textbf{false}, \varphi \wedge \varphi', \forall x.\varphi$ and the modal box operator $[\alpha]\varphi$ which stands for $\neg\langle\alpha\rangle\neg\varphi$.

Using the shorthand notations for actions we can specify safety properties with $[\textsf{allAct}^*]\varphi$; deadlock freeness is expressed by $[\textsf{allAct}^*]\langle\textsf{allAct}\rangle\textbf{true}$. Liveness properties, like "whenever an action a has happened, an action b can eventually occur", can be expressed by $[\textsf{allAct}^*; a]\langle\textsf{allAct}^*; b\rangle\textbf{true}$. We can also express that an action b must never occur when an action a has happened before: $[\textsf{allAct}^*; a; \textsf{allAct}^*; b]\textbf{false}$.

Definition 1 (Ensemble specification). *An* ensemble specification *$ESpec = (E\Sigma, \Phi)$ consists of an ensemble signature $E\Sigma$ and a set $\Phi \subseteq \text{Fm}(E\Sigma, X)$ of ensemble formulas, called* axioms of ESpec.

Example 4. We provide a requirements specification $ESpec_0 = (E\Sigma_{\textsf{Rescue}}, \Phi_0)$ for robot rescue ensembles. The specification relies on the ensemble signature $E\Sigma_{\textsf{Rescue}}$ of Example 3. Φ_0 consists of the formula in Fig. 2 which uses the predicate π_{help} explained in Example 2. The specification requires for all victims $\textsf{v}$: "Whenever $\textsf{v}$ issues the first time a $\textsf{help}$ message transmitting the victim's position to a set of receivers such that the predicate π_{help} holds (i.e. the receivers are landmarks or rescuers within the broadcast distance of $\textsf{v}$), then it is eventually possible that a rescuer arrives at $\textsf{v}$'s position notifying $\textsf{v}$ about its rescue." (Semantically component instances will be assigned to variables $\textsf{receivers}$ and $\textsf{rescuer}$ such that the predicates π_{help} and π_{rescue} are satisfied.)

```
∀v. Victim(v) ⟹
[(-help)* ; π_help:(v → upd receivers).help(v.pos)]
   ⟨allAct* ; π_rescue:(upd rescuer → {v}).rescue()⟩ true

where π_rescue is: Rescuer(rescuer) ∧ rescuer.pos = v.pos
```

Fig. 2. Requirements specification for robot rescue ensembles

It would be undesired if the first help message would be sent by a landmark (and hence not by a victim). To forbid such behaviours can be expressed by:

$$[(-help)^* ; \text{Landmark}(s) : (\textbf{upd}\ s \rightarrow \textbf{upd}\ rs).help(\textbf{upd}\ p)]\,\textbf{false}$$

4 Semantics of Ensemble Specifications

For the semantic interpretation of ensemble specifications we use ensemble transition systems. Let $E\Sigma = (mts, C\Sigma(CT))$ be an ensemble signature.

Ensemble states. An $E\Sigma$-ensemble state is a pair

$$e\sigma = (ctrl, c\sigma)$$

where $ctrl$ is a global control state recording the current execution state of an ensemble and $c\sigma$ is a component system state over $C\Sigma$. The set of ensemble states over $E\Sigma$ is denoted by $States(E\Sigma)$. In the following we implicitly assume that the control part of an ensemble state $e\sigma$ is $ctrl$ and its component system state is $c\sigma$, and likewise for ensemble states $e\sigma'$, etc.

Labels. In an ensemble transition system two kinds of labels are used on transitions which provide semantic interpretations of the atomic (syntactic) actions (a) and (b) defined in Sect. 3. They use semantic values, in particular component instances and sets of component instances, instead of variables.

(a) A *communication label* $(v_1 \rightarrow v_2).mt(v_3, \dots, v_n)$ expresses a synchronous multi-cast communication where v_1 is a sending component instance transmitting a message of type $mt : n\text{-}2$ with parameter values $v_3, \dots, v_n$ simultaneously to each member of a set v_2 of receiving component instances.

(b) An *operation invocation label* $v_1.op(v_2, \dots, v_n)$ expresses that operation op with arity $n\text{-}1$ is invoked for component instance v_1 with actual parameter values $v_2, \dots, v_n$.

The set of (semantic) labels over $E\Sigma$ is denoted by $Lab(E\Sigma)$.

Ensemble transition systems provide the semantic domain for ensemble-based systems and thus for the interpretation of (logical) ensemble specifications. Their transitions are labelled by communication and operation invocation labels. The former model the coordination between ensemble participants by multi-cast message exchange. They do not modify component system states (but usually the control state of the ensemble). Component system states can be changed by executing component operations.

Definition 2 (Ensemble transition system). *Let $E\Sigma = (mts, C\Sigma(CT))$ be an ensemble signature. An $E\Sigma$-ensemble transition system (ETS) is a tuple*

$$T = (ES, e\sigma_0, Lab(E\Sigma), \rightarrow) \quad \text{such that}$$

- *$ES \subseteq States(E\Sigma)$ is a set of ensemble states such that, for all $e\sigma, e\sigma' \in ES$, $|c\sigma| = |c\sigma'|$[1];*
- *$e\sigma_0 \in ES$ is the initial ensemble state;*
- *$\rightarrow \subseteq ES \times Lab(E\Sigma) \times ES$ is a transition relation such that, for all $e\sigma \xrightarrow{l} e\sigma'$,*
  (a) if l is of the form $(v_1 \rightarrow v_2).mt(v_3, \ldots, v_n)$ then
     (pre) $v_1 \in \mathsf{cmp}^c\sigma$, $v_2 \in \mathsf{cmps}^c\sigma \backslash \{v_1\}$, $v_3, \ldots, v_n \in |c\sigma|$ and there exists a message type $mt \in mts$ with arity $n\text{-}2$,
     (post) $c\sigma' = c\sigma$;
  (b) if l is of the form $v_1.op(v_2, \ldots, v_n)$ then there exists $ct \in CT$ such that $op : n\text{-}1 \in \mathsf{opns}[ct]$, $v_1 \in cstate^{ct}$, and $v_2, \ldots, v_n \in |c\sigma|$.

The class of all ensemble transition systems for $E\Sigma$ is denoted by $Trans(E\Sigma)$.

Let us now define the satisfaction relation between ETS and ensemble formulas. For this purpose we have to consider environments providing values for the variables in formulas. Assume given an $E\Sigma$-ETS $T = (ES, e\sigma_0, Lab(E\Sigma), \rightarrow)$ with initial ensemble state $e\sigma_0 = (ctrl_0, c\sigma_0)$. By definition, for each ensemble state $e\sigma = (ctrl, c\sigma) \in ES$, the carrier set $|c\sigma|$ must coincide with $|c\sigma_0|$. Hence, variable environments are elements of $Env(X, |c\sigma_0|)$, i.e. partial functions $\rho : X \rightarrow |c\sigma_0|$. To define the satisfaction relation for ensemble formulas we derive from the semantic transition relation of T a syntactic transition relation
$$\twoheadrightarrow \subseteq (ES \times Env(X, |c\sigma_0|)) \times Act(E\Sigma) \times (ES \times Env(X, |c\sigma_0|))$$
inductively constructed according to the rules in Fig. 3. The first two rules have transitions of T, denoted by $\rightarrow$ and labelled with communication and operation invocation labels, in their premises. The third rule treats assignments in the usual way but taking care of undefined term interpretations. The remaining rules reflect the construction of relations for structured actions in dynamic logic.

The transition relation $\twoheadrightarrow$ is used to define satisfaction of modal formulas $\langle \alpha \rangle \varphi$. For any $E\Sigma$-ensemble transition system $T = (ES, e\sigma_0, Lab(E\Sigma), \rightarrow)$ with initial state $e\sigma_0 = (ctrl_0, c\sigma_0)$, for any ensemble state $e\sigma = (ctrl, c\sigma) \in ES$ and environment $\rho \in Env(X, |c\sigma_0|)$ the satisfaction of ensemble formulas by T is inductively defined as follows:

- $T, e\sigma, \rho \models \mathbf{true}$;
- $T, e\sigma, \rho \models p(t_1, \ldots, t_n)$ if $c\sigma, \rho \models_{c\Sigma} p(t_1, \ldots, t_n)$, cf. Sect. 2;
- $T, e\sigma, \rho \models \neg\varphi$ if not $T, e\sigma, \rho \models \varphi$;
- $T, e\sigma, \rho \models \varphi \vee \psi$ if $T, e\sigma, \rho \models \varphi$ or $T, e\sigma, \rho \models \psi$;

---

[1] We do not allow here that the set of existing component instances can change during a state transition. This could, however, be incorporated along the lines of [11,14]. The other parts of a component system state are anyway considered as fixed data types.

- $T, e\sigma, \rho \models \exists x.\varphi$ if there exists $v \in |c\sigma_0|$ such that $T, e\sigma, \rho[x \mapsto v] \models \varphi$;
- $T, e\sigma, \rho \models \langle \alpha \rangle \varphi$ if there exists $(e\sigma', \rho') \in ES \times Env(X, |c\sigma_0|)$ such that $(e\sigma, \rho) \overset{\alpha}{\twoheadrightarrow} (e\sigma', \rho')$ and $T, e\sigma', \rho' \models \varphi$.

T *satisfies* an ensemble formula $\varphi \in \mathrm{Fm}(E\Sigma, X)$, denoted by $T \models \varphi$, if $T, e\sigma_0, \rho_\perp \models \varphi$.

(comm)	$$\cfrac{e\sigma \xrightarrow{(v1 \to v2).mt(v_3,\ldots,v_n)} e\sigma'}{(e\sigma, \rho) \xrightarrow{\pi:(a_1 \to a_2).mt(a_3,\ldots,a_n)} \twoheadrightarrow (e\sigma', \rho')}$$ whenever $I_\rho^{c\sigma}(a_i) = v_i$ for all $i \in \{1,\ldots,n\}$ such that $a_i \in T(C\Sigma, X)$, $\rho' = \rho[x_i \mapsto v_i \mid$ for all $i \in \{1,\ldots,n\}$ such that $a_i = \mathbf{upd}\, x_i]$ and $c\sigma, \rho' \models_{C\Sigma} \pi$
(op invoke)	$$\cfrac{e\sigma \xrightarrow{v_1.op(v_2,\ldots,v_n)} e\sigma'}{(e\sigma, \rho) \xrightarrow{\pi:a_1.op(a_2,\ldots,a_n)} \twoheadrightarrow (e\sigma', \rho')}$$ whenever $I_\rho^{c\sigma}(a_i) = v_i$ for all $i \in \{1,\ldots,n\}$ such that $a_i \in T(C\Sigma, X)$, $\rho' = \rho[x_i \mapsto v_i \mid$ for all $i \in \{1,\ldots,n\}$ such that $a_i = \mathbf{upd}\, x_i]$ and $c\sigma, \rho' \models_{C\Sigma} \pi$
(assignment)	$(e\sigma, \rho) \xrightarrow{\mathbf{upd}\, x := e} \twoheadrightarrow (e\sigma, \rho[x \mapsto I_\rho^{c\sigma}(e)])$ for all $(e\sigma, \rho) \in ES \times Env(X, \sigma_0)$ such that $I_\rho^{c\sigma}(e)$ is defined
(test)	$(e\sigma, \rho) \xrightarrow{\pi?} \twoheadrightarrow (e\sigma, \rho)$ for all $(e\sigma, \rho) \in ES \times Env(X, \sigma_0)$ such that $c\sigma, \rho \models_{C\Sigma} \pi$
(seq. composition)	$$\cfrac{(e\sigma, \rho) \overset{\alpha}{\twoheadrightarrow} (\hat{e}\sigma, \hat{\rho}), (\hat{e}\sigma, \hat{\rho}) \overset{\beta}{\twoheadrightarrow} (e\sigma', \rho')}{(e\sigma, \rho) \overset{\alpha;\beta}{\twoheadrightarrow} (e\sigma', \rho')}$$
(union)	$$\cfrac{(e\sigma, \rho) \overset{\alpha}{\twoheadrightarrow} (e\sigma', \rho')}{(e\sigma, \rho) \overset{\alpha+\beta}{\twoheadrightarrow} (e\sigma', \rho')} \qquad \cfrac{(e\sigma, \rho) \overset{\beta}{\twoheadrightarrow} (e\sigma', \rho')}{(e\sigma, \rho) \overset{\alpha+\beta}{\twoheadrightarrow} (e\sigma', \rho')}$$
(iteration refl.)	$(e\sigma, \rho) \overset{\alpha^*}{\twoheadrightarrow} (e\sigma, \rho)$ for all $(e\sigma, \rho) \in ES \times Env(X, \sigma_0)$
(iteration trans.)	$$\cfrac{(e\sigma, \rho) \overset{\alpha^*}{\twoheadrightarrow} (\hat{e}\sigma, \hat{\rho}), (\hat{e}\sigma, \hat{\rho}) \overset{\alpha}{\twoheadrightarrow} (e\sigma', \rho')}{(e\sigma, \rho) \overset{\alpha^*}{\twoheadrightarrow} (e\sigma', \rho')}$$

Fig. 3. Generation of syntactic transitions with environments from an ETS

Definition 3 (Semantics of ensemble specifications and refinement).
Let ESpec = (EΣ, Φ) be an ensemble specification. A model of ESpec is an ETS which satisfies Φ. The semantics of ESpec is given by its model class

$$Mod(ESpec) = \{T \in Trans(E\Sigma) \mid T \models \varphi \text{ for all } \varphi \in \Phi\}.$$

An ensemble specification ESpec' = (EΣ, Φ') is a refinement *of ESpec if Mod(ESpec') ⊆ Mod(ESpec).*

Example 5. We are going to develop a more concrete specification for global behaviours of robot rescue ensembles. For this purpose we construct a refinement $ESpec_1$ of the requirements specification $ESpec_0$ in Example 4. The specification $ESpec_1 = (E\Sigma_{\mathsf{Rescue}}, \Phi_1)$ contains an axiom Φ_1 shown in Fig. 4. This axiom describes a possible scenario how victims can be rescued by spreading help messages from victims to landmarks, from landmarks to landmarks, and finally to rescuers. In the best case a victim's message has immediately reached a rescuer. Each sender can only reach receivers within its broadcast distance. It is assumed that landmarks are walking around until they receive a help message. Then they start sending help messages further. Once a rescuer has received such a message, it moves to the victim's position and notifies the victim about its rescue. Our scenario description uses a while-loop; see Sect. 3. The program is highly non-deterministic and relies on the concurrent execution of the distributed components. The scenario requires that it is eventually possible to inform a rescuer. It starts whenever a victim has issued the first time a help message with its position. It is easy to see that $ESpec_1$ is a refinement of $ESpec_0$ since the scenario specialises the loosely specified actions in the diamond modality in Fig. 2.

```
∀v. Victim(v) ⟹
[(-help)* ; π_help:(v → upd receivers).help(v.pos)]
  ⟨ Scenario ⟩ true

where Scenario is the following structured action (program)

upd senders:={v}∪(receivers∩Landmark.allInst);
while (receivers ∩ Rescuer.allInst = ∅)
   π_walk:upd walker.walk() +
   ( π_help':(upd sender → upd receivers).help(v.pos);
     upd senders:=senders∪(receivers∩Landmark.allInst) )
od;
π_move:upd rescuer.move(v.pos);
π_rescue':(rescuer → {v}).rescue()

where
π_walk is: Landmark(walker) ∧ walker∉senders
π_help' is: sender∈senders ∧
            ∀x.(x∈receivers ⟺ x∉senders ∧ (Landmark(x) ∨ Rescuer(x)) ∧
                              dist(sender.pos,x.pos) ≤ sender.bdist )
π_move is: Rescuer(rescuer) ∧ rescuer∈receivers
π_rescue' is: rescuer.pos = v.pos
```

Fig. 4. Refined specification for robot rescue ensembles

5 Ensemble Realisations

Ensemble specifications describe properties of collaborating ensemble participants from a global perspective. In this section we consider ensemble realisations which define, for each component type ct of an ensemble signature, a local behaviour to be respected by all instances of ct. Behaviours are described by process expressions. Given an ensemble signature $E\Sigma = (mts, C\Sigma(CT))$ process expressions and (local) actions are defined by the following grammar similar to the AbC calculus [1,2]. We omit parallel composition of local processes, which anyway will run concurrently per instance when a system is built, and model the awareness construct by guards for operation invocations. We extend AbC actions by local operation calls which can perform attribute updates as in AbC as a special case. Differently from AbC, our predicates π range over first-order formulas and we use message (type) names for making interactions more explicit.

$$P ::= \mathbf{nil} \mid a.P \mid P_1 + P_2 \mid K$$
$$a ::= mt(e_1, \ldots, e_n)@\pi \mid (\pi)mt(x_1, \ldots, x_n) \mid \pi : op(e_1, \ldots, e_n)$$

In the grammar K is a process name, $\pi \in \mathrm{Fm}(C\Sigma, X)$ a first-order formula, $mt \in mts$ a message type of arity n, $x_i \in X$ are variables, $e_i \in T(C\Sigma, X)$ terms, and $op \in \mathsf{opns}(C\Sigma)$ is an operation of arity n. The set of process expressions over $E\Sigma$ is denoted by $PExp(E\Sigma)$. $\mathbf{nil}$ denotes the null process, $a.P$ action prefix, $P_1 + P_2$ non-deterministic choice and K a possibly recursive call to a process with name K. In contrast to global communication actions in $Act(E\Sigma)$, there are distinguished receive and send actions seen from the perspective of a single component instance. A send action $mt(e_1, \ldots, e_n)@\pi$ expresses that the current instance, say c, is enabled to send a message, transmitting the values of $e_1, \ldots, e_n$, to all component instances which satisfy π under the current local variable environment of c. In π the special variable $\mathbf{this}$ can be used to refer to c and $\mathbf{target}$ to refer to any component instance satisfying π. A receive action $(\pi)mt(x_1, \ldots, x_n)$ expresses that the current instance c is enabled to receive a message of type mt if the sender satisfies π. Again $\mathbf{this}$ refers to c and a special variable $\mathbf{source}$ is used to refer to the sending component instance. The transmitted parameters are stored in the local variables $x_1, \ldots, x_n$ of c.

An action $\pi : op(e_1, \ldots, e_n)$ represents the invocation of an operation with actual parameters $e_1, \ldots, e_n$ by the current component instance c. It is only executed in the ensemble if the guard π is satisfied in the current component system state under the local variable environment of c; again $\mathbf{this}$ can be used in π to refer to c. In contrast to processes we do not provide a special syntax for operation implementations but describe their effect semantically. Given an operation $op : n \in \mathsf{opns}(C\Sigma)$ an *operation realisation* of op is a set of relations

$$OpR_{v.op(v_1, \ldots, v_n)} \subseteq States(C\Sigma) \times States(C\Sigma),$$

such that for all $(c\sigma, c\sigma') \in OpR_{v.op(v_1, \ldots, v_n)}$ it holds $v, v_1, \ldots, v_n \in |c\sigma|$ and $|c\sigma| = |c\sigma'|$.

An ensemble realisation provides an implementation for each component type in terms of a process description. It also provides an operation realisation for each operation and an initial component system state which determines the component instances running in parallel during ensemble execution.

Definition 4 (Ensemble realisation). *An* ensemble realisation *is a tuple*

$$EReal = (E\Sigma, CReals, OpReals, c\sigma_0) \quad \text{such that}$$

- $E\Sigma = (mts, C\Sigma(CT))$ *is an ensemble signature,*
- *CReals is a set of process declarations* $K = P$ *with* $P \in PExp(E\Sigma)$ *containing, for each* $ct \in CT$, *a unique process declaration* $ct = P_{ct}$,
- *OpReals is a set of operation realisations, one for each* $op : n \in \mathsf{opns}(C\Sigma)$,
- $c\sigma_0 \in States(C\Sigma)$ *is an initial component system state.*

The semantics of an ensemble realisation is given in terms of an ensemble transition system. In this case the global control state $ctrl$ of an ensemble state $e\sigma = (ctrl, c\sigma)$ has a particular form: it is a function $ctrl : \mathsf{cmp}^{c\sigma} \to LStates(E\Sigma)$ assigning to each component instance $c \in \mathsf{cmp}^{c\sigma}$ a local state. A *local state* is a pair $l = (\rho, P)$ where $\rho : X \to |c\sigma|$ is an environment of the local variables of c and $P \in PExp(E\Sigma)$ is a process expression recording the current computation state of c. We write $\mathsf{env}[l]$ for ρ and $\mathsf{proc}[l]$ for P. The set of all local states over $E\Sigma$ is denoted by $LStates(E\Sigma)$.

In contrast to the loose semantics of ensemble specifications, an ensemble realisation $EReal = (E\Sigma, CReals, OpReals, c\sigma_0)$ determines a unique ensemble transition system. Its initial ensemble state is $e\sigma_0 = (ctrl_0, c\sigma_0)$ where the control state $ctrl_0$ is given by the function $ctrl_0 : \mathsf{cmp}^{c\sigma} \to LStates(E\Sigma)$ such that for all $ct \in CT$ and $c \in ct^{c\sigma}$, $ctrl_0(c) = (\rho_\perp[\mathbf{this} \mapsto c], P_{ct})$ if $ct = P_{ct} \in Reals$.

Structural operational semantics (SOS) rules generate the ensemble transitions. We pursue an incremental approach, similar to the Fork Calculus [10] and other calculi like SCEL [6], Helena [13], and AbC [1,2], by splitting the semantics into two different layers. The first layer describes how processes evolve according to the given constructs for process expressions. Figure 5 provides the corresponding SOS rules. We use the symbol $\hookrightarrow$ for transitions on process level.

On the second level we consider ensemble states and their transitions denoted by $\to$ in Fig. 6. Rule (com) describes that a (global) communication, exchanging message $mt(v_1, \ldots, v_n)$, happens if the local process state of a sender is enabled to send the message and the set of receivers is a maximal set of component instances whose local processes are enabled to receive the message such that, in the current component system state, each receiver satisfies the predicate of the sender and the sender satisfies the predicate of each receiver. Additionally, the values of the actual parameters must be taken into account when evaluating receiver predicates. Rule (op) says that an operation invocation $c.op(v_1, \ldots, v_n)$ happens on ensemble level if the local process of component instance c is enabled to invoke op and if the guard π is (currently) satisfied by the sender. The execution of the operation is then performed in accordance with the given operation realisation.

(action prefix)	$a.P \overset{a}{\hookrightarrow} P$
(choice-left)	$\dfrac{P_1 \overset{a}{\hookrightarrow} P_1'}{P_1 + P_2 \overset{a}{\hookrightarrow} P_1'}$
(choice-right)	$\dfrac{P_2 \overset{a}{\hookrightarrow} P_2'}{P_1 + P_2 \overset{a}{\hookrightarrow} P_2'}$
(process invocation)	$\dfrac{K = P,\ P \overset{a}{\hookrightarrow} P'}{K \overset{a}{\hookrightarrow} P'}$

Fig. 5. SOS rules for process expressions

(comm)

$$\dfrac{P \xrightarrow{mt(e_1,\ldots,e_n)@\pi} P',\ \{P_j \xrightarrow{(\pi_j)mt(x_{j,1},\ldots,x_{j,n})} P_j' \mid j \in J\}}{(ctrl,\, c\sigma) \xrightarrow{(c \to \{c_j \mid j \in J\}).mt(v_1,\ldots,v_n)} (ctrl',\, c\sigma')}$$

whenever J is a maximal index set such that :

$c \in \mathsf{cmp}^{c\sigma}, \{c_j \mid j \in J,\, c_j \neq c\} \in \mathsf{cmps}^{c\sigma}, v_1, \ldots, v_n \in |c\sigma|,$

$\mathsf{proc}[ctrl(c)] = P,\ I_\rho^{c\sigma}(e_i) = v_i$ for $\rho = \mathsf{env}[ctrl(c)]$ and $i = 1, \ldots, n,$

$\mathsf{proc}[ctrl(c_j)] = P_j$ for all $j \in J,$

$c\sigma, \rho[\mathbf{target} \mapsto c_j] \models_{C\Sigma} \pi$ for all $j \in J,$

$c\sigma, \rho_j[\mathbf{source} \mapsto c][x_{j,i} \mapsto v_i \mid i = 1, \ldots, n] \models_{C\Sigma} \pi_j$

  for $\rho_j = \mathsf{env}[ctrl(c_j)]$ and all $j \in J,$

$ctrl' = ctrl[c \mapsto (\rho, P')][c_j \mapsto (\rho_j[x_{j,i} \mapsto v_i \mid i = 1, \ldots, n], P_j') \mid j \in J],$

$c\sigma' = c\sigma$

(op)

$$\dfrac{P \xrightarrow{\pi : op(e_1,\ldots,e_n)} P'}{(ctrl,\, c\sigma) \xrightarrow{c.op(v_1,\ldots,v_n)} (ctrl',\, c\sigma')}$$

whenever there exists $ct \in CT$ such that :

$op : n \in \mathsf{opns}[ct], c \in c\sigma^{ct}, v_1, \ldots, v_n \in |c\sigma|,$

$\mathsf{proc}[ctrl(c)] = P,\ I_\rho^{c\sigma}(e_i) = v_i$ for $\rho = \mathsf{env}[ctrl(c)]$ and $i = 1, \ldots, n,$

$c\sigma, \rho \models_{C\Sigma} \pi$, and

$ctrl' = ctrl[c \mapsto (\rho, P')], (c\sigma, c\sigma') \in OpR_{c.op(v_1,\ldots,v_n)}.$

Fig. 6. SOS rules for deriving an ETS from an ensemble realisation

Definition 5 (Semantics of an ensemble realisation). *The semantics of an ensemble realisation* $EReal = (E\Sigma, CReals, OpReals, c\sigma_0)$ *is the ensemble transition system*

$$[\![EReal]\!] = (ES, e\sigma_0, Lab(E\Sigma), \rightarrow)$$

where $e\sigma_0$ *is the initial ensemble state (derived from EReal as explained above) and* $ES, \rightarrow$ *are inductively generated from* $e\sigma_0$ *by applying the rules in Fig. 5 and Fig. 6.*

Note that the rules in Fig. 6 guarantee the constraints for an ensemble transition system formulated in Definition 2. Our semantic concepts lead to an obvious correctness notion for ensemble specifications and their realisations:

Definition 6 (Correct ensemble realisation). *Let ESpec be an ensemble specification and EReal be an ensemble realisation over the same signature. EReal is a* correct realisation *of ESpec if* $[\![EReal]\!] \in Mod(ESpec)$.

Example 6. We provide a realisation for robot rescue ensembles. Figure 7 shows the process declarations for each component type. We assume that our ensemble is started in an initial component system state $c\sigma_0$ with one victim, one rescuer and $n > 0$ landmarks. Moreover, we assume given operation realisations for walk and move such that the latter moves a rescuer to a given target position. A victim process sends recursively help messages transmitting its position to components within its broadcast distance. This behaviour is stopped once the victim receives a rescue message from a component arrived at the victim's position. Any landmark is continuously walking until it receives a help message. From that point on it forwards recursively the message (and the received value) to components within its broadcast distance. A rescuer becomes active when it receives a help message with parameter vp. Then it executes the move operation towards position vp and sends rescue to the components at that position.

```
Victim =
  (help(this.pos)@dist(this.pos,target.pos) ≤ this.bdist).Victim
  +
  (source.pos = this.pos).rescue().nil

Landmark =
  ((true)this.walk()).Landmark + (true)help(vp).SendHelp
SendHelp =
  (help(vp)@dist(this.pos,target.pos) ≤ this.bdist).SendHelp

Rescuer =
  (true)help(vp).(true)this.move(vp).(rescue@target.pos = this.pos).nil
```

Fig. 7. Realisation of the robot rescue ensemble

To discuss the correctness of our realisation w.r.t. the specification $ESpec_1$ of Example 5 we must check that our ensemble, starting with the $n + 2$ component instances in $c\sigma_0$, can, after the victim has asked for help, eventually reach a state where a rescuer arrives at the victim's position to rescue it. For this we must assume that, depending on the size of the exploration area, there are sufficiently many landmarks around whose `walk` operation is implemented in such a way that an appropriate distribution of the landmarks is reachable where the broadcast distance of each sender is sufficient to transfer the messages. Then the interactions that are possible due to our ensemble implementation guarantee that there is a possibility to execute the specified global interaction scenario. □

6   Conclusion

We have proposed a logical framework and methodology for developing collective systems starting from abstract requirements specifications of global interactions down to constructive ensemble realisations in terms of local processes. In contrast to our previous work, communication partners are not explicitly linked but specified by predicates in a multi-cast fashion. Several extensions of our approach are interesting, e.g., creating new component instances on demand [6,14], asynchronous communication as in HELENA [17], integrating statistical methods [8,18], proof techniques and tools [13], as well as larger case studies.

References

1. Abd Alrahman, Y., De Nicola, R., Loreti, M.: A calculus for collective-adaptive systems and its behavioural theory. Inf. Comput. **268**, 104457 (2019)
2. Abd Alrahman, Y., De Nicola, R., Loreti, M.: Programming interactions in collective adaptive systems by relying on attribute-based communication. Sci. Comput. Program. **192**, 102428 (2020)
3. Abeywickrama, D., Bicocchi, N., Mamei, M., Zambonelli, F.: The SOTA approach to engineering collective adaptive systems. Int. J. Softw. Tools Technol. Transfer **22**, 399–415 (2020). https://doi.org/10.1007/s10009-020-00554-3
4. Bortolussi, L., et al.: CARMA: collective adaptive resource-sharing Markovian agents. In: Bertrand, N., Tribastone, M. (eds.) Proceedings Thirteenth Workshop on Quantitative Aspects of Programming Languages and Systems, QAPL 2015, EPTCS, vol. 194, pp. 16–31 (2015)
5. Bruni, R., Corradini, A., Gadducci, F., Melgratti, H., Montanari, U., Tuosto, E.: Data-driven choreographies à la Klaim. In: Boreale, M., Corradini, F., Loreti, M., Pugliese, R. (eds.) Models, Languages, and Tools for Concurrent and Distributed Programming. LNCS, vol. 11665, pp. 170–190. Springer, Cham (2019). https://doi.org/10.1007/978-3-030-21485-2_11
6. De Nicola, R., Loreti, M., Pugliese, R., Tiezzi, F.: A formal approach to autonomic systems programming: the SCEL language. ACM Trans. Auton. Adapt. Syst. (TAAS) **9**(2), 1–29 (2014)
7. Ebbinghaus, H.-D.: Über eine Prädikatenlogik mit partiell definierten Prädikaten und Funktionen. Arch. Math. Logik Grundlagenforschung **12**, 39–53 (1969)
8. Forejt, V., Kwiatkowska, M., Norman, G., Parker, D.: Automated verification techniques for probabilistic systems. In: Bernardo, M., Issarny, V. (eds.) SFM 2011. LNCS, vol. 6659, pp. 53–113. Springer, Heidelberg (2011). https://doi.org/10.1007/978-3-642-21455-4_3

9. Harel, D., Kozen, D., Tiuryn, J. (eds.): Dynamic Logic. MIT Press, Cambridge (2000)
10. Havelund, K., Larsen, K.G.: The fork calculus. In: Lingas, A., Karlsson, R., Carlsson, S. (eds.) ICALP 1993. LNCS, vol. 700, pp. 544–557. Springer, Heidelberg (1993). https://doi.org/10.1007/3-540-56939-1_101
11. Hennicker, R.: Role-based development of dynamically evolving esembles. In: Fiadeiro, J.L., Tutu, I. (eds.) Recent Trends in Algebraic Development Techniques - 24th IFIP WG 1.3 International Workshop, WADT 2018, Revised Selected Papers. LNCS, vol. 11563, pp. 3–24. Springer, Cham (2018). https://doi.org/10.1007/978-3-030-23220-7_1
12. Hennicker, R., Klarl, A.: Foundations for ensemble modeling – the HELENA approach. In: Iida, S., Meseguer, J., Ogata, K. (eds.) Specification, Algebra, and Software. LNCS, vol. 8373, pp. 359–381. Springer, Heidelberg (2014). https://doi.org/10.1007/978-3-642-54624-2_18
13. Hennicker, R., Klarl, A., Wirsing, M.: Model-checking HELENA ensembles with spin. In: Martí-Oliet, N., Ölveczky, P.C., Talcott, C. (eds.) Logic, Rewriting, and Concurrency. LNCS, vol. 9200, pp. 331–360. Springer, Cham (2015). https://doi.org/10.1007/978-3-319-23165-5_16
14. Hennicker, R., Wirsing, M.: Dynamic logic for ensembles. In: Margaria, T., Steffen, B. (eds.) ISoLA 2018. LNCS, vol. 11246, pp. 32–47. Springer, Cham (2018). https://doi.org/10.1007/978-3-030-03424-5_3
15. Honda, K., Yoshida, N., Carbone, M.: Multiparty asynchronous session types. In: Proceedings of the 35th Annual ACM SIGPLAN-SIGACT Symposium on Principles of Programming Languages (POPL 2008), pp. 273–284. ACM (2008)
16. Kernbach, S., Schmickl, T., Timmis, J.: Collective adaptive systems: challenges beyond evolvability. CoRR abs/1108.5643 (2011)
17. Klarl, A.: HELENA: Handling massively distributed systems with ELaborate ENsemble Architectures. Ph.D. thesis, LMU Munich, Germany (2016)
18. Latella, D., Loreti, M., Massink, M., Senni, V.: Stochastically timed predicate-based communication primitives for autonomic computing. In: Bertrand, N., Bortolussi, L. (eds.) QAPL 2014. EPTCS, vol. 154, pp. 1–16 (2014)
19. Nicola, R., et al.: The SCEL language: design, implementation, verification. In: Wirsing, M., Hölzl, M., Koch, N., Mayer, P. (eds.) Software Engineering for Collective Autonomic Systems. LNCS, vol. 8998, pp. 3–71. Springer, Cham (2015). https://doi.org/10.1007/978-3-319-16310-9_1
20. Pinciroli, C., Bonani, M., Mondada, F., Dorigo, M.: Adaptation and awareness in robot ensembles: scenarios and algorithms. In: Wirsing, M., Hölzl, M., Koch, N., Mayer, P. (eds.) Software Engineering for Collective Autonomic Systems. LNCS, vol. 8998, pp. 471–494. Springer, Cham (2015). https://doi.org/10.1007/978-3-319-16310-9_15
21. Vassev, E., Hinchey, M.: Engineering requirements for autonomy features. In: Wirsing, M., Hölzl, M., Koch, N., Mayer, P. (eds.) Software Engineering for Collective Autonomic Systems. LNCS, vol. 8998, pp. 379–403. Springer, Cham (2015). https://doi.org/10.1007/978-3-319-16310-9_11
22. Wirsing, M., Banâtre, J.-P., Hölzl, M., Rauschmayer, A. (eds.): Software-Intensive Systems and New Computing Paradigms. LNCS, vol. 5380. Springer, Heidelberg (2008). https://doi.org/10.1007/978-3-540-89437-7
23. Wirsing, M., Hölzl, M., Koch, N., Mayer, P. (eds.): Software Engineering for Collective Autonomic Systems. LNCS, vol. 8998. Springer, Cham (2015). https://doi.org/10.1007/978-3-319-16310-9

24. Wirsing, M., Hölzl, M., Tribastone, M., Zambonelli, F.: ASCENS: engineering autonomic service-component ensembles. In: Beckert, B., Damiani, F., de Boer, F.S., Bonsangue, M.M. (eds.) FMCO 2011. LNCS, vol. 7542, pp. 1–24. Springer, Heidelberg (2013). https://doi.org/10.1007/978-3-642-35887-6_1

25. Würtz, R.P.: Organic Computing. UCS. Springer, Heidelberg (2008). https://doi.org/10.1007/978-3-540-77657-4

Abstractions for Collective Adaptive Systems

Omar Inverso[1](✉), Catia Trubiani[1](✉), and Emilio Tuosto[1,2](✉)

[1] Gran Sasso Science Institute, L'aquila, Italy
{omar.inverso,catia.trubiani,emilio.tuosto}@gssi.it
[2] University of Leicester, Leicester, England

Abstract. This paper advocates behavioural abstractions for the coordination of *collective adaptive systems* (CAS). In order to ground the discussion in a concrete framework, we sketch mechanisms based on behavioural types for some recently proposed calculi that formalise CAS. We analyse new typing mechanisms and show that such mechanisms enable formal specifications of CAS that cannot be easily attained through existing behavioural types. We illustrate how a quantitative analysis can be instrumented through our behavioural specifications by means of a case study in a scenario involving autonomous robots. Our analysis is auxiliary to our long term aim which is three-fold: (i) study suitable typing mechanisms for CAS, (ii) identify basic properties of CAS that may be enforced by typing, and (iii) consider quantitative properties of CAS.

1 Introduction

Collective adaptive systems (CAS) consist of computational agents that collaborate and take decisions to achieve some goals [17]. Typically, agents of CAS are autonomous units that coordinate distributively. Namely, there is no central unit and the overall state of the computation is fragmented in the local state of agents. Also, these agents execute in a cyber-physical context and are supposed to adapt to changes of these open-ended environments. Hence, at a given moment, agents have a partial knowledge about the overall state of the computation. For each agent, such knowledge is made of information possibly acquired autonomously (e.g., by sensing and elaborating information about the surrounding environment) or communicated by other agents. Decisions are *local*: agents use their knowledge to establish the next course of action.

We will use a simple scenario to illustrate some key features of CAS. The scenario is centred around the *stable marriage problem* [20] (SM), that finds applications in many domains to determine matching of resources. Given two equally-sized sets of elements, each having individual preferences (in form of an ordered list) on

Research partly supported by the EU H2020 RISE programme under the Marie Skłodowska-Curie grant agreement No 778233. Work partly funded by MIUR projects PRIN 2017FTXR7S *IT MATTERS* and PRIN 2017TWRCNB *SEDUCE*. .

T. Margaria and B. Steffen (Eds.): ISoLA 2020, LNCS 12477, pp. 243–260, 2020.
https://doi.org/10.1007/978-3-030-61470-6_15

the elements of the other group, Stable Marriage (SM) amounts to finding a stable matching between the elements of the two groups. The original formulation was described in terms of groups of women and men, whence the word marriage originates; in the following, we retain the original terminology.

The SM protocol can be solved by pairing men to women so that no man and woman would rather prefer each other to their current partner. In the classical solution of [20] each man proposes himself to his most favourite woman, according to his preferences. When a man's offer is rejected or a woman drops her current partner due to a better pretender, the man tries with his next preferred woman. A woman accepts any proposal when single or, depending on her preferences, she chooses the best man between her current partner and the one making advances, abandoning her current partner in the second case. The SM protocol guarantees the existence of a unique stable matching.

The following python-like pseudocode describes the use of the algorithm of [20] for the classical SM protocol where agents use preference lists to take their decisions.

```
def B(prefs, myID):                def C(aID, aPID):
    ... # code to handle prefs         while true:
    for charger in prefs:                  recv("p", idNew)
        send("p", myID) at charger         if choose(aPID, idNew):
        recv(res)                              send("no") to aPID
                                           else: send("no") to idNew
```

Assume that the parameter *ID is used to identify agents; for instance, B communicates its identifier myID to C and the latter may use it in further communications.

In a CAS scenario, we can imagine a number of agents executing either (or both) the snippets above in order to "pair up": for instance, an autonomous agent roaming in a smart city in need to recharge its battery may execute B to search for a charger agent executing C. Now suppose that chargers are not available in the immediate proximity of an agent needing a recharge.

In such a scenario, a key element for *correctness*[1] is therefore *how* information spreads among agents. For instance, the message sent by B should reach a charger. Simple communication mechanisms such as point-to-point (p2p) communications present some limitations in this application domain. The main drawback of these mechanisms is that they impose the design of ad-hoc communication protocols to (1) identify partners, (2) disseminate information, (3) update local knowledge of agents. In the snippet above, partners include identifiers and it is assumed that the communication infrastructure delivers messages properly. This requires to configure agents appropriately: the identifiers used must exist, be unique, and immutable. For instance, malfunctions can arise when renaming chargers or assigning the same name to different chargers. Moreover, the deployment of new chargers would go "unnoticed" to existing agents unless updating their preference list. Besides p2p communications have an overhead since multi-party interactions are commonplace in CAS.

As reviewed in Sect. 7, a number of proposals have indeed been made to provide suitable communication mechanism. Those approaches aim to provide suitable linguistic abstractions to specify CAS. For instance, the calculus of

---

[1] We will come back to correctness soon.

attribute-based communication (AbC) [1] allows one to specify the scenario above by addressing agents according to their attributes so that, e.g., B can send a request to *any* charger within a given distance and with a given amperage and cost. However, those mechanisms are complex and often hard to enforce in communication infrastructures. Also, it is difficult to understand how those mechanisms can be used to guarantee interesting properties of CAS (cf. Sect. 7). This point can be explained with an analogy. Synchronous communications allow the designer to assume that after an interaction the receiving agent has acquired the information. Said differently, this type of interaction allows the sender to make safe assumptions on the state of the receiver. This has important consequences on the way one can reason about the system. So, fixed a sophisticated communication mechanism, natural questions to ask are:

1. "What can be safely assumed about the distributed state of the system after an interaction among agents?"
2. "What (behavioural) properties a given communication mechanism enforces?"
3. "How can one *statically* validate such properties?"
4. "Can behavioural abstractions support or improve run-time execution?"
5. "Can behavioural specifications foster quantitative analysis of CAS?"

This paper discusses the characteristics of behavioural abstractions for CAS. We argue that existing frameworks are not suitable for the specification or the static analysis of CAS. For the sake of the argument we will use AbC as an illustrative language and sketch behavioural abstractions tailored on the linguistic mechanisms of AbC. Giving a full fledged typing discipline is out of the scope of this paper. Our main goal is to discuss what are the main features that behavioural types for CAS should provide and how such features can be used to support quantitative analysis of CAS.

Outline. Section 2 surveys AbC using the SM protocol. Section 3 sketches a behavioural type for CAS. For the sake of the presentation, we will refrain from technical definitions and give only informal descriptions to motivate our proposal in Sect. 4. Section 5 uses the simple examples in Sect. 3 and a case study from the robotic domain for examing the questions above. Section 6 shows how the behavioural types discussed here could be helpful for quantitative analysis of CAS. Related and future work are discussed in Sect. 7 together with concluding remarks.

2   A Bird-Eye View of **AbC**

The calculus of attribute-based communication [1] (AbC), was initially conceived as a simplified version of SCEL [16]. Intuitively, AbC can be seen as a generalisation of traditional message-passing. In message-passing, communication is typically restricted to either one-to-one (point-to-point) or one-to-all (broadcast). AbC relaxes this restriction by allowing one-to-many communication via attribute-based send and receive constructs. Interestingly, communication across dynamically-formed many-to-many groups can take place. This allows to model effortlessly several different classes of distributed systems, which would be harder to do under more traditional formalisms, such as Actors [3], channels [27], or broadcast [29], that rely on the identity of the communicating peers.

Informally, an AbC system consists of multiple communicating *components*. Depending on the domain and the interaction patterns of interest, each component exposes some *attributes*. A send operation can thus target all the components satisfying a given *predicate* on such attributes. Every component satisfying the sending predicate is thus selected as a potential receiver. At the other end, similarly, each potential receiver performing a receive operation eventually gets messages depending on its receiving predicate. Any other message is discarded. For instance, cooperating robots in a swarm may be modelled as separate components that expose their battery level and location. A robot can ask cooperation to robots within a certain distance and with a minimum battery level. However, a robot which is already busy may want to discard this invitation.

More concretely, the core syntax of (our variant of) AbC is as follows

$$C ::= \Gamma : P \mid C_1 \parallel C_2 \qquad\qquad\qquad \text{Components}$$

$$P ::= 0 \mid \alpha.P \mid [\mathsf{a} := E]P \mid \langle \Pi \rangle P \mid P_1 + P_2 \mid P_1 \mid P_2 \mid K \qquad \text{Processes}$$

$$E ::= \mathsf{v} \mid x \mid \mathsf{a} \mid \mathsf{this.a} \mid \_x \mid (E) \qquad\qquad \text{Expressions}$$

$$\alpha ::= E@\Pi \mid \Pi(E) \qquad\qquad\qquad\qquad \text{Actions}$$

$$\Pi ::= \mathsf{true} \mid \mathsf{false} \mid E_1 \bowtie E_2 \mid \Pi_1 \wedge \Pi_2 \mid \neg\Pi \mid \{\Pi\} \qquad \text{Predicates}$$

An AbC system consists of multiple *components*. A component is either the parallel composition of two components, or a pair $\Gamma : P$, where Γ denotes the attribute environment of the component, and P a process describing its behaviour. Processes exchange expressions E which may be a constant value v, a variable x, an attribute name a, a reference $\mathsf{this.a}$ to an attribute a of the *local* environment, or a placeholder $\_x$ used by the pattern matching mechanism. Values include basic data types (e.g., atoms $\mathsf{'v'}$, numeric or boolean values), arithmetic expressions, and tuples $(\!|E_1, \ldots, E_n|\!)$ including the empty tuple $(\!|\,|\!)$.

The *attribute environment* Γ is a mapping from attribute names to values. As mentioned, attributes expresses specific features of the components that are relevant for communication, for example the position of an agent on a grid, the battery level of a robot, the role of the component or its identity, etc. The set of attributes exposed by each component is statically fixed upfront.

A *process* P can be the inactive process 0 (hereafter omitted where possible), an action prefixing process $\alpha.P$, an *update* process $[\mathsf{a} := E]P$, an *awareness* process $\langle \Pi \rangle P$. Processes can be composed using the usual non-deterministic choice $P_1 + P_2$ and parallel composition constructs $P_1|P_2$, and invocation K.

The prefixing process executes *action* α and continues as P. The update process sets attribute a to the value of expression E. The awareness process blocks the execution of process P until predicate Π holds. Non-deterministic choice and parallel composition work as usual. Note that the awareness construct may be combined with non-deterministic choice to express branching.

An *attribute-based send* action $E@\Pi$ sends the evaluation of expression E to those components whose attributes satisfy predicate Π. An *attribute-based receive* action $\Pi(E)$ uses expressions E to pattern match expressions in send actions. More precisely, the occurrences of a placeholder $\_x$ are bound in E and the continuation of the receive prefix; upon communication, $\_x$ is assigned the corresponding values in the message received from any component whose attributes (and possibly values communicated in the body of the message) satisfy predicate Π. Send operations are asynchronous while receive are blocking.

An update operation is performed atomically with the action following it, if the component under the updated environment can perform that action. It is possible to model an update operation in isolation $[a := E]$ via an empty send action $(\!|\!)@\texttt{false}$ to obtain $[a := E](\!|\!)@\texttt{false}$.

A predicate Π can be either $\texttt{true}$, a comparison between two expressions $E_1 \bowtie E_2$ (e.g., $x + y \leq 2z$), a logical conjunction of two predicates $\Pi_1 \wedge \Pi_2$ or a negation of a predicate $\neg \Pi$.

Back to our example, the behaviour of the robot looking for help can be partially sketched by the following fragment:

$$(\!|\,\text{`help'}, \text{this.pos}\,|\!)@\{\texttt{distance}(\text{this.pos}, pos) < k \wedge \text{battery} > 0.5\}$$

where the robot sends an '`help`' message along with its position to all robots within distance k and with at least 50% battery charge left. For simplicity, we use $\texttt{distance}$ as a shorthand for a more complex expression that computes the distance between any two given positions. Note that the robot uses this.pos to indicate the local attribute which refers to its own position. A possible reaction of a robot at the other end could be:

$$\langle\neg\text{this.busy}\rangle(\text{message} = \text{`help'})(\text{message}).\cdots +$$
$$\langle\text{this.busy}\rangle(\text{message} = \text{`help'})(\text{message})$$

To further illustrate the effectiveness of AbC in describing non-trivial interaction patterns, we consider the stable marriage protocol (cf. Sect. 1) and its attribute-based implementation [13, 14].

In AbC, we can model men and women as components whose attributes are the identifier id, the preference list prefs, and the current partner. A man updates his attribute partner to the first element of prefs, and then sends a propose message to components whose id attribute coincide with the partner attribute; he then waits for a no message to reset the partner, and so on:

$$M = [\text{this.partner} := \texttt{head}(\text{this.prefs}), \text{this.prefs} := \texttt{tail}(\text{this.prefs})]$$
$$(\text{propose}, \text{this.id})@(\text{id} = \text{this.partner}).\text{Wait}$$
$$\text{Wait} = [\text{this.partner} := \texttt{null}](no)(\_m).M$$

Women wait for incoming proposals (Handle process), and either prefer the proposer to her current partner (process A), or otherwise (process R). Note that immediately after receiving a proposal, women can handle other proposals. Notice that both R and A use a reversed form of preference lists to compare identifier of the current partner with one of a new proposer:

$$\text{Handle} = (\textbf{propose})(\text{Handle} \mid (\textbf{propose}, \_id).(A(id) + R(id)))$$
$$A(id) = \langle \texttt{this.prefs[this.partner]} < \texttt{this.prefs}[id] \rangle$$
$$[ex := \texttt{this.partner}, \texttt{this.partner} := id](no)@(\textsf{id} = ex)$$
$$R(id) = \langle \texttt{this.prefs[this.partner]} > \texttt{this.prefs}[id] \rangle (no)@(\textsf{id} = id)$$

3 AbC-inspired Behavioural Types

We scribble a few abstractions for CAS that we dub AbC-*inspired behavioural types* (ABeT for short). Basically, ABeT mix together ideas from session types [23] in order to support the specification, verification, and analysis of CAS. In particular, ABeT blend *global choreographies* [22,31], and *klaimographies* [8]. Instead of appealing to formal syntax and semantics, we opt for an intuitive visual description. To this purpose, we use diagrams (see Fig. 1) depicting the communication pattern of the SM protocol. We now survey the core features of ABeT.

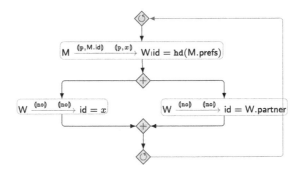

Fig. 1. A behavioural abstraction of the SM protocol

The diagram in Fig. 1 represents a distributed workflow of *interactions*, which are the atomic elements of ABeT; the general form of an interaction for CAS is inspired by AbC and takes the form

$$A_{|\rho} \xrightarrow{e \quad e'} B_{|\rho'}$$

(1)

The intuitive meaning of the interaction in (1) is as follows:

any agent, say A, *satisfying* ρ generates an expression e for *any* agents satisfying ρ', dubbed B, provided that expression e' *matches* e.

We anticipate that A and B here are used just for convenience and may be omitted for instance writing $\rho \xrightarrow{\ e\ \ e'\ } B_{|}\rho'$ or $\rho \xrightarrow{\ e\ \ e'\ } \rho'$. Also, we abbreviate $A_{|}\rho$ with @ when P is a tautology. This allows us to be more succinct. For instance, the top-most interaction in Fig. 1 specifies that

- all "man" agents propose to the "woman" who is top in their preference list by generating a tuple made of the constant value p and their identifier M.id
- any "woman" agent (denoted as W in the rest of the diagram) whose identifier equals the head hd(M.prefs) of her preference list pattern matches the tuple sent by M and records in the variable x the identity of the proposer.

Interactions such as (1) introduce already some abstractions:

- Similarly to global choreographies, (1) abstracts away from asynchrony; interactions are supposed to be atomic
- As in klaimographies, (1) abstracts away from the number of agents in execution
- As behavioural types, (1) abstracts away from the local behaviour of the agents; for instance, it does not tell if/how the local state of agents are changed (if at all) by the interaction

Interactions are the basic elements of an algebra of protocols [31] that allows us to iterate them or compose them in non-deterministic choices or in parallel. In Fig. 1, the ◇-gates mark the entry and exit points of the loop of the SM protocol. Likewise, the ◇-gates mark the branching and merging points of a non-deterministic choice. The "body" of the loop in Fig. 1 yields the choice specified by the SM protocol. We will also use ⊞-gates to mark forking and joining points of parallel protocols.

These abstractions are "compatible" with the pseudocode in Sect. 1. In fact, one could assign[2] B the communication pattern of M in Fig. 1 and to C the communication pattern of W. Besides, other "implementations" of the SM protocol could be given those types. For instance, M can also be the type of an agent that puts back in its list of preferences the identifier of a charger which denies the service (so to try again later).

4   Speculating on ABeT

We advocate new behavioural types for CAS. In the following we argue why "standard" behavioural types fall short of the requirements imposed by CAS.

Communication, roles & instances. As discussed in Sec. 1, point-to-point communications are not ideal for CAS. In particular, features such as attribute-based communications would be unfeasible with point-to-point interactions. Since the communication mechanism adopted in ABeT is inspired by AbC, it seems natural

---

[2] A suitable typing discipline, out of the scope of this paper, could do the assignment.

to get inspiration from klaimographies which, as far as we know, are the only behavioural abstractions that are not based on point-to-point communication. Klaimographies indeed are based on generative communication [9]. We envisage attribute-based communication as a further abstraction of generative communication. In fact, it would be interesting to look at ABeT as a mechanism to support the realisation of CAS by realising AbC specifications with distributed tuple spaces. We will return to this point in Sect. 7.

A basic abstraction borrowed from klaimographies is the notion of *role*. For instance, Fig. 1 describes the communication pattern of the "male" and "female" roles of SM protocol. Such roles are then enacted by *instances* of agents. The distinction between roles and instances is instrumental to abstract away from the number of agents, which is a paramount aspect of CAS. This is also a reason why we believe that standard behavioural type systems are not suitable to capture the complexity of CAS. For instance, *parameterised session types* [12] use indexed roles that can be rendered with a given number of instances. However, parameterised session types can only handle point-to-point communications.

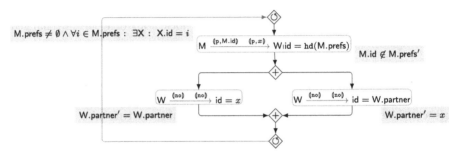

Fig. 2. Pre- and post-conditions in ABeT

Another peculiarity of CAS is that agents may play more than one role in the protocol. This will be indeed the case for the scenario considered in Sect. 5. We are not aware of any existing behavioural type framework allowing this.

Correctness. The agent R described at the end of Sect. 3 has a drastically different behaviour than agent B in Sect. 1. In fact, provided that preferences satisfy some properties, the latter has been shown in [20] to "stabilises" in a state where agents B are deadlocked waiting for a message from a charger C that is never sent and that each male agent pairs up with a female one and vice versa. The former CAS can instead diverge if e.g., the identifier of an agent B is not in the preference list of any charger agent.

The previous example suggests that ABeT do not guarantee progress. This is a distinctive difference from standard behavioural types, where the usual theorem is that well-typed programs are (dead)lock-free. Notice though, that progress (at least the strong variant usually taken in behavioural type theories) is not necessarily desirable in CAS. For instance, agents B *must* deadlock in order to successfully run the protocol. These observations immediately impose the following questions

– what notion of correctness suits CAS?
– what behavioural property do typed CAS enjoy?
– what features should ABeT have to capture such properties?

We argue that, to address these questions, it is not enough to capture the control-flow of CAS in behavioural abstractions. Basically, to some extent ABeT should also allow one to model the local behaviour of agents, at least to some extent. To illustrate this we use the variant of SM protocol in Fig. 2 where the top-most interaction is now decorated with some pre- and post-conditions. The idea is that these conditions constraint the local behaviour of agents. Intuitively,

– the pre-condition in Fig. 2 requires that, before sending a proposal, all the identifiers in the preference list of an agent M are assigned to some agent
– the post-condition in Fig. 2 states that, after being used for a proposal, the identifier is removed from the preference list of M.

Likewise, the post-conditions on the interactions of each branch state that the partner of W is set to the agent to whom the message no is not sent. Using pre- and post-conditions we can assign the decorated ABeT of Fig. 2 to agent B but not to agent R.

Asserted interactions have been proposed in [7] in order to specify relations among data exchanged by participants. We advocate the use of assertions also to specify local behaviour of CAS agents. For instance, the post-conditions on the branches in Fig. 2 is a mere assertion on the state of W and it does not involve any communication.

Progress & well-formedness. Related to correctness is the problem of identifying suitable notions of progress for CAS. The classical SM protocol is designed so that agents are actually suppose to deadlock. This is inconceivable in all the behavioural type systems but klaimographies, which brings us to a fundamental peculiarity of ABeT.

The typical result of behavioural type theories is the definition of *well-formedness* conditions that guarantee some form of progress. The idea is that well-formedness constraints are conditions on the choreography sufficient to ensure that the protocol deadlocks only if all participants terminates. For instance, all the known well-formed conditions of behavioural types would reject the SM protocol as ill-typed. In fact, the choice in the SM protocol is not prop-agated well according to the canons of behavioural types. This is due to the following reason. Behavioural types require that branches of a distributed choice to be "alternative", namely only one of them should be enacted by *all* the involved agents. Well-formedness conditions are usually imposed to guarantee that all the agents involved in a distributed choice unequivocally agree on which branch to follow. The rationale is to avoid mismatches in the communications when some participants follow a branch while other execute another branch of the choice. This is exactly what happens in the SM protocol. The choice involves the agent W, M, and W.partner. However, W communicates her decision only to one between M and W.partner.

Run-time support. An advantage of behavioural abstraction is that they allow us to *project* specifications to lower down levels of abstraction. For instance, one can obtain specification of each role by projecting the ABeT of Fig. 1 similarly to what done for klaimographies in [8]. Most behavioural types are amenable of being projected on executable code [21] as well as monitors to enforce some run-time properties [6,18,28]. These projections are "simple" since the communication model in the behavioural types is very close to existing ones (such as those of message-oriented middlewares or programming languages such as Erlang or GoLang). Attaining such projection operations for ABeT would not be that straightforward. Attribute-based communication requires some ingenuity to be effectively realised on the common communication infrastructures available for distributed systems.

We think that ABeT can support the run-time execution of CAS systems. The idea is to generate *ghost* components that decide how to spread the information among agents. The ghost of an agent can be statically derived by projection a global type in order to regulate the spread of the information across CAS. For instance, a static analysis could determine that some roles are not interested receiving some data, hence the ghosts of agents willing to synchronise on those patterns would spread the relevant information among themselves before sending it to any other agents. Similarly, the ghost of an agent that has to spread some information to other agents can prioritise the ones that are more likely to need that information in the near future than those that will not access it soon.

5   Autonomous Robots

To highlight other features of ABeT, in this section we consider a more complex scenario. Initially, we assume that agents can play two roles for simplicity but one can easily imagine that more roles could be involved.

5.1   A Coordination Protocol

Consider a decentralised system where robots roam a physical environment to delivery some goods. When a robot is in operational state, its battery depletes according to some factors (such as its load, speed, etc.). Therefore, robots collaborate to optimise the use of energy by *offering* and *requiring* energy. More precisely, a robot can offer other robots a recharging service when e.g., its energy is above a given threshold or seek for a recharge of its battery from other robots when its battery consumption becomes high. This way, energy is exchanged among robots, and it is less likely that robots cannot terminate their delivery tasks due to battery drain. This means that all the robots simultaneously assume the role of being consumers and suppliers of energy. The collective behaviour of robots is a strategy to accomplish their goal.

We now design a protocol that robots may use to administer their batteries. Let us assume that Sue and Rick are two robots of our delivery system enacting a specific role for our scenario. Namely, Sue behaves as energy supplier while Rick looks for a recharge, respectively. The robots repeatedly behave as follows.

Initially, Sue advertises her offer by sending to every potential consumer the available charge of the battery, and her contact details. She then waits for incoming answers from any interested robot. When Rick receives an offer of energy, he decides whether to make a request. For instance, this decision depends on the quantity of energy offered and the quantity of energy needed. If Rick is interested to acquire a certain amount of energy from Sue, it makes a request to Sue and sends his contact details. Rick then waits for Sue to confirm or to cancel the offer of energy; this is necessary because in the meantime Sue may have committed to supply some energy to other robots or she may have switched to a consumer modality depending on the level of her battery. Therefore, upon Rick's request, Sue decides whether the offer is still valid. If that is the case, Sue notifies Rick with the amount of energy she is willing to supply. Otherwise, Sue tells Rick that the offer is no longer available. For simplicity, we will assume that robots have identifiers that encompass all their contact details.

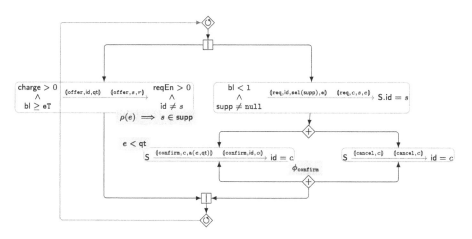

Fig. 3. ABeT specification of robots

5.2   A Specification in ABeT

The protocol in Fig. 3 captures the scenario in Sect. 5.1. The protocol is a loop in which robots manage energy through two parallel threads. In the left-most thread, energy offers are advertised by robots whose local state is such that they can offer a recharge (charge > 0) and have a battery level above a fixed threshold (bl $\geq$ eT). This advert is addressed to any robot requiring energy (reqEn > 0). Those robots may not consider the offer if they deem it inconvenient; this is modelled by the conditional post-condition $c(e) \implies s \in \mathsf{supp}$ where the proposition $c(\_)$ establishes whether the energy e offered is "convenient"; only if this is the case the robot updates its local state adding the supplier's identifier in its list of potential suppliers. Notice that the condition $id \neq s$ avoids adding the consumer's identity in supp; this avoids dealing with self-offers.

Once advertisements are out, a robot in need of energy can contact one of the suppliers chosen from those stored in its supp attribute ($\mathsf{sel}(\mathsf{supp})$). At this point the contacted supplier decides whether to confirm the offer (left-most branch of the choice) or cancel it. The former case requires that the amount of requested energy is lower than the supplier's energy level (pre-condition $e < \mathsf{qt}$). In our specification the actual amount of offered energy is a function of the required energy and the available quantity ($\mathsf{a}(e, \mathsf{qt})$); in the simplest case this may just equal e, but one could think of a lower amount if the local state of the supplier had changed between the advertisement and the current request of energy. Upon confirmation of the offer, the consumer updates its local state accordingly; this is modelled with the post-condition $\phi_{\mathtt{confirm}}$ that reads as

$$\mathsf{S.charge} = \mathsf{S.qt} - o \qquad \wedge \qquad \mathsf{C.bl} = \mathsf{C.bl} + o \wedge \mathsf{C.reqEn} = \mathsf{C.reqEn} - o$$

namely, the supplier is supposed to subtract the offered energy from its quantity while the consumer has to add the same amount to its battery level and updates its reqEn attribute accordingly. This scenario offers the possibility of a few remarks, besides the general ones in Sect. 4.

The protocol describes the behaviour of robots in need of energy and, *at the same time*, their behaviour when offering energy. In other words, the same agent can play both roles and behave according to a "supplier-" or "consumer-modality". Crucially, the specification in Fig. 3 does not constraint *a-priori* when or how these modalities can be played. For instance, the following would be all valid implementations:

- some robots act purely as suppliers (e.g., to model charging stations) while others act purely as consumers (e.g., mobile robots);
- robots can behave according to either of the modalities at a time;
- robots can offer or require energy at the same time.

This variability is not possible in most existing settings based on behavioural types where single-threadness is necessary. Notice that the behaviours mentioned above may determine different roles, e.g., a recharging station pursues a different goal than robots and it follows different communication patterns.

Another observation is that the protocol can be configured to obtain different emerging behaviours by tuning up some parameters such as the thresholds, the function a used when confirming the offers, or the proposition c used when accepting offers. For instance, one could set the battery level so that a robot acting just as charging station continuously makes offers (e.g., $\mathsf{bl} = 0$). Likewise, the protocol is permissive on local computations. For example, the criteria used by a robot to select the supplier to contact are abstracted away by the function `sel(_)` which can be implemented in a myriad of different ways. To mention but a few options, consider solutions where

- the attribute `supp` just contains the latest received offer and `sel(_)` is just the identity function;
- `sel(_)` treats the attribute `supp` as a priority list;
- the robot may store information about the amount of energy offered by suppliers or its physical position and select the one closest to its needs.

In principle, one could be more specific on those aspects by tuning up pre- and post-conditions of interactions.

6 Quantitative Analysis

We now discuss how to derive a quantitative analysis for CAS using the ABeT specification of the robots case study of Sect. 5. Starting from the specification of the interaction protocol, we build a quantitative abstraction that provides some analysis of the system under study. To this end, in this paper we propose to adopt Queuing Network (QN) models [25] which are widely applied in the software performance engineering community [5, 24, 30].

A QN model is a collection of *service centres* each regulated by a *rate*. Intuitively, service centres represent resources shared by a set of *jobs*, also called *customers* [25]. Incoming workload can be modelled as: (i) a *closed* class (i.e., a constant number of customers in each class and a think time regulating the delay of performing a system request), or (ii) an *open* class (i.e., the customer arrival rate). The former workload class is modelled through *delay* centres, whereas the latter required the specification of *source* and *sink* nodes for indicating the start and the completion, respectively, of requests. Delay centres, unlike service centres, do not have a queue. They are intended to model delays occurring when specifying closed workloads (i.e., requests re-iterate in the network in a loop-based fashion) or communication networks.

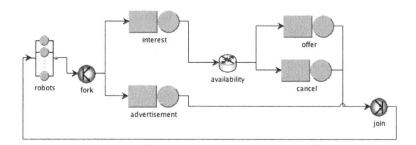

Fig. 4. QN model for the Exchange of resources among robots.

Service and delay centres are connected through *links* that form the network topology; a service centre consists of a *server* and a (possibly unbound) *queue*.

Servers process *jobs* scheduled from their queues according to a specific policy (e.g., FIFO). Each processed request is then routed to another service centre through links. More precisely, each server picks the next job (if any) from its queue, processes it, and sends the result on its outgoing link; a link may go through a *router node* which forwards it to the queue of another service centre according to a given probability.

In order to capture parallelism, QN models feature *fork* and *join* nodes. The former nodes are used to split the jobs into several tasks to be executed in parallel while a join node represents the point where these tasks are synchronized. Summarizing, a QN model can be interpreted as a directed graph whose nodes are service centres and their connections are the graph edges. Jobs go through edges set on the basis of the behaviour of customers' requests.

Figure 4 depicts the QN model obtained from the ABeT specification given in Sect. 5.2. More precisely, the topology of the model tightly correspond to the structure of specification given in Fig. 3 as follows:

- each interaction becomes a service centre;
- each parallel and join gate of the type in Fig. 3 respectively becomes a fork and a join node of the QN model;
- the non-deterministic choice becomes a router node;
- the delay centre can be used to model network delays in the communication among agents, however we decided to skip such modelling and to insert one delay centre only that is representative of the system closed workload (i.e., number of robots and their thinking time, if any).

The delay node namely *robots* represents the incoming requests, and for our case study we have three classes of jobs: suppliers, consumers, supp&cons, i.e., robots simultaneously acting as suppliers and consumers. In parallel, as showed by the *fork* node, robots can (i) put their offers, as modelled by the *advertisement* queuing centre, or (ii) verify if an offer matches their request, as modelled by the *interest* queuing centre. A router node, namely *availability* regulates the probability with which robots send an *offer* or a *cancel* message. In case of a confirmed offer, it is necessary to update the attributes, as modelled by the *offer* queueing centre. In case of cancel, it is also possible to specify a service time denoting the check of the corresponding message. All the requests outcoming from *offer*, *cancel*, and *advertisement* are routed to the *join* node modelling the completion of the iteration so that robots can re-iterate their behaviour.

To run a model-based performance analysis, we set the values for the parameters of the QN model. Table 1 shows an example of parameters' setting; the analysis is later performed by varying the parameter *robots*. The delay centre is associated with the specification of the closed workload. In particular, we set a workload population (wp) equal to 30 robots for the three classes of jobs (i.e., suppliers, consumers, supp&cons), thus considering 10 robots for each of the classes. The service centres are associated with parameters drawn from exponential distributions with average λ. For example, if the *advertisement* node is assigned $\lambda = 10$, the inter-arrival time drawn from the distribution averages one request every 0.1 time units (i.e., milliseconds in this case). Here we give

Parameter	Value
robots	wp=30
advertisement	$\lambda = 10$
interest	$\lambda = 10$
offer	$\lambda = 10$
cancel	$\lambda = 10$
availability	$\pi = 0.5$

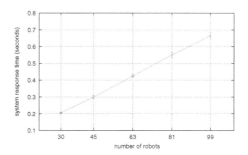

Table 1. Setting of parameters   **Fig. 5.** QN model results

a flavour of the type of analysis that can be performed in such scenarios. Note that the router node is associated with a π value denoting the probability associated to the branching points set with equal probabilities. Of course other values can be set to evaluate the behaviour under different assumptions. The obtained QN model has been analysed with the Java Modeling Tool (JMT) [11]. Figure 5 presents simulation results for the timing analysis, varying the population of robots, on the x-axis, up to 99, i.e., denoting up to 33 robots of each type.

As expected, the system response time (reported on the y-axis) increases as the number of robots increases going from 0.21 to 0.67 s. For example, a population of 45 robots (i.e., 15 robots for each type), results in a mean response time of 0.299 seconds and maximal and minimal values estimated to be 0.308 and 0.291 s, respectively.

7 Conclusions, Related and Future Work

We outlined some ideas for behavioural abstractions of CAS in the context of the AbC calculus. By means of some examples we argued for a new class of behavioural specifications tailored on CAS. In the following, we review the state-of-the-art by focusing on behavioural and quantitative abstractions for CAS.

Behavioural Abstractions. In the past thirty years behavioural types [23] have been widely adopted to reason about and support the development of communicating systems. Extensive research yielded important results for distributed systems where channel-based communications are adopted. To the best of our knowledge, klaimographies [8] are the only attempt to develop behavioural types for generative communication [9], recently applied to event-notification systems [19]. This recent results inspired the ideas described in this paper. In fact, CAS coordination mechanisms are often reduced to some sorts of event-notification mechanisms. In fact, we believe that event-notification is probably the most suitable approach to implement languages used to specify CAS.

Linguistic mechanisms. A recent work on modelling the interactions of CAS is [2] where a language-based approach is introduced for building groups of communicating partners by considering their attributes. The same attribute-based communication (AbC) paradigm has been also used in our previous work [13, 15] in which different forwarding strategies for message passing together with Erlang are exploited for dealing with scalability issues. The precursor of AbC is represented by SCEL [16] aimed to model the dynamic formation of ensembles of interacting autonomic components, and to verify some system properties (e.g., reachability). Programming actor-based CAS is discussed in [10] where global-level system specifications are translated into Scala/Akka actors with the goal of carrying coordination tasks that involve large sets of devices.

Quantitative Abstractions. The idea of proposing a quantitative evaluation of CAS finds its root in [32] where ordinary differential equations (ODEs) are adopted as trade-off between expressiveness and efficiency of the analysis. The modelling and quantitative verification of CAS is also proposed in [26] where a language (i.e., CARMA) aims to capture the timing and the probabilistic behaviour of agents. In [4] the focus is on verifying the robustness of CAS, against various classes of attacks, by embedding trust models of communication, i.e., reputation and trust relationships among the agents' exchanged information. Engineering resilient CAS is tackled in [33] with the goal of providing reusable blocks of distributed behaviour that can be substituted by functionally equivalent ones, possibly more efficient in terms of performance or showing desirable dynamics, i.e., without affecting the overall system behaviour and resilience. These works mostly focus on specific aspects, such as efficiency [32, 33] dependability [26], and reputation [4]. As opposite to these approaches, we aim to narrowing the behavioural and quantitative abstractions within CAS, thus to quantify the impact of design choices acting on the communication among agents with their non-functional properties.

Future work. The obvious next step is the precise formalisation of behavioural type systems that capture the ideas sketched in the previous sections. A natural starting point is the elaboration of klaimographies. We plan to refine the types described here and identify relevant properties for CAS that could be statically checked. For instance, a system that allows us to check that AbC implementations type check against type specifications such as those seen for the scenario of Sect. 5. This would require the identification of suitable local types as well as the definition of suitable projection operations. We are also interested in translating the results of the behavioural type systems into insights for their quantitative analysis. As long term goal, we aim to bridge behavioural abstractions with their quantitative counterpart, thus to provide a deeper analysis of CAS.

References

1. Abd Alrahman, Y., De Nicola, R., Loreti, M.: A calculus for collective-adaptive systems and its behavioural theory. Inf. Comput. **268**, 104457 (2019)
2. Abd Alrahman, Y., De Nicola, R., Loreti, M.: Programming interactions in collective adaptive systems by relying on attribute-based communication. Sci. Comput. Program. **192**, 102428 (2020)

3. Agha, G.: Actors: A Model of Concurrent Computation in Distributed Systems. MIT Press, Cambridge (1986)
4. Aldini, A.: Design and verification of trusted collective adaptive systems. ACM Trans. Model. Comput. Simul. **28**(2), 1–27 (2018)
5. Balsamo, S., Marzolla, M.: Performance evaluation of UML software architectures with multiclass queueing network models. In: Workshop on Software and Performance (2005)
6. Bocchi, L., Chen, T.-C., Demangeon, R., Honda, K., Yoshida, N.: Monitoring networks through multiparty session types. In: Beyer, D., Boreale, M. (eds.) FMOODS/FORTE -2013. LNCS, vol. 7892, pp. 50–65. Springer, Heidelberg (2013). https://doi.org/10.1007/978-3-642-38592-6_5
7. Bocchi, L., Honda, K., Tuosto, E., Yoshida, N.: A theory of design-by-contract for distributed multiparty interactions. In: Gastin, P., Laroussinie, F. (eds.) CONCUR 2010. LNCS, vol. 6269, pp. 162–176. Springer, Heidelberg (2010). https://doi.org/10.1007/978-3-642-15375-4_12
8. Bruni, R., Corradini, A., Gadducci, F., Melgratti, H.C., Montanari, U., Tuosto, E.: Data-driven choreographies à la Klaim. In: Boreale, M., Corradini, F., Loreti, M., Pugliese, R. (eds.) Models, Languages, and Tools for Concurrent and Distributed Programming. LNCS, vol. 11665, pp. 170–190. Springer, Cham (2019). https://doi.org/10.1007/978-3-030-21485-2_11
9. Carriero, N., Gelernter, D.: Linda in context. CACM **32**(4), 444–458 (1989)
10. Casadei, R., Viroli, M.: Programming actor-based collective adaptive systems. In: Ricci, A., Haller, P. (eds.) Programming with Actors. LNCS, vol. 10789, pp. 94–122. Springer, Cham (2018). https://doi.org/10.1007/978-3-030-00302-9_4
11. Casale, G., Serazzi, G.: Quantitative system evaluation with Java modeling tools. In: International Conference on Performance Engineering (2011)
12. Castro, D., Hu, R., Jongmans, S., Ng, N., Yoshida, N.: Distributed programming using role-parametric session types in go: statically-typed endpoint APIs for dynamically-instantiated communication structures. PACMPL **3**(POPL), 1–30 (2019)
13. De Nicola, R., Duong, T., Inverso, O., Trubiani, C.: AErlang at work. In: Steffen, B., Baier, C., van den Brand, M., Eder, J., Hinchey, M., Margaria, T. (eds.) SOFSEM 2017. LNCS, vol. 10139, pp. 485–497. Springer, Cham (2017). https://doi.org/10.1007/978-3-319-51963-0_38
14. De Nicola, R., Duong, T., Inverso, O., Trubiani, C.: AErlang: empowering erlang with attribute-based communication. In: Jacquet, J.-M., Massink, M. (eds.) COORDINATION 2017. LNCS, vol. 10319, pp. 21–39. Springer, Cham (2017). https://doi.org/10.1007/978-3-319-59746-1_2
15. De Nicola, R., Duong, T., Inverso, O., Trubiani, C.: AErlang: empowering erlang with attribute-based communication. Sci. Comput. Program. **168**, 71–93 (2018)
16. De Nicola, R., Loreti, M., Pugliese, R., Tiezzi, F.: A formal approach to autonomic systems programming: the SCEL language. ACM Trans. Auton. Adapt. Syst. **9**(2), 1–29 (2014)
17. Ferscha, A.: Collective adaptive systems. In: International Joint Conference on Pervasive and Ubiquitous Computing and Symposium on Wearable Computers (2015)
18. Francalanza, A., Mezzina, C.A., Tuosto, E.: Reversible choreographies via monitoring in Erlang. In: Bonomi, S., Rivière, E. (eds.) DAIS 2018. LNCS, vol. 10853, pp. 75–92. Springer, Cham (2018). https://doi.org/10.1007/978-3-319-93767-0_6

19. Frittelli, L., Maldonado, F., Melgratti, C., Tuosto, E.: A choreography-driven approach to APIs: the OpenDXL case study. In: Bliudze, S., Bocchi, L. (eds.) COORDINATION 2020. LNCS, vol. 12134, pp. 107–124. Springer, Cham (2020). https://doi.org/10.1007/978-3-030-50029-0_7

20. Gale, D., Shapley, L.S.: College admissions and the stability of marriage. Am. Math. Monthly **68**(1), 9–15 (1962)

21. Gay, S., Ravara, A. (eds.): Behavioural Types: From Theory to Tools. Automation, Control and Robotics. River, Gistrup (2009)

22. Guanciale, R., Tuosto, E.: An abstract semantics of the global view of choreographies. In: Interaction and Concurrency Experience (2016)

23. Hüttel, H., et al.: Foundations of session types and behavioural contracts. ACM Comput. Surv. **49**(1), 1–36 (2016)

24. Kleinrock, L.: Theory, Volume 1, Queueing Systems. Wiley-Interscience, Hoboken (1975)

25. Lazowska, E.D., Zahorjan, J., Scott Graham, G., Sevcik, K.C.: Computer System Analysis Using Queueing Network Models. Prentice-Hall Inc., Englewood Cliffs (1984)

26. Loreti, M., Hillston, J.: Modelling and analysis of collective adaptive systems with CARMA and its tools. In: Bernardo, M., De Nicola, R., Hillston, J. (eds.) SFM 2016. LNCS, vol. 9700, pp. 83–119. Springer, Cham (2016). https://doi.org/10.1007/978-3-319-34096-8_4

27. Milner, R., Parrow, J., Walker, D.: A Calculus of Mobile Processes, I and II. Inf. Comput. **100**(1), 1–40 (1992)

28. Neykova, R., Bocchi, L., Yoshida, N.: Timed runtime monitoring for multiparty conversations. Formal Aspects Comput. **29**(5), 877–910 (2017). https://doi.org/10.1007/s00165-017-0420-8

29. Prasad, K.V.S.: A calculus of broadcasting systems. Sci. Comput. Program. **25**(2–3), 285–327 (1995)

30. Smith, C.U., Williams, L.G.: Performance and scalability of distributed software architectures: an SPE approach. Scalable Comput. Pract. Exp. **3**(4), 74106–0700 (2000)

31. Tuosto, E., Guanciale, R.: Semantics of global view of choreographies. J. Logical Algebraic Methods Program. **95**, 17–40 (2018)

32. Vandin, A., Tribastone, M.: Quantitative abstractions for collective adaptive systems. In: Bernardo, M., De Nicola, R., Hillston, J. (eds.) SFM 2016. LNCS, vol. 9700, pp. 202–232. Springer, Cham (2016). https://doi.org/10.1007/978-3-319-34096-8_7

33. Viroli, M., Audrito, G., Beal, J., Damiani, F., Pianini, D.: Engineering resilient collective adaptive systems by self-stabilisation. ACM Trans. Model. Comput. Simul. **28**(2), 1–28 (2018)

Verifying AbC Specifications via Emulation

Rocco De Nicola[1]([⊠]), Tan Duong[1]([⊠]), and Omar Inverso[2]

[1] IMT School for Advanced Studies, Lucca, Italy
rocco.denicola@imtlucca.it, tan.duong@imtlucca.it
[2] Gran Sasso Science Institute, L'Aquila, Italy
omar.inverso@gssi.it

Abstract. We propose a methodology for verifying specifications written in AbC, a process calculus for collective systems with a novel communication mechanism relying on predicates over attributes exposed by the components. We emulate the execution of AbC actions and the operators that compose them as programs where guarded sequential functions are non-deterministically invoked; specifically, we translate AbC specifications into sequential C programs. This enables us to use state-of-the-art bounded model checkers for verifying properties of AbC systems. To vindicate our approach, we consider different case studies from different areas and model them as AbC systems, then we translate these AbC specifications into C and instrument the resulting program for verification, finally we perform actual verification of properties of interest.

Keywords: Attribute-based communication · Formal analysis · Bounded model checking

1 Introduction

Collective adaptive systems (CAS) [1] are typically characterised by a massive number of interacting components and by the absence of central control. Examples of these systems can often be found in many natural and artificial systems, from biological systems to smart cities. Guaranteeing the correctness of such systems is very difficult due to the dynamic changes in the operating environment and the delay or loss of messages that at any time may trigger unexpected behaviour. Due to interleaving, explicit-state analysis and testing may not always be appropriate for studying these systems. Rigorous theories, methods, techniques, and tools are being developed to formally reason about their chaotic behaviour and verifying their emergent properties [2].

Process calculi, traditionally seen as paradigms for studying foundational aspects of a particular domain have also been used as specification languages [3]. This is due to their well-specified operational semantics, which enables formal verification and compact descriptions of systems under consideration. On

This work is partially funded by MIUR project PRIN 2017FTXR7S *IT MATTERS* (Methods and Tools for Trustworthy Smart Systems).

T. Margaria and B. Steffen (Eds.): ISoLA 2020, LNCS 12477, pp. 261–279, 2020.
https://doi.org/10.1007/978-3-030-61470-6_16

the other hand, due to minimalism in their designs, encoding complex agents behaviour could be tedious. Our work aims at offering a tool for studying CAS by using AbC [4], a kernel calculus centered on attribute-based communication [5], specifically designed to model complex interactions in collective systems. AbC takes into account the runtime status of the components while forming communication groups. Each component is equipped with a set of attributes whose values may be affected by the communication actions. Components interact according to their mutual interests, specified as predicates over the attributes of the potential communication partners. This way, complex interactions can be expressed in a natural way. The AbC communication model is defined on top of broadcast following a style similar to [6]. A distinctive feature is that only components whose attributes satisfy the predicate of a sender can receive the communicating message, provided that they are willing to do so and that the sender attributes also satisfy the predicates specified by the receiving components.

In this paper, we show how AbC can be used to specify different kinds of systems and how some of their emergent properties can be verified. Specifically, we translate AbC specifications into C programs, instrument the latter with properties of interest, and finally analyse the programs by means of classical verifiers for C.

Our translation turns AbC actions into a set of emulation functions guarded by appropriate enabling conditions that, when satisfied, make it possible for the functions to be non-deterministically executed. Since the actions are originally composed by process-algebraic operators, our translation works out such enabling conditions by taking into account the semantics of process operators, and possibly specific code extracted from the actions themselves. A main function plays the role of a scheduler that orchestrates the non-deterministic invocation of the emulation functions. The evolution of the original system is emulated according to the *lock-step* semantics of AbC, which in turn is modelled in the form of a loop. The encoding at each emulation step allows for non-deterministic selection of a single component such that any of its output actions is able to initiate a multi-party synchronization.

Having obtained the C programs for a set of systems from different contexts, we manually annotate them with appropriate assertions that encode properties of interest in the form of expressions over the attributes of the components. We then focus on under-approximate analysis, exploiting mature bounded model checkers, traditionally used for bug hunting in C programs [7,8], to analyse the translated AbC specifications. We have implemented a tool to automatically translate all the examples in this paper. The translator, the source AbC specifications, and the target C programs are available at http://github.com/ArBITRAL/AbC2C.

The rest of the paper is organised as follows. In Sect. 2 we briefly present the fragment of the AbC calculus that we consider in the rest of the paper, present our translation from AbC to C, and describe how to instrument state-based properties of interest. In Sect. 3 we use AbC to model a number of systems borrowed from classical papers in the literature and show how some of their key properties can be verified by means of two bounded model checkers for C. The final section recaps the work done, draws some conclusions, briefly describes related works and suggests directions for future research.

2   Translating AbC into C

Before going into the details of the translation, we briefly review the syntax and semantics of AbC with the help of a running example, namely the two-phase commit protocol [9]. The reader is referred to [4,10] for the full description of the calculus.

2.1   AbC in a Nutshell

An AbC *component* (C) is either a pair $\Gamma : P$, where Γ is an attribute environment and P a process, or the parallel composition $C_1 \parallel C_2$ of two components. The environment Γ is a mapping from a set of attribute names $a \in \mathcal{A}$ to ground values $v \in \mathcal{V}$; $\Gamma(a)$ indicates the value of a in Γ.

Let us now consider the two-phase commit protocol (2PC), where a *manager* asks a number of participants for their votes on either "commit" or "abort" a transaction. The transaction is aborted if at least one *participant* votes "abort", and is committed in case all participants vote "commit".

In AbC we can model the manager as a component $M \triangleq \Gamma_m : P_m$. The attribute environment Γ_m has three attributes: role, initially set to 1 and representing the manager role in the protocol; n, initially set to the number of participants; c, a counter used for counting participant votes, initially set to 0. Each participant is modelled by a component $C_j \triangleq \Gamma_j : P_p$ and three attributes: role, initially set to 0 representing the participant role, vote specifying the vote, i.e., "commit" or "abort" casted by the participant, and d, used for storing the final decision sent by the manager. A scenario consisting of n participants and one manager is then rendered as an AbC system: $M \parallel C_1 \parallel \ldots \parallel C_n$.

In the general case, an AbC process (P) is defined by the following grammar that involves standard constructors such as inactive process (0), action prefixing (.), non-deterministic choice (+), interleaving (|), and invocation of a unique process identifier K.

$$P ::= 0 \mid Q \mid P + P \mid P|P \mid K \quad Q ::= \langle \Pi \rangle P \mid \alpha.P \mid \alpha.[\tilde{a} := \tilde{E}]P \quad \alpha ::= \Pi(\tilde{x}) \mid (\tilde{E})@\Pi$$

We use $\tilde{\ }$ to denote a finite sequence whose length is not relevant. Process P in the construct $\langle \Pi \rangle P$ is blocked until the awareness predicate Π is satisfied within the local environment. In a prefixed process, an action α may be associated with an attribute update $[\tilde{a} := \tilde{E}]$ that, when the action is executed, sets the values of attributes $\tilde{a}$ to that of expressions $\tilde{E}$. Output action $(\tilde{E})@\Pi$ is used to send the values of expressions $\tilde{E}$ to all components whose attributes satisfy the sending predicate Π. Input action $\Pi(\tilde{x})$ is used to receive a message (to be bound to $\tilde{x}$) from any sending component whose attributes (and the message) satisfy the receiving predicate Π.

A predicate Π can be either *true*, a comparison $\bowtie$ (e.g., $<, >, =, \leq, \ldots$) on two expressions E, a logical conjunction of two predicates, or the negation of a predicate. Other logical connectives may be built from these. An expression E is either a value v, a variable x, an attribute name a or an attribute of the current component *this.a*. A component must use *this.a* in its communication predicates (sending or receiving) for distinguishing its own attributes from other different components.

$$\Pi ::= true \mid E \bowtie E \mid \Pi \wedge \Pi \mid \neg\Pi \qquad E ::= v \mid x \mid a \mid this.a \mid \ldots$$

Larger expressions can also be built using binary operators such as $+, -$, etc. Expressions E can be evaluated under Γ $\{\!|E|\!\}_\Gamma$. The satisfaction relation $\models$ defines when a predicate Π is satisfied in an environment Γ.

$\Gamma \models true$ for all Γ $\qquad\qquad\qquad \Gamma \models \Pi_1 \wedge \Pi_2$ if $\Gamma \models \Pi_1$ and $\Gamma \models \Pi_2$

$\Gamma \models E_1 \bowtie E_2$ if $\{\!|E_1|\!\}_\Gamma \bowtie \{\!|E_2|\!\}_\Gamma$ $\quad \Gamma \models \neg\Pi$ if not $\Gamma \models \Pi$

Continuing with our example, the behaviour P_m of the manager component is specified as: $P_m \triangleq A|B$, where $A \triangleq (\text{``}req\text{''})@(\texttt{role} = 0).0$ and

$$\begin{aligned}
B \triangleq \ & \langle \texttt{c} < \texttt{n} \rangle (x = \text{``}commit\text{''})(x).[\texttt{c} := \texttt{c} + 1]B \\
& + \langle \texttt{c} = \texttt{n} \rangle (\text{``}commit\text{''})@(\texttt{role} = 0).0 \\
& + (x = \text{``}abort\text{''})(x).(\text{``}abort\text{''})@(\texttt{role} = 0).0.
\end{aligned}$$

Process A sends a request to all participants using the predicate ($\texttt{role} = 0$), and terminates. Process B is a choice between different behaviours. The first branch stores the number of "commit" votes in $\texttt{c}$ using recursion. The second branch deals with the case when all votes are of "commit", i.e., the counter $\texttt{c}$ is equal to the number of participants $\texttt{n}$. The third branch enforces early termination: as soon as an "abort" arrives, the manager can send an "abort" message regardless of the other votes.

All participants have the same behaviour P_p which is specified as:

$$\begin{aligned}
P_p \triangleq \ & (x = \text{``}req\text{''})(x).((\textbf{vote})@(\texttt{role} = 1).(\texttt{role} = 1)(x).[\texttt{d} := x]0 \\
& + (\texttt{role} = 1)(x).[\texttt{d} := x]0)
\end{aligned}$$

Upon receiving a vote request from the manager, a participant faces two possibilities encoded as a choice $(+)$ in the continuation of P_p: it may reply with its $\texttt{vote}$ and continue to wait for a final decision to arrive, or it may receive the decision before sending $\texttt{vote}$. Either possibility updates the final decision to attribute $\texttt{d}$ and terminates.

Communication. In AbC, output actions are non-blocking while input actions must wait to synchronize on available messages. If multiple components are willing to offer output actions at the same time, only one of them is allowed to move. Communication among components takes place in a broadcast fashion: when a component sends a message, all other receiving components take part in the synchronization by checking the satisfactions of both sending and receiving predicates for reception. Components that accept the message evolve together with the sending component. Components who are not offering a successful input action or reject the message stay unchanged.

As a side note, we mention that since AbC is an untyped calculus, it is the responsibility of the modeller to specify appropriately attributes values, expressions, and predicates so that their evaluations make sense.

2.2   Emulating *AbC* Systems in C

Our translation takes as input an AbC specification, possibly composed of multiple component specifications. Each component specification is in the form $\langle \Gamma_i, P_{init_i}, D_i \rangle$ where Γ_i is the attribute environment, P_{init_i} the component's top-level behaviour, and D_i the set of process definitions. For example, the specification of the manager component illustrated in the previous section would be $\langle \Gamma_m, P_m, \{ P_m \triangleq A|B, A \triangleq \ldots, B \triangleq \ldots \} \rangle$.

The translation produces a single C program whose structure follows a pre-designed template (Fig. 1). The encoding is parameterized in the total number of components (N), and the maximum number of parallel processes, of process definitions, and of input-bindings variables across all component specifications (P_MAX, D_MAX, and V_MAX, respectively). These constants are extracted from the input specification and defined at the beginning of the output program. The components' attributes are represented as global vectors (line 4), so that each component can access the attributes via its index. Note that, as shown in the figure, we encode the values of the attributes as integers. For each component i, we declare a vector of program counters pc[i] for keeping track of the executions of the component's actions during the emulation, a vector bound[i] for storing inbound messages, and vector tgt to store the indexes of potential receivers when a component sends a message (line 7).

For each (specification of) component i, we translate its behaviour, i.e., $\langle P_{init_i}, D_i \rangle$ into a set of emulation functions. In particular, each action α is translated into a uniquely named function, denoted as $Name_\alpha$, parameterized (among others) with the component index (lines 10–17). The function body is guarded by an enabling condition whereas a return value indicates whether it is executed.

In order to emulate the executions of all functions in the set with respect to P_{init_i}, the translation visits all actions reachable from the process (by using D_i for looking up process code when necessary); while traversing, it calculates for each action α an index j_α, used for accessing program counter pc[i][j_α] and two execution points, namely entry point en_α and exit point ex_α used for controlling the action's execution. A guard pc[i][j_α] == en_α, called *entry condition* means that the function body may be executed, among other conditions, if the program counter of α satisfies such condition. At the end of the function, the program counter is set to ex_α, i.e., its *exit condition*, to enable the next set of feasible actions. Intuitively, the entry and exit conditions of the translated functions must behave according to the intended behavior of the corresponding process operators $(., +, |)$. For example, in a prefix process $\alpha.P$, the exit point of α must be equal to the entry point of the continuation process P. In a choice process $P_1 + P_2$, the entry points of both P_1 and P_2 must be the same but those of their continuations are not. In a parallel process $P_1|P_2$, the entry conditions of the subprocesses must be independent. For additional details on how to determine entry and exit conditions, we refer the reader to [11].

Whether or not an action can really be executed, however, does not depend only on the guarding mechanisms just described, but it depends also on action-

```
1    #define ...   // define key constants N,P_MAX,D_MAX,V_MAX
2
3    ... //other declarations
4    int attr₁[N]; int attr₂[N]; ... ; // attributes
5
6    /* program counter, input-binding variables, receiving components */
7    int pc[N][P_MAX]; int bound[N][D_MAX][V_MAX]; int tgt[N];
8
9    /* A function Nameα emulates action α of component i */
10   int Nameα(int i, ...) {
11      if (pc[i][jα] == enα && ...) {
12         ... // action code
13         pc[i][jα] = exα;
14         return 1;
15      }
16      return 0;
17   }
18   ... // all other actions
19
20   /* lookup table for the translated input and output actions */
21   struct {...} lookup[N];
22
23   /* initializations for attributes environments and lookup table */
24   void init() { ... } ;
25
26   /* Driver functions  */
27   int Schedule() { //non deterministic scheduling
28      int i = nondet_int();
29      assume(i >= 0 && i < N);
30      return i;
31   };
32
33   int Evolve(int i) { // lock-step evolution
34      int ns = ...; // lookup for the number of output actions of i
35      pts* sa = ...; // lookup for the vector of output actions of i
36      // nondeterministically selects an index
37      int k = nondet_int();
38      assume(k >= 0 && k < ns);
39      return (sa[k])(i,1); // executes the kth output action of i
40   };
41
42   int Available() {...};   //check the existence of enabled output actions
43
44   void Sync(int i, int *m); {...}; // multi-party synchronization
45
46   /* Emulation loop */
47   int main() {
48      int i;       // selected component index
49      init();
50      while (Available()) {   //there exists enabled output actions
51         i = Schedule();      // choose one component
52         assume(Evolve(i)); // perform lock-step evolution, assuming i sending
53      }
54      return 0;
55   }
```

Fig. 1. Structure of the output C program.

specific aspects, such as satisfactions of awareness and receiving predicates. In fact, the emulation function will have different input parameters and body, depending on whether the action being encoded is an input or an output action. More on this will be explained later.

All the emulation functions are organized in a `lookup` table to conveniently invoke them using the component index. Intuitively, each entry i in the table contains, among others, the sets of (pointers to the emulation functions of) input and output actions of component i. The `init()` function (line 24) is responsible for initializing all attribute environments by translating $\Gamma_0, \Gamma_1, \ldots$ and for filling up the `lookup` table.

Towards the end of the output program, we provide several fixed driver functions whose functionalities are as follows.

- `Schedule()`: non-deterministically selects a component index and returns it;
- `Evolve(i)`: non-deterministically selects an output action of component i and returns the result of performing the action;
- `Available()`: checks whether there exists an enabled output action;
- `Sync(i,m)`: delivers message m of component i to potential receiving components (used by output actions).

The source of non-determinism in an AbC system is due to non-deterministic choice and to the possibility that different components or different processes within a component perform output actions. To model such non-determinism in the target program, we rely on the common library functions supported by C verifiers: i) `nondet_int` to choose a non-deterministic value from the `int` data type; and ii) `assume` to restrict non-deterministic choices made by the program according to a given condition. We use these primitives in `Schedule()`, as shown in lines 27–31. The implementation of `Evolve(i)` additionally relies on `lookup` to non-deterministically execute an output action of component i (lines 33–40). Other driver functions do not consider nondeterminism; their implementation (omitted for brevity) is straightforward by relying on `lookup` and taking advantage of the fact that the number of components N is known.

Using the above functions, we emulate the evolution of the translated system through a loop, as shown in lines 50–53. Since an AbC system can only evolve when there are components willing to send, the loop iterations are guarded by `Available()`.

At each iteration, an index i is selected by `Schedule` and passed to `Evolve` which in turn performs actual computation. The output action called by `Evolve` relies on `Sync` for sending its message, allowing multi-party synchronization in one pass. Moreover, the emulation considers only non-deterministic choices over component index and the corresponding output action that results in valid computations, i.e., the selected output action can actually be executed. This is achieved by wrapping `Evolve` in the library function `assume` (line 52). Our scheduling mechanism based on the idea of non-deterministically selecting the emulation functions has been inspired from [12].

In the rest of the section, we describe the translation for input and output actions in detail. Note that an action may be associated with a preceding awareness predicate and a following attribute update. For example, process B of the component manager (Sect. 2.1) contains such an action. Thus we consider the general form of an action α to be $\langle \Pi \rangle \alpha.[\tilde{a} := \tilde{E}]$. If no awareness construct $\langle \Pi \rangle$ is present, we just consider $\langle \Pi \rangle = true$. If no attribute updates occurs, $[\tilde{a} := \tilde{E}]$ is regarded as an empty assignment. In the following, we write Π_g, Π_s, Π_r to differentiate between the three kinds of predicates: awareness, sending and receiving, respectively.

An output action $\langle \Pi_g \rangle(\tilde{E})@\Pi_s.[\tilde{a} := \tilde{E}]$, where the first $\tilde{E}$ is the expression(s) to be sent, is translated into a function depicted in Fig. 2 (left).

```
int Nameₐ(int i, int f) {                    int Nameₐ(int i, int j, int* m) {
  if (!f) return (pc[i][jₐ] == enₐ && ‖Πg‖);    if (pc[i][jₐ] == enₐ && ‖Πg‖ && ⟦Πr⟧ˣ̃) {
  if (pc[i][jₐ] == enₐ && ‖Πₐ‖) {                 // receive
    for (int j = 0; j < N; j++)                    bound[i][d][jₓ₀] = m[0]; ...
      if (j != i && ⟦Πₛ⟧) tgt[j] = 1;             //--- attr update ---
      else tgt[j] = 0;                             ‖ã := Ẽ‖;
    int m[|Ẽ|]; // a vector of size |Ẽ|           pc[i][jₐ] = exₐ;
    m[0] = ‖E₀‖; ...                               return 1;}
    Sync(i,m); // sending                        return 0;}
    ‖ã := Ẽ‖; // attr update
    pc[i][jₐ] = exₐ;
    return 1;}
  return 0;}
```

Fig. 2. The translation of output (left) and input (right)

The translation generates a unique identifier Name_α for the function. The two function parameters are the index i of the component containing α, and a flag f used to check the enabled condition of the action/function without actually executing it. This flag is specifically used by the driver function $\texttt{Available()}$ mentioned before.

The enabling condition of an output action, besides the guard on its program counter, includes the satisfaction of the associated awareness predicate, if any. Note that we use two auxiliary translations $\|\cdot\|$ for translating Π_g and local expressions and $\llbracket\cdot\rrbracket$ for translating Π_s. In the function body, the set $\texttt{tgt}$ of potential receivers is calculated based on the satisfaction of Π_s. Since all components' attributes are globally declared in the emulation program, the output action can evaluate its sending predicate immediately.

After that, a message is prepared as a vector $\texttt{m}$ that contains the values of output expressions, and sent via driver function $\texttt{Sync}$. This function retrieves the set of potential receivers in $\texttt{tgt}$ and invokes their receiving functions. $\texttt{Sync}$ stops delivering $\texttt{m}$ to a potential component when one of its receiving functions returns success (i.e., the message is accepted), or none of them do (i.e., the potential component rejects the message). The translation is completed by a sequence of assignments to model attribute updates, if any.

An input action, whose general form is $\langle \Pi_g \rangle \Pi_r(\tilde{x}).[\tilde{a} := \tilde{E}]$, is translated into a function depicted in Fig. 2 (right).

The function takes as input the second argument as sending component index and the third as a communicated message. The enabling condition for executing this function includes satisfaction of awareness and receiving predicates. Here we denote by $[\![\Pi_r]\!]^{\tilde{x}}$ the translation of Π_r parameterized with input-binding variables $\tilde{x}$. In order to model variable binding, we store the inbound message m in vector $\mathtt{bound[i][d]}$ where d is (the index of) the *process definition* that contains α. Moreover, all input-binding variables y in d are also indexed according to their names, denoted by j_y. In this way, the message is stored by assigning each of its element k to $\mathtt{bound[i][d][j_{x_k}]}$, where x_k is the kth variable in the sequence $\tilde{x}$.

In the above translation, we have used $\lfloor\!\lfloor\cdot\rfloor\!\rfloor$ for translating awareness predicates and local expressions. This function is defined as follows:

$$\lfloor\!\lfloor\Pi_1 \wedge \Pi_2\rfloor\!\rfloor = \lfloor\!\lfloor\Pi_1\rfloor\!\rfloor \ \&\& \ \lfloor\!\lfloor\Pi_2\rfloor\!\rfloor \qquad \lfloor\!\lfloor a\rfloor\!\rfloor = \mathtt{attr[i]}$$
$$\lfloor\!\lfloor\neg\Pi\rfloor\!\rfloor = ! \ \lfloor\!\lfloor\Pi\rfloor\!\rfloor \qquad\qquad\quad \lfloor\!\lfloor this.a\rfloor\!\rfloor = \mathtt{attr[i]}$$
$$\lfloor\!\lfloor true\rfloor\!\rfloor = \mathtt{true} \qquad\qquad\qquad \lfloor\!\lfloor v\rfloor\!\rfloor = \mathtt{v}$$
$$\lfloor\!\lfloor E_1 \bowtie E_2\rfloor\!\rfloor = \lfloor\!\lfloor E_1\rfloor\!\rfloor \bowtie \lfloor\!\lfloor E_2\rfloor\!\rfloor \qquad \lfloor\!\lfloor x\rfloor\!\rfloor = \mathtt{bound[i][d][j_x]}$$

The functions $[\![\cdot]\!]$ and $[\![\cdot]\!]^{\tilde{x}}$ are used for translating the sending and receiving predicates, respectively. They have the same definition as above, except when translating attributes and variables:

$$[\![a]\!] = [\![a]\!]^{\tilde{x}} = \mathtt{a[j]} \qquad [\![this.a]\!] = [\![this.a]\!]^{\tilde{x}} = \mathtt{attr[i]}$$

$$[\![y]\!]^{\tilde{x}} = \begin{cases} \mathtt{m[k]} \text{ if } y \in \tilde{x} \text{ and } y = x_k \\ \mathtt{bound[i][d][j_y]} \text{ otherwise} \end{cases}$$

Thus, $\lfloor\!\lfloor\cdot\rfloor\!\rfloor$ does not differentiate between a and $this.a$ whereas $[\![\cdot]\!]$ and $[\![\cdot]\!]^{\tilde{x}}$ do. In $[\![y]\!]^{\tilde{x}}$, if a variable appears in the list of input-binding variables then it is translated into the corresponding element of the communicated message. In all other cases, the variable is already bound and its value can be looked up in vector $\mathtt{bound[i][d]}$.

2.3   Encoding Properties

The evolution of an AbC system over time can be viewed as a tree rooted at the initial state, i.e., the union of all the components' initial states. An edge from a node to a child represents a lock-step evolution in which a component sends and others receive (hence, changing the overall system state). From a node there may be multiple edges, each corresponding to a synchronization initiated by a non-deterministically selected sending component.

Typically, program verifiers do not allow to directly express temporal logics for specifying properties; users must use `assert` statements to check that their intentions hold. We use assertions to express state-based formulae, e.g., conditions over the components' attributes. In practice, we encode such a formula as a boolean-valued C expression, denoted as p, and insert a statement `assert(p)` within the emulation loop of the main function.

Notice that, due to the emulation mechanism explained in previous section, the C program emulates all possible execution paths of the translated AbC system. This means that checking the assertions at every iteration of the emulation loop in the C program corresponds to checking whether p holds in (every state of) all possible execution traces of the initial AbC system. Naturally, in this way the system is verified against a safety property denoted as $S\ p$. In this paper, we focus on bounded analysis, i.e., limit the emulation up to a given number B of system evolutions of the AbC system by bounding the number of iterations of the emulation loop. Thus, in practice we only analyse safety up to the given bound. In other words, we deal with bounded safety $(S\ p)^B$.

For AbC systems one may also be interested in eventual properties, e.g., "good" system states that eventually emerge from the interactions of individual components. Since we focus on bounded analysis, we must resort to a bounded variant of liveness, and reduce liveness checking to safety checking [13] by expressing the former via the latter. We consider three (bounded) versions of eventuality and describe their encodings in the following.

"Possibly" - $(P\ p)^B$ is encoded as $(S\ \neg p)^B$: we simply assert the negation of p inside the emulation loop, and wait for the model checker to report a counter example (of $\neg p$) that would be the evidence that there is at least one execution trace that satisfies p.

"Eventually" - $(E\ p)^B$. We translate this property into safety by following the idea of [13], the intuition being that if the formula p fails, it must do so within B steps. Thus, when the bound is reached, we need to assert whether p has been true at least once. Our encoding is illustrated in the left of Fig. 3. A variable `step` counts the number of steps performed by the system up to that point. In each step of the emulation, the truth value of p is accumulated into a boolean variable `live` via alternation. The `assert` statement checks the value of `live` when the emulation stops, i.e., either the bound B is reached or there are no available sending components.

```
int step = 0;                          int step = 0;
_Bool aa = Available();                _Bool aa = Available();
_Bool live = false;                    _Bool live = false, saved = false;
while (aa) {                           while (aa) {
    step = step + 1;                       step = step + 1;
    ... //AbC system's evolution           ... // Abc system's evolution
    live = live || p();                    live = saved?(live && p()):(live || p());
    aa = Available();                      if (!saved && live) saved = true;
    assert((!(step == B) && aa) || live);  aa = Available();
}                                          assert((!(step == B) && aa)|| live);
                                       }
```

Fig. 3. Encoding of $(E\ p)^B$ (left), and $(EI\ p))^B$ (right)

"Eventually then Inevitably" - $(EI\ p)^B$. Compared to "Eventually", this property further requires that once p holds, it remains true afterward. The encoding is shown on the right of Fig. 3 where we extend the previous code snippet to enforce this additional requirement. Specifically, we use a variable `saved` to record the first time when p holds. When this happens, `live` is conjuncted with p rather than alternating. Because of this p must remain true after `saved` is set, otherwise the property fails.

3   Experimental Evaluation

We now illustrate the effectiveness of the proposed method by considering some case studies and systematically verifying their properties.

3.1   Case Studies

Max-Element. This system is an attribute-based variant of the one presented in [14]. Given N agents, each associated with an integer $\in \{1, \ldots N\}$, we wish to find an agent holding the maximum value. This problem can be modeled in AbC by using one component type with two attributes, namely s, initially set to 1, indicating that the current component is the max, and n, that stores the component's value. The behavior of a component is specified by the following choice process P:

$$P \triangleq \langle s = 1 \rangle (n)@(n \leq this.n).0 + (x \geq this.n)(x).[s := 0]0.$$

Thus, a component either announces its own value by sending its attribute n to all other components with smaller numbers, or non-deterministically accepts a greater value from another. In addition, upon receiving a greater value a component sets its flag s to 0 since it can not possibly be the max.

   For this system, we are interested in verifying whether eventually there exists only one component whose attribute s is equal to 1, and that holds the maximum value of n.

Or-Bit. This example and the next one are adapted from [15]. Given a number of agents, where each agent is given an input bit, the agents must collaborate with each other in order to compute the logical disjunction of all their bits. We model this system with an AbC component with two attributes ib and ob, representing the input and output bits, respectively. Initially, ob is set to 0, but this may change during interactions. The behaviour of a component is specified by a choice process P:

$$P \triangleq \langle ib = 1 \rangle (ib)@(ib = 0).[ob := 1]0 + \langle ib = 0 \rangle (x = 1)(x).[ob := 1]0.$$

The first branch of P controls the behaviour of components whose input bits is equal to 1. These announce the bits and update their outputs to 1. In other cases, components with 0 input bits keep waiting for any positive bit to arrive in order to update their outputs to 1. For this example, we are interested in checking whether each component correctly calculates (in ob) the disjunction of all the bits.

Majority. Given a system composed of *dancers* and *followers*, we would like to determine whether the dancers are the majority, i.e., no less than the number of followers, without any centralized control.

   This scenario is rendered in AbC by using two types of components, representing dancers and followers respectively. The approach is to design a protocol for matching pairs of dancers and followers. Eventually, by looking at the ones without partners, we can conclude about the majority of one type over the other. For both kinds of components, we introduce an attribute r for representing the component's role, where value 1 encodes a dancer, an attribute p indicating if a current component is already paired up with another member of the other role. Furthermore, for dancers that are responsible for initiating the matching, we add an additional attribute u, used as a unique tag when sending messages.

A dancer starts by announcing a unique message (using u) and waits for a follower to show up. The first branch in the choice process D below illustrates this behaviour:

$$D \triangleq (\mathbf{u})@(true).(x = this.\mathbf{u})(x).[\mathbf{p} := 1]0 + (\mathbf{r} = this.\mathbf{r})(x).(y \neq this.\mathbf{u})(y).D.$$

The second branch of D instead models the situation in which the dancer's turn to announce has been preempted by some other dancer, i.e., the input action with a receiving predicate $(\mathbf{r} = this.\mathbf{r})$ is executed. In that case, it has to listen to (and discards silently) a reply from some follower (to the announcer) in order to try again.

Any announcements sent by process D is broadcast but only followers answer. A follower listens to the announcements, i.e., via the predicate $(\mathbf{r} \neq this.\mathbf{r})$, then it either replies to the sender using the sender's message tag or silently discards a message from some other follower (who has replied to this sender before it). The process F defined below captures the described intuition:

$$F \triangleq (\mathbf{r} \neq this.\mathbf{r})(x).((x)@(true).[\mathbf{p} := 1]0 + (y = x \wedge \mathbf{r} = this.\mathbf{r})(y).F).$$

For this case study, we check for the majority of dancers by asserting that either there is at least one dancer left without partner or everyone has a partner.

Two-Phase Commit. This example has already been described in Sect. 2. The property of interest is that all participants consistently agree on either abort or commit the concerned transaction. In the latter case, we must check that all participants voted for commit.

Debating Philosophers. This example is taken from [16]. A number N of philosophers hold two different opinions on a thesis, possibly against it ($^-$) or in favor of it ($^+$). Each philosopher has also a physical condition, either rested (R) or tired (T). When two philosophers with different opinions debate, a rested philosopher convinces the tired one of his opinion; if the two philosophers are in the same physical condition, the positive one convinces the negative one and both get tired afterwards. On the other hand, philosophers holding the same opinion do not debate.

Each philosopher has the following attributes: attribute u, a unique identifier used for announcement, attribute $o \in \{0, 1\}$ is the initial opinion with a value 1 indicating positive opinion ($^+$), and attribute $c \in \{0, 1\}$ represent the initial physical condition with a value 1 denoting rested (R). We design the behaviour for philosophers to interact with each other by a parallel process $P \triangleq F \mid A$. The property of interest is a majority one which states that the number of positive philosophers is not less than that of negative ones. Our protocol is as follows. Any philosopher supporting the thesis repeatedly convince the members of the other group by using process F, specified as:

$$F \triangleq \langle o = 1 \rangle (\mathsf{u}, \mathsf{c}) @(\mathit{true}).((\mathit{this}.\mathsf{u} = x \wedge y \neq \mathit{this}.\mathsf{c})(x, y).[\mathsf{o} := \mathsf{c}] F$$
$$+ (\mathit{this}.\mathsf{u} = x \wedge y = \mathit{this}.\mathsf{c})(x, y).[\mathsf{c} := 0] F)$$
$$+ \langle \mathsf{o} = 1 \rangle (\mathsf{o} = \mathit{this}.\mathsf{o})(x, y).(\mathsf{o} \neq \mathit{this}.\mathsf{o})(x, y).F$$

Each branch of F is guarded by an awareness predicate $\langle \mathsf{o} = 1 \rangle$. In the first branch, a positive philosopher announces its unique message u and the physical condition c. It waits for a message from a negative one by checking on the condition $(\mathit{this}.\mathsf{u} = x)$, and additionally consider two possibilities of the opponent's physical condition y. The following choice process implements concisely the first two debate rules described above for this philosopher where his opinion o or condition c is updated. In the second branch, the philosopher receives an announcement from another positive one, i.e., $(\mathsf{o} = \mathit{this}.\mathsf{o})$. When this happens, it must listen silently until the debate started by the sender finishes.

Philosophers who are against (or negative about) the thesis listen to the opinion of the others and debate according to process A as follows:

$$A \triangleq \langle \mathsf{o} = 0 \rangle (\mathsf{o} \neq \mathit{this}.\mathsf{o})(x, y).((\langle y \neq \mathsf{c} \rangle (x, \mathsf{c}) @(\mathit{true}).[\mathsf{o} := y] A$$
$$+ \langle y = \mathsf{c} \rangle (x, \mathsf{c}) @(\mathit{true}).[\mathsf{o} := 1, \mathsf{c} := 0] A$$
$$+ (z = x)(z, y).A).$$

A is guarded by an awareness predicate $\langle \mathsf{o} = 0 \rangle$ to limit such behavior to negative philosophers. When a negative philosopher receives an announcement, he may involve into the debate with the sender by replying with the sender's unique value, stored in x and its current physical condition. During this action, changes to opinion and physical conditions (in the form of attribute updates) are implemented by following the first two debate rules. On the other hand, there may happen that another negative one is already engaged into the debate with the same sender, in such case the philosopher waits for another announcement.

Experimental Setup. We developed a translator implementing the method described in Sect. 2 and used it on the AbC specifications of the case studies. We manually instrumented the generated C programs with appropriate assertions to express the properties of interest described above. While instrumenting, we applied the scheme shown in the right of Fig. 3 (Sect. 2.3) for all case studies, i.e., to consider the "Eventually then Inevitability" properties. Additionally, we applied the other two schemes "Eventually" and "Possibly" for the last case study. Hereafter for brevity we refer to the instrumented properties by using their versions, i.e., EI, E and P respectively.

We used two mature bounded model checkers, namely CBMC v5.11[1] and ESBMC v6.2[2] respectively SAT- and SMT-based, for the actual analysis of the

---

[1] http://www.cprover.org/cbmc/.
[2] https://github.com/esbmc/esbmc/releases/tag/v6.2.

instrumented C programs up to different bounds of the emulation loop. Note that all the other loops in the program (namely, those within the driver functions) are always bounded by constants, and thus are fully unrolled by the model checker in any case.

3.2   Verification Results

The verification results of the three case studies Maximum Element (max), Or Bit (bit) and Two-Phase Commit (2pc) are presented in Fig. 4. The subtable on the left contains the results obtained from CBMC; the right one corresponds to ESBMC. In the tables, we include the numbers of components (N), the unwinding bound for the emulation loop (B), the property, the verification times (in seconds), and the verification result. A [✓] means that the verification succeeds, i.e., when the property holds, otherwise [×].

For each of these case studies, we fix a number N of components and experiment by verifying the property EI of interest while varying B. Figure 4 shows that when B is sufficiently large both verifiers confirm that all considered instances satisfy their properties EI. This means that, within the considered number of evolution steps, the behaviour of the system is guaranteed to preserve the property of interest. Furthermore, we have that once the property is guaranteed within a bound B, it continues to hold with a larger bound. This confirms our intuition on the encoding scheme of property EI.

CBMC	N	B	Property	Time	Result
	10	9	EI	12	×
Max	10	10	EI	15	✓
	10	11	EI	241	✓
	8	7	EI	6	×
Bit	8	8	EI	10	✓
	8	9	EI	12	✓
	7	7	EI	187	×
2pc	7	8	EI	252	✓
	7	9	EI	325	✓

ESBMC	N	B	Property	Time	Result
	7	6	EI	46	×
Max	7	7	EI	106	✓
	7	8	EI	108	✓
	8	7	EI	11	×
Bit	8	8	EI	13	✓
	8	9	EI	15	✓
	5	5	EI	70	×
2pc	5	6	EI	127	✓
	5	7	EI	265	✓

Fig. 4. Experiments with Max Elem, Or Bit and Two Phase Commit

As for the Majority example, we experimented with a few input configurations. A configuration is completely defined as a pair (D,F) indicating the number of dancers and followers. For each considered pair we experiment with varying the bound B and present the relevant results in Fig. 5. The first column of each table represents input configurations whereas other columns have the same meaning as before.

The results show that for configurations with at least as many dancers as followers, the verification of majority returns success across different values of bound B. When considering minority configurations, i.e., (3,4) and (3,5), the verification succeeds with small values of B but fails with larger values. To see why, we note it takes steps to match one dancer with one follower (i.e., one request and one response). Thus, for example, with $B = 4$ the systems can only match two pairs, leaving one dancer un-matched; this results in a majority of dancers. When increasing the bound to at least 6, we have that all three dancers are paired, but the property fails because not everybody has a partner.

CBMC	N	B	Property	Time	Result
(3,5)	8	4	EI	10	✓
(3,5)	8	6	EI	22	✗
(3,5)	8	8	EI	41	✗
(4,4)	8	6	EI	23	✓
(4,4)	8	8	EI	42	✓
(4,4)	8	10	EI	78	✓
(5,3)	8	6	EI	25	✓
(5,3)	8	8	EI	46	✓
(5,3)	8	10	EI	74	✓

ESBMC	N	B	Property	Time	Result
(3,4)	7	4	EI	23	✓
(3,4)	7	6	EI	75	✗
(3,4)	7	8	EI	246	✗
(3,3)	6	4	EI	15	✓
(3,3)	6	6	EI	43	✓
(3,3)	6	8	EI	67	✓
(4,3)	7	4	EI	19	✓
(4,3)	7	6	EI	31	✓
(4,3)	7	8	EI	50	✓

Fig. 5. Experiments with Majority example

We use the case study Debating Philosophers to experiment with different property encodings. An input configuration is a pair consisting of the numbers of positive and negative philosophers equipped with their physical conditions (i.e., either R or T). Furthermore, in each element of the pair, we may use a $-$ to separate the rested philosophers from tired ones. We analyzed the properties "Eventually then Inevitably" (EI), "Eventually" (E) and "Possibly" (P) for several configurations, and report some interesting cases in the Fig. 6.

CBMC	N	B	Property	Time	Result
(2R,2R)	4	4	EI	37	✓
(2R,2R)	4	8	EI	165	✗
(2R,2R)	4	10	EI	257	✗
(1T,6T)	7	6	EI	289	✓
(3R,3R)	6	10	E	605	✓
(2T,3R)	5	8	E	250	✗
(1R,2R-4T)	7	4	P	101	✓
(1R,2R-4T)	7	6	P	273	✗

ESBMC	N	B	Property	Time	Result
(2R,2R)	4	2	EI	17	✓
(2R,2R)	4	4	EI	122	✓
(2R,2R)	4	6	EI	462	✗
(1T,5T)	6	4	EI	359	✓
(2R,2R)	4	10	E	205	✓
(2T,3R)	5	8	E	1120	✗
(1R,2R-3T)	6	2	P	27	✓
(1R,2R-3T)	6	4	P	206	✗

Fig. 6. Experiments with Philosophers example

When verifying property EI for configuration (2R,2R), we observe that the property only holds for small values of B. Similar to Majority, in this case study the systems need two steps in order to accomplish one debate. Thus, for example, with $B = 4$, there can only happen two debates which results in majority of the positive opinions. However, when we allow for at least three debates to happen, the majority property will not hold any longer. A counter example returned by one of the tools explain the following trace. First, $1R^+$ convinces $1R^-$, which leads to $2T^+$. It is followed that each of $2T^+$ is convinced by the other $1R^-$ to join him. Then, the resulting configuration (1R,1R-2T) does not satisfy majority.

When verifying the property for somewhat trivial configurations, i.e., (1T,5T), (1T,6T) both tools confirm that when the bound B is large enough a single positive philosopher can convince any set of tired negative ones.

We also tried with E property, i.e., allowing the majority property to fail after it became true. Then, the property E holds for a previously failed configuration, in particular, configurations of the same number of positive and negative philosophers (in the Fig. 6 (2R,2R) and (3R,3R)). In another configuration, eventually a number of positive philosophers cannot convince a bigger group of negative philosophers to get to majority of positive opinions.

Finally, we experimented with verifying property P for the configurations of the form (1R, 2R-4T), for CBMC and (1R, 2R-3T) for ESBMC. By checking P, we are interested to see whether the majority can happen by using only one rested, positive philosopher. As shown in Fig. 6, when the bound is too low the only $1R^+$ does not have enough time to convince the others; the verifications succeed and no counter example is reported. However with the bound increased enough to afford one more debate, the verifications fail. By inspecting the returned counter examples, we observed expected traces in which the only positive philosopher continuously convinces the others without being interfered by (at least) $1R^-$.

In summary, the verifications results obtained from the two model checkers are consistent in all considered instances of all case studies. This demonstrates the feasibility of our approach. In addition, between the two tools CBMC seems a bit more efficient when analyzing our programs.

4   Concluding Remarks

We have presented a translation from AbC process specifications to C programs. The translation enables us to reduce automated checking of (some classes of) properties of interest for the AbC system under consideration to simple reachability queries on the generated C program. To experiment with our method on a series of naturally challenging examples, we have first encoded them as AbC systems, then translated their specifications into C programs, and finally instrumented the programs to express properties of interest of the initial AbC system. We have reported and discussed our experimental evaluation on the automated analysis of such programs via SAT- and SMT-based bounded model checking, under different execution bounds and parameters of the initial system. Our work suggests that the novel communication style of the attribute-based calculus, complemented with appropriate verification techniques, can be effective for studying complex systems.

Our work is closely related to the encoding proposed in [11], which models systems evolutions by entry and exit conditions on the individual actions. In that work, AbC specifications are transformed into doubly-labelled transition systems and then analyzed via the UMC explicit-state model checker [17]. That approach does support a more expressive logic for properties than the current one, that also requires additional effort for instrumenting properties of interest with assertions and for interpreting counter examples associated to C programs. This is less of a burden in [11], since the target formalism has a direct correspondence with the initial specifications. In [11], however, the target representation can grow very quickly in size, for instance to model non-deterministic initialisation of an attribute (e.g., the initial position of an agent on a grid), for which an explicit transition will be added for each possible value of the attribute. In our translation we can introduce a non-deterministic variable (by using the non-deterministic initialisation construct) to represent this symbolically. A similar argument holds for value passing in general. We plan to compare our approach with [11] in terms of efficiency.

Another work closely related to ours is [12]; it uses a mechanism similar to the one used in [11] to guard the actions of a component and to transform the initial system into a sequential C program with a scheduling mechanism similar to the one proposed here. However, the input language of the translation is quite different from AbC, especially for the primitives for components interaction, which are based on stigmergy.

The SCEL language [5] has been the main source of inspiration for AbC. In [18], SCEL specifications are translated into Promela and analyzed by the SPIN model checker to prove safety and liveness properties. Promela has a C-like syntax and supports the dynamic creation of threads and message passing. Because of this, the modelling in [18] is more straightforward than ours. However, in [18] only a fragment of SCEL is considered while we consider full AbC systems; moreover, the program produced by our encoding is sequential, and because of this some ingenuity is required for emulating processes and for encoding properties.

The considered experiments seem to provide some evidence that the proposed encoding favors the use of specific tools. As future work, we would like to reconsider it in order to make the use of other verification back-ends possible. It would be interesting to see whether the SAT-based parallel bounded model checking technique proposed in [19] could be adapted to our case, given the similarity between the programs generated from AbC by our translation and the sequentialised programs considered in [19]. Completeness thresholds for bounded model checking [20] would allow to adapt our technique to unbounded analysis.

We also plan to develop an interactive simulator for AbC to explore specifications through simulations. This would enable one to remove coding errors introduced during the early steps of the design and to gain confidence about specifications before formally verifying them against the properties of interest.

Finally, we would like to use our approach to consider more interesting case studies, e.g., those that involve spatial reasoning, such as flocks. However, to do this, we think that it is important to extend AbC with a notion of globally-shared environment and global awareness, thereby facilitating reasoning about agents locations which is considered as an important feature of CAS [21].

References

1. Anderson, S., Bredeche, N., Eiben, A., Kampis, G., van Steen, M.: Adaptive collective systems: herding black sheep. In: BookSprints for ICT Research (2013)

2. De Nicola, R., Jähnichen, S., Wirsing, M.: Rigorous engineering of collective adaptive systems: special section. Int. J. Softw. Tools Technol. Transf. **22**(4), 389–397 (2020). https://doi.org/10.1007/s10009-020-00565-0

3. De Nicola, R., Ferrari, G.L., Pugliese, R., Tiezzi, F.: A formal approach to the engineering of domain-specific distributed systems. J. Logic Algebraic Methods Program. **111**, 100511 (2020)

4. Abd Alrahman, Y., De Nicola, R., Loreti, M.: A calculus for collective-adaptive systems and its behavioural theory. Inf. Comput. **268**, 104457 (2019)

5. De Nicola, R., Loreti, M., Pugliese, R., Tiezzi, F.: A formal approach to autonomic systems programming: the SCEL language. ACM Trans. Auton. Adapt. Syst. **9**(2), 7:1–7:29 (2014)

6. Ene, C., Muntean, T.: A broadcast-based calculus for communicating systems. In: IPDPS, p. 149. IEEE Computer Society (2001)

7. Clarke, E., Kroening, D., Lerda, F.: A tool for checking ANSI-C programs. In: Jensen, K., Podelski, A. (eds.) TACAS 2004. LNCS, vol. 2988, pp. 168–176. Springer, Heidelberg (2004). https://doi.org/10.1007/978-3-540-24730-2_15

8. Gadelha, M.Y.R., Monteiro, F.R., Morse, J., Cordeiro, L.C., Fischer, B., Nicole, D.A.: ESBMC 5.0: an industrial-strength C model checker. In: ASE, pp. 888–891. ACM (2018)

9. Lampson, B., Sturgis, H.E.: Crash recovery in a distributed data storage system (1979). https://www.microsoft.com/en-us/research/publication/crash-recovery-in-a-distributed-data-storage-system/

10. Abd Alrahman, Y., De Nicola, R., Loreti, M.: Programming interactions in collective adaptive systems by relying on attribute-based communication. Sci. Comput. Program. **192**, 102428 (2020)

11. De Nicola, R., Duong, T., Inverso, O., Mazzanti, F.: Verifying properties of systems relying on attribute-based communication. In: Katoen, J.-P., Langerak, R., Rensink, A. (eds.) ModelEd, TestEd, TrustEd. LNCS, vol. 10500, pp. 169–190. Springer, Cham (2017). https://doi.org/10.1007/978-3-319-68270-9_9

12. De Nicola, R., Di Stefano, L., Inverso, O.: Multi-agent systems with virtual stigmergy. Sci. Comput. Program. **187**, 102345 (2020)

13. Biere, A., Artho, C., Schuppan, V.: Liveness checking as safety checking. Electron. Notes Theor. Comput. Sci. **66**(2), 160–177 (2002)

14. Prasad, K.V.S.: Programming with broadcasts. In: Best, E. (ed.) CONCUR 1993. LNCS, vol. 715, pp. 173–187. Springer, Heidelberg (1993). https://doi.org/10.1007/3-540-57208-2_13

15. Aspnes, J., Ruppert, E.: An introduction to population protocols. In: Garbinato, B., Miranda, H., Rodrigues, L. (eds.) Middleware for Network Eccentric and Mobile Applications, pp. 97–120. Springer, Heidelberg (2009). https://doi.org/10.1007/978-3-540-89707-1_5

16. Esparza, J., Ganty, P., Leroux, J., Majumdar, R.: Verification of population protocols. In: CONCUR. LIPIcs, vol. 42, pp. 470–482. Schloss Dagstuhl - Leibniz-Zentrum für Informatik (2015)

17. ter Beek, M.H., Fantechi, A., Gnesi, S., Mazzanti, F.: A state/event-based model-checking approach for the analysis of abstract system properties. Sci. Comput. Program. **76**(2), 119–135 (2011)

18. De Nicola, R., et al.: Programming and verifying component ensembles. In: Bensalem, S., Lakhneck, Y., Legay, A. (eds.) ETAPS 2014. LNCS, vol. 8415, pp. 69–83. Springer, Heidelberg (2014). https://doi.org/10.1007/978-3-642-54848-2_5

19. Inverso, O., Trubiani, C.: Parallel and distributed bounded model checking of multi-threaded programs. In: PPoPP, pp. 202–216. ACM (2020)

20. Kroening, D., Ouaknine, J., Strichman, O., Wahl, T., Worrell, J.: Linear completeness thresholds for bounded model checking. In: Gopalakrishnan, G., Qadeer, S. (eds.) CAV 2011. LNCS, vol. 6806, pp. 557–572. Springer, Heidelberg (2011). https://doi.org/10.1007/978-3-642-22110-1_44
21. Loreti, M., Hillston, J.: Modelling and analysis of collective adaptive systems with CARMA and its tools. In: Bernardo, M., De Nicola, R., Hillston, J. (eds.) SFM 2016. LNCS, vol. 9700, pp. 83–119. Springer, Cham (2016). https://doi.org/10.1007/978-3-319-34096-8_4

Adaptive Security Policies

Flemming Nielson[1]([✉]), René Rydhof Hansen[2], and Hanne Riis Nielson[1]

[1] Department of Mathematics and Computer Science,
Technical University of Denmark, Kgs. Lyngby, Denmark
{fnie,hrni}@dtu.dk
[2] Department of Computer Science, Aalborg University, Aalborg, Denmark
rrh@cs.aau.dk

Abstract. We develop an approach to security of adaptive agents that is based on respecting the local security policies of agents rather than imposing a global security policy on all agents. In short, an agent can be assured, that it will not be able to observe any violation of its own security policy due to the changing presence of other agents in its environment. The development is performed for a version of Dijkstra's Guarded Commands with relocation primitives, channel based communication, and explicit non-determinism. At the technical level a type system enforces local security policies whereas a reference monitor ensures that relocation is permissible with local security of all agents.

1 Introduction

In a traditional IT system, security is usually taken care of by a central security policy enforced on all components of the IT system. Security policies may range from simple discretionary access control policies over mandatory access control policies to decentralised control policies. In keeping with this approach, designs like the ones based on XACML [14] presuppose the existence of a central access control server for mandating whether or not access operations can be permitted throughout the possibly distributed IT system.

To fully support collective adaptive systems it seems overly demanding to enforce that they all adhere to the same security policy. Rather a framework needs to be found, where individual agents can define their own security policy and get some assurance that their own security policy is not compromised due to the changing presence of other agents in its environment. Examples might include visitors with mobile phones entering the premises of a corporation, customers changing their service providers, or a robot entering from one legislative domain to another.

This paper proposes a framework ensuring that agents will never be able to observe that information flows throughout the system in a manner that violates their own security policies. The basic idea being that an agent must accept its environment as long as it cannot observe any violation of its own security policy. We consider this to be a realistic proposal, because in real systems one would never have any guarantees against the internal behaviour of other agents on the

© Springer Nature Switzerland AG 2020
T. Margaria and B. Steffen (Eds.): ISoLA 2020, LNCS 12477, pp. 280–294, 2020.
https://doi.org/10.1007/978-3-030-61470-6_17

system, including providers of social media channels and national intelligence services. As an example, if another agent receives confidential information and decides to make it public on a medium that can also be accessed from the agent in question, then this would constitute a violation of our framework. We consider it acceptable that we cannot detect if information is collected by other agents in a closed group, such as a company like Google or a national intelligence service.

The approach is highly motivated by considerations of *non-interference*; here it is ensured that there is no information flow from data at a higher security level to data at a lower security level. This is usually formulated for a deterministic system as the condition that two executions whose start states agree above a certain 'secret' security level also produce resulting states that agree above that 'secret' security level. (For non-deterministic systems the sets of possible outcomes need to be the same; for probabilistic systems the probability distributions on possible outcomes need to be the same.) This is a global condition focusing on terminating computations, so we will need to rephrase it as a local condition on what can be observed during a possibly non-terminating computation. We therefore aim at a situation where no agent in the collective adaptive system will be able to observe an information flow from data at a higher security level *in its own security lattice* to data at a lower security level *in its own security lattice*.

Motivated by [4] this paper develops the syntax and semantics of a language supporting this development. We then clarify our notion of security at the agent level and at the system level and finally we consider how to make this practical by precomputing the security checks. We conclude with directions for further work and a comparison with the literature.

2   Syntax

We extend Dijkstra's Guarded Commands language [6] with parallelism, communication and security domains and allow agents to dynamically modify their location in the environment. This could be change of physical location or merely change of logical location by changing its contact point in the environment (for example the internet provider); our syntax will be more suggestive of the latter.

The main syntactic category of *Adaptive Guarded Commands* is that of systems (denoted S). A system

$$\texttt{par } L_1 \, D_1 \, C_1 \, [] \, \cdots \, [] \, L_n \, D_n \, C_n \, \texttt{rap}$$

consists of a number of parallel agents, each with their own security lattice (L_i) for expressing their local security policy, their own declarations (D_i) of local variables and channels to the environment, and their own command (C_i) for controlling its behaviour. The fundamental idea is that the partial order ($\sqsubseteq_i$ or just $\sqsubseteq$) of the security lattice indicates the direction in which the security level of data may freely change; in approaches based on the Decentralised Label Model [11] this is called 'restriction'. The syntax is summarised in Fig. 1 and explained below; for simplicity of presentation we shall assume that any two security lattices (L_i and L_j) are either disjoint or equal ($L_i \cap L_j = \emptyset$ or $L_i = L_j$) so that we can use the union of lattices rather than the disjoint union of lattices.

systems:	$S ::= \mathbf{par}\, L_1\, D_1\, C_1\, \square\, \cdots\, \square\, L_n\, D_n\, C_n\, \mathbf{rap}$	$(n > 0)$
declarations:	$D ::= D; D \mid x : t\ell \mid c? : t\ell \mid c! : t\ell$	
commands:	$C ::= x := e \mid c!e \mid c?x \mid C_1 ; C_2$	
	$\quad\mid\ \mathbf{if}\ e_1 \to C_1\, \square\, ...\, \square\, e_n \to C_n\ \mathbf{fi}$	$(n > 0)$
	$\quad\mid\ \mathbf{do}\ e_1 \to C_1\, \square\, ...\, \square\, e_n \to C_n\ \mathbf{od}$	$(n > 0)$
	$\quad\mid\ \mathbf{sum}\ C_1\, \square\, ...\, \square\, C_n\ \mathbf{mus}$	$(n > 0)$
	$\quad\mid\ \mathtt{relocate}(l)$	
expressions:	$e ::= x \mid \mathtt{loc} \mid n \mid e_1 + e_2 \mid \cdots$	
	$\quad\mid\ \mathtt{true} \mid e_1 = e_2 \mid \cdots \mid e_1 \wedge e_2 \mid \cdots$	
data types:	$t ::= \mathtt{int} \mid \mathtt{bool} \mid \mathtt{data} \mid \cdots$	
security level:	$\ell \in \bigcup_i L_i$	

Fig. 1. Syntax of Adaptive Guarded Commands.

Each agent will have a number of declarations. It may be a variable (x) of some type (t) and security level (ℓ). It may be a channel (c) used for input accepting data of some type and security level. It may be a channel (c) used to output data of some type and security level.

The commands include those of Dijkstra's Guarded Commands so we have the basic command of assignment $(x := e)$ in addition to sequencing $(C_1 ; C_2)$ and constructs for conditionals (if $e_1 \to C_1\ \square\ ...\ \square\ e_n \to C_n$ fi) and iteration (do $e_1 \to C_1\ \square\ ...\ \square\ e_n \to C_n$ od). On top of this we follow [13] and introduce basic commands for output $(c!e)$ and input $(c?x)$ over a channel (c) and a command performing an 'external' non-deterministic choice among commands (sum $C_1\ \square\ ...\ \square\ C_n$ mus); although it will typically be the case that each C_i in sum $C_1\ \square\ ...\ \square\ C_n$ mus takes the form $c!e; C$ or $c?x; C$ we shall not formally impose this. Finally, we have a relocation construct ($\mathtt{relocate}(l)$) for allowing an agent to dynamically relocate to another contact point (l) in its environment.

The details of the expressions (e) are of little interest to us but they are likely to include variables (x), a special token indicating the current location ($\mathtt{loc}$), numbers (n), arithmetic operations (e.g. $e_1 + e_2$), truth values (e.g. $\mathtt{true}$), relational operations (e.g. $e_1 = e_2$), and logical operations (e.g. $e_1 \wedge e_2$).

We do not need to go deeply into the structure of datatypes (t) but assume that they contain integers ($\mathtt{int}$) and booleans ($\mathtt{bool}$) and a more interesting type of data ($\mathtt{data}$). We shall leave the syntax of security levels (ℓ), channels (c), and locations (l) to the concrete examples.

3   Semantics

Expressions. Expressions are evaluated with respect to a memory σ that assigns values to all variables of interest and following [13] the semantic judgement takes the form

$$\sigma \vdash e \rhd v$$

$$\frac{}{\sigma \vdash n \triangleright n} \qquad \frac{}{\sigma \vdash \mathtt{true} \triangleright \mathtt{tt}} \qquad \frac{}{\sigma \vdash \mathtt{loc} \triangleright \sigma(\mathtt{loc})} \qquad \frac{}{\sigma \vdash x \triangleright \sigma(x)} \text{ if } \sigma(x) \text{ defined}$$

$$\frac{\sigma \vdash e_1 \triangleright v_1 \quad \sigma \vdash e_2 \triangleright v_2}{\sigma \vdash e_1 + e_2 \triangleright v_1 + v_2} \qquad \frac{\sigma \vdash e_1 \triangleright v_1 \quad \sigma \vdash e_2 \triangleright v_2}{\sigma \vdash e_1 = e_2 \triangleright v_1 = v_2} \qquad \frac{\sigma \vdash e_1 \triangleright v_1 \quad \sigma \vdash e_2 \triangleright v_2}{\sigma \vdash e_1 \wedge e_2 \triangleright v_1 \wedge v_2}$$

Fig. 2. Semantics of expressions.

$$\frac{\sigma \vdash e \triangleright v}{(x := e, \sigma) \to^\tau (\sqrt{}, \sigma[x \mapsto v])} \text{ if } \sigma(x) \text{ is defined}$$

$$\frac{\sigma \vdash e \triangleright v}{(c!e, \sigma) \to^{c!v} (\sqrt{}, \sigma)} \qquad \frac{}{(c?x, \sigma) \to^{c?v} (\sqrt{}, \sigma[x \mapsto v])} \text{ if } \sigma(x) \text{ is defined}$$

$$\frac{(C_1, \sigma) \to^\varphi (C_1', \sigma')}{(C_1 ; C_2, \sigma) \to^\varphi (C_1' ; C_2, \sigma')} \text{ if } C_1' \neq \sqrt{} \qquad \frac{(C_1, \sigma) \to^\varphi (\sqrt{}, \sigma')}{(C_1 ; C_2, \sigma) \to^\varphi (C_2, \sigma')}$$

$$\frac{\sigma \vdash e_i \triangleright \mathtt{tt}}{(\mathtt{if} \ e_1 \to C_1 \ \square \ \cdots \ \square \ e_n \to C_n \ \mathtt{fi}, \sigma) \to^\tau (C_i, \sigma)}$$

$$\frac{\sigma \vdash e_i \triangleright \mathtt{tt}}{(\mathtt{do} \ \cdots \ \square \ e_i \to C_i \ \square \ \cdots \ \mathtt{od}, \sigma) \to^\tau (C_i ; \mathtt{do} \ \cdots \ \square \ e_i \to C_i \ \square \ \cdots \ \mathtt{od}, \sigma)}$$

$$\frac{\sigma \vdash e_1 \triangleright \mathtt{ff} \quad \cdots \quad \sigma \vdash e_n \triangleright \mathtt{ff}}{(\mathtt{do} \ e_1 \to C_1 \ \square \ \cdots \ \square \ e_n \to C_n \ \mathtt{od}, \sigma) \to^\tau (\sqrt{}, \sigma)}$$

$$\frac{(C_i, \sigma) \to^\varphi (C_i', \sigma')}{(\mathtt{sum} \ C_1 \ \square \ \cdots \ \square \ C_n \ \mathtt{mus}, \sigma) \to^\varphi (C_i', \sigma')}$$

$$\frac{}{(\mathtt{relocate}(l), \sigma) \to^{go \ l} (\sqrt{}, \sigma)}$$

Fig. 3. Semantics of commands.

and the details are provided by the axiom schemes and rules of Fig. 2 and are mostly straightforward and uninteresting; note that the token $\mathtt{loc}$ is treated as a variable.

Commands. Commands are interpreted relative to a local memory σ for each agent in question and may update it as needed. The semantic judgement takes the form

$$(C, \sigma) \to^\varphi (C', \sigma')$$

where the superscript (φ) indicates whether the action is silent (τ), an input ($c?v$), an output ($c!v$) or a relocation (go l).

The details are provided in Fig. 3 and we use C and C' to range both over the commands of Fig. 1 and the special symbol $\sqrt{}$ indicating a terminated configuration. Communication will be taken care of at system level by means of synchronous communication so the rules for output and input merely indicate

$$\frac{(C_i, \sigma_i) \to^\tau (C_i', \sigma_i')}{\begin{array}{l}(\mathbf{par} \cdots \mathbb{0}\, L_i\, D_i\, C_i\, \mathbb{0} \cdots \mathbf{rap}, \cdots \sigma_i \cdots) \\ \to (\mathbf{par} \cdots \mathbb{0}\, L_i\, D_i\, C_i'\, \mathbb{0} \cdots \mathbf{rap}, \cdots \sigma_i' \cdots)\end{array}} \qquad \text{if } \sigma_i \text{ covers } D_i$$

$$\frac{(C_i, \sigma_i) \to^{c!v} (C_i', \sigma_i') \qquad (C_j, \sigma_j) \to^{c?v} (C_j', \sigma_j')}{\begin{array}{l}(\mathbf{par} \cdots L_i\, D_i\, C_i\, \mathbb{0}\, L_j\, D_j\, C_j \cdots \mathbf{rap}, \cdots \sigma_i \sigma_j \cdots) \\ \to (\mathbf{par} \cdots L_i\, D_i\, C_i'\, \mathbb{0}\, L_j\, D_j\, C_j' \cdots \mathbf{rap}, \cdots \sigma_i' \sigma_j' \cdots)\end{array}} \qquad \text{if } \begin{cases} \sigma_i \text{ covers } D_i \\ \sigma_j \text{ covers } D_j \\ i \neq j \\ c? : t\,\ell \text{ in } D_i \\ \text{and } \ell \neq \perp_i \\ c! : t'\,\ell' \text{ in } D_j \\ \sigma_i(\mathtt{loc}) = \sigma_j(\mathtt{loc}) \end{cases}$$

$$\frac{(C_i, \sigma_i) \to^{\mathsf{go}\ l} (C_i', \sigma_i')}{\begin{array}{l}(\mathbf{par} \cdots \mathbb{0}\, L_i\, D_i\, C_i\, \mathbb{0} \cdots \mathbf{rap}, \cdots \sigma_i \cdots) \\ \to (\mathbf{par} \cdots \mathbb{0}\, L_i\, D_i\, C_i'\, \mathbb{0} \cdots \mathbf{rap}, \cdots \sigma_i'' \cdots)\end{array}} \qquad \text{if } \begin{cases} \sigma_i \text{ covers } D_i \\ \cdots \end{cases}$$

$$\text{where } \sigma_i''(\mathtt{loc}) = l \text{ and } \sigma_i''(x) = \begin{cases} \sigma_i'(x) \text{ if } x : t\,\ell \text{ in } D_i \text{ and } \ell = \perp \\ 0_t \qquad \text{if } x : t\,\ell \text{ in } D_i \text{ and } \ell \neq \perp \end{cases}$$

Fig. 4. Semantics of systems (with an incomplete rule for relocation).

the action taking place (as a superscript on the arrow). The same approach is taken for the relocation construct. The remaining constructs are in line with [13] and are generally straightforward.

Systems. The agents of a system have disjoint local memories so they can only exchange values by communicating over the channels. More precisely this means that for each process we will have a local memory assigning values to the variables of interest and we shall be based on synchronous communication. The judgement takes the form

$$\begin{array}{l}(\mathbf{par}\ L_1\, D_1\, C_1\, \mathbb{0} \cdots \mathbb{0}\, L_n\, D_n\, C_n\ \mathbf{rap}, \sigma_1 \cdots \sigma_n) \\ \to \quad (\mathbf{par}\ L_1\, D_1\, C_1'\, \mathbb{0} \cdots \mathbb{0}\, L_n\, D_n\, C_n'\ \mathbf{rap}, \sigma_1' \cdots \sigma_n')\end{array}$$

where once more we allow C and C' to range both over commands and the special symbol $\sqrt{}$ indicating a terminated configuration.

The details are provided in Fig. 4. The first rule takes care of a constituent agent performing a silent step and we use 'σ_i covers D_i' as a shorthand for the condition that the domain of σ_i contains all variables declared in D_i as well as the token $\mathtt{loc}$.

The second rule takes care of synchronous communication between two distinct agents. We require that $i \neq j$ and the rule should *not* be read to suggest that $i+1 = j$. On top of ensuring that channels are locally declared in a manner consistent with their use for output and input we also ensure that both agents are located at the same point in their environment. In case a declaration contains multiple declarations of the form $c? : t\,\ell$ we use '$c? : t\,\ell$ in D_i' as a shorthand for the condition that the rightmost occurrence of any declaration of $c? : t'\,\ell'$ is

c? : $t\,\ell$; similar considerations apply to c! : $t\,\ell$ (and x : $t\,\ell$ below). The decision not to allow the reception of data at security level $\perp$ will be explained below.

The third rule takes care of relocation. Since the semantics of systems needs to ensure that our overall notion of security is maintained we cannot provide the full details of the rule before having developed our notion of security in the subsequent sections. However, already now we can record that the location information of the agent relocating is being updated. Also, that the agent relocating is only allowed to retain its data at the lowest security level; at higher security levels some constant element 0_t of type t will replace any previous value.

Example 1. The condition in the rule for communication that data cannot be received at the lowest security level, and the condition in the rule for relocation that only data at the lowest security level can be retained, jointly prevent certain information flows due to relocation that are not captured by our security checks developed in the next sections.

To illustrate this point let us suppose we have locations LOC1 and LOC2 and a parallel system composed of processes *procA* (initially located at LOC1 with security lattice $\boldsymbol{L}_1$: $\mathsf{U} \sqsubseteq_1 \mathsf{C} \sqsubseteq_1 \mathsf{S}$), *procB* (initially located at LOC1 with security lattice $\boldsymbol{L}_2$: $\mathsf{L} \sqsubseteq_1 \mathsf{H}$) and *procC* (initially located at LOC2 with security lattice $\boldsymbol{L}_3$: $\mathsf{N} \sqsubseteq_1 \mathsf{P}$) defined as follows:

$$procA = \boldsymbol{L}_1 \ (\mathsf{c}_1! : \mathsf{data\ S};\ \mathsf{c}_3? : \mathsf{data\ C};\ \mathsf{tmpS} : \mathsf{data\ S};\ \mathsf{tmpC} : \mathsf{data\ C})$$
$$\mathsf{c}_1 \ ! \ \mathsf{tmpS};\ \mathsf{c}_3 \ ? \ \mathsf{tmpC}$$

$$procB = \boldsymbol{L}_2 \ (\mathsf{c}_1? : \mathsf{data\ H};\ \mathsf{c}_2! : \mathsf{data\ H};\ \mathsf{tmpH} : \mathsf{data\ H})$$
$$\mathsf{c}_1 \ ? \ \mathsf{tmpH};\ \mathsf{relocate}(\mathsf{LOC2});\ \mathsf{c}_2 \ ! \ \mathsf{tmpH}$$

$$procC = \boldsymbol{L}_3 \ (\mathsf{c}_2? : \mathsf{data\ P};\ \mathsf{c}_3! : \mathsf{data\ P};\ \mathsf{tmpP} : \mathsf{data\ P})$$
$$\mathsf{c}_2 \ ? \ \mathsf{tmpP};\ \mathsf{relocate}(\mathsf{LOC1});\ \mathsf{c}_3 \ ! \ \mathsf{tmpP}$$

The system can then be defined as:

$$\textbf{par}\ procA \ [] \ procB \ [] \ procC \ \textbf{rap}$$

Here there would be an information flow from the security level S to the security level C if we would allow this program to execute without the two conditions in the rules for communication and relocation.   □

In all cases, note that if one of the processes terminates then the corresponding component in the configuration will contain $\sqrt{}$ and it will not be able to evolve further.

4   Agent-Level Security

We begin by developing an information flow type system for ensuring that each agent can be assured that it adheres to its own security policy. The development borrows from that of [13] and is inspired by traditional approaches such as those of [15,16] but are extended to deal with parallelism and non-determinism.

$$\overline{\rho \vdash n : \mathtt{int} \perp} \qquad \overline{\rho \vdash \mathtt{true} : \mathtt{bool} \perp} \qquad \overline{\rho \vdash \mathtt{loc} : \mathtt{data} \perp} \qquad \overline{\rho \vdash x : t\,\ell} \; \text{if } \rho(x) = (t, \ell)$$

$$\frac{\rho \vdash e_1 : \mathtt{int}\,\ell_1 \quad \rho \vdash e_2 : \mathtt{int}\,\ell_2}{\rho \vdash e_1 + e_2 : \mathtt{int}\,(\ell_1 \sqcup \ell_2)} \qquad \frac{\rho \vdash e_1 : t\,\ell_1 \quad \rho \vdash e_2 : t\,\ell_2}{\rho \vdash e_1 = e_2 : \mathtt{data}\,(\ell_1 \sqcup \ell_2)} \qquad \frac{\rho \vdash e_1 : \mathtt{bool}\,\ell_1 \quad \rho \vdash e_2 : \mathtt{bool}\,\ell_2}{\rho \vdash e_1 \wedge e_2 : \mathtt{bool}\,(\ell_1 \sqcup \ell_2)}$$

Fig. 5. Types and security levels for expressions.

Well-typed Expressions. For expressions the judgement takes the form

$$\rho \vdash e : t\,\ell$$

where ℓ is intended to indicate the 'highest' security level of a variable used in the expression (but we need to be a bit more precise for security lattices that are not totally ordered).

The details are provided by the axiom schemes and rules of Fig. 5 and will be explained below. The judgement makes use of a type environment ρ that assigns types and security levels to all variables; if the expression e occurs in some agent then it will become clear shortly that ρ is constructed from the declarations local to that agent and that the only security levels considered are the local ones. The overall idea is that $\rho \vdash e : t\,\ell$ should ensure that the type of the expression e is t and that the security level is $\ell = \bigsqcup_i \rho(x_i)_2$ where x_i ranges over all free variables of e and $\rho(x)_2 = \ell$ whenever $\rho(x) = (t, \ell)$. This is in line with the development in [15, 16].

Well-typed Commands. For commands the typing judgement takes the form

$$\rho \vdash C : L$$

where $L = [\ell_1, \ell_2]$ is intended to be a pair of security levels: ℓ_1 is the 'lowest' security level of a variable assigned in the command and ℓ_2 is the 'highest' security level a variable assigned in the command (but we need to be a bit more precise for security lattices that are not totally ordered). This tells us all we will need about the set of security levels for variables assigned in the command, as it will allow us to demand that the set contains exactly one element by imposing $\ell_1 = \ell_2$, and that it contains at most one element by imposing $\ell_1 \sqsupseteq \ell_2$; we shall do the latter to prevent information flows due to non-determinism.

The typing judgement is defined by the axiom schemes and rules of Fig. 6 to be explained shortly. We shall allow to write $\ell \sqsubseteq [\ell_1, \ell_2]$ for $\ell \sqsubseteq \ell_1$ and define

$$[\ell_1, \ell_2] \sqcap [\ell_1', \ell_2'] = [\ell_1 \sqcap \ell_1', \ell_2 \sqcup \ell_2']$$

(which is the greatest lower bound operation with respect to a partial order $\sqsubseteq'$ defined by $[\ell_1, \ell_2] \sqsubseteq' [\ell_1', \ell_2']$ whenever $\ell_1 \sqsubseteq \ell_1'$ and $\ell_2 \sqsupseteq \ell_2'$). We shall write $\mathtt{uniq}([\ell_1, \ell_2])$ for the condition that $\ell_1 \sqsupseteq \ell_2$ and we shall write $L_{\mathsf{null}} = [\top, \perp]$. The intuition is, that if $\mathcal{L}$ is the set of security levels of variables modified in

$$\frac{\rho \vdash e : t\,\ell}{\rho \vdash x := e : [\ell', \ell']} \ \text{if} \ \begin{cases} \rho(x) = (t, \ell') \\ \ell \sqsubseteq \ell' \end{cases} \qquad \frac{\rho \vdash C_1 : L_1 \quad \rho \vdash C_2 : L_2}{\rho \vdash C_1 ; C_2 : L_1 \sqcap L_2}$$

$$\frac{\rho \vdash e : t\,\ell}{\rho \vdash c!e : [\ell', \ell']} \ \text{if} \ \begin{cases} \rho(c!) = (t, \ell') \\ \ell \sqsubseteq \ell' \end{cases} \qquad \frac{}{\rho \vdash c?x : [\ell', \ell']} \ \text{if} \ \begin{cases} \rho(c?) = (t, \ell) \\ \rho(x) = (t, \ell') \\ \ell \sqsubseteq \ell' \end{cases}$$

$$\frac{\bigwedge_i \rho \vdash e_i : \text{bool}\,\ell_i \quad \bigwedge_i \rho \vdash C_i : L_i}{\rho \vdash \text{if } e_1 \rightarrow C_1 \ \square \ \cdots \ \square \ e_n \rightarrow C_n \ \text{fi} : L_1 \sqcap \cdots \sqcap L_n} \ \text{if} \ \begin{cases} \bigwedge_i \ell_i \sqsubseteq L_i \\ \bigwedge_{(i,j) \in \text{cosat}} \ell_j \sqsubseteq L_i \\ \bigwedge_{(i,j) \in \text{cosat}} \text{uniq}(L_i) \end{cases}$$

$$\frac{\bigwedge_i \rho \vdash e_i : \text{bool}\,\ell_i \quad \bigwedge_i \rho \vdash C_i : L_i}{\rho \vdash \text{do } e_1 \rightarrow C_1 \ \square \ \cdots \ \square \ e_n \rightarrow C_n \ \text{od} : L_1 \sqcap \cdots \sqcap L_n} \ \text{if} \ \begin{cases} \bigwedge_i \ell_i \sqsubseteq L_i \\ \bigwedge_{(i,j) \in \text{cosat}} \ell_j \sqsubseteq L_i \\ \bigwedge_{(i,j) \in \text{cosat}} \text{uniq}(L_i) \end{cases}$$

$$\frac{\bigwedge_i \rho \vdash C_i : L_i}{\rho \vdash \text{sum } C_1 \ \square \ \cdots \ \square \ C_n \ \text{mus} : L_1 \sqcap \cdots \sqcap L_n} \ \text{if} \ \bigwedge_i \text{uniq}(L_i)$$

$$\frac{}{\rho \vdash \text{relocate}(l) : [\bot, \bot]}$$

Fig. 6. Types and pairs of security levels for commands.

C then $L = [\bigsqcap \mathcal{L}, \bigsqcup \mathcal{L}]$; it follows that $\text{uniq}(L)$ holds whenever $\mathcal{L}$ contains at most one element, and $L = L_{\text{null}}$ whenever $\mathcal{L}$ is empty (as would be the case for any skip statement we might add to the language). The first component of a security label $L = [\ell_1, \ell_2]$ is in line with the development in [15,16] whereas the second component is responsible for dealing with non-determinism [13].

The rule for assignment records the security level of the variable modified and checks that the explicit information flow is admissible. The rule for sequencing is straightforward given our explanation of $\rho \vdash C : L$ and the operation $L_1 \sqcap L_2$. The rule for output and the axiom scheme for input are somewhat similar to the one for assignment, essentially treating output $c!e$ as an assignment $c := e$, and input $c?x$ as an assignment $x := c$. One might consider to adopt a more permissive type system by using L_{null} for output (rather than $[\ell', \ell']$) but this would open for some mild information flow due to communication.

The rule for 'external' non-deterministic choice takes care of correlation flows [12,13]. It makes use of $\text{uniq}(L_i)$ to ensure that all modified variables (if any) have the same security level. The rules for conditional and iteration are essentially identical and make use of guards of the form $e_1 \rightarrow C_1 \ \square \ \cdots \ \square \ e_n \rightarrow C_n$. They take care of implicit flows by checking that $\ell_i \sqsubseteq L_i$ whenever $\bigwedge_i \rho \vdash e_i : \text{bool}\,\ell_i$ and $\bigwedge_i \rho \vdash C_i : L_i$. They take care of bypassing flows [12,13] whenever some $e_i \wedge e_j$ is satisfiable for $i \neq j$. This is expressed using the set cosat that contains those *distinct* pairs (i,j) of indices such that $e_i \wedge e_j$ is satisfiable; it may be computed using a Satisfaction Modulo Theories (SMT) solver such as Z3 [5] or it may be approximated using the DAG-based heuristics described in

$$\frac{\rho \vdash C : L}{\vdash \boldsymbol{L} D C : \checkmark} \quad \text{where} \quad \begin{cases} \rho(x) = (t, \ell) \text{ whenever } x : t\ell \text{ in } D \\ \rho(c!) = (t, \ell) \text{ whenever } c! : t\ell \text{ in } D \\ \rho(c?) = (t, \ell) \text{ whenever } c? : t\ell \text{ in } D \\ D \text{ only mentions security levels in } \boldsymbol{L} \\ \text{all } c? : t\ell \text{ in } D \text{ have } \ell \neq \bot \end{cases}$$

$$\frac{\bigwedge_i \vdash \boldsymbol{L}_i \, D_i \, C_i : \checkmark}{\vdash \mathbf{par} \ \boldsymbol{L}_1 \, D_1 \, C_1 \ \text{\textlbrackdbl} \ \cdots \ \text{\textlbrackdbl} \ \boldsymbol{L}_n \, D_n \, C_n \ \mathbf{rap} : \checkmark} \quad \text{where} \quad \begin{cases} t_i = t_j \\ \text{whenever } c? : t_i \, \ell_i \text{ in } D_i \\ \text{whenever } c! : t_j \, \ell_j \text{ in } D_j \end{cases}$$

Fig. 7. Well-formedness of agents and systems.

[12]. Whenever this is the case, the condition $\ell_j \sqsubseteq L_i$ checks that the bypassing flows are admissible, and the condition $\mathtt{uniq}(L_i)$ checks the correlation flows are admissible.

In the rule for relocation one might consider to adopt a more permissive type system by using L_{null} for relocation (rather than $[\bot, \bot]$) but this would open for some mild information flow due to relocation.

Well-typed Agents. To finish the considerations of security at the agent-level we may consider a judgement that takes the form

$$\vdash \boldsymbol{L} D C : \checkmark$$

and that is defined by the topmost rule in Fig. 7. In addition to ensuring that the command is well-typed, it ensures that the variables, channels and security level occurring in a command are only the local ones, in line with the semantics not admitting any variables shared between agents, and it ensures that no information is received at the lowest security level as discussed previously.

5   System-Level Security

For systems we might extend the judgement $\vdash \cdots : \checkmark$ from agents to systems as suggested in the bottommost rule in Fig. 7. In addition to ensuring that each agent is well-formed, it ensures that all information about a channel agree with respect to the type given to it. Clearly, there is no similar condition on the security levels because they are likely to come from different security domains. We shall only allow to use the semantics on well-typed systems S (i.e. satisfying $\vdash S : \checkmark$) which means that a few of the conditions in Fig. 4 about the security levels of channels become superfluous.

Our current setup creates the risk that the communications between an agent and its environment (i.e. the other agents) give rise to information flow that would not be admitted within the agent itself. Hence there is the risk that communication leads to local information flow not captured by the type system of the previous section.

$$\frac{\ell' \sqsubseteq_i \ell''\qquad i \in \Sigma}{\Sigma \vdash (i,\ell') \mapsto (i,\ell'')} \qquad \frac{\Sigma \vdash (i',\ell') \mapsto (i,\ell)\qquad \Sigma \vdash (i,\ell) \mapsto (i'',\ell'')}{\Sigma \vdash (i',\ell') \mapsto (i'',\ell'')} \qquad \frac{c? : t\,\ell'' \text{ in } D_{i''}\qquad c! : t\,\ell' \text{ in } D_{i'}\qquad i',i'' \in \Sigma}{\Sigma \vdash (i',\ell') \mapsto (i'',\ell'')}$$

Fig. 8. System-Level Information Flow.

$$\frac{(C_i,\sigma_i) \to^{\text{go } l} (C_i',\sigma_i')}{(\text{par} \cdots [\!] \; L_i\,D_i\,C_i \; [\!] \; \cdots \text{rap}, \cdots \sigma_i \cdots) \to (\text{par} \cdots [\!] \; L_i\,D_i\,C_i' \; [\!] \; \cdots \text{rap}, \cdots \sigma_i'' \cdots)} \quad \text{if} \quad \left\{ \begin{array}{l} \sigma_i \text{ covers } D_i \\ \forall j \in \Sigma : \\ \quad (\Sigma \vdash_j \ell' \mapsto \ell'') \Rightarrow \ell' \sqsubseteq_j \ell'' \\ \text{where} \\ \quad \Sigma = \{i\} \cup \{j \mid \sigma_j(\text{loc}) = l\} \end{array} \right.$$

$$\text{where } \sigma_i''(\text{loc}) = l \text{ and } \sigma_i''(x) = \left\{ \begin{array}{ll} \sigma_i'(x) & \text{if } x : t\,\ell \text{ in } D_i \text{ and } \ell = \bot \\ 0_t & \text{if } x : t\,\ell \text{ in } D_i \text{ and } \ell \neq \bot \end{array} \right.$$

Fig. 9. Semantics of relocation (dynamic version).

We shall be interested in recording when the declaration of channels in the system may give rise to an information flow from some $\ell' \in L_{i'}$ to some $\ell'' \in L_{i''}$. We shall write this as

$$\Sigma \vdash (i',\ell') \mapsto (i'',\ell'')$$

where $\Sigma \subseteq \{1, \cdots, n\}$ records the agents at the location of interest including $i', i'' \in \Sigma$. The definition is given in Fig. 8 where we write $\sqsubseteq_i$ for the partial order of L_i.

The definition specialises to the case where $\ell' \in L_i$ and $\ell'' \in L_i$ for $i \in \Sigma$ and motivates defining

$$\Sigma \vdash_i \ell' \mapsto \ell'' \quad \text{iff} \quad \Sigma \vdash (i,\ell') \mapsto (i,\ell'') \wedge \ell' \in L_i \wedge \ell'' \in L_i$$

and we say that there is a *global information flow* from $\ell' \in L_i$ to $\ell'' \in L_i$ via Σ. We are now ready to define our notion of when a system S is secure but shall do so in two steps.

Definition 1. *A system* par $L_1\,D_1\,C_1 \; [\!] \; \cdots \; [\!] \; L_n\,D_n\,C_n$ rap *is secure with respect to Σ whenever every global information flow from $\ell' \in L_i$ to $\ell'' \in L_i$ via Σ is consistent with L_i: $\forall i \in \Sigma : \forall \ell', \ell'' \in L_i : (\Sigma \vdash_i \ell' \mapsto \ell'') \Rightarrow \ell' \sqsubseteq_i \ell''$.*

To incorporate our notion of a system being secure into the well-formedness rules for systems would require us to fix the set Σ and hence limit the possibility of the system to adapt as agents are allowed to roam throughout the system.

Instead, we shall incorporate our notion of a system being secure into the semantics by allowing an agent to relocate only if security is not jeopardised. This gives rise to the completion of the semantics (of Fig. 4) that is shown in Fig. 9. Here the placement information Σ is computed from the local memories and we require security for all agents at the location to which the agent relocates (including the agent itself).

This motivates the following definition and proposition stating that the semantics of Fig. 9 preserves security.

Definition 2. *A configuration* (par $L_1 D_1 C_1$ □ $\cdots$ □ $L_n D_n C_n$ rap, $\sigma_1 \cdots \sigma_n$) *is secure whenever* par $L_1 D_1 C_1$ □ $\cdots$ □ $L_n D_n C_n$ rap *is secure with respect to* $\Sigma_l = \{j \mid \sigma_j(\text{loc}) = l\}$ *for all locations l.*

Example 2. The system in Example 1 in an initial state located as stated in Example 1, yields a configuration that is secure. However, the dynamic semantics guards against any information flow from S to C due to relocation.   □

Proposition 1. *Security is preserved under evaluation by the semantics of Figs. 4 and 9.*

Proof. Suppose that (par $L_1 D_1 C_1$ □ $\cdots$ □ $L_n D_n C_n$ rap, $\sigma_1 \cdots \sigma_n$) is secure and that

$$
\begin{aligned}
& (\text{par } L_1 D_1 C_1 \ \square \ \cdots \ \square \ L_n D_n C_n \text{ rap}, \sigma_1 \cdots \sigma_n) \\
\to \ & (\text{par } L_1 D_1 C_1' \ \square \ \cdots \ \square \ L_n D_n C_n' \text{ rap}, \sigma_1' \cdots \sigma_n')
\end{aligned}
$$

The resulting configuration (par $L_1 D_1 C_1'$ □ $\cdots$ □ $L_n D_n C_n'$ rap, $\sigma_1' \cdots \sigma_n'$) is trivially secure if one of the first two rules in Fig. 4 was used for the transition. In the case where the rule of Fig. 9 is used for the transition we note that removing the i'th agent from the location $\sigma_i(\text{loc})$ does not jeopardise security, and adding the i'th agent to the location l does not jeopardise security either, because of the tests present in Fig. 9.

Although our approach is motivated by the development of [4] (as mentioned in the Introduction) there are a substantial number of differences. In [4] programs are only allowed to be straight-line programs, so that there are no implicit flows into constructs that exchange data between different security domains, and the permissible flows are constrained to be determined by partial functions; we allow implicit, bypassing and correlation flows, we support the dynamic relocation of processes, and we do not require the permissible flows to be constrained by partial functions. With respect to security policies the approach of [4] applies the framework of Lagois connections [9] which forces them to impose additional technical[1] constraints on top of those needed in our development.

6   Precomputing Security Checks

It is possible to check for security in cubic time with respect to the size of the system S. To see this, first note that the number of security levels and channels considered is linear in the size of the system S. Next note that using Fig. 8 to

---

[1]   In the terminology of [4] we impose constraints similar to their SC1(=LC1) and SC2(=LC2) but do not require any of their PC1, PC2, LC3, LC4, CC1, CC2 which are purely needed to stay within the framework of [9].

compute $\Sigma \vdash (i,\ell) \mapsto (i',\ell')$ amounts to computing the transitive closure of binary relations and that this can be done in cubic time.

Hence the application of the transition in Fig. 9 can also be done in cubic time. We might expect to do better because we only perform the check for one location but it seems unfeasible to state a better worst-case complexity bound. This might make the approach unfeasible in practice in case n is very large.

To circumvent these problems we shall assume that while there might be many agents they will fall in a smaller number of groups sharing security lattices and channels. This seems a very realistic assumption for large collective adaptive systems. Define two agents indexed by i and j to be equivalent, written $i \sim j$, whenever

$$L_i = L_j$$
$$c! : t\,\ell \text{ in } D_i \Leftrightarrow c! : t\,\ell \text{ in } D_j$$
$$c? : t\,\ell \text{ in } D_i \Leftrightarrow c? : t\,\ell \text{ in } D_j$$

(for all choices of c, t, and ℓ). This requires the two agents to agree on the security lattice and their channels but not necessarily on their local variables.

This gives rise to equivalence classes $E_1, \cdots, E_N$ covering $\{1, \cdots, n\}$. For each equivalence class E_j we further choose a representative member $e_j \in E_j$ (say the least element of E_j). For an agent $i \in \{1, \cdots, n\}$ we next define $[i] \in \{1, \cdots, N\}$ to be the index of the equivalence class containing i, i.e. $i \in E_{[i]}$.

Lemma 1. *A system is secure with respect to Σ if and only if the system is secure with respect to $\{e_{[i]} \mid i \in \Sigma\}$.*

Proof. This follows from observing that we have $i \sim e_{[i]}$ and $i \sim j \Leftrightarrow [i] = [j]$ for all i, j.

While this result can be used to make the semantics more feasible (in case N is considerably smaller than n) we can go even further in obtaining a practical semantics. To do so we shall make use of a mapping

$$\Delta : \mathsf{Loc} \times \{1, \cdots, N\} \to \mathbb{N}$$

that for each location and (index of an) equivalence class gives the number of agents of that equivalence class that are currently at that location. We further define

$$\Delta \bullet l = \{e_k \mid \Delta(l, k) > 0\}$$

to be the set of representative members of agents present at the location l.

Restricting our attention from $\{1, \cdots, n\}$ to the representative members $\{e_1, \cdots, e_N\}$, and letting Σ range over subsets of the latter rather than the former, it makes sense to precompute the collection of Σ's, where the global information flow is consistent with the security lattices:

$$\mathcal{S} = \{\Sigma \subseteq \{e_1, \cdots, e_N\} \mid \forall j \in \Sigma : (\Sigma \vdash_j \ell' \mapsto \ell'') \Rightarrow \ell' \sqsubseteq_j \ell''\}$$

For small N it makes sense to represent this set as a list of bit-vectors of length N as there will be at most 2^N of these; if N is not small, symbolic datastructures can be used for checking $\Sigma \in \mathcal{S}$ efficiently.

$$\frac{(C_i, \sigma_i) \to^\tau (C'_i, \sigma'_i)}{(\Delta, \mathbf{par} \cdots \mathbb{[} \boldsymbol{L_i} D_i C_i \mathbb{]} \cdots \mathbf{rap}, \cdots \sigma_i \cdots)} \quad \text{if } \sigma_i \text{ covers } D_i$$
$$\to (\Delta, \mathbf{par} \cdots \mathbb{[} \boldsymbol{L_i} D_i C'_i \mathbb{]} \cdots \mathbf{rap}, \cdots \sigma'_i \cdots)$$

$$\frac{(C_i, \sigma_i) \to^{c!\,v} (C'_i, \sigma'_i) \qquad (C_j, \sigma_j) \to^{c?\,v} (C'_j, \sigma'_j)}{(\Delta, \mathbf{par} \cdots \boldsymbol{L_i} D_i C_i \mathbb{]} \boldsymbol{L_j} D_j C_j \cdots \mathbf{rap}, \cdots \sigma_i \sigma_j \cdots)} \quad \text{if} \begin{cases} \sigma_i \text{ covers } D_i \\ \sigma_j \text{ covers } D_j \\ i \neq j \\ c? : t\ell \text{ in } D_i \\ \text{and } \ell \neq \perp_i \\ c! : t'\,\ell' \text{ in } D_j \\ \sigma_i(\texttt{loc}) = \sigma_j(\texttt{loc}) \end{cases}$$
$$\to (\Delta, \mathbf{par} \cdots \boldsymbol{L_i} D_i C'_i \mathbb{]} \boldsymbol{L_j} D_j C'_j \cdots \mathbf{rap}, \cdots \sigma'_i \sigma'_j \cdots)$$

$$\frac{(C_i, \sigma_i) \to^{\mathbf{go}\ l} (C'_i, \sigma'_i)}{(\Delta, \mathbf{par} \cdots \mathbb{[} \boldsymbol{L_i} D_i C_i \mathbb{]} \cdots \mathbf{rap}, \cdots \sigma_i \cdots)} \quad \text{if} \begin{cases} \sigma_i \text{ covers } D_i \\ \Delta' \bullet l \in \mathcal{S} \end{cases}$$
$$\to (\Delta', \mathbf{par} \cdots \mathbb{[} \boldsymbol{L_i} D_i C'_i \mathbb{]} \cdots \mathbf{rap}, \cdots \sigma''_i \cdots)$$

$$\text{where } \Delta' = \begin{cases} \Delta & \text{if } \sigma_i(\texttt{loc}) = l \\ \Delta \begin{bmatrix} (\sigma_i(\texttt{loc}), [i]) \mapsto \Delta(\sigma_i(\texttt{loc}), [i]) - 1 \\ (l, [i]) \mapsto \Delta(l, [i]) + 1 \end{bmatrix} & \text{if } \sigma_i(\texttt{loc}) \neq l \end{cases}$$

$$\sigma''_i(\texttt{loc}) = l \text{ and } \sigma''_i(x) = \begin{cases} \sigma'_i(x) & \text{if } x : t\ell \text{ in } D_i \text{ and } \ell = \perp \\ 0_t & \text{if } x : t\ell \text{ in } D_i \text{ and } \ell \neq \perp \end{cases}$$

Fig. 10. Semantics of systems (with precomputed security checks).

This then motivates the semantics of Fig. 10 that differs from our previous semantics in using the precomputed set $\mathcal{S}$ to check the permissibility of relocation more efficiently than before. The main idea is to extend a configuration with the mapping Δ and to devise a constant time operation for updating Δ in the case of relocation. This provides an essentially constant time semantics that is equivalent to the dynamic one.

Proposition 2. *The semantics of Fig. 10 is equivalent to that of Figs. 4 and 9:*

- *if $(\Delta, S, \boldsymbol{\sigma}) \to (\Delta', S', \boldsymbol{\sigma}')$ then $(S, \boldsymbol{\sigma}) \to (S', \boldsymbol{\sigma}')$*
- *if $(S, \boldsymbol{\sigma}) \to (S', \boldsymbol{\sigma}')$ then $(\Delta^S_{\boldsymbol{\sigma}}, S, \boldsymbol{\sigma}) \to (\Delta^{S'}_{\boldsymbol{\sigma}'}, S', \boldsymbol{\sigma}')$*

where $\Delta^S_{\boldsymbol{\sigma}}(l, k)$ is the number of elements in $\{i \mid \sigma_i(\texttt{loc}) = l \wedge [i] = k\}$.

7   Conclusion

We have adapted elements of non-interference to the setting of collective adaptive systems. The basic idea being that an agent must accept its environment as long as it cannot observe any violation of its own security policy. We consider this to be a realistic proposal, because in real systems one would never have any guarantees against the internal behaviour of other agents on the system, including providers of social media channels and national intelligence services. We have made an attempt at capturing the flows observable to an agent but do not fully guarantee against the exclusion from certain services; while exclusion from services is clearly observable, the reasons seldom are, and we do therefore not consider this a major drawback of our proposal.

Our notion of *relocation* requires agents to be sanitised before they relocate, i.e. our insistence that they can only retain information at the lowest security level. It would be interesting to consider a more flexible notion of *migration* where such sanitisation is not imposed. We believe this to be feasible by creating equivalence classes of the locations amongst which migration (as opposed to relocation) might take place; however, it is not clear that the precomputation semantics can be adapted to be semantically equivalent rather than just an approximation (where only the first condition in Proposition 2 would be ensured).

Enforcing security in a distributed system with data sharing and mobile code is a notoriously hard problem. In [7] the *myKlaim* calculus is proposed as a way to model and reason about *open* systems in which external, third-party code may be allowed inside a system to then be executed in a 'sandbox' environment to maintain security. If the mobile code can be proven to comply with the local security policy, through static analysis or certification, the code is also allowed to execute outside the sandbox. The security policies considered are access control policies rather than policies for secure information flow.

The *Fabric* framework, described in [1,8], is an ambitious effort to develop a language and underlying system for designing and implementing distributed systems in a safe and secure manner. The system supports computational models based on both mobile code and data replication with strong security guarantees. Here the security policies are based on an extended version of the *decentralised label model* [10,11]. This allows *principals*, essentially programs, to specify degrees of trust in other (remote) programs and thereby bound the potential security impact if that node should be compromised.

The main problems, insights, and solutions concerning the relationship between secure information flow and trust are distilled and further explored in the *Flow-Limited Authorization Model* [2] and the *Flow-Limited Authorization Calculus* [3] for reasoning about dynamic authorisation decisions.

Acknowledgement. The first author was supported in part by the EU H2020-SU-ICT-03-2018 Project No. 830929 CyberSec4Europe (`cybersec4europe.eu`). The third author is currently on leave from the Department of Mathematics and Computer Science, Technical University of Denmark, Kgs. Lyngby, Denmark.

References

1. Arden, O., George, M.D., Liu, J., Vikram, K., Askarov, A., Myers, A.C.: Sharing mobile code securely with information flow control. In: Proceedings of the Symposium on Security and Privacy (SP 2012), pp. 191–205 (2012)

2. Arden, O., Liu, J., Myers, A.C.: Flow-limited authorization. In: Proceedings of the 28th Computer Security Foundations Symposium (CSF 2015), pp. 569–583 (2015)
3. Arden, O., Myers, A.C.: A calculus for flow-limited authorization. In: Proceedings of the 29th Computer Security Foundations Symposium (CSF 2016), pp. 135–149 (2016)
4. Bhardwaj, C., Prasad, S.: Only connect, securely. In: Pérez, J.A., Yoshida, N. (eds.) FORTE 2019. LNCS, vol. 11535, pp. 75–92. Springer, Cham (2019). https://doi.org/10.1007/978-3-030-21759-4_5
5. de Moura, L., Bjørner, N.: Z3: an efficient SMT solver. In: Ramakrishnan, C.R., Rehof, J. (eds.) TACAS 2008. LNCS, vol. 4963, pp. 337–340. Springer, Heidelberg (2008). https://doi.org/10.1007/978-3-540-78800-3_24
6. Dijkstra, E.W.: Guarded commands, nondeterminacy and formal derivation of programs. Commun. ACM **18**(8), 453–457 (1975)
7. Hansen, R.R., Probst, C.W., Nielson, F.: Sandboxing in myKlaim. In: Proceedings of the International Conference on Availability, Reliability and Security (ARES 2006), pp. 174–181 (2006)
8. Liu, J., Arden, O., George, M.D., Myers, A.C.: Fabric: building open distributed systems securely by construction. J. Comput. Secur. **25**(4–5), 367–426 (2017)
9. Melton, A., Schröder, B.S.W., Strecker, G.E.: Lagois connections - a counterpart to galois connections. Theor. Comput. Sci. **136**(1), 79–107 (1994)
10. Myers, A.C., Liskov, B.: A decentralized model for information flow control. In: Proceedings of the 16th ACM Symposium on Operating Systems Principles (SOSP 1997) (1997)
11. Myers, A.C., Liskov, B.: Protecting privacy using the decentralized label model. ACM Trans. Softw. Eng. Methodol. **9**(4), 410–442 (2000)
12. Nielson, F., Nielson, H.R.: Lightweight information flow. In: Boreale, M., Corradini, F., Loreti, M., Pugliese, R. (eds.) Models, Languages, and Tools for Concurrent and Distributed Programming. LNCS, vol. 11665, pp. 455–470. Springer, Cham (2019). https://doi.org/10.1007/978-3-030-21485-2_25
13. Nielson, F., Nielson, H.R.: Secure guarded commands. In: Di Pierro, A., Malacaria, P., Nagarajan, R. (eds.) From Lambda Calculus to Cybersecurity Through Program Analysis. LNCS, vol. 12065, pp. 201–215. Springer, Cham (2020). https://doi.org/10.1007/978-3-030-41103-9_7
14. Ramli, C.D.P.K., Nielson, H.R., Nielson, F.: The logic of XACML. Sci. Comput. Program. **83**, 80–105 (2014)
15. Volpano, D.M., Irvine, C.E.: Secure flow typing. Comput. Secur. **16**(2), 137–144 (1997)
16. Volpano, D.M., Irvine, C.E., Smith, G.: A sound type system for secure flow analysis. J. Comput. Secur. **4**(2/3), 167–188 (1996)

Capturing Dynamicity and Uncertainty in Security and Trust via Situational Patterns

Tomas Bures[1]([✉]), Petr Hnetynka[1]([✉]), Robert Heinrich[2], Stephan Seifermann[2], and Maximilian Walter[2]

[1] Charles University, Prague, Czech Republic
{bures,hnetynka}@d3s.mff.cuni.cz
[2] Karlsruhe Institute of Technology (KIT), Karlsruhe, Germany
{robert.heinrich,stephan.seifermann,maximilian.walter}@kit.edu

Abstract. Modern smart systems are highly dynamic and allow for dynamic and ad-hoc collaboration not only among devices, but also among humans and organizations. Such a collaboration can introduce uncertainty to a system, as behavior of humans cannot be directly controlled and the system has to deal with unforeseen changes. Security and trust play a crucial role in these systems, especially in domains like Industry 4.0 and similar. In this paper we aim at providing situational patterns for tackling uncertainty in trust – in particular in access control. To do so, we provide a classification of uncertainty of access control in Industry 4.0 systems and illustrate this on a series of representative examples. Based on this classification and examples, we derive situational patterns per type of uncertainty. These situational patterns will serve as adaptation strategies in cases when, due to uncertainty, an unanticipated situation is encountered in the system. We base the approach on our previous work of autonomic component ensembles and security ensembles.

Keywords: Dynamic systems · Security · Access control · Uncertainty

1 Introduction

Smart systems (such as smart manufacturing in Industry 4.0, smart traffic, smart buildings, etc.) are becoming more and more ubiquitous. With this advent and their direct influence on human lives, also the problem of their security and trust in them is becoming highly relevant.

As the smart systems strive towards being more intelligent and being able to cope with various situations, they are becoming highly dynamic and rely on dynamic and ad-hoc collaboration not only among devices constituting a single system, but also among systems, humans and organizations. Such a collaboration typically introduces uncertainty in the system, due to faults in system components, unexpected behavior of humans, and not fully understood behavior of other systems and the environment. This all means that a smart system increasingly needs to deal with unforeseen situations and changes.

© Springer Nature Switzerland AG 2020
T. Margaria and B. Steffen (Eds.): ISoLA 2020, LNCS 12477, pp. 295–310, 2020.
https://doi.org/10.1007/978-3-030-61470-6_18

This uncertainty has a significant impact on the security and overall trust. While the security and trust are normally modeled in rather a strict (and often static) manner, the introduction of uncertainty demands loosening the strict boundaries of security and requires a system to inventively self-adapt to meet new and not fully foreseen situations.

In this paper, we take a first step towards such self-adaptation of security to not fully foreseen situations. We scope our work to access control in Industry 4.0 settings (as here we can derive experience from our completed project Trust4.0 and our ongoing project FluidTrust). To create a frame for such self-adaptation, we provide a classification of uncertainty of access control in Industry 4.0 systems and illustrate this on a series of representative examples. Based on this classification and examples, we derive situational patterns per type of uncertainty. These situational patterns will serve as adaptation strategies in cases when, due to uncertainty, an unanticipated situation is encountered in the system. We base the approach on our previous work of autonomic ensembles and security ensembles [4].

The structure of the paper is as follows. Section 2 analyzes state of the art and related work and then presents a classification of uncertainty. In Sect. 3, we discuss and analyze the representative examples of uncertainty and then, based on the classification and analysis of the examples, Sect. 4 defines the adaptation patterns. Section 5 overviews the adaptation framework where the patterns are employed and Sect. 6 concludes the paper.

2   Classification of Uncertainty in Security and Trust

In this section, we first discuss existing related approaches and then, based on them, we build a classification of uncertainty regarding access control. The classification will serve as a foundation of run-time analyses.

2.1   State of the Art in Access Control and Uncertainty

As confirmed in [33], security is a critical attribute in dynamic and adaptive systems (among whose Industry 4.0 systems belong). The need for dynamicity and self-adaption in these systems stems from the constantly changing context in which the system operates. The survey in [29] discusses context-based middlewares targeting systems like Internet of Things (which are a special type of dynamic and adaptive systems). Security and privacy is dealt only by three middlewares out of eleven. As access control is one of most important aspects of security and confidentiality, RBAC and similar approaches are discussed below.

Access Control is one of established means to enable security and trust. The classical access control systems are DAC [40] and MAC [17] but they are applicable to the simplest solutions only. More advance is Role-based access control (RBAC) [1], which employs groups to gather access rights for similar users. Through this abstraction, the rules are more comprehensible. However, the strict static relationship from groups to rules does not fit dynamic situations and there is no horizontal composition supported between multiple organization.

Thus, the Organisational Based Access Control (OrBAC) has been introduced and recently enhanced by support of horizontal composition [9]. However, it does not support the inclusion of confidentiality analysis and uncertainty. Another well-known access control system is Attribute Based Access Control (ABAC) [25], where access is managed over attributes, which need to be satisfied for accessing data. In [7], an approach based on ABAC is described, which targets also dynamic situations, nevertheless only unexpected and uncommon user behavior (that might represent an attack) is considered. In [39], an approach targeting access policies generation for dynamically established coalitions is described, nevertheless, the coalitions are meant only as groups of people with the same goal but by themselves are not dynamically described. In [42], an approach for security and access control in health care IoT systems is described, but from the point of dealing with uncertainty, it supports only emergency like situations, for which it offers a "break-glass key" approach, i.e., there is a predefined set of persons that know the particular "break-glass key" and in the case of unexpected emergency situation, they have to be contacted. In [36], an adaptive access control approach based on answer set programming targeting context-based systems is shown, but uses predefined access control policies with predefined exceptions.

In summary, there are approaches targeting dynamic access control but only for anticipated changes (i.e., no uncertainty) and with rigid and predefined access rules. However, the increase in dynamicity leads to not anticipated changes, which results in uncertainty. Thus, it is important to take a look to at the uncertainty research area and try to combine it with access control approaches.

An important step to quantify the uncertainty is to realize its source. Depending on the classifications presented on [31], the uncertainty exists on different levels of the system, which are in modeling phase, adaptation functions, goal, environmental and resource uncertainty. Regarding the uncertainty in adaption, the authors in [19] define an uncertainty taxonomy, classify the uncertainty types and match them to MAPE-K stages. These requires to investigate the source of uncertainty and involve the uncertainty handling in the current techniques for performing self-adaptation [27], which are based on using parameters that change the behavior, changing the structure (i.e., reconfiguration), or changing the context. For instance, some frameworks [8,37] investigate the context that introduces uncertainty in behavior. In [30], the authors present a context taxonomy in addition to a 3-layer framework to design context-aware systems. The authors in [32] aim at reducing the impact of uncertainty in quality evaluation. This is done by defining uncertainty taxonomy and study their sources. The study shows that multiple uncertainties could impact model-based quality evaluation. In [34], the study aims at defining taxonomy of uncertainty types, template for their sources, occurrence, and their effect on requirement, design and runtime levels.

Regarding uncertainty in requirements engineering, the classical RELAX [41] approach captures weakening requirements according to environmental conditions (i.e., uncertainty) in runtime. Even though combing RELAX with SysM-LKaos [2] allows the developer to consider non-functional requirements, it does not consider the development of the system nor provides mechanisms to fulfill the conditional requirements.

In self-adaptive systems, many works are handling different kinds of uncertainty using probabilities and learning. For instance, the Stitch language [14] is used in Rainbow framework [16] that employs MAPE-K model. It introduces tactics and strategies as basic concepts for supporting dynamicity. It allows the developer to describe the likelihood of evaluating the condition of strategy selection to true. Using formal approach, [38] presents stochastic multi-mode systems (SMMS) that approximate the action of a moving vehicle, so it satisfies almost-sure reachability, which is the movement within a certain safety corridor. As for uncontrollable entities, [6] introduced a proactive adaptation to capture possible dangerous situations using prediction over historical data (i.e., fire prediction). For unforeseen situations, NiFti project [26] uses human-robot cooperation to achieve the goal in rescue missions. More specifically, the robots can alter a pre-defined plan to utilize the resources, and depending on robot updates on a 3D map the rescue can change the path for robots to avoid obstacles. Even though the previous work considered controllable/uncontrollable entities, they do not consider evaluating the risk/loss tradeoff.

Systems of the Industry 4.0 domain can be seen as a special case of Smart Cyber-Physical Systems (sCPS) [11], which also exhibit a high level of uncertainty. This has been already partially studied, e.g., in the scopes of the ASCENS and Quanticol projects [28,35]. Also, we partially addressed statistical modeling of human behavior in sCPS [10] and adaptation via meta-adaptation strategies [21] however a complete approach for sCPS is yet missing.

In summary, there are classifications and approaches for uncertainty. However, so far to our knowledge no combination of access control approaches and uncertainty exists.

2.2   Classification of Uncertainty in Access Control

We applied, adopted, and condensed the classification of uncertainty from Perez-Palacin et al. [32] to better fit the needs of uncertainty in access control in Industry 4.0 systems. The adapted classification consists of three dimensions: Levels of uncertainty, Nature, and Source. The first two dimensions are taken from [32]. The last one is added to better categorize software architecture.

Levels of uncertainty categorize uncertainty by the degree of awareness. There are four levels. We removed the fifth from the original classification because it is—in our eyes—not practically applicable. The first level is that no uncertainty exists. In our case, this means that the system can decide without guessing what the correct access rules are. The second level introduces uncertainty but the system is aware of it and has appropriate measures to handle it. One solution to handle this is fuzzy logic for access control like used in [13]. The third level adds situations where the system is unaware of the existence of uncertainty. In the field of security, a component of an access control system can fail and deny access for everyone. In that case, the uncertainty is about the operability of the access control system. One solution for this might be a continuous monitoring approach similar to [23], which will trigger an adaptation process. This moves the uncertainty to level two because the system becomes aware of the uncertainty. The fourth and last level is that there exists no process to find out that the system has uncertainties. In general, this should be avoided [32].

Nature distinguishes between epistemic and aleatory. We reuse this category from [32] unchanged. Epistemic means that uncertainty exists because there is not enough data available. In policy mining approaches such as the one in [15], uncertainty might exist if the log data does not consist of every necessary case. Aleatory describes a situation, which is too random to consider. For instance, this might be the break-down of a security sensor because of vandalism.

Source describes where uncertainty for access control can be found in the modeled system. We distinguish between *system structure*, *system behavior*, and *system environment*. We used this three subcategories, since systems consist of at least a structure, a behavior and an environment and in everyone of these uncertainty can exist. However, this is not an exclusive categorization, because scenarios could fall into multiple of these categories. System structure is comparable to the *model structure* from [32]. The *system structure* describes the design of the system. It consists of for example components, hardware resources, the wiring of components via required and provided interfaces. The *system behavior* describes the uncertainty in the actual behavior of the system. This can be for example the uncertainty about the intended usage. In access control the behavior is often regulated by access control rules. These rules might introduce uncertainty, if they are incorrect. However, they might also help to handle uncertainty. Therefore, we would count access control rules to the system behavior. The last subcategory is the *system environment*. The *system environment* describes the context in which a system is executed. This includes also the input data for the system. For instance this might be that due to bad sensor data, which is the input data the system cannot produce an accurate result for the location of an user and therefore decides s/he is not in compound and marks her/him as unauthorized.

3   Representative Examples/Use-Cases

As a basis of representative examples, we are using a use-case [5] from our previous project Trust4.0[1], which focused on dynamic security. The use-case is simple however fully realistic as it has been developed together with and is based on interviews with industrial experts in the project. Within the project we created an approach for managing access control suitable for highly dynamic environment of Industry 4.0. The approach is based on application of dynamic security rules. Nevertheless, during the project we encountered several important situations, where uncertainty prevented formulating or even foreseeing strict access control rules. This requires a foundational change in the approach how the access control rules can be designed, verified and enforced, such that the uncertainty can be explicitly represented, tackled and reasoned about.

---

[1] http://trust40.ipd.kit.edu/home/.

In the light of the classification shown in Sect. 2.2, we compare these categories against experiences of these situations we gathered together with our industry partners. We examined how the different types of uncertainty in the scenarios can be located within the given categories. We are focusing on the second and third *level* of uncertainty (the first level represents no uncertainty whereas in the fourth, uncertainty cannot be managed). As for *nature*, we handle both epistemic and aleatory uncertainty – this is necessary because if in a decentralized system an unexpected situation occurs, it is imperative to make a reaction regardless whether the situation is completely random or just not fully known. Importantly, we also assume that as the reaction typically has to be immediate there is no scope to obtain unknown data which would normally be one way to handle epistemic uncertainty. Similarly, we address the different subcategories in the *source* section. We describe the application of the *source* categorization with each example.

The use-case [5] assumes a factory with multiple working places where groups of workers work in shifts. The workers have access only to the workplace to which they have been assigned. Also, before the shift, they have to collect protective gear from a dispenser, without which they are not allowed to enter the workplace. The workplace is equipped with machines that can monitor their state and also can be reconfigured. The actual detailed log of what the machine did and what its internal settings are is confidential as it constitutes the intellectual property of the factory. To support the production in the factory, there is a constant inflow of trucks bringing in material and taking out finished products. The truck is allowed to enter the factory only when it is designated so in the schedule and to enter the factory it must use a designated gate within a designated time interval.

Primarily, the access-control permissions are of two kinds: *allow* and *deny* (in a case of inconsistencies, evaluation order is allow–deny).

The identified examples of situations, in which the system encounters a state that was not anticipated and the access-control rules do not count with it, are as follows:

Example 1. A dispenser breaks and stops distributing the protective gear which is required to enter a shift. The system has to allow a foreman to open the dispenser so as to distribute the protective gear manually. Applying our source categorization, this falls into system structure and behavior, since the failing dispenser would be a structure problem and the opening and the distribution of gear by the foreman would be a different system behavior.

Example 2. An access gate is disconnected from the central authorization service and thus prohibits anyone to pass through because the access cannot be verified (this is actually quite a commons situation of gates letting the trucks inside the factory). The system has to allow the security personnel on the gate to manually define who can pass through. This would also fall into the system structure since the access gate would be a missing component and the system behavior category since the default behavior is changed.

Example 3. A machine is broken and repair requires that a third-party repairman has access to internal machine logs. In order to do the job, the repairman requires access data summaries which are anonymized over several shifts. As the repairman arrives at the place, it turns out that access to the data cannot be given because the data cannot be properly anonymized because the last operation was not long enough to collect the required data points that are needed to ensure proper anonymization. The source categorization would categorize this example into system structure since the broken machine introduces uncertainty, and system environment since the input data adds uncertainty whether machine can be repaired by the technician or not.

Example 4. An unexpected and unauthorized person appears at a workplace. By the system design this cannot happen because the person would have to pass a security gate. In this case, the system should dynamically enable the foreman or some other trusted person in the vicinity to access information allowing them to determine the person identity and reason to be there before the security personnel is called. As for our source categorization this would be in the category environment, since the context (here attendance of person) introduces uncertainty to the system.

In all the examples above, the system needs to autonomously take a decision which is beyond its pre-designed access control rules. In doing so, it has to evaluate how the access-control rules should be adapted in order to minimize the potential risk and loss (i.e., what is risked if the access-control rules are weakened and what can be lost, if the rules are strictly followed and not weakened).

3.1   Examples Analysis

Here, we analyze the presented situations from multiple different views in order to build the situational patterns in the next section.

In *Example* 1, the system gives rights to someone, who is already trustworthy. Particularly, the foreman is responsible for the whole shift and has rights to access personal information about all the workers in his/her shift and has overall responsibility of the shift. Thus, assigning him/her the rights for the dispenser does not represent a significant security issue. On the other hand, not to assign the rights means that the shift cannot be executed without the protective gear and there might be a significant loss for the company.

In *Example* 2, the situation is similar from the risk/loss view. Again, the access right (for the gate now) is assigned to someone, who is trustworthy and in fact already has a superior access right (the security personnel is responsible for all the entries to the factory area anyway).

Nevertheless, there is an important difference between *Example* 1 and *Example* 2 which is characterized by the question which component in the security chains is broken. In the *Example* 1, the dispenser is a terminal component in the chain. Thus, the foreman needs to be assigned with a additional access right (open the dispenser), however no one (foreman, workers) has it currently assigned. In *Example* 2, the gate is disconnected and cannot verify access rights. The broken part here is an intermediate component in the security chain which assigns the access rights. The security personnel thus replaces a component (the gate) in the chain and the scenario is as before.

The *Example* 3 is a different one. Here, the security risk is that the repairman can see unanonymized data and the loss is that the shift cannot proceed (which can lead to loss of profit for the company). However, the repairman typically has signed a kind of NDA (non-disclosure agreement) as even only via his/her presence in the company, he/she is eligible see proprietary information. Thus, relaxing on having the access right for seeing unanonymized data does not represent a significant issue (the anonymized data are a second level of protection—the first one is NDA).

Example 4 is quite close to *Example* 1. Here, the system has to give additional rights to someone, who is already trustworthy (the foreman is responsible for the whole shift and all workers in the shift).

3.2 Summary

Based on the analysis from the previous section, we can identify two dimensions defining a space, in which new rules are created: (i) whether something is allowed or denied (ii) what is done with access rights.

For the first dimension, the options are obvious, either the new rule works with: (1) the *allow* permission, or with (2) the *deny* permission.

For the second dimension, the options are: (A) a permission is given to a component, (B) decision about a permission assignment is delegated to a component, (C) a permission is removed.

Table 1 maps the examples to the space of above defined dimensions. The cases not covered by the examples above, can be exemplified as follows (in the table marked as *Post-hoc* examples): For the 1xC case (removing the *allow* permission, *Post-hoc C* example)—if the foreman tries to read information not accessible to him/her, it is evaluated as a potential security attack and all his/her access rights are removed. For the 2xA case (adding the *deny* permission to a component, *Post-hoc A* example)—if the repairman starts to read data unrelated to the machine/shift, new rule with the deny permission for him/her is created. For the 2xB case (delegating the *deny* permission to a component, *Post-hoc B* example)—as in the previous one, if the repairman starts to read data unrelated to the machine/shift, new rule delegating the *deny* permission to the foremen is created.

Table 1. 1st vs 2nd dimension

	A	B	C
1	Example 1, 4	Example 2	Post-hoc C
2	Post-hoc A	Post-hoc B	Example 3

Also, from the analysis, we can observe that the typical reasons that someone obtains new permissions is

(a) he/she already has a role that implies governance over part of a system for which the new permission is to be granted – thus the new permission does not extend the scope of governance of the subject, it only completes it,

(b) he/she has an equivalent role to someone who already has the permission,
(c) a risk connected with obtaining the new permission is low compared to the
     loss connected with not obtaining the permission.

Similarly, we can observe that the typical reasons that someone is loosing permissions is that he/she is trying to perform a suspicious operation and thus, as a preventive measure, he/she looses access.

   Note that item (c) subsumes (a) and (b). However, we still list (a) and (b) separately because these conditions are easier to establish. Whereas the comparison of risk vs. loss is typically difficult to do. In situations when this ratio cannot be reliably done, it is necessary to assume that the risk is too high.

4   Situational Patterns for Uncertainty

With the analysis performed, we can define the situational patterns, which serve as a strategy for dynamic adaptation of security access rules.

   For describing the patterns, we use a format inspired by the classical books on patterns [12,18], however we have updated the format to our needs (which is a common and recommended practice [20], i.e., to update the format to own needs as the content is more important than the form). Our format is: (i) *Name of the pattern*, (ii) *Solution* (description of the pattern), (iii) *Context* (determination of components and their behavior where the pattern is applied), (iv) *Consequences* (in our cases, mainly the risk discussion), and (v) *Example*.

   There are three identified patterns following the second dimension from Sect. 3. Plus, there are sub-variants following the first dimension in those case where the division is necessary.

4.1   Pattern 1a – Adding an *allow* Rule

Solution A new situation cannot be handled with currently assigned permissions—a new *allow* permission needs to be assigned, i.e., a new security access rule assigning the *allow* to a component is added to the system.

Context The *allow* permission, i.e., a rule with the *allow* permission, is assigned to a component, which either has: (a) such a role in the system that the new rule does not fall outside the component's area of competence, or (b) a similar role in the system as a component that already has the same rule.

Consequences By adding the *allow* permission, the affected component can have higher access within the system than originally intended and it might lead to a potentially dangerous situations. Thus the trade-off has to be greater for adding the *allow* permission than for not adding it (and therefore leaving the system in a non-functional state).

Example The *Examples* 1 and 4 are direct representatives of this pattern.

4.2   Pattern 1b – Adding a *deny* Rule

Solution A potentially dangerous situation occurs in the system. The *deny* permission is assigned to the component (i.e., a new security access rule assigning the *deny* to a component is added to the system).

Context A component has started to misbehave—accessing more than is usual and/or necessary for it. As a security measure, the *deny* rule is assigned to the component.

Consequences The situation here is reversed to the *Pattern 1a*, i.e., the trade-off has to be greater for limiting access right for the affected component.

Example The *Post-hoc A* example is direct representative of this pattern.

4.3   Pattern 2a – Removing an *allow* Rule

Solution A potentially dangerous situation occurs in the system. The *allow* permission is removed from the component (i.e., an existing security access rule assigning the *allow* to a component is removed from the system).

Context A component has started to misbehave and or is broken. As a security measure, the *allow* rule is removed from the component. The pattern is very similar to the *Pattern 1b*—the difference is that the *Pattern 1* is used when there is no rule to be removed.

Consequences The situation here is the same as for the *Pattern 1b*

Example The *Post-hoc C* example is direct representative of this pattern.

4.4   Pattern 2b – Removing a *deny* Rule

Solution The system runs in a situation that is blocked by a rule with the *deny* permission. The *deny* permission is removed from the component (i.e., an existing security access rule assigning the *deny* to a component is removed from the system).

Context The system can continue in the common operations only if a component can access an entity (e.g., another component) but there is a rule *denying* the access. The rule is removed.

Consequences The rule can be removed only in the case the rule represents redundancy in the security chain.

Example The *Example 3* is direct representative of this pattern.

4.5   Pattern 3 – A New Access Rule Validator

Summary The system runs in a situation that is blocked by a component that validates access for other components (e.g., the component is broken). Another component is chosen as a replacement and serves as a new validator.

Context The selected component has to already have a supervisor-like role in the system.

Consequences As the selected component has to already have a supervisor-like role, the risk of assigning additional permissions to it is minimized.

Example The *Example 2* is direct representative of this pattern for the *allow* permission and the *Post-hoc B* for the *deny* permission.

5   Applying Patterns in an Adaptation Framework

As we described in [3], we model dynamic security rules as ensembles. This allows us to target dynamic security in collective adaptive systems. Ensembles are instantiated dynamically to reflect ever changing situations and collaborations in a system.

An ensemble definition is static in terms which permission it assigns and the predicate identifying components it applies to (i.e., subjects and objects of the permissions). The dynamicity comes from the fact that an ensemble is instantiated at runtime for each group of components that match the roles and constraints in the ensemble. The components are identified by their state. As this state changes throughout the lifetime of the system, the selection is dynamic.

From the architecture perspective, we model the system as an adaptive system, where security ensembles generate access control rules that are understood by legacy systems. This is the first-level of adaptation as shown in Fig. 1 – controlled by an Adaptation Manager. In this paper, we see the adaptation as decentralized. As such, we assume multiple Adaptation Managers, each of which instantiates ensembles in its domain of control and determines access control rules pertaining to particular subjects and objects.

To account uncertainty that is addressed by the situational patterns as presented in this paper, we build on our approach to architectural homeostasis [22] and incorporate the patterns described in this paper as a meta-adaptation layer (i.e., a layer that adapts the ensembles themselves) as visualized in Fig. 1.

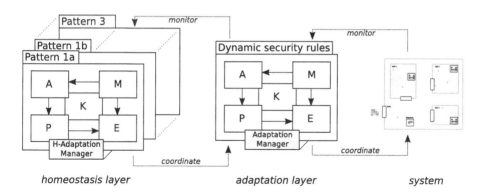

Fig. 1. Meta-adaptation framework

The idea is that each pattern is reflected as one strategy of the meta-adaptation layer. The strategy modifies existing ensembles that implement the dynamic security of the collective adaptive system. This extra layer extends the adaptation space of the system and helps tackling situations that were not fully anticipated and lie beyond the scope of the system states addressed by the security ensembles (i.e., the middle layer in Fig. 1).

Each pattern is represented as a MAPE-K adaptation loop that monitors the system for unanticipated situations targeted by the particular pattern. The pattern also determines the dynamic security rules that have to be introduced to tackle the unanticipated situation.

Listing 1 shows a brief excerpt of the security specification via ensembles for our factory use-case. The specification is written in our DSL, which is created as an internal DSL in the Scala language.

```
 1  class TestScenario() extends Model {
 2    object CAS extends Component { /*...*/ }
 3    class Gate(/*...*/) extends Component { /*...*/ }
 4    /* ... */
 5    class FactorySystem(factory: Factory) extends RootEnsemble {
 6      class GateAccess(gate: Gate) extends Ensemble {
 7        initiatedBy(CAS)
 8        val assignedTransports = transports.filter(tr => tr.assignedGate == gate)
 9        class TransportAccessThroughGate(transport: Transport) extends Ensemble {
10          situation {
11            (now isEqualOrAfter (transport.scheduledArrival minusMinutes 5)) &&
12              (now isEqualOrBefore (transport.scheduledArrival plusMinutes 15)) &&
13                transport.assignedGate == gate
14          }
15          allow(transport, Enter, gate)
16        }
17        val transportAccesses = rules(transports.filter(tr => tr.assignedGate == gate).map(tr => new
                TransportAccessThroughGate(tr)))
18      }
19
20      class ShiftTeam(shift: Shift) extends Ensemble {
21        initiatedBy(CAS)
22        object AccessToFactory extends Ensemble {
23          situation {
24            (now isEqualOrAfter (shift.startTime minusMinutes 45)) &&
25              (now isEqualOrBefore (shift.endTime plusMinutes 45))
26          }
27          allow(shift.foreman, Enter, shift.workPlace.factoryBuilding)
28          allow(assignedWorkers, Enter, shift.workPlace.factoryBuilding)
29        }
30        object AccessToDispenser extends Ensemble {
31          situation {
32            (now isEqualOrAfter (shift.startTime minusMinutes 40)) &&
33              (now isEqualOrBefore shift.endTime)
34          }
35          allow(shift.foreman, Use, shift.workPlace.factoryBuilding.dispenser)
36          allow(assignedWorkers, Use, shift.workPlace.factoryBuilding.dispenser)
37        }
38        object AccessToWorkplace extends Ensemble { /* ... */ }
39        object AccessToMachine extends Ensemble { /* ... */ }
40        object NoAccessToMachineSensitiveDataOtherThanFromWorkplace extends Ensemble { /* ... */ }
41        object AccessToBrokenMachine extends Ensemble {
42          val assignedRepairmen = repairmen.filter(rm => rm.machine == shift.workPlace.machine)
43          allow(assignedRepairmen, Read("logs"), shift.workPlace.machine)
44        }
45        deny(repairmen, Read("*"), shift.workPlace.machine, PrivacyLevel.SENSITIVE)
46        /* ... */
47        rules(
48          AccessToFactory, AccessToDispenser, AccessToWorkplace,
49          AccessToMachine, AccessToBrokenMachine, CancellationOfWorkersThatAreLate
50        )
51      }
52      val shiftTeams = rules(shifts.filter(shift => shift.workPlace.factoryBuilding.factory ==
                factory).map(shift => new ShiftTeam(shift)))
53      val gateAccessRules = rules(gates.map(gate => new GateAccess(gate)))
54    }
55    val factoryTeam = root(new FactorySystem(factory))
56  }
```

Listing 1: Original security specification

Below, we overview the parts of the specification important to this paper. Details about the syntax and semantics of DSL for security ensemble specifications are available at [24].

Components are used to represent entities in the system that (a) can be assigned access control, (b) are subject of access control, or (c) can determine the access control by controlling formation of security ensembles (i.e., acting as the Adaptation Manager in the middle layer).

The components are listed in lines 2–4. These represent components for the Gate, Factory, Workplace, Central−Access−System (CAS), etc. but also components that cannot be directly controlled by the system, but still are relevant to access control—like Workman, Repairman, etc.

Then, the ensembles representing security specifications are defined. The ensembles are hierarchical, which allows for more simple definition thanks to decomposition. The FactorySystem ensemble (line 5) represent the whole system. The GateAccess (line 6) ensemble controls access through the gate to the factory. This ensemble is initiated (i.e., its instantiation is controlled by) the CAS component and it has a single further subensemble TransportAccessThroughGate (line 9), which is instantiated for each transport coming to the factory. Here, if the transport satisfies the condition defined in the situation (line 10), it is allowed to enter through the gate via the allow rule (line 15). Similarly to the GateAccess ensemble, the ShiftTeam ensemble (line 20) controls access of workers (and other persons) to and within the factory. It is also decomposed to several subensmbles controlling access to individual elements of the factory, i.e., the AccessToFactory ensemble controlling access to the factory, the AccessToDispenser controlling access to the dispenser for headgear, and so on.

In addition to the allow rules, the specification also lists deny rules. The semantics is allow-deny, meaning that a deny rule overrides any allow rules. The deny rules are used in the specification to express cross-cutting policies—e.g., that no external repairman should get access to sensitive data. We assume that all the security to be primarily specified via the allow rules. The deny rules thus act more as assertions to detect inconsistencies in the specification.

As mentioned above, the H-adaptation manager monitors the system for unanticipated situations and introduces new ensembles and rules to the security specification of the system. Particularly for our use-case, if the H-adaptation manager detects a situation corresponding to the *Example* 1 (the broken dispenser, i.e., the **Pattern 1a**), it updates the AccessToDispenser ensemble with the additional allow rule and thus, the ensemble rules will look as follows:

```
1  object AccessToDispenser extends Ensemble {
2    /* ... */
3    allow(shift.foreman, Use, shift.workPlace.factoryBuilding.dispenser)
4    allow(shift.foreman, Open, shift.workPlace.factoryBuilding.dispenser) // ADDED
5    allow(assignedWorkers, Use, shift.workPlace.factoryBuilding.dispenser)
6  }
```

Listing 2: Updated specification based on Pattern 1a

Similarly, if the H-manager detects a situation corresponding to the *Example* 3 (the broken machine, i.e., the **Pattern 2b**), it removes the deny rule at line 45 (in Listing 1) disallowing the repairman to read sensitive data.

If the H-manager detects a situation corresponding to the *Example* 2 (the disconnected gate, i.e., the **Pattern 3**), it updates the GateAccess ensemble so it is initiated not by the CAS component but by the security personnel, i.e., it starts as follows:

```
1 class GateAccess(gate: Gate) extends Ensemble {
2   initiatedBy(gateSecurityHeads(gate)) // instead of initiatedBy(CAS)
```

Listing 3: Updated specification based on Pattern 3

6   Conclusion

In this paper, we have presented access-control related situational patterns, which serve as meta-adaptation strategies in cases when an unanticipated situation is encountered in the system. The patterns primarily target the domain of Industry 4.0, however they are applicable to other similar domains of modern smart cyber-physical system. They are based on our experience gained from participating in industrial projects. The patterns represent a first step for self-adaptation of security management.

Currently, we are continuing with the implementation of the adaptation framework and incorporating the patterns there. As an ongoing work, we investigate further industrial-based examples and update the patterns correspondingly.

Acknowledgment. This work has been funded by the DFG (German Research Foundation) – project number 432576552, HE8596/1-1 (FluidTrust), supported by the Czech Science Foundation project 20-24814J, and also partially supported by Charles University institutional funding SVV 260451.

References

1. Abreu, V., Santin, A.O., Viegas, E.K., Stihler, M.: A multi-domain role activation model. In: Proceedings of ICC 2017, Paris, France, pp. 1–6. IEEE (2017)
2. Ahmad, M., Gnaho, C., Bruel, J.-M., Laleau, R.: Towards a requirements engineering approach for capturing uncertainty in cyber-physical systems environment. In: Abdelwahed, E.H., et al. (eds.) MEDI 2018. CCIS, vol. 929, pp. 115–129. Springer, Cham (2018). https://doi.org/10.1007/978-3-030-02852-7_11
3. Al Ali, R., Bures, T., Hnetynka, P., Krijt, F., Plasil, F., Vinarek, J.: Dynamic security specification through autonomic component ensembles. In: Margaria, T., Steffen, B. (eds.) ISoLA 2018. LNCS, vol. 11246, pp. 172–185. Springer, Cham (2018). https://doi.org/10.1007/978-3-030-03424-5_12
4. Al Ali, R., Bures, T., Hnetynka, P., Matejek, J., Plasil, F., Vinarek, J.: Toward autonomically composable and context-dependent access control specification through ensembles. Int. J. Softw. Tools Technol. Transfer **22**(4), 511–522 (2020). https://doi.org/10.1007/s10009-020-00556-1
5. Al-Ali, R., et al.: Dynamic security rules for legacy systems. In: Proceedings of ECSA 2019 - Volume 2, Paris, France, pp. 277–284. ACM (2019)
6. Anaya, I.D.P., Simko, V., Bourcier, J., Plouzeau, N., Jézéquel, J.M.: A prediction-driven adaptation approach for self-adaptive sensor networks. In: Proceedings of SEAMS 2014, Hyderabad, India, pp. 145–154 (2014)

7. Argento, L., Margheri, A., Paci, F., Sassone, V., Zannone, N.: Towards adaptive access control. In: Kerschbaum, F., Paraboschi, S. (eds.) DBSec 2018. LNCS, vol. 10980, pp. 99–109. Springer, Cham (2018). https://doi.org/10.1007/978-3-319-95729-6_7

8. Baudry, G., Macharis, C., Vallée, T.: Range-based multi-actor multi-criteria analysis: a combined method of multi-actor multi-criteria analysis and Monte Carlo simulation to support participatory decision making under uncertainty. Eur. J. Oper. Res. **264**(1), 257–269 (2018)

9. Ben Abdelkrim, I., Baina, A., Feltus, C., Aubert, J., Bellafkih, M., Khadraoui, D.: Coalition-OrBAC: an agent-based access control model for dynamic coalitions. In: Rocha, Á., Adeli, H., Reis, L.P., Costanzo, S. (eds.) WorldCIST'18 2018. AISC, vol. 745, pp. 1060–1070. Springer, Cham (2018). https://doi.org/10.1007/978-3-319-77703-0_103

10. Bures, T., Plasil, F., Kit, M., Tuma, P., Hoch, N.: Software abstractions for component interaction in the Internet of Things. Computer **49**(12), 50–59 (2016)

11. Bures, T., Weyns, D., Schmer, B., Fitzgerald, J.: Software engineering for smart cyber-physical systems: models, system-environment boundary, and social aspects. ACM SIGSOFT Softw. Eng. Not. **43**(4), 42–44 (2019)

12. Buschmann, F. (ed.): Pattern-Oriented Software Architecture: A System of Patterns. Wiley, Hoboken (1996)

13. Cheng, P.C., Rohatgi, P., Keser, C., Karger, P.A., Wagner, G.M., Reninger, A.S.: Fuzzy multi-level security: an experiment on quantified risk-adaptive access control. In: Proceedings of SP 2007, Berkeley, USA, pp. 222–227 (2007)

14. Cheng, S.W., Garlan, D.: Stitch: a language for architecture-based self-adaptation. J. Syst. Softw. **85**(12), 2860–2875 (2012)

15. Cotrini, C., Weghorn, T., Basin, D.: Mining ABAC rules from sparse logs. In: Proceedings of EURO S&P 2018, London, UK, pp. 31–46 (2018)

16. Cámara, J., Garlan, D., Kang, W.G., Peng, W., Schmerl, B.R.: Uncertainty in self-adaptive systems categories, management, and perspectives. Report CMU-ISR-17-110, Institute for Software Research School of Computer Science Carnegie Mellon University, Pittsburgh, PA 15213 (2017)

17. De Capitani di Vimercati, S., Samarati, P.: Mandatory access control policy (MAC). In: van Tilborg, H.C.A., Jajodia, S. (eds.) Encyclopedia of Cryptography and Security, p. 758. Springer, Boston (2011). https://doi.org/10.1007/978-1-4419-5906-5_822

18. Gamma, E., Helm, R., Johnson, R., Vlissides, J.: Design Patterns: Elements of Reusable Object-Oriented Software. Addison Wesley Professional, Boston (1994)

19. Esfahani, N., Malek, S.: Uncertainty in self-adaptive software systems. In: de Lemos, R., Giese, H., Müller, H.A., Shaw, M. (eds.) Software Engineering for Self-Adaptive Systems II. LNCS, vol. 7475, pp. 214–238. Springer, Heidelberg (2013). https://doi.org/10.1007/978-3-642-35813-5_9

20. Fowler, M.: Writing Software Patterns (2006). https://www.martinfowler.com/articles/writingPatterns.html

21. Gerostathopoulos, I., Bures, T., Hnetynka, P., Hujecek, A., Plasil, F., Skoda, D.: Strengthening adaptation in cyber-physical systems via meta-adaptation strategies. ACM Trans. Cyber-Phys. Syst. **1**(3), 1–25 (2017)

22. Gerostathopoulos, I., Škoda, D., Plášil, F., Bureš, T., Knauss, A.: Tuning self-adaptation in cyber-physical systems through architectural homeostasis. J. Syst. Softw. **148**, 37–55 (2019)

23. Heinrich, R.: Architectural runtime models for integrating runtime observations and component-based models. J. Syst. Softw. **169**, 110722 (2020)

24. Hnetynka, P., Bures, T., Gerostathopoulos, I., Pacovsky, J.: Using component ensembles for modeling autonomic component collaboration in smart farming. In: Proceedings of SEAMS 2020, Seoul, Republic of Korea (2020)
25. Hu, V.C., Kuhn, D.R., Ferraiolo, D.F.: Attribute-based access control. Computer **48**(2), 85–88 (2015)
26. Kruijff, G., et al.: Designing, developing, and deploying systems to support human-robot teams in disaster response. Adv. Robot. **28**(23), 1547–1570 (2014)
27. Krupitzer, C., Roth, F.M., VanSyckel, S., Schiele, G., Becker, C.: A survey on engineering approaches for self-adaptive systems. Pervasive Mob. Comput. **17**, 184–206 (2015)
28. Latella, D., Loreti, M., Massink, M., Senni, V.: Stochastically timed predicate-based communication primitives for autonomic computing. In: Electronic Proceedings in Theoretical Computer Science, vol. 154, pp. 1–16 (2014)
29. Li, X., Eckert, M., Martinez, J.F., Rubio, G.: Context aware middleware architectures: survey and challenges. Sensors **15**(8), 20570–20607 (2015)
30. Lu, Y.: Industry 4.0: a survey on technologies, applications and open research issues. J. Ind. Inf. Integration **6**, 1–10 (2017)
31. Mahdavi-Hezavehi, S., Avgeriou, P., Weyns, D.: A classification framework of uncertainty in architecture-based self-adaptive systems with multiple quality requirements. In: Managing Trade-Offs in Adaptable Software Architectures, pp. 45–77. Elsevier (2017)
32. Perez-Palacin, D., Mirandola, R.: Uncertainties in the modeling of self-adaptive systems: a taxonomy and an example of availability evaluation. In: Proceedings of ICPE 2014, Dublin, Ireland, pp. 3–14 (2014)
33. Peruma, A., Krutz, D.E.: Security: a critical quality attribute in self-adaptive systems. In: Proceedings of SEAMS 2018, Gothenburg, Sweden, pp. 188–189 (2018)
34. Ramirez, A.J., Jensen, A.C., Cheng, B.H.C.: A taxonomy of uncertainty for dynamically adaptive systems. In: Proceedings of SEAMS 2012, Zurich, Switzerland, pp. 99–108 (2012)
35. Reijsbergen, D.: Probabilistic modelling of station locations in bicycle-sharing systems. In: Milazzo, P., Varró, D., Wimmer, M. (eds.) STAF 2016. LNCS, vol. 9946, pp. 83–97. Springer, Cham (2016). https://doi.org/10.1007/978-3-319-50230-4_7
36. Sartoli, S., Namin, A.S.: Modeling adaptive access control policies using answer set programming. J. Inf. Secur. Appl. **44**, 49–63 (2019)
37. Sharif, M., Alesheikh, A.A.: Context-aware movement analytics: implications, taxonomy, and design framework: context-aware movement analytics. Wiley Interdiscip. Rev. Data Min. Knowl. Discov. **8**(1), e1233 (2018)
38. Somenzi, F., Touri, B., Trivedi, A.: Almost-sure reachability in stochastic multi-mode system. arXiv:1610.05412 (2016)
39. Verma, D., et al.: Generative policy model for autonomic management. In: Proceedings of IEEE SmartWorld 2017, San Francisco, USA, pp. 1–6 (2017)
40. Vimercati, S.D.C.: Discretionary access control policies (DAC). In: van Tilborg, H.C.A., Jajodia, S. (eds.) Encyclopedia of Cryptography and Security, pp. 356–358. Springer, Boston (2011). https://doi.org/10.1007/978-1-4419-5906-5_817
41. Whittle, J., Sawyer, P., Bencomo, N., Cheng, B.H., Bruel, J.M.: RELAX: incorporating uncertainty into the specification of self-adaptive systems. In: Proceedings of RE 2009, Atlanta, USA, pp. 79–88 (2009)
42. Yang, Y., Zheng, X., Guo, W., Liu, X., Chang, V.: Privacy-preserving smart IoT-based healthcare big data storage and self-adaptive access control system. Inf. Sci. **479**, 567–592 (2019)

Guaranteeing Type Consistency in Collective Adaptive Systems

Jonas Schürmann, Tim Tegeler$^{(\boxtimes)}$, and Bernhard Steffen

Chair for Programming Systems, TU Dortmund University, Dortmund, Germany
{jonas2.schuermann,tim.tegeler,bernhard.steffen}@tu-dortmund.de

Abstract. Collective adaptive systems whose entities are loosely coupled by their exchange of complex data structures became a very common architecture for distributed web-based systems. As HTTP-based APIs transfer data as plain text, this exchange is very error prone: API changes and malicious data modifications may remain unnoticed. GraphQL addresses this concern at the server side with strong typing but leaves the clients untouched. In this paper we present an approach to align the type schemas provided by GraphQL and type definitions at the client side on three levels during the systems' life cycles: At generation time by verifying queries against the GraphQL schema, at compile time by leveraging TypeScript's type system, and at run time by using decoders to validate payloads. Key to our solution are a functional, type-safe domain-specific language for the definition of GraphQL queries and a corresponding generator implementation providing the GraphQL queries and TypeScript artefacts. Together they ensure that clients become aware of and are able to react to changes of the (evolving) GraphQL schema, a precondition for maintaining the consistency of the overall collective adaptive system. We will illustrate our approach along a popular GitHub-based, collaborative development scenario.

Keywords: Domain-Specific Language · GraphQL · Type Safety · TypeScript · Web Service

1 Introduction

Modern information exchange on the internet increasingly relies upon decentralized web services. The ubiquity of mobile devices and the continuing growth of the *Internet of Things* (IoT) have contributed to the trend [8,17] of using web-based *Application Programming Interfaces* (APIs). Almost every major platform (e.g., GitHub[1]) either provides a separate web service to their users or design their architecture completely by an *API first* strategy. Web services are treated as *first-class citizens* and become the pivotal part of modern web-based systems. This trend is influenced by the era of agile software development and DevOps [1,10], where the *time to market* has a major impact on the success of a product and, automation, reliability and validation is key. Although the

---

[1] https://docs.github.com.

© Springer Nature Switzerland AG 2020
T. Margaria and B. Steffen (Eds.): ISoLA 2020, LNCS 12477, pp. 311–328, 2020.
https://doi.org/10.1007/978-3-030-61470-6_19

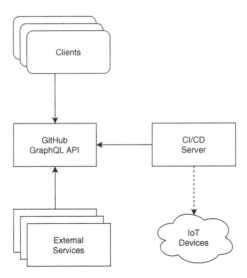

Fig. 1. Example of a web-based collective adaptive system

adoption of data types can contribute to satisfying these requirements, a large part of collective adaptive systems (CAS) on the web are built upon weakly typed scripting languages (e.g., JavaScript). Historically, JavaScript is very popular for developing browser-based *Graphical User Interfaces* (GUI) [9], but the introduction of the Node.js run time made it also available for server-side applications [24]. Different approaches exist to bring compile time type checking to the JavaScript ecosystem. Languages like TypeScript[2] [15] extend JavaScript with static typing and libraries like Flow [9,15] perform static type checking. Even with those approaches or strongly typed languages like Java for server-side applications, the communication on the web stays untyped. The widely used form of web-based communication is based on the *Hypertext Transfer Protocol* (HTTP) as the application protocol and the *JavaScript Object Notation* (JSON) as the data interchange format. Malformed data, like JSON objects/arrays, may produce unpredictable behaviors [11,13] in the consuming application. In contrast to JSON, where at least (de)serialization is natively supported by most languages, queries in modern APIs (i.e., GraphQL) are completely formulated in plain text and are often composed by string concatenation at run time. Developers won't receive any feedback about the correctness of the queries until running them against a matching GraphQL server.

A prominent class of collective adaptive systems is characterized by interaction solely by exchanging data via a common data space in a client-server fashion. In fact, this system structure dominates the design of modern distributed web-based systems, where the vulnerability typically lies in the complex, deeply nested data structures that are collaboratively manipulated in a

---

[2] https://www.typescriptlang.org.

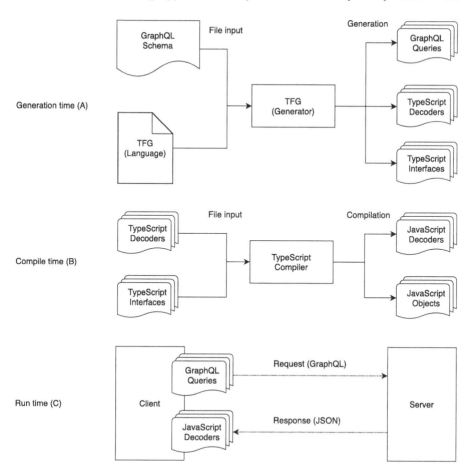

Fig. 2. Type consistency on three levels. c.f., (A) → Sect. 4, (B) → Subsect. 6.1, (C) → Subsect. 6.2

service-oriented [21] fashion by entities in an uncontrolled and unsecure environment: new entities may be added at any time, others evolve, and the communication via the internet is hard to control and open to various forms of attacks. In particular, HTTP-based communication, where structured data is simply encoded as text and then decoded at the receivers side gives a lot of room for data structures to get out of sync, be it because of a (run time) update of an API or malicious modifications.

In this paper we present an approach[3] that brings together GraphQL queries and GraphQL schemas to align the communication between the entities of the above described data-centric collective systems by guaranteeing type consistency at three levels: (c.f., Fig. 2).

---

[3] https://gitlab.com/scce/typesafe-functional-graphql.

– At *generation time* by a custom *Domain-Specific Language* (DSL) [14] for GraphQL queries. The included generator utilizes the typed GraphQL schema to validate query definitions and generate (plain text) GraphQL queries, TypeScript interfaces and decoders.

– At *compile time* by compiling the generated TypeScript interfaces and decoders to JavaScript. It utilizes the TypeScript compiler to perform static type checking and to make sure generated interfaces and decoders match.

– At *run time* by using the generated GraphQL queries and the compiled decoders. The prior validation against the GraphQL schema guarantees the type-correctness of the requests. JSON objects/arrays from server responses will be validated by the decoders to anonymous but valid (i.e., correctly typed) JavaScript objects/arrays.

We will illustrate our approach along the example scenario shown in Fig. 1 which incorporates the popular GitHub services. GitHub is a platform for collaborative software development, including features like version control, issue tracking and continuous practices. It is quite common for smaller software companies to collaboratively use GitHub for the entire software development lifecycle (e.g., for IoT-Devices), including continuous integration and deployment (CI/CD). Centerpiece of the example is the GraphQL API of GitHub, which abstracts from the internal, distributed structure of GitHub.[4] We choose this example of a collective adaptive system, because GitHub is very popular[5], a single point of failure for dependent systems, and can itself be used as a platform to develop other collective adaptive system.

In Sect. 2 we introduce the key technologies, the basic concept and an overview of the single components. Section 3, 4, 5 and 6 illustrate the components in detail. Related work is addressed in Sect. 7, before we conclude the paper in Sect. 8.

2 Overview

GraphQL is a query and mutation language that allows clients to exchange data with a web service [16,26]. It is an alternative to other forms of client-server communication, like the popular approach of *Representational State Transfer* (REST). Its key innovation compared to previous resource-centric approaches [26] to this problem is the ability of the client to shape the data that is requested; making GraphQL data-centric [26]. In most other systems, as it is in RESTful web services, the form of the data returned from one endpoint is fixed (i.e., usually one endpoint only returns one entity or a flat list of entities), leading to under- and over-fetching issues [26]. In consequence, clients will have to run multiple parallel or sequential queries to assemble associated data, each with a fixed constant overhead. GraphQL gives the client the freedom to choose which fields of an entity and which associated objects are to be

---

[4] https://github.blog/2009-10-20-how-we-made-github-fast.
[5] https://octoverse.github.com/.

```
query repositoryListing($organization: String!, $length: Int!) {
    organization(login: $organization) {
        repositories(
            first: $length,
            orderBy: {field: PUSHED_AT, direction: DESC}
        ) {
            nodes {
                name
                languages(
                    first: 100,
                    orderBy: {field: SIZE, direction: DESC}
                ) {
                    edges {
                        size
                        node {
                            name
                        }
                    }
                }
            }
        }
    }
}
```

Fig. 3. Example query against the GitHub GraphQL server

included in the response. This makes it possible to request complex data structures efficiently and minimize overall traffic, which is important especially in slow mobile networks. As the name implies, GraphQL uses a graph model to represent the server-side database and employs a query DSL to select entity fields and navigate between associated graph nodes. Figure 3 shows a query against the GitHub GraphQL API that selects the repositories of an organization. The data returned from the server (as shown in Fig. 4) is encoded in JSON and matches the requested form.

In addition, a GraphQL server includes a self-describing schema of the data store. It describes all interfaces that can be queried and the types of their properties. Figure 5 shows an excerpt from the schema of the GitHub GraphQL API. On its own, it's a good documentation of the web service and can be used by the server to validate incoming queries. Unfortunately these type definitions are unavailable during the development of web clients, where the queries are formulated. Developers have to manually analyze and understand these type definitions as a whole, before being able to transfer the knowledge to queries on the client side. Especially in collective adaptive systems where requirements of the participants and the specification of the communication frequently change, this is an error-prone process. If changes in the server specification are not correctly transferred to the clients, miscommunication and system errors are the

```
{
    "organization": {
        "repositories": {
            "nodes": [
                {
                    "name": "grammars-v4",
                    "languages": {
                        "edges": [
                            {"node": {"name": "ANTLR"}, "size": 3802132},
                            {"node": {"name": "Assembly"}, "size": 398661},
                            ...
                        ]
                    }
                },
                {
                    "name": "antlr4",
                    "languages": {
                        "edges": [
                            {"node": {"name": "Java"}, "size": 2948093},
                            {"node": {"name": "Python"}, "size": 1421237},
                            ...
                        ]
                    }
                },
                ...
            ]
        }
    }
}
```

Fig. 4. JSON response to the GraphQL query

consequence. The GraphQL schema alone does not provide any validation of client-server interactions.

To close this gap we present a language with accompanying typechecker and generators. As Fig. 6 shows, this makes it possible to bring the type information provided by the GraphQL schema into the type system of the client-side programming language. First, we introduce a new DSL called *Type-Safe Functional GraphQL* (TFG) that will be used to formulate queries against GraphQL servers. This language is built on top of GraphQL to achieve compositionality and type safety during development. The typechecker TFG/Typed validates queries written in TFG by consolidating a GraphQL schema file and produces an *intermediate representation* (IR) enriched with type information. From there, two generators build the artifacts of the compilation process. The GraphQL generator TFG/GraphQL reduces TFG queries back to GraphQL so that they can be sent to GraphQL servers. TFG/TypeScript generates TypeScript source code. It includes interfaces for request and response data to enable static type checking and decoders for server responses to assure run time type safety. This paper

```
type Query {                          type Repository {
    organization(                         name: String!
        login: String!                    languages(
    ): Organization                           first: Int,
    ...                                       orderBy: LanguageOrder,
}                                             ...
                                          ): LanguageConnection
type Organization {                   }
    repositories(
        first: Int,                   type LanguageConnection {
        orderBy: RepositoryOrder,         edges: [LanguageEdge]
        ...                               ...
    ): RepositoryConnection!          }
    ...
}                                     type LanguageEdge {
                                          size: Int!
type RepositoryConnection {               node: Language!
    nodes: [Repository]               }
    ...
}                                     type Language {
                                          name: String!
                                          ...
                                      }
```

Fig. 5. Relevant excerpts from the GitHub GraphQL schema

illustrates our approach with TypeScript as target language. The adaptation to other suitable, typed programming languages like Elm, Reason and PureScript is straightforward.

3   The TFG Language

The TFG language is, just like GraphQL, an external DSL to define queries and mutations against a GraphQL server. It borrows much of the syntax from GraphQL, but introduces a new concept for the construction of queries for nested data structures. In GraphQL, all subqueries for nested objects are included within a single nested query. The only way[6] to split up queries and reuse parts of it is given by a native feature called *fragments*. Figure 7 shows how the fragment `language` is spliced into the `repositoryListing` query to reassemble the previously introduced GraphQL query. In contrast, TFG queries describe selections of flat data objects that can be functionally composed by application using TFG's arrow operator <-. When a property is not of a basic type but references

---

[6] Other approaches to reuse based on auxiliary technologies like templating at run time, won't be discussed in this paper. Due to their missing type safety and error-proneness, we don't consider them resilient solutions.

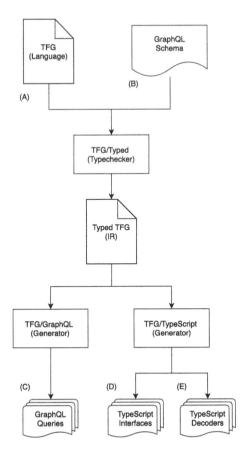

Fig. 6. Workflow of TFG components; from source files to generated artifacts. c.f., (A) → Fig. 8, (B) → Fig. 5, (C) → Fig. 3, (D) → Fig. 11, (E) → Fig. 12

another collection in the graph model, a subquery is applied to determine further selections on that collection. Figure 8 shows a translation of the previous GraphQL query (c.f., Fig. 3) to TFG, using the arrow operator to compose four queries.

With query composition, every subtree of a complex data object has a proper readable name. This is valuable later in the TFG/TypeScript generator when typed interfaces of the server responses are generated. If query definitions are nested like it is the case in GraphQL, there would only be one big nested TypeScript interface that describes the whole response. The interface would be so specialized to the related response that it makes reuse impossible. But when flat queries are composed, it also becomes possible to generate flat interfaces that reference each other to build up nested types. And when responses are taken apart in the frontend application, there is a well-named typed interface readily available to describe every possible subtree. This form of composition works

```
query repositoryListing {            fragment languages on Repository {
    organization {                       languages {
        repositories {                       edges {
            nodes {                              size
                name                             node {
                    ...languages                     name
                }                                }
            }                                }
        }                                }
    }                                }
}
```

Fig. 7. Fragments in GraphQL

well in the TFG language and in the type system of client applications. And with it come the usual benefits of composition like reuse, maintainability, and the elimination of redundancy; when writing queries, but also in the generated client source code.

The example query against the GitHub API (c.f., Fig. 3) demonstrates that responses can become quite nested as a result of the graph model design. The response object in this case is seven layers deep. A good part of the nesting is unnecessary for this particular query. A data model that represents a language could be modelled by a flat object with just two properties, name and size, but in the query response it is an object that is nested three layers deep. Because TFG only allows flat queries, this would require seven separate queries that are to be composed. And the data object would still be needlessly complex. To remedy this situation, TFG introduces *deep queries*. When selecting properties, a query is allowed to reach down into the graph model and pull up properties using the dot operator. Using the dot operator, the repositoryForListing query can eliminate the extra layer of the edge property and in the languageWithSize query can eliminate the extra layer of the node property. This results in a perfect representation of languages as a flat data object that just holds the name and the size. In addition, an alias can be specified before a colon to rename the property in the response data object. Despite the fact that the response returned by the GraphQL server is seven layers deep, only four separate TFG queries are needed and the response data object for the frontend application is greatly simplified.

GraphQL queries can declare input variables and whenever a query is sent to the server, an object of input values is sent along to parameterize the query. Within the GraphQL query these variables can be applied to the properties that are selected, e.g. to provide the ID of the entity that should be fetched. TFG additionally allows variables to be applied to subqueries with the arrow operator to pass along values during composition. This can be seen in the repositoryListing query, which applies the $length variable to the organizationForListing query.

```
query repositoryListing($organization: String!, $length: Int!) {
    organization(login: $organization) <-
        organizationForListing(length: $length)
}

query organizationForListing($length: Int!) {
    repositories(
        first: $length, orderBy: {field: PUSHED_AT, direction: DESC}
    ).nodes <- repositoryForListing
}

query repositoryForListing {
    name
    languages(first: 100, orderBy: {field: SIZE, direction: DESC}).edges <-
        languageWithSize
}

query languageWithSize  {
    size
    node.{
        name
    }
}
```

Fig. 8. TFG query for a repository listing (c.f., generated interfaces in Fig. 11, generated decoders in Fig. 12)

We used ANTLR[7] for the implementation of the TFG language. The corresponding grammar definition[8] alone is enough for ANTLR to provide a parser that can turn TFG text files into complete parse trees [23].

4   Type-Checking TFG

After a TFG file was parsed TFG/Typed type-checks the *abstract syntax tree* (AST) against a GraphQL schema. This validates the TFG query, making sure that the formulated queries are correctly typed and match the schema of the GraphQL server, already at generation time (c.f., Fig. 2). If the type-checking fails, TFG/Typed provides a list of all reachable type errors. Possible type errors include references to undefined properties, argument applications of the wrong type or the application of subqueries that target the wrong interface.

Besides validation, the type-checker also produces an intermediate representation that enriches the AST with type information from the GraphQL schema. It records the type of every property selected by a query as defined by the

---

[7] https://www.antlr.org/.

[8] https://gitlab.com/scce/typesafe-functional-graphql/-/blob/d63df0ed1146eabd664
32c4115a86534c6b03772/src/main/antlr/GraphQLSelection.g4.

$$\frac{\forall i \in [n].\, \text{target} : \sigma, \{v_j : \rho_j\}_{j \in [m]} \,\vdash\, s_i : \text{selection } x_i\, \tau_i \text{ on } \sigma}{\vdash \text{query q } (\$v_j : \rho_j)_{j \in [m]} \text{ on } \sigma \left\{ s_i \right\}_{i \in [n]} : \text{query } (\rho_j)_{j \in [m]} \to \{ x_i : \tau_i \}_{i \in [n]} \text{ on } \sigma} \quad \text{(QI)}$$

$$\frac{\Gamma, \text{target} : \sigma \vdash a : \text{anchor } x\, T \text{ on } \sigma \qquad \vdash q : \text{query } (\rho_i)_{i \in [n]} \to \tau \text{ on } T \qquad \forall i \in [n].\, \Gamma, \text{target} : \sigma \vdash e_i : \rho_i}{\Gamma, \text{target} : \sigma \vdash a \leftarrow q(e_i)_{i \in [n]} : \text{selection } x\, \tau \text{ on } \sigma} \quad \text{(QE)}$$

$$\frac{\Gamma, \text{target} : \sigma \vdash a : \text{anchor } x\, \tau \text{ on } \sigma \qquad \text{basic type}(\tau)}{\Gamma, \text{target} : \sigma \vdash a : \text{selection } x\, \tau \text{ on } \sigma} \quad \text{(BE)}$$

$$\frac{\vdash \text{Schema}[\sigma] : \{ p : (\rho_i)_{i \in [n]} \to \tau, \dots \}}{\vdash p : \text{property } (\rho_i)_{i \in [n]} \to \tau \text{ on } \sigma} \quad \text{(PI)}$$

$$\frac{\vdash p : \text{property } (\rho_i)_{i \in [n]} \to \tau \text{ on } \sigma \qquad \forall i \in [n].\, \Gamma \vdash e_i : \rho_i}{\Gamma \vdash p(e_i)_{i \in [n]} : \text{anchor } p\, \tau \text{ on } \sigma} \quad \text{(PE)}$$

Fig. 9. Excerpt from the type inference rules of TFG (The full set of inference rules is available at https://gitlab.com/scce/typesafe-functional-graphql/-/raw/d63df0ed1146eabd66432c4115a86534c6b03772/documentation/type-system.pdf)

GraphQL schema. It also includes if a property returns a list of values and whether values returned from a property can be null. The subsequent TypeScript generator relies on this information to generate typed interfaces and decoders, providing type safety and validation at run time.

The type system of TFG follows the type system that is used for GraphQL schema files, but extends it with typing rules for query applications and deep selections. Every query is an abstraction that defines variables which are then, together with literal values, applied to properties and subqueries. The GraphQL specification only describes the syntax of the language formally and leaves the type system to informal specification. In contrast, the type system of TFG is formally specified (c.f., Fig. 9).

- *Query Introduction* (QI) takes a query definition and brings the target collection σ and all query arguments into the context. It requires all listed selections to type-check under these conditions.
- *Query Elimination* (QE) applies a subquery to an anchor in the body of a query to determine the selection of complex associated objects. The targets of the anchor and the subquery have to match and all arguments passed to the subquery must be of the correct type.
- *Basic Type Elimination* (BE) is used in the case that an anchor points to a field of a basic type. In that case no further query specifications are needed.
- *Property Introduction* (PI) provides property definitions by consulting the GraphQL schema for the required signature.
- *Property Elimination* (PE) applies the required values to a property to provide an anchor that points to a field in the current interface. The argument types must match the signature acquired from the GraphQL schema.

TFG   → GraphQL
                                            ↦
```
query rootQuery on Query {                query rootQuery {
   property <- subquery(aⱼ)ⱼ∈[m]              property {
}                                                subproperty(
                                                    eᵢ[vⱼ := aⱼ]ⱼ∈[m]
query subquery(vⱼ)ⱼ∈[m] on T {                  )ᵢ∈[n]
     subproperty(eᵢ)ᵢ∈[n]                     }
}                                         }
```

Fig. 10. Composition synthesis by insertion and syntactic substitution

5   GraphQL Generator

The first generator, TFG/GraphQL, reduces TFG queries back to plain GraphQL. This step is always required, no matter which client programming language is targeted. GraphQL queries can be treated as simple strings and are meant to be sent in the body of a HTTP request to a GraphQL server. Because the TFG language is quite similar to GraphQL, this transformation is relatively easy.

The hardest part is the elimination of composition by subquery application, a feature that is not supported in GraphQL. But GraphQL supports nested queries, so query application will be realized by nesting all the referenced subqueries into one big GraphQL query. Figure 10 shows the process. On the left are two TFG queries, rootQuery and subquery and the second query is applied to a property of the first one, a structure that cannot directly be expressed GraphQL (c.f. Sect. 3). Rather, the selections of the second query need to be inserted at the point where they were referenced, melting the two queries together into one nested GraphQL query. In Fig. 10, subquery defined the variables $(v_j)_{j\in[m]}$ that have been instatiated with the values $(a_j)_{j\in[m]}$ s in the rootQuery. These variables can't exist anymore in GraphQL, so every variable v_j of subquery has to be syntactically substituted by the assigned value a_j wherever it was used in an expression e_i. If the whole query is several layers deep, this step has to be repeated recursively. This is how TFG query definitions are reduced back to GraphQL, ready to be sent to a GraphQL server.

6   TypeScript Generator

The second generator, TFG/TypeScript, creates a client application library from the typed intermediate representation. The generated TypeScript code provides static type definitions for request and response data of TFG queries and decoders that validate responses received from the server. This generator implementation takes the example of TypeScript, but it can be simply replaced by any other code generator targeting a different statically typed language.

6.1   Static Type-Checking in the Generated Client

```
interface RepositoryListing {
    organization: OrganizationForListing | null
}

interface OrganizationForListing {
    repositories: [RepositoryForListing | null] | null
}

interface RepositoryForListing {
    name: string
    languages: [LanguageWithSize | null] | null
}

interface LanguageWithSize {
    size: number
    name: string | null
}
```

Fig. 11. Generated TypeScript interfaces (c.f., TFG source code in Fig. 8)

When a GraphQL query is performed the client includes an object of input arguments and the server responds with a data object that matches the query. TFG/TypeScript generates TypeScript interfaces for both, the input argument objects and the response data objects. All the type information comes from the typed intermediate representation of the AST that has been produced by the type-checker (c.f., Fig. 6). This way all interactions with the GraphQL server are statically checked for type correctness.

Instead of generating deeply nested interfaces for the response data objects, TFG/TypeScript takes advantage of the compositionality of TFG. It generates one flat interface for every TFG query definition, as described in Sect. 3. And when queries are composed by query application, the interfaces are composed by referencing the respective other query to reflect the whole query response. Figure 11 illustrates this: The interface RepositoryListing describes the whole server response for the query and it references other interfaces with each layer of the data structure. This helps when individual parts of a large response are passed around in the client application. Having a properly named interface for each layer (following the principle of readable code [2]) makes it easy to specify types for these interactions and aids possible debugging of the code as a side effect.

```
function repositoryForListingDecoder(): Decoder<RepositoryForListing> {
    return object({
        languages: field(
            "languages",
            field(
                "edges",
                nullable(array(nullable(languageWithSizeDecoder()))),
            ),
        ),
    })
}

function languageWithSizeDecoder(): Decoder<LanguageWithSize> {
    return object({
        size: number(),
        name: field("node", field("name", nullable(string()))),
    })
}
```

Fig. 12. Two type-safe decoders for server responses (c.f., TFG source code in Fig. 8)

6.2   Assuring Type Safety at Run Time

The previous section assumed correct response data from the server to assure type safety. But there are several reasons why the server might answer with malformed data. E.g., the client and server might have become out of sync or the server uses a different GraphQL schema from the one that the client assumes. The server might also just behave faulty because of a software error or an attacker, tries to foist altered data to the client by a *man in the middle* attack [7]. Without any further guards, these broken responses would possibly make it deep into the application and cause errors at unexpected places. Thus server responses should be validated as early as possible at the edge of the API (i.e., fail-fast [4]) so that the static types always match the actual data.

This is why the TFG generator additionally creates a decoder for each TypeScript interface. The decoder accepts the deserialized, but untyped JSON object received from the server and returns a result object. The result object is a sum that either contains a correctly typed object or an error message describing what is wrong with the server response. When these decoders are used, errors are handled early and properly.

Figure 12 shows the generated decoders matching the previous interfaces. The decoders compose just like the interfaces, referencing each other by name for nested objects. The decoders are interpreted by the json-bouncer TypeScript library[9]. That is where the primitives like object, array and string come from. json-bouncer brings another guarantee to improve program correctness:

---

[9] https://gitlab.com/MazeChaZer/json-bouncer.

By leveraging the type system of TypeScript during compile time (c.f., Fig. 2), it makes sure that only valid decoders can be constructed and that every decoder really provides a result that matches the annotated `Decoder`-type. This is an additional layer of safety to assure that the generation of interfaces and decoders is in sync.

7   Related Work

Most CAS languages like SCEL [12], DEECo [5] and TCOEL [6] focus either on the general architecture of collective adaptive systems or on the collective behaviour of ensembles based on the autonomous behaviour of their entities. In contrast, TFG assumes a fixed client server architecture and focusses on the consistent and efficient exchange of complex data between the clients and the server. Type checking ensures that the data models of all involved entities remain in sync and deep querying the efficiency of the data transfer even in response of complex nested queries.

Although GraphQL is a relatively new technology (released as open source in 2015) there are several mature projects that are related to the approach presented in this paper. The *Apollo CLI*[10] is a toolset for development and production workflows and part of the popular *Apollo Data Graph Platform*. Besides Apollo-specific tasks, it provides the ability to generate client-side static types derived from a GraphQL schema. The *GraphQL Code Generator*[11] is a plugin-driven generator for front- and backend code. It is built on top of pre-defined and user-defined templates for different target languages. The *TypeGraphQL*[12] project leverages decorators (e.g., in combination of DTO classes) as an internal DSL to generate native GraphQL files, focused on TypeScript. It uses TypeScript as the carrier language [14] of the DSL and the target language.

To our knowledge, TFG is unique in not only providing compile time type safety (c.f., Fig. 2) by generating static types (c.f., Subsect. 6.1), but also run time type safety by generating decoders (c.f., Subsect. 6.2). In addition, our approach has the following unique structural advantages that aim at simplicity [19,20,22]:

1. Instead of just reutilizing GraphQL schema and operations files, TFG conceptual introduces a higher level external DSL (c.f. Sect. 3). This enables us to enhance GraphQL by introducing new concepts (e.g., *query composition*) and syntactic sugar (e.g., *deep selections*), resulting in a more convenient programming experience.
2. An intermediate representation enables the substitution of whole generators (instead of just templates) for different target languages (c.f. Sect. 6) which simplifies the adoption of adopt new target languages.
3. Convention over configuration further reduces the effort for the setup. Native Type- or JavaScript packages that are delivered by the *Node Package Manager* (NPM), often depend on multiple libraries due to *dependency chains* [18].

---

[10] https://github.com/apollographql/apollo-tooling.
[11] https://github.com/dotansimha/graphql-code-generator.
[12] https://github.com/MichalLytek/type-graphql.

They require the dedicated installation of those dependencies before execution. In contrast, TFG is distributed with all dependencies in a single binary, which makes it easy to install (and uninstall) in your system's PATH.

4. Despite the fact that generated code can be seen as a disposable artefact, TFG focuses on generating readable code (c.f. Fig. 11). It follows aspects like "simplify naming [...] and formatting" as well as "reduce complexity and confusion" [2].

8   Conclusion

We have presented an approach to synthesize type-safe communication interfaces for loosely coupled collective adaptive systems, which are solely synchronised by exchanging complex untyped data structures. This form of communication between collaborative entities is common for distributed systems on the web. One popular technology for realizing corresponding APIs is GraphQL. Centerpiece of our approach is TFG, a type-safe, functional DSL for the definition of GraphQL queries. The simplicity of the DSL eases the tailored access to deeply nested content, and supports reuse in a compositional fashion. TFG overcomes certain shortcomings of GraphQL, enabling us to leverage GraphQL schema definitions to support the type-safe development of client side applications and contributing to the robustness of entire distributed systems. It helps, e.g., to catch version issues or corrupted data transfer that may be due to erroneous components or even third party attacks.

Building on the GraphQL schema definition, TFG offers three layers of type safety. First, programs written in the TFG language are statically type-checked before they get instantiated by the generators. Second, the generated client library is using a type-safe language and exposes a type-safe public interface to other parts of the application. Third, the generated client library decodes all data the application receives from the server, ensuring type safety at run time.

These properties are particularly valuable for the development of collective adaptive systems, as they help to maintain the consistency of the common data space along the system's life cycles: TFG allows one to automate the propagation of specification changes across participants and type-checks the participant's implementation against the specification of the data exchange.

In combination with modern collaborative software development and system operating (like the popular DevOps practices [1]), TFG can have an even greater impact on robustness, reliability and security. One of the central aspects of DevOps is known as *shift left*, where issues (e.g., incompatibilities and vulnerabilities) are identified earlier [3] in the development life-cycle. The generator-based technology of TFG supports this aspect by introducing another level of validation preceding traditional build and test processes. In the future, we want to make TFG compatible with *Continuous Practices* [25] to execute code generation as a stage in automated continuous deployment pipelines. The meta-level technology of the TFG language allow us to generate entire custom-tailored test-suites which validate the correctness of opposing GraphQL servers. They cannot only be manually used during development, but also automatically in the entire development life-cycle by integrating them in continuous integration pipelines. Those artifacts would speed up the entire development life-cycle of collective adaptive systems and decrease the failure rate.

References

1. Bass, L., Weber, I.M., Zhu, L.: DevOps: A Software Architect's Perspective. The SEI Series in Software Engineering. Addison-Wesley, Boston (2015)
2. Boswell, D., Foucher, T.: The Art of Readable Code. O'Reilly Series. O'Reilly Media Incorporated, Sebastopol (2011)
3. Brown, A., Forsgren, N., Humble, J., Kersten, N., Kim, G.: 2016 state of DevOps report. Technical report (2016). https://services.google.com/fh/files/misc/state-of-devops-2016.pdf
4. Bugayenko, Y.: Elegant Objects. No. v. 2 in Elegant Objects, CreateSpace Independent Publishing Platform, Scotts Valley (2017)
5. Bures, T., Gerostathopoulos, I., Hnetynka, P., Keznikl, J., Kit, M., Plasil, F.: DEECO: an ensemble-based component system. In: Proceedings of the 16th International ACM Sigsoft Symposium on Component-Based Software Engineering, CBSE 2013, pp. 81–90. Association for Computing Machinery, New York (2013)
6. Bures, T., et al.: A language and framework for dynamic component ensembles in smart systems. Int. J. Softw. Tools Technol. Transf. **22**(4), 497–509 (2020). https://doi.org/10.1007/s10009-020-00558-z
7. Callegati, F., Cerroni, W., Ramilli, M.: Man-in-the-middle attack to the HTTPS protocol. IEEE Secur. Priv. **7**(1), 78–81 (2009)
8. Campinhos, J., Seco, J.C., Cunha, J.: Type-safe evolution of web services. In: 2017 IEEE/ACM 2nd International Workshop on Variability and Complexity in Software Design (VACE), pp. 20–26 (2017)
9. Chaudhuri, A., Vekris, P., Goldman, S., Roch, M., Levi, G.: Fast and precise type checking for JavaScript. Proc. ACM Program. Lang. **1**(OOPSLA) (2017)
10. Cohn, M.: Succeeding with Agile: Software Development Using Scrum, 1st edn. Addison-Wesley Professional, Boston (2009)
11. Costantini, G., Ferrara, P., Cortesi, A.: A suite of abstract domains for static analysis of string values. Softw. Pract. Exper. **45**(2), 245–287 (2015)
12. De Nicola, R., et al.: The SCEL language: design, implementation, verification. In: Wirsing, M., Hölzl, M., Koch, N., Mayer, P. (eds.) Software Engineering for Collective Autonomic Systems. LNCS, vol. 8998, pp. 3–71. Springer, Cham (2015). https://doi.org/10.1007/978-3-319-16310-9_1
13. Dhar, A., Purandare, R., Dhawan, M., Rangaswamy, S.: CLOTHO: saving programs from malformed strings and incorrect string-handling. In: Proceedings of the 2015 10th Joint Meeting on Foundations of Software Engineering, ESEC/FSE 2015, pp. 555–566. Association for Computing Machinery (2015)
14. Fowler, M.: Domain-Specific Languages. Addison-Wesley Signature Series (Fowler). Pearson Education, Boston (2010)
15. Gao, Z., Bird, C., Barr, E.T.: To type or not to type: quantifying detectable bugs in JavaScript. In: 2017 IEEE/ACM 39th International Conference on Software Engineering (ICSE), pp. 758–769 (2017)
16. Hartig, O., Perez, J.: Semantics and complexity of GraphQL. In: Proceedings of the 2018 World Wide Web Conference, WWW 2018, International World Wide Web Conferences Steering Committee, pp. 1155–1164 (2018)

17. Kizza, J.M.: Internet of Things (IoT): growth, challenges, and security. Guide to Computer Network Security. TCS, pp. 517–531. Springer, Cham (2020). https://doi.org/10.1007/978-3-030-38141-7_24

18. Kula, R.G., Ouni, A., German, D.M., Inoue, K.: On the impact of micro-packages: an empirical study of the NPM JavaScript ecosystem. CoRR abs/1709.04638 (2017)

19. Margaria, T., Hinchey, M.: Simplicity in it: the power of less. Computer **46**(11), 23–25 (2013)

20. Margaria, T., Steffen, B.: Simplicity as a driver for agile innovation. Computer **43**(6), 90–92 (2010)

21. Margaria, T., Steffen, B., Reitenspieß, M.: Service-oriented design: the roots. In: Benatallah, B., Casati, F., Traverso, P. (eds.) ICSOC 2005. LNCS, vol. 3826, pp. 450–464. Springer, Heidelberg (2005). https://doi.org/10.1007/11596141_34

22. Merten, M., Steffen, B.: Simplicity driven application development. J. Integr. Des. Process Sci. **17**, 9–23 (2013)

23. Parr, T.: The definitive ANTLR 4 reference. In: Pragmatic Bookshelf (2013)

24. Schiavio, F., Sun, H., Bonetta, D., Rosa, A., Binder, W.: NodeMOP: runtime verification for Node.js applications. In: Proceedings of the 34th ACM/SIGAPP Symposium on Applied Computing, SAC 2019, pp. 1794–1801. Association for Computing Machinery (2019)

25. Stahl, D., Martensson, T., Bosch, J.: Continuous practices and DevOps: beyond the buzz, what does it all mean? In: 2017 43rd Euromicro Conference on Software Engineering and Advanced Applications (SEAA), pp. 440–448 (2017)

26. Taskula, T.: Advanced data fetching with GraphQL: case bakery service. Master's thesis, Aalto University, 11 March 2019

Epistemic Logic in Ensemble Specification

Jan Sürmeli$^{(\boxtimes)}$ (iD)

FZI Forschungszentrum Informatik, Karlsruhe, Germany
suermeli@fzi.de

Abstract. Different logics are used to specify the structure, life cycle and interaction of dynamically forming ensembles. Specified aspects include the construction and finalization of an ensemble, joining and leaving of collaborators, acceptable and forbidden behaviors of the ensemble, local and global goals and boundaries, and the permission to access resources. As ensembles are dynamically formed from heterogeneous agents, it is reasonable to assume an evolving information asymmetry between its collaborators. Epistemic logic explicitly considers the concepts of knowledge, as held and developed by the different agents in a scope. In this paper, we explore the idea of applying epistemic logic in the specification of different aspects of an ensemble.

Keywords: Epistemic logic · Formal methods · Distributed systems

1 Introduction

An *ensemble* [14] is a distributed system – a dynamically formed collaboration of heterogeneous agents that interact with one another to reach a goal. They operate in challenging environments, interacting with humans or other software systems, adapting to new challenges as they arise, without interruption of system functionality (cf. [13], §1.1). In order to ensure its functionality at runtime, the principles of software engineering encourage to specify and model a system before its deployment, and ensembles are no exception to this rule. While an ensemble can be specified in different ways, a few commonalities persist between the approaches. Central aspects comprise the ensemble's membership relations, that is, characterizations of the possible collaborators of an ensemble, and its behavior, that is, the internal actions, its interaction between the collaborators and its reaction to the environment. Those aspects can be specified locally based on properties of each collaborating agent, or globally by requiring a certain interplay of the collaborators. Existing approaches focus on the interfaces and capabilities of the agents, and their exposed behavior, such as the SCEL-Language [5], or logical representations [9].

In this paper, we focus on the *knowledge of agents* and the inherent information asymmetry between them. While an agent can presumably observe its full internal state, it can only make *assumptions* about other agents' internal state or the environment, based on interactions and observations. Hence, there is a

© Springer Nature Switzerland AG 2020
T. Margaria and B. Steffen (Eds.): ISoLA 2020, LNCS 12477, pp. 329–343, 2020.
https://doi.org/10.1007/978-3-030-61470-6_20

wanted or unwanted information asymmetry between agents. In *epistemic (and doxastic) logic*, this is expressed by concepts of knowledge (and belief) held by an agent or groups of agents. A few examples:

- An agent knows that a certain internal variable has a specific value.
- An agent knows that under the assumption of adherence to a certain protocol, all ensemble members will eventually gain knowledge of this value.
- An agent believes that another agent knows about the belief of a third agent.
- A group of agents believes that at least one of their members has knowledge over some proposition.
- A certain proposition is (or becomes) common knowledge inside a group of agents, that is, every agent knows it, knows that all of the agents in the group know it, knows that they all know that, etc.

As the agents and their environment evolve, new observations are made, and knowledge may become outdated or updated, and beliefs may be revised.

We note that while the concepts of knowledge and belief – particularly the latter – are originally associated with human agents, the aforementioned information asymmetry also applies to technical components. For instance, it is not feasible for a technical system to have access to the internal states of all other systems in its environment, and the issues of observing the actions or transitions of other systems is a well-known problem in the area of distributed systems. Similarly, while executing an image recognition algorithm on camera recordings may yield a single result, it is usually associated with non-total confidence. As such, the concepts of knowledge and belief can be extended to technical components.

Our approach is to apply the core concepts of epistemic knowledge to ensemble specifications. Our goal is not to invent a new specification paradigm or language, but to find aspects of epistemic logic that could enrich existing methods. In the following, we briefly present a few promising cases for the application of epistemic logic:

Requiring initial knowledge. It could be that an ensemble only accepts such agents that have a certain initial knowledge. Depending on the actual gatekeeping mechanism, this could mean that the agent needs to convince some group of agents of their knowledge, that is, makes the group revise their belief regarding the knowledge of the candidate.

Dissemination. An ensemble could wish that certain propositions become common knowledge or belief between its collaborators. This is particularly interesting if new agents can join the ensemble after its initial foundation.

Preservation. Common knowledge is not always necessary or desirable. Assume that a collaborator α_1 of an ensemble has certain knowledge, important for the ensemble. When α_1 leaves the ensemble, it could be that the knowledge leaves with them – depending on whether α_1 shared the knowledge with other collaborators. If so, it might be crucial for the other collaborators to notice this. Example: Assume that α_1 has acted as a gatekeeper to a safe data storage, knowing how to access it. Whenever other collaborators require access to the data storage, they post a request to α_1, and α_1 fulfills the request but never shares the knowledge on how to access the data storage. If α_1 leaves, the remainder of the ensemble loses access to the data storage.

Knowledge and belief as a trigger. Once a collaborator α_1 gains knowledge about a certain fact, or revises their belief towards it, α_1 might be triggered to act upon it: perform an internal action, or interact with another collaborator or the environment. Knowledge or belief revision can also lead to structural changes in the ensembles: α_1 could leave the ensemble as a consequence. Similarly, knowledge or belief can lead to some collaborators forcing others out of the ensemble, e.g. if the majority of an ensemble believes that a certain set of collaborators shows harmful behavior.

As classic propositional logic, epistemic formulas are built from atomic propositions (which can be valuated *true* or *false*), and Boolean operators. To capture the aspects of agents and their knowledge, epistemic logic comprises further operators. The goal of this paper is to present ideas how epistemic logic can be applied ensemble specification. Instead of creating a new specification method, first concepts are developed aiming to be applicable in a minimally invasive manner. To this end, after a short primer on our main concepts and epistemic logic (Sect. 2), we present a collection of atomic propositions and related epistemic axioms tailored for use in ensemble specifications in Sect. 3. Then, we discuss the topic of ensembles with changing sets of collaborators in Sect. 4 before concluding in Sect. 5.

2 Preliminaries

2.1 Ensembles, Worlds, Information Asymmetry

In this section, we informally introduce the basic assumptions for this paper.

Agents. Agents are entities that interact with one another. They have their own views of the world, goals and requirements. They can collaborate in an ensemble. Examples for agents are persons, sensors, vehicles, software systems. In this paper, agents are treated as atomic entities.

Ensembles. An ensemble encompasses a dynamic set of collaborating agents. Here, dynamic means two things: First, the set of agents is not fixed before the ensemble is created, and second, agents may join or leave over the lifecycle of an ensemble.

Worlds. A *world* is a global state that effectively valuates every proposition with either true or false. A world itself is free of contradictions. In general, every agent has only a limited understanding of a given world. That is, given one agent α and a world w, there generally exists another world w', so that α cannot distinguish between w and w'.

Knowledge. Given a proposition ϕ, its truth value is established by a given world. An agent *knows* the truth value of ϕ in a given world w, if and only if, the truth value of ϕ in w is the same in all worlds w' that α cannot distinguish from w.

Information Asymmetry. This assumption means that, given two different agents α, α' and a world w, there exists at least one proposition ϕ such that α knows the truth value of ϕ in w, but α' does not.

Confluent Knowledge. We note that, for the scope of this paper, agents cannot "err". If α knows ϕ to be true in a world w, then ϕ *is* true in w. Every other agent then either also knows that ϕ is true in w, or simply has no knowledge of the truth value of ϕ in w. That is, if two agents know the truth value of ϕ in a world, then they have the same truth value in mind.

2.2 A Short Primer to Epistemic Logics

We recall the notions of epistemic logic most relevant to this paper. For a more sophisticated introduction and definition of syntax and semantics, we kindly point the reader to literature, e.g. [4,6]. We provide more detailed formal definitions in Sect. 6.

The basis for epistemic logic is propositional logic over a universe $\mathcal{P}$ of atomic propositions, and a finite universe $\mathcal{A}$ of agents. In addition to negation ($\neg\phi$), conjunction ($\phi \wedge \psi$) and disjunction ($\phi \vee \psi$), the language $\mathbb{L}$ of epistemic logic adds a *knowledge operator* K_α for each agent α, as well as a *group knowledge operator* K_A and a *common knowledge operator* CK_A for each set A of agents:

$$\mathbb{L} ::= p \mid \mathbb{L} \vee \mathbb{L} \mid \neg\mathbb{L} \mid \mathsf{K}_\alpha \mathbb{L} \mid \mathsf{K}_A \mathbb{L} \mid \mathsf{CK}_A \mathbb{L} \qquad (p \in \mathcal{P}, \alpha \in \mathcal{A}, A \subseteq \mathcal{A})$$

The semantics of $\mathbb{L}$ is defined based on *Kripke Structures* (e.g. [10], cf. 6.1): Each state is a world w, providing a valuation of all atomic propositions. The transitions are labeled with agents; an α-labeled transition from w to w' means that α cannot distinguish between w and w'. Every formula $\phi \in \mathbb{L}$ is then evaluated in a pair $(\mathbf{W}, w)$ of a Kripke structure $\mathbf{W}$ and a world w of $\mathbf{W}$. The propositional operators follow the classic semantics. A formula $\mathsf{K}_\alpha \phi$ holds in a world w iff ϕ holds in all worlds indistinguishable from w for agent α. For a more detailed description, we point the reader to Sect. 6.2. We note that the knowledge operator can be arbitrarily nested, e.g. $\mathsf{K}_\alpha \mathsf{K}_{\alpha'} \phi$ means that α knows that α' knows ϕ. The concept that α knows the truth value of ϕ can be written as $\mathsf{K}_\alpha \phi \vee \mathsf{K}_\alpha \neg\phi$, abbreviated by $\mathsf{K?}_\alpha \phi$ to increase readability.

Group Knowledge and Common Knowledge. Let $A \subseteq \mathcal{A}$ be a set of agents. The group knowledge operator $\mathsf{K}_A \phi$ abbreviates $\bigwedge_{\alpha \in A} \mathsf{K}_\alpha \phi$. Group knowledge of a fact ϕ does not imply that every agent in the group is aware that ϕ is known in the group. This motivates the introduction of the *common knowledge operator* $\mathsf{CK}_A \phi$: Intuitively, a fact ϕ is common knowledge to A iff each agent $\alpha \in A$ knows ϕ, and each of the agent knows that each agent knows, and so on. Hence, $\mathsf{CK}_A \phi$ abbreviates $\mathsf{K}_A \phi \wedge \mathsf{K}_A \mathsf{K}_A \phi \wedge \dots$. Due to the finite length of formulas, the common knowledge operator cannot be characterized by the other operators.

Relationship with Belief Logics. While an agent not necessarily knows about every fact, they cannot "falsely know" something: We always have $\mathsf{K}_\alpha \phi \Rightarrow \phi$.

This is where *belief logic* comes into play, which introduce an unary operator B_α, where $B_\alpha \phi$ means that $\alpha \in \mathcal{A}$ believes ϕ to be a fact, and ϕ could be false. Combining the two kinds of logics, while tempting, bears problems of its own, depending on the underlying axiomizations, and we leave the treatment of belief logic for future work.

Knowledge Update. Assuming an evolving system described by epistemic logic, it is feasible that the knowledge of an agent, or the truth value of an atomic proposition change, through the occurrence of events. Different mechanisms exist to capture this, such as public or secret announcements.

3   Ensemble-Specific Atomic Propositions and Axioms

Using epistemic logic in ensemble specifications means to instantiate the general framework of epistemic logic for the scenario to be specified. Looking at the definition of $\mathbb{L}$, this ensues the definition of a set of atomic propositions as building blocks of formulae. However, atomic propositions alone do not carry any semantics. For instance, one could require that two formulas ϕ and ψ should not be true at the same time. Generally, there are two possible approaches:

1. One assumes that all worlds (as described by the Kripke structure) need to adhere to the proposition. Then, every agent implicitly knows about the proposition – missing knowledge always requires two indistinguishable worlds with contradicting valuations.
2. One assumes that the Kripke structure also contains worlds that do not adhere to the proposition, but add the proposition as an axiom to the specification. Then, some agents might lack the knowledge about the proposition.

In this paper, we specify such propositions by axioms to describe the semantics of newly introduced atomic propositions, and the relationships between one another. Thereby, our goal is to propose a set of atomic propositions and axioms that are so general that they are applicable in many ensemble specifications. Before presenting such atomic propositions and axioms, we briefly discuss our approach.

The examples presented here follow the pattern to encode n-ary relations over fixed finite domains as atomic propositions. Thereby, *fixed* means that even if the relation may change over the lifecycle of an ensemble, the domains stay constant. Let R be a symbol and $S_1, \ldots, S_n$ be finite sets of symbols. Then, we can introduce atomic propositions $R(s_1, \ldots, s_n)$ for all $(s_1, \ldots, s_n) \in S_1 \times \cdots \times S_n$. Every world w then interprets the symbol R as the relation $R_w \subseteq S_1 \times \cdots \times S_n$, where $(s_1, \ldots, s_n) \in R_w$ iff w valuates $R(s_1, \ldots, s_n)$ to true. We note that this does not add to the expressivity of $\mathbb{L}$: From the viewpoint of $\mathbb{L}$, an atomic proposition $R(s_1, \ldots, s_n)$ is no different from any other atomic proposition, that is, the structure of the proposition is disregarded. Similarly, this way of encoding relations does not encompass any further semantics of the relation. For instance, if there are two relations that should be mutually exclusive, then the above encoding does not prevent a world from violating this condition by valuating the atomic propositions accordingly. This can be approached by adding further *axioms* to the specification. For instance, if two unary relations R and R' over the same set S should be mutually exclusive in every world, one could add an axiom of the form:

X1 $\bigwedge_{s \in S} \neg(R(s) \wedge R'(s))$.

We stress that as we assume relations over finite domains, we can encode universal and existential quantification over the domains by using $\bigwedge_{s \in S}$ or $\bigvee_{s \in S}$, respectively.

We note that an axiom ϕ does not directly imply agents knowing about it, but it is possible to introduce another axiom $\mathsf{K}_\alpha \phi$ for some or every agent α (or even add common knowledge, if desired). For example, we can add the following axiom for an agent α:

X2 $\mathsf{K}_\alpha \bigwedge_{s \in S} \neg(R(s) \wedge R'(s))$.

We draft how axioms can help reasoning about the specification. Assume that the question is whether α knows whether some $s \in S$ is in the unary relation $R' \subseteq S$ if α knows that s is in the unary relation R. Put differently: *Can we (dis-)prove $\mathsf{K}_\alpha \neg R'(s)$ from $\mathsf{K}_\alpha R(s)$?*

– If we have the axiom X1 (but not axiom X2), we can prove $\neg R'(s)$: From $\mathsf{K}_\alpha R(s)$, we know $R(s)$, and together with X1 this implies $\neg R'(s)$. However, we cannot prove $\mathsf{K}_\alpha \neg R'(s)$ – intuitively, there could be another world with $R'(s)$, indistiguishable for α.
– Enriching our specification with X2 allows proving $\mathsf{K}_\alpha \neg R'(s)$ by applying the following epistemic tautology $\mathsf{K}_\alpha(\psi_1 \wedge \psi_2) \Leftrightarrow \mathsf{K}_\alpha \psi_1 \wedge \mathsf{K}_\alpha \psi_2$.

In the remainder of this section, we instantiate the framework, by introducing atomic propositions for the peer relationship (Sect. 3.1), the membership relationship (Sect. 3.2), and ensemble lifecycle (Sect. 3.3).

3.1 Peer Relationship

In a loosely coupled network of agents, generally not every agent is aware of the existence of every other agent. Similarly, there could be pairs of agents without a communication channel between them. This motivates the notion of a *peer*: Two agents are peers, if they are aware of one another, and share some communication channel. We suggest to add an atomic proposition $Peers(\alpha, \alpha')$ for any pair $\alpha, \alpha' \in \mathcal{A}$. Then, α and α' are peers in a world w iff w valuates $Peers(\alpha, \alpha')$ to true.

As the peer relationship is reflexive and symmetric, we suggest the following (non-epistemic) axioms:

P0 $\bigwedge_{\alpha \in \mathcal{A}} Peers(\alpha, \alpha)$.
P1 $\bigwedge_{\alpha, \alpha' \in \mathcal{A}} Peers(\alpha, \alpha') \Leftrightarrow Peers(\alpha', \alpha)$.

As P0 and P1 describe two very basic structural properties of the peer relationship, we suggest to add the following epistemic axiom:

P2 $CK_{\mathcal{A}} P0 \wedge P1$

We note that P2 makes everyone aware of the general rules of the peers relationship, but P2 does not imply that agents are aware of being each others peers. Given that peers should be aware of one another, we suggest the following epistemic axiom:

P3 $\bigwedge_{\alpha,\alpha' \in \mathcal{A}} K?_\alpha \, Peers(\alpha, \alpha')$.

The peers atomic proposition can also be used to specify further properties of the network topology. For instance, the following axiom can be used to express that all agents are peers of one another:

P4 $\bigwedge_{\alpha,\alpha' \in \mathcal{A}} Peers(\alpha, \alpha')$.

Discussion. The above definitions to do not take the exact topology of a network into account. Often, it is difficult to make any further assumptions. However, depending on the use case, further axioms could be useful, e.g. to model hierarchies between agents, or to reason about the distance between them. An example for a more refined notion of a relationship between agents are sensors inside a vehicle: Each sensor is an agent that communicates with other agents inside the vehicle, and the vehicle in turn could communicate with other vehicles. Another example are mutually trusted instances, such as financial institutes or administrative services. These are connected with other agents following a star pattern.

3.2   Collaboration and Membership

We now model the concept of an ensemble by means of membership propositions. For every ensemble $e \in \mathcal{E}$ in a finite universe $\mathcal{E}$, and every agent α, we assume an atomic proposition $member_e(\alpha)$, stating that α is a collaborator of e. Epistemic logic allows us to add axioms that consider the mutual awareness of collaborators in an ensemble.

As a starting point, it is reasonable to state that an agent is aware of its own membership in an ensemble: For each ensemble e add:

M0 $\bigwedge_{\alpha \in \mathcal{A}, e \in \mathcal{E}} K?_\alpha \, member_e(\alpha)$, that is, every agent α knows whether α is a member of e or not.

Given that ensembles can be a collaboration of a large number of heterogenous agents, even the members of one ensemble are not necessarily aware of each others membership. If desired, however, such awareness of between collaborators can be specified like this:

M1 $\bigwedge_{\alpha,\alpha' \in \mathcal{A}, e \in \mathcal{E}} member_e(\alpha) \Rightarrow K?_\alpha \, member_e(\alpha')$, that is, every collaborator of e knows who the collaborators of e are.

If the use case requires, this can be further liberalized by allowing by making membership "public knowledge". This could be feasible if the ensemble is to follow certain rules of transparency:

M2 $\bigwedge_{\alpha,\alpha' \in \mathcal{A}, e \in \mathcal{E}}$ K?$_\alpha$ $member_e(\alpha')$, that is, every agent knows who the collaborators of every ensemble are.

The axioms M1 and M2 do not take into account whether two agents are peers. If awareness of other agents is bound to the peer-relationship, it might be reasonable to require that agents only have knowledge about their own peers. If so, the following axioms can be used instead of M1 and M2:

M1P $\bigwedge_{\alpha,\alpha' \in \mathcal{A}, e \in \mathcal{E}}$ $Peers(\alpha, \alpha') \wedge member_e(\alpha) \Rightarrow$ K?$_\alpha$ $member_e(\alpha')$, that is, every collaborator α of e knows which α's peers are collaborators of e.
M2P $\bigwedge_{\alpha,\alpha' \in \mathcal{A}, e \in \mathcal{E}}$ $Peers(\alpha, \alpha') \Rightarrow$ K?$_\alpha$ $member_e(\alpha')$, that is, every agent knows in which ensembles their peers collaborate.

We note that given P4, M1 and M2 collapse with M1P and M2P, respectively.

We stress that the above axioms are mere implications of the form "If non-epistemic proposition ϕ is a fact then some agent knows that proposition ψ is a fact." Such implications do not prevent that ψ holds, that is, an agent α know that ψ holds without ϕ being fulfilled. If such additional knowledge is to be excluded, the converse has to be stated as well. As an example, the following axiom is the converse of M2P:

M2PC $\bigwedge_{\alpha,\alpha' \in \mathcal{A}, e \in \mathcal{E}}$ K?$_\alpha$ $member_e(\alpha') \Rightarrow Peers(\alpha, \alpha')$.

Similar axioms can be created to further restrict knowledge. However, we note that generally, our approach to add axioms is that of an open world assumption. Unless an axiom excludes certain knowledge for an agent, the agent could have it (or not).

Discussion. The simple membership proposition may not be sufficient to describe the structure of an ensemble. For instance, some collaborators inside an ensemble could have specific roles or responsibilities. This is also discussed in Sect. 4.2. In general, as the network of agents can have a certain topology, this holds true for ensembles as well.

3.3   Ensemble Lifecycle and State Mapping

So far, the suggested atomic propositions and axioms have focused on the role of agents. Now, we put the ensemble itself into the spotlight, and discuss its *lifecycle*, that is, the states that an ensemble could be in, as well as the transitions between them.

In a first step, we define the respective state spaces for ensembles. We assume that the state space (for the sake of the specification) is finite. In some applications that could require that an infinite state space is reduced or abstracted to a finite set of states, which could be achieved by methods such as predicate abstraction, abstract interpretation, refinement, or similar formal methods. Assuming a finite set of ensembles, we define the following propositions based on a finite universe $\mathcal{S}$ of states.

For every ensemble e and state $s \in \mathcal{S}$, we add an atomic proposition $state_e(s)$, encoding that s is in the state space of e in the current world.

Based thereon, we can define that every ensemble is in exactly one state at the same time. To this end, we add an atomic proposition $current_e(s)$ for each state $s \in \mathcal{S}$ and ensemble e, encoding that e is currently in state s. Then, we add the following axioms:

C0 $\bigwedge_{s \in \mathcal{S}, e \in \mathcal{E}} current_e(s) \Rightarrow state_e(s)$.
C1 $\bigwedge_{e \in \mathcal{E}} \bigvee_{s \in \mathcal{S}} current_e(s)$.
C2 $\bigwedge_{s \neq s' \in \mathcal{S}, e \in \mathcal{E}} \neg(current_e(s) \wedge current_e(s'))$.

Based thereon, we can now add axioms describing the knowledge of agents. If every member of an ensemble knows about the current state of an ensemble, one could add the following axiom:

S0 $\bigwedge_{\alpha \in \mathcal{A}, e \in \mathcal{E}, s \in \mathcal{S}} member_e(\alpha) \Rightarrow \mathsf{K}?_\alpha current_e(s)$.

Similar to reasoning about the current state, it is also possible to reason about future states. Arguably the simplest notion regarding future states is reachability. We can encode reachability of one state s' from a source state s into an atomic proposition $reachable_e(s, s')$ for every pair s, s' of states and ensemble e. Usually, reachability is reflexive and transitive, motivating the following axioms:

R0 $\bigwedge_{e \in \mathcal{E}, s \in \mathcal{S}} reachable_e(s, s)$ (Reflexivity).
R1 $\bigwedge_{e \in \mathcal{E}, s, s', s'' \in \mathcal{S}} reachable_e(s, s') \wedge reachable_e(s', s'') \Rightarrow reachable_e(s, s'')$ (Transitivity).
R2 Only states of an ensemble are reachable: $\bigwedge_{e \in \mathcal{E}, s, s' \in \mathcal{S}} reachable_e(s, s') \Rightarrow state_e(s) \wedge state_e(s')$.

To constitute these axioms as "ground rules" can be achieved by making the axioms Ri ($i = 0, \ldots, 2$) universally known to agents, yielding axiom RiK:

RiK $\bigwedge_{\alpha \in \mathcal{A}} \mathsf{K}_\alpha$ Ri ($i = 1, 2, 3$).

We can also introduce an atomic proposition $currentlyReachable_e(s)$ to state that s is reachable from the current state of the ensemble e:

RC $\bigwedge_{e \in \mathcal{E}, s \in \mathcal{S}} currentlyReachable_e(s) \Leftrightarrow \bigvee_{s' \in \mathcal{S}} current_e(s') \wedge reachable_e(s', s)$.
RCK $\bigwedge_{\alpha \in \mathcal{A}} \mathsf{K}_\alpha$ RC.

Now, we could state that members of an ensemble e have sufficient knowledge to reason about reachability of states in e:

RM $\bigwedge_{\alpha \in \mathcal{A}, e \in \mathcal{E}, s, s' \in \mathcal{S}} member_e(\alpha) \Rightarrow \mathsf{K}?_\alpha reachable_e(s, s')$.

Based thereon, we can prove that every member of an ensemble knows which states are reachable from the current state, that is, the following proposition is a fact:

$$\bigwedge_{\alpha \in \mathcal{A}, s \in \mathcal{S}, e \in \mathcal{E}} member_e(\alpha) \Rightarrow \mathsf{K}?_\alpha \ currentlyReachable_e(s)$$

Intuitively, if α is a member of e, then by S0, α knows the current state of e, by RM knows which states are reachable from the current state, and by RCK knows that states reachable from the current state are those currently reachable.

Discussion. The above introduced concepts assume a global state of an ensemble. In reality, global state is usually composed from various local states, particularly given the heterogeneity of agents. It could thus be required to refine the above concepts accordingly. Thereby, one could e.g. follow the Petri net [11] approach. Global states could still be applied for the more general "life phases" of an ensemble, e.g. "formed", "running", "terminated", and so on. Even then, the problem remains that agents do not necessarily observe such transitions between life phases synchronously. In addition, some specification approaches do not start from a finite state system but instead describe the behavior by means of temporal logics (cf. e.g. [1]). One existing knowledge-based approach to temporal logic is [2]. There, the main idea is to define which actions a set of agents can take given that they have common knowledge of a specific fact.

4 Epistemic Logic and Dynamic Ensembles

We first introduce a new epistemic operator to specify group and common knowledge for ensembles (Sect. 4.1), and then explore a role/instance approach in Sect. 4.2. Finally, we briefly discuss the issue of evolving knowledge and factual change in Sect. 4.3.

4.1 A New Knowledge Operator: Ensemble Knowledge

It may be desirable to express group knowledge and common knowledge in terms of an ensemble instead of a fixed set of agents. If an ensemble has a fixed set of members, this does not require any further operators. However, if membership is valuated differently in different worlds, a new solution is required. To this end, we introduce an *ensemble knowledge operator* K_e and an *ensemble common knowledge operator* CK_e, yielding a new language $\mathbb{L}_e \supset \mathbb{L}$:

$$\mathbb{L}_e ::= p \mid \mathbb{L}_e \vee \mathbb{L}_e \mid \neg \mathbb{L}_e \mid \mathsf{K}_\alpha \mathbb{L}_e \mid \mathsf{K}_A \mathbb{L}_e \mid \mathsf{CK}_A \mathbb{L}_e \mid \mathsf{K}_e \mathbb{L}_e \mid \mathsf{CK}_e \mathbb{L}_e$$
$$(p \in \mathcal{P}, \alpha \in \mathcal{A}, A \subseteq \mathcal{A})$$

We can define the semantics for $\mathbb{L}_e$ by extending the semantics of $\mathbb{L}$ by the following tautologies (cf. 6.3):

EK0 $\mathsf{K}_e \phi \Leftrightarrow (\bigwedge_{\alpha \in \mathcal{A}} member_e(\alpha) \Rightarrow \mathsf{K}_\alpha \phi)$.

EK1 $CK_e \phi \Leftrightarrow K_e \phi \wedge K_e K_e \phi \wedge \ldots .$

We study the special case where the membership relation is static in a Kripke structure $\mathbf{W}$. For every $\alpha \in \mathcal{A}$, let $member_e(\alpha)$ have the same truth value in every world of $\mathbf{W}$. In particular, let $A \subseteq \mathcal{A}$ be the set of agents α, such that $member_e(\alpha)$ is true in every world of $\mathbf{W}$. Then, $\mathbb{L}$ and $\mathbb{L}_e$ coincide on $\mathbf{W}$ in the following sense: For every $\phi \in \mathbb{L}_e$, there exists $\phi_A \in \mathbb{L}$ with

1. ϕ_A can be obtained from ϕ by replacing each occurrence of K_e and CK_e by K_A and CK_A, respectively, and
2. Every world of $\mathbf{W}$ satisfies $\phi \Leftrightarrow \phi_A$.

Studying further properties of K_e and CK_e is subject for future work.

4.2 Instantiation of Roles

So far, our framework captured the particular knowledge on the level of collaborators. However, some ensembles form dynamically for a situation at run time, effectively drawing their collaborators from a pool of available agents. As such, at the time of specifying an ensemble, the actual collaborators are often unknown. Instead, a more abstract approach is followed, where collaborators are specified by constraints, e.g. on their interfaces, behavior or capabilities. Likewise, the specific number of collaborators is not necessarily known beforehand, as collaborators can fulfill several tasks at once, or the number of required collaborators depends on the real time situation.

This can be captured by a role/instantiation model: The specification encompasses roles which capture the requirements for collaborators. At runtime, these roles are instantiated by actual collaborators. We can apply this to our epistemic logic approach as well: Instead of reasoning about knowledge of specific collaborators, we instead knowledge of roles. It is quite natural to then reason about the relationship of knowledge on role level and knowledge on collaborator level. Here, we face the challenge that the role-instance-relationship is generally not one-to-one but many-to-many. In particular, we can observe the following:

One-to-Many. There can be multiple collaborators fulfilling the same role. For instance, a set of collaborators could be required to carry an object, and their exact number could depend on the individual agents and the properties of the object.

Many-to-One. The same collaborator could fulfill different roles at once. For instance, a collaborator that offers multiple functionalities could both participate in the carrying process and fulfill a navigator role.

One-to-None. Some roles could be optional to be instantiated in specific situations. For instance, a specific class of objects could require an additional supervisor, which is not required in other cases.

In the remainder of this section, we reason about the relationship between knowledge of roles and knowledge of collaborators. In particular, we look for a model that encompasses both the role-level and the collaborator-level, and allows expressing their relationships. While it might be tempting to approach this with first-order logic, this paper stays inside the scope of propositional logic. To this end, we make the following assumption: We draw the roles from the universe of agents. That is, for every role, we make use of a "paragon agent" that represents the role, but is never a member of the instantiated ensemble. We formalize this by an atomic proposition $inst(e', e)$ encoding that e' is an instance of e. We add the following axioms:

RI0 $\bigwedge_{\alpha \in \mathcal{A}, e, e' \in \mathcal{E}} inst(e, e') \Rightarrow \neg(member_e(\alpha) \wedge member_{e'}(\alpha))$.
RI1 $\bigwedge_{\alpha, \alpha' \in \mathcal{A}, e, e' \in \mathcal{E}} member_e(\alpha) \wedge member_{e'}(\alpha') \wedge inst(e, e') \Rightarrow \neg Peers(\alpha, \alpha')$.

We can now add the role/instance concept: For each $e, e' \in \mathcal{E}$, $\alpha, \alpha' \in \mathcal{A}$, we introduce the atomic proposition $instanceOf_{e,e'}(\alpha, \alpha')$ encoding that α' from e' instantiates α from e.

RI2 $\bigwedge_{\alpha, \alpha' \in \mathcal{A}, e, e' \in \mathcal{E}} instanceOf_{e,e'}(\alpha, \alpha') \Rightarrow inst(e, e') \wedge member_e(\alpha) \wedge member_{e'}(\alpha')$.

Using this framework, we can express statements of the form "all instances of role r in any instance of ensemble e know proposition ϕ" as follows:

$$\bigwedge_{\alpha' \in \mathcal{A}, e' \in \mathcal{E}} instanceOf_{e,e'}(\alpha, \alpha') \Rightarrow \mathsf{K}_{\alpha'} \phi.$$

Similarly, one can express that in each instance of e, at least one instance of role α knows ϕ:

$$\bigwedge_{e' \in \mathcal{E}} inst(e, e') \Rightarrow \bigvee_{\alpha' \in \mathcal{A}} instanceOf_{e,e'}(\alpha, \alpha') \wedge \mathsf{K}_{\alpha'} \phi.$$

4.3   Evolution of Ensembles and Their Environments

Given a formula $\phi \in \mathbb{L}$ and a world w in a Kripke structure $\mathbf{W}$, the truth value of ϕ is immutable. While useful for reasoning about a certain "snapshot" in time, it is not as suitable to specify the evolution of an ensemble or its environment over time. For instance, a collaborator joins/leaves an ensemble, a fact becomes known to a collaborator, or some environmental value changes.

From the point of view of epistemic logic, there are two kinds of changes:

1. *The world changes.* This embodies factual change: An atomic proposition changes its truth value in a transition from a source world w to a target world w'. The step from w to w' not only changes the valuation of atomic propositions but might also blur or clarify the knowledge of agents.
2. *An agent changes their "world view".* Usually by gaining information, an agent evolves to be able to distinguish between more worlds.

When specifying ensembles, both types of change must be considered: By their very definition, ensembles exist in volatile environments (that are subject to change), and agents may gain information by exchanging messages between one another or with the environment.

Looking at the Kripke structure semantics, evolution means to transition from one world w in a Kripke structure $\mathbf{W}$ to another world w' in a Kripke structure $\mathbf{W'}$, There are different approaches to address these transitions in literature, summarized under the notion of *dynamic epistemic logic* [5]. Their applicability in the specification of ensembles needs to be further studied. We generally suggest that the exact evolution method should be chosen based on the way the evolution of the ensemble and its environment is specified.

5   Conclusion and Future Work

In this paper, we presented first ideas for using epistemic logic in the specification of ensembles. We can envision the following next steps. To deepen the understanding of the application of epistemic logics in ensemble specification, the properties of the logics itself could be studied. A discussion on existing theorems on classical properties, such as decidability or completeness, could enable the discovery of refined, setting-specific properties. If one uses epistemic knowledge inside existing specification approaches, it could be valuable to explore properties that link different approaches together, such as equivalences or coincidence theorems. This could then serve as a foundation for proving properties of the method resulting from adding epistemic logics to an existing specification method. As a first evaluation, one could enrich existing ensemble specifications by the concepts presented in this paper. This could then lead to a more thorough connection of epistemic logic with existing approaches, such as the SCEL-Language, where it would be particularly interesting to relate the respective concepts of knowledge. This also includes an evaluation of different approaches of dynamic epistemic logic with respect to the chosen ensemble specification method. As ensembles consist of many heterogenous agents and exist in volatile environments, trust in received information cannot be guaranteed. Thus, Doxastic logic and belief revision (complementing certain knowledge and the acquisition thereof) should be studied. One particular direction could be the *logic of lying* [3] in the field of ensemble specification in order to specify malevolent collaborators or environments. Current approaches in the implementation of distributed systems, such as distributed ledger technologies, also touch the field of zero-knowledge proofs [7,8,12], which could yield an interesting link from the here developed approach into practice.

6   Appendix

6.1   Kripke Structures

An epistemic Kripke structure $\mathbf{W} = (W, Sat, (\equiv_\alpha)_{\alpha \in \mathcal{A}})$ over atomic propositions $\mathcal{P}$ and agents A is a vertex- and edge-labeled, directed graph, where

- each vertex $w \in W$ is called a *world*,
- $Sat : \mathcal{P} \to 2^W$ is the valuation function, mapping atomic proposition $p \in \mathcal{P}$ to the set $Sat(p)$ of worlds in which p is true, and
- each $\equiv_\alpha \subseteq W \times W$ is a reflexive, symmetric relations specifying that if in world w, α also considers w' as the current world iff $w \equiv_\alpha w'$.

For an agent α and a world $w \in W$, we define the set $Ind_{\mathbf{W}}(w, \alpha) := \{w' \mid w' \in W, w \equiv_\alpha w'\}$ of worlds indistinguishable from w by α in $\mathbf{W}$, observing $w \in Ind_{\mathbf{W}}(w, \alpha)$.

6.2   Semantics of $\mathbb{L}$

The semantics of a formula are defined by the set of worlds in which the formula holds, formalized as the function $Worlds(\mathbf{W}, \cdot) : \mathbb{L} \to 2^W$ where for each $\phi, \psi \in \mathbb{L}$:

1. $Worlds(\mathbf{W}, p) = Sat(p)$ for all $p \in \mathcal{P}$.
2. $Worlds(\mathbf{W}, \neg\phi) = W \setminus Worlds(\mathbf{W}, \phi)$.
3. $Worlds(\mathbf{W}, \phi \vee \psi) = Worlds(\mathbf{W}, \phi) \cup Worlds(\mathbf{W}, \psi)$.
4. $Worlds(\mathbf{W}, \mathsf{K}_\alpha \phi) = \{w \in W \mid Ind_{\mathbf{W}}(w, \alpha) \subseteq Worlds(\mathbf{W}, \phi)\}$.
5. $Worlds(\mathbf{W}, \mathsf{K}_A \phi) = \bigcap_{\alpha \in A} Worlds(\mathbf{W}, \mathsf{K}_\alpha \phi)$.
6. $Worlds(\mathbf{W}, \mathsf{CK}_A \phi)$
   $\qquad = Worlds(\mathbf{W}, \phi) \cap Worlds(\mathbf{W}, \mathsf{K}_A \phi) \cap Worlds(\mathbf{W}, \mathsf{K}_A \mathsf{K}_A \phi) \ldots$.

From $w \in Ind_{\mathbf{W}}(w, \alpha)$, we get $Worlds(\mathbf{W}, \mathsf{K}_\alpha \phi) \subseteq Worlds(\mathbf{W}, \phi)$. Hence, $\mathsf{K}_\alpha \phi \Rightarrow \phi$ is a tautology: α knows that the formula ϕ is a fact, that is, ϕ is true, and α knows that ϕ is true.

6.3   Semantics of $\mathbb{L}_e$

The semantics of a formula $\phi \in \mathbb{L}_e$ are defined by the set of worlds in which the formula holds, formalized as the function $Worlds_e(\mathbf{W}, \cdot) : \mathbb{L}_e \to 2^W$ where for each $\phi, \psi \in \mathbb{L}$:

1. $Worlds_e(\mathbf{W}, p) = Sat(p)$ for all $p \in \mathcal{P}$.
2. $Worlds_e(\mathbf{W}, \neg\phi) = W \setminus Worlds_e(\mathbf{W}, \phi)$.
3. $Worlds_e(\mathbf{W}, \phi \vee \psi) = Worlds_e(\mathbf{W}, \phi) \cup Worlds_e(\mathbf{W}, \psi)$.
4. $Worlds_e(\mathbf{W}, \mathsf{K}_\alpha \phi) = \{w \in W \mid Ind_{\mathbf{W}}(w, \alpha) \subseteq Worlds_e(\mathbf{W}, \phi)\}$.
5. $Worlds_e(\mathbf{W}, \mathsf{K}_A \phi) = \bigcap_{\alpha \in A} Worlds_e(\mathbf{W}, \mathsf{K}_\alpha \phi)$.
6. $Worlds_e(\mathbf{W}, \mathsf{CK}_A \phi)$
   $\qquad = Worlds_e(\mathbf{W}, \phi) \cap Worlds_e(\mathbf{W}, \mathsf{K}_A \phi) \cap Worlds_e(\mathbf{W}, \mathsf{K}_A \mathsf{K}_A \phi) \ldots$.
7. $Worlds_e(\mathbf{W}, \mathsf{K}_e \phi) = \bigcap_{\alpha \in A} Worlds_e(\mathbf{W}, \phi_\alpha)$ where $\phi_\alpha = member_e(\alpha) \Rightarrow \mathsf{K}_\alpha \phi$.
8. $Worlds_e(\mathbf{W}, \mathsf{CK}_A \phi)$
   $\qquad = Worlds_e(\mathbf{W}, \phi) \cap Worlds_e(\mathbf{W}, \mathsf{K}_e \phi) \cap Worlds_e(\mathbf{W}, \mathsf{K}_e \mathsf{K}_e \phi) \ldots$.

References

1. Bieber, P.: A logic of communication in hostile environment. In: [1990] Proceedings, The Computer Security Foundations Workshop III, pp. 14–22 (1990)
2. Clarke, E.M., Henzinger, T.A., Veith, H., Bloem, R. (eds.): Handbook of Model Checking. Springer, Cham (2018). https://doi.org/10.1007/978-3-319-10575-8
3. van Ditmarsch, H., van Eijck, J., Sietsma, F., Wang, Y.: On the logic of lying. In: van Eijck, J., Verbrugge, R. (eds.) Games, Actions and Social Software. LNCS, vol. 7010, pp. 41–72. Springer, Heidelberg (2012). https://doi.org/10.1007/978-3-642-29326-9_4
4. van Ditmarsch, H., Halpern, J.Y., van der Hoek, W., Kooi, B.P.: An introduction to logics of knowledge and belief. CoRR abs/1503.00806 (2015). http://arxiv.org/abs/1503.00806
5. van Ditmarsch, H., van der Hoek, W., Kooi, B.: Dynamic Epistemic Logic. SYLI, vol. 337, 1st edn. Springer, Dordrecht (2007). https://doi.org/10.1007/978-1-4020-5839-4
6. Fagin, R., Moses, Y., Halpern, J.Y., Vardi, M.Y.: Reasoning About Knowledge. MIT Press, Cambridge (2003)
7. Goldwasser, S., Micali, S., Rackoff, C.: The knowledge complexity of interactive proof systems. SIAM J. Comput. 18(1), 186–208 (1989). https://doi.org/10.1137/0218012
8. Groth, J.: Short pairing-based non-interactive zero-knowledge arguments. In: Abe, M. (ed.) ASIACRYPT 2010. LNCS, vol. 6477, pp. 321–340. Springer, Heidelberg (2010). https://doi.org/10.1007/978-3-642-17373-8_19
9. Hennicker, R., Wirsing, M.: Dynamic logic for ensembles. In: Margaria, T., Steffen, B. (eds.) ISoLA 2018. LNCS, vol. 11246, pp. 32–47. Springer, Cham (2018). https://doi.org/10.1007/978-3-030-03424-5_3
10. Hughes, G.E., Cresswell, M.J.: A New Introduction to Modal Logic. Routledge, London (1996)
11. Reisig, W.: Understanding Petri Nets. Modeling Techniques, Analysis Methods, Case Studies. Translated from the German by the author (07 2013). https://doi.org/10.1007/978-3-642-33278-4
12. Sasson, E.B., et al.: Zerocash: decentralized anonymous payments from bitcoin. In: 2014 IEEE Symposium on Security and Privacy, pp. 459–474. IEEE (2014)
13. Wirsing, M., Hölzl, M., Tribastone, M., Zambonelli, F.: ASCENS: engineering autonomic service-component ensembles. In: Beckert, B., Damiani, F., de Boer, F.S., Bonsangue, M.M. (eds.) FMCO 2011. LNCS, vol. 7542, pp. 1–24. Springer, Heidelberg (2013). https://doi.org/10.1007/978-3-642-35887-6_1
14. Wirsing, M., Hölzl, M., Koch, N., Mayer, P. (eds.): Software Engineering for Collective Autonomic Systems. LNCS, vol. 8998. Springer, Cham (2015). https://doi.org/10.1007/978-3-319-16310-9

FSCAFI: A Core Calculus for Collective Adaptive Systems Programming

Roberto Casadei[1], Mirko Viroli[1(✉)], Giorgio Audrito[2],
and Ferruccio Damiani[2]

[1] Alma Mater Studiorum–Università di Bologna, Cesena, Italy
{roby.casadei,mirko.viroli}@unibo.it
[2] Università di Torino, Turin, Italy
{giorgio.audrito,ferruccio.damiani}@unito.it

Abstract. A recently proposed approach to the rigorous engineering of
collective adaptive systems is the aggregate computing paradigm, which
operationalises the idea of expressing collective adaptive behaviour by
a global perspective as a functional composition of dynamic computational fields (i.e., structures mapping a collection of individual devices
of a collective to computational values over time). In this paper, we
present FSCAFI, a core language that captures the essence of exploiting field computations in mainstream functional languages, and which is
based on a semantic model for field computations leveraging the novel
notion of "computation against a neighbour". Such a construct models expressions whose evaluation depends on the same evaluation that
occurred on a neighbour, thus abstracting communication actions and,
crucially, enabling deep and straightforward integration in the Scala programming language, by the SCAFI incarnation. We cover syntax and
informal semantics of FSCAFI, provide examples of collective adaptive
behaviour development in SCAFI, and delineate future work.

1 Introduction

The Internet of Things (IoT), Cyber-Physical Systems (CPS), and related ini-
tiatives point out a trend in informatics where computation and interaction are
increasingly pervasive and ubiquitous, and carried on by a potentially huge and
dynamic set of heterogeneous devices deployed in physical space. To address
the intrinsic complexity of these settings, a new viewpoint is emerging: a large-
scale network of devices, situated in some environment (e.g., the urban area of
a smart city), can be seen as a computational overlay of the physical world, to
be programmed as a "collective" exhibiting robustness and resiliency by inherent adaptation processes. These kinds of systems are sometimes referred to as
Collective Adaptive Systems (CAS) [1], to emphasise that computational activities are collective (i.e., they involve multiple coordinated individuals), and that
a main expected advantage is inherent adaptivity of behaviours to unforeseen
changes (e.g., as induced by changes/faults in the computational environment
or interactions with humans or other systems).

T. Margaria and B. Steffen (Eds.): ISoLA 2020, LNCS 12477, pp. 344–360, 2020.
https://doi.org/10.1007/978-3-030-61470-6_21

Aggregate Computing [2] is an approach to CAS engineering that takes a global stance to design and programming and where coordinated adaptation is a key feature. Hence, it targets problems and application domains such as crowd engineering, complex situated coordination, robot/UAV swarms, smart ecosystems and the like [3]. Its key idea is to *program a large system as a whole*, that is, to directly consider an ensemble of devices as the target machine to be programmed, and provide under-the-hood, automatic global-to-local mapping: once the desired system-level behaviour is expressed by a global program, then individual computational entities of an aggregate are bound to play a derived, contextualised local behaviour of that program. Prominently, the distinguishing characteristic of Aggregate Computing as a "macro-approach" [4] lies in the ability to formally represent the adaptive behaviour of an ensemble *in a compositional and declarative way*, namely, by combination of functional coordination operators and high-level building blocks expressing the outcome of a collective task.

One fundamental enabling abstraction for specifying the dynamics of situated collectives is that of a *computational field* (or simply, field) [5–7]: a distributed data structure that maps devices to computational objects across time. Accordingly, *Aggregate Programming* is about describing (dynamic) field computations, namely, how input fields (data coming from sensors) turn into output fields (actions feeding actuators)—computations that can be conveniently expressed using the functional paradigm.

A modern implementation of the aggregate programming paradigm is SCAFI[1] (SCala FIelds) [8]. It is a toolkit, tightly integrated with the Scala programming language, that comprises a Domain-Specific Language (DSL), a library, and platform tools for specifying and running (distributed) systems by leveraging computational fields. SCAFI provides a number of key advantages with respect to previous implementation attempts which were standalone DSLs (PROTELIS [9] and Proto [6]), such as: *(i) familiar programming environment*, by coherently supporting field constructs within the ecosystem as well as the syntactic and semantic model of a mainstream language like Scala; *(ii) lightweight type safety*, by leveraging Scala's powerful type system and type inference; and *(iii) seamless reuse of functionality*, by providing unrestricted access to both Scala features (e.g., lightweight components, implicits) and existing libraries on the JVM.

Technically, such a smooth integration with Scala has been achieved thanks to a semantic variation of previous formalisation attempts, which were based on the *field calculus* [5]: the notion of "neighbouring value" (a map from neighbours to data values), used in field calculus to locally express outcome of message reception from neighbours, is replaced with that of "computation against a neighbour", namely, by expressions whose evaluation depends on the same evaluation occurring on a neighbour. This change leads to a new computational model that we reify by a calculus called FEATHERWEIGHT SCAFI (FSCAFI) and present in this paper.

---

[1] https://scafi.github.io.

The content is structured as follows. Section 2 provides motivation for SCAFI and covers related work. Section 3 describes syntax and informal semantics of FSCAFI. Section 4 provides examples, showing how FSCAFI can be used to develop collective adaptive behaviour. Section 5 ends up the paper with a wrap-up and discussion of future work.

2   Background

Scenarios like the IoT, CPS, smart cities, and the like, foster a vision of rich computational ecosystems providing services by leveraging strict cooperation of large collectives of smart devices, which mostly operate in a contextual way. Engineering complex behaviour in these settings calls for approaches providing some abstraction through the notion of *ensemble*, neglecting as much as possible the more traditional view of focussing on the single device and the messages it exchanges with peers.

2.1   Aggregate Computing

Aggregate computing is the main theme of this paper. A recent survey of its historical development and state-of-the-art is provided in [3]. The essence of the approach is captured by the field calculus [5], a core language grounding semantics and formal analysis of field computations [10,11].

Programming languages to work with computational fields have been introduced in the past, with Proto [6] as common ancestor (Lisp-based), and PROTELIS [9] as its Java-oriented, standalone DSL version. These approaches however have the drawback of not smoothly integrating field computations in the syntactic, semantic, and typing structures of a modern, conventional language—to fully remedy this problem, in this paper we shall present some key semantic changes to the field calculus.

To address this problem, a prominent, modern approach is to devise an "internal" or "embedded" DSL [12] that provides mechanisms to support the new features on top of an adequate host programming language. Of course, with embedded DSLs, both the syntax and the semantics are limited by the constraints exerted by the host language. However, the model can sometimes be slightly adjusted in order to favour the embedding, considering the common syntactic, typing, and semantic features of the candidate set of host languages.

When conceiving this DSL, we took into account the following requirements and desiderata for the host language: *pragmatism* (supporting easy reuse of existing programming mechanisms); *reliability* (intercepting errors early—cf., type checking); *expressivity* (offering an eloquent syntax); and *functional paradigm support* (all the significant features of functional programming must be cleanly available). All the above considerations led us towards the Scala programming language as the host. Then, to well design the key constructs and provide a framework for rigorous analysis of programs and properties, we came up with

FSCAFI model of field computations. Its peculiarity is to handle standard values has been the local representative of a computational field, which provides a simplified setting for DSL embedding. To achieve this, we introduced a local notion of "computation against a neighbour", namely, a computation whose outcome depends on the most recent, local view of the result of computation in that neighbour (unlike in the standard field calculus, this allows smooth application of host typing mechanisms to any field expression)—as detailed in Sect. 3.

Such a model, and related tooling, is implemented in the SCAFI aggregate computing DSL and platform [8,13]. SCAFI achieves the goal of providing an environment to streamline and support effective development of systems based on the Aggregate Computing paradigm, leveraging the solid basis provided by a mainstream programming language such as Scala and its ecosystem. In fact, Scala: runs on the JVM and thus enables straightforward interaction with the Java ecosystem; offers a powerful type system, with type inference, that helps to build type-safe libraries with minimal overhead; has a flexible syntax (convenient for creation of elegant APIs/DSLs). Moreover, Scala has great popularity in the distributed computing arena: it is the implementation language for several distributed computing toolkits, such as Apache Kafka[2] and the Akka actor framework[3]. Hence, our choice of Scala also fosters the construction of a platform-level support on top of SCAFI, in the form of a middleware for running distributed and situated systems [13,14].

2.2   Related Work

Aggregate programming languages. Prior aggregate programming languages are standalone (also called external) DSLs and include PROTO [6], the Lisp-like progenitor, and its evolution PROTELIS [9]. PROTELIS is based on an untyped, standalone DSL able to interoperate with existing Java code. This approach has some limitations: aligning the syntax and semantics, as well as providing training and documenting for a *distinct* language w.r.t. the one used to develop the execution platform can be burdensome; extra development and maintenance effort is needed to adequately support editing tools (e.g., plugins are required for common IDE features like syntax highlighting and refactoring); activities that span both the DSL and the target language (e.g., static analysis and debugging) may be hard to implement; and finally, the ability to smoothly reuse the features and libraries of the target language can be limited. Though language tools greatly improved recently (cf. the Xtext language workbench [15] and its Xbase extension [16], to name a popular one), practically, with an external DSL it may be difficult to come up with a cohesive design of the resulting software system (cf. Generation gap pattern [17]), since parts written in the DSL need to bidirectionally refer and interact with other parts of the system [18].

Ensemble approaches. In *Helena* [19] components can dynamically participate in multiple ensembles and adapt according to different *roles* whose behaviour

---

[2] https://kafka.apache.org.
[3] https://akka.io.

is given by a process expression. *DEECo* [20] is another CAS model where components can only communicate by dynamically binding together through ensembles; DEECo ensemble is formed according to a *membership condition* and consists of one *coordinator* and multiple *members* interacting by implicit *knowledge exchange*; DEECo has a Java implementation called jDEECo which enables the definition of components and ensembles through Java annotations. The *GCM/ProActive* [21] framework supports the development of large-scale ensembles of adaptable autonomous devices through a hierarchical component model where components have a non-functional membrane and "collective interfaces", and a programming model based on active objects. *SCEL* [22] is a kernel language to specify the behaviour of autonomic components, the logic of ensemble formation, as well interaction through attribute-based communication (which enables implicit selection of a group of recipients). *Attribute-based communication* [23] is an approach to CAS coordination that leverages implicit multicasts towards recipients matched by predicates over attributes. The approach has been formalised by the *AbC calculus* [23] and implemented as an Erlang DSL in the so-called AErlang library [24]. Generally speaking, it is worth noting that the field calculus fits useful device abstractions (such as neighbourhood, message exchange, attribute-based filtering) into a purely functional approach, which can then smoothly interoperate with more traditional programming frameworks and languages. More specifically, attribute-based communication can be achieved in the field calculus (and hence in FSCAFI) both at the receiver and the sender side, via construct `branch` (see Sect. 4), by which one can define subcomputations carried on by a subset of nodes—those that execute the same branch and hence remain actually "observable" by operator `nbr`. In a more programmatically expressible way, a notion of ensemble can be captured as a field computation on a dynamic domain of devices, denoted by the concept of an *aggregate process* [25].

Spatial computing and macro-programming. An extensive survey on spatial computing can be found in [4]. Indeed, multiple classes of approaches address (at least in part) the problem of organising a collective of computational entities. These include *topological and geometrical languages* like *GPL* [26] (exploiting the botanical metaphor of "growing points") and *OSL* [27] (focussing on programming "computational surfaces" through folding operations); *languages abstracting communication and networks*, like TOTA [7] and Linda-$\sigma\tau$ [28] (supporting diffusion and aggregation of tuples on a network of agents), Logical Neighbourhoods [29] (supporting virtual connectivity), and SpatialViews [30] (abstracting a network into *spatial views* that can be iterated on to visit nodes and request services); and *macro-programming languages*, like *SpaceTime Oriented Programming (STOP)* [31] (providing abstractions to support collection and processing of past or future network data in arbitrary spatio-temporal resolutions) and *Regiment* [32] (modelling network state and regions as spatially distributed, time-varying signals). Aggregate Computing belongs to the class of so-called general-purpose spatial computing languages, all addressing the problem of engineering distributed (or parallel) computing by providing mechanisms to manipulate data structures diffused in space and evolving in time. Other notable examples include the SDEF programming system inspired by systolic computing [33], and topological computing with MGS [34]. They typically provide specific abstractions that significantly differ from that of computational fields: for instance, MGS defines computations over manifolds, the goal of which is to alter the manifold itself as a way to represent input-output transformation.

3   FEATHERWEIGHT SCAFI: A Core Calculus for SCAFI

In this section, we present FEATHERWEIGHT SCAFI (FSCAFI), a minimal core calculus that models the aggregate computing aspects of SCAFI—much as FJ [35] models the object-oriented aspects of Java.

In the aggregate computing model, devices undergo computation in rounds. When a round starts, the device gathers information about messages received from neighbours (only the last message from each neighbour is actually considered), performs an evaluation of the program, and finally emits a message to all neighbours with information about the outcome of computation. The scheduling policy of such rounds is abstracted in this formalisation, though it is typically considered fair and non-synchronous.

FSCAFI is a core subset of SCAFI, *strictly retaining its syntax* (with the exception of typing annotations, which are not here presented). The syntax of FSCAFI is given in Fig. 1. Following [35], the overbar notation denotes metavariables over sequences and the empty sequence is denoted by $\bullet$; e.g., for expressions, we let $\bar{e}$ range over sequences of expressions, written $e_1, e_2, \ldots e_n$ $(n \geq 0)$. FSCAFI focuses on aggregate programming constructs. In particular:

- it neglects the many orthogonal Scala features that one can use (object-oriented constructs, and the like), and
- it is parametric in the built-in data constructors and functions.

Note that – apart from specific Scala syntax – the examples of SCAFI code given in Sect. 4 are actually examples of FSCAFI code. In particular, in order to turn SCAFI functions (such as foldhoodPlus, gradient and branch—covered in Sect. 4) into FSCAFI functions, it is enough to drop type annotations and default parameters.

A program P consists of a sequence $\bar{F}$ of function declarations and a main expression e. A function declaration F defines a (possibly recursive) function; it consists of a name d, $n \geq 0$ variable names $\bar{x}$ representing the formal parameters, and an expression e representing the body of the function.

Expressions e are the main entities of the calculus, modelling a whole field computation. An expression can be: a variable x, used as function formal parameter; a value v; an anonymous function $(\bar{x})$ $\overset{\tau}{=>}$ @@{e} (where $\bar{x}$ are the formal parameters, e is the body, and τ is a *tag*); a function call $e(\bar{e})$; a rep-expression rep(e){e}, modelling time evolution; an nbr-expression nbr{e}, modelling neighbourhood interaction; or a foldhood-expression foldhood(e)(e){e} which combines values obtained from neighbours.

$$
\begin{array}{llr}
\text{P} & ::= \bar{\text{F}}\ \text{e} & \text{program} \\
\text{F} & ::= \texttt{def}\ \text{d}(\bar{\text{x}}) =\ \texttt{@@\{e\}} & \text{function declaration} \\
\text{e} & ::= \text{x}\ \mid\ \text{v}\ \mid\ (\bar{\text{x}}) \overset{\tau}{=>} \texttt{@@\{e\}}\ \mid\ \text{e}(\bar{\text{e}}) & \text{expression} \\
& \mid\ \texttt{rep(e)\{e\}}\ \mid\ \texttt{nbr\{e\}}\ \mid\ \texttt{foldhood(e)(e)\{e\}} \\
\hline
\text{v} & ::= \text{c}(\bar{\text{v}})\ \mid\ \text{f} & \text{value} \\
\text{f} & ::= \text{b}\ \mid\ \text{d}\ \mid\ (\bar{\text{x}}) \overset{\tau}{=>} \texttt{@@\{e\}} & \text{function value}
\end{array}
$$

Fig. 1. Syntax of FSCAFI.

Tags τ of anonymous functions $(\bar{\text{x}}) \overset{\tau}{=>} \texttt{@@\{e\}}$ do not occur in source programs: when the evaluation starts each anonymous function expression $(\bar{\text{x}}) => \texttt{@@\{e\}}$ occurring in the program is given a distinguished tag τ—for instance, two occurrences of the same anonymous function expression get different tags. In the following we will use the phrase *name of a function* to refer both to the tag of an anonymous function, or to the name of a built-in or declared function. As we will see below, names are used to define function equality.

The set of the *free variables* of an expression e, denoted by $\mathbf{FV}(\text{e})$, is defined as usual (the only binding construct is $(\bar{\text{x}}) \overset{\tau}{=>} \texttt{@@\{e\}}$). An expression e is *closed* if $\mathbf{FV}(\text{e}) = \bullet$. The main expression of any program must be closed.

A value can be either a *data value* $\text{c}(\bar{\text{v}})$ or a *functional value* f. A data value consists of a *data constructor* c of some arity $m \geq 0$ applied to a sequence of m data values $\bar{\text{v}} = \text{v}_1, ..., \text{v}_m$. A data value $\text{c}(\text{v}_1, ..., \text{v}_m)$ is written c when $m = 0$. Examples of data values are: the Booleans True and False, numbers, pairs (like $\text{Pair}(\text{True}, \text{Pair}(5, 7))$) and lists (like $\text{Cons}(3, \text{Cons}(4, \text{Null}))$).

Functional values f comprise:

- declared function names d;
- closed anonymous function expressions $(\bar{\text{x}}) \overset{\tau}{=>} \texttt{@@\{e\}}$ (i.e., such that $\mathbf{FV}(\text{e}) \subseteq \{\bar{\text{x}}\}$);
- built-in functions b, which can in turn be:
  - *pure operators* o, such as functions for building and decomposing pairs (pair, fst, snd) and lists (cons, head, tail), the equality function (=), mathematical and logical functions (+, &&, ...), and so on;
  - *sensors* s, which depend on the current environmental conditions of the computing device δ, such as a temperature sensor—modelling construct sense in SCAFI;
  - *relational sensors* r, modelling construct nbrvar in SCAFI, which in addition depend also on a specific neighbour device δ' (e.g., nbrRange, which measures the distance with a neighbour device).

In case e is a binary built-in function b, we shall write e_1 b e_2 for the function call $\text{b}(\text{e}_1, \text{e}_2)$ whenever convenient for readability of the whole expression in which it is contained.

The key constructs of the calculus are:

- *Function call:* $e(e_1, \ldots, e_n)$ is the main construct of the language. The function call evaluates to the result of applying the function value f produced by the evaluation of e to the value of the parameters $e_1, \ldots, e_n$ *relatively to the aligned neighbours*, that is, relatively to the neighbours that in their last execution round have evaluated e to a function value with the *same name* of f. For instance, suppose to have defined a function def $plus(a, b)$ = @@$\{a + b\}$; then, function call $plus(5, 2)$ yields a field that is 7 in every point of space and time (i.e., the expression evaluates to 7 in each round of every device).
- *Time evolution:* $\text{rep}(e_1)\{e_2\}$ is a construct for dynamically changing fields through the "repeated" application of the functional expression e_2. At the first computation round (or, more precisely, when no previous state is available—e.g., initially or at re-entrance after state was cleared out due to branching), e_2 is applied to e_1, then at each other step it is applied to the value obtained at the previous step. For instance, $\text{rep}(0)\{(x) \Rightarrow$ @@$\{x + 1\}\}$ counts how many rounds each device has computed (from the beginning, or more generally, since that piece of state was missing). Another example is an expression $\text{snd}(\text{rep}(\text{Pair}(x, \text{False}))\{(x_R) \Rightarrow$ @@$\{\text{Pair}(x, x == \text{fst}(x_R))\}\})$ that evaluates to True when some value x changes w.r.t. the previous round; it is common to use tuples when dealing with multiple pieces of state/result.
- *Neighbourhood interaction:* $\text{foldhood}(e_1)(e_2)\{e_3\}$ and $\text{nbr}\{e\}$ model device-to-device interaction. The foldhood construct evaluates expression e_3 *against every aligned neighbour*[4] (including the device itself), then aggregates the values collected through e_2 together with the initial value e_1. The nbr construct tags expressions e signalling that (when evaluated against a neighbour) the value of e has to be gathered from neighbours (and not directly evaluated). Such behaviour is implemented via a conceptual broadcast of the values evaluated for e. Subexpressions of e_3 not containing nbr are *not* gathered from neighbours instead.
As an example, consider the expression

$$\text{foldhood}(2)(+)\{\min(\text{nbr}\{\text{temperature}()\}, \text{temperature}())\}$$

evaluated in device δ_1 (in which $\text{temperature}() = 10$) with neighbours δ_2 and δ_3 (in which $\text{temperature}()$ gave 15 and 5 in their last evaluation round, orderly). The result of the expression is then computed adding 2, $\min(10, 10)$, $\min(15, 10)$ and $\min(5, 10)$ for a final value of 27.

Note that, according to the explanation given above, calling a declared or anonymous function acts as a branch, with each function in the range applied only on the subspace of devices holding a function with the same tag. In fact, a branching construct $\text{branch}(e_1)\{e_2\}\{e_3\}$ (which computes e_2 or e_3 depending on the value of e_1) can be defined through function application as $\text{mux}(e_1, () \Rightarrow$ @@$\{e_2\}, () \Rightarrow$ @@$\{e_3\})()$, where mux is a built-in function selecting among its second and third argument depending on the value of the first.

---

[4] This is where FSCAFI differs from classical field calculus, where instead neighbouring fields are explicitly manipulated.

Notice that the semantics of this language is compositional and message exchanges are performed under the hood by nbr constructs within a foldhood; with an automatic matching of each message from a neighbour to a specific nbr construct, determined through a process called *alignment* [36]. Basically, each nbr construct produces an "export" (i.e., a data value to be sent to neighbours) tagged with the coordinates of the node in the evaluation tree (i.e., the structure arising from the dynamic unfolding of the main expression evaluation) up to that construct. All exports are gathered together into a message which is broadcast to neighbours, and which can be modelled as a *value tree*: an ordered tree of values obtained during evaluation of each sub-expression of the program. The alignment mechanism then ensures that each nbr is matched with corresponding nbr reached by neighbours with an identical path in the evaluation tree.

4   Showcasing FSCAFI: Programming Examples

In this section, we provide examples of FSCAFI programs, showing how to represent and manipulate fields to implement collective adaptive functionality, using the SCAFI syntax.

4.1   Scala Syntax

In SCAFI, the FSCAFI constructs introduced in Sect. 3 are represented as object-oriented methods through the following Scala trait (interface):

```
trait Constructs {
  def rep[A](init: => A)(fun: (A) => A): A
  def foldhood[A](init: => A)(aggr: (A, A) => A)(expr: => A): A
  def nbr[A](expr: => A): A
  def @@[A](b: => A): A
}
```

This is mostly a straightforward Scala encoding of the syntax of Fig. 1. The main different is given by the presence of *typing information* and, in particular, the use of *by-name parameters*, of type =>T, which provide syntactic sugar for 0-ary functions: these enable to capture expressions at the call site, pass them unevaluated to the method, and evaluate them lazily every time the parameter is used. This turns out very useful to implement the FSCAFI semantics while providing a very lightweight syntax for the DSL. Moreover, note that method signatures do not include field-like type constructors: in fact, in FSCAFI, fields are not reified explicitly but only exist at the semantic level.

4.2   Programming Examples

When thinking at field programs, one can adopt two useful viewpoints: the *local* viewpoint, typically useful when reasoning about low-level aspects of field computations, which considers a field expression as the computation carried on by a specific individual device; and the *global* viewpoint, typically more useful when focussing on higher-level composition of field computations, which regards a specification at the aggregate level, as a whole spatio-temporal computation evolving a field. So, an expression (e.g., 1+3 of type Int) can represent the outcome of execution of a computation locally (4), or globally as the program producing a field (a field of 4s). Note, however, that the global field is not accessed computationally: a local computation will only access a *neighbouring* field (which is actually a *view*, given by the messages received from neighbours, of the actual, asynchronously evolving field).

In the following, we incrementally describe the constructs introduced in Sect. 3 and the design of higher-level building blocks of collective adaptive behaviour through examples. In SCAFI, a usual literal such as, for instance, tuple

```
("hello", 7.7, true)
```

is to be seen as a *constant* (i.e., not changing over time) and *uniform* (i.e., not changing across space) field holding the corresponding local value at any point of the space-time domain. By analogy, an expression such as

```
1 + 2
```

denotes a global expression where a field of 1s and a field of 2s are summed together through the field operator +, which works like a point-wise application of its local counterpart. Indeed, literal + can also be thought of as representing a constant, uniform field of (binary) functions, and function application can be viewed as a global operation that applies a function field to its argument fields.

A constant field does not need to be uniform. For instance, given a static network of devices, then

```
mid()
```

denotes the field of device identifiers, which does not change across time but does vary in space. On the other hand, expression

```
sense[Double]("temperature") // type can be omitted if can be inferred
```

is used to represent a field of temperatures (as obtained by collectively querying the local temperature sensors over space and time), which is in general non-constant and non-uniform.

Fields changing over time can also be programmatically defined by the rep operator; for instance, expression

```
// Initially 0; state is incremented at each round
rep(0){ x => x + 1 } // Equally expressed in Scala as: rep(0)(_ + 1)
```

counts how many rounds each device has executed: it is still a non-uniform field since the update phase and frequency of the devices may vary both between devices and across time for a given device.

Folding can be used to trigger the important concept of neighbour-dependent expression. As a simple initial example, expression

```
foldhood(0) (_ + _) { 1 }
```

counts the number of neighbours at each device (possibly changing over time if the network topology is dynamic). Note that folding collects the result of the evaluation of 1 against all neighbours, which simply yields 1, so the effect is merely the addition of 1 for each existing neighbour.

The key way to define truly neighbour-dependent expressions is by the nbr construct, which enables to "look around" just one step beyond a given locality. Expression

```
foldhood(0) (_+_) {nbr{sense[Double]("temperature")}} / foldhood(0)(_+_){1}
```

evaluates to the field of average temperature that each device can perceive in its neighbourhood. The numerator sums temperatures sensed by neighbours (or, analogously, it sums the neighbour evaluation of the temperature sensor query expression), while the denominator counts neighbours as described above. As another example, the following expression denotes a Boolean field of warnings:

```
val warningTh: Double = 42.0 // temperature threshold for warning
foldhood(false) (_ || _) { nbr { sense[Double]("temperature") } > warningTh }
```

This is locally true if any neighbour perceives a temperature higher than some topical threshold. Notice that by moving the comparison into the nbr block,

```
foldhood(false) (_ || _) { nbr { sense[Double]("temperature") > warningTh } }
```

then the decision about the threshold (i.e., the responsibility of determining when a temperature is dangerous) is transferred to the neighbours, and hence warnings get blindly extended by 1-hop. Of course, provided warningTh is uniform, the result would be the same in this case.

Functions can be defined to capture and give a name to common field computation idioms, patterns, and domain-specific operations. For instance, by assuming a mux function that implements a strictly-evaluated version of if:

```
def mux[A, B<:A, C<:A] (cond: Boolean) (th: B) (el: C) : A = if(cond) th else el
```

A variation of foldhood, called foldhoodPlus[5], which does not take "self" (the current device) into account, can be implemented as follows:

```
def foldhoodPlus[A] (init: => A) (aggr: (A, A) => A) (expr: => A) : A =
  foldhood(init) (aggr) (mux(mid==nbr{mid}){ init }{ expr })
```

Notice that the identity init is used when considering a neighbour device whose identifier (nbr{mid}) is the same as that of the current device (mid). As another example, one can give a label to particular sensor queries, such as:

---

[5] The "Plus" suffix is to mimic the mathematical syntax R^+ of the transitive closure of a (neighbouring) relation R.

```
def temperature = sense[Double]("temperature")
def nbrRange = nbrvar[Double]("nbr-range")
```

The second case uses construct nbrvar, which is a neighbouring sensor query operator providing, for each device, a sensor value for each corresponding neighbour: e.g., for nbrRange, the output value is a floating-point number expressing the estimation of the distance from the currently executing device to that neighbour—so, it is usually adopted as a metric for "spatial algorithms". Based on the above basic expressions, one can define a rather versatile and reusable building block of Aggregate Programming, called *gradient* [37–39]. A gradient (see Figure 2) is a numerical field expressing the minimum distance (according to a certain metric) from any device to source devices; it is also interpretable as a surface whose "slope" is directed towards a given source. In ScAFI, it can be programmed as follows:

```
def gradient(source: Boolean, metric: () => Double = nbrRange): Double =
  rep(Double.PositiveInfinity){ distance =>
    mux(source) { 0.0 }{
      foldhoodPlus(Double.PositiveInfinity)
                  (Math.min(_,_)) { nbr{distance} + metric }
  } }
```

The rep construct allows one to keep track of the distances across rounds of computations: source devices are at a null distance from themselves, and the other devices take the minimum value among those of neighbours increased by the corresponding estimated distances as given by metric—defaulting to nbrRange. Notice that foldhoodPlus (i.e., a version of foldhood that does not consider the device itself) must be used to prevent devices from getting stuck to low values because of self-messages (as it would happen when a source node gets deactivated): with it, gradients dynamically adapt to changes in network topology or position/number of sources, i.e., it is self-stabilising [11].

Another key operation on fields is splitting computation into completely separate parts or sub-computations executed in isolated space-time regions. An example is computing a gradient in a space that includes obstacle nodes so that gradient slopes circumvent the obstacles. The solution to the problem needs to leverage aggregate functions, and their ability of acting as units of alignment. That is, we can use a different aggregate function for normal and obstacle nodes:

```
(mux(isObstacle){ () => @@{ Double.PositiveInfinity } }
                { () => @@{ gradient(isSource) } }
)()
```

Calling such functions effectively restricts the domain to the set of devices executing them, thanks to the space-time branching enacted by construct @@ wrapping *the bodies* of the corresponding literal functions; by calling them exclusively in any device, the system gets partitioned into two sub-systems, each one exe-

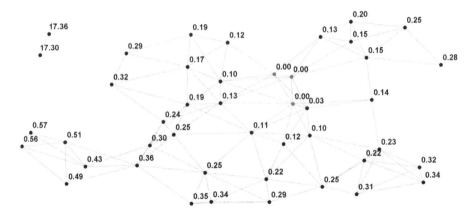

Fig. 2. Snapshot of a gradient field from a simulation in SCAFI. The red nodes are the sources of the gradient. The nodes at the top-left have parted from the network and their values increase unboundly. The gray lines represent device connectivity according to a proximity-based neighbouring relationship.

cuting a different sub-computation. For convenience, SCAFI provides as built-in function, called branch, defined as:

```
def branch[A](cond: => Boolean)(th: => A)(el: => A): A =
  mux(cond)(() => @@{ th })(() => @@{ el })()
```

With it, a gradient overcoming an obstacle is properly written as

```
branch(isObstacle){ Double.PositiveInfinity }{ gradient(isSource) } // correct
```

which is cleaner and hides some complexity while better communicating the intent: branching computation. Generally, notation @@ has to be used for bodies of literal functions that include aggregate behaviour, i.e., functions which (directly or indirectly) call methods of the Constructs trait—other uses have no effects on the result of computation. We remark that the above field calculus expression (gradient avoiding obstacles) effectively creates a distributed data structure that is rigorously self-adaptive [11]: independently of the shape and dynamics of obstacle area(s), source area(s), metric and network structure, it will continuously bring about formation of the correct gradient, until eventually stabilising to it. For instance, it could be used in a wireless sensor network scenario to let devices equipped with sensors transmit local perception on a hop-by-hop basis until all information reaches the gradient source. Generally, gradients can be used as building block for more complex behaviour, to which the self-adaption properties will be transferred, by simple functional composition.

An example of more complex behaviour is the *self-healing channel* [40], i.e., the field of Booleans that self-stabilises to a true value in the devices belonging to the minimal path connecting source with target devices. This functionality can be implemented as follows:

```
def channel(source: Boolean, target: Boolean, width: Double): Boolean =
  gradient(source) + gradient(target) <=
    distanceBetween(source, target) + width
```

i.e., by applying the triangle inequality property (with some tolerance as captured by parameter width), and exploiting a block distanceBetween that calculates the distance between source and target (e.g., using a gradient) and broadcasts that value to the whole network (e.g., by gossiping or along another gradient).

5   Conclusion and Future Work

Aggregate Computing is a recent paradigm for "holistically" engineering CASs and smart situated ecosystems, which aims to exploit, both functionally and operationally, the increasing computational capabilities of our environments—as fostered by driver scenarios like IoT, CPS, and smart cities. It formally builds on computational fields and corresponding calculi to functionally compose macro behavioural specifications that capture, in a declarative way, the adaptive logic for turning local activity into global, resilient behaviour. In this paper, we have introduced FSCAFI, a core calculus that captures the essential features of SCAFI, a recently developed Scala-internal aggregate programming DSL. In particular, it leverages a novel notion of "computation against a neighbour" which enabled seamless integration in the Scala language and type system.

In future work, we will formalise the FSCAFI semantics (informally sketched in this paper), its properties, and relation with the field calculus—mainly aimed at proving analogous properties such as those in [10,11,41,42]. Additionally, work on SCAFI is part of the research agenda for Aggregate Computing as comprehensively covered in [3], which includes the study of dynamic field computations, or aggregate processes [25] as well as the design and implementation of aggregate computing runtime platforms [13,14]. Together, they could lead to the emergence of a new platform for large-scale distributed systems deployment over phyisical environments (such as the IoT), whereby distributed computations can be dynamically injected, executed in a distributed way, and cooperate and compete with each other to realise an ecosystem of adaptive services—developing on the the vision of, e.g., [43].

References

1. Anderson, S., Bredeche, N., Eiben, A., Kampis, G., van Steen, M.: Adaptive collective systems: herding black sheep (2013)
2. Beal, J., Pianini, D., Viroli, M.: Aggregate programming for the Internet of Things. IEEE Comput. **48**(9), 22–30 (2015)
3. Viroli, M., Beal, J., Damiani, F., Audrito, G., Casadei, R., Pianini, D.: From distributed coordination to field calculus and aggregate computing. J. Logical Algebraic Methods Program. **109**, 100486 (2019). https://doi.org/10.1016/j.jlamp.2019.100486

4. Beal, J., Dulman, S., Usbeck, K., Viroli, M., Correll, N.: Organizing the aggregate: languages for spatial computing. In: Mernik, M. (ed.) Formal and Practical Aspects of Domain-Specific Languages: Recent Developments, chap. 16, pp. 436–501. IGI Global (2013). https://doi.org/10.4018/978-1-4666-2092-6.ch016
5. Audrito, G., Viroli, M., Damiani, F., Pianini, D., Beal, J.: A higher-order calculus of computational fields. ACM Trans. Comput. Logic **20**(1), 5:1–5:55 (2019). https://doi.org/10.1145/3285956
6. Beal, J., Bachrach, J.: Infrastructure for engineered emergence in sensor/actuator networks. IEEE Intell. Syst. **21**, 10–19 (2006)
7. Mamei, M., Zambonelli, F.: Programming pervasive and mobile computing applications: the TOTA approach. ACM Trans. Softw. Eng. Methodol. **18**(4), 1–56 (2009). https://doi.org/10.1145/1538942.1538945
8. Casadei, R., Pianini, D., Viroli, M.: Simulating large-scale aggregate MASs with alchemist and scala. In: 2016 Federated Conference on Computer Science and Information Systems (FedCSIS), pp. 1495–1504. IEEE (2016)
9. Pianini, D., Viroli, M., Beal, J.: Protelis: practical aggregate programming. In: 2015 ACM Symposium on Applied Computing, pp. 1846–1853 (2015)
10. Beal, J., Viroli, M., Pianini, D., Damiani, F.: Self-adaptation to device distribution in the Internet of Things. ACM Trans. Auton. Adapt. Syst. **12**(3), 12:1–12:29 (2017). https://doi.org/10.1145/3105758
11. Viroli, M., Audrito, G., Beal, J., Damiani, F., Pianini, D.: Engineering resilient collective adaptive systems by self-stabilisation. ACM Trans. Model. Comput. Simul. **28**(2), 16:1–16:28 (2018). https://doi.org/10.1145/3177774
12. Voelter, M.: DSL Engineering: Designing, Implementing and Using Domain-Specific Languages. CreateSpace Independent Publishing Platform, Scotts Valley (2013)
13. Viroli, M., Casadei, R., Pianini, D.: On execution platforms for large-scale aggregate computing. In: Proceedings of the 2016 ACM International Joint Conference on Pervasive and Ubiquitous Computing: Adjunct, pp. 1321–1326. ACM (2016)
14. Casadei, R., Viroli, M.: Programming actor-based collective adaptive systems. In: Ricci, A., Haller, P. (eds.) Programming with Actors. LNCS, vol. 10789, pp. 94–122. Springer, Cham (2018). https://doi.org/10.1007/978-3-030-00302-9_4
15. Bettini, L.: Implementing Domain-Specific Languages with Xtext and Xtend. Packt, Birmingham (2016)
16. Efftinge, S., et al.: Xbase: implementing domain-specific languages for Java. In: ACM SIGPLAN Notices, vol. 48, pp. 112–121. ACM (2012)
17. Vlissides, J.M.: Pattern Hatching: Design Patterns Applied. Addison-Wesley, Reading (1998)
18. Ghosh, D.: DSL for the uninitiated. Commun. ACM **54**(7), 44–50 (2011). https://doi.org/10.1145/1965724.1965740
19. Hennicker, R., Klarl, A.: Foundations for ensemble modeling – the HELENA approach. In: Iida, S., Meseguer, J., Ogata, K. (eds.) Specification, Algebra, and Software. LNCS, vol. 8373, pp. 359–381. Springer, Heidelberg (2014). https://doi.org/10.1007/978-3-642-54624-2_18
20. Bures, T., Gerostathopoulos, I., Hnetynka, P., Keznikl, J., Kit, M., Plasil, F.: DEECO: an ensemble-based component system. In: Proceedings of the 16th International ACM Sigsoft symposium on Component-Based software engineering, pp. 81–90. ACM (2013). https://doi.org/10.1145/2465449.2465462
21. Baude, F., Henrio, L., Ruz, C.: Programming distributed and adaptable autonomous components-the GCM/ProActive framework. Softw.: Pract. Exp. **45**(9), 1189–1227 (2015). https://doi.org/10.1002/spe.2270

22. De Nicola, R., Loreti, M., Pugliese, R., Tiezzi, F.: A formal approach to autonomic systems programming: the SCEL language. ACM Trans. Auton. Adapt. Syst. (TAAS) **9**(2), 7:1–7:29 (2014). https://doi.org/10.1145/2619998
23. Alrahman, Y.A., De Nicola, R., Loreti, M., Tiezzi, F., Vigo, R.: A calculus for attribute-based communication. In: Proceedings of the 30th Annual ACM Symposium on Applied Computing, pp. 1840–1845 (2015)
24. De Nicola, R., Duong, T., Inverso, O., Trubiani, C.: AErlang: empowering erlang with attribute-based communication. Sci. Comput. Program. **168**, 71–93 (2018)
25. Casadei, R., Viroli, M., Audrito, G., Pianini, D., Damiani, F.: Aggregate processes in field calculus. In: Riis Nielson, H., Tuosto, E. (eds.) COORDINATION 2019. LNCS, vol. 11533, pp. 200–217. Springer, Cham (2019). https://doi.org/10.1007/978-3-030-22397-7_12
26. Coore, D.: Botanical computing: a developmental approach to generating interconnect topologies on an amorphous computer. Ph.D. thesis, MIT (1999)
27. Nagpal, R.: Programmable pattern-formation and scale-independence. In: Minai, A.A., Bar-Yam, Y. (eds.) Unifying Themes in Complex Systems IV, pp. 275–282. Springer, Heidelberg (2008). https://doi.org/10.1007/978-3-540-73849-7_31
28. Viroli, M., Pianini, D., Beal, J.: Linda in space-time: an adaptive coordination model for mobile ad-hoc environments. In: Sirjani, M. (ed.) COORDINATION 2012. LNCS, vol. 7274, pp. 212–229. Springer, Heidelberg (2012). https://doi.org/10.1007/978-3-642-30829-1_15
29. Mottola, L., Picco, G.P.: Logical neighborhoods: a programming abstraction for wireless sensor networks. In: Gibbons, P.B., Abdelzaher, T., Aspnes, J., Rao, R. (eds.) DCOSS 2006. LNCS, vol. 4026, pp. 150–168. Springer, Heidelberg (2006). https://doi.org/10.1007/11776178_10
30. Ni, Y., Kremer, U., Stere, A., Iftode, L.: Programming ad-hoc networks of mobile and resource-constrained devices. ACM SIGPLAN Not. **40**(6), 249–260 (2005)
31. Wada, H., Boonma, P., Suzuki, J.: A spacetime oriented macroprogramming paradigm for push-pull hybrid sensor networking. In: 2007 16th International Conference on Computer Communications and Networks, pp. 868–875. IEEE (2007)
32. Newton, R., Welsh, M.: Region streams: functional macroprogramming for sensor networks. In: Workshop on Data Management for Sensor Networks, pp. 78–87 (2004)
33. Engstrom, B.R., Cappello, P.R.: The SDEF programming system. J. Parallel Distrib. Comput. **7**(2), 201–231 (1989)
34. Giavitto, J.-L., Michel, O., Cohen, J., Spicher, A.: Computations in space and space in computations. In: Banâtre, J.-P., Fradet, P., Giavitto, J.-L., Michel, O. (eds.) UPP 2004. LNCS, vol. 3566, pp. 137–152. Springer, Heidelberg (2005). https://doi.org/10.1007/11527800_11
35. Igarashi, A., Pierce, B.C., Wadler, P.: Featherweight Java: a minimal core calculus for Java and GJ. ACM Trans. Program. Lang. Syst. **23**(3), 396–450 (2001)
36. Audrito, G., Damiani, F., Viroli, M., Casadei, R.: Run-time management of computation domains in field calculus. In: IEEE International Workshops on Foundations and Applications of Self* Systems, pp. 192–197. IEEE (2016). https://doi.org/10.1109/FAS-W.2016.50
37. Lin, F.C.H., Keller, R.M.: The gradient model load balancing method. IEEE Trans. Softw. Eng. **13**(1), 32–38 (1987). https://doi.org/10.1109/TSE.1987.232563
38. Beal, J., Bachrach, J., Vickery, D., Tobenkin, M.: Fast self-healing gradients. In: 2008 Proceedings of ACM SAC, pp. 1969–1975. ACM (2008)

39. Audrito, G., Casadei, R., Damiani, F., Viroli, M.: Compositional blocks for optimal self-healing gradients. In: 11th IEEE International Conference on Self-Adaptive and Self-Organizing Systems, SASO, pp. 91–100. IEEE Computer Society (2017). https://doi.org/10.1109/SASO.2017.18

40. Viroli, M., Beal, J., Damiani, F., Pianini, D.: Efficient engineering of complex self-organising systems by self-stabilising fields. In: 2015 IEEE 9th International Conference on Self-Adaptive and Self-Organizing Systems (SASO), pp. 81–90. IEEE, September 2015. https://doi.org/10.1109/SASO.2015.16

41. Damiani, F., Viroli, M.: Type-based self-stabilisation for computational fields. Logical Methods Comput. Sci. **11**(4) (2015). https://doi.org/10.2168/LMCS-11(4: 21)2015

42. Audrito, G., Beal, J., Damiani, F., Viroli, M.: Space-time universality of field calculus. In: Di Marzo Serugendo, G., Loreti, M. (eds.) COORDINATION 2018. LNCS, vol. 10852, pp. 1–20. Springer, Cham (2018). https://doi.org/10.1007/978-3-319-92408-3_1

43. Montagna, S., Viroli, M., Fernandez-Marquez, J.L., Di Marzo Serugendo, G., Zambonelli, F.: Injecting self-organisation into pervasive service ecosystems. Mobile Netw. Appl. **18**(3), 398–412 (2013). https://doi.org/10.1007/s11036-012-0411-1

Writing Robotics Applications
with X-Klaim

Lorenzo Bettini[1](✉) ⓘ, Khalid Bourr[2](✉), Rosario Pugliese[1](✉) ⓘ,
and Francesco Tiezzi[2](✉) ⓘ

[1] Dipartimento di Statistica, Informatica, Applicazioni,
Università degli Studi di Firenze, Florence, Italy
{lorenzo.bettini,rosario.pugliese}@unifi.it
[2] School of Science and Technology, Computer Science Division,
Università di Camerino, Camerino, Italy
{khalid.bourr,francesco.tiezzi}@unicam.it

Abstract. Developing robotics applications is a demanding software engineering challenge. Such a software has to perform multiple cooperating tasks in a well-coordinated manner in order to avoid unsatisfactory behavior. In this paper, we define an approach for developing robot software based on the integration of the programming language X-Klaim and the popular robotics framework ROS. X-Klaim is a programming language specifically devised to design distributed applications consisting of software components interacting through multiple distributed tuple spaces. Advantages of using X-Klaim in the robotics domain derive from its high abstraction level, that allows developers to focus on robots' behavior, and from its computation and communication model, which is especially suitable for dealing with the distributed nature of robots' architecture. We show the feasibility and the effectiveness of the proposed approach by implementing a scenario involving a robot looking for potential victims in a disaster area.

Keywords: Robotics applications · X-Klaim · Tuple spaces · ROS

1   Introduction

Autonomous robots are versatile machines increasingly used in many fields in today's society, while their capabilities are becoming ever more complex and heterogeneous. They are software-intensive systems, whose software components are typically deployed on a distributed and heterogeneous computing infrastructure, possibly with limited resources. Such software components interact in real-time with a highly dynamic and uncertain environment through sensors and actuators.

Developing robotics applications is currently among the most demanding software engineering challenges [12,14,18,23]. Indeed, such a software has to

The work was supported by the PRIN project "SEDUCE" n. 2017TWRCNB.

T. Margaria and B. Steffen (Eds.): ISoLA 2020, LNCS 12477, pp. 361–379, 2020.
https://doi.org/10.1007/978-3-030-61470-6_22

perform the multiple cooperating tasks in a well-coordinated manner in order to avoid unsatisfactory behavior that can even cause economic losses and threaten safety. Moreover, since low-level details must be considered in the early phases, robotic experts need very good programming skills or the help of programming experts. In general, expertise from multiple domains needs to be integrated conceptually and technically. Finally, robotic software is difficult to adapt to hardware changes.

In the last few years, a variety of software libraries and middlewares have been specifically developed by different research laboratories and universities to assist and simplify the rapid prototyping of robotic applications. They offer mechanisms for, e.g., real-time control, synchronous and asynchronous communication, abstract access to sensors and actuators. Many researchers have also proposed using higher-level abstractions to drive the software development process and then resorting to some tools for automatic generation of executable code and system configuration files. This permits hiding the lower-level programming details to robotic experts and helping them to focus on their own field of expertise rather than on implementation. The use of a suitably abstract level also supports better maintainability and reusability of software components, and reduces the effort in understanding and modifying the software. Many proposals in the literature are surveyed in [23]. We mention the domain-specific language RobotML [14], enabling to describe robotics concerns with concepts and notations closer to the respective problem domain and to automate code generation. We also mention the prototype framework CommonLang [26], exploiting model-driven software engineering techniques to abstract away from underlying technologies and create executable code for different robotics platforms using code generation.

Along this direction, in this paper we propose an approach for developing robotics applications based on the integration of the programming language X-KLAIM, and its effective Eclipse-based IDE, with the ROS middleware.

X-KLAIM[1] (eXtended KLAIM, originally introduced in [6] and reimplemented from scratch in [8]) is based on the coordination language KLAIM [13] specifically devised to design distributed applications consisting of (possibly mobile) software components interacting through multiple distributed tuple spaces. X-KLAIM code is compiled into Java code and executed on a standard JVM. Because of its specific features, we envisage possible exploitation of the renewed X-KLAIM as a coordination language for developing modern ICT systems, in such domains as robotics, IoT, Smart Cities, e-Health, etc. As a language, X-KLAIM provides a high level of abstraction, allowing developers to focus on robots' behavior while abstracting from technical details (e.g., the low-level commands sent to robots' actuators and the management of events and data coming from robots' sensors). Moreover, as argued below, X-KLAIM features many advantages for different kinds of software architectures used in robotics systems [20]. Its computation and communication model, inherited from KLAIM, is particularly suitable for dealing with the distributed nature of robots architecture, where the components

---

[1] https://github.com/LorenzoBettini/xklaim.

(e.g. actuators and sensors) execute concurrently. Indeed, the X-KLAIM computation model permits to distribute an application across multiple threads of execution or even multiple hardware platforms. Each application component may have its own *tuple space*, that is a repository for storing *anonymous* data and *associatively* retrieving them by means of a pattern-matching mechanism. Application components communicate by means of their distributed tuple spaces, where all data are stored and accessed by the components that are responsible for performing specific tasks. This model features ease of implementation and low computational overhead. It ensures that components can operate *independently*, and gather *asynchronously* the required data by accessing it from a tuple space, without having to communicate directly with each other. If necessary, the same data can be read by multiple components, without the need to replicate them. Appropriate synchronizations among the application components can be implemented still through the tuple spaces. By exchanging request and response messages through the tuple spaces, a component can also act as a service that replies with a response message once another component sends a request message.

ROS[2] (Robot Operating System [24]) is a well-known set of software libraries and tools to build robotics applications. Since X-KLAIM code is compiled into Java and can interact with any existing Java library, we make use of *java_rosbridge*[3] to connect the code generated from an X-KLAIM program with the ROS server that enacts the publish/subscribe interactions of ROS components. This allows us to use X-KLAIM only for writing the code that controls the robot's behavior in a compact and readable way. We also abstract the typical robot behaviors, described at ROS level by large pieces of code. Our framework can be thought of as a proof-of-concept implementation for experimenting with the applicability of the tuple space-based paradigm to robotics applications. For illustrating the proposed approach, we consider a simple disaster scenario. To show the execution of the generated code we use Gazebo[4], an open-source simulator of robot behaviors in complex environments that is based on a robust physics engine and provides a high-quality 3D visualization of simulations.

The rest of the paper is organized as follows. In Sect. 2, we provide some background notions concerning the languages and the technologies at the basis of our approach, while in Sect. 3 we present our approach. In Sect. 4 we (partially) illustrate the implementation of a simple robotics scenario according to the proposed approach. In Sect. 5 we discuss more strictly related work, while in Sect. 6 we conclude and touch upon directions for future work.

---

[2] https://www.ros.org/.
[3] https://github.com/h2r/java_rosbridge.
[4] http://gazebosim.org/.

2   Background Notions

In this section, we briefly summarize some background notions concerning the languages and the technologies at the basis of our approach. We refer the interested reader to the referred sources for a full account of each of them.

2.1   KLAIM

KLAIM (Kernel Language for Agents Interaction and Mobility, [13]) is a formal language specially devised to design distributed applications consisting of (possibly mobile) software components deployed over the nodes of a network infrastructure. Although KLAIM is based on process algebras [22], it builds on the notion of *generative communication* introduced by the coordination language Linda [19] and generalizes it to multiple distributed tuple spaces. A *tuple space* is a shared data repository consisting of a multiset of tuples. *Tuples* are *anonymous* sequences of data items that are associatively retrieved from tuple spaces by means of a *pattern-matching* mechanism. Interprocess communication occurs through *asynchronous* exchange of tuples via tuple spaces: processes can indeed *insert, read* and *withdraw* tuples into/from tuple spaces. Communicating processes are thus decoupled both in space and time as there is no need for producers (i.e., senders) and consumers (i.e., receivers) of a tuple to synchronize. Tuple spaces are identified by means of *localities*, that are symbolic addresses of network nodes where processes and tuples can be allocated. Localities can be exchanged through interprocess communication. They provide the naming mechanism to represent the notion of administrative domain: computations at a given locality are under the control of a specific authority.

A computational *node* of a KLAIM network is characterized by its locality and a collection of running processes.[5] *Processes*, i.e., the active computational units of KLAIM, can be executed concurrently, either at the same locality or at different localities. They are built up by composing basic actions acting on network nodes, process variables and process calls, either sequentially or in parallel. Process variables support *higher-order communication*, namely the capability to exchange (the code of) a process and possibly execute it. Recursive behaviors are modeled via calls to process definitions.

Figure 1 depicts a generic KLAIM node and the basic *actions* which processes are made of. In these actions, processes can use the distinguished locality self to refer to their current hosting node. Action **out**(tuple)@nodeLocality adds the tuple resulting from the evaluation of the argument tuple to the tuple space of the target node identified by the (possibly remote) locality nodeLocality. A tuple is a sequence of actual fields, i.e., expressions, localities, or pro-

---

[5] For the sake of presentation, we omit from the description of KLAIM nodes the distinction between physical and logical localities and, hence, the so called *allocation environment*. The latter is a component of a node that acts as a name solver binding logical localities, occurring in the processes hosted in the node, to specific physical localities.

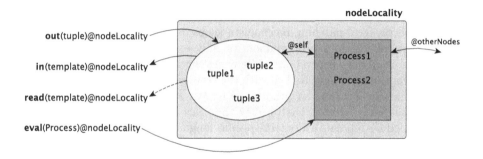

Fig. 1. A KLAIM node.

cesses. In general, any of these fields can contain variables. Instead, an evaluated tuple must not contain variables. Thus, tuple evaluation only succeeds when a tuple does not contain variables and amounts to computing the values of the expressions occurring in the tuple. Action **in**(template)@nodeLocality (resp. **read**(template)@nodeLocality) withdraws (resp. reads) tuples from the tuple space hosted at the (possibly remote) locality nodeLocality. If matching tuples are found, one is non-deterministically chosen, otherwise, the process is blocked. These retrieval actions exploit templates as patterns to select tuples in a tuple space. *Templates* are sequences of *actual* and *formal* fields, where the latter are used to bind variables to values, localities, or processes. Templates must be evaluated before they can be used for retrieving tuples. Their evaluation is like that of tuples, where formal fields are left unchanged by the evaluation. Intuitively, an evaluated template matches against an evaluated tuple if both have the same number of fields and corresponding fields do match; two values/localities match only if they are identical, while formal fields match any value of the same type. A successful matching returns a substitution function mapping the variables contained in the formal fields of the template to the values contained in the corresponding actual fields of the accessed tuple. Such a substitution is then applied to the process syntactically following the action. Action **eval**(Process)@nodeLocality sends Process for execution to the (possibly remote) node identified by nodeLocality. Finally, KLAIM also provides an action for creating new network nodes, but we do not present it here as it is not exploited in the paper.

2.2   KLAVA and X-KLAIM

The implementation of KLAIM basically consists of two main components:

- the Java package KLAVA (KLAIM in Java, originally introduced in [4]);
- the programming language X-KLAIM.

KLAVA provides the implementation of the KLAIM tuple space operations and concepts (such as *nodes*, *nets*, *processes*, etc.) in terms of classes and methods, relying on the IMC framework [3] for the communication infrastructure.

Any Java object can be stored into and retrieved from a KLAVA tuple and the implemented pattern matching mechanism keeps Java subtyping into consideration. KLAVA allows Java programmers to fully exploit Java mechanisms and the libraries of its huge ecosystem, while using the KLAIM programming model. However, programmers have to deal with the verbosity of Java, which also makes it hard to directly use KLAIM primitives. KLAVA strives for making Java programmers' life easier, but it has to obey the rules of Java. For this reason, we also developed X-KLAIM, a domain-specific language that is closer to KLAIM while providing typical high-level programming constructs. The X-KLAIM compiler translates X-KLAIM programs into Java code that uses the Java package KLAVA. The produced Java code can be then compiled and executed using the standard Java toolchain.

The versions of X-KLAIM and KLAVA used in this paper are available as an open source project. Sources and links to Eclipse update site and to complete Eclipse distributions are available from: https://github.com/LorenzoBettini/xklaim.

For the new implementation of X-KLAIM we relied on XTEXT [5], an Eclipse framework for the development of programming languages and DSLs. XTEXT also provides a complete IDE support based on Eclipse: editor with syntax highlighting, code completion, error reporting and incremental building, just to mention a few. Furthermore, we made use of another mechanism provided by XTEXT, that is, XBASE [17], an extensible and reusable expression language. By using XBASE in X-KLAIM, besides a rich Java-like syntax, we also inherit its interoperability with Java and its type system. In fact, an X-KLAIM program can seamlessly access any Java type and Java library available in the classpath of the project. The interoperability with Java allowed us to seamlessly integrate X-KLAIM with *java_rosbridge*.

The syntax of XBASE is similar to Java, thus it should be easily understood by Java programmers, but it removes much "syntactic noise" from Java. For example, terminating semicolons are optional, as well as other syntax elements like parenthesis when invoking a method without arguments. Moreover, XBASE comes with a powerful type inference mechanism, compliant with the Java type system: the programmer can avoid specifying types in declarations when they can be inferred from the context. The X-KLAIM compiler is completely integrated into Eclipse: typical IDE mechanisms like content assist and code navigation are available in the X-KLAIM editor. The same holds for the automatic building mechanisms of Eclipse: saving an X-KLAIM file automatically triggers the Java code generation, which in turns triggers the generation of Java byte-code. Notably, the X-KLAIM integration in Eclipse, allows the programmer to debug an X-KLAIM program.

In the rest of this section we briefly describe the main features of X-KLAIM that are relevant for this paper. Thus, for example, we will not describe code mobility features, as they are not used in this paper (the interested reader is referred to [8] for more details).

An X-KLAIM program can contain process, node and net definitions. All these components can also be defined in separate files and can be referred through a Java-like *import* mechanism.[6]

A *process* definition consists of a name, a list of parameters (using the Java syntax for declaring parameters) and a body:

proc aProcess(... parameters ...) { ... body ... }

The body consists of XBASE expressions, whose syntax has been extended with KLAIM operations (that we will show in Sect. 4). Typical programming structures such as if, while and OOP Java-like mechanisms, such as object creation and method invocation, are already part of XBASE.

An X-KLAIM network definition consists of *net* and *node* definitions as shown in the following example:

net ANet {
    node Node1 { ... start code ... }
    node Node2 { ... start code ... }
    ...
}

In particular, the name of a node also represents its locality within the network. Each node can specify some initialization code for creating and running a few processes, as we will see in the example of Sect. 4. This is the simplest way of specifying a *flat* network. X-KLAIM also implements the hierarchical version of the KLAIM model as presented in [7], but we will not use it in this paper.

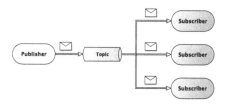

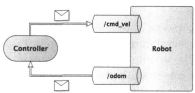

Fig. 2. ROS publish/subscribe mechanism.

Fig. 3. Interaction with ROS robot.

2.3 ROS

Robotic Operating System (ROS)[7] is one of the most sophisticated and popular frameworks for writing robot software. It provides tools and libraries for simplifying the development of complex and robust robot controllers while abstracting from the underlying hardware. ROS works with more than a hundred robots,

---

[6] Code completion is provided in the X-KLAIM Eclipse editor for imports as well as standard "Organize imports" mechanisms.

[7] https://www.ros.org/.

ranging from autonomous cars to drones and humanoid robots, and integrates a multitude of sensors.

The core element of the ROS framework is the message-passing middleware, which enables hardware abstraction for a wide variety of robotic platforms. The processes of a robotics application can exchange data, being agnostic with respect to the source of the data. The communicated data can be sensor readings or actuator commands, formatted in a standardized way, produced by or directed to robot's devices.

Although ROS supports different communication mechanisms, in this paper we only use the most common one: the anonymous and asynchronous publish/-subscribe mechanism. For sending a message, a process has to publish it in a *topic*, which is a named and typed bus. A process that is interested in such message has to subscribe to the topic. Whenever a new message is published in the topic, the subscriber will be notified. This decouples the production of data from its consumption. Multiple publishers and subscribers for the same topic are allowed. The diagram in Fig. 2 illustrates this concept, while the one in Fig. 3 shows how a robot controller interacts with the devices of a mobile robot in a black-box, hardware-independent fashion. In the latter diagram, the controller acts as both publisher and subscriber: it sends a message directed to the wheels actuator and receives back a message containing the position the robot has moved to. The topic `/cmd_vel` stands for *command velocity*. The topic `/odom` stands for *odometry*, the technique used to estimate the change in position over time from robot sensors data.

3   Our Approach and Framework

In this section we illustrate our approach, and the resulting software framework, for programming robotics applications using X-KLAIM and ROS.

The architecture of autonomous robots has a distributed nature, as it typically consists of different components, in particular sensors and actuators, that cooperate with each other making use of a communication infrastructure. Their software architecture reflects such a distribution and partitions the robot's software into parts, with specific relationships among them, working together as a coherent whole. Robot components are thus managed by specialized processes that may need to work on local data and can demand dedicated machines for their execution.

This distributed architecture of the robot's software is naturally rendered in X-KLAIM as a network where the different parts are deployed. As depicted in Fig. 4, we typically have a controller node and several sensor and actuator nodes. The latter nodes are not fixed once and for all. Rather, they can be dynamically added or removed, and even equipped with different processes, in order to represent different robot types and configurations. To concretely program with the X-KLAIM language the behaviors of robots, we have integrated it with the ROS middleware. The communication infrastructure of the integrated framework is graphically depicted in Fig. 5.

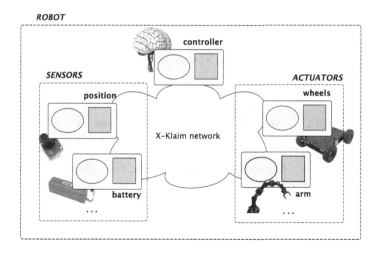

Fig. 4. Software architecture of robots in X-KLAIM.

Specifically, X-KLAIM applications are indirectly connected with the ROS framework by means of the Java library *java_rosbridge*. It provides Java objects supporting publishing and subscribing over ROS topics. In its own turn, *java_rosbridge* communicates with the ROS Bridge server, via the WebSocket protocol, by means of the Jetty web server.[8] The ROS Bridge server, indeed, provides via WebSocket a JSON API to ROS functionality for external programs. This way, ROS receives and executes commands on the physical robot, and gives feedback and sensor data. In addition, ROS can optionally interact with the Gazebo simulator,[9] via the ROS commutation mechanism (e.g., by launching the simulator as a ROS node). The use of the simulator is not mandatory when ROS is deployed in a real robot; however, even in such a case, the

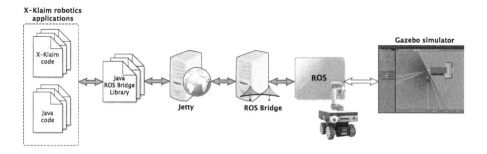

Fig. 5. The integrated framework.

---

[8] Jetty 9: https://www.eclipse.org/jetty/.
[9] This interaction is denoted in Fig. 5 by a white arrow, to stress its optionality.

```
{ "topic": "/robot_base_velocity_controller/cmd_vel",
  "msg": {
    "linear": { "x": 0.0013, "y": 0.0, "z": 0.0 },
    "angular": { "x": 0.0, "y": 0.0, "z": 0.0029 }
  }
}
```

Fig. 6. Example of a JSON message for the /cmd_vel topic.

design activity of the robot's controller may benefit from the use of a simulator, to save time and reduce the development cost.

A crucial role in the framework described above is played by JSON messages. Indeed, the use of JSON enables the interoperability of ROS with most programming languages, including Java. As an example, we report in Fig. 6 a Twist message in the JSON format published on the ROS topic /cmd_vel, providing information for moving the robot. This message expresses the velocity in terms of its linear and angular parts, each of which defined as a vector.

4   X-Klaim at Work on a Robotics Scenario

For illustrating the proposed approach, in this section we show and briefly comment a few interesting parts of the implementation of a simple robotics scenario. The full source code can be found at https://github.com/LorenzoBettini/ xklaim-ros-example. It consists of an Eclipse/Maven project with X-Klaim code (and its generated Java code), using *java_rosbridge*.[10]

The scenario that we consider involves a robot looking for potential victims in a disaster area. By following a random walk, the robot explores an unknown, flat environment where a number of obstacles are present while avoiding collisions with them. As soon as the robot has localized a potential victim, it stops near the victim and signals its position. The robot has a limited battery lifetime and the battery's state of charge is monitored during the course of the robot's activities. If the state of charge drops under a given threshold value, then the robot stops searching for a victim and rather moves towards a charging station whose position is known to it.

In Fig. 7 we show the whole network for our implementation of the scenario. As discussed in Section 3, each part of the robot is rendered as an X-Klaim node, whose name represents its locality (see Sect. 2.2). For each node we have one or several processes that deal with the robot's sensors (e.g., PositionSensor) or with the robot's moving parts (e.g., WheelsActuator). Each node creates processes locally and executes them concurrently by means of the Klaim operation eval. We have made a few processes parametric with respect to the localities, so that they can be easily relocated to any node. This way, we could experiment with different network configurations (see also Sect. 6). The most interesting

---

[10] We 'consume' *java_rosbridge* and X-Klaim runtime libraries as Maven artifacts.

```
net RobotNet {
  node Position {
    eval(new PositionSensor())@self
  }
  node Wheels {
    eval(new WheelsActuator())@self
    eval(new GoToActuator(Position))@self
  }
  node Controller {
    eval(new RobotController(Wheels, Position, Battery, ObstacleAvoidance))@self
  }
  node Battery {
    eval(new LowBatterySensor(Controller))@self
    eval(new BatteryConsumption())@self
    eval(new BatteryCharge(Position))@self
  }
  node ObstacleAvoidance {
    eval(new LaserSensor())@self
    eval(new CalculateOrientation(Wheels))@self
  }
  node Victim {
    eval(new VictimSensor(Controller, Position))@self
  }
}
```

Fig. 7. The X-KLAIM net of our example.

process under that respect is `RobotController`, which has to deal with several robot's components and so it takes such components' localities as parameters.

The source code of the process `RobotController` is shown in Fig. 8. The code should be easily readable by a Java programmer. Such types as `Double`, `Locality` and `Random` (note the `import` statement) are actually Java types, since, as mentioned above, X-KLAIM programs can refer directly to Java types. Note also that `nextFloat` is actually the Java method of the Java class `Random`. Java static methods, like `String.format`, can be used as well; `println` is a shortcut for the standard `System.out.println`. Variable declarations in XBASE start with `val` or `var`, for final and non-final variables, respectively. The types of variables can be omitted if they can be inferred from the initialization expression. Note how XBASE removes much syntactic noise of Java. It also treats safely operators such as `==`, which, for objects like `String`, actually translates to a call `equals` in the generated Java code. Here we also see the typical KLAIM operations, `read`, `in` and `out`, acting on possibly distributed tuple spaces. Formal fields in a tuple are specified as variable declarations, since formal fields implicitly

import java.util.Random

```
proc RobotController(Locality wheels, Locality position,
              Locality battery, Locality obstacleAvoidance) {
  val rand = new Random()
  out("control step", "random walking")@self // initial control step tuple
  while (true) {
    read("control step", var String stepType)@self // read the control step tuple
    if (stepType == "random walking") {
      val angularVelocity = rand.nextFloat() * 10 − 5 // a random angular velocity
      val linearVelocity = 1.5
      out("velocity", linearVelocity, angularVelocity)@obstacleAvoidance
    } else if (stepType == "low battery") {
      read("charge station position", var Double x, var Double y)@battery
      out("go to", x, y)@wheels
      in("battery charged")@battery
      in("control step", stepType)@self
      out("control step", "random walking")@self
    } else if (stepType == "victim detected") {
      out("velocity", 0.0, 0.0)@wheels
      read("position", var Double x, var Double y, var Double anyTheta)@position
      println(String.format("victim detected at position: %f, %f", x, y))
      return
    }
  }
}
```

Fig. 8. The X-KLAIM RobotController process.

declare variables that are available in the code after **in** and **read** operations (just like in KLAIM).[11]

Besides that, the code of Fig. 8 basically relies on the KLAIM tuple space based communication. The controller first reads a local tuple containing the "type" of step to perform and acts accordingly. The 'normal' behavior consists of random walking in the working area. The controller creates the tuple indicating the velocity broken in its linear and angular part, and inserts it in the obstacle avoidance's tuple space. If the level of the robot's battery is too low, the robot goes to a charging station. The controller retrieves the charge station position, moves the robot to the charge station and waits for the completion of the charge. Then, it replaces the low battery control step with the random walking one. If a victim is found, the controller stops the movement by sending velocity 0 to the wheels actuator. It then sends the current position to the rescuers (here it simply prints out a message in the console with the position of the victim) and the process terminates. During these actions the controller communicates with other

---

[11] Non-blocking versions of **in** and **read** are also available: **in_nb** and **read_nb**, respectively.

```
import ros.*
import ros.msgs.geometry_msgs.Twist

proc WheelsActuator() {
  val bridge = new RosBridge()
  bridge.connect("ws://0.0.0.0:9090", true)
  val publisher = new Publisher(
    "/robot_base_velocity_controller/cmd_vel", "geometry_msgs/Twist", bridge)
  while (true) {
    in("velocity", var Double x, var Double z)@self
    val twistMsg = new Twist();
    twistMsg.linear.x = x
    twistMsg.angular.z = z
    publisher.publish(twistMsg);
  }
}
```

Fig. 9. The X-KLAIM `WheelsActuator` process.

parts of the robot (i.e., with the corresponding X-KLAIM processes) by means of tuples inserted into or retrieved from specific tuple spaces, whose localities are received as parameters. The localities `wheels` and `positions` correspond to the next two processes we are going to describe.

The code of the process `WheelsActuator` is shown in Fig. 9. Here we can see that X-KLAIM code can also interact with Java libraries, like *java_rosbridge*. In fact, we establish a bridge with the ROS Bridge WebSocket. In this case, we create a ROS publisher (see Sect. 2.3) and we publish `Twist` messages (as the one in Fig. 6). We do that after consuming a tuple containing the velocity data.

The code of the process `PositionSensor` is shown in Figure 10.

As before, we use the Java API provided by *java_rosbridge*. This time we subscribe for a specific topic (we refer to *java_rosbridge* documentation for the used API). The last argument is an XBASE lambda. XBASE *lambda expressions* have the shape: [`param1`, `param2`, ... | `body`]. The types of the parameters can be omitted if they can be inferred from the context. The lambda will be executed when an event for the subscribed topic is received. In particular, the lambda reads some data from the event (in JSON format) concerning "position" and "orientation", performs some computation (again, by using the standard Java library) and uses the computed information to update the tuple space. The JSON message format is dictated by ROS. On the contrary, for the tuples inserted in the tuple space, we could have also defined a Java class, e.g., `RobotPosition`, as a datatype for "position" tuples. Indeed, as explained in Section 2.2, any Java object can be inserted in a tuple.

As already discussed in Sect. 3, the execution of an X-KLAIM robotics application requires the ROS Bridge server to run, providing a WebSocket connection at a given URI. In the code of our example application, we consider the ROS Bridge server running on the local machine (0.0.0.0) at the port 9090. Similarly,

```
proc PositionSensor() {
    val bridge = new RosBridge()
    bridge.connect("ws://0.0.0.0:9090", true)
    out("position", 5.0, 4.5, 0.0)@self // initial position and orientation tuple
    bridge.subscribe( // Subscribe to the Pose topic of the robot
        SubscriptionRequestMsg.generate("/robot_base_velocity_controller/odom")
            .setType("nav_msgs/Odometry").setThrottleRate(1).setQueueLength(1),
        [ data, stringRep |
            val pose = data.get("msg").get("pose").get("pose")
            val position = pose.get("position")
            val x = position.get("x").asDouble()
            val y = position.get("y").asDouble()
            val orientation = pose.get("orientation")
            val qx = orientation.get("x").asDouble()
            val qy = orientation.get("y").asDouble()
            val qz = orientation.get("z").asDouble()
            val qw = orientation.get("w").asDouble()
            val siny_cosp = 2 * (qw * qz + qx * qy)
            val cosy_cosp = 1 − 2 * (qy * qy + qz * qz)
            val theta = Math.atan2(siny_cosp, cosy_cosp)
            in("position", var Double anyX, var Double anyY, var Double anyTheta)@self
            out("position", x, y, theta)@self
        ])
}
```

Fig. 10. The X-KLAIM `PositionSensor` process (imports are omitted).

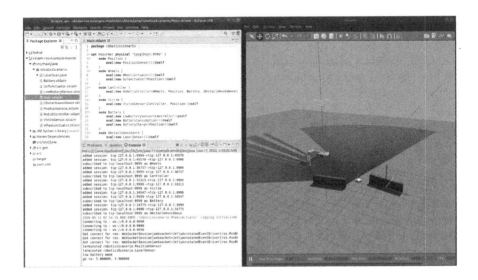

Fig. 11. Execution of an X-KLAIM robotics application.

to execute the code in a simulated environment and obtain a 3D visualization of the execution, the Gazebo simulator has to be launched with the corresponding robot description. At this point, our application can be executed by running the Java class `Main`, which has been generated by the X-KLAIM compiler. The screenshot in Fig. 11 shows our X-KLAIM robotics application in execution. Of course, since the robot explores the disaster area randomly, executions are different from each other.

5   Related Work

More strictly related works are a couple of proposals using high-level languages for producing ROS applications. In [1], an approach is proposed that aims at creating nodes of ROS applications using a DSL based on the Python language. This DSL can be used interactively, through the Python command line interface, to create brand new ROS nodes and to reshape existing ROS nodes by wrapping their communication interfaces. In [21], the tool ROSGen is described, which, given as an input a specification of a ROS system architecture, generates a ROS node model. This is a glue code written in a DSL, which specifies the ROS nodes that compose the system and the topics that the nodes subscribe to and publish on. This paper also proposes a demonstration that the code generation process is amenable to formal verification, using the theorem prover Coq.

Other less specific works regard applications of Model-Driven Engineering (MDE) and development of DSL for robotics applications. MDE [28] is considered by many robotics researchers to be a promising approach for simplifying design, implementation and execution of software for robotics systems. MDE advocates the use of domain-specific modeling languages (DSMLs) for expressing robotics models through concepts that abstract away from the underlying technology and are closer to the problem domain. Many proposals in the literature instantiate this approach, like e.g. the domain-specific language RobotML [14], the model-based framework SafeRobots [25] and the prototype framework CommonLang [26]. In [15], a family of domain-specific languages for specifying missions of multi-robot systems is introduced. The proposed languages are organized in different layers comprising languages conceived for the end-user describing missions and the environmental context, an intermediate language describing the detailed behavior of each robot (hidden to the user), and the robot language containing the hardware and low-level specification of each type of robot within the team. The authors claim that the layer managing the robot controller is implemented using Java and ROS, which interact via *java_rosbridge* as in our work. In [16], a domain-specific language for developing robot arm applications is defined. Special attention is paid to the automatic generation of robot control logic and to the validation and certification of software components. In [27], the relationships between MDE and the service-oriented component-based development approach in the robotics domain are discussed, and a software engineering approach, called SmartSoft, resulting from their combination is illustrated. All required and provided services of a SmartSoft component are built on top of a small set of communication patterns, which connect the externally visible services with the internally visible set of access methods for these services. This provides a completely middleware-independent view on the component ports and on the communication interfaces visible to the user. From the modeling perspective, the approach is supported by a UML-based notation, called SmartMARS, representing the SmartSoft concepts independently of any implementation technology. In [2], a model-driven toolchain for robotics software development, based on the 3-View Component Meta-Model V^3CMM, is introduced. It provides designers with an expressive, yet simple, platform-independent modeling language for component-based application design. The MDE approach permits generating the code for specific platforms via model transformations, which allow programmers to progressively include application-dependent details. In [10], the BRICS model-based development paradigm is proposed. This paradigm aims at providing robotics developers with a set of guidelines, meta-models and tools for structuring the development of robotics software systems, without introducing any framework or application-specific details. In [9], several MDE-based solutions for software development in robotics are illustrated. This paper focuses specifically on the architectural model as the central artifact of almost all software development activities. In [23], the state of the art in DSMLs in robotics is surveyed. This paper also provides an overview of subdomains relevant for programming and simulation of robotics applications that are already supported through the MDE approach. Finally, [29] shows that by relying on a suitably designed transformation and verification architecture it is possible, also in such critical environments like robotics systems, to mitigate the additional risk resulting from the automatic transformation from DSLs to code through the use of so-called *language workbenches*.

We leave for future work a systematic comparison with the related literature, also aimed at identifying the requirements of robotic applications and showing the benefits of our approach. Anyhow, we want to point out that our work differs from the ones discussed above for the use of a high-level language with a tuple-based communication mechanism. X-KLAIM computation and communication model is particularly suitable for programming robot's behavior. Indeed, X-KLAIM natively supports concurrent programming, which is required by the distributed nature of robots' software. In addition, communicating processes are decoupled both in space and time and X-KLAIM tuples permit to model both raw data produced by sensors and aggregated information obtained from such data. This allows programmers to specify the robot's behavior at different levels of granularity.

6   Concluding Remarks and Future Work

In this paper we have introduced an approach for developing robotics applications based on the programming language X-KLAIM and the ROS middleware. We consider this as a first exploratory attempt. We think that X-KLAIM has proved expressive enough to implement this first scenario. In particular,

X-Klaim integration with Java allowed us to seamlessly use the *java_rosbridge* API directly in the X-Klaim code.

Further experimentation will be needed with application scenarios typical of the robotics domain to allow us to assess whether the linguistic primitives of X-Klaim are already sufficiently expressive or whether we need to equip the language with further abstractions which better fit the problem domain. In addition, a usability evaluation of the X-Klaim language will be also needed to assess the benefits of using it in place of the traditional solutions for ROS-based robotics applications (i.e., C++ and Python). Our long-term goal is the design of a domain specific language for the robotics domain which, besides being used for generating executable code, is integrated with automated reasoning tools that can support application verification and analysis.

We also plan to extend our approach from single robot scenarios to collective ones. In this respect, we believe that the form of communication offered by tuple spaces, supported by X-Klaim, which permits decoupling communicating processes both in space and time, brings benefits for the scalability of collective robotics systems in terms of the number of components and robots that can be dynamically added. This would also permit to meet the open-endedness requirement (i.e., robots can dynamically enter or leave the system), which is crucial in collective systems. The tuple space-based paradigm supported by X-Klaim relies on Klava, which abstracts from the actual implementation of the tuple space. Klava itself provides a default implementation where all tuples are stored in a list, which has to be scanned sequentially when looking for a matching tuple. Other optimized and ad-hoc implementations of tuple spaces can be injected into Klava. We plan to experiment with such optimizations along the lines of [11].

In the extension from single to multi robots systems, we can take advantage of the hierarchical version of the network model presented in [7], which is already implemented in X-Klaim, as mentioned in Sect. 2.2. For example, this feature will allow us to organize the components of a single robot in a flat network (as in the current implementation of the example), and to structure the collective system as a network of networks. Note that, as we stressed in Sect. 4, even in the current shape, our processes are already independent from the actual physical positions of the nodes, since they are parametric with respect to tuple space localities.

Since runtime adaptation is another important capability of collective systems, we also plan to investigate to what extent we can benefit from X-Klaim code mobility mechanisms to achieve adaptive behaviors in robotics applications. For example, an X-Klaim process (a controller or an actuator) could dynamically receive code from other possibly distributed processes containing the logic to continue the execution.

Finally, in this work we have used the version 1 of ROS as a reference middleware for the proposed approach, because currently this seems to be most adopted in practice. We plan anyway to extend our approach to the version 2 of ROS, which features a more sophisticated publish/subscribe system based on the OMG DDS standard.

References

1. Adam, S., Schultz, U.P.: Towards interactive, incremental programming of ROS nodes. In: Workshop on Domain-Specific Languages and Models for Robotic Systems (2014)
2. Alonso, D., Vicente-Chicote, C., Ortiz, F., Pastor, J., Álvarez, B.: V^3CMM: a 3-view component meta-model for model-driven robotic software development. J. Softw. Eng. Rob. **1**, 3–17 (2010)
3. Bettini, L., De Nicola, R., Falassi, D., Lacoste, M., Loreti, M.: A flexible and modular framework for implementing infrastructures for global computing. In: Kutvonen, L., Alonistioti, N. (eds.) DAIS 2005. LNCS, vol. 3543, pp. 181–193. Springer, Heidelberg (2005). https://doi.org/10.1007/11498094_17
4. Bettini, L., De Nicola, R., Pugliese, R.: KLAVA: a Java package for distributed and mobile applications. Softw. Pract. Experience **32**(14), 1365–1394 (2002)
5. Bettini, L.: Implementing Domain-Specific Languages with Xtext and Xtend, 2nd edn. Packt Publishing, Birmingham (2016)
6. Bettini, L., De Nicola, R., Pugliese, R., Ferrari, G.L.: Interactive mobile agents in X-Klaim. In: WETICE, pp. 110–117. IEEE Computer Society (1998)
7. Bettini, L., Loreti, M., Pugliese, R.: An infrastructure language for open nets. In: SAC, pp. 373–377. ACM (2002)
8. Bettini, L., Merelli, E., Tiezzi, F.: X-KLAIM is back. In: Boreale, M., Corradini, F., Loreti, M., Pugliese, R. (eds.) Models, Languages, and Tools for Concurrent and Distributed Programming. LNCS, vol. 11665, pp. 115–135. Springer, Cham (2019). https://doi.org/10.1007/978-3-030-21485-2_8
9. Brugali, D.: Model-driven software engineering in robotics: Models are designed to use the relevant things, thereby reducing the complexity and cost in the field of robotics. IEEE Robot. Autom. Mag. **22**(3), 155–166 (2015)
10. Bruyninckx, H., Klotzbücher, M., Hochgeschwender, N., Kraetzschmar, G.K., Gherardi, L., Brugali, D.: The BRICS component model: a model-based development paradigm for complex robotics software systems. In: SAC, pp. 1758–1764. ACM (2013)
11. Buravlev, V., De Nicola, R., Mezzina, C.A.: Evaluating the efficiency of Linda implementations. Concurr. Comput. Pract. Exp. **30**(8) (2018)
12. De Nicola, R., Di Stefano, L., Inverso, O.: Toward formal models and languages for verifiable multi-robot systems. Front. Rob. AI **5**, 94 (2018)
13. De Nicola, R., Ferrari, G.L., Pugliese, R.: KLAIM: a kernel language for agents interaction and mobility. IEEE Trans. Software Eng. **24**(5), 315–330 (1998)
14. Dhouib, S., Kchir, S., Stinckwich, S., Ziadi, T., Ziane, M.: RobotML, a domain-specific language to design, simulate and deploy robotic applications. In: Noda, I., Ando, N., Brugali, D., Kuffner, J.J. (eds.) SIMPAR 2012. LNCS (LNAI), vol. 7628, pp. 149–160. Springer, Heidelberg (2012). https://doi.org/10.1007/978-3-642-34327-8_16
15. Di Ruscio, D., Malavolta, I., Pelliccione, P.: A family of domain-specific languages for specifying civilian missions of multi-robot systems. In: Proceedings of MORSE@STAF. CEUR Workshop Proceedings, vol. 1319, pp. 16–29 (2014)
16. Djukic, V., Popovic, A., Tolvanen, J.: Domain-specific modeling for robotics: from language construction to ready-made controllers and end-user applications. In: Proceedings of MORSE@RoboCup, pp. 47–54. ACM (2016)
17. Efftinge, S., et al.: Xbase: implementing domain-specific languages for Java. In: GPCE, pp. 112–121. ACM (2012)

18. Frigerio, M., Buchli, J., Caldwell, D.G.: A domain specific language for kinematic models and fast implementations of robot dynamics algorithms. In: Proceedings of DSLRob'11. CoRR, vol. abs/1301.7190 (2013)
19. Gelernter, D.: Generative Communication in Linda. ACM Trans. Program. Lang. Syst. **7**(1), 80–112 (1985)
20. Houliston, T., et al.: NUClear: a loosely coupled software architecture for humanoid robot systems. Front. Rob. and AI **3**, 20 (2016)
21. Meng, W., Park, J., Sokolsky, O., Weirich, S., Lee, I.: Verified ROS-based deployment of platform-independent control systems. In: Havelund, K., Holzmann, G., Joshi, R. (eds.) NFM 2015. LNCS, vol. 9058, pp. 248–262. Springer, Cham (2015). https://doi.org/10.1007/978-3-319-17524-9_18
22. Milner, R.: Communication and Concurrency. PHI Series in Computer Science. Prentice Hall, Upper Saddle River (1989)
23. Nordmann, A., Hochgeschwender, N., Wigand, D., Wrede, S.: A survey on domain-specific modeling and languages in robotics. J. Softw. Eng. Rob. **7**, 75–99 (2016)
24. Quigley, M., et al.: ROS: an open-source robot operating system. In: ICRA Workshop on Open Source Software (2009)
25. Ramaswamy, A., Monsuez, B., Tapus, A.: SafeRobots: a model-driven approach for designing robotic software architectures. In: Proceedings of CTS, pp. 131–134. IEEE (2014)
26. Rutle, A., Backer, J., Foldøy, K., Bye, R.T.: CommonLang: a DSL for defining robot tasks. In: Proceedings of MODELS 2018 Workshops. CEUR Workshop Proceedings, vol. 2245, pp. 433–442 (2018)
27. Schlegel, C., Steck, A., Lotz, A.: Model-driven software development in robotics: communication patterns as key for a robotics component model. In: Introduction to Modern Robotics, pp. 119–150. iConcept Press (2011)
28. Schmidt, D.C.: Guest editor's introduction: model-driven engineering. IEEE Comput. **39**(2), 25–31 (2006)
29. Voelter, M.: Using language workbenches and domain-specific languages for safety-critical software development. In: Proceedings of SE/SWM. LNI, vol. P-292, pp. 143–144. GI (2019)

Measuring Adaptability and Reliability
of Large Scale Systems

Valentina Castiglioni[1]([⊠]), Michele Loreti[2]([⊠]), and Simone Tini[3]([⊠])

[1] Reykjavik University, Reykjavik, Iceland
`valentinac@ru.is`
[2] University of Camerino, Camerino, Italy
`michele.loreti@unicam.it`
[3] University of Insubria, Como, Italy
`simone.tini@uninsubria.it`

Abstract. In this paper we propose a *metric approach* to the analysis and verification of large scale self-organising collective systems. Typically, these systems consist of a large number of agents that have to interact to coordinate their activities and, at the same time, have to adapt their behaviour to the dynamic surrounding environment. It is then natural to apply a probabilistic modelling to these systems and, thus, to use a metric for the comparison of their behaviours. In detail, we introduce the *population metric*, namely a pseudometric measuring the differences in the probabilistic evolution of two systems with respect to some given requirements. We also use this metric to express the properties of *adaptability* and *reliability* of a system, which allow us to identify potential critical issues with respect to perturbations in its initial conditions. Then we show how we can combine our metric with *statistical inference* techniques to obtain a mathematically tractable analysis of large scale systems. Finally, we exploit *mean-field approximations* to measure the adaptability and reliability of large scale systems.

1 Introduction

The ever increasing complexity of the digital world has moved the focus of researchers to new classes of systems that are characterised by a large number of interacting components, or *agents*. These agents, when considered in isolation from the system, usually show a rather simple behaviour. However, the interaction of a massive number of them enables the desired complex behaviour of the system. Most prominent examples of this class of systems are IoT systems [19], wireless sensors networks, and *self-organising collective systems* [2] (SCS). The latter ones are characterised by a large number of interacting agents that coordinate their activities in a decentralised and often implicit way. Each agent may change its behaviour according to the current status of the other agents in order to make the system reach its objectives. However, the dynamic behaviour of a massive number of agents, and the potential interaction of the system with users and physical phenomena, make these changes subject to uncertainties and unpredictable events. For simplicity, given one agent, we call environment the ensemble of all other agents, users and phenomena that can affect its behaviour. We are interested in ensuring that the system, and thus each agent, is able to adjust its behaviour with respect to the current environmental conditions in order to fulfil its tasks.

© Springer Nature Switzerland AG 2020
T. Margaria and B. Steffen (Eds.): ISoLA 2020, LNCS 12477, pp. 380–396, 2020.
https://doi.org/10.1007/978-3-030-61470-6_23

Due to the unpredictable behaviour of the environment, it is natural to employ a probabilistic model for the formal specification of the behaviour of these systems. In particular, we can use a *discrete-time Markov chain* (DTMC) to model the semantics of each agent and, thus, of the system (see, e.g., [20]). When quantitative aspects of systems behaviour are considered, we can use metrics for verification purposes [4, 6, 8, 14, 15, 23], as they allow us to quantify how far the current behaviour of a system is from its intended one. In the literature, several formal frameworks have been proposed for modelling and analysing SCS (see among others [7, 13, 25, 31]). However, to the best of our knowledge, so far there have been no proposals of a metric semantics for SCS.

Hence, our first contribution consists in filling this gap as we propose a *metric approach* to the analysis and verification of large scale SCS. For the specification, we consider the probabilistic model from [20]: agents are identical, at any point in time each agent can be in any of finitely many states, and the evolution of the system proceeds in a clock-synchronous fashion. As each agent can change its state probabilistically, at each time step we obtain a probability distribution over the possible configurations of the system. Therefore, we express system's semantics in terms of its *evolution sequence*, i.e., the sequence of probability distributions so obtained. Then, we introduce the *population metric*, a (time-dependent) pseudometric measuring the differences between the evolution sequences of systems. Besides the disparities in the probabilistic behaviour, the distance considers the ability of systems to fulfil their tasks. The population metric consists of two components: a *metric on global states* and the *Wasserstein metric* [29]. The former considers the *global state* of the system, i.e. the identification of the current state of each agent, and is defined in terms of a (time-dependent) *penalty function* comparing two global states only on the base of the objectives of the system (at a given time). The latter lifts this metric to a metric on distributions over global states, and thus on the evolution sequences of systems. We then exploit the population metric to define the notions of *adaptability* and *reliability* of a system, allowing us to analyse its ability to adjust its behaviour to perturbations in the initial environmental conditions.

As systems are constituted by a large number of agents, a direct evaluation of the population metric is generally unfeasible. Hence, as our second contribution, we provide a *randomised algorithm*, based on statistical inference and on results in [26, 28, 30], to compute the distance between two systems in time $O(TR\log(R))$, where R is the number of samples used to estimate the evolution sequences of the two systems, and T denotes the number of comparisons performed between the estimated evolution sequences, each one at a different time step. We then show an application of our algorithm to evaluate the adaptability of a system in the balancing scenario from [5].

Nevertheless, when the number of agents increases dramatically, the proposed empirical technique falls short of efficiency. For this reason, as our third contribution, we propose a modification of our randomised algorithm based on *mean-field approximation* and the results in [21]. We express system's evolution in terms of the changes in its *occupancy vector*, whose elements correspond to the fraction of agents in a particular state. In [21] it was proven that when the number of agents goes to infinity, the DTMC capturing the evolution of the occupancy vector of the system can be approximated by a deterministic process. This process corresponds to the deterministic solution of a set of difference equations called mean-field, and it can be exploited to obtain a good estimation of the behaviour of the entire system. As an application example, we evaluate the adaptability of the system in the balancing scenario with an infinite number of agents.

2 Background

As general notational conventions, given a set $\mathcal{X}$ we let $|\mathcal{X}|$ denote its cardinality, and given a vector $\mathbf{x} \in \mathcal{X}^n$, we let $\mathbf{x}_{[i]}$ denote the i-th component of $\mathbf{x}$.

Metrics. A *metric* on a set $\mathcal{X}$ is a function $m \colon \mathcal{X} \times \mathcal{X} \to \mathbb{R}^{\geq 0}$ with $m(x_1, x_2) = 0$ iff $x_1 = x_2$, $m(x_1, x_2) = m(x_2, x_1)$, and $m(x_1, x_2) \leq m(x_1, x_3) + m(x_3, x_2)$, for all $x_1, x_2, x_3 \in \mathcal{X}$. We obtain a *pseudometric* by relaxing the first property to $m(x_1, x_2) = 0$ if $x_1 = x_2$. As elsewhere in the literature, as the difference in the two notions is not relevant for our purposes, we will not distinguish between metrics and pseudometrics and use the term *metric* as a general term to denote both. A metric m is *l-bounded* if $m(x_1, x_2) \leq l$ for all $x_1, x_2 \in \mathcal{X}$.

Probability distributions. Given a countable set $\mathcal{X}$, a *discrete probability distribution*, henceforth simply *distribution*, over $\mathcal{X}$ is a mapping $\mu \colon \mathcal{X} \to [0,1]$ such that $\sum_{x \in \mathcal{X}} \mu(x) = 1$. The *support* of μ is the set $\mathrm{supp}(\mu) = \{x \in \mathcal{X} \mid \mu(x) > 0\}$. By $\Delta(\mathcal{X})$ we denote the set of all distributions over $\mathcal{X}$, ranged over by $\mu, \pi, \mu', \ldots$ Given an element $x \in \mathcal{X}$, we let δ_x denote the *Dirac* (or *point*) *distribution on x*, defined by $\delta_x(x) = 1$ and $\delta_x(y) = 0$ for all $y \neq x$. For a finite set of indexes I, weights $p_i \in (0, 1]$ with $\sum_{i \in I} p_i = 1$ and distributions $\mu_i \in \Delta(\mathcal{X})$ with $i \in I$, the distribution $\sum_{i \in I} p_i \mu_i$ is defined by $(\sum_{i \in I} p_i \mu_i)(x) = \sum_{i \in I} p_i \cdot \mu_i(x)$, for all $x \in \mathcal{X}$.

Discrete-time Markov chains. A *discrete-time Markov chain* (DTMC) is a pair $\mathcal{M} = \langle \mathcal{X}, \mathbf{P} \rangle$ consisting in a countable set of *states* $\mathcal{X}$ and a $|\mathcal{X}| \times |\mathcal{X}|$ *one step probability matrix* $\mathbf{P}$ such that $\mathbf{P}_{x,y}$ expresses the probability of reaching state y from state x in one computation step. Equivalently, we can define a Markov chain $\mathcal{M}$ as a *stochastic process* $\{\mathbf{X}_t\}_{t \in \mathbb{N}}$ satisfying the Markov property, i.e., the probability of moving to the next state depends only on the current state and not on the previous ones. Formally,

$$\Pr(\mathbf{X}_{t+1} = x \mid \mathbf{X}_0 = x_0, \ldots, \mathbf{X}_t = x_t) = \Pr(\mathbf{X}_{t+1} = x \mid \mathbf{X}_t = x_t) = \mathbf{P}_{x_t, x}.$$

3 A Calculus of Interacting Agents

In this section we present a simple formalism that can be used to describe the behaviour of N identical interacting agents. At any point in time, each agent can be in any of its *finitely many* states and the evolution of the system proceeds in a *clock-synchronous* fashion: at each clock tick each member of the population must either execute one of the transitions that are enabled in its current state, or remain in such a state. The presented formalism is a simple adaptation of the one introduced first in [21] and in [20].

Agent specifications. An *agent specification* consists of a triple $\langle \mathcal{S}, \mathrm{Act}, \mathcal{D} \rangle$, where:

- $\mathcal{S}$ is a *finite* non-empty set of *state constants*, ranged over by $A, A', A_1, \ldots$;
- Act is a countable non-empty set of *actions*, ranged over by $a, a', a_1, \ldots$;
- $\mathcal{D}$ is a set of *agent definitions* associating each state constant $A_i \in \mathcal{S}$ with a *summation* of enabled actions:

$$A_i := \sum_{j \in J_i} a_{ij}.A_{ij},$$

with J_i a finite index set, $A_i, A_{ij} \in \mathcal{S}$, and $a_{ij} \in \mathrm{Act}$, for $i \in I$ and $j \in J_i$.

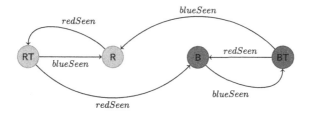

Fig. 1. Behaviour of agents in Example 1.

We let $\mathsf{Act}(A_i) = \{a_{ij} \mid j \in J_i\}$ denote the set of *actions enabled* in state A_i. Notation $\sum_{j \in J_i} a_{ij}.A_{ij}$ can be thought of as the n-ary extension of the standard binary nonde-terministic choice operator. We assume that $a_{ij} \neq a_{ij'}$ whenever $j \neq j'$ for $j, j' \in J_i$. Since $\mathcal{S}$ is finite we can assume, without loss of generality, that the state constants are ordered and univocally identified by their index, namely $\mathcal{S} = \{A_1, \ldots, A_{|\mathcal{S}|}\}$.

In order to show how this simple formalism can be used to model the behaviour of a population of agents, and as a running example for an application of our results, we consider the following *balancing scenario* from [5].

Example 1 (Balancing scenario). Let us consider a group of agents that can be either *red* or *blue*. We want to guarantee that the two groups are *balanced* in size, without any centralised control. Each agent can change its colour only by interacting with the other participants in the systems. An agent of a given colour starts a *transitional phase* when it meets another agent of the same colour. In this phase, if another agent with the same colour is met, the agent *changes* its own. The transitional phase is cancelled when an agent with a different colour is found. As typical of SCS, this procedure may never end.

The above behaviour is rendered via state constants B, R, RT and BT. The first two states indicate a *blue* and a *red* agent, respectively; while the last two states describe an agent in a *transition* phase. We let $\mathcal{D}_{RB}$ be the following set of *agent definitions*:

$$\mathsf{B} := blueSeen.\mathsf{BT} \qquad \mathsf{BT} := redSeen.\mathsf{B} + blueSeen.\mathsf{R}$$
$$\mathsf{R} := redSeen.\mathsf{RT} \qquad \mathsf{RT} := redSeen.\mathsf{B} + blueSeen.\mathsf{R}$$

where action $redSeen$ is performed when a *red* agent is met, while $blueSeen$ indicates that the colour of encountered agent is *blue*.

Finally, the agent specification Σ_{RB} is $\Sigma_{RB} = \langle \mathcal{S}_{RB}, \mathsf{Act}_{RB}, \mathcal{D}_{RB} \rangle$, where $\mathcal{S}_{RB} = \{\mathsf{B}, \mathsf{R}, \mathsf{BT}, \mathsf{RT}\}$, $\mathsf{Act}_{RB} = \{blueSeen, redSeen\}$, and $\mathcal{D}_{RB}$ is the one defined above.

An agent specification can be also depicted via a graph as reported in Fig. 1. As common in the literature, for $A_i := \sum_{j \in J} a_j.A_j$, we write $A_i \xrightarrow{a_j} A_j$ to denote that if an agent in state A_i performs action a_j then its state changes to A_j, for each $j \in J$.

Global states and occupancy vectors. An agent specification $\langle \mathcal{S}, \mathsf{Act}, \mathcal{D} \rangle$ describes the behaviour of a set of agents operating in a system. A *configuration* of a system consists of any representation of the current states of the N agents in it. Two different levels of abstraction for modelling configurations can be considered. The basic, and more detailed, one is based on *global states*. This consists of a sequence $\mathbf{A}$ in $\mathcal{S}^N$ of the form $(A_{i_1}, \ldots, A_{i_N})$, where A_{i_k} is the current state of agent k, for each $k = 1, \ldots, N$. We refer to N as the *population size*, and we let $\mathbf{A}_{[k]}$ denote the k-th element in $\mathbf{A}$. The state of each agent operating in the system is then univocally identified. Appropriate syntactical shorthands will be used to denote system configurations. For instance, we let $\langle \mathsf{B}[1000], \mathsf{R}[0], \mathsf{BT}[0], \mathsf{RT}[0] \rangle$ denote the configuration with only 1000 blue agents.

However, sometimes we can abstract from the precise state of each single agent while we are interested in considering only the fraction of agents in each state. For this reason, a configuration can be also represented via an *occupancy vector* associating each *state* with the fraction of *agents* in that state. An occupancy vector $\mathbf{o}$ is then an element in $\mathcal{U}^{|\mathcal{S}|} = \{\mathbf{u} \in [0,1]^{|\mathcal{S}|} \mid \sum_{i=1}^{|\mathcal{S}|} \mathbf{u}_{[i]} = 1\}$, namely the *unit simplex* of dimension $|\mathcal{S}|$. We let $\mathrm{OF}_{\mathcal{S},N}$ denote the function mapping each global state in $\mathcal{S}^N$ to the corresponding occupancy vector: $\mathrm{OF}_{\mathcal{S},N} : \mathcal{S}^N \to \mathcal{U}^{|\mathcal{S}|}$ is defined for all $\mathbf{A} \in \mathcal{S}^N$ by:

$$\mathrm{OF}_{\mathcal{S},N}(\mathbf{A})_{[i]} = \frac{1}{N} \sum_{k=1}^{N} \mathbf{1}_{[\mathbf{A}_{[k]} = A_i]}$$

where $\mathbf{1}_{[\mathbf{A}_{[k]} = A_i]}$ is 1 if $\mathbf{A}_{[k]} = A_i$, and it is 0 otherwise, $i = 1, \ldots, |\mathcal{S}|$.

We call $\mathrm{OF}_{\mathcal{S},N}$ the *occupancy function* on $\mathcal{S}^N$. We shall drop the subscripts $\mathcal{S}$ and N from $\mathrm{OF}_{\mathcal{S},N}$ when no confusion shall arise.

Probability functions. Let us consider an agent specification $\langle \mathcal{S}, \mathsf{Act}, \mathcal{D} \rangle$ and a global state $\mathbf{A} \in \mathcal{S}^N$. The behaviour of $\mathbf{A}$ is modelled via a probabilistic process. Each agent in $\mathbf{A}$ selects probabilistically the next action to perform. The probability of an agent in a given state A_i to perform an action $a \in \mathsf{Act}(A_i)$ in the current time step depends on the distribution of the current states of the other agents, and thus on $\mathrm{OF}(\mathbf{A})$. Clearly, the changes in the distribution of the states of the agents induced by each computation step entail a modification of the (probabilistic) behaviour of each agent at the next step until an equilibrium is eventually reached.

Formally, as a first step in the definition of the dynamic behaviour of agents, we assign a *weight* to each action in a global state $\mathbf{A}$ by means of a *weight function* $\mu_{\mathcal{S}} : \mathcal{U}^{|\mathcal{S}|} \times \mathsf{Act} \to \mathbb{R}$. The weight function is built on the *weight expressions* $E \in \mathsf{Exp}$, defined according to the following grammar:

$$E ::= v \mid \mathsf{frc}\,(A) \mid \langle \mathsf{uop} \rangle E \mid E \langle \mathsf{bop} \rangle E \mid (E)$$

Above $v \in [0,1]$ and for each state $A \in \mathcal{S}$, $\mathsf{frc}\,(A)$ denotes the fraction of agents in the system that are currently in state A out of the total number of objects N. Operators $\langle \mathsf{uop} \rangle$ and $\langle \mathsf{bop} \rangle$ are standard arithmetic unary and binary operators.

Each expression is interpreted over a $\mathbf{u} \in \mathcal{U}^{|\mathcal{S}|}$ by means of an expressions interpretation function $[\![\cdot]\!]_{\mathbf{u}} : \mathsf{Exp} \to \mathbb{R}$ defined as follows:

$$[\![v]\!]_{\mathbf{u}} = v \qquad [\![\mathsf{frc}\,(A_i)]\!]_{\mathbf{u}} = \mathbf{u}_{[i]} \qquad [\![\langle \mathsf{uop} \rangle E]\!]_{\mathbf{u}} = \langle \mathsf{uop} \rangle ([\![E]\!]_{\mathbf{u}})$$

$$[\![E_1 \langle \mathsf{bop} \rangle E_2]\!]_{\mathbf{u}} = ([\![E_1]\!]_{\mathbf{u}}) \langle \mathsf{bop} \rangle ([\![E_2]\!]_{\mathbf{u}}) \qquad [\![(E)]\!]_{\mathbf{u}} = ([\![E]\!]_{\mathbf{u}})$$

Hence, we can associate each action $a \in \text{Act}$ with a weight expression E_a and define the weight of action a with respect to an occupancy vector $\mathbf{o}$ by $\mu_S(\mathbf{o}, a) = [\![E_a]\!]_{\mathbf{o}}$.

We say that a state $A \in S$ is *probabilistic* in an occupancy vector $\mathbf{o}$ if

$$0 \leq \sum_{a \in \text{Act} \,:\, A \xrightarrow{a} A'} \mu_S(\mathbf{o}, a) \leq 1,$$

i.e., if the total weight assigned by μ_S to the actions enabled for A with respect to $\mathbf{o}$ is non-negative and smaller than 1. Then, we say that μ_S is a *probability function* if all the states in S are probabilistic in $\mathbf{o}$, for any $\mathbf{o} \in \mathcal{U}^{|S|}$. In the remainder of the paper we shall consider only functions μ_S that are probability functions.

We shall drop the subscript S from μ_S when no confusion shall arise.

Example 2. For the *red blue* balancing scenario of Example 1, given an occupancy vector $\mathbf{o}$, we can consider the probability function $\mu_{S_{RB}}$ defined as follows:

$$\mu_{S_{RB}}(\mathbf{o}, blueSeen) = [\![\alpha \cdot (\text{frc}\,(\text{B}) + \text{frc}\,(\text{BT}))]\!]_{\mathbf{o}}$$
$$\mu_{S_{RB}}(\mathbf{o}, redSeen) = [\![\alpha \cdot (\text{frc}\,(\text{R}) + \text{frc}\,(\text{RT}))]\!]_{\mathbf{o}},$$

with α a parameter in $[0, 1]$ expressing the probability of an agent *to see another agent*.

Systems semantics. A *system specification* Σ is a tuple of the form $\langle S, \text{Act}, \mathcal{D}, \mu_S \rangle$, where $\langle S, \text{Act}, \mathcal{D} \rangle$ is an agent specification and μ_S is a *probability* function. We let Σ^N denote a system Σ composed by N agents.

As outlined above, the behaviour of a *global state* $\mathbf{A} \in S^N$ can be described in terms of the (probabilistic) evolution of the states of the agents. To this end, let us focus on the behaviour of a single agent in its interaction with the others. Let $\mathbf{o}$ be an occupancy vector in $\mathcal{U}^{|S|}$. The *agent transition function* $\mathbf{K}$ is used to express the probability under $\mathbf{o}$ of an agent in state A_i to change its state to A_j after one computation step. Formally, we define $\mathbf{K} \colon \mathcal{U}^{|S|} \times S \times S \to [0, 1]$ as follows:

$$\mathbf{K}(\mathbf{u})_{A_i, A_j} = \begin{cases} \displaystyle\sum_{a \in I(A_i)} \mu_S(\mathbf{u}, a) & \text{if } A_i \neq A_j \\ 1 - \displaystyle\sum_{a \in I(A_i)} \mu_S(\mathbf{u}, a) & \text{if } A_i = A_j \end{cases},$$

where $I(A_i) = \{a \in \text{Act} \mid \exists A_j \in S \colon A_i \xrightarrow{a} A_j \wedge A_i \neq A_j\}$.

As we are assuming that all the states in S are probabilistic in any occupancy vector $\mathbf{o}$, we can interpret $\mathbf{K}(\mathbf{o})$ as a one step $|S| \times |S|$ transition probability matrix, and call it the *agent transition matrix*. Then, the second case in the definition of $\mathbf{K}(\mathbf{o})$ expresses the probability of an agent in state A_i to remain in that state after the clock tick.

Starting from $\mathbf{K}$, we can define the probabilistic behaviour of global states via the *global state transition matrix* $\mathbf{P}^{(N)} \colon S^N \times S^N \to [0, 1]$ defined for all $\mathbf{A}, \mathbf{A}' \in S^N$ as

$$\mathbf{P}^{(N)}_{\mathbf{A}, \mathbf{A}'} = \prod_{k=1}^{N} \mathbf{K}(\text{OF}(\mathbf{A}))_{\mathbf{A}_{[k]}, \mathbf{A}'_{[k]}} \tag{1}$$

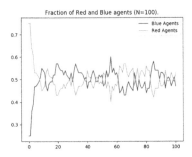

Fig. 2. Single simulation run of red-blue scenario. (Color figure online)

Since all states in $\mathcal{S}$ are probabilistic in any occupancy vector $\mathbf{o}$, the $|\mathcal{S}^N| \times |\mathcal{S}^N|$ matrix $\mathbf{P}^{(N)}$ corresponds to the one step transition probability matrix of the (finite state) DTMC modelling a possible single step of the system as result of the parallel execution of a single step of each of the N agents In detail, given a *global state* $\mathbf{A} \in \mathcal{S}^N$, we define the *evolution sequence* of $\mathbf{A}$ as the sequence $\pi_{\mathbf{A},0}, \dots, \pi_{\mathbf{A},t}, \dots$ of probability distributions over $\mathcal{S}^N$ such that $\pi_{\mathbf{A},0} = \delta_{\mathbf{A}}$ and $\pi_{\mathbf{A},t+1} = \pi_{\mathbf{A},t}\mathbf{P}^{(N)}$, for each $t > 0$. In this case, we let $\mathbf{X}_{\mathbf{A}}^{(N)}(t)$ denote the Markov chain with transition probability matrix $\mathbf{P}^{(N)}$ as above and $\mathbf{X}_{\mathbf{A}}^{(N)}(0) = \mathbf{A}$, i.e. with initial probability distribution $\delta_{\mathbf{A}}$. From the Markov chain $\{\mathbf{X}_{\mathbf{A}}^{(N)}(t)\}_{t \in \mathbb{N}}$ we can obtain the *occupancy DTMC* $\{\mathbf{O}_{\mathbf{A}}^{(N)}(t)\}_{t \in \mathbb{N}}$, namely the Markov chain modelling the evolution in time of the occupancy vector of the system. Intuitively, and with a slight abuse of notation, $\mathbf{O}_{\mathbf{A}}^{(N)}(t)$ corresponds to $\mathrm{OF}(\mathbf{X}_{\mathbf{A}}^{(N)}(t))$ and its transition probability is defined by:

$$\Pr\{\mathbf{O}_{\mathbf{A}}^{(N)}(t+1) = \mathbf{o}' \mid \mathbf{O}_{\mathbf{A}}^{(N)}(t) = \mathrm{OF}(\mathbf{A})\} = \sum_{\mathbf{A}' : \mathrm{OF}(\mathbf{A}')=\mathbf{o}'} \mathbf{P}_{\mathbf{A},\mathbf{A}'}^{(N)} \qquad (2)$$

Notice that $\mathbf{O}^{(N)}$ is well-defined: if $\mathrm{OF}(\mathbf{A}) = \mathrm{OF}(\mathbf{A}'')$, then $\mathbf{A}$ and $\mathbf{A}''$ are two permutations of the same local states. Hence, for all $\mathbf{A}'$ we have $\mathbf{P}_{\mathbf{A},\mathbf{A}'}^{(N)} = \mathbf{P}_{\mathbf{A}'',\mathbf{A}'}^{(N)}$.

Example 3. We can use the presented semantics to generate the stochastic process of our system of Example 1. The result of the simulation of a single computational path is reported in Fig. 2. There we consider an initial state composed by $N = 100$ agents out of which 75 are in the state R and 25 are in the state B. We consider $\alpha = 0.5$ (see Example 2). We can observe that, after few steps, the system is able to evolve to balanced configurations. (Data have been obtained by using Spear Tool available at https://github.com/quasylab/spear.)

4   Measuring the Adaptability and Reliability of Systems

In this section we provide the tools necessary to study and analyse the differences in the dynamics of the systems described in the previous section. More precisely, we introduce a *metric* over systems, called the *population metric* m, that quantifies the dissimilarities over the evolution sequences of the initial configurations of the systems. The definition of the population metric will then make use of a *(time-dependent) metric on global states*, measuring the differences of each pair of global states with respect to some parameters of interest, and of the *Wasserstein metric*, allowing for lifting the former metric to probability distributions over global states. We then exploit the population metric to define the notions of *adaptability* and *reliability* of a system, expressing how well the system can adjust its behaviour with respect to changes in the initial conditions.

4.1 A Metric over Systems: The population Metric

A metric over global states. We start by proposing a *metric over global states*. This metric expresses the distance between two given configurations by comparing them with respect to some parameters representing the ideal, optimal behaviour of a system. To this end, we introduce a *penalty function* $\rho\colon \mathcal{S}^N \to [0,1]$, namely a function assigning to each global state $\mathbf{A} \in \mathcal{S}^N$ a penalty in $[0,1]$ expressing how far the values of the parameters on interest in $\mathbf{A}$ are from their desired ones. Intuitively, $\rho(\mathbf{A}) = 0$ if $\mathbf{A}$ respects all the parameters. Since some parameters can be time-dependent, so is the penalty function: at any time step t, the t-penalty function ρ_t compares the global states with respect to the values of the parameters expected at time t.

Example 4. In Example 1 one is interested in verifying that *blue* and *red* agents are balanced. It is then natural to define a penalty function on $\mathcal{S}_{RB}^N$ such that: (i) the penalty is zero if the number of *red* agents is equal to the number of the *blue* ones; (ii) the penalty is higher for less balanced systems, (iii) the penalty does not depend on time, (iv) the penalty is a value in $[0,1]$.

Given the occupancy function OF of $\mathcal{S}_{RB}^N$, we set

$$\rho_t(\mathbf{A}) = \big|\big(\mathrm{OF}(\mathbf{A})[\mathsf{B}] + \mathrm{OF}(\mathbf{A})[\mathsf{BT}]\big) - \big(\mathrm{OF}(\mathbf{A})[\mathsf{R}] + \mathrm{OF}(\mathbf{A})[\mathsf{RT}]\big)\big|,$$

for all $t \in \mathbb{N}$, where, with a slight abuse of notation, we let $\mathrm{OF}(\mathbf{A})[\mathsf{A}]$ denote the component of the occupancy vector corresponding to state A, for $\mathsf{A} \in \mathcal{S}_{RB}$.

The *(timed) metric over global states* is then defined as the difference between the values assigned to them by the penalty function.

Definition 1 (Metric over global spaces). *For any time step t, let $\rho_t\colon \mathcal{S}^N \to [0,1]$ be the t-penalty function on $\mathcal{S}^N$. The* timed metric over global states *in $\mathcal{S}^N$, $m_{\rho,t}\colon \mathcal{S}^N \times \mathcal{S}^N \to [0,1]$, is defined, for all global states $\mathbf{A}_1, \mathbf{A}_2 \in \mathcal{S}^N$, by*

$$m_{\rho,t}(\mathbf{A}_1, \mathbf{A}_2) = |\rho_t(\mathbf{A}_1) - \rho_t(\mathbf{A}_2)|.$$

When no confusion shall arise, we shall drop the ρ, t subscript. It is not hard to see that for all $\mathbf{A}_1, \mathbf{A}_2, \mathbf{A}_3 \in \mathcal{S}^N$ we have that (i) $0 \leq m(\mathbf{A}_1, \mathbf{A}_2) \leq 1$, (ii) $m(\mathbf{A}_1, \mathbf{A}_1) = 0$, (iii) $m(\mathbf{A}_1, \mathbf{A}_2) = m(\mathbf{A}_2, \mathbf{A}_1)$, and (iv) $m(\mathbf{A}_1, \mathbf{A}_2) \leq m(\mathbf{A}_1, \mathbf{A}_3) + m(\mathbf{A}_3, \mathbf{A}_2)$, thus ensuring that m is well defined.

Proposition 1. *Function m is a 1-bounded pseudometric over $\mathcal{S}^N$.*

We remark that the use of the penalty functions allows us to define the distance between two global states, which are elements in $\mathcal{S}^N$, in terms of a distance on $\mathbb{R}$. As we will discuss in Sect. 5, this feature significantly lowers the complexity of the evaluation of the population metric. Moreover, thanks to the penalty function, the metric on global states m could be directly generalised to a metric over $\mathcal{S}^{N_1} \times \mathcal{S}^{N_2}$ with $N_1 \neq N_2$, i.e., a metric over global states of different dimensions. However, to simplify the presentation in the upcoming sections and ease of notation, we preferred to consider only the case of global states of the same dimension.

Lifting m to distributions. The second step in the definition of the population metric consists in lifting m to a metric over probability distributions over global states. In the literature, we can find a wealth of notions of distances over probability measures (see [22] for a survey). For our purposes, the most suitable one is the *Wasserstein metric* [29]. This metric has been applied in several different contexts, from image processing to economics, and it is known under different names, accordingly. Among the most prominent ones, we recall its use in optimal transport problems [30], where it is called the *Earth mover's distance*, and in the definition of bisimulation metrics (see among others [6,10,14,15]), where it is usually referred to as the *Kantorovich metric* [18]. More recently, the Wasserstein metric has been successfully implemented in privacy problems [9,11] and has found a wealth of applications in machine learning for improving the stability of generative adversarial networks training [3,17,27].

Definition 2 (Wasserstein metric). *For any two probability distributions μ, ν on $\mathcal{S}^N$, the* Wasserstein lifting *of m to a distance between μ and ν is defined by*

$$\mathbf{W}(m)(\mu, \nu) = \min_{\mathfrak{w} \in \mathfrak{W}(\mu, \nu)} \sum_{\mathbf{A}, \mathbf{A}' \in \mathcal{S}^N} \mathfrak{w}(\mathbf{A}, \mathbf{A}') \cdot m(\mathbf{A}, \mathbf{A}')$$

where $\mathfrak{W}(\mu, \nu)$ is the set of the couplings for μ and ν, i.e., the set of joint distributions $\mathfrak{w}$ over the product space $\mathcal{S}^N \times \mathcal{S}^N$ having μ and ν as left and right marginal respectively, i.e., $\sum_{\mathbf{A}' \in \mathcal{S}^N} \mathfrak{w}(\mathbf{A}, \mathbf{A}') = \mu(\mathbf{A})$ and $\sum_{\mathbf{A}' \in \mathcal{S}^N} \mathfrak{w}(\mathbf{A}', \mathbf{A}) = \nu(\mathbf{A})$, for all $\mathbf{A} \in \mathcal{S}^N$.

Thus, the infimum in Definition 2 is always achieved and it is, in fact, a minimum.

Due to the convexity of the Wasserstein lifting and in light of Proposition 1, we are guaranteed that $\mathbf{W}(m)$ is a well-defined pseudometric.

Proposition 2. *Function $\mathbf{W}(m)$ is a 1-bounded pseudometric over $\Delta(\mathcal{S}^N)$.*

The population metric. We are now ready to lift the distance $\mathbf{W}(m)$ to a distance over systems, which we call the *population metric*. This is obtained from the comparison of the evolution sequences of the initial configurations of two systems. To favour computational tractability, we will *not* compare *all* the probability distributions in the evolution sequences, but *only* those that are reached at certain time steps, called the *observation times* (OT). To perform such a comparison, we propose a sort of *weighted infinity norm* of the tuple of the Wasserstein distances between the distributions in the evolution sequences. More precisely, we consider a non-increasing function $\lambda: \text{OT} \to (0, 1]$

allowing us to express how much the distance at time t, namely $\mathbf{W}(m_{\rho,t})(\pi_{\mathbf{A}_1,t}, \pi_{\mathbf{A}_2,t})$, affects the overall distance between global states $\mathbf{A}_1$ and $\mathbf{A}_2$. Following the terminology used for behavioural metrics [1, 16], we refer to λ as to the *discount function*, and to $\lambda(t)$ as to the *discount factor at time t*.

Definition 3 (Population metric). *Assume a finite set* OT *of observation times, a penalty function* $\rho_t \colon \mathcal{S}^N \to [0,1]$ *for each* $t \in$ OT *and a discount function* $\lambda \colon$ OT $\to$ $(0,1]$. *The* λ-population metric *over* OT, $\mathfrak{m}_{\mathrm{OT}}^\lambda \colon \mathcal{S}^N \times \mathcal{S}^N \to [0,1]$ *is defined, for all* $\mathbf{A}_1, \mathbf{A}_2 \in \mathcal{S}^N$, *by*

$$\mathfrak{m}_{\mathrm{OT}}^\lambda(\mathbf{A}_1, \mathbf{A}_2) = \sup_{t \in \mathrm{OT}} \lambda(t) \cdot \mathbf{W}(m_{\rho,t})\left(\pi_{\mathbf{A}_1,t}, \pi_{\mathbf{A}_2,t}\right).$$

We remark that although both $m_{\rho,t}$ and $\mathfrak{m}_{\mathrm{OT}}^\lambda$ are formally defined as metrics over global states in $\mathcal{S}^N$, their expressive power is totally different. On one hand, $m_{\rho,t}$ compares the global states $\mathbf{A}_1$ and $\mathbf{A}_2$ seen as *static* objects. In fact, $m_{\rho,t}(\mathbf{A}_1, \mathbf{A}_2)$ is based on the evaluation of ρ_t on the current states of $\mathbf{A}_1$ and $\mathbf{A}_2$. On the other hand, $\mathfrak{m}_{\mathrm{OT}}^\lambda$ compares $\mathbf{A}_1$ and $\mathbf{A}_2$ as *dynamic* objects. The distance $\mathfrak{m}_{\mathrm{OT}}^\lambda(\mathbf{A}_1, \mathbf{A}_2)$ is in fact evaluated by considering the evolution sequences of the two global states.

The following proposition is a direct consequence of Proposition 2.

Proposition 3. *Function* $\mathfrak{m}_{\mathrm{OT}}^\lambda$ *is a 1-bounded pseudometric over* $\mathcal{S}^N$.

Notice that if λ is a *strictly* decreasing function, then it specifies how much the distance of *future events* is mitigated and, moreover, it guarantees that to obtain upper bounds on the population metric only a *finite* number of observations is needed.

Furthermore, as for the metric m, the population metric could be easily generalised to a metric over systems composed by a different number of agents. For consistency with the choice made for Definition 1, we considered only the simple case of systems having the same number of agents. We leave as future work an in-depth analysis of the population metric over $\mathcal{S}^{N_1} \times \mathcal{S}^{N_2}$, for $N_1 \neq N_2$. In particular, our metric could be used to measure the differences between the systems Σ^N and Σ^{N+1}, namely to analyse the impact of the addition (or removal) of a single agent from the system.

4.2 System Adaptability and Reliability

We now apply the population metric to verify whether a system is able to *adjust* its behaviour to changes in the initial conditions. For instance, we are interested in verifying whether a small perturbation to the initial distribution of states produces a controlled perturbation to the dynamics of the system. We express this kind of properties in terms of the notions of *adaptability* and *reliability* of a system. The main difference between these notions is in how time is taken into account.

The notion of adaptability imposes some constraints on the *long term* behaviour of systems, disregarding their possible initial dissimilarities. Given the thresholds $\eta_1, \eta_2 \in [0,1)$ and an observable time $\tilde{t}$, we say that a system Σ^N is adaptable around a *global state* $\mathbf{A}_0$ if whenever the computation is started from a global state $\mathbf{A}'$ that differs from $\mathbf{A}_0$ for at most η_1, then we are guaranteed that the distance that we can observe between the evolution sequences of the two systems after time $\tilde{t}$ is bounded by η_2.

```
 1: function ESTIMATE(A, T, R)
 2:     ∀t : (0 ≤ t ≤ T) : 𝒪_t ← ∅
 3:     counter ← 0
 4:     while counter ≤ R do
 5:         (A_0, ..., A_T) ← SIMULATE(A, T)
 6:         ∀t : 𝒪_t ← 𝒪_t, A_t
 7:         counter ← counter + 1
 8:     end while
 9:     return 𝒪_0, ..., 𝒪_T
10: end function
```

Fig. 3. Function giving R samples of the evolution sequence of **A** with time horizon T.

Definition 4 (Adaptability). *Consider a system specification Σ over N agents. Let $\tilde{t} \in OT$ and $\eta_1, \eta_2 \in [0, 1)$. We say that Σ^N is $(\tilde{t}, \eta_1, \eta_2)$-adaptable around $\mathbf{A}_0$ if*

$$\forall \mathbf{A}' \in \mathcal{S}^N \text{ with } m_{\rho,0}(\mathbf{A}_0, \mathbf{A}') \leq \eta_1 \text{ it holds } \mathsf{m}^\lambda_{\{t \in OT | t \geq \tilde{t}\}}(\mathbf{A}_0, \mathbf{A}') \leq \eta_2.$$

Roughly, Σ^N is adaptable if whenever the starting conditions are changed, then Σ^N is able to return *close* to the original behaviour within the time threshold $\tilde{t}$. The notion of reliability strengthens that of adaptability by bounding the distance on the evolution sequences of systems from the beginning. A system is reliable if it ensures that small variations in the initial conditions cause only bounded variations in its evolution.

Definition 5 (Reliability). *Consider a system specification Σ over N agents. Let $\eta_1, \eta_2 \in [0, 1)$. We say that Σ^N is (η_1, η_2)-reliable around state $\mathbf{A}_0$ if*

$$\forall \mathbf{A}' \in {}^N \text{ with } m_{\rho,0}(\mathbf{A}_0, \mathbf{A}') \leq \eta_1 \text{ it holds } \mathsf{m}^\lambda_{OT}(\mathbf{A}_0, \mathbf{A}') \leq \eta_2.$$

5   Statistical Estimation of Adaptability and Reliability

Given two evolution sequences one could explicitly compute the distance among them. However, this approach is unfeasible when the number of agents in the involved states increases. For this reason, in this section, we discuss an empirical technique that given two global states $\mathbf{A}_1$ and $\mathbf{A}_2$ allows us to generate their evolution sequences and then evaluate the distance between them. The same technique will be used to verify the *adaptability* and *reliability* of a system *around* a given global state **A**.

5.1   Computing Empirical evolution sequences

To compute the *empirical evolution sequence* of a global state **A** the function ESTIMATE in Fig. 3 can be used. This function invokes R times function SIMULATE, i.e., any simulation algorithm sampling a sequence of global states $\mathbf{A}_0, ..., \mathbf{A}_T$, modelling T steps of a computation from $\mathbf{A} = \mathbf{A}_0$. Then, a sequence of observations $\mathcal{O}_0, ..., \mathcal{O}_T$ is computed, where each $\mathcal{O}_t$ is the tuple $\mathbf{A}_t^1, ..., \mathbf{A}_t^R$ of global states observed at time t in each of the R sampled computations. Each $\mathcal{O}_t$ can be used to

```
1: function DISTANCE(A₁, A₂, ρ, λ, OT, R, ℓ)    1: function COMPUTEW(O₁, O₂, ρ)
2:     T ← max_OT                                2:     (A₁¹, ..., A₁ᴿ) ← O₁
3:     O₁¹, ..., O_T¹ ← ESTIMATE(A₁, T, R)        3:     (A₂¹, ..., A₂^{ℓR}) ← O₂
4:     O₁², ..., O_T² ← ESTIMATE(A₂, T, ℓR)       4:     ∀l : (1 ≤ l ≤ R) : ω_l ← ρ(A₁ˡ)
5:     m ← ∞                                      5:     ∀h : (1 ≤ h ≤ ℓR) : ν_h ← ρ(A₂ʰ)
6:     for all t ∈ OT do                          6:     re index {ω_l} such that ω_l ≤ ω_{l+1}
7:         m_t ← COMPUTEW(O_t¹, O_t², ρ_t)        7:     re index {ν_h} such that ν_h ≤ ν_{h+1}
8:         m ← min{m, λ(t) · m_t}                 8:     return (1/ℓR) Σ_{h=1}^{ℓR} |ω_⌈h/ℓ⌉ − ν_h|
9:     end for                                    9: end function
10:    return m
11: end function
```

Fig. 4. Functions used to estimate the population metric on systems.

estimate the real probability distribution $\pi_{\mathbf{A},t}$. For any t, with $0 \leq t \leq T$, we let $\hat{\pi}_{\mathbf{A},t}^R$ be the probability distribution such that, for any $\mathbf{A}' \subseteq \mathcal{S}^N$, $\hat{\pi}_{\mathbf{A},t}^R(\mathbf{A}') = \frac{|\mathbf{A}'|_{\mathcal{O}_t}}{R}$ where $|\mathbf{A}'|_{\mathcal{O}_t}$ denotes the number of occurrences of $\mathbf{A}'$ in $\mathcal{O}_t$. Since the R samples are i.i.d., we can apply to them the weak law of large numbers, obtaining that $\hat{\pi}_{\mathbf{A},t}^R$ converges weakly to $\pi_{\mathbf{A},t}$:

$$\lim_{R \to \infty} \hat{\pi}_{\mathbf{A},t}^R = \pi_{\mathbf{A},t}. \tag{3}$$

5.2 Computing Distance Between Two Configurations

We now evaluate the distance between the evolution sequences of two global states $\mathbf{A}_1$ and $\mathbf{A}_2$ by exploiting the independent samples collected via function ESTIMATE. To this end, we apply the approach of [26] to estimate the Wasserstein distance between two (unknown) distributions. In order to approximate the distance $\mathbf{W}(m_{\rho,t})(\pi_{\mathbf{A}_1,t}, \pi_{\mathbf{A}_2,t})$, for any $0 \leq t \leq T$, we consider R independent samples $\mathcal{O}_{1,t} = \{\mathbf{A}_1^1, ..., \mathbf{A}_1^R\}$ taken from $\pi_{\mathbf{A}_1,t}$ and ℓR samples $\mathcal{O}_{2,t} = \{\mathbf{A}_2^1, ..., \mathbf{A}_2^{\ell R}\}$ taken from $\pi_{\mathbf{A}_2,t}$. We then apply the t-penalty function ρ_t to them, obtaining the two sequences of values $\{\omega_l = \rho_t(\mathbf{A}_1^l) \mid 1 \leq l \leq R\}$ and $\{\nu_h = \rho_t(\mathbf{A}_2^h) \mid 1 \leq h \leq \ell R\}$. Without loss of generality, we can assume that $\omega_l \leq \omega_{l+1}$ and $\nu_h \leq \nu_{h+1}$, i.e., the two sequences are ordered. In light of the next theorem, which is based on results from [26,28,30], we have that $\mathbf{W}(m_{\rho,t})(\pi_{\mathbf{A}_1,t}, \pi_{\mathbf{A}_2,t})$ can be approximated by $\frac{1}{\ell R} \sum_{h=1}^{\ell R} |\omega_{\lceil \frac{h}{\ell} \rceil} - \nu_h|$, and that the latter value converges to the real distance when $R \to \infty$.

Theorem 1. *Let $\pi_{\mathbf{A}_1,t}, \pi_{\mathbf{A}_2,t} \in \Delta(\mathcal{S}^N)$ be unkonwn. Let $\{\mathbf{A}_1^1, ..., \mathbf{A}_1^R\}$ be independent samples taken from $\pi_{\mathbf{A}_1,t}$, and $\{\mathbf{A}_2^1, ..., \mathbf{A}_2^{\ell R}\}$ independent samples taken from $\pi_{\mathbf{A}_2,t}$. Let $\{\omega_l = \rho_t(\mathbf{A}_1^l) \mid 1 \leq l \leq R\}$ and $\{\nu_h = \rho_t(\mathbf{A}_2^h) \mid 1 \leq h \leq \ell R\}$ be the ordered sequences obtained from the samples and the t-penalty function. Then*

$$\mathbf{W}(m_{\rho,t})(\pi_{\mathbf{A}_1,t}, \pi_{\mathbf{A}_2,t}) \overset{a.s.}{=} \lim_{R \to \infty} \frac{1}{\ell R} \sum_{h=1}^{\ell R} |\omega_{\lceil \frac{h}{\ell} \rceil} - \nu_h|.$$

Functions DISTANCE and COMPUTEW in Fig. 4 realise the procedure outlined above. The former takes as input the two global states to compare, the penalty function (seen as the sequence of the t-penalty functions), the discount function λ, the bounded set OT of observation times, and the parameters R and ℓ used to obtain the samplings of the computations. It calls function ESTIMATE to collect the samples $\mathcal{O}_t$ of possible computations during the observation period $[0, \max_{OT}]$. Then, for each observation time $t \in OT$, the distance at time t is computed via the function COMPUTEW$\mathcal{O}_{1,t}, \mathcal{O}_{2,t}, \rho_t$. Since the penalty function allows us to evaluate the Wasserstein distance on $\mathbb{R}$, the complexity of function COMPUTEW is $O(\ell R \log(\ell R))$ due to the sorting of $\{\nu_h \mid h \in [1, \dots, \ell R]\}$ (cf. [26]).

Example 5. We use function COMPUTEW to evaluate the impact of a perturbation in the initial configuration of the system in Example 3. There, we have considered an initial state of the form $\mathbf{A}_1 = \langle \mathsf{B}[25], \mathsf{R}[75], \mathsf{BT}[0], \mathsf{RT}[0] \rangle$. Consider the new initial configuration $\mathbf{A}_2 = \langle \mathsf{B}[0], \mathsf{R}[100], \mathsf{BT}[0], \mathsf{RT}[0] \rangle$. Figure 5(a) shows the variation in time of the distance between $\mathbf{A}_1$ and $\mathbf{A}_2$, for $R = 100$ and $\ell = 10$: after around 10 steps, the two systems cannot be distinguished. Therefore, we can infer that, after around 10 steps, the actual distance between the two systems will be bounded by the approximation error $e_{\mathbf{W}} = |\, \mathbf{W}(m_{\rho,10})(\hat{\pi}^{100}_{\mathbf{A}_1,10}, \hat{\pi}^{1000}_{\mathbf{A}_2,10}) - \mathbf{W}(m_{\rho,10})(\pi_{\mathbf{A}_1,10}, \pi_{\mathbf{A}_2,10})|$. We refer the interested reader to [24, Corollary 3.5, Equation (3.10)] for an estimation of $e_{\mathbf{W}}$.

5.3 Estimating Adaptability and Reliability

We can use a randomised algorithm to verify the adaptability and reliability of a system. Given a global state $\mathbf{A}$, a set OT of observation times and a given threshold $\eta_1 \geq 0$, we can sample M variations $\{\mathbf{A}_1, \dots, \mathbf{A}_M\}$ of $\mathbf{A}$ such that, for any $i = 1, \dots, M$, $m_{\rho,0}(\mathbf{A}, \mathbf{A}_i) \leq \eta_1$. Then, for each sample we can estimate the distance between $\mathbf{A}$ and $\mathbf{A}_i$ at the different time steps in OT, namely $\mathfrak{m}^\lambda_{\{t \in OT | t \geq \tilde{t}\}}(\mathbf{A}, \mathbf{A}_i)$ for any $\tilde{t} \in OT$. Finally, for each $\tilde{t} \in OT$, we let $L_{\tilde{t}} = \max_i \{\mathfrak{m}^\lambda_{\{t \in OT | t \geq \tilde{t}\}}(\mathbf{A}, \mathbf{A}_i)\}$. We can observe that, for the chosen η_1, each $L_{\tilde{t}}$ gives us a lower bound to the $\tilde{t}$-adaptability of our system. Similarly, for $t_{\min} = \min_{OT} t$, $L_{t_{\min}}$ gives a lower bound for its reliability.

Example 6. Figure 5(b) shows the evaluation of $L_{\tilde{t}}$ for configuration $\mathbf{A}_1$ from Example 3 with parameters $M = 20$ and $\eta_1 = 0.25$. Observe that the initial perturbation is not amplified and after 15 steps it is less than 0.05. Hence, our system of Example 3 is $(15, 0.25, \eta_2)$-adaptable around $\mathbf{A}_1$ for any $\eta_2 \geq e_{\mathbf{W}}$.

6 Mean-Field Approximation of Adaptability and Reliability

When the number of agents increases dramatically, sampling the behaviour of each global state may become unfeasible. Hence, in this section we strengthen our randomised algorithm by means of *mean-field approximation* [21]. We have seen in Sect. 3 that we can express the behaviour of a system via the Markov chain $\{\mathbf{X}^{(N)}_{\mathbf{A}}(t)\}_{t \in \mathbb{N}}$ taking values in $\mathcal{S}^N$. However, we can also abstract from the identity of each single agent while focusing only on the fraction of agents in a given state, and model systems behaviour via the occupancy DTMC, namely the Markov chain $\{\mathbf{O}^{(N)}_{\mathbf{A}}(t)\}_{t \in \mathbb{N}}$ taking

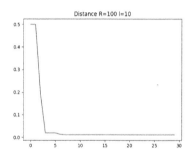

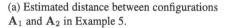

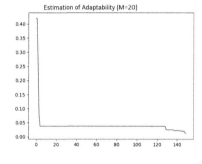

(a) Estimated distance between configurations A_1 and A_2 in Example 5.

(b) Adaptability of A_1 (Example 3) for $M = 20$, $\eta_1 = 0.25$.

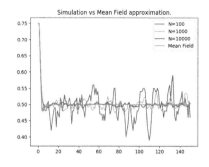

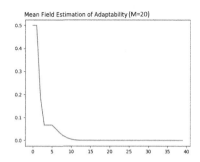

(c) Simulation vs Mean-Field Approximation

(d) Mean-field adaptability of A_1 (Example 3) for $M = 20$, $\eta_1 = 0.25$.

Fig. 5. Some experiments carried out with the Spear Tool.

values in $\mathcal{U}^{|\mathcal{S}|}$. We recall that, for each N, the occupancy DTMC $\{O_A^{(N)}(t)\}_{t \in \mathbb{N}}$ is given by $O_A^{(N)}(t) = OF_{\mathcal{S},N}(X_A^{(N)}(t))$, with initial distribution $\delta_{OF_{\mathcal{S},N}(A)}$.

In the following we use the fundamental result due to Le Boudec et al. [21] that guarantees that when N goes to infinite, the Markov chain $O_A^{(N)}(t)$ converges to a *deterministic behaviour*. Given a global state $A \in \mathcal{S}^N$, we let cA denote the *global state* in $\mathcal{S}^{cN}$ such that $(cA)_{[\gamma \cdot N+k]} = A_{[k]}$ for any $1 \leq k \leq N$ and $0 \leq \gamma < c$. Intuitively, cA consists of c copies of A and it is called a *c-scale* of A. We can observe that for any $A \in \mathcal{S}^N$ and for any $c \geq 1$, $OF_{\mathcal{S},N}(A) = OF_{\mathcal{S},cN}(cA)$. Hence, for all $A_i, A_j \in \mathcal{S}$, $K(OF_{\mathcal{S},N}(A))_{A_i,A_j} = K(OF_{\mathcal{S},cN}(cA))_{A_i,A_j}$. Consequently, *scaling* a state by a factor c has no effect on the behaviour of an agent since the probability to select an action does not change. We can consider the sequence of occupancy DTMCs $\{O_{cA}^{(cN)}(t)\}$ obtained by increasing the scale c of our system. By Theorem 4.1 of [21], this sequence converges *almost surely* to the following deterministic process in $\mathcal{U}^{|\mathcal{S}|}$:

- $D_A(0) = O_A^{(N)}(0)$;
- $D_A(t+1) = D_A(t) \cdot K(D_A(t))$.

In other words,

$$\lim_{c \to \infty} \mathbf{O}_{c\mathbf{A}}^{(cN)}(t) = \mathbf{D}_{\mathbf{A}}(t) \tag{4}$$

Example 7. In Fig. 5c we can observe how when the scale of the system of Example 3 is increased (we consider $N = 100$, $N = 1000$ and $N = 10000$), the single sampled simulation run gets close to the mean-field approximation.

We say that a penalty function $\rho : \mathcal{S}^N \to [0, 1]$ is *scale invariant* if there exists a function $\rho_{\mathbf{o}} : \mathcal{U}^{|\mathcal{S}|} \to [0, 1]$ such that $\rho(\mathbf{A}) = \rho_{\mathbf{o}}(\mathrm{OF}_{\mathcal{S},N}(\mathbf{A}))$. We can use mean-field approximation to study the *adaptability* and *reliability* around a given state $\mathbf{A}$ with respect to a scale invariant penalty function.

Proposition 4. *Assume a penalty function ρ_t that is scale invariant for each $t \in \mathbb{N}$. Let* $\mathfrak{m}_{\mathrm{OT}}^{\lambda}$ *be the population metric defined on $m_{\rho,t}$. Then,*

$$\lim_{c \to \infty} \mathfrak{m}_{\mathrm{OT}}^{\lambda}(c\mathbf{A}_1, c\mathbf{A}_2) = \sup_{t \in \mathrm{OT}} \lambda(t) \cdot |\rho_{\mathbf{o}}(\mathbf{D}_{\mathbf{A}_1}(t)) - \rho_{\mathbf{o}}(\mathbf{D}_{\mathbf{A}_2}(t))|. \tag{5}$$

We let $\mathfrak{mf}_{\mathrm{OT}}^{\lambda}(\mathbf{A}_1, \mathbf{A}_2) = \sup_{t \in \mathrm{OT}} \lambda(t) \cdot |\rho_{\mathbf{o}}(\mathbf{D}_{\mathbf{A}_1}(t)) - \rho_{\mathbf{o}}(\mathbf{D}_{\mathbf{A}_2}(t))|$.

The same randomised algorithm outlined in Sect. 5.3 can be adapted to estimate adaptability and reliability via mean-field approximation. Given a global state $\mathbf{A}$, a set OT of observation times and a threshold $\eta_1 \geq 0$, we can sample M variations $\{\mathbf{A}_1, \ldots, \mathbf{A}_M\}$ of $\mathbf{A}$, such that for any i, $m_{\rho,0}(\mathbf{A}, \mathbf{A}_i) \leq \eta_1$. Then, for each sampled global state we can compute the distance between $\mathbf{A}$ and $\mathbf{A}_i$ by using their *mean field* approximants $\mathbf{D}_{\mathbf{A}_1}(t)$ and $\mathbf{D}_{\mathbf{A}_2}(t)$. Finally, a *lower bound* to the $\tilde{t}$-adaptability of our system can be computed as $L_{\tilde{t}} = \max_i \{\mathfrak{mf}_{\{t \in \mathrm{OT} | t \geq \tilde{t}\}}^{\lambda}(\mathbf{A}, \mathbf{A}_i)\}$. Similarly, for $t_{\min} = \min_{\mathrm{OT}} t$, $L_{t_{\min}}$ gives a lower bound for its reliability.

Example 8. Figure 5d shows the evaluation of $L_{\tilde{t}}$ for configuration $\mathbf{A}_1$ from Example 3 with parameters $M = 20$ and $\eta_1 = 0.25$. Observe that the initial perturbation is not amplified and after 15 steps it is absorbed. Hence, while we increase the scale of our system, we can guarantee that it is $(15, 0.25, \eta_2)$-adaptable around $\mathbf{A}_1$ for any $\eta_2 \geq e_{\mathbf{W}}$.

7   Concluding Remarks

We have proposed the population metric, a pseudometric allowing us to compare the behaviour of self-organising collective systems. This metric quantifies the differences in the evolution sequences of two systems, i.e., the sequences of probability distributions over global states describing the (probabilistic) behaviour of each system. Then we have provided a randomised algorithm for the evaluation of the metric over large scale systems. Moreover, we have shown how we can use the population metric to verify the properties of adaptability and reliability of system, expressing its ability of adjusting its behaviour to perturbations in its initial configuration. We have then modified our algorithm to obtain an estimation of the adaptability and reliability of a system via mean-field approximations.

In this work we have considered a discrete-time approach to systems modelling. Hence, as future work, it would be interesting to provide an adaptation of our framework to system with a continuous model of time. In particular, we could exploit the *fluid-flow* approximation based on [12], in place of the mean-field one, to deal with system with a dramatically large population. Another interesting direction for future research, would be to use our metric to analyse systems with a different number of agents. From the technical point of view, our definitions and results can be directly lifted to cover this case. However, it would allow us to analyse the impact of a new agent (or a new set of agents) on the dynamics of the system. Finally, we could extend our metric approach to study other properties than adaptability and reliability, and thus obtain some measures on systems performance.

References

1. de Alfaro, L., Henzinger, T.A., Majumdar, R.: Discounting the future in systems theory. In: Baeten, J.C.M., Lenstra, J.K., Parrow, J., Woeginger, G.J. (eds.) ICALP 2003. LNCS, vol. 2719, pp. 1022–1037. Springer, Heidelberg (2003). https://doi.org/10.1007/3-540-45061-0_79

2. Anderson, S., Bredeche, N., Eiben, A., Kampis, G., van Steen, M.: Adaptive collective systems: herding black sheep. Bookprints (2013)

3. Arjovsky, M., Chintala, S., Bottou, L.: Wasserstein generative adversarial networks. In: Proceedings of ICML 2017, pp. 214–223 (2017). http://proceedings.mlr.press/v70/arjovsky17a.html

4. Bacci, G., Bacci, G., Larsen, K.G., Mardare, R.: On the total variation distance of semi-Markov chains. In: Pitts, A. (ed.) FoSSaCS 2015. LNCS, vol. 9034, pp. 185–199. Springer, Heidelberg (2015). https://doi.org/10.1007/978-3-662-46678-0_12

5. Bortolussi, L., Hillston, J., Loreti, M.: Fluid approximation of broadcasting systems. Theoret. Comput. Sci. **816**, 221–248 (2020). https://doi.org/10.1016/j.tcs.2020.02.020

6. Breugel, F.: A behavioural pseudometric for metric labelled transition systems. In: Abadi, M., de Alfaro, L. (eds.) CONCUR 2005. LNCS, vol. 3653, pp. 141–155. Springer, Heidelberg (2005). https://doi.org/10.1007/11539452_14

7. Bures, T., Plasil, F., Kit, M., Tuma, P., Hoch, N.: Software abstractions for component interaction in the internet of things. Computer **49**(12), 50–59 (2016)

8. Castiglioni, V.: Trace and testing metrics on nondeterministic probabilistic processes. In: Proceedings of EXPRESS/SOS 2018. EPTCS, vol. 276, pp. 19–36 (2018). https://doi.org/10.4204/EPTCS.276.4

9. Castiglioni, V., Chatzikokolakis, K., Palamidessi, C.: A logical characterization of differential privacy via behavioral metrics. In: Bae, K., Ölveczky, P.C. (eds.) FACS 2018. LNCS, vol. 11222, pp. 75–96. Springer, Cham (2018). https://doi.org/10.1007/978-3-030-02146-7_4

10. Castiglioni, V., Loreti, M., Tini, S.: The metric linear-time branching-time spectrum on non-deterministic probabilistic processes. Theoret. Comput. Sci. **813**, 20–69 (2020). https://doi.org/10.1016/j.tcs.2019.09.019

11. Chatzikokolakis, K., Gebler, D., Palamidessi, C., Xu, L.: Generalized bisimulation metrics. In: Baldan, P., Gorla, D. (eds.) CONCUR 2014. LNCS, vol. 8704, pp. 32–46. Springer, Heidelberg (2014). https://doi.org/10.1007/978-3-662-44584-6_4

12. Darling, R., Norris, J.: Differential equation approximations for Markov chains. Probab. Surv. **5**, 37–79 (2008). https://doi.org/10.1214/07-PS121

13. De Nicola, R., Loreti, M., Pugliese, R., Tiezzi, F.: A formal approach to autonomic systems programming: the SCEL language. ACM Trans. Auton. Adapt. Syst. **9**(2), 7:1–7:29 (2014). https://doi.org/10.1145/2619998

14. Deng, Y., Chothia, T., Palamidessi, C., Pang, J.: Metrics for action-labelled quantitative transition systems. Electron. Not. Theoret. Comput. Sci. **153**(2), 79–96 (2006). https://doi.org/10.1016/j.entcs.2005.10.033

15. Desharnais, J., Gupta, V., Jagadeesan, R., Panangaden, P.: Metrics for labeled Markov systems. In: Baeten, J.C.M., Mauw, S. (eds.) CONCUR 1999. LNCS, vol. 1664, pp. 258–273. Springer, Heidelberg (1999). https://doi.org/10.1007/3-540-48320-9_19

16. Desharnais, J., Gupta, V., Jagadeesan, R., Panangaden, P.: Metrics for labelled Markov processes. Theoret. Comput. Sci. **318**(3), 323–354 (2004). https://doi.org/10.1016/j.tcs.2003.09.013

17. Gulrajani, I., Ahmed, F., Arjovsky, M., Dumoulin, V., Courville, A.C.: Improved training of Wasserstein GANs. In: Proceedings of Advances in Neural Information Processing Systems, pp. 5767–5777 (2017). http://papers.nips.cc/paper/7159-improved-training-of-wasserstein-gans

18. Kantorovich, L.V.: On the transfer of masses. Dokl. Akad. Nauk **37**(2), 227–229 (1942)

19. Kopetz, H.: Internet of things. In: Kopetz, H. (ed.) Real-Time Systems. Real-Time Systems Series, pp. 307–323. Springer, Boston (2011). https://doi.org/10.1007/978-1-4419-8237-7_13

20. Latella, D., Loreti, M., Massink, M.: On-the-fly PCTL fast mean-field approximated model-checking for self-organising coordination. Sci. Comput. Program. **110**, 23–50 (2015). https://doi.org/10.1016/j.scico.2015.06.009

21. Le Boudec, J.Y., McDonald, D., Mundinger, J.: A generic mean field convergence result for systems of interacting objects. In: Proceedings of QEST 2007, pp. 3–18. IEEE Computer Society (2007). https://doi.org/10.1109/QEST.2007.8

22. Rachev, S.T., Klebanov, L.B., Stoyanov, S.V., Fabozzi, F.J.: The Methods of Distances in the Theory of Probability and Statistics. Springer, New York (2013). https://doi.org/10.1007/978-1-4614-4869-3

23. Song, L., Deng, Y., Cai, X.: Towards automatic measurement of probabilistic processes. In: Proceedings of QSIC 2007, pp. 50–59 (2007). https://doi.org/10.1109/QSIC.2007.65

24. Sriperumbudur, B.K., Fukumizu, K., Gretton, A., Schölkopf, B., Lanckriet, G.R.G.: On the empirical estimation of integral probability metrics. Electron. J. Stat. **6**, 1550–1599 (2021). https://doi.org/10.1214/12-EJS722

25. Talcott, C., Nigam, V., Arbab, F., Kappé, T.: Formal specification and analysis of robust adaptive distributed cyber-physical systems. In: Bernardo, M., De Nicola, R., Hillston, J. (eds.) SFM 2016. LNCS, vol. 9700, pp. 1–35. Springer, Cham (2016). https://doi.org/10.1007/978-3-319-34096-8_1

26. Thorsley, D., Klavins, E.: Approximating stochastic biochemical processes with Wasserstein pseudometrics. IET Syst. Biol. **4**(3), 193–211 (2010). https://doi.org/10.1049/iet-syb.2009.0039

27. Tolstikhin, I.O., Bousquet, O., Gelly, S., Schölkopf, B.: Wasserstein auto-encoders. In: Proceedings of ICLR 2018 (2018). https://openreview.net/forum?id=HkL7n1-0b

28. Vallender, S.S.: Calculation of the Wasserstein distance between probability distributions on the line. Theory Probab. Appl. **18**(4), 784–786 (1974)

29. Vaserstein, L.N.: Markovian processes on countable space product describing large systems of automata. Probl. Peredachi Inf. **5**(3), 64–72 (1969)

30. Villani, C.: Optimal Transport: Old and New, vol. 338. Springer, Heidelberg (2008). https://doi.org/10.1007/978-3-540-71050-9

31. Wirsing, M., Hölzl, M., Koch, N., Mayer, P. (eds.): Software Engineering for Collective Autonomic Systems. LNCS, vol. 8998. Springer, Cham (2015). https://doi.org/10.1007/978-3-319-16310-9

Centrality-Preserving Exact Reductions of Multi-Layer Networks

Tatjana Petrov$^{(\boxtimes)}$ (iD) and Stefano Tognazzi$^{(\boxtimes)}$

University of Konstanz, Konstanz, Germany
{tatjana.petrov,stefano.tognazzi}@uni-konstanz.de

Abstract. Multi-Layer Networks (MLN) generalise the traditional, single layered networks, by allowing to simultaneously express multiple aspects of relationships in collective systems, while keeping the description intuitive and compact. As such, they are increasingly gaining popularity for modelling Collective Adaptive Systems (CAS), e.g. engineered cyber-physical systems or animal collectives. One of the most important notions in network analysis are centrality measures, which inform us about the relative importance of nodes. Computing centrality measures is often challenging for large and dense single-layer networks. This challenge is even more prominent in the multi-layer setup, and thus motivates the design of efficient, centrality-preserving MLN reduction techniques. Network centrality does not naturally translate to its multi-layer counterpart, since the interpretation of the relative importance of nodes and layers may differ across application domains. In this paper, we take a notion of eigenvector-based centrality for a special type of MLNs (multiplex MLNs), with undirected, weighted edges, which was recently proposed in the literature. Then, we define and implement a framework for exact reductions for this class of MLNs and accompanying eigenvector centrality. Our method is inspired by the existing bisimulation-based exact model reductions for single-layered networks: the idea behind the reduction is to identify and aggregate nodes (resp. layers) with the same centrality score. We do so via efficient, static, syntactic transformations. We empirically demonstrate the speed up in the computation over a range of real-world MLNs from different domains including biology and social science.

Keywords: Multi-Layer Networks · Centrality measures · Model reduction · Efficient algorithms

1 Introduction

Traditional network analysis has facilitated key developments in research on Collective Adaptive Systems (CAS). CAS are a focus of important research efforts of today, such as ensuring the safety of cyber-physical systems, planning for smart cities, or understanding animal collective behaviour. These systems consist of a large number of entities which continuously interact with each other and the

T. Margaria and B. Steffen (Eds.): ISoLA 2020, LNCS 12477, pp. 397–415, 2020.
https://doi.org/10.1007/978-3-030-61470-6_24

environment, they self-organise and often give rise to a system-level dynamics, *emergent behaviours*, which can not be seen by studying individuals in isolation. Network representation of a collective system is intuitive, and it allows to reason over the different aspects of the modelled system, e.g. information flows, or its evolution over time. Network analysis often centers around classification of network components – nodes, edges etc. – wrt. different importance notions. Importance is defined through a *centrality* measure, and different algorithms for computing such measures have been proposed over time. A centrality measure is a real-valued function which associates nodes to their importance and, therefore, allows to rank them accordingly. Historically, the Bonacich index [5,6] (most often referred to as *eigenvector centrality*) and other extensions inspired by the Bonacich index such as Katz centrality [31] and PageRank [42] played a prominent role in network analysis. Other measures of centrality are based accordingly on different factors such as shortest paths [28], diffusion capability [1] and nodes with high contagion potential [14]. Although each of these notions measure different features of the nodes, they share common mathematical traits [4].

However, the traditional, single-layered networks allow to capture only one type of interaction among nodes. In many real-world scenarios, relations among individuals have multiple facets: in social networks, the same individuals may communicate via multiple communication platforms (i.e., they can use different online social networks to spread and gather information [54]). During epidemics, individuals interact both in the physical world, in which they spread the infection, and in a virtual communication network, where awareness about the disease is spread [26]. Moreover, animals belonging to the same collective (herd, fish school, etc.) can relate to each other differently through different activities such as grooming, social aggregation, foraging, as shown for baboons [2,23], dolphins [25] and birds [21].

Any finite, discrete number of different communication aspects among a set of agents, can be formally captured by adding typed edges or edge colours to the network description. Enriching the network formalism with multiple views/layers results in a multi-layer network (MLN) [17]. MLNs offer a novel way to model interactions among the components of a system as connected layers of different types of interactions. General MLNs allow for stacking up a collection of graphs over possibly different node-sets, through arbitrary coupling relationships between pairs of layers. In this work, we focus on a class of MLNs called *multiplex networks*. A multiplex is a collection of graphs over the same set of nodes but different edge sets, each of which is modelling a different type of interaction. Single-layer Networks are conveniently represented as matrices and many tools from matrix analysis have proven to be useful in identifying important network components. Along these lines, multiplex MLNs can be represented using tensors.

Carrying over the theory from network analysis to MLNs is desirable but non-trivial: most of the notions and concepts that are fundamental for single-layer network centrality do not naturally translate to its multi-layer counterpart, since the interpretation of the relative importance of nodes and layers may differ across application domains. For instance, in an effort to extend the Bonacich index to MLNs, several eigenvector-based centrality measures have been defined for multiplexes in the last few years [3,18,19,46]. In this work, we focus on the extension presented in [50] which is based on eigenvector centrality for undirected and (potentially) weighted multiplex MLNs. Among the large variety of methodologies for single-layer network analysis [29] such as clustering [7], blockmodeling [8] and role-equivalent partitioning [35,53], we here aim for exact, centrality-preserving network reduction. In general, model reduction techniques aim to provide a smaller or simpler dynamical model from the original one. Reductions are *exact*, when they guarantee an exact, provable relationship between their respective solutions, without error (otherwise, the reductions are *approximate*, when the error is either guaranteed or estimated). Exact, centrality-preserving network reduction was proposed in the context of single-layer networks [48]. This method is based on efficient model reduction framework for more general dynamical systems [27,49]; The core of these frameworks is based on an efficient partition-refinement procedure of Paige and Tarjan [43]. More specifically, some model reduction techniques based on lumping states have shown to preserve centrality properties of single-layer networks (such as Eigenvector centrality, Katz centrality and PageRank centrality) while, at the same time, relating to a variety of notions from different fields: exact role assignment [53], equitable partitions [37,38], lumpability [22,24] and bisimulation [44,51].

In this work, we define and implement a framework for exact model reduction of multiplex MLNs, by lumping states and layers. Reduction is designed so to preserve the eigenvector centrality for multiplex MLNs, defined in [50] (i.e., two nodes equivalent in the ODEs enjoy the same eigenvector centrality). While our proposed framework directly extends the concept used in [48] for single-layer networks, the major technical challenge arising in the multi-layer setup is that the iterative scheme for computing eigenvector centrality for MLNs contains non-linear terms. In addition, two real-valued exponents, introduced to guarantee convergence, require additional care when lifting from the reduced solution to the original one. The relevance of our framework is demonstrated by benchmarking over a number of real-world multiplex MLNs.

Paper outline. Section 2 reviews the background notions, while Sect. 3 introduces the proposed model reduction framework. Section 4 features an experimental evaluation on real-world multiplex MLNs. Section 5 concludes the paper.

2   Background

In this section we provide an overview of the notions that will be used throughout the paper: single- and multi-layer networks (MLNs), eigenvector centrality measure for MLNs, IDOL programs for specifying dynamical systems and model reduction techniques based on Backward Differential Equivalence.

Notation. Throughout this work, when clear from context, we will use x_i both to denote the i-th element of vector $\boldsymbol{x}$ or the value of the map $x(i)$ (following Definition 3). For a partition $\mathcal{H}$ over a variable set $V_p \subseteq \{\mathsf{x}_1, \mathsf{x}_2, \ldots\}$, induced by an equivalence relation $\sim_{\mathcal{H}} \subseteq V_p \times V_p$, we will denote elements of a partition class $H \in \mathcal{H}$ by $\mathsf{x}_{H,1}, \mathsf{x}_{H,2}, \ldots, \mathsf{x}_{H,|H|}$. We denote by $\|\cdot\|_1$ the 1-norm. We will denote with $V_N = \{1, \ldots, N\}$, $V_L = \{1, \ldots, L\}$ the set of nodes and layers, respectively. Vectors will be assumed to be written in column notation.

2.1   Networks and Multiplex Multi-Layer Networks

Definition 1. A (weighted, directed) *graph* is a pair $G = (V_N, E)$, where V_N is a set of $N \geq 1$ nodes and $E : V_N \times V_N \to \mathbb{R}_{\geq 0}$ is an edge-weighting function, such that $E(i, j) = 0$ reflects that there is no edge in the graphical representation of the network. In matrix notation, a graph is given by a non-negative *adjacency matrix* $\boldsymbol{A} = (A_{ij}) \in \mathbb{R}_{\geq 0}^{N \times N}$. Graph G is *undirected*, if the matrix $\boldsymbol{A}$ is symmetric.

In this paper, we will work with a generalisation of networks called *multiplex networks* or *edge-colored-graphs*, which are useful for simultaneously representing different kinds of relationships over the same set of nodes. This paper will focus on weighted, undirected multiplex networks.

Definition 2. A *multiplex network* with L layers is an ordered collection of L graphs over the same set of nodes:

$$\mathcal{G} = \{G^{(l)} = (V_N, E^{(l)})\}_{l \in V_L},$$

where $E^{(l)} : V_N \times V_N \to \mathbb{R}_{\geq 0}$ are the edge weights at layer $l \in V_L$. For every layer l, we denote the non-negative adjacency matrix of the graph $G^{(l)}$ by $\boldsymbol{A}^{(l)} = (A_{ij}^{(l)}) \in \mathbb{R}_{\geq 0}^{N \times N}$. Then, the multiplex network can be represented by a 3rd-order *adjacency tensor*:

$$\boldsymbol{\mathcal{A}} = (\mathcal{A}_{ijl}) \in \mathbb{R}_{\geq 0}^{N \times N \times L}, \text{ such that } \mathcal{A}_{ijl} := A_{ij}^{(l)} = E^{(l)}(i, j),$$

that is, $\mathcal{A}_{ijl}$ is the weight of the edge from node i to node j in layer l.

Example 1. The adjacency tensor for the multiplex depicted in Fig. 1 left is given by layers $\boldsymbol{\mathcal{A}}^{(1)} = \begin{pmatrix} 0 & 1 & 1 \\ 1 & 0 & 0 \\ 1 & 0 & 0 \end{pmatrix}$ and $\boldsymbol{\mathcal{A}}^{(2)} = \begin{pmatrix} 0 & 1 & 0 \\ 1 & 0 & 1 \\ 0 & 1 & 0 \end{pmatrix}$.

Remark 1. While in this work we will focus on multiplex networks, they are a special case of a more general notion of interconnected *multilayer networks* (MLNs), where layers can have different node sets, and, moreover, they can be coupled across layers in arbitrary ways. For example, modelling public transport by different means (e.g. bus, train or metro) requires such a model.

2.2 Centrality Measures

Given an undirected graph $G = (V_N, E)$ and its adjacency matrix $A \in \mathbb{R}_{\geq 0}^{N \times N}$, we first recall the definition of eigenvector centrality for single-layer networks [39].

Definition 3. *Eigenvector centrality* $x : V_N \to \mathbb{R}_{\geq 0}$ maps each node to the weighted sum of eigenvector centralities of all nodes directly reachable from it: for $i \in V_N$, $x(i) = \frac{1}{\lambda} \sum_{j \in V_n} A_{ij} x(j)$, where $\frac{1}{\lambda}$ is some positive constant. In vector notation, the eigenvector centrality vector $x \in \mathbb{R}_{\geq 0}^{V_N}$ is such that $Ax = \lambda x$, that is, x is the right eigenvector wrt. the adjacency matrix A.

For a given graph with adjacency matrix A, eigenvector centrality may not be well-defined, that is, there may exist no unique non-negative right eigenvector (up to linear scaling). By the famous Perron-Frobenius result, whenever the largest real eigenvalue of A is unique, eigenvector centrality is guaranteed to be well-defined, and it is the respective eigenvector, with all non-negative entries. When eigenvector centrality is well-defined, it can be efficiently computed with the power iteration scheme. We restate this well-known result, for the sake of transparent analogy with the case of MLN's, which we introduce next.

Theorem 1 ([39]). *If there exists a unique, non-negative eigenvector centrality on A, denoted by x^*, and such that $\|x^*\|_1 = 1$, it can be computed as a limit of the power iteration sequence $x^{(k)} = \frac{A x^{(k-1)}}{\|A x^{(k-1)}\|_1}$ for $k \geq 0$ and initially $x^{(0)} = \mathbf{1}^N$.*

In this paper, we will use one possible extension of eigenvector centrality for multiplex MLNs, proposed in [50]. The authors propose a 2-map, f-*eigenvector centrality*, in which the first component of the map represents the centrality associated to the *nodes*, while the second component is centrality associated to the *layers*.

Definition 4 ([50]). Let $\mathcal{A} \in \mathbb{R}_{\geq 0}^{N \times N \times L}$ be the adjacency tensor of an MLN with weighted, undirected layers, and let $\alpha, \beta > 0$ be such that $\frac{2}{\beta} < (\alpha - 1)$. Then, define $f = (f_1, f_2) : \mathbb{R}_{\geq 0}^N \times \mathbb{R}_{\geq 0}^L \to \mathbb{R}_{\geq 0}^N \times \mathbb{R}_{\geq 0}^L$ as follows:

$$f_1(x, t)_i = \left(\sum_{j=1}^{N} \sum_{l=1}^{L} A_{ijl} x_j t_l \right)^{\frac{1}{\alpha}} \text{ for } i \in V_N, \quad f_2(x, t)_l = \left(\sum_{i=1}^{N} \sum_{j=1}^{N} A_{ijl} x_i x_j \right)^{\frac{1}{\beta}} \text{ for } l \in V_L.$$

In words, the centrality x_i of node i is a sum of the centralities of each of its neighbouring nodes, weighted by the product of the edge-weight and the centrality of the layer at which that connection lies. At the same time, the centrality of a layer t_l is a sum of the centrality of all edges at that layer, where an importance of an edge is, in addition to its own weight, weighted by the centrality of the two nodes which constitute it. The parameters α and β are introduced in order to guarantee convergence and respectively well-definedness in case of undirected MLNs. Further discussion is beyond the scope of this manuscript and we refer the interested reader to [50].

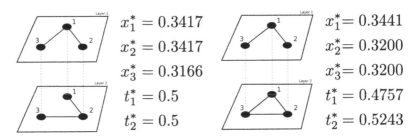

$$x_1^* = 0.3417$$
$$x_2^* = 0.3417$$
$$x_3^* = 0.3166$$
$$t_1^* = 0.5$$
$$t_2^* = 0.5$$

$$x_1^* = 0.3441$$
$$x_2^* = 0.3200$$
$$x_3^* = 0.3200$$
$$t_1^* = 0.4757$$
$$t_2^* = 0.5243$$

Fig. 1. An example with two MLNs and their respective f-eigenvector centralities.

Similarly as in the case of single-layer networks, a power iteration scheme for computing f-centrality is desired. Throughout the rest of the work, we will use a normalised version of f-mapping, denoted by g:

$$g(x,t) = \left(\frac{f_1(x,t)}{\|f_1(x,t)\|_1}, \frac{f_2(x,t)}{\|f_2(x,t)\|_1} \right)$$

We now restate a result from [50], that, for a given MLN with undirected layers, f-centrality is well-defined and it can be computed as a limit of a power iterative sequence.

Theorem 2 ([50]). There exists a unique, non-negative fixed point of the mapping g. Moreover, this fixed point, denoted by $(x^*, t^*) \in \mathbb{R}^N_{\geq 0} \times \mathbb{R}^L_{\geq 0}$, is a limit of the following iterative scheme[1]:

$$(x^{(k)}, t^{(k)}) = g(x^{(k-1)}, t^{(k-1)}) \text{ for } k \geq 1 \text{ and initially } (x^{(0)}, t^{(0)}) = (\mathbf{1}^N, \mathbf{1}^L) \tag{1}$$

Notice that, from the definition of g, independently of $k \geq 0$, it holds that $\|x^{(k)}\|_1 = \|t^{(k)}\|_1 = 1$, including the limit value (x^*, t^*).

Example 2. Consider the MLN depicted in Fig. 1 (left). The iterative scheme to compute the f-eigenvector centrality (Definition 4) is the following:

$$x_1^{(k+1)} = (1x_2^{(k)}t_1^{(k)} + 1x_3^{(k)}t_1^{(k)} + 1x_2^{(k)}t_2^{(k)})^{\frac{1}{\alpha}}/\|f_1(x,t)\|_1$$
$$x_2^{(k+1)} = (1x_1^{(k)}t_1^{(k)} + 1x_1^{(k)}t_2^{(k)} + 1x_3^{(k)}t_2^{(k)})^{\frac{1}{\alpha}}/\|f_1(x,t)\|_1$$
$$x_3^{(k+1)} = (1x_1^{(k)}t_1^{(k)} + 1x_2^{(k)}t_2^{(k)})^{\frac{1}{\alpha}}/\|f_1(x,t)\|_1$$
$$t_1^{(k+1)} = (2x_1^{(k)}x_2^{(k)} + 2x_1^{(k)}x_3^{(k)})^{\frac{1}{\beta}}/\|f_2(x,t)\|_1$$
$$t_2^{(k+1)} = (2x_1^{(k)}x_2^{(k)} + 2x_2^{(k)}x_3^{(k)})^{\frac{1}{\beta}}/\|f_2(x,t)\|_1$$

---

[1] We refer the interested reader to the original reference, for a discussion on the error and rate of convergence.

Example 3. In Fig. 1 we show two different MLNs and their respective $\boldsymbol{f}$-eigenvector centralities. Adding an edge at Layer 2 changes both the node centrality and the layer centrality scores. More specifically, Node 1 and 3 gain importance while Node 2 loses importance. Moreover, if in the left example the two layers had equivalent centralities, in the right one, Layer 2 becomes more important because it contains more connections between high-centrality-nodes. This shows that when we choose $\boldsymbol{f}$-eigenvector centrality as the measure of choice, the role played by the nodes and layers is intertwined and therefore the two aspects of the $\boldsymbol{f}$ mapping can not be computed independently.

2.3 Intermediate Drift Oriented Language (IDOL)

The Intermediate Drift Oriented Language (IDOL) is a language for describing non-linear, first-order, autonomous and explicit finite systems of coupled ordinary differential equations (ODEs). We here report the fragment of the syntax and semantics of IDOL which is useful for presenting this work.

Syntax. An IDOL program p over a set of variables V_p is written in the following syntax:

$$p ::= \varepsilon \mid \mathrm{x}'_i = \eta, p$$

$$\eta ::= n \mid \mathrm{x}_i \mid \eta + \eta \mid \eta \cdot \eta$$

where $\mathrm{x}_i \in V_p$, $n \in \mathbb{Z}$ and ε is used to define the end of the program.

Semantics. We will consider conventional ODE semantics for a given IDOL program p, as the solution of the system of ODE's that it represents. The solution map $[\![\cdot]\!] : \mathbb{R}_{\geq 0}^{|V_p|} \to (V_p \to ([0, T) \to \mathbb{R}_{\geq 0}))$ will (deterministically) map each initial condition and a variable to a trace from the time domain with horizon $T \in \mathbb{R}_{\geq 0}$ to a value. For simplicity, we will denote the solution for variable x_i by $[\![\mathrm{x}_i]\!]_{x_0}$, and we omit the dependency on initial condition $x_0 \in \mathbb{R}_{\geq 0}^{|V_p|}$ when clear from context.

2.4 Backward Differential Equivalence

Backward differential equivalence (BDE) is a model reduction technique for dynamical systems written in IDOL [9,12]. BDE groups IDOL variables which are *exact fluid lumpable* - they have the same ODE semantics whenever they are given the same initial assignment. Finding the (largest) BDE amounts to finding the coarsest partition over the variable set, which ensures that the semantic criterion is met. This criterion allows to construct a smaller IDOL program, using only one representative variable from each partition class. The reduction algorithms proposed in [9,12] are only syntactically manipulating the IDOL program, and they are of polynomial complexity in the number of variables of the program. We propose in this paper to use BDE reductions, to reduce the computation of $\boldsymbol{f}$-centrality measure for MLNs.

Definition 5. We call $\boldsymbol{x} \in \mathbb{R}_{\geq 0}^{|V_p|}$ *constant on* $\mathcal{H}$ if for all $H \in \mathcal{H}$ and all $x_i, x_j \in H$, it holds that $x_i = x_j$.

Definition 6. Let p be an IDOL program and $\mathcal{H}$ a partition over the variable set V_p. Then, the IDOL program p is *exact fluid lumpable wrt. partition* $\mathcal{H}$, if $[\![\boldsymbol{x}]\!]_{\boldsymbol{x}_0}(t)$ is constant on $\mathcal{H}$ for all $t \geq 0$, whenever $\boldsymbol{x}_0$ is constant on $\mathcal{H}$. Then, we will call $\mathcal{H}$ a *BDE partition* of V_p.

Following [9], the coarsest BDE partition can be computed in polynomial time complexity, for any IDOL program which corresponds to a set of chemical reactions with mass-action kinetics.

We now state the result which shows how to use a BDE to construct a reduced IDOL program, operating over only the representative variables (BDE quotient).

Theorem 3 ([10]). *Let p be an IDOL program and $\mathcal{H}$ a BDE partition over its variable set V_p, and $T > 0$ a time horizon. The backward reduced program of p with respect to $\mathcal{H}$, denoted by $\tilde{p}_{\mathcal{H}}$, is defined over a set of variables $V_{p_{\mathcal{H}}} = \{\tilde{\mathsf{x}}_1, \dots, \tilde{\mathsf{x}}_{|\mathcal{H}|}\}$, and with the following update functions:*

$$\tilde{\mathsf{x}}_H' = \eta_{H,1}[\mathsf{x}_{\bar{H},1}/\tilde{\mathsf{x}}_{\bar{H}}, \dots, \mathsf{x}_{\bar{H},|\bar{H}|}/\tilde{\mathsf{x}}_{\bar{H}} : \bar{H} \in \mathcal{H}], \quad \text{for } H \in \mathcal{H},$$

where, $\mathsf{x}_{\bar{H},i}/\tilde{\mathsf{x}}_{\bar{H}}$ *denotes the action of renaming variable* $\mathsf{x}_{\bar{H},i}$ *by* $\tilde{\mathsf{x}}_{\bar{H}}$.

Originally designed for reducing ODEs, BDE techniques have also been applied for reducing single-layer networks, continuous-time Markov chains (CTMCs) and differential algebraic equations. In particular, in [48], a property-preserving exact model reduction algorithm for networks is shown. The given network is first transformed into an IDOL program, and then a BDE reduction ensuring exact fluid lumpability is applied. We restate a Theorem showing that BDE reduction also preserves the measure of eigenvector centrality.

Theorem 4 ([48]). *Given a graph $G = (V_N, E)$ with adjacency matrix $\boldsymbol{A}$, let p_G be the IDOL program over the set of variables V_N:*

$$\mathsf{x}_i' = \sum_{1 \leq j \leq n} A_{ij} \cdot \mathsf{x}_j \,, \quad \text{for all } i \in V_N.$$

Let x_i^* denote the eigenvector centrality of node i. Then, $\mathcal{H}$ is a BDE of p_G if and only if, for all $H \in \mathcal{H}$ and for all $x_i, x_j \in H$, it holds that $x_i^* = x_j^*$.

In words, the transformation from network to IDOL program is such that the equation for the derivative of variable x_i is the weighted sum of its direct (outgoing) edges[2]. So, the key idea in the transformation from the network to an IDOL program is that the equations in the IDOL program exactly match the iterative scheme for computing the centrality measure of interest.

Notice that the obtained IDOL program contains only linear transformations over its variables. We next propose an analogue of Theorem 4 for multiplex MLNs. The translation to an IDOL program will encode the iterative scheme for computing $\boldsymbol{f}$-centrality, which involves non-linear terms (of second order).

---

[2] In case of symmetric graphs, ingoing and outgoing edges will be indistinguishable and overall neighbours are accounted for.

3   Centrality-Preserving MLN Reduction

Given a multi-layered network, its f-centrality can be computed with the iterative scheme g presented in Theorem 2 (Eq. 1). Our aim is to bypass the direct computation and instead compute the f-centrality indirectly, by first detecting sets of variables which evolve equivalently throughout the iterations, and then proposing a reduced iterative scheme $\tilde{g}$, where only one representative variable is kept for each set of equivalent ones.

To do so, we first introduce an assignment of an IDOL program to a given MLN. Then, given an IDOL program, we compute its BDE-equivalent quotient, as described in Sect. 2. BDE equivalence guarantees that the original and smaller IDOL programs have the same differential, continuous-step semantics. On the other hand, the iterative scheme g defines a discrete-step semantics over the variables of the MLN. Our proposal is to compute the centrality measure of the original MLN using the smaller IDOL program. To do so, we need to show that the reduced iterative scheme $\tilde{g}$ over the BDE-quotient of the original IDOL program, preserves the solutions of the iterative scheme g. A diagram of the workflow of the proposed framework is presented in Fig. 2.

The following theorem shows which are the quantities that we should account for when we search for equivalences among the centrality scores.

Theorem 5. For $i \in V_N$, define the quantity of interest

$$\bar{x}_i^{(k)} := \sum_{a=1}^{N} \sum_{l=1}^{L} A_{ial} x_a^{(k)} t_l^{(k)},$$

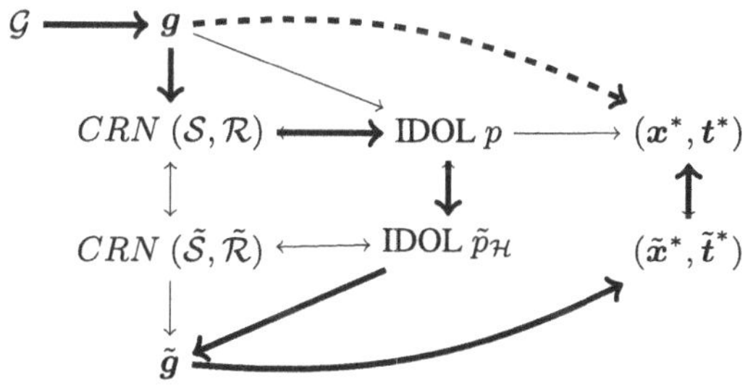

Fig. 2. An illustration of the proposed methodology. The arrows are used for illustrative purpose and they are not to be formally interpreted. For a given MLN $\mathcal{G}$, its f-centrality vector $(\boldsymbol{x}^*, \boldsymbol{t}^*)$ can be computed directly through the iterative map g (dotted line). Alternatively, as depicted with thick full arrows, the equations in g can first be translated into an IDOL program p with variables, and its BDE quotient program $p_\mathcal{H}$ is used to define a reduced iterative scheme $\tilde{g}$ over a reduced set of variables, the solution of which, $(\tilde{\boldsymbol{x}}^*, \tilde{\boldsymbol{t}}^*)$, allows to exactly reconstruct the f-centrality of the original MLN.

which is the right hand side of the mapping $\boldsymbol{f}$ from Definition 4, without the exponential operator α. Then, for all pairs of nodes $i, j \in V_N$, it holds that

$$\text{if } \bar{x}_i^{(k)} = \bar{x}_j^{(k)} \text{ then } x_i^{(k+1)} = x_j^{(k+1)}, \text{ for all } k \geq 0.$$

The key idea is to go from the definition of the multilayer network eigenvector centrality obtained with the iterative scheme (1) to an IDOL program p such that there is a correspondence between the node and the layer eigenvector centrality and the variables of the IDOL program.

Definition 7. (IDOL translation) Let $\mathcal{G}$ be a multiplex network and let $\mathcal{A}_{ijl}$ be the 3-rd order adjacency tensor of the multiplex $\mathcal{G}$. We define an IDOL program p, with $V_p = V_N \cup V_L$, as follows:

$$\mathsf{x}_i' = \sum_{j=1}^{N} \sum_{l=1}^{L} \mathcal{A}_{ijl} \mathsf{x}_j \mathsf{t}_l \quad \mathsf{t}_l' = \sum_{i=1}^{N} \sum_{j=1}^{N} \mathcal{A}_{ijl} \mathsf{x}_i \mathsf{x}_j$$

for all $i \in V_N$ and for all $l \in V_L$. With $\boldsymbol{x}_0 = \mathbb{1}^N$ and $\boldsymbol{t}_0 = \mathbb{1}^L$.

We now want to identify which nodes in the MLN have identical $\boldsymbol{f}$-eigenvector centrality. This holds if they follow equivalent equations in the iterative scheme used for computing them. Similarly to the result presented in Theorem 4 which shows a similar translation for single layer networks, the iterative scheme equations used to compute the $\boldsymbol{f}$-eigenvector centralities on MLNs can be translated to an IDOL program. The major technical difference is that the MLN translation contains non-linear terms, and the exponents α and β. Once we have obtained the corresponding IDOL program we can apply the general technique for computing the equivalences among its variables.

The next Theorem shows how to write an IDOL program, such that if two variables have the same semantics in the dynamical system of the IDOL program, then, the respective nodes in the iterative scheme of a given MLN have identical centrality scores over all the steps of the computation, provided the equivalence over initial conditions.

Theorem 6. Let $\mathcal{G}$ be a multiplex network and let $\mathcal{A}_{ijl}$ be the 3-rd order adjacency tensor of the multiplex network $\mathcal{G}$. Let $\boldsymbol{f}$ be the mapping as defined in Definition 4, and let $\boldsymbol{g}$ its normalized version. Let $(\boldsymbol{x}^*, \boldsymbol{t}^*)$ be the unique solution (the centrality scores). Given any initial conditions $(\boldsymbol{x}^{(0)}, \boldsymbol{t}^{(0)}) \in \mathbb{R}_{\geq 0}^N \times \mathbb{R}_{\geq 0}^L$ and $(\boldsymbol{x}^{(k+1)}, \boldsymbol{t}^{(k+1)}) = \boldsymbol{g}(\boldsymbol{x}^{(k)}, \boldsymbol{t}^{(k)})$, the following holds:

$$\lim_{k \to \infty} (\boldsymbol{x}^{(k)}, \boldsymbol{t}^{(k)}) = (\boldsymbol{x}^*, \boldsymbol{t}^*)$$

Then, in the IDOL program p obtained via Definition 7, for some $i, j \in \{1, \ldots, N\}$ and $l, q \in \{1, \ldots, L\}$, the following holds:

- If $\forall t \in [0, T) \, . \, [\![\mathsf{x}_i]\!](t) = [\![\mathsf{x}_j]\!](t)$ in the IDOL program p, then $\forall k \in \mathbb{N} \, . \, x_i^{(k)} = x_j^{(k)}$
- If $\forall t \in [0, T) \, . \, [\![\mathsf{t}_l]\!](t) = [\![\mathsf{t}_q]\!](t)$ in the IDOL program p, then $\forall k \in \mathbb{N} \, . \, t_l^{(k)} = t_q^{(k)}$

From Theorem 6 we now know that we can build a non-linear IDOL program p such that if two variables are equal in the IDOL program then, the corresponding nodes (or layer) centrality are equal. Now, we can use the established results on the IDOL program and calculate the BDE partition $\mathcal{H}$ on the IDOL program p generated with Theorem 6. With the next Theorem we show that, because of the relationship established by Theorem 6 and the established results on the notion of BDE, we can carry over the results that we obtain on the IDOL program to the procedure to calculate the multilayer node (or layer) centrality.

Up to this point, starting from a multiplex graph $\mathcal{G}$ we provided a procedure to translate it into an IDOL program and we provided a technique to calculate a BDE partition $\mathcal{H}$ on the IDOL program. Now, we introduce the following lemma and definition to formally translate partition $\mathcal{H}$, which is defined over the IDOL program's variables, to its counterpart $\mathcal{H}^*$ defined over the nodes and the layers of the multiplex graph $\mathcal{G}$.

Lemma 1. Let $\mathcal{G}$ be a multiplex network and let p be the IDOL program defined in Theorem 6 and let $\mathcal{H} = (\mathcal{H}_x, \mathcal{H}_t)$ be a BDE partition over the set of variables such that there is no overlap between the nodes and the layers, i.e. $\mathcal{H}_x$ is a partition over the node variables $\{x_1, \ldots, x_N\}$ and $\mathcal{H}_t$ is a partition over the layer variables $\{t_1, \ldots, t_L\}$. Then, for all initial conditions the following holds:

- $\forall t \in [0, T), \forall x_i, x_j \in H_x, \forall H_x \in \mathcal{H}_x \; . \; [\![x_i]\!](t) = [\![x_j]\!](t) \implies \forall k \in \mathbb{N} \; . \; x_i^{(k)} = x_j^{(k)}$
- $\forall t \in [0, T), \forall t_l, t_q \in H_t, \forall H_t \in \mathcal{H}_t \; . \; [\![t_l]\!](t) = [\![t_q]\!](t) \implies \forall k \in \mathbb{N} \; . \; t_l^{(k)} = t_q^{(k)}$

Moreover, let $\mathcal{G}$ be the corresponding multiplex graph and we define $\mathcal{H}^* = (\mathcal{H}_x^*, \mathcal{H}_t^*)$ as the corresponding partition over the node and layer variables $\{x_1, \ldots, x_N, t_1, \ldots, t_L\}$ of $\mathcal{G}$. We define $\mathcal{H}^*$ as follows:

$$\forall i, j \in \{1, \ldots, N\}, H_{a,x} \in \mathcal{H}_x \; . \; x_i, x_j \in H_{a,x} \implies H_{a,x}^* \in \mathcal{H}^* \; . \; x_i, x_j \in H_{a,x}^*$$
$$\forall i, j \in \{1, \ldots, L\}, H_{a,t} \in \mathcal{H}_t \; . \; t_i, t_j \in H_{a,t} \implies H_{a,t}^* \in \mathcal{H}^* \; . \; t_i, t_j \in H_{a,t}^*$$

Example 4. If we go back to the running example presented in the left of Fig. 1 and we apply Theorem 6 we obtain the following IDOL program p:

$$
\begin{aligned}
x_1' &= 1x_2t_1 + 1x_3t_1 + 1x_2t_2 & t_1' &= 2x_1x_2 + 2x_1x_3 \\
x_2' &= 1x_1t_1 + 1x_1t_2 + 1x_3t_2 & t_2' &= 2x_1x_2 + 2x_2x_3 \\
x_3' &= 1x_1t_1 + 1x_2t_2
\end{aligned}
$$

We consider the following partition $\mathcal{H} = \{\{x_1, x_2\}, \{x_3\}, \{t_1\}, \{t_2\}\}$, which is a BDE of p and we shall use $\tilde{x}_1$ as the representative of block $\{x_1, x_2\}$, $\tilde{x}_2$ as the representative of block $\{x_3\}$ and r_1, r_2 representatives of the blocks $\{t_1\}, \{t_2\}$, respectively. The IDOL quotient of p given $\mathcal{H}$ is the following:

$$
\begin{aligned}
y_1' &= 1y_1r_1 + 1y_2r_1 + 1y_1r_2 & r_1' &= 2y_1y_1 + 2y_1y_2 \\
y_2' &= 1y_1r_1 + 1y_1r_2 & r_2' &= 2y_1y_1 + 2y_1y_2
\end{aligned}
$$

Now that we established the relationship between the partitions we proceed to define the proper reduced system to calculate the multiplex node and layer centrality as follows.

Definition 8. Let $(\boldsymbol{x}^{(k)}, \boldsymbol{t}^{(k)}) = g(\boldsymbol{x}^{(k-1)}, \boldsymbol{t}^{(k-1)})$ be the iterative scheme and let $\mathcal{H} = (\mathcal{H}_x, \mathcal{H}_t)$ be the BDE partition on the IDOL program p obtained using Theorem 6 and Lemma 1. Let $\mathcal{H}^* = (\mathcal{H}_x^*, \mathcal{H}_t^*)$ be the corresponding partition on the iterative scheme as defined in Lemma 1. We define $(\boldsymbol{y}^{(k)}, \boldsymbol{r}^{(k)}) = \tilde{g}(\boldsymbol{y}^{(k-1)}, \boldsymbol{r}^{(k-1)})$ as the *Reduced iterative scheme* with respect to $\mathcal{H}^*$:

$$\tilde{f}_1 = f_1[x_{H_x,1}/y_{H_x}, \ldots, x_{H_x,|H_x|}/y_{H_x}, t_{H_t,1}/r_{H_t}, \ldots, t_{H_t,|H_t|}/r_{H_t} : H_x \in \mathcal{H}_x, \; H_t \in \mathcal{H}_t]$$

$$\tilde{f}_2 = f_2[x_{H_x,1}/y_{H_x}, \ldots, x_{H_x,|H_x|}/y_{H_x}, t_{H_t,1}/r_{H_t}, \ldots, t_{H_t,|H_t|}/r_{H_t} : H_x \in \mathcal{H}_x, \; H_t \in \mathcal{H}_t]$$

Next, we define $\bar{y}_i^{(k)}$, similarly as we previously defined $\bar{x}_i^{(k)}$, and the reduced computation to retrieve the values of $\boldsymbol{x}^{(k)}$:

$$\bar{y}_i^{(k)} = \sum_{j=1}^{N} \sum_{l=1}^{L} A_{ijl} y_{H_x,j}^{(k-1)} r_{H_t,l}^{(k-1)}, \quad \boldsymbol{x}^{(k)} = \frac{\bar{x}^{(k)}}{\|\bar{x}^{(k)}\|_1} = \frac{\bar{y}^{(k)}}{\sum_{j=1}^{m} |H_{x,j}| \bar{y}_j^{(k)}} = \boldsymbol{y}^{(k)}.$$

where, $H_{x,j} = i$ if $x_j \in H_{x,i}$ and $H_{t,q} = l$ if $t_q \in H_{t,l}$. We can now focus on the second component of the mapping and we define $\bar{r}_l^{(k)}$ and its reduced computation:

$$\bar{r}_l^{(k)} = \sum_{i=1}^{N} \sum_{j=1}^{N} A_{ijl} y_{H_x,i}^{(k-1)} y_{H_x,j}^{(k-1)}, \quad \boldsymbol{t}^{(k)} = \frac{\bar{t}^{(k)}}{\|\bar{t}^{(k)}\|_1} = \frac{\bar{r}^{(k)}}{\sum_{j=1}^{Q} |H_{t,j}| \bar{r}_j^{(k)}} = \boldsymbol{r}^{(k)}.$$

where, $H_{x,j} = i$ if $x_j \in H_{x,i}$.

Example 5. If we consider the running example presented in the left of Fig. 1, we know that the partition $\mathcal{H} = \{\{x_1, x_2\}, \{x_3\}, \{t_1\}, \{t_2\}\}$ is a BDE of the IDOL program p and we obtained the following reduced IDOL program:

$$y_1' = 1y_1 r_1 + 1y_2 r_1 + 1y_1 r_2 \qquad r_1' = 2y_1 y_1 + 2y_1 y_2$$
$$y_2' = 1y_1 r_1 + 1y_1 r_2 \qquad r_2' = 2y_1 y_1 + 2y_1 y_2$$

In order to compute the original $\boldsymbol{f}$-eigenvector centrality values we set up the following iterative scheme:

$$\bar{y}_1^{(k)} = 1y_1^{(k-1)} r_1^{(k-1)} + 1y_2^{(k-1)} r_1^{(k-1)} + 1y_1^{(k-1)} r_2^{(k-1)} \qquad \bar{r}_1^{(k)} = 2y_1^{(k-1)} y_1^{(k-1)} + 2y_1^{(k-1)} y_2^{(k-1)}$$
$$\bar{y}_2^{(k)} = 1y_1^{(k-1)} r_1^{(k-1)} + 1y_1^{(k-1)} r_2^{(k-1)} \qquad \bar{r}_2^{(k)} = 2y_1^{(k-1)} y_1^{(k-1)} + 2y_1^{(k-1)} y_2^{(k-1)}$$

4 Experimental Results

In this section we present the results of our experimental evaluation on some real world case studies. We measure the performance of our approach in terms of model reduction ratio and we measure the speed up in the computation of the desired centrality measures.

Implementation and Environment. The tools used for the experiments are MAT-LAB and ERODE [11], a state-of-the-art tool for model reduction for systems of ODEs and Chemical Reaction Networks. The input is the list of edges $E^{(l)}$ for all $l \in \{1, ..., L\}$ representing a multiplex network $\mathcal{G} = \{G^{(l)} = (V_N, E^{(l)})\}_{l \in V_L}$. ERODE accepts the input as a file that encodes an ODE system or a Chemical Reaction Network (CRN). Due to a bottleneck in the processing of files in the ODE format we had to input the files in the CRN format. A MATLAB script translates the list of edges in the CRN. ERODE then proceeds with the model reduction and provides the reduced CRN as its output. The centrality scores are computed with a MATLAB script and another MATLAB script is used to convert the reduced CRN into the reduced model and used to calculate the centrality score on the reduced model. All the experiments have been conducted on a MacBook Pro with a 2.6 GHz Intel Core i7 with 16 GB of RAM.

The Instances. In order to provide some real-world case studies we ran our proposed reduction technique on multiplex MLNs retrieved from the CoMuNe Lab repository (https://comunelab.fbk.eu). The results for both undirected and directed instances are presented in Table 1. We first present the *undirected graphs* instances. These instances are undirected in the repository.

- *Padgett-Florentine-Families* (1): this multiplex describes the relationships between Florentine families in the Renaissance, the two layers represent marriage alliances and business relationships, respectively [41].
- *CS-Aarhus* (2): this multiplex social network consists of five kinds of relationships between the employees of the Computer Science department at Aarhus university. The layers represent the following relationships: Facebook, Leisure, Work, Co-Authorship and Lunch [36].
- *London-Transport* (3): the nodes in this multiplex represent the train stations in London and edges encode existing routes between stations. The layers represent the Underground, Overground and DLR stations, respectively [16].
- *EUAirTrainsportation* (4): the multilayer network is composed by thirty-seven different layers each one corresponding to a different airline operating in Europe [13].
- *PierreAuger* (5): this instance represents the different working tasks carried out over a two years span within the Pierre Auger Collaboration between the CoMuNe Lab and the Pierre Auger observatory. Each layer represents 16 different topics based on the keywords and the content of each submission [20].
- *arxiv-netscience* (6): this multiplex consists of layers corresponding to different arXiv categories. Nodes represent authors and edges represent the weighted co-authorship relationship [20].

Due to the fact that many of the undirected instances are small we do not obtain sensible reductions nor speed up in the computation. Despite this, we can observe a meaningful reduction for the largest of the undirected instances, namely the *arxiv-netscience* instance. We now present the instances that in the repository are *directed*. It is worth noting that, because of the fact that the centrality measure we considered throughout this paper is defined for the undirected case only, we modified these instances to make them undirected in order to prove the effectiveness of our proposed methodology. Another reason to do so is the fact that there is a small number of undirected instances. Moreover, the undirected instances present a limited variety of nodes, edges and layer sizes.

- *Krackhardt-High-Tech* (7): this multiplex social network describes the relationships between managers of an high-tech company. The layers represent advice, friendship and "reports to" relationships, respectively [33].
- *Vickers-Chan-7thGraders* (8): this data was collected from 29 seventh grade students in a school in Victoria, Australia. Students were asked to nominate their classmates on a number of relations including the following three (layers): Who do you get on with in the class? Who are your best friends in the class? Who would you prefer to work with? [52].
- *Kapferer-Tailor-Shop* (9): this instance represents the interactions in a tailor shop in Zambia over a period of ten months. The layers represent two different types of interactions, recorded at two different times. The relationships captured by this multiplex are *instrumental* (work-related) and *sociational* (friendship, socio-emotional) interactions [30].
- *Lazega-Law-Firm* (10): this multiplex social network consists of three kinds of relationships between partners and associates of a corporate law partnership. The layers represent co-work, friendship and advice relationships, respectively [34,45].
- *Genetic interaction instances* (11-28): we consider a variety of genetic interactions networks that are present in the CoMuNe Lab repository [15]. In turn, these instances were taken from the Biological General Repository for Interaction Datasets (BioGRID) and represent different types of genetic interactions for organisms [47]. More specifically, according to the nomenclature used in the repository we present experimental results on the following instances: HepatitusC (11), DanioRerio (12), HumanHerpes4 (13), CElegans Connectome (15), Bos (16), Candida (17), Xenopus (18), HumanHIV1 (19), Plasmodium (20), Rattus (21), CElegans (22), Sacchpomb (23), Sacchere (24), Arabidopsis (25), Mus (26), Drosophila (27), Homo (28).
- *CKM-Physicians-Innovation* (14): this multiplex describes how new drugs adoption spreads in a community of physicians.
- *Fao-Trade* (29): this multiplex describes different types of trade relationships among countries, it was originally obtained from the Food and Agriculture Organization of the United Nations. The worldwide food import/export network is an economic network in which layers represent products, nodes are countries and edges at each layer represent import/export relationships of a specific food product among countries. It is worth pointing out that, due to the nature of this instance, it has the peculiarity that there are more layers than nodes [15].
- *MoscowAthletics2013* (30): this multiplex represents the different types of social relationships among Twitter users during the 2013 World Championships in Athletics. The three layers correspond to retweets, mentions and replies over the time frame of the event. These are the relationships that will be also used for the following Twitter instances [40].

- *NYClimateMarch2014* (31): this instance describes the Twitter interactions among the users during the People's Climate March in 2014 [40].
- *MLKing2013* (32): this instance describes the Twitter interactions among the users during the 50th anniversary of Martin Luther King's speech in 2013 [40].
- *Cannes2013* (33): this instance describes the Twitter interactions among the users during the Cannes Film Festival in 2013 [40].

As expected, similarly to the undirected instances, the small instances do not provide much insight on the effectiveness of the methodology but, as the size of the instance increases we can see significant reductions and speed ups. Notably, when tackling the big instances the proposed methodology yields reductions that reduce the size of the network to half of its original size and, in the case of the largest instance we can obtain a reduction that at least provides some information about which nodes have the same centrality. Such information could not be retrieved by calculating the centrality directly on the original multiplex because of the computational cost.

Table 1. Experimental results. Columns show the ID of the instance, the number of nodes (N), the number of layers (L), the number of nodes in the reduced model (rN), the number of layers in the reduced model (rL), the time spent to compute the centrality measure using the original model (Cen), the time spent to do the BDE reduction (BDE) and the time spent to compute the centrality measure using the reduced model (rCen).

	Undirected instances							Directed instances						
ID	N	L	rN	rL	Cen(s)	BDE(s)	rCen(s)	ID	N	L	rN	rL	Cen(s)	BDE(s)	rCen(s)
(1)	16	2	16	2	0.26	0.00	-	(18)	461	5	276	5	0.18	0.01	0.08
(2)	61	5	61	5	0.07	0.01	-	(19)	1005	5	137	5	0.51	0.02	0.13
(3)	368	3	366	3	0.14	0.01	0.15	(20)	1203	3	994	3	1.04	0.04	0.94
(4)	450	37	374	37	0.67	0.03	0.55	(21)	2640	6	1264	6	3.50	0.06	1.19
(5)	514	16	351	16	1.28	0.18	0.52	(22)	3879	6	2372	6	7.90	0.10	4.16
(6)	14488	13	8008	13	192.53	0.66	83.71	(23)	4092	7	3613	7	53.71	0.75	59.47

	Directed Instances														
ID	N	L	rN	rL	Cen(s)	BDE(s)	rCen(s)								
(7)	21	3	21	3	0.05	0.00	-	(24)	6570	7	6087	7	494.21	10.14	428.68
(8)	29	3	29	3	0.06	0.00	-	(25)	6980	7	4527	7	32.74	0.11	17.21
(9)	39	4	39	4	0.07	0.01	-	(26)	7747	7	4887	7	35.99	0.30	19.58
(10)	71	3	71	3	0.14	0.02	-	(27)	8215	7	7397	7	76.42	0.45	72.34
(11)	105	3	11	3	0.06	0.00	0.03	(28)	18222	7	13978	7	747.52	1.97	562.42
(12)	155	5	90	5	0.08	0.00	0.04	(29)	214	364	214	364	49.17	0.50	–
(13)	216	4	46	4	0.09	0.00	0.03	(30)	88804	3	37773	3	3359.26	6.68	1316.53
(14)	246	3	242	3	0.21	0.01	0.18	(31)	102439	3	48018	3	6188.51	5.36	3296.76
(15)	279	3	279	3	0.70	0.05	-	(32)	327707	3	63136	3	21289.98	2.51	1806.65
(16)	325	4	162	4	0.12	0.01	0.09	(33)	438537	3	180443	3	>10 h	12.05	>3 h
(17)	367	7	62	7	0.13	0.00	0.09								

5   Conclusions and Future Work

In this paper we have related an extension of eigenvector centrality on undirected and (possibly) weighted multiplex MLNs to BDE, an exact model reduction technique for dynamical systems. We have shown that we can use a BDE-inspired technique to introduce a framework that allows to reduce MLNs while preserving the f-eigenvector centrality measure. The relevance of the result was demonstrated by efficiently computing reduction of real-world MLNs and by showing a speed up in the computation of such measure of interest. Throughout this work we considered exact reductions although it is worth noting that one of the possible future directions is to consider approximate reductions which are already prominent in the study of clustering in networks [7] and approximate lumping in agent-based models [32]. Future work will focus on the extension of these results to multiplex MLNs that feature directed layers. Other directions will include extending the framework to other centrality measures and other families of MLNs. Thanks to the theory established in this paper, we can naturally approach the study of approximate versions of this reduction technique because it is known that exact reductions might not yield significant reductions in very asymmetric real-world case studies. Moreover, this framework is a very versatile cornerstone work that, with few appropriate changes, can be easily modified to deal with other types of notions such as extensions of role equivalence on MLNs.

Acknowledgements. The authors' research is supported by the Ministry of Science, Research and the Arts of the state of Baden-Württemberg, and the DFG Centre of Excellence 2117 'Centre for the Advanced Study of Collective Behaviour' (ID: 422037984). The authors would like to thank Ulrik Brandes and Giacomo Rapisardi for the inspiring discussions on the topic, Andrea Vandin for the support and the insights on the use of the tool ERODE and the anonymous reviewers for their suggestions and comments.

References

1. Banerjee, A., Chandrasekhar, A., Duflo, E., Jackson, M.: The diffusion of microfinance. Science **341**, 1236498 (2013)
2. Barrett, L., Henzi, P., Lusseau, D.: Taking sociality seriously: the structure of multi-dimensional social networks as a source of information for individuals. Phil. Trans. Roy. Soc. Lond. Ser. B Biol. Sci. **367**, 2108–2118 (2012)
3. Battiston, F., Nicosia, V., Latora, V.: Structural measures for multiplex networks. Phys. Rev. E Stat. Nonlinear Soft Matter Phys. **89**, 032804 (2014)
4. Bloch, F., Jackson, M., Tebaldi, P.: Centrality measures in networks. SSRN Electron. J. (2016)
5. Bonacich, P.: Factoring and weighting approaches to status scores and clique identification. J. Math. Sociol. **2**(1), 113–120 (1972)
6. Bonacich, P.: Power and centrality: a family of measures. Am. J. Sociol. **92**(5), 1170–1182 (1987)
7. Brandes, U., et al.: On modularity clustering. IEEE Trans. Knowl. Data Eng. **20**, 172–188 (2008)

8. Brandes, U., Lerner, J.: Structural similarity: spectral methods for relaxed block-modeling. J. Classif. **27**(3), 279–306 (2010)
9. Cardelli, L., Tribastone, M., Tschaikowski, M., Vandin, A.: Efficient syntax-driven lumping of differential equations. In: Chechik, M., Raskin, J.-F. (eds.) TACAS 2016. LNCS, vol. 9636, pp. 93–111. Springer, Heidelberg (2016). https://doi.org/10.1007/978-3-662-49674-9_6
10. Cardelli, L., Tribastone, M.,Tschaikowski, M., Vandin, A.: Symbolic computation of differential equivalences. In: 43st ACM SIGPLAN-SIGACT Symposium on Principles of Programming Languages (POPL) (2016)
11. Cardelli, L., Tribastone, M., Tschaikowski, M., Vandin, A.: ERODE: a tool for the evaluation and reduction of ordinary differential equations. In: Legay, A., Margaria, T. (eds.) TACAS 2017. LNCS, vol. 10206, pp. 310–328. Springer, Heidelberg (2017). https://doi.org/10.1007/978-3-662-54580-5_19
12. Cardelli, L., Tribastone, M., Tschaikowski, M., Vandin, A.: Maximal aggregation of polynomial dynamical systems. PNAS **114**(38), 10029–10034 (2017)
13. Cardillo, A., et al.: Emergence of network features from multiplexity. Sci. Rep. **3**, 1344 (2013)
14. Christakis, N., Fowler, J.: Social network sensors for early detection of contagious outbreaks. PloS One **5**, e12948 (2010)
15. De Domenico, M., Nicosia, V., Arenas, A., Latora, V.: Structural reducibility of multilayer networks. Nat. Commun. **6**, 6864 (2015)
16. De Domenico, M., Solé-Ribalta, A., Gómez, S., Arenas, A.: Navigability of interconnected networks under random failures. Proc. Natl. Acad. Sci. **111**, 8351–8356 (2014)
17. De Domenico, M., et al.: Mathematical formulation of multi-layer networks. Phys. Rev. X **3**, 07 (2013)
18. De Domenico, M., Solé-Ribalta, A., Omodei, E., Gomez, S., Arenas, A.: Centrality in interconnected multilayer networks. Phys. D Nonlinear Phenom. **323**, 11 (2013)
19. De Domenico, M., Solé-Ribalta, A., Omodei, E., Gomez, S., Arenas, A.: Ranking in interconnected multilayer networks reveals versatile nodes. Nat. Commun. **6**, 6868 (2015)
20. De Domenico, M., Lancichinetti, A., Arenas, A., Rosvall, M.: Identifying modular flows on multilayer networks reveals highly overlapping organization in social systems. ArXiv, abs/1408.2925 (2015)
21. Farine, D., Aplin, L., Sheldon, B., Hoppitt, W.: Interspecific social networks promote information transmission in wild songbirds. Proc. Biol. Sci. Roy. Soc. **282**, 20142804 (2015)
22. Feret, J., Henzinger, T., Koeppl, H., Petrov, T.: Lumpability abstractions of rule-based systems. Theor. Comput. Sci. **431**, 137–164 (2012)
23. Franz, M., Altmann, J., Alberts, S.: Knockouts of high-ranking males have limited impact on baboon social networks. Curr. Zool. **61**, 107–113 (2015)
24. Ganguly, A., Petrov, T., Koeppl, H.: Markov chain aggregation and its applications to combinatorial reaction networks. J. Math. Biol. **69**(3), 767–797 (2014)
25. Gazda, S., Iyer, S., Killingback, T., Connor, R., Brault, S.: The importance of delineating networks by activity type in bottlenose dolphins (Tursiops truncatus) in cedar key, Florida. Roy. Soc. Open Sci. **2**, 140263 (2015)
26. Granell, C., Gomez, S., Arenas, A.: Dynamical interplay between awareness and epidemic spreading in multiplex networks. Phys. Rev. Lett. **111**, 128701 (2013)
27. Iacobelli, G., Tribastone, M., Vandin, A.: Differential bisimulation for a markovian process algebra. In: MFCS, pp. 293–306 (2015)

28. Jackson, M.: Social and Economic Networks (2008)
29. Johnson, J., Borgatti, S., Everett, M.: Analyzing Social Networks (2013)
30. Kapferer, B.: Strategy and transaction in an African factory: African workers and Indian management in a Zambian town. Manchester Univ. Press **43**(4), 362–363 (1972)
31. Katz, L.: A new status index derived from sociometric analysis. Psychometrika **18**(1), 39–43 (1953)
32. KhudaBukhsh, W.R., Auddy, A., Disser, Y., Koeppl, H.: Approximate lumpability for markovian agent-based models using local symmetries. J. Appl. Probab. **56**, 04 (2018)
33. Krackhardt, D.: Cognitive social structures. Social Netw. **9**(2), 109–134 (1987)
34. Lazega, E.: The Collegial Phenomenon: The Social Mechanisms of Cooperation among Peers in a Corporate Law Partnership. Oxford University Press, Oxford (2001)
35. Lerner, J.: Role assignments. In: Network Analysis: Methodological Foundations [Outcome of a Dagstuhl Seminar, 13–16 April 2004], pp. 216–252 (2004)
36. Magnani, M., Micenková, B., Rossi, L.: Combinatorial analysis of multiple networks. CoRR, abs/1303.4986 (2013)
37. McKay, B.: Practical graph isomorphism. Congressus Numerantium **30**, 45–87 (1981)
38. McKay, B., Piperno, A.: Practical graph isomorphism, II. J. Symb. Comput. **6009**, 94–112 (2013)
39. Newman, M.: Networks: An Introduction. Oxford University Press Inc., New York (2010)
40. Omodei, E., De Domenico, M., Arenas, A.: Characterizing interactions in online social networks during exceptional events. Front. Phys. **3**, 06 (2015)
41. Padgett, J.F., Ansell, C.K.: Robust action and the rise of the medici, 1400–1434. Am. J. Sociol. **98**(6), 1259–1319 (1993)
42. Page, L., Brin, S., Motwani, R., Winograd, T.: The pagerank citation ranking: bringing order to the web. In: WWW 1999 (1999)
43. Robert Paige and Robert Endre Tarjan: Three partition refinement algorithms. SIAM J. Comput. **16**(6), 973–989 (1987)
44. Pappas, G.J.: Bisimilar linear systems. Automatica **39**(12), 2035–2047 (2003)
45. Snijders, T.A.B., Pattison, P.E., Robins, G.L., Handcock, M.S.: New specifications for exponential random graph models. Sociol. Methodol. **36**(1), 99–153 (2006)
46. Conde, L.S., Romance, M., Herrero, R., Flores, J., del Amo, A.G., Boccaletti, S.: Eigenvector centrality of nodes in multiplex networks. Chaos (Woodbury, N.Y.) **23**, 033131 (2013)
47. Stark, C., Breitkreutz, B.-J., Reguly, T., Boucher, L., Breitkreutz, A., Tyers, M.: Biogrid: a general repository for interaction datasets. Nucleic Acids Res. **34**, D535–D539 (2006)
48. Tognazzi, S., Tribastone, M., Tschaikowski, M., Vandin, A.: Differential equivalence yields network centrality. In: Margaria, T., Steffen, B. (eds.) ISoLA 2018, Part III. LNCS, vol. 11246, pp. 186–201. Springer, Cham (2018). https://doi.org/10.1007/978-3-030-03424-5_13
49. Tschaikowski, M., Tribastone, M.: Exact fluid lumpability for Markovian process algebra. In: CONCUR, pp. 380–394 (2012)
50. Tudisco, F., Arrigo, F., Gautier, A.: Node and layer eigenvector centralities for multiplex networks. SIAM J. Appl. Math. **78**(2), 853–876 (2018)
51. van der Schaft, A.J.: Equivalence of dynamical systems by bisimulation. IEEE Trans. Autom. Control **49**, 2160–2172 (2004)

52. Vickers, M., Chan, M.: Representing classroom social structure. Victoria Institute of Secondary Education, Melbourne (1981)
53. Stanley, W., Katherine, F.: Social Network Analysis: Methods and Applications, vol. 8. Cambridge University Press, Cambridge (1994)
54. Wei, X., Valler, N.B., Prakash, A., Neamtiu, I., Faloutsos, M., Faloutsos, C.: Competing memes propagation on networks: a case study of composite networks. ACM SIGCOMM Comput. Commun. Rev. **42**, 5–11 (2012)

Towards Dynamic Dependable Systems Through Evidence-Based Continuous Certification

Rasha Faqeh[1]([⊠]), Christof Fetzer[1]([⊠]), Holger Hermanns[2,3]([⊠]),
Jörg Hoffmann[2]([⊠]), Michaela Klauck[2]([⊠]), Maximilian A. Köhl[2]([⊠]),
Marcel Steinmetz[2]([⊠]), and Christoph Weidenbach[4]([⊠])

[1] Technische Universität Dresden, Dresden, Germany
{rasha.faqeh,christof.fetzer}@tu-dresden.de
[2] Saarland University, Saarland Informatics Campus, Saarbrücken, Germany
{hermanns,hoffmann,klauck,mkoehl,steinmetz}@cs.uni-saarland.de
[3] Institute of Intelligent Software, Guangzhou, China
[4] Max Planck Institute for Informatics, Saarland Informatics Campus,
Saarbrücken, Germany
weidenbach@mpi-inf.mpg.de

Abstract. Future cyber-physical systems are expected to be dynamic, evolving while already being deployed. Frequent updates of software components are likely to become the norm even for safety-critical systems. In this setting, a full re-certification before each software update might delay important updates that fix previous bugs, or security or safety issues. Here we propose a vision addressing this challenge, namely through the evidence-based continuous supervision and certification of software variants in the field. The idea is to run both old and new variants of component software inside the same system, together with a supervising instance that monitors their behavior. Updated variants are phased into operation after sufficient evidence for correct behavior has been collected. The variants are required to explicate their decisions in a logical language, enabling the supervisor to reason about these decisions and to identify inconsistencies. To resolve contradictory information, the supervisor can run a component analysis to identify potentially faulty components on the basis of previously observed behavior, and can trigger micro-experiments which plan and execute system behavior specifically aimed at reducing uncertainty. We spell out our overall vision, and provide a first formalization of the different components and their interplay. In order to provide efficient supervisor reasoning as well as automatic verification of supervisor properties we introduce SupERLog, a logic specifically designed to this end.

Authors are listed alphabetically. This work was partially supported by the ERC Advanced Investigators Grant 695614 (POWVER), by DFG Grant 389792660 as part of TRR 248 (see https://perspicuous-computing.science), and by the Key-Area Research and Development Program Grant 2018B010107004 of Guangdong Province.

T. Margaria and B. Steffen (Eds.): ISoLA 2020, LNCS 12477, pp. 416–439, 2020.
https://doi.org/10.1007/978-3-030-61470-6_25

Keywords: Certification · Dependability · Model checking · Planning · Supervision

1   Introduction

The complexity of constructing dependable systems is increasing dramatically, as future cyber-physical systems – like those used in the context of autonomous vehicles – are expected to change *dynamically*: they need to evolve not only to changing needs, but also according to lessons learned in the field. Systems where *software components* are constantly updated in the field are likely to become the norm, together with a general acceptance of the fact that it seems outright impossible to upfront guarantee safety-by-design. Over the last years, Tesla has been pioneering this approach with apparent success [24, 34] and other companies will follow.

Safety certification of such systems requires a process combining formal guarantees, statistical methods, in-field testing, simulation and proven-in-practice arguments. This is doomed to be a lengthy process. The update of any component requires, however, a new certification so as to assure absence of safety violations. Such a re-certification is costly and might delay important updates that are meant to fix previous bugs. Rapid deployment of fixes is imperative especially for security-relevant bugs since adversaries notoriously attempt to attack systems that are not yet patched, and because security loopholes make any safety guarantee void.

In this paper, we are thus exploring how to enable the immediate deployment of new software variants without time-intensive re-certification. Software updates might take the form of device drivers and microcode updates relating to hardware components, so we are factually facing variability of software as well as hardware(-induced) behavior.

In this setting, the primary goal is to ensure that new variants for system components do not cause safety violations, e.g., by the introduction of new bugs. Our vision is the *evidence-based continuous supervision and certification of software variants* in the field. At its core is the idea to run multiple variants of the component software inside the same system, together with a *supervising instance* that monitors and compares the variants' behaviors. The supervising instance itself is trusted, i.e., it is formally verified. Ideally, the verification can be done fully automatically. Furthermore, the supervisor reasoning needs to be effective and efficient to fulfill the monitoring and decision task of the supervisor. The logic SupERLog, (Sup)ervisor (E)ffective (R)easoning (Log)ics, supports all these requirements: it is decidable, so properties of the supervisor can be automatically verified. SupERLog enables fast reasoning on ground facts, the typical situation when the supervisor is run on the evidence (ground facts) provided by the different components. The supervisor itself is expected to not evolve regularly during the lifetime of the system. If it were to evolve, this would require a re-certification. The supervisor can be designed *fail-operational*, i.e., it tolerates failures and hence is considered not to be a single point of failure in the system.

Note that the supervisor can not use the traditional majority voting to handle the variants because the variants are expected to be non-deterministic in behavior. Therefore, there might not be any majority despite all variants being correct. And even if a majority exists, it is not guaranteed that the majority is correct. In our approach, each variant has to deliver evidence for its decisions and a majority that does not provide sufficient evidence will lose to a minority that provides sufficient evidence.

To explain why variants need to be treated as non-deterministic, consider that a new variant might be putting different emphasis on the different sensor types like video vs. LIDAR signals. Moreover, a new variant might have added new features or have fixed some bugs or deficiencies in the older variants. However, a new variant might also introduce new bugs that could violate the safety of the system.

Our approach is meant to enable the continuous certification of variants of component software, by collecting in-field evidence demonstrating the safety of new variants while at the same time using the older variants to safeguard critical activities.   Of course, the older variant of a component software is not always the one to trust. In order to determine the ground truth despite component misbehavior, we envision an approach to resolve contradictory information arriving from different components and their variants: a *component analysis* and *micro-experiments*. *Component analysis* identifies potentially faulty components based on previously observed behavior; and, in case previous observations are insufficient to disambiguate between faulty vs. correct variants, *micro-experiments* generate behavior specifically aimed to achieve such disambiguation.

We will first introduce our generic architecture and then give a more formal and detailed description of our approach.

2   Approach

A component is *dependable* if and only if reliance can justifiably be placed on the service it delivers [7,30]. Intuitively, we are justified in placing reliance on a component, provided the body of available evidence suggests it to be dependable. Stronger evidence enables us to place more reliance on a component or system. We apply a staged approach to continuously certify variants of component software, centered on the collection of evidence to show the safety of a new variant.[1] New component variants are introduced after bug fixes or after the addition of new features. Updates are executed in *shadow mode*, to test their behavior while older variants are still in charge. In this way, the system can fail-over to an updated but not yet certified variant in case the behavior of an older variant is considered to be unsafe. Updates are phased into operation after sufficient evidence for correct behavior was collected.

We envision this process to be orchestrated by a central *supervisor* component. All component variants $V_1, V_2, \ldots$ of a component are assumed to produce

---

[1] The idea is not limited to software components but expands to hardware components as well.

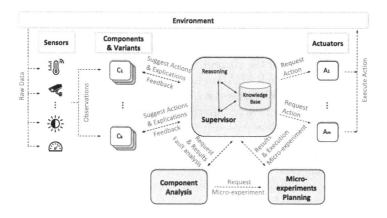

Fig. 1. Architecture overview.

outputs, but only the output of one variant is forwarded to other components of the system. The supervisor is responsible for the decision on which output to forward. It monitors the outputs received, and selects one. So a component variant can never expect to be *in charge*, i.e., that its outputs are the ones forwarded. Note that such arrangements are already being used in practice:

Example 1 (Component not in Charge). Modern cars have software components to assist in the steering of the car, but the human driver can always overwrite the decision of the software. So the outputs are controlled by the human driver and the software components are robust enough to adjust their future actions to the behavior that is imposed by the driver.

Figure 1 sketches our architectural vision. The supervisor component is the central decision entity. It monitors the different variants of each component, and decides which variant is in charge. It can at any point switch from one variant to another. To support these decisions, each component variant must be able to *explicate* its decision for a given output to the supervisor, which cross-checks the explications. We envision that these explications will be based on predicate logics extended with theories. The supervisor maintains a knowledge base, and reasons about the explications using standard as well as sophisticated reasoning mechanisms tailored to the efficacy needs in a running system.

The supervisor reasoning connects and compares outputs produced by different variants of individual components, and across components. Leveraging the explications in combination with the supervisor's knowledge base, the supervisor thus attempts to resolve any contradictions that may exist between variants.

If the supervisor reasoning can resolve the relevant contradictions, a unique decision is obtained. But that will not always be the case:

Example 2 (Conflicting Sensors). Assume we have updated the software component responsible for lane changing maneuvers in an autonomous vehicle. The new variant of the component proposes to change to the left lane and explains its decision to the supervisor by a LIDAR sensor reading indicating that there is an obstacle ahead but the left lane is free. The older variant of the component instead proposes to stay on the current lane and explains its decision by a reading of a different sensor, a RADAR sensor, indicating the lane is free but the left lane is blocked. To resolve this conflict, the supervisor needs to know which sensor to trust - unless there is an alternative on which all variants agree upon like changing to the right lane instead.

To allow the supervisor to determine the ground truth despite component misbehavior, we envision machinery to resolve contradictory information and decisions arriving from different component variants. The supervisor can trigger this machinery when needed.

The first step in the machinery is *component analysis*, which identifies faulty components based on previously observed behavior. Component analysis compares models of component behavior to system-trace observations collected in the past, and based on this evidence reduces the set of component models to those that are indeed compatible with the observations, including possible fault models. The latter information can be qualitative ("which faults are possible?") or quantitative ("which faults are most likely?"). This feeds back to the supervisor, fostering its ability to decide which actions are safe to be carried out and which components to trust.

However, previous observations may not be enough to sufficiently disambiguate between faulty vs. correct components. For such cases, we envision the use of *micro-experiments* as a second, more radical, step. Based on the possible model information as derived by component analysis, micro-experiment planning then identifies behavior – system actions – optimized to minimize the uncertainty about the actual model employed by the components, and thus about which components are faulty in which way. The supervisor executes the micro-experiment (in an execution-and-replanning loop) and draws conclusions from the observed behaviors. Micro-experiments are limited to "small" activities (hence the name) which do not endanger the mission performance, nor, of course, the safety of the system.

Example 3 (Micro-experiment). In the above situation, we keep a model that among others estimates the distance to obstacles with two different sensors, LIDAR and RADAR. Assuming that the alleged obstacle is fixed, e.g., a traffic cone, deceleration and acceleration has a very specific effect on the sensor reading. If we now make the vehicle decelerate slightly, we can predict the distance change if the respective sensors were behaving correctly. So we carry out the deceleration (which is not a risk maneuver) while observing the sensor changes, so as to draw conclusions about the sensor believed to be faulty.

Notably, component analysis and micro-experiments can be performed only under particular circumstances. Component analysis is a complex time-consuming process. The same is true for micro-experiment planning, and actually executing a micro-experiment can of course be done only when circumstances allow, i.e., when the system is safe. Our vision therefore is for component analysis and micro-experiment planning to be triggered and executed alongside system execution whenever computational resources are available (locally or via communication with an external server), and for the supervisor to execute safe fallback actions (like pulling over to the right-hand side of the road) if conflicts cannot be resolved on the spot. Supervisor reasoning about explications, in this context, serves as a quick means to detect and resolve simple conflicts online, without the need to embark on more complex analyses.

The role of the supervisor in a dynamic software deployment process is analogous to the role of a certifier for a sophisticated algorithm. Verification of a sophisticated algorithm is beyond the scope of any automatic verification technology. Certifiers are rather small, far less complicated components that check the correctness of the output of the sophisticated algorithm. They can often be addressed by automatic verification technology. For example, while the verification of modern SAT solving technology is still at the level of effort of a PhD thesis using an interactive theorem prover [17], the implementation and verification of a proof certifier for SAT in an interactive theorem prover is a standard exercise and even leads to code that outperforms hand-written certifiers [29]. In the same vein, the software deployed into a cyber-physical system is beyond the scope of automatic verification, but the safety of its suggested actions can be controlled by reasoning on its explications, effectuated by a far simpler supervisor, for which we envision a logic, called *SupERLogs* for (Sup)ervisor (E)ffective (R)easoning (Log)ics, as a standard knowledge representation framework maintained by the supervisor. Reasoning about the explications will use standard reasoning mechanisms, with satisfiability of the relevant SupERLogs fragments being decidable, and their Horn fragments serving as an efficient rule-based programming language to ensure efficacy in the running system.

In the sequel, we will shed more light on the challenges and intricacies of this vision. We will first discuss related literature, then detail the concepts needed for the three major system components, i.e., supervisor, component analysis, and micro-experiments.

3   Related Work

Dependable systems. Dependable systems must detect and tolerate failures at different levels of abstraction such as hardware, architecture, systems software and application level [41]. Traditional dependable systems are usually static [6], i.e., there will be at most minor changes after deployment. Their correctness needs to be certified prior to the use in operations, e.g., [3,37]. This certification is mostly process-based in the sense that one ensures the quality of a newly developed system by assessing the quality of the development processes [13]. Recent software systems tend to be more dynamic and require continuous updates, fast and cost effective deployment [1] which is hard to achieve with such traditional certification process [12]. Therefore, an alternative approach for the certification of dependable systems is an evidence-based approach [9]: one collects sufficient evidence to show that a system is safe in a given environment and safety cases attest to the safety of the system based on the given evidence.

Online updates of dependable software in the field is a double-edged sword as it can increase safety, fixing critical vulnerabilities, but can also decrease safety through the introduction of new bugs. Dynamic software updates require mechanisms for robust software management [15]. System failures can differ substantially in impact [21]. Avoiding system failures that violate safety, i.e., put human lives at risk, has the highest priority. System failures that reduce system availability have lower priority, but higher priority than failures that merely result in inconveniences. This can be achieved with multiple mechanisms like proactive fault management [40] and failure transformation [44].

Ensuring system integrity online. Our approach focuses on collecting evidence during run-time from different variants using explications. We depend on a supervisor component that cross-checks explications and conducts online experiments to obtain additional information to identify faulty components when required. Related work investigates the use of agents testing each other [20] requiring a predefined number of agents to confirm an agent faulty. Agents check the information collected from the environment in addition to generating test events and evaluating the reaction of their peers. Similarly, we test multiple, diverse components at run-time using explications and using micro-experiments but we rely on the centralized supervisor component. This centralized unit allows to overcome the problem of having multiple agents failing by which the predefined number of agents may no longer be in reach.

The supervisor is required to be fail-operational, otherwise, it would potentially be a single point of failure. In addition to the traditional approaches to ensure that the supervisor is correctly designed, we also need to ensure that it is correctly executed. Specifically, related work investigates the correct execution of the supervisor when executed on potentially unreliable hardware [25], under security attacks [5,27,28] or even protect its integrity despite the existence of CPU design faults [26].

Supervisory control. Supervisory control theory, rooted in the work of Ramadge and Wonham [38] is a method for automatically synthesizing controllers based on formal models of hardware and control requirements. The supervisory controller observes machine behavior by receiving signals from ongoing activities, upon which it sends back control signals about allowed activities [10]. Assuming that the controller reacts sufficiently fast on machine input, this feedback loop is modeled as a pair of synchronizing processes. The model of the machine, referred to as plant, is restricted by synchronization with the model of the controller, referred to as supervisor. This theory has been the nucleus for a plethora of foundational and applied work, reaching out to the SCADA (supervisory control and data acquisition) framework in process industry, but also linking to the context of reactive synthesis, where cyber-physical systems are abstracted as discrete transition systems subject to specifications expressed in temporal logic. Notably, while our setup has a conceptual similarity with that setting, we address supervision at a higher architectural level. Our supervisors are software artifacts (of considerable complexity) that are manually crafted in a SupERLog, not synthesized; they supervise several other software artifacts each of which is meant to play the role of a partial plant controller; our machinery of explications, reasoning about these, and formal methods for component analysis and micro-experiment planning are used to achieve supervision at this level.

4   Formal Underpinning

To set the stage for the discussion that follows, we now provide details on the formal models needed to conceptualize supervisor, component analysis, and micro-experiments.

4.1   SupERLog

In order to allow for a sketch of our supervisor architecture in a generic form (Sect. 5.2), we introduce the basics of a SupERLog based on a function-free predicate logic with integer arithmetic. The logic supports the modeling of supervisor behavior via rules. Reasoning in SupERLog is effective in the sense that verification of supervisor properties is decidable, and that consequence finding, can be efficiently done in a bottom-up reasoning style. Consequence finding is the main task of the supervisor.

Predicates of SupERLog range over abstract objects (constants) as well as numbers with respect to an integer arithmetic theory. Constant symbols identify the objects of interest, function symbols are not required. Abstract objects identify particles of the real world such as technical components, a sensor, or a car. Integer numbers represent sensor input or calibration data of the supervisor. The resulting logic can be viewed (i) as an extension of basic datalog with integer arithmetic, potentially non-Horn rules and unsafe variables [11], (ii) as an extension of SMT (Satisfiability Modulo Theory) by universally quantified variables [36], and (iii) as an instance of function-free first-order logic extended with integer arithmetic [22,43]. Satisfiability in this logic is undecidable in general [23]. However, it is decidable if integer variables are of bounded range in all rules. We assume this as a typical property in a technical environment. The prerequisite of finitely bounded variables also enables SupERLog support for rich arithmetic operations, as we will demonstrate in Example 5.

Definition 1 (SupERLog Signature). *A SupERLog signature* $\Sigma = (\Omega, \Pi,$ *IA) consists of a finite set* Ω *of predicate symbols, a finite set* Π *of constant symbols, and the symbols IA from integer arithmetic.*

Each $P \in \Omega$ *is associated with its* arity *k. We also write* $P(x_0, \ldots, x_{k-1})$ *to indicate the predicate's arguments explicitly. Variables may either range over finite domains generated by constants from* Π *or over integer numbers.*

Definition 2 (SupERLog Rules). *Given a SupERLog signature Σ, a rule*

$$H_1, \ldots, H_n \leftarrow B_1, \ldots, B_m \parallel \Lambda$$

for $H_i = P_i(\vec{x}_i, \vec{c}_j)$, $B_i = Q_i(\vec{y}_i, \vec{d}_i)$, $Q_i, P_i \in \Omega$, $c_j, d_j \in \Pi$, and Λ is an arithmetic IA constraint over variables $\bigcup_i(\vec{x}_i, \vec{y}_i)$.

Definition 3 (Facts). *Given a SupERLog signature $\Sigma = (\Omega, \Pi, IA)$ and an atom $P(x_0, \ldots, x_{k-1})$, $P \in \Omega$, for any tuple $\vec{c} = (c_0, \ldots, c_{k-1}) \in (\Pi \cup \text{const}(IA))^k$ we say that the instantiation of $P(x_0, \ldots, x_{k-1})$ with $\vec{c}$, written $P(c_0, \ldots, c_{k-1})$, is a (ground) fact. We denote by $F[\Sigma]$ the set of all facts in Σ.*

In case $n = 1$ a SupERLog rule becomes a Horn rule. Such rules are used to define supervisor behavior, because of their unique minimal model semantics. In this case reasoning is complete in a datalog-style, hyper-resolution fashion: the premises B_i are matched against ground facts A_i by a ground substitution σ and if the respective constraint $\Lambda\sigma$ is satisfied, the head H_1 is inferred. Given a finite set R of SupERLog Horn rules, we say that a fact H is derivable from R if there exists an iteratively applicable sequence of (grounded) rules from R whose outcome contains H. The derivation $F[[R]] \subseteq F[\Sigma]$ from F with R is the set of all such H. Obviously, because Π is finite and integer variables appear only bounded, the above bottom-up reasoning terminates and $F[[R]]$ is finite.

The case of general SupERLog rules ($n > 1$) results from verification. For example, a component model typically includes non-deterministic behavior expressible by disjunction. Then, bottom-up reasoning is no longer complete and we stick to model-driven reasoning [16] which is also terminating for SupERLog non-Horn clause sets.

4.2   System Model

We will be working in a setting with components interacting through input/output synchronization. We use a very natural extension of the I/O-automata formalism [33] to a setting with probabilistic transition effects, known as probabilistic I/O systems [19]. Probabilistic I/O automata give us the opportunity to model in a very natural manner typical cyber-physical systems (CPS) which are built up of components that interact and exchange information. In addition, CPS often occur in only partially controllable or known environments and also the modelling is bounded by technical and physical challenges which can be represented in the design of probabilistic automata.

Definition 4 (PIOS [19]). *A probabilistic I/O atom is a tuple $(S, Act, G, R, \bar{s})$, where S is a finite set of states, Act is a finite set of action labels, $G \subseteq S \times \mathcal{D}(Act \times S)$ is a generative output transition relation, $R: S \times Act \to \mathcal{D}(S)$ is a reactive transition function, and $\bar{s} \in S$ is an initial state.*

A probabilistic I/O system (PIOS) *is a finite vector* $\mathcal{P} = (\alpha_1, \ldots, \alpha_n)$ *of probabilistic I/O atoms* $\alpha_i = (S_i, Act_i, G_i, R_i, \bar{s}_i)$ *for* $i \in \{1, \ldots, n\}$. *The set of states of the system is the product of the component states* $S(\mathcal{P}) := \bigtimes_i S_i$ *and* $\bar{s}(\mathcal{P}) := (\bar{s}_1, \ldots, \bar{s}_n)$ *is the system's initial state. Let* $\mathcal{A} := \mathcal{D}(\bigcup_i Act_i)$ *be the set of transition labels. We define a transition relation* $\rightarrow \subseteq S(\mathcal{P}) \times \mathcal{A} \times \mathcal{D}(S(\mathcal{P}))$ *such that* $((s_1, \ldots, s_n), \kappa, \mu) \in \rightarrow$ *if and only if there exists an* $i \in \{1, \ldots, n\}$ *and* $\kappa_i \in \mathcal{D}(Act_i \times S_i)$ *such that* $(s_i, \kappa_i) \in G_i$, *for all* $a \in Act_i$, $\kappa(a) = \sum_{s \in S_i} \kappa_i(a, s)$, *and for all* $(s'_1, \ldots, s'_n) \in S(\mathcal{P})$:

$$\mu(s'_1, \ldots, s'_n) = \sum_{a \in Act_i} \kappa(a, s'_i) \prod_{j \neq i} \begin{cases} R_j(s_j, a)(s'_j) & a \in Act_j \\ \delta(s_j)(s'_j) & a \notin Act_j \end{cases}$$

Executions of CPS modelled as probabilistic I/O systems can be described and observed by traces which include the actions taken in the system and paths which in addition contain the system states which occurred during the execution. Having these information one can reconstruct what happened during the execution and what was the reason.

Definition 5 (Paths and Traces). *For a given PIOS* $\mathcal{P} = (\alpha_1, \ldots, \alpha_n)$, *a finite* path *is an alternating sequence of states and transitions* $s_0 t_0 s_1 t_1 \ldots t_{k-1} s_k$ *where* $s_i \in S(\mathcal{P})$ *for* $0 \leq i \leq k$ *and for each index* $j \in \{0, 1, \ldots, k-1\}$, $t_j = (s_j, \kappa_j, \mu_j) \in \rightarrow$ *such that* $\mu(s_{j+1}) > 0$. *For such a path, the sequence of actions* $\kappa_1 \kappa_2 \ldots \kappa_k$ *is called its* trace. *Each such trace is a word* $\hat{\rho} \in \mathcal{A}^*$. *Let* $\mathbb{T}[\mathcal{P}]$ *denote the set of all traces of PIOS* $\mathcal{P}$.

The supervisor is a special component of the complete PIOS defining the CPS under investigation. This component contains only one state and repeatedly executes control actions and thereby fully determines the system's behavior. This is later needed for conducting the micro-experiments.

Definition 6 (Supervisor Model). *We model the supervisor as a component* $\alpha_s = (S_s, Act_s, G_s, R_s, \bar{s}_s)$ *with* $S_s := \{\bar{s}_s\}$, $G_s := \{(\bar{s}_s, \delta((a, \bar{s}_s))) \mid a \in Act_C\}$ *for some set of* control actions $Act_C \subseteq Act_s$, *and* $R_s(\bar{s}_s, a) := \delta(\bar{s}_s)$.

The set Act_C will correspond to a certain set of facts under the control of the supervisor.

4.3   Observers and Boolean Monitors

We assume that a system perceives its environment through sets of facts which are provided by an *observer* based on an execution trace as defined in Definition 5. The action sequences given by execution traces contain information such as sensor readings which the observer translates into facts:

Definition 7. *An* observer *is a function mapping traces to sets of facts:*

$$O : \mathcal{A}^* \rightarrow 2^{F[\Sigma]}$$

To formally specify observers, we harvest results from the area of runtime verification. Runtime verification techniques allow to check whether a trace of a system under scrutiny satisfies or violates a given property [32] usually specified in a formal specification language e.g., [8,14]. Work in the area also expands to the computation of quantitative properties e.g., [2,31]. We abstract from the concrete specification language and introduce the following framework-agnostic notion of boolean monitors:

Definition 8. *A* boolean monitor *is a function mapping traces to booleans:*

$$M_{\mathbb{B}} : \mathcal{A}^* \to \mathbb{B}$$

The property observed by a boolean monitor then provides a verdict regarding a particular ground fact. For instance, there may be a boolean monitor that determines whether a lane is free based on information provided by a LIDAR sensor extracted from the current execution trace. We capture this correspondence between boolean monitors and ground facts formally as follows.

Definition 9 ($\mathcal{M}$-Observer). *Let $\mathcal{M}$ be a set of pairs $\langle M_{\mathbb{B}}, p(\vec{c}) \rangle$ of boolean monitors and grounded facts. For each $\mathcal{M}$ we define an observer:*

$$O[M_{\mathbb{B}}](\hat{\rho}) := \{\, p(\vec{c}) \mid \langle M_{\mathbb{B}}, p(\vec{c}) \rangle \in \mathcal{M} \text{ s.t. } M_{\mathbb{B}}(\hat{\rho}) = \top \,\}$$

The boolean monitors making up $\mathcal{M}$ can be based on any work in the area of runtime verification that is suitable for computing boolean properties over traces as defined in Definition 5. This includes specification languages for quantitative properties as long as they *also* allow the computation of boolean properties. While this setup is very general, there are some practical constraints. In particular, the set $\mathcal{M}$ must be finite or at least finitely representable such that we can actually compute the set of facts for a given trace.

5   The Supervisor

With its central role in our envisioned architecture, the supervisor has to fulfill a variety of tasks. Most prominent is the reasoning about component explications, but the coordination role requires also other activities. We first give an overview of the supervisor role as a whole, then delve into the details of reasoning. Component analysis and micro-experiments are tackled by separate components, and will be addressed in Sect. 6 and Sect. 7 respectively.

The supervisor itself is assumed to be a reusable, dependable component. It is designed using state-of-the-art dependability approaches like formal proofs and fault-tolerance mechanisms, like [42], to *prevent* that the supervisor becomes a single point of failure.

5.1   Overall Role and Tasks

Consider again the architecture overview in Fig. 1. The supervisor is the entity communicating with all other components and emitting the action decisions to be executed in the system's environment. It makes use of a knowledge base and a reasoning engine for reasoning about component explications. From this central position and design, the following tasks arise:

(i) *Knowledge base maintenance.* The supervisor needs to update its knowledge of the environment and its behavior, adjusting, e.g., for environment changes and low-probability events that were not observed before deployment. This knowledge base might be shared with the supervisors of other systems.

(ii) *Reasoning about explications.* As previously outlined, the supervisor needs to check component outputs, and in particular suggested action decisions, for contradictions given its knowledge.

(iii) *Synchronization with component variants.* The supervisor needs to continuously inform the component variants about the state of affairs, i.e., which action decisions were executed, which variants are in charge, which outputs have been forwarded to other components.

(iv) *Observations statistics maintenance.* The supervisor must collect and maintain the system execution data relevant for component analysis and, indirectly, micro-experiments.

(v) *Taking action decisions.* The supervisor is responsible for deciding whether the outcome of reasoning is sufficient to take an action decision, whether a safe fallback action should be executed, or whether further investigation through component analysis or micro experiments should be triggered.

(vi) *Executing micro-experiments.* Micro-experiments are used to identify action strategies that minimize uncertainty about faulty components. The supervisor is responsible for executing these strategies.

(vii) *Taking analysis results into account.* The supervisor must be able to incorporate the results from component analysis and micro-experiments into its decisions as per (v).

While items (i), (iii), and (iv) can be based on well-understood principles (e.g., [35, 39]), items (ii), (v) and (vi) need more discussion. For reasoning about explications (ii) we employ SupERLog reasoning, as outlined below. This comes with a trade-off between expressivity and efficiency paving a controlled way to the use of online, real-time decision making in dynamic systems.

For the core of item (v), a straightforward solution consists of hardcoded rules like "execute an action only if proved safe" or "trigger component analysis if uncertainty greater than threshold". A more advanced and robust solution is to formulate the entire decision-making process – encompassing regular actions, fallback actions and whether to trigger component analysis – as a single overall reasoning process. Our SupERLog reasoning mechanism is suited for this purpose.

Micro-experiment execution in item (vi) takes the form of re-planning [18], based on an action policy suggested by the micro-experiment planner (see Sect. 7). In each execution step, this policy suggests an action A to execute to the supervisor. The supervisor decides whether to execute A or another action (like a fallback action, or a decision to remain idle and just observe the environment behavior). The supervisor communicates its decision back to the micro-experiment planner, which re-plans an adapted policy if needed.

For taking analysis results into account (vii), Micro-experiment execution generates new observations (feeding into the supervisor like all observations, via an $\mathcal{M}$-Observer cf. next sub-section), while component analysis results need to be directly fed into the supervisor knowledge base. A canonical instance of the latter is to feed back assessments classifying component variants as "correct" vs. "potentially faulty" vs. "definitely faulty" (which we shall specify formally in Sect. 6). If required, more detailed properties can be communicated by including corresponding predicates and knowledge about fault-model specifics.

5.2   Reasoning About Component Explications

A central issue in logical reasoning is the trade-off between expressivity and efficiency: more powerful logics allow to express more complex phenomena, but are more complex to reason about and quickly become undecidable. Reasoning in Horn SupERLog terminates and can be efficiently implemented making it a perfect choice for online decision making in dynamic systems. We next specify a possible form of a supervisor model based on SupERLog and introduce different modes of reasoning along these lines, using SupERLog deduction over ground facts. We first address component variants, then the supervisor itself. For the implementation of the supervisor we employ a Horn SupERLog rule base.

Component variants are components in system control, working together to choose actions (from the action set Act_C in our system model). At the abstraction level in our supervisor model here, they are collections of functions on facts over a signature, implemented by Horn rules of the supervisor, where the target signature contains an encoding of system control information:

Definition 10 (Variant). *Given the set of actions Act_C, a (component) variant V is a finite set $\{V_1, \ldots, V_k\}$ of functions $V_i : 2^{F[\Sigma^I]} \mapsto 2^{F[\Sigma_i^O]}$, where Σ^I and Σ_i^O are SupERLog signatures. We require that $\Pi^I \supseteq Act_C$ and that, for all i, $\Pi_i^O \supseteq \Pi^I \cup \{V\}$ and $\Omega_i^O \supseteq \Omega^I \cup \{p_i^{ctrl}\}$. We will refer to p_i^{ctrl} as V_i's control predicate.*

Note that the set Act_C comprises the actions in control of the supervisor, cf. Definition 6. The input $2^{F[\Sigma^I]}$ common to all functions V_i here connects to observations on the trace of the system, i.e., the facts in $F[\Sigma^I]$ are associated with boolean monitors in an $\mathcal{M}$-Observer as per Definition 9. That $\mathcal{M}$-Observer is permanently associated with the supervisor, serving to connect its representation of facts to the system trace observations in the model underlying component analysis.

A component variant is a collection of functions, rather than a single function, to allow to distinguish its outputs with respect to individual control predicates. Such predicates encode outputs that form part of the system control, i.e., that provide information about which actions Act_C should be chosen. This includes direct control information through predicates like $doAction(V, a)$ and $illegalAction(V, a)$ where variant V decides to execute a or deems that action to be illegal in the current situation. It also includes intermediate information like $emergencyBreakNeeded(V)$ indicating that one part of the machinery suggests an action (like an emergency-break unit which raises a need to break whenever an obstacle is detected ahead) which will be combined with other information in the supervisor before taking an actual decision (like changing the lane instead). The remaining (non-control-predicate) output of each individual function V_i is an *explication* in terms of the subset of relevant *input facts* responsible for the control-predicate decision made by V_i.

Naturally, for every input fact set F, the output $V_i(F)$ of each function should be a subset of F (the explication) plus exactly one control fact, and the control facts should not contradict each other across different $V_i(F)$. Our definition does not make these restrictions to permit exceptions, and to allow the model to capture faulty components where implementation bugs may disvalidate these properties. It is the supervisor's task to reason about inconsistencies in component variants' outputs. Furthermore, our defined predicate logic enables effective computation of guarantees such as the existence of single control facts.

The functions V_i are arbitrary in our definition to keep our concepts generic and as the internal working of the component variant is not of interest in the supervisor specification (it is, instead, the subject of faulty component analysis and micro-experiments). In practice, implementations of the component variants must, for use in our framework, be extended with an implementation of the functions V_i describing their behavior in terms of predicates as specified above to support supervisor reasoning. As an example, the emergency-break unit as above, reacting to obstacles detected in front-camera pictures, requires to have simple adaptors that translate the relevant signals ("obstacle detected", "control: break") into suitable ground facts.

The supervisor now simply takes as input the component variants' outputs, and processes this information with its SupERLog rules set.

Definition 11 (Supervisor). *Given a set of actions Act_C and a set $\mathcal{V}$ of variants, a supervisor is defined by a SupERLog signature Σ_s where $\bigcup_{V \in \mathcal{V}, V_i \in V} \Omega_i^O \subseteq \Omega_s$, as well as a finite set R_s of SupERLog Horn rules for Σ_s.*

Given a set of facts $F \subseteq F[\Sigma^I]$ for each variant V, the supervisor computes the SupERLog derivation $F^O[[R_s]]$ from the union of outputs $F^O := \bigcup_{V \in \mathcal{V}, V_i \in V} V_i(F)$. It takes decisions based on that derivation.

For example, a simple situation is that where the supervisor checks for contradictions when dealing with a variant V that is already certified, and another variant V' with recent security updates that we want to certify. To this end, we include a predicate $contradiction(x, y)$ into P_s, and the rule

$contradiction(x, y) \leftarrow doAction(x, a), illegalAction(y, a)$ into R_s. We then check for ground instances $contradiction(x, y) \in F^O[[R_s]]$. The absence of such a contradiction between V and V' for a long period of time increases confidence in the safety of V'. If there is a contradiction however, there are two possible cases. First, $contradiction(V', V)$ where V forbids an action suggested by V', indicating that V' is unsafe. Second, vice versa $contradiction(V, V')$, which results in an ambiguous situation as V' is not yet certified yet may have an important security update. In both cases, the supervisor may decide to take an emergency action, like a handover to the human operator. Or, given sufficient time is available, it may invoke component analysis, and transitively micro-experiments, to gain more confidence in which of V and V' is correct.

In the latter case, the supervisor uses the explications delivered by V and V' as part of their output. Namely, say the reason for V's decision is the input fact $p \in F$ and that for V''s decision is $q \in F$. We assume that the integrity of the inputs can be verified by the supervisor, i.e., a variant can neither generate inputs nor can it modify inputs. This can be achieved, for example, by digitally signing all inputs. Each of p and q are associated with boolean monitors in the supervisor's $\mathcal{M}$-Observer, $\langle M_\mathbb{B}^p, p(\vec{c})\rangle$ and $\langle M_\mathbb{B}^q, q(\vec{c})\rangle$. The supervisor communicates $M_\mathbb{B}^p$ and $M_\mathbb{B}^q$ to component analysis, which makes use of this information about system traces to narrow down the possible fault models as we shall specify in the next section.

Example 4 (Conflicting Sensors: Supervisor Reasoning). Consider, as in Example 2, an update to the software component responsible for lane changing maneuvers in an autonomous vehicle. Say the vehicle is currently driving in the right lane. The old variant V outputs a control predicate $doAction(V, gostraight) \in V_i(F)$ while the new variant V' outputs $illegalAction(V', gostraight) \in V_j'(F)$. With the above simple reasoning, the supervisor concludes $contradiction(V, V')$, indicating a conflict. Say the supervisor decides to handover to the human operator and, simultaneously, to trigger component analysis. The explications provided by V_i and V_j' are $p = free(rightlane)$ and $q = blocked(rightlane)$ respectively.[2] The supervisor maps these to boolean monitors $M_\mathbb{B}^p$ and $M_\mathbb{B}^q$ in its $\mathcal{M}$-Observer.

From a SupERLog reasoning perspective, action-contradiction checking as above is extremely simple. More complex reasoning arises, for example, in meta-reasoning about which decision to take given mixed evidence (go ahead? bail out? trigger component analysis?); and when components do not output actions directly, but pieces of information that will need to be assembled by the supervisor reasoning to arrive at an action decision. The latter makes sense, for example, in the context of a lane change scenario, where what is a safe distance depends on road conditions:

---

[2] Note that, for the sake of efficiency, SupERLog reasoning may not explicitly handle negation. Instead, the relevant contradictory fact combinations can be identified via appropriate extra rules.

Example 5 (Lane Change). The supervisor calculates a safe distance ahead of car depending on wet or dry road conditions using the explications provided by the variants $(speed(S), distance(D))$. For example, the supervisor decides based on following rules if the distance between the car x and a car y in front of it is safe $(Safe\_Distance\_Ahead(SDA))$. Specifically, the distance should be large enough $(Base\_Safe\_Distance\_Ahead(BSDA))$ in addition to extra space required if the road is wet $(Extra\_Distance(ED))$. Note that $BSDA$ rules varies depending on the speed of the car x compared to the speed of car y.

$$\frac{\mathrm{SDA}(x,y,sx,sy,z) \leftarrow \mathrm{BSDA}(x,y,sx,sy,v), \mathrm{ED}(x,sx,w), \| \ z > v + w}{\mathrm{BSDA}(x,y,sx,sy,v) \leftarrow \mathrm{S}(x,sx), \mathrm{S}(y,sy), \mathrm{D}(z,x,y) \ \| \ sx > sy, z > sx * 10}$$
$$\frac{}{\mathrm{BSDA}(x,y,sx,sy,v) \leftarrow \mathrm{S}(x,sx), \mathrm{S}(y,sy), \mathrm{D}(z,x,y) \ \| \ sx \leqslant sy, z > sx}$$
$$\mathrm{ED}(x,sx,w) \leftarrow \mathrm{S}(x,sx), \mathrm{Wet}(u) \ \| \ w = \mathrm{div}(sx * u, 10)$$

6 Component Analysis

Given a formal and componentwise model of the system, the component analysis identifies potentially faulty components in the system.

Definition 12 (System Configuration). *Let* $\langle C_1, \dots, C_n \rangle$ *be a finite vector of components and* $\mathcal{M}_i := \{\alpha_1^i, \dots, \alpha_{k_i}^i\}$ *be a set of PIOS atoms for each component* C_i. *A system configuration is a PIOS* $c = \langle \alpha^1, \dots, \alpha^n \rangle$ *such that* $\alpha^i \in \mathcal{M}_i$. *Let* $\mathcal{C}$ *be the set of all system configurations. Then* $\mathbb{T}[\mathcal{C}] := \bigcup_{c \in \mathcal{C}} \mathbb{T}[c]$ *is the set of all finite traces over all system configurations.*

Definition 13 (Observation Function). *Let Obs be a potentially infinite set of observables. An observation function* $\mathcal{O} : \mathbb{T}[\mathcal{C}] \to Obs$ *maps traces to observables* $o \in Obs$. *For each system configuration* $c \in \mathcal{C}$ *the set* $Obs(c) = \{\mathcal{O}(\hat{\pi}) \mid \hat{\pi} \in \mathbb{T}[c]\} \subseteq Obs$ *is the set of observables consistent with c.*

Given an observation of an observable $o \in Obs$ we seek to explain o in virtue of a system configuration which is consistent with o, i.e., a system configuration that may result in an observation of o. The different models α_x^i for each component C_i enable us to ask and answer model-based *what-if* questions.

Example 6. Returning to Example 2, imagine a distance sensor component C_i measuring the distance to obstacles in the present lane based on which a boolean monitor concluded that there is an obstacle ahead. Now, given an observation o and different models α_N^i and α_F^i for sensor C_i where α_N^i describes the behavior of a perfectly functioning and α_F^i the behavior of a faulty sensor, we may ask: what if the sensor were faulty, would that explain the observation o? To answer this question, we check whether o is consistent with a configuration where the sensor behaves normally versus a configuration where the sensor is faulty. The answer allows the supervisor to determine which components to trust.

Definition 14 (Faulty Components). *With respect to an observable o, we call a component potentially faulty if and only if there exists a configuration c consistent with o such that the component's model in c describes faulty behavior. We call a component definitely faulty if and only if for all configurations c consistent with o, the component's model in c describes faulty behavior.*

Note that if there is a failure mode of the component that may still produce the correct behavior in some execution, e.g., a sensor which non-deterministically provides values, then Definition 14 always considers the sensor potentially faulty. This matches our intuition that in such a case we can never be certain that the sensor is not already faulty until it actually misbehaves.

In case of probabilistic systems one may further assign a (minimal/maximal) probability to each configuration c with respect to a given observable o capturing how probable it is to observe o if the system were configured according to c. Such probabilities provide the supervisor with insights about the likelihood of certain components being faulty and can be a further basis for its decision.

With regard to the architecture displayed in Fig. 1, the environment, each sensor, and the actuators are represented as components. Treating them as components allows us to capture interactions between actuator commands and expected sensor readings.

For instance, if the obstacle in Example 2 is fixed then acceleration and deceleration should have a specific effect on the slope of the measured distance.

Example 7 (Component Analysis). Recapitulating Example 2 and Example 3, we model the system as four components, the LIDAR sensor C_L, the RADAR sensor C_R, the environment C_E, and the supervisor C_S. For the environment, we define a single probabilistic I/O atom with digital clock semantics describing how the distance of the car changes in response to (discrete) speed changes of the supervisor. The supervisor is modeled as per Definition 6 which results in non-determinism in the model regarding the acceleration and deceleration decisions. Those acceleration and deceleration actions are, however, provided by the observation and thereby resolved by the actual system. For both sensors, we have a nominal model capturing the measured distance with respect to changes in the environment. In addition, we have the following failure models: (1) the measured distance is non-deterministically stuck and does not change and (2) the measured distance is multiplied by 5. Now, if the car decelerates slightly, the correct measurements are described by the nominal models. Our model predicts that given an observation of a deceleration action this should be followed by a specific change in distance. If the observed value for a sensor does not change at all, then this is in line with what the failure model (1) would predict. If the value changes over-proportionally by a factor of 5, then this is in line with what the failure model (2) would predict.

For the observation function, we assume that a subset $\mathcal{A}_O \subseteq \mathcal{A}$ of the transition labels in the PIOS are directly observable, e.g., sensor readings and actuator commands. The set *Obs* of observables is the set of finite words over $\mathcal{A}_O$, i.e.,

$Obs = \mathcal{A}_O^*$. For a finite trace $\hat{\rho} = \kappa_0\kappa_1\ldots\kappa_n \in \mathcal{A}^*$ of a PIOS $(\alpha_1,\ldots,\alpha_n)$ we define the observation function O as follows:

$$\mathcal{O}(\kappa_0\kappa_1\ldots\kappa_n) = \mathcal{O}(\kappa_0)\mathcal{O}(\kappa_1)\ldots\mathcal{O}(\kappa_n) \quad \text{with } \mathcal{O}(\kappa) := \begin{cases} \kappa & \text{if } \kappa \in \mathcal{A}_O \\ \epsilon & \text{otherwise} \end{cases}$$

The supervisor provides the component analysis with the boolean monitors responsible for the contradiction. We assume that some of the boolean monitors respond to specific transition labels generated by particular components. For example, the I/O atoms modeling a LIDAR sensor have generative transitions for specific *LIDAR-sensor-reading* actions which are the basis for the monitor's verdict regarding the distance to obstacles on the lanes. Based on this information, we prioritize different sets of system configurations we consider for the analysis. Note, however, that a contradiction of facts may not only be caused by malfunctioning of the components which are directly connected via monitors to those facts. Hence, the information provided by the supervisor is merely used as a hint to quickly identify potential faults by assuming that all other components except those involved in the contradiction are functioning nominally.

If the component analysis is not able to determine which of the components is faulty because there are multiple configurations consistent with a given observation, then the component analysis invokes micro-experiment planning. To this end, the micro-experiment planner is provided with a set of *possible* configurations $\mathcal{C}_\Diamond \subseteq \mathcal{C}$ and the given observation o.

7 Micro-Experiments

The purpose of a micro-experiment is to provide the supervisor with specific instructions that, when followed, will allow to distinguish between the system models $\mathcal{C}_\Diamond$ still considered possible after component analysis. Ultimately, upon the completion of a micro-experiment, a unique possible model is identified. We next define what a micro-experiment is (in terms of an action selection function), and outline the use within the supervisor framework.

As previously discussed, the supervisor resolves action choices, as captured by actions in our model (cf. Sect. 4.2). For instance, in our lane change example, a component could request a lane change in either left or right direction in order to evade an obstacle on the current lane. We formalize micro-experiments based on these action choices, as a function of observations.

Concretely, in the system model formalization, Definition 4, the supervisor is represented abstractly via atom α_s. The supervisor's control actions are Act_C. For ease of presentation, we assume that the control actions available in a specific situation can be observed by the supervisor directly, i.e., $Act_C \subseteq \mathcal{A}_O$. Intuitively, components must explicitly request the supervisor to make a decision. For that request to make sense, the supervisor must be able to know (and thus to observe) the available options. Given this, micro-experiments are defined as follows:

Definition 15 (Micro-Experiment). *The* observation histories $\mathcal{H}$ *denote the set of all finite sequences of pairs* $\mathcal{A}_O \times \{\top, \bot\}$. *A micro-experiment is a (partial) function* $\pi : \mathcal{H} \mapsto \mathcal{A}_O \cup \{\square\}$.

Observation histories allow to track and to accordingly react to observations made since the beginning of the micro-experiment execution. Micro-experiments are hence decision strategies that inform the supervisor what to do next depending on what has been observed so far.

This is non-trivial in two aspects. First, the uncertainty about system models entails uncertainty which actions are enabled. Indeed, applicability of observable actions is the information at our disposal to distinguish between different system models. Definition 15 reflects this with the annotation symbols $\top$ and $\bot$, which encode applicability and inapplicability respectively. Second, the supervisor can control only some, not all, of the observable actions. Non-controlled observable actions must be taken into account as signals for the execution of a micro-experiment, i.e., they must be added to the observation history. Definition 15 hence permits arbitrary observable actions as the micro-experiment output.

The micro-experiment execution is structured accordingly. It consists of a loop, where in each iteration the supervisor queries the micro-experiment with the current observation history h. The history is initially empty, and is extended by one more element in each step. Each loop iteration has an active or passive nature depending on whether the suggested action $a := \pi(h)$ is (a) a control action $a \in Act_C$ or (b) a non-control action $a \in \mathcal{A}_O \setminus Act_C$. In case (a), the supervisor checks whether a is enabled. If yes, the supervisor executes a and updates the observation history to $h \circ \langle \pi(h), \top \rangle$; if no, the supervisor updates the observation history to $h \circ \langle \pi(h), \bot \rangle$. In case (b), the supervisor takes a passive role, merely monitoring the system behavior and updating the history accordingly. The micro-experiment at such a point essentially asks the supervisor whether the next action executed by the system is a. The supervisor updates h to $h \circ \langle \pi(h), \top \rangle$ if the observed action indeed matches the requested action a, and to $h \circ \langle \pi(h), \bot \rangle$ otherwise. The micro-experiment terminates when $\pi(h) = \square$. The observation history h collected until this point allows to remove those models from $\mathcal{C}_\Diamond$ that are inconsistent with h.

Example 8. In continuation of Examples 2, 3, and 7, assume that our system contains a potentially faulty distance sensor C_S. Let α_N (nominal), α_V (errors at higher speeds), and α_A (errors at certain view angles to the obstacle) be our models of C_S that are consistent with the current observations. The supervisor now wishes to obtain additional information about the potential faultiness of C_S. Figure 2 illustrates a possible micro-experiment π for that purpose. The control actions here are those actions that actively change the state of the car. The non-control actions represent sensor outputs. The distinguish between the two, the latter are shown in *italic*. The gray sets reflect how the possible models of C_S change according to the observations made during micro-experiment execution.

Assume that the car is currently moving on a straight road with a speed of $14\frac{m}{s}$. Let there be a static obstacle detected by C_S with a distance of 100 m. π immediately requests the supervisor to slightly decelerate (step i). If this is not possible, i.e., the supervisor answers with "$\perp$", the execution of π is stopped without obtaining additional information about the models. If it is possible "$\top$", π requests the supervisor to observe how the distance measurement of C_S changes when decelerating (step ii). The amount of deceleration is chosen large enough to assure that even under fault model α_V, the sensor now measures the correct distance. Consequently, if the new measurement does not agree with what would be expected given the initial distance estimate, the "$\perp$" case, then the initial distance estimate must have been wrong. Thus, the chosen control action implies that α_V has to be the model of C_S.

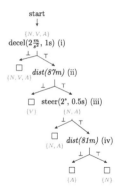

Fig. 2. An example micro-experiment π.

Vice versa, for "$\top$" we know that α_V cannot be underlying C_S since the change in speed was indeed adequately represented in the distance measurement. The execution of π then continues from the reduced model set α_N and α_A as further depicted in Fig. 2.

The question of course is how to construct a suitable micro-experiment in the first place. We conjecture that this can be done via standard tools based on an encoding into partially observable Markov decision processes (POMDP) [45]. Specifically, the uncertainty about system models can be encoded into POMDP state uncertainty by making the true system model an unobservable part of the state, and defining the transition behavior according to the true model. Observable actions in such a POMDP then decrease state uncertainty by distinguishing states where the action is enabled from ones where it is not. The objective of maximally decreasing uncertainty can be encoded as a reward dependent on the POMDP's belief state, as in so-called ρPOMDPs [4]. It remains a topic for future work to spell out this approach.

8 Discussion and Outlook

Cyber-physical systems that evolve dynamically through in-field component updates are clearly a grand challenge to dependability, especially when facing insufficient time for full re-certification of the updates. Our approach brings together five key ideas to design an architecture addressing that challenge:

(i) Not a single but several component variants are maintained, and a *supervisor* monitors and arbitrates their behavior.

(ii) Component variants must provide *explications* for their decisions.

(iii) Effective and verifiable *reasoning* is used by the supervisor to identify inconsistencies across components and component variants.

(iv) In-field *component analysis* identifies possible faults from past system observations.

(v) In-field *micro-experiments* disambiguate between faults through injection of dedicated system behavior.

In short, our proposed architecture safeguards uncertified component variants through a certifiable control layer, and offers the system the possibility to self-diagnose (autonomously, if necessary) in the field. Each of the ideas (i) – (v) draws on established concepts in different areas of computer science. Our contribution lies in bringing them together, and providing a first formalization of the constituents and their interplay.

At this stage, our contribution is a vision. It remains to implement and evaluate the envisioned architecture.

Observe that, to this end, for (i), (iii), (iv), and (v) one can draw on established techniques in dependability, logics, verification, and artificial intelligence respectively. The present paper brings together these areas and outlines a possible architecture instance together with its formalization. Many other instantiations are conceivable given the wealth of concepts available in each area.

For (ii), the computation of explications, matters are somewhat different as the process of explicating decisions remains in itself a grand challenge for classical software engineering as well as for machine learning (ML) systems. For ML this is commonly known as the Explainable AI challenge. While for now we assume a relatively benign form of explications, namely identifying the relevant subset of the input which led to the output, we expect that our architecture vision will profit from progress in that highly active area.

Our next steps will be to spell out different aspects of our architecture, to be implemented and evaluated in individual use cases, paving the way to the vision of a full integrated system. We believe that this opens a new sub-area of dependable systems research, which we hope will inspire other researchers as well.

References

1. Aizpurua, J., Muxika, E., Papadopoulos, Y., Chiacchio, F., Manno, G.: Application of the D3H2 methodology for the cost-effective design of dependable systems. Safety **2**(2), 9 (2016). https://doi.org/10.3390/safety2020009
2. Alur, R., Fisman, D., Raghothaman, M.: Regular programming for quantitative properties of data streams. In: Thiemann, P. (ed.) ESOP 2016. LNCS, vol. 9632, pp. 15–40. Springer, Heidelberg (2016). https://doi.org/10.1007/978-3-662-49498-1_2
3. Alvaro, A., de Almeida, E.S., de Lemos Meira, S.R.: Software component certification: a survey. In: 31st EUROMICRO Conference on Software Engineering and Advanced Applications, pp. 106–113 (2005)
4. Araya, M., Buffet, O., Thomas, V., Charpillet, F.: A POMDP extension with belief-dependent rewards. In: Lafferty, J.D., Williams, C.K.I., Shawe-Taylor, J., Zemel, R.S., Culotta, A. (eds.) Advances in Neural Information Processing Systems 23, pp. 64–72. Curran Associates, Inc. (2010)

5. Arnautov, S., Trach, B., Gregor, F., Knauth, T., Martin, A., Priebe, C., Lind, J., Muthukumaran, D., O'Keeffe, D., Stillwell, M.L., Goltzsche, D., Eyers, D., Kapitza, R., Pietzuch, P., Fetzer, C.: SCONE: secure Linux containers with intel SGX. In: 12th USENIX Symposium on Operating Systems Design and Implementation (OSDI 2016), Savannah, GA, pp. 689–703. USENIX Association (2016). https://www.usenix.org/conference/osdi16/technical-sessions/presentation/arnautov

6. Avizienis, A., Laprie, J.C., Randell, B., Landwehr, C.: Basic concepts and taxonomy of dependable and secure computing. IEEE Trans. Dependable Secur. Comput. **1**(1), 11–33 (2004). https://doi.org/10.1109/TDSC.2004.2

7. Avizienis, A., Laprie, J.C., Randell, B., et al.: Fundamental concepts of dependability. University of Newcastle upon Tyne, Computing Science (2001)

8. Bauer, A., Leucker, M., Schallhart, C.: Monitoring of real-time properties. In: Arun-Kumar, S., Garg, N. (eds.) FSTTCS 2006. LNCS, vol. 4337, pp. 260–272. Springer, Heidelberg (2006). https://doi.org/10.1007/11944836_25

9. Bishop, P., Bloomfield, R.: A methodology for safety case development, February 1998. https://doi.org/10.1007/978-1-4471-1534-2_14

10. Cassandras, C.G., Lafortune, S.: Introduction to Discrete Event Systems, 2nd edn. Springer, Heidelberg (2010)

11. Ceri, S., Gottlob, G., Tanca, L.: What you always wanted to know about datalog (and never dared to ask). IEEE Trans. Knowl. Data Eng. **1**(1), 146–166 (1989)

12. Council, N.R.: Software for Dependable Systems: Sufficient Evidence? The National Academies Press, Washington, DC (2007). https://doi.org/10.17226/11923. https://www.nap.edu/catalog/11923/software-for-dependable-systems-sufficient-evidence

13. Currit, P.A., Dyer, M., Mills, H.D.: Certifying the reliability of software. IEEE Trans. Softw. Eng. **SE–12**(1), 3–11 (1986)

14. D'Angelo, B., Sankaranarayanan, S., Sanchez, C., Robinson, W., Finkbeiner, B., Sipma, H.B., Mehrotra, S., Manna, Z.: LOLA: runtime monitoring of synchronous systems. In: 12th International Symposium on Temporal Representation and Reasoning (TIME 2005), pp. 166–174 (2005)

15. Felser, M., Kapitza, R., Kleinöder, J., Schröder-Preikschat, W.: Dynamic software update of resource-constrained distributed embedded systems. In: Rettberg, A., Zanella, M.C., Dömer, R., Gerstlauer, A., Rammig, F.J. (eds.) IESS 2007. ITIFIP, vol. 231, pp. 387–400. Springer, Boston, MA (2007). https://doi.org/10.1007/978-0-387-72258-0_33

16. Fiori, A., Weidenbach, C.: SCL with theory constraints. CoRR abs/2003.04627 (2020). https://arxiv.org/abs/2003.04627

17. Fleury, M.: Formalization of logical calculi in Isabelle/HOL. Ph.D. thesis, Saarland University, Saarbrücken, Germany (2020)

18. Ghallab, M., Nau, D., Traverso, P.: Automated Planning and Acting. Cambridge University Press, Cambridge (2016)

19. Giro, S., D'Argenio, P.R., Fioriti, L.M.F.: Distributed probabilistic input/output automata: expressiveness, (un)decidability and algorithms. Theoret. Comput. Sci. **538**, 84–102 (2014). Quantitative Aspects of Programming Languages and Systems (2011–2012). https://doi.org/10.1016/j.tcs.2013.07.017. http://www.sciencedirect.com/science/article/pii/S0304397513005203

20. Heck, H., Rudolph, S., Gruhl, C., Wacker, A., Hähner, J., Sick, B., Tomforde, S.: Towards autonomous self-tests at runtime. In: 2016 IEEE 1st International Workshops on Foundations and Applications of Self* Systems (FAS*W), pp. 98–99 (2016)

21. Heimerdinger, W., Weinstock, C.: A conceptual framework for system fault tolerance. Technical report CMU/SEI-92-TR-033, Software Engineering Institute, Carnegie Mellon University, Pittsburgh, PA (1992). http://resources.sei.cmu.edu/library/asset-view.cfm?AssetID=11747

22. Horbach, M., Voigt, M., Weidenbach, C.: On the combination of the Bernays–Schönfinkel–Ramsey fragment with simple linear integer arithmetic. In: de Moura, L. (ed.) CADE 2017. LNCS (LNAI), vol. 10395, pp. 77–94. Springer, Cham (2017). https://doi.org/10.1007/978-3-319-63046-5_6

23. Horbach, M., Voigt, M., Weidenbach, C.: The universal fragment of Presburger arithmetic with unary uninterpreted predicates is undecidable. CoRR abs/1703.01212 (2017)

24. Kessler, A.M.: Elon musk says self-driving tesla cars will be in the US by summer. The New York Times **19**, 1 (2015). https://www.nytimes.com/2015/03/20/business/elon-musk-says-self-driving-tesla-cars-will-be-in-the-us-by-summer.html

25. Kuvaiskii, D., Faqeh, R., Bhatotia, P., Felber, P., Fetzer, C.: HAFT: hardware-assisted fault tolerance. In: Proceedings of the Eleventh European Conference on Computer Systems, EuroSys 2016. Association for Computing Machinery, New York (2016). https://doi.org/10.1145/2901318.2901339

26. Kuvaiskii, D., Fetzer, C.: δ-encoding: Practical encoded processing (2015)

27. Kuvaiskii, D., Oleksenko, O., Arnautov, S., Trach, B., Bhatotia, P., Felber, P., Fetzer, C.: SGXBOUNDS: memory safety for shielded execution. In: Proceedings of the Twelfth European Conference on Computer Systems, EuroSys 2017, pp. 205–221. Association for Computing Machinery, New York (2017). https://doi.org/10.1145/3064176.3064192

28. Kuvaiskii, D., Oleksenko, O., Bhatotia, P., Felber, P., Fetzer, C.: ELZAR: triple modular redundancy using intel AVX (practical experience report). In: 2016 46th Annual IEEE/IFIP International Conference on Dependable Systems and Networks (DSN), June 2016. https://doi.org/10.1109/dsn.2016.65

29. Lammich, P.: Efficient verified (UN)SAT certificate checking. J. Autom. Reason. **64**(3), 513–532 (2020)

30. Laprie, J.C.: Dependability: basic concepts and terminology. In: Laprie, J.C. (ed.) Dependability: Basic Concepts and Terminology. DEPENDABLECOMP, vol. 5, pp. 3–245. Springer, Vienna (1992). https://doi.org/10.1007/978-3-7091-9170-5_1

31. Leucker, M., Sánchez, C., Scheffel, T., Schmitz, M., Schramm, A.: TeSSLa: runtime verification of non-synchronized real-time streams. In: ACM Symposium on Applied Computing (SAC), France. ACM, April 2018

32. Leucker, M., Schallhart, C.: A brief account of runtime verification. J. Logic Algebraic Program. **78**(5), 293–303 (2009). The 1st Workshop on Formal Languages and Analysis of Contract-Oriented Software (FLACOS '07)

33. Lynch, N.: Input/output automata: basic, timed, hybrid, probabilistic, dynamic, In: Amadio, R., Lugiez, D. (eds.) CONCUR 2003. LNCS, vol. 2761, pp. 191–192. Springer, Heidelberg (2003). https://doi.org/10.1007/978-3-540-45187-7_12

34. Lyyra, A.K., Koskinen, K.M.: With software updates, Tesla upends product life cycle in the car industry. LSE Bus. Rev. (2017)

35. Moore, E.F., et al.: Gedanken-experiments on sequential machines. Automata Stud. **34**, 129–153 (1956)

36. Nieuwenhuis, R., Oliveras, A., Tinelli, C.: Solving SAT and SAT modulo theories: from an abstract Davis-Putnam-Logemann-Loveland procedure to DPLL(T). J. ACM **53**, 937–977 (2006)

37. Palin, R., Ward, D., Habli, I., Rivett, R.: ISO 26262 safety cases: Compliance and assurance, vol. 2011, September 2011. https://doi.org/10.1049/cp.2011.0251
38. Ramadge, P., Wonham, W.: Supervisory control of a class of discrete event processes, **25**, 206–230 (1987). https://doi.org/10.1007/BFb0006306
39. Russell, S., Norvig, P.: Artificial Intelligence: A Modern Approach, 3rd edn. Prentice Hall, Upper Saddle River (2010)
40. Salfner, F., Malek, M.: Architecting dependable systems with proactive fault management. In: Casimiro, A., de Lemos, R., Gacek, C. (eds.) WADS 2009. LNCS, vol. 6420, pp. 171–200. Springer, Heidelberg (2010). https://doi.org/10.1007/978-3-642-17245-8_8
41. Saltzer, J.H., Reed, D.P., Clark, D.D.: End-to-end arguments in system design. ACM Trans. Comput. Syst. **2**(4), 277–88 (1984). https://doi.org/10.1145/357401.357402
42. Schneider, F.B.: Implementing fault-tolerant services using the state machine approach: a tutorial. ACM Comput. Surv. (CSUR) **22**(4), 299–319 (1990)
43. Voigt, M.: The Bernays–Schönfinkel–Ramsey fragment with bounded difference constraints over the reals is decidable. In: Dixon, C., Finger, M. (eds.) FroCoS 2017. LNCS (LNAI), vol. 10483, pp. 244–261. Springer, Cham (2017). https://doi.org/10.1007/978-3-319-66167-4_14
44. Wu, W., Kelly, T.: Safety tactics for software architecture design. In: Proceedings of the 28th Annual International Computer Software and Applications Conference 2004, COMPSAC 2004, vol. 1, pp. 368–375 (2004)
45. Åström, K.: Optimal control of Markov processes with incomplete state information. J. Math. Anal. Appl. **10**(1), 174–205 (1965). https://doi.org/10.1016/0022-247X(65)90154-X

Forming Ensembles at Runtime: A Machine Learning Approach

Tomáš Bureš[1(✉)], Ilias Gerostathopoulos[1,2(✉)], Petr Hnětynka[1(✉)], and Jan Pacovský[1(✉)]

[1] Charles University, Prague, Czech Republic
{bures,hnetynka,pacovsky}@d3s.mff.cuni.cz
[2] Vrije Universiteit Amsterdam, Amsterdam, Netherlands
i.g.gerostathopoulos@vu.nl

Abstract. Smart system applications (SSAs) built on top of cyber-physical and socio-technical systems are increasingly composed of components that can work both autonomously and by cooperating with each other. Cooperating robots, fleets of cars and fleets of drones, emergency coordination systems are examples of SSAs. One approach to enable cooperation of SSAs is to form dynamic cooperation groups—ensembles—between components at runtime. Ensembles can be formed based on predefined rules that determine which components should be part of an ensemble based on their current state and the state of the environment (e.g., "group together 3 robots that are closer to the obstacle, their battery is sufficient and they would not be better used in another ensemble"). This is a computationally hard problem since all components are potential members of all possible ensembles at runtime. In our experience working with ensembles in several case studies the past years, using constraint programming to decide which ensembles should be formed does not scale for more than a limited number of components and ensembles. Also, the strict formulation in terms of hard/soft constraints does not easily permit for runtime self-adaptation via learning. This poses a serious limitation to the use of ensembles in large-scale and partially uncertain SSAs. To tackle this problem, in this paper we propose to recast the ensemble formation problem as a classification problem and use machine learning to efficiently form ensembles at scale.

Keywords: Adaptation · Ensembles · Cooperative systems · Machine learning

1 Introduction

Smart system applications (SSAs) are cyber-physical and socio-technical systems that comprise a number of components that cooperate towards a common goal. These systems are increasingly popular and include wide range of applications spanning from smart building management (coordinating heat, ventilation, air

© Springer Nature Switzerland AG 2020
T. Margaria and B. Steffen (Eds.): ISoLA 2020, LNCS 12477, pp. 440–456, 2020.
https://doi.org/10.1007/978-3-030-61470-6_26

conditioning with physical access control, etc.), smart traffic, emergency response systems, up to smart farming or smart underwater exploration.

The cooperation among components is a key feature of these systems. The cooperation is typically governed by certain application-specific collaboration rules. For instance, in the smart farming domain, the drones monitoring the crop on fields may coordinate to keep three drones in the air patrolling the surveyed area while the rest of the drones recharges or stays idle on the ground. This naturally leads to describing the coordination in these systems using a set of constraints (both hard constraints and soft constraints) that govern which components should cooperate at a particular point in time and what their task is. For instance, such constraints would assign the three drones the task to patrol the fields. The selection would be based on the battery level of the drone and its distance to the patrolled area. Formally speaking, the correct and optimal operation of such a system is then reduced to the problem of finding the assignment of components to collaboration groups that satisfy the constraints and optimize the soft-optimization rules.

In our work we use the architectural concept of autonomic component ensemble to model the collaboration group. The ensemble defines its potential members and stipulates the set of hard constraints and optimization rules that govern which components are eventually selected as members. As multiple ensembles can co-exist at the same time, there are naturally also constraints across the ensembles—for enforcing that the same component may be a member of only one of several ensembles of the same type. The problem of finding such assignment of components to ensembles (we term this *ensemble resolution*) is inherently exponential and cannot be easily overcome even with state-of-the-art SMT or CSP solvers.

The problem is even aggravated by the fact that the solution to the problem has to be found repeatedly—essentially whenever the state of the components or the environment changes. This is because the constraints controlling the membership of components in ensembles typically directly depend on the state of the components and the environment. As this state constantly changes, ensembles have to be continuously re-resolved at runtime. This puts hard practical limits on the time needed to complete the ensemble resolution to be in order of seconds (up to minutes), and consequently on the maximum size of the system (which, based on our experiments [9], depends on the complexity of ensembles often limited to a dozen or a few dozens of components). Longer waiting times means that the system cannot flexibly react to ever changing situations in its environment.

In this position paper, we thus explore an approach to address the problem of ensemble resolution that does not require exponential time at runtime. In particular, we show how the problem of ensemble resolution can be recast to a classification problem. In our work we use both neural networks and decision trees as classifiers. After training the classifier offline, we can execute it quickly at runtime, thus significantly cutting down the time needed to resolve ensembles.

As we discuss further in the text, using the classifier conceptually changes the problem from crisp solutions that strictly follow the hard constraints to fuzzied solutions that do not necessarily have to strictly obey the hard constraints.

As it turns out, if well designed, such a system with approximate solutions still works. This requires a bit more robust design that balances well the responsibilities in the system among autonomously operating components (meaning that the components themselves are responsible for ensuring their safe and reliable operation) and ensemble-level decisions that deal with high-level coordination of components. However, such a design is overall necessary to make the system more robust to uncertainty and to facilitate decentralization.

In this paper we report on our initial experiments in this direction. To demonstrate and evaluate the idea, we adopt a use-case inspired by our work in a smart farming project [9]. We use the agent-based simulator of the use-case scenario to draw indicative results pointing to the feasibility of our approach.

We describe our running example inspired by our work in the smart farming project [9] in Sect. 2. Then we explain how to recast the problem of ensemble formation to a classification problem in Sect. 3. Section 4 provides an initial evaluation of the feasibility of our prediction-based ensemble resolution. Finally, Sect. 5 positions the work w.r.t related ones, and Sect. 6 concludes with a summary and outlook.

2   Running Example

As a motivational example, we use an actual scenario taken from our ECSEL JU project AFarCloud[1], which focuses on smart-farming and efficient usage of cyber-physical and cloud-systems in agriculture. Figure 1 shows a screenshot from our simulator developed to demonstrate the scenario.

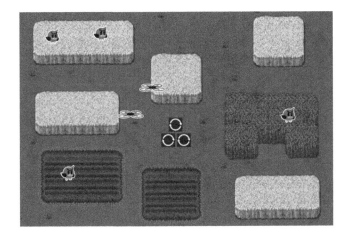

Fig. 1. Example

---

[1] https://www.ecsel.eu/projects/afarcloud.

In the scenario, there is a farm with several fields—the yellow ones represent fields with crop requiring a protection from birds (which can damage the crop) while the brown and dark-green ones require no protection. The whole farm is continuously monitored by a fleet of autonomous drones. The drones perform environment monitoring (humidity, temperature, etc.) and also detection of flocks of birds. In case a flock is detected, the drones are used to scare the flock away from the crop fields to the birds-insensitive farm areas. To be effective in scaring, the drones have to form a group (depending on the size of the flock). Additionally, the drones can operate for a limited time only (depending on the battery capacity) and need to periodically recharge in the charger (the rounded arrow blocks at the center), but which can charge only a limited number of drones at the same time. Thus in order to be effective as a whole, the system has to balance between the number of drones monitoring the farm, scaring the birds, and charging themselves. Plus, the system needs to select the most suitable drones for individual tasks (i.e. the closest ones, with a sufficient amount of energy, etc. depending on the task).

To model and run dynamic and autonomous systems (like this one), we use our approach based on autonomic ensembles [13]. In this approach, entities of a system are modeled as components and cooperation among the components is modeled via ensembles, which are dynamic context-dependent (time and space bound) groups of components. For simple and easy development and experimentation with ensembles, we have created a Scala-based internal domain-specific language (DSL) to specify components and ensembles.

Listing 1.1 shows an excerpt of the specification of the example in DSL. Both the component and ensemble types are modeled as classes, while the actual component and ensemble instances are instantiations of these classes (there can be a number of instances of a particular type). In the example, there are four component types—DroneComponent, FieldComponent, ChargerComponent and FlockComponent (lines 1–23). A component state (called component knowledge) is modeled via the class fields. The FieldComponent and FlockComponent are non-controllable components, i.e., they cannot be directly controlled by the system and their state is observed only.

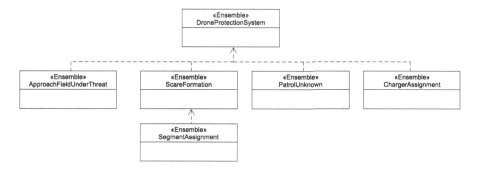

Fig. 2. Ensembles hierarchy in the running example.

There are six ensemble types—the top level one and five nested ones (the structure is shown in Fig. 2). An ensemble is formed dynamically in order to execute a group-level behavior (e.g., scare the flock). Only the top-level ensemble instance (called the *root ensemble*) exists for the whole lifetime of the system (it is instantiated at line 97). The component instances grouped in the ensemble are not defined statically but via its membership condition, which is a conjunction of predicates over the component instances and their knowledge and which is continuously evaluated. For instance, in the DroneProtectionSystem ensemble, the lines 30–33 of Listing 1.1 identify component instances in the system and categorize them by mode. These groups of components are then used in ensembles to declare potential members. The declaration of potential members is done via oneOf (e.g. line 65) and subsetOfComponents (e.g. line 41). These two declarations differ only in cardinality constraints.

A particular component instance can be a member of several ensemble instances at the same time. If additional conditions have to be hold, the constraint construct can be used (e.g., at line 91 in the DroneProtectionSystem). The utility construct (e.g., at line 85 in the DroneProtectionSystem) represents a soft condition, which is an optimization function for forming ensembles (i.e., in the case, there are several possibilities to choose component instances for the ensemble). Finally, the tasks construct assigns responsibilities to component instances which are members of a particular ensemble instance.

As already mentioned, ensembles can be nested; members (i.e. component instances) of an ensemble are also members of a parent ensemble. The meaning of nesting is that the root ensemble (the one without any parent) defines the overall goal of the system while the nested ones represent particular sub-goals. The DroneProtectionSystem ensemble is the root and represents the whole system. The ApproachFieldUnderThreat ensemble is used to direct the necessary number of drones to the field with detected birds. When the necessary number of drones is above the field, an instance of the ScareFormation ensemble replaces the instance of the previous ensemble and tries to scare birds away from the field by moving drones above the field in a formation that equally spreads the drones over the field. To simplify definition of assignment of the drones to positions over the affected field, the ensemble contains the sub-ensembles SegmentAssignment. The PatrolUnknown ensemble is used to guide a drone to a field that has unknown status (no information about birds). And finally, the ChargerAssignment ensemble is instantiated per charger place and assigns a drone that has a low energy level to the charger.

The sub-ensembles are declared using ensembles (e.g. line 80) and rules (e.g. line 70). The former declares a potential ensemble instance (i.e. such that will be instantiated if constraints allow it), the latter declares a mandatory ensemble instance (i.e. such that has to exist if its parent ensemble instance gets instantiated).

```scala
 1  case class DroneComponent(
 2      id: String, mode: DroneMode.DroneMode, position: Position, energy: Double,
 3      chargingInChargerId: Option[ChargerId], observedFields: Map[String, FieldObservation]
 4    ) extends Component {
 5    name(id)
 6  }
 7
 8  case class FieldComponent(idx: Int, flocks: Map[String, FlockState]) extends Component {
 9    name(s"Field ${idx}")
10    val center = FieldIdHelper.center(idx), val area = FieldIdHelper.area(idx)
11    val isUnknown = false, val isUnderThreat = flocks.values.exists(flock => area.contains(flock.position))
12    val requiredDroneCountForProtection = FieldIdHelper.protectingDroneCountRequired(idx)
13    val protectionCenters = FieldIdHelper.centers(idx, requiredDroneCountForProtection)
14  }
15
16  case class ChargerComponent(idx: Int, isFree: Boolean) extends Component {
17    name(s"Charger ${idx}")
18    val chargerId = ChargerId(idx), val position = chargerId.position
19  }
20
21  case class FlockComponent(position: Position) extends Component {
22    name(s"Flock @ ${position}")
23  }
24
25  class Scenario(simulationState: SimulationState) extends /*....*/ {
26
27    class DroneProtectionSystem extends Ensemble {
28      name(s"Root ensemble of the protection system")
29
30      val operationalDrones = allDrones.filter(drone => drone.mode != DroneMode.DEAD &&
                drone.mode != DroneMode.CHARGING && drone.energy > Drone.chargingThreshold)
31      val dronesInNeedOfCharging = allDrones.filter(drone => drone.mode != DroneMode.DEAD &&
                drone.mode != DroneMode.CHARGING && drone.energy < Drone.chargingThreshold)
32      val fieldsWithUnknownStatus = allFields.filter(_.isUnknown)
33      val fieldsUnderThreat=allFields.filter(_.isUnderThreat), val freeChargers=allChargers.filter(_.isFree)
34
35      class ApproachFieldUnderThreat(val field: FieldComponent) extends Ensemble {
36        name(s"ApproachFieldUnderThreat ensemble for field ${field.idx}")
37
38        val flocksInField = allFlocks.filter(x => field.area.contains(x.position))
39        val dronesInField = operationalDrones.filter(x => field.area.contains(x.position))
40        val droneCount = field.requiredDroneCountForProtection, val center = field.center
41        val drones = subsetOfComponents(operationalDrones, _ <= droneCount)
42
43        utility {drones.sum(x=>if (field.area.contains(x.position)) 10 else dist2Utility(x.position, center))}
44
45        tasks {
46          if (flocksInField.isEmpty) {
47            for (drone <- drones.selectedMembers) moveTask(drone, center)
48          } else {
49            val selectedDronesInFieldCount = drones.selectedMembers.count(x =>
                    field.area.contains(x.position))
50            /* ... */
51          }
52        }
53      }
54
55      class ScareFormation(val field: FieldComponent) extends Ensemble {
56        name(s"ScareFormation ensemble for field ${field.idx}")
57
58        val dronesInField = operationalDrones.filter(x => field.area.contains(x.position))
59        val droneCount = field.requiredDroneCountForProtection
60        val segmentCenters = field.protectionCenters
61
62        class SegmentAssignment(val segmentCenter: Position) extends Ensemble {
63          name(s"Assignment for field ${field.idx} @ ${segmentCenter.x},${segmentCenter.y}")
64
65          val drone = oneOf(operationalDrones)
66
67          utility { drone.sum(x => dist2Utility(x.position, segmentCenter)) }
```

```
68          tasks { moveTask(drone, segmentCenter) }
69        }
70        val protectionSegmentAssignments = rules(segmentCenters.map(new SegmentAssignment(_)))
71
72        utility { protectionSegmentAssignments.sum(assignment => assignment.utility) / droneCount }
73        constraint( protectionSegmentAssignments.map(_.drone).allDisjoint )
74      }
75
76      class PatrolUnknown(val field: FieldComponent) extends Ensemble { /* ... */ }
77
78      class ChargerAssignment(charger: ChargerComponent) extends Ensemble { /* ... */ }
79
80      val patrolUnknown = ensembles(fieldsWithUnknownStatus.map(new PatrolUnknown(_)))
81      val chargerAssignments = ensembles(freeChargers.map(new ChargerAssignment(_)))
82      val approachFieldsUnderThreat =
              ensembles(fieldsUnderThreat.filter(ApproachFieldUnderThreat.isInSituation(_)).map(new
              ApproachFieldUnderThreat(_)))
83      val scareFormations = ensembles(fieldsUnderThreat.filter(ScareFormation.isInSituation(_)).map(new
              ScareFormation(_)))
84
85      utility {
86        approachFieldsUnderThreat.sum(assignment => assignment.utility) +
87        scareFormations.sum(assignment => assignment.utility) +
88        patrolUnknown.sum(assignment => assignment.utility) / 4 +
89        chargerAssignments.sum(assignment => assignment.utility)
90      }
91      constraint(
92        (patrolUnknown.map(_.drone) ++ approachFieldsUnderThreat.map(_.drones) ++
              scareFormations.map(_.drones)).allDisjoint &&
93        chargerAssignments.map(_.drone).allDisjoint
94      )
95    }
96
97    val root = EnsembleSystem(new DroneProtectionSystem)
98  }
```

Listing 1.1. Running example in DSL

The more complete version of the example is available in [9] together with details of the ensemble definition and DSL definition. The complete code of the example is available at https://github.com/smartarch/afcens.

3   Methods

3.1   As a Constraint Satisfaction Problem

Our existing approach to instantiating ensembles (described, e.g., in [13]) is to cast it as a constraint satisfaction (CSP) and optimization problem. That is, how to assign given component instances to ensemble instances such that the cardinality restrictions (e.g., line 65 or line 41 in Listing 1.1) and constraint blocks in ensembles (e.g., line 91) are satisfied and such that the utility function of the root ensemble instance is maximized.

The ensemble specification (Listing 1.1) describes all potential ensemble instances and for each potential ensemble instance, it defines its potential member component instances. However, not all of these potential ensemble instances are eventually created. Only those are created that together satisfy the constraints while maximizing the utility function. Technically, existence of each potential ensemble instance is represented in the constraint optimization problem by a Boolean variable. Similarly, membership of a component instance in a particular ensemble instance is again represented by a Boolean variable. Constraints are formed to reflect the structural constraints between ensemble component instances (such as those that existence of a sub-ensemble instance implies existence of the parent ensemble instance) and the constraints expressed in the specification. The result of the constraint optimization is the assignment of Boolean variables that indicate which ensemble instances are to be created and which components are their members. We perform the constraint optimization using an existing CSP solver (in particular Choco Solver[2]).

An obvious problem with this approach is that the constraint optimization has by its nature exponential complexity. We performed several test on various scenarios and all indicate that while the approach works well and has clear and crisp semantics, it does not scale beyond a dozen or several dozens of component instances (depending on the complexity of the specification). Beyond such limit, the CSP solver requires minutes or even hours to run, which makes it impractical for forming ensembles at runtime as this requires periodic re-evaluation of ensembles (for instance every couple of seconds or minutes). As such, we explore further in this section an alternative way to decide on which ensembles to instantiate by re-casting the ensemble forming as a classification problem. Though the training phase of the classifier takes long, the actual execution of the classifier is almost instantaneous—thus very suitable for constant re-evaluation of the situation at runtime.

3.2 As a Classification Problem

When casting the ensemble resolution as a classification problem, we take the inputs and outputs of the CSP solver as a starting point and, instead of invoking a CSP solver to determine the assignment of component instances to ensemble instances, we train classifiers to predict such assignment given the same inputs as the CSP solver. Our approach is application of supervised learning where each classifier is trained on a number of examples of inputs and outputs provided by the historical invocations of the CSP solver.

The inputs of the classification problem are identical to the CSP problem inputs and comprise the component knowledge (Listing 1.1) that influences in any way the ensemble resolution process, i.e. is considered in the constraints expressed in the specification. In our running example, the knowledge fields included are the ones presented in Table 1.

---

[2]https://choco-solver.org/.

Table 1. Inputs of classification problem.

Component	Field	Domain	Example
Charger	occupied	Boolean	True
Drone	energy	float	0.82
	x	float	113.125
	y	float	53.375
	mode	enum	CHARGING
Flock	x	float	157.875
	y	float	66.187

The outputs of the CPS problem are the Boolean variables that represent membership of a component instance to an ensemble instance. For the classification problem, we use as outputs nominal variables that represent the membership of component instances to ensembles.

Since there are several outputs and the outputs follow a nominal scale, the overall classification problem we need to solve to assign component instances to ensemble instances in our setting is a multi-output, multi-class problem. Such problems can be solved by training either *one* multi-output, multi-class classifier (which simultaneously predicts all outputs) or *several* independent single-output, multi-class classifiers (one for each output). In our experiments, we used both single-output and multi-output classifiers and different learning methods, namely decision trees and neural networks, overviewed next.

Decision Trees (DT) represent a supervised learning method that can be used both for classification and regression. Its operation is based on creating a tree structure where leaves represent class labels (in case of classification) or continuous values (in regression) and branches represent decision rules inferred from the values of the inputs that lead to the leaves. In the case of multi-output problems, leaves represent a set of class labels, one for each output. A DT is iteratively constructed by an algorithm that selects, at each iteration, a value for an input that splits the output dataset into two subsets and uses a metric to evaluate the homogeneity of the output within the subsets. In our experiments, we used the Gini impurity metric [12]. We did not use any pruning or set a maximum depth to the derived trees. Finally, since we deal with unbalanced data (Fig. 5), we use class weighting in training, with the inverse of the class distribution in our training sets. We experimented with two DT variants: the *multi-output* variant, in which a single DT was trained to predict the decisions of four drones (we used this number of drones for all our experiments, see Sect. 4.1) and the *single-output* variant, in which four separate DTs were trained, one for each drone.

Neural networks (NN). In our experiments, we used fully connected feed-forward NNs with residual connections that connect layers that are not adjacent. In between the dense layers and within the first layer we regularize the outputs with batch normalization [10]. As a optimizer we use LAMB [16]—(stochastic gradient descent method that is based on Layer-wise adaptive estimation of first-order and second-order moments) with multiple steps of logarithmic learning decay. We used a batch size of 50.000 and trained the NNs for 50 epochs. We experimented with different network architectures—Fig. 3 shows the architecture of the best performing NN (called *large NN* henceforth), Fig. 4 a shows less complex, but only slightly worse performing network, which we term *small NN*. Both networks have four outputs corresponding to the decisions of the four drones.

4 Evaluation

In this section, we provide an initial evaluation of the feasibility of our prediction-based ensemble resolution approach. First, we describe the experimental setup used for both obtaining historical data and for evaluating the use of the trained classifiers at runtime. Then, we overview the classification performance of the different learning methods using different metrics. Finally, we describe the results obtained when using the trained classifiers, together with the CSP solver, for ensemble resolution at runtime.

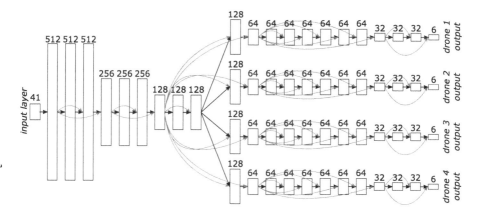

Fig. 3. Architecture of *large NN* with emphasized residual connections. Numbers denote width of the fully connected layers.

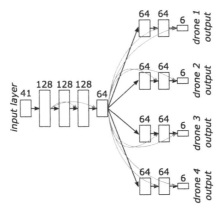

Fig. 4. Architecture of *small NN* with emphasized residual connections. Numbers denote width of the fully connected layers.

4.1   Experimental Setup

Our experimental setup consists of a simulation that runs the smart farming system described in Sect. 2. In all our experiments, we have used the following number of component instances: four `drones`, five `fields`, three `chargers`, and five `flocks`. Instead of considering all the component instances and all the potential ensembles in the evaluation of our prediction-based approach, in our preliminary experiments we focused on the `drone` component and the `ApproachFieldUnderThreat` ensemble. We created classifiers to predict four output variables, each corresponding to one `drone` in the simulation, capturing whether the `drone` belongs to the `ApproachFieldUnderThreat` ensemble formed for the protection of a particular field. So, each output variable takes one of six values: "no field", "field 1", "field 2", "field 3", "field 4", "field 5".

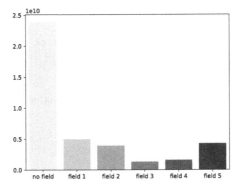

Fig. 5. Distribution of dataset in different classes.

4.2 Evaluation of Classification Performance

To evaluate the performance of the different classifiers we trained, we used the metrics of balanced accuracy, precision, recall, and F1-score. These metrics are computed as follows. We count true positives (TP), true negatives (TN), false positives (FP), and false negatives (FN) that characterize whether a class has been correctly predicted by a classifier. In particular, for each of the six classes ("no field", "field 1", "field 2", "field 3", "field 4", "field 5") and for each output variable, TP, TN, FP, and FN numbers are calculated in the following way. Given a predicted value y_{pred} and a real value y_{real} and considering a class c:

(a) TP_c is increased by one if $y_{pred} = c$ and $y_{real} = c$;
(b) TN_c is increased by one if $y_{pred} \neq c$ and $y_{real} \neq c$;
(c) FP_c is increased by one if $y_{pred} = c$ and $y_{real} \neq c$;
(d) FN_c is increased by one if $y_{pred} \neq c$ and $y_{real} = c$.

Given the above, the following metrics can be defined for a class c:(i) $accuracy_c = \frac{TP_c+TN_c}{TP_c+TN_c+FP_c+FN_c}$, capturing the ratio of correct predictions; (ii) $precision_c = \frac{TP_c}{TP_c+FP_c}$, capturing the time a positive prediction was also correct; (iii) $recall_c = \frac{TP_c}{TP_c+FN_c}$, capturing the times a positive value was also predicted as such; and (iv) $F1score_c = \frac{2*precision_c*recall_c}{precision_c+recall_c}$, the harmonic mean of precision and recall.

To give a single indicator of classification performance, the above metrics can be averaged over the different six classes in our dataset. A popular overall metric in multi-class classification is the average accuracy calculated by simply averaging the accuracy from all classes. However, such calculation can lead to biased estimates of classifier performance when tested on imbalanced datasets. In our case, we indeed have a imbalanced datasets, since the "no ensemble" class appears much more often than the other classes (Fig. 5). We have thus opted for calculating the *balanced accuracy* by first dividing each class accuracy by the number of instances of that class and then taking the average [6].

Table 2 depicts the balanced accuracy of the different classifiers we have trained, averaged over the four outputs. The testing set was always set to 100 million samples. A first observation is that the four separate single-output decision tree classifiers outperform the multi-output decision tree one (which performed overall very poorly). Another observation is that the two neural networks

Table 2. Average balanced accuracy of the different classifiers, calculated with testing set of 100 million samples, for three sizes of training sets.

Training samples (million)	1	10	100
multi-output decision tree	49.11%	62.29%	72.33%
single-output decision trees	70.18%	77.21%	83.01%
small neural network	71.87%	94.02%	97.03%
large neural network	75.55%	95.86%	98.77%

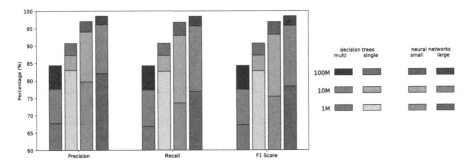

Fig. 6. Weighted averages of precisions, recalls, and F1-scores for different classifiers and training set sizes, in million (10M depicts the delta between the result obtained with 10M and 1M samples and 100M the delta between 100M and 10 M samples).

outperform the decision tree classifiers in all cases, while big improvements are seen compared to the decision trees when trained with 10 and 100 million samples. Finally, for all classifiers, there is always an improvement when trained with more data; however, while for decision trees the improvement is linear (e.g. ~7% from one to 10 million and ~6% from 10 to 100 million for the single-output case), for the neural networks it is more profound when going from one to 10 million (~20–23%) compared to going from 10 to 100 million (~3%).

We also calculated the weighted average of precision, recall, and F1 score for each drone. The weighted average is calculated by weighting each class according to its inverse prevalence (Fig. 5). Figure 6 shows the weighted averages of the three metrics, averaged over the four drones. We observe that the single-output classifiers perform universally better than the multi-output one; similarly, the large neural network performs slightly better than the small one across the board. Also, we see the same pattern as with weighted averages: in neural networks, there is a large gain when using 10 instead of 1 million data; this gain is much

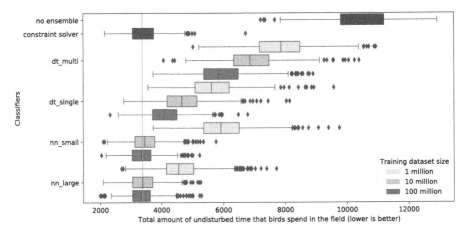

Fig. 7. Boxplots of overall utilities (undisturbed time for birds) when plugging the different predictors in the simulation of our running example.

smaller when using 100 instead of 10 million data. Instead, for decision trees, there is an almost equal gain when using 10 times more data. Finally, contrary to the balanced accuracy results, the single-output decision tree classifier outperforms the other classifiers (including the neural network ones) in all metrics when trained with 1 million data.

4.3 Experiments Using Classifiers for Ensemble Resolution

To evaluate how effective the trained classifiers are when used together with the CSP solver in ensemble resolution, we plugged them in the simulation of our running example and evaluated the overall utility of a run, given by the amount of undisturbed time that birds spend on fields. We compared the following cases:

- Runs where the drones were never participating in the ApproachFieldUnderThreat ensemble. This serves as the overall baseline.
- Runs with ensemble resolution every 1 min of simulation time by invoking the CSP solver.
- Runs with ensemble resolution every 1 min of simulation time by means of invoking a respective predictor to determine the participation of each drone in ApproachFieldUnderThreat. (As the other ensembles were not handled by the predictor, we still formed them based on the CSP solver.)

Each run had a duration of 600 min of simulated time; we performed 1000 runs (randomizing the starting position of flocks and drones) for each case, with the results depicted in Fig. 7.

The boxplots show that, for each predictor, using more training data resulted in higher overall utility. Also, while in most of the cases, using the predictor with the CSP resulted in a reduction of the system utility w.r.t using only the CSP solver, all cases performed better than not participating in ensembles at all. Also, in two cases (nn_small and nn_large trained with 100 million samples) there was a marginal improvement over the CSP case. We believe this happens due to the classifier being able to generalize over the solution provided in the form of hard/soft constraints and was able to improve on corner cases which lead for instance to short intervals of oscillation when a drone was switching between two targets and, as the result, did not move. Another interesting observation is that higher balanced accuracy does not always translates to higher utility in the simulation: e.g. even though the small_nn on 1 million samples had slightly higher balanced accuracy than the respective dd_single (Table 2), its overall utility is slightly lower, as can be seen in Fig. 7.

5   Related Work

The original idea of ensembles is based on the SCEL language [11]. In its implementation JRESP[3] [11], the ensembles are formed implicitly, as they are

---

[3] http://jresp.sourceforge.net/.

abstractions capturing groups of components and dynamically determined by their attribute-based communication. Almost the same approach is used in the Ab^aCuS [2] (which is not strictly an ensemble-based framework however it is built on the principles of the attribute-based communication). Another ensemble-based framework is Helena [8] but here, the ensembles are formed explicitly, i.e., the components indicate, to which the ensemble they belong. In our implementation [13] of ensemble-based system, we have used the constraint solver for forming ensembles but its issues have been already mentioned in Sect. 3.

The concept of ensembles targets emergent configurations. In the implementation of the ECo-IoT [1] approach, the emergent configurations are solved using a state space planner, nevertheless its performance is also hindered by exponential complexity. The planner is also employed in [7], where the linear complexity is claimed. However, measurements are done with respect to the growing number of adaptations in a system (and not the size of the system).

Machine learning has been recently used in different ways to replace heavy computations that are part of constraint satisfaction and combinatorial optimization problems by fast approximations using machine learning, as overviewed in a recent survey [4]. For example, decision trees have been used in predicting the satisfiability of SAT instances [15], while deep neural networks have been used in predicting the satisfiabilities of random Boolean binary CSPs with high prediction accuracies (>99.99%) [14]. Other approaches have tried to embed neural networks, but also decision trees and random forests, in constraint programming [3,5]. The idea is to learn part of the combinatorial optimization model and embed the learned piece of knowledge in the combinatorial model itself. We too train classifiers to overcome computational issues associated with ensemble resolution, where constraint programming is the host technology.

6   Conclusion

In this paper, we proposed a new approach for formation of ensembles at runtime. Instead of relying on a constraint solver to decide on optimal placement of components to ensembles, we employed machine learning. This allows us to tackle the problem of exponential time needed by the constraint solver, which is especially a problem since ensembles have to be formed at runtime (typically in real-time). When employing machine learning, we can (after the initial training stage) decide on placement of components into ensembles with linear time.

In our approach, we casted the problem of ensemble formation to a classification problem. To give comparison how well this approach works, we implemented two different classifiers—decision trees and neural networks. We show that with enough data, we were able to train the predictor with high enough accuracy. Not only that, when we plugged the predictor in the simulation of our running example and evaluated the overall utility, we observed that some classifiers even perform marginally better than the original solution that employed the constraint solver. We attribute this to the fact that the classifier was able to generalize the solution provided in the form of ensemble specification (i.e., logical predicates and optimization function).

This paper provided the initial idea and indicative experiments. In future work, we would like to focus on generalization which would allow the predictors to be trained on smaller models and generalize them to larger scope. Also, we are looking into how to further improve the prediction and how to include reinforcement learning to take also into account the overall end-to-end utility function (e.g. the time that the birds spend undisturbed in the field – as used in our running example).

Acknowledgment. This paper is part of a project that has received funding from the European Research Council (ERC) under the European Union's Horizon 2020 research and innovation programme (grant agreement No 810115). Also, the research leading to these results has received funding from the ECSEL Joint Undertaking (JU) under grant agreement No 783221 and was partially supported by Charles University institutional funding SVV 260451.

We are also grateful to Milan Straka from Institute of Formal and Applied Linguistics at Faculty of Mathematics and Physics at Charles University for valuable input in the field of deep networks that improved the training speed and results significantly.

References

1. Alkhabbas, F., Spalazzese, R., Davidsson, P.: ECo-IoT: an architectural approach for realizing emergent configurations in the Internet of Things. In: Cuesta, C.E., Garlan, D., Pérez, J. (eds.) ECSA 2018. LNCS, vol. 11048, pp. 86–102. Springer, Cham (2018). https://doi.org/10.1007/978-3-030-00761-4_6

2. Abd Alrahman, Y., De Nicola, R., Loreti, M.: Programming of CAS systems by relying on attribute-based communication. In: Margaria, T., Steffen, B. (eds.) ISoLA 2016. LNCS, vol. 9952, pp. 539–553. Springer, Cham (2016). https://doi.org/10.1007/978-3-319-47166-2_38

3. Bartolini, A., Lombardi, M., Milano, M., Benini, L.: Neuron constraints to model complex real-world problems. In: Lee, J. (ed.) CP 2011. LNCS, vol. 6876, pp. 115–129. Springer, Heidelberg (2011). https://doi.org/10.1007/978-3-642-23786-7_11

4. Bengio, Y., Lodi, A., Prouvost, A.: Machine learning for combinatorial optimization: a methodological tour d'Horizon. arXiv: 1811.06128 [cs, stat], March 2020

5. Bonfietti, A., Lombardi, M., Milano, M.: Embedding decision trees and random forests in constraint programming. In: Michel, L. (ed.) CPAIOR 2015. LNCS, vol. 9075, pp. 74–90. Springer, Cham (2015). https://doi.org/10.1007/978-3-319-18008-3_6

6. Brodersen, K.H., Ong, C.S., Stephan, K.E., Buhmann, J.M.: The balanced accuracy and its posterior distribution. In: Proceedings of ICPR 2010, Istanbul, Turkey, pp. 3121–3124. IEEE, August 2010. https://doi.org/10.1109/ICPR.2010.764

7. Bucchiarone, A.: Collective adaptation through multi-agents ensembles: the case of smart urban mobility. ACM Trans. Auton. Adapt. Syst. **14**(2), 1–28 (2019). https://doi.org/10.1145/3355562

8. Hennicker, R., Klarl, A.: Foundations for ensemble modeling – the HELENA approach. In: Iida, S., Meseguer, J., Ogata, K. (eds.) Specification, Algebra, and Software. LNCS, vol. 8373, pp. 359–381. Springer, Heidelberg (2014). https://doi.org/10.1007/978-3-642-54624-2_18

9. Hnetynka, P., Bures, T., Gerostathopoulos, I., Pacovsky, J.: Using component ensembles for modeling autonomic component collaboration in smart farming. In: Proceedings of SEAMS 2020, Seoul, Korea (2020, accepted)

10. Ioffe, S., Szegedy, C.: Batch normalization: accelerating deep network training by reducing internal covariate shift. arXiv:1502.03167 [cs], March 2015

11. Nicola, R.D., Loreti, M., Pugliese, R., Tiezzi, F.: A formal approach to autonomic systems programming: the SCEL language. ACM Trans. Auton. Adapt. Syst. **9**(2), 7:1–7:29 (2014). https://doi.org/10.1145/2619998

12. Raileanu, L.E., Stoffel, K.: Theoretical comparison between the Gini index and information gain criteria. Ann. Math. Artif. Intell. **41**(1), 77–93 (2004). https://doi.org/10.1023/B:AMAI.0000018580.96245.c6

13. Bures, T., et al.: A language and framework for dynamic component ensembles in smart systems. Int. J. Softw. Tools Technol. Transfer **22**(4), 497–509 (2020). https://doi.org/10.1007/s10009-020-00558-z

14. Xu, H., Koenig, S., Kumar, T.K.S.: Towards effective deep learning for constraint satisfaction problems. In: Hooker, J. (ed.) CP 2018. LNCS, vol. 11008, pp. 588–597. Springer, Cham (2018). https://doi.org/10.1007/978-3-319-98334-9_38

15. Xu, L., Hoos, H.H., Leyton-Brown, K.: Predicting satisfiability at the phase transition. In: Proceedings of the Twenty-Sixth AAAI Conference on Artificial Intelligence. AAAI 2012, pp. 584–590. AAAI Press, Toronto, July 2012

16. You, Y., et al.: Large batch optimization for deep learning: training BERT in 76 minutes. arXiv:1904.00962 [cs.LG] (2019)

Synthesizing Control for a System with Black Box Environment, Based on Deep Learning

Simon Iosti[1(✉)], Doron Peled[2(✉)], Khen Aharon[2(✉)], Saddek Bensalem[1(✉)], and Yoav Goldberg[2(✉)]

[1] University Grenoble Alpes VERIMAG, 38410 St. Martin d'Héres, France
iosti.simon@gmail.com, saddek.bensalem@gmail.com
[2] Department of Computer Science, Bar Ilan University, 52900 Ramat Gan, Israel
doron.peled@gmail.com, khen.aharon@gmail.com, yoav.goldberg@gmail.com

Abstract. We study the synthesis of control for a system that interacts with a black-box environment, based on deep learning. The goal is to minimize the number of interaction failures. The current state of the environment is unavailable to the controller, hence its operation depends on a limited view of the history. We suggest a reinforcement learning framework of training a Recurrent Neural Network (RNN) to control such a system. We experiment with various parameters: loss function, exploration/exploitation ratio, and size of lookahead. We designed examples that capture various potential control difficulties. We present experiments performed with the toolkit DyNet.

1 Introduction

Deep learning (DL) [8] led to a huge leap in the capabilities of computers. Notable examples include speech recognition, natural language processing, image recognition and calculating strategies for difficult games, like Chess [5] and Go [4].

We study the deep-learning based synthesis of control for finite state systems that interact with black-box environments. In the studied model, the internal structure of the environment is not provided and its current state is not observable during the execution. In each step, the system makes a choice for the next action, and the environment must follow that choice if the action is enabled. Otherwise, a failed interaction occurs and the system does not move while the environment makes some independent progress. The control enforces the next

S. Iosti and S. Bensalem—The research performed by these authors was partially funded by H2020-ECSEL grants CPS4EU 2018-IA call - Grant Agreement number 826276.

D. Peled and K. Aharon—The research performed by these authors was partially funded by ISF grants "Runtime Measuring and Checking of Cyber Physical Systems" (ISF award 2239/15) and "Efficient Runtime Verification for Systems with Lots of Data and its Applications" (ISF award 1464/18).

T. Margaria and B. Steffen (Eds.): ISoLA 2020, LNCS 12477, pp. 457–472, 2020.
https://doi.org/10.1007/978-3-030-61470-6_27

action of the system based on the available partial information, which involves the sequence of states and actions that occurred so far of the system and the indication of success/failure to interact at each point. The control goal is to minimize the number of times that the system will offer an action that will result in a failed interaction.

The motivation for this problem comes from the challenge to construct distributed schedulers for systems with concurrent processes that will lower the number of failed interactions between the participants. In this case, the environment of each concurrent thread is the collection of all other threads, interacting with it. An alternative approach for constructing schedulers that is based on distributed knowledge was presented in [2].

Algorithmic synthesis of control for enforcing temporal constraints on interacting with an environment was studied in [12,13]. It includes translating a temporal logic specification into an automaton [7], determinizing it [14], and computing a winning strategy for a game defined over that automaton [18]. Reinforcement learning (RL) [15] suggests algorithmic solutions for synthesizing control for systems where the goal is to maximize (minimize, respectively) some accumulated future reward (penalty, respectively) over the interaction with the environment. In RL, a complete model of the environment does not have to be given, and in this case control can be synthesized through experimenting with it. However, often the current state of the environment is fully observable; this is not the case in our studied problem.

One approach for constructing control of a system that interacts with a black-box environment is to first apply automata learning techniques [1] in order to obtain a model of the environment. However, a complete learning of a model for the environment is sometimes infeasible for various reasons, e.g., when one cannot interface directly with the environment in isolation for making the needed experiments, or due to high complexity.

We study the construction of control based on neural networks, where after training, the neural network is used to control the system. This control construction is *adaptive*, which is important in the cases where the environment can change its typical behavior or where the tradeoff between further training and improved performance is not clear in advance; we can resume the training after deploying the system, and collecting runtime statistics.

We employ Recurrent Neural Networks (RNN), which include a feedback loop that returns part of the internal state as additional input. This allows the output to depend on the history of inputs rather than only on the last input. An RNN is well suited to provide the control strategy due to the invisibility of the structure and the immediate state of the environment; the controller's choice for the next step of the system needs to be based on its limited view of the past execution history.

Neural networks have been used within reinforcement learning for finding strategies for difficult board games such as Chess and Go. They were trained to provide the *quality* function Q from the current state of the game to a numeric value. The obtained game strategy chooses the move that maximizes the current quality function. Our model cannot calculate a Q function, since the current state of the environment, corresponding to the game board in those examples, is not visible. Instead, we exploit a summary of the visible part of the execution so far, as calculated by the trained neural network. Notable work that involve training an RNN includes playing Atari games such as *space invaders* or *breakout* [9]. The reason for using the RNN architecture for these games is that the strategy depends on a limited number of preceding states (specifically for these games, four states are used); this permits the strategy to be influenced by the speed and trajectory of the movement. By contrast, our study involves training an RNN to produce a strategy that depends on a long history of the interaction between the system and the environment.

In [11] we compared the potential use of automata learning, deep learning and genetic programming for control synthesis. In this paper we focus on deep learning and present a full study of a methodology for synthesizing control to a system that interacts with a black-box environment. We study the required architecture and training parameters and present experiments using the DyNet tool [6].[1]

2   Preliminaries

We study the construction of control for a finite state reactive system that interacts with black-box environment.

System and Environment. We study systems that are modeled as finite state automata. Let $\mathcal{A} = (G, \iota, T, \delta)$ be an automaton, where

- G is a finite set of *states* with $\iota \in G$ its *initial state*.
- T is a finite set of *actions* (often called the *alphabet*).
- $\delta : (G \times T) \rightarrow G \cup \{\bot\}$ is a partial *transition function*, where $\bot$ stands for *undefined*. We denote $en(g) = \{t \mid t \in T \wedge \delta(g, t) \neq \bot\}$, i.e., $en(g)$ is the set of actions *enabled* at the state g. We assume that for each $g \in G$, $en(g) \neq \emptyset$.
- An optional component is a probabilistic distribution on the selection of actions $d : G \times T \rightarrow [0, 1]$ where $\Sigma_{\tau \in T} d(g, \tau) = 1$. Then, the model is called a *Markov Chain*. In this case, $\delta(g, t) = \bot$ iff $d(g, t) = 0$.

The *asymmetric combination* of a system and an environment $\mathcal{A}^s \lceil \mathcal{A}^e$ involves the *system automaton* $\mathcal{A}^s = (G^s, \iota^s, T^s, \delta^s)$, and the *environment* automaton $\mathcal{A}^e = (G^e, \iota^e, T^e, \delta^e)$, where $T^s \cap T^e \neq \emptyset$. The two components progress synchronously starting with their initial state. The system offers an action that is enabled from its current state. If this action is enabled also from the current state of the environment automaton, then the system and the environment change their respective states, making a *successful* interaction. If the action is

---

[1] DyNet is a python package for automatic differentiation and stochastic gradient training, similar to PyTorch, and TensorFlow but which is also optimized for strong CPU performance.

not currently enabled by the environment, the interaction *fails*; in this case, the system remains at its current state, and the environment chooses randomly some enabled action and moves accordingly. After a failed interaction, the system can offer the same or a different action.

Formally,

$$\mathcal{A}^s \lceil \mathcal{A}^e = (G^s \times G^e, (\iota^s, \iota^e), T^s \times T^e, \delta)$$

where

$$\delta((g^s, g^e), (t^s, t^e)) = \begin{cases} (\delta^s(g^s, t^s), \delta^e(g^e, t^s)), & \text{if } t^s \in en(g_e) \\ (g^s, \delta^e(g^e, t^e)), & \text{otherwise} \end{cases}$$

An environment with a probabilistic distribution on selecting actions makes a probabilistic choice only if the action offered by the system is currently disabled. In this case, $\delta((g^s, g^e), (t^s, t^e)) = (g^s, \delta^e(g^e, t^e))$ with probability $d(g^e, t^e)$. We restrict ourselves to non-probabilistic (and deterministic) systems.

An execution ξ of $\mathcal{A}^s \lceil \mathcal{A}^e$ is a finite or infinite alternating sequence

$$(g_0^s, g_0^e)\,(t_0^s, t_0^e)\,(g_1^s, g_1^e) \ldots$$

of pairs of states and pairs of actions, where $g_0^s = \iota^s$, $g^e = \iota^e$ and $(g_{i+1}^s, g_{i+1}^e) = \delta((g_i^s, g_i^e), (t_i^s, t_i^e))$. According to the definitions, if $t_i^s \neq t_i^e$, then $g_i^s = g_{i+1}^s$; this is the case where the interaction failed. We denote by $\xi|_i$ the prefix of ξ that ends with the states (g_i^s, g_i^e).

Consider the system in Fig. 2 (left) and its environment (middle). This system can always make a choice between the actions a, b and c, and the environment has to agree with that choice if it is enabled from its current state. If the system selects actions according to $(abc)^*$, then the environment can follow that selection with no failures. On the other hand, if the system selects actions according to $(baa)^*$, the system will never progress, while the environment keeps changing states.

Supervisory control studies the problem of constructing a controller that restricts the behavior of a system; the combination guarantees additional requirements [16]. Our work is related to two methods for supervisory control, *reinforcement learning* and *deep learning*.

Reinforcement Learning. Reinforcement learning includes methods for controlling the interaction with an environment [15]. The goal is to maximize the expected utility value that sums up the future rewards/penalties; these can be discounted by γ^n with respect to its future distance n from the current point, with $0 < \gamma \leq 1$, or be summed up with respect to a finite distance (horizon). Typically, the model for RL is a Markov Decision Process (MDP), where there is a probability distribution on the states that are reached by taking an action from a given state. When the current state of the environment is not directly known to the controller during the execution, the model is a Partially Observable MDP (POMDP).

A *value-based* control policy (strategy) can be calculated by maximizing either a state value function $V(s)$ or a state-action value $Q(s, a)$. When the structure of the environment is known, a procedure based on Bellman's equation [15] can be used. If the structure is unknown, a randomized-based (*Monte Carlo*) exploration method can be used to update the value function and convert towards the optimal policy.

Policy based RL methods avoid calculating the optimal utility value directly at each state, hence are more effective when the number of possible states is huge. The policy is parametric and its parameters are optimized based on gradient descent. Such parameters can be, in particular, the weights of a neural network.

The training data is either selected *a priori*, according to some predefined scheme, or using the output of the partially trained neural network. In *mixed* training mode, we perform with probability ϵ an *exploration step* based on a random choice with uniform probability and with probability $1-\epsilon$ an *exploitation* step, based on the selection of the partially trained network. The value of ϵ may diminish with the progress of the training.

Deep Learning. Deep learning is a collection of methods for training *neural networks*, which can be used to perform various tasks such as image and speech recognition or playing games at an expert level. A neural network consists of a collection of nodes, the *neurons*, arranged in several layers, each neuron connected to all the neurons in the previous and the next layer. The first layer is the *input layer* and the last layer is the *output layer*. The other layers are *hidden*.

The value x_i of the ith neuron at layer $j + 1$ is computed from the column vector $\mathbf{y} = (y_1, \ldots, y_m)$ of all the neurons at layer j. To compute x_i, we first apply a transformation $t_i = \mathbf{w}_i \mathbf{y} + b_i$ where $\mathbf{w}_i$ is a line vector of *weights*, and b_i is a number called *bias*. Then we apply to the vector $\mathbf{t} = (t_1, \ldots, t_n)$ an *activation function*, which is usually non-linear, making the value of each neuron a function of the values of neurons at the preceding layer. Typical activation functions include the sigmoid and tanh functions, as well as the softmax.

The softmax activation function takes a vector of values and normalizes it into a corresponding vector of probability distributions, i.e., with values between 0 and 1, summing up to 1.

$$\texttt{softmax}(\mathbf{t_1}, \ldots, \mathbf{t_n}) = \left(\frac{e^{t_1}}{\Sigma_i e^{t_i}}, \ldots, \ldots, \frac{e^{t_n}}{\Sigma_i e^{t_i}} \right)$$

Given values for all neurons in the input layer, we can compute the values for all neurons in the network, and overall a neural network represents a function $\mathbb{R}^n \to \mathbb{R}^m$ where n is the size of the input layer, and m the size of the output layer.

The values of the weights w_i and the biases b_i are initially random, and modified through *training*. A *loss function* provides a measurement on the distance between the actual output of the neural net and the desired output. The goal of training is to minimize the loss function. Optimizing the parameters is performed from the output layer backwards based on gradient descent.

For applications where sequences of inputs are analyzed, as e.g. in language recognition, one often uses a form of network called *Recurrent Neural Network* (RNN). An RNN maintains a feedback loop, where values of some neurons are returned to the network as additional inputs in the next step. In this way an RNN has the capability of maintaining some long term memory that summarizes the input sequence so far. The backward propagation of the gradient descent is applied not only once to the RNN, but continues to propagate backwards according to the length of the input sequence, as the RNN has been activated as many times as the length of the input so far. This allows training the RNN with respect to the input sequence instead of the last input. However the long propagation increases the problem of vanishing/exploding gradient. A more specific type of RNN that intends to solve this problem is a *Long Short-Term Memory*, LSTM. It includes components that control what (and how much) is erased from the memory layer of the network and what is added.

3   Controlling a System Interfacing with a Black Box

We seek to construct a controller for the system that will reduce the number of failed interactions. This is based on the information visible to the system (hence also to the controller), which is the executed sequence of system states, actions offered and the success/failure status of these interactions. The controller maintains and uses a summary of visible part of the execution so far. In addition, it receives the information about the latest execution step: the state of the system, the action selected by the system and whether the interaction succeeded or not. It then updates the summary and selects an enabled action; see Fig. 1.

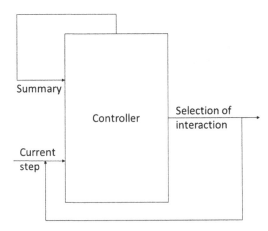

Fig. 1. A contoroller for the system

We now formally define the particular control problem. The *view* (visible part) $v(\xi)$ of an execution $\xi = (g_0^s, g_0^e)(t_0^s, t_0^e)(g_1^s, g_1^e)\ldots$ is the alternating sequence $g_0^s(t_1^s, b_1)g_1^s(t_2^s, b_2)\ldots$, where $b_i = (t_i^s = t_i^e)$. $v(\xi|_i)$ is the prefix of $v(\xi)$ that ends with g_i^s. The control output is a function from the visible part of an execution to an action that is enabled in the current state of the system and will be offered to the environment in the next step.

Due to the invisibility of the environment structure and the state, there can be multiple histories (i.e., prefixes of an execution) that correspond to the same view. Future failing actions can cause the environment to make choices that are invisible to the controller; there can be multiple continuation from the current state. The goal of adding control is to minimize the sum of *penalties* due to failed interactions up to some fixed horizon.

The length of the current execution prefix, and subsequently the view, can grow arbitrarily. Instead, we maintain a finite *summary* of the view $m(v(\xi|_i))$ that we can use instead of $v(\xi|_i)$ itself. We seek a control function that is based on a summary of the view of the current prefix of the execution, and in addition the most recent information about the action selected by the system.

We assume a fixed probability on the selection of actions by the environment, in case of an interaction failure; for the experiments, we will assume a uniform distribution. We limit ourselves to *deterministic* policies, where at each point there is a unique selection of an enabled action. After training, our RNN will output some probability distribution on the selection of the next action, and the system will select the action with the highest probability.

A Suite of Examples

The following examples present for constructing a controller. They were used to select the loss function needed for training the neural networks used as controllers.

In Example **permitted** in Fig. 2, the system allows actions a, b and c. A controller that has the same structure as the environment would guarantee that the system never makes an attempt to interact that will fail, restricting the system to the single sequence $(abc)^*$. The action that appears in the figure next to a state of the controller is the action it enforces to select.

Note that the finite state controllers suggested in the figures of this section are *not* the actual ones that are implemented using neural networks trained through deep-learning.

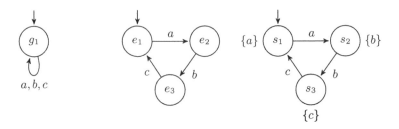

Fig. 2. `permitted`: System (left), Environment (middle) and Controller (right)

In Example `schedule` in Fig. 3, the controller must make sure that the system will never choose an a. Otherwise, after interacting on a, the environment will progress to e_3, and no successful interaction with b will be available further. A controller with two states that alternates between b and c, i.e., allows exactly the sequence of interactions $(bc)^*$ is sufficient to guarantee that no failure ever occurs.

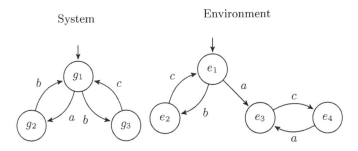

Fig. 3. `schedule`: The control needs to avoid the action a as its initial choice

In Example `cases` in Fig. 4 the system is obliged to offer an a from its initial state. The environment allows initially only b or c. Hence, the interaction will fail, the system will stay at the same state and the environment will progress to e_2 or to e_3, according to its choice, which is not visible to the system. After the first a, the system does not change state, hence it is again the only action that it offers. The controller that appears in Fig. 4 (left) moves after offering the first a, which is due to fail, from s_1 to s_2. It checks now whether offering a fails again; if not, it moves to s_3 and restricts the environment to offer $(ba)^*$. Otherwise, it moves to s_4 and will restrict the environment to offer $(ac)^*$.

In Example `strategy` in Fig. 5, the system offers initially only the interaction a, which necessarily fails, and consequently the environment makes a choice that is invisible to the system. After that, the system and the environment synchronize on an a. At this point, if the system chooses, by chance, an action that is enabled by the environment, making a successful interaction (b or c, respectively), it will

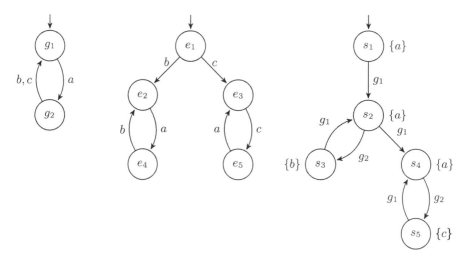

Fig. 4. cases: Needs to check if a succeeded

necessarily lead to entering self loops that are incompatible (at g_3 and e_7, or at g_4 and e_6, respectively), and no further successful interaction will happen. On the other hand, if the system chooses an interaction that immediately fails, it must repeat that same choice; This leads to compatible loops (g_3 and e_6, or g_4 and e_7), and there will be no further failures; flipping to the other choice after that will lead again to the incompatible loops.

Unfortunately, because of the invisible choice of the environment at the beginning of the execution, no controller can guarantee to restrict the number of failures in every execution. However, a weaker goal can be achieved, restricting the number of failures with some probability, which depends on the probability p of the environment to choose an b over c from its initial state. If we can learn the probability p, we may guarantee restricting the number of failures to two in at least $max(p, 1 - p) \geq 0.5$ of the cases.

The Training Process

We will now show how an RNN of type LSTM can be trained to control a system in order to reduce the overall number of failures. The input layer is a vector of size $q \times |T|$, where q is the number of states of the system and $|T|$ is the number of transitions. The output of the last layer is passed through a softmax function to give the actual output of the network.

Let us consider the situation after a partial execution, where the RNN is fed the input and produces an output w. The system uses this output to choose an action a_j among its available actions. Let t be the number of such currently enabled actions. We distinguish two cases:

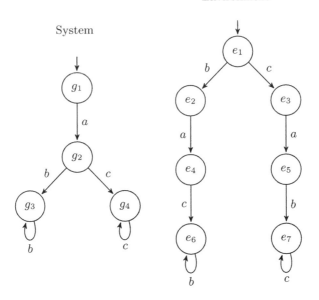

Fig. 5. strategy: Fail next, or succeed and fail forever

– If action a_j is *successful*, then the loss is defined to be

$$-log(\texttt{softmax}(\texttt{w})_j)$$

where $\texttt{softmax}(\texttt{w})_j$ is the jth coordinate of the softmax of the output w.
– If action a_j is *failed*, then the loss is defined to be

$$\Sigma_{1 \leq i \leq t, i \neq j} - \frac{1}{t-1} log(\texttt{softmax}(\texttt{w})_i)$$

Note that in the failed case, if there is only one available action ($t = 1$), then the loss is 0, which is not problematic since there is only one action to choose from. A backward propagation pass in then done through the RNN using this loss formula.

This loss function can initially seem counter-intuitive because of the second case, i.e., of a failed action. When offering action a_j fails, we chose to interpret this failure as meaning that *any other* choice would have been equally good. Consequently, we update their probabilities towards this. In other words, when a_j fails, instead of reducing its probability, we "even out" the probabilities of all other actions towards a uniform distribution among them. This effectively results in a reduction of the probability of a_j, but with more control over the probabilities of other actions.

We compare the above loss with another loss function (which we used in earlier experiments) that follows a more direct approach. It is computed in the same way as the one described in the case of a successful action. In the case where action a_j is failed, the loss is computed as

$$log(\texttt{softmax}(\texttt{w})_j)$$

This results in effectively "punishing" the choice of selecting a_j, lowering its probability, instead of rewarding all other actions. We will call this loss the *naive* loss. Experiments show that this loss function has a tendency to learn less efficiently than the other one, and sometimes does not learn an optimal behavior at all.

Training Pattern with Fixed Lookahead. We fix a lookahead number $l \geq 0$ (where $l = 0$ corresponds to use the simple training pattern described above). We train the network at step n only when the execution reaches step $n + l$, and the loss is computed according to the same formulas as above, except that the l last steps of the execution are taken into account to compute the loss at step n. When the current partial execution of length $n + l$, we observe the output w that the RNN has generated at step n, with action a_j that was chosen by the system. Let successes be the number of successful actions taken by the system between step n and step $n + l$, and failures to be the number of failures between the same steps.

The loss is then computed as:

$$\text{successes} \times -log(\texttt{softmax}(\texttt{w})_j) + \text{failures} \times -\Sigma_{1 \leq i \leq t}log(\texttt{softmax}(\texttt{w})_i)$$

The backward propagation is then applied to this loss at step n (and not at step $n + l$).

We also experimented with fixing a probability ϵ for exploring actions randomly, not based on the output of the partially trained RNN, both with a fixed ϵ and with diminishing the value of ϵ as training progressed. Another variant we experiment with is using a dual network, where, for diminishing instability of the updates, one is used for the exploitation of the partial training, and the other is updated. Switching between them each fixed number of steps.

The output provided by our RNN after training is, as a result of the softmax activation function, a probability distribution among the actions that can be taken from the current state. After training, we choose the action suggested by the controller with the highest probability. In many cases the training will converge towards a non probabilistic control policy, but will be limited due to the duration of the training. It is known from RL theory that for an environment that is deterministic or a Markov Chain, there exists an optimal deterministic policy that guarantees the highest expected discounted-sum utility from each state.

The fact that the environment is a black box does not change the situation, and a deterministic optimal control policy still exists. Yet, if we do not know how many states the environment has, we cannot even bound the size of such a policy. The number of states affects the number of required experiments and their length. A further complication occurs because the state of the environment, and its selection in case of a failure, are unobservable. Based on a given finite view, the environment can be in one of several states according to some probability distribution (which we cannot calculate, since the environment is a black box). In fact, it is possible that there can be infinitely many such distributions for different views.

Even when there exists an optimal deterministic strategy, we have no guarantee that the deep learning training will converge towards a deterministic strategy. For consider again Example **strategy** in Fig. 5. In case that the environment makes its choice from e_1 with *uniform* probability, any probabilistic choice between b and c by the system will make as good (or bad) policy as making a fixed choice between these two actions.

4   Experiments

We describe several experiments with the examples from the training suite. The experiments show testing different training patterns on each individual example. All results have been obtained using a similar structure for the RNN associated to the network. The size of the LSTM layer is 10. Initializing the non-recurrent parameters of the network is according to the Glorot initialization. The training passes have been done in every case by generating training sequences of increasing size, from 1 to 50, and repeating this 50 times.

Comparison of the Actual and the Naive Loss. The aim of this section is to show the advantage of using our actual loss described in the previous section over using the naive loss.

We present in Table 1 the results of experiments on four examples from the training suite, with various values for the lookahead and ϵ. The rows correspond to the different environments, and the columns to the pair (l, ϵ), where l is the lookahead in the training, and ϵ is the probability of performing an exploration step. Shaded lines correspond to the results when using the naive loss, while unshaded lines show the results for our actual loss. The entries in the table show the average percentage of failures when generating 100 executions of size 200.

Table 1. Summary of Experiments; shaded results are obtained using the naive loss

%failures \ (l, ϵ)	$(0,0)$	$(0,0.2)$	$(0,0.5)$	$(3,0)$	$(3,0.2)$	$(3,0.5)$	$(20,0)$	$(20,0.2)$	$(20,0.5)$
permitted	0.0	0.0	0.0	0.0	0.0	7.6	15.9	22.2	27.0
	15.69	18.62	18.68	43.79	55.01	61.44	65.56	65.32	67.39
schedule	98.5	98.4	98.5	9.9	0.2	0.0	0.5	0.3	78.5
	98.39	96.47	97.08	0	0	0	0	0	94.75
cases	1.7	1.6	6.9	1.5	1.5	1.6	34.5	38.9	45.6
	3.04	1.78	2	1.56	1.54	1.94	56.06	42.98	47.04
choice-scc	46.7	49.6	44.9	80.1	85.0	85.0	28.7	22.3	4.5
	46.22	54.2	64.0	80.2	73.7	70.5	36.8	30.3	33.5

We first discuss the results concerning our actual loss function (unshaded lines in the table).

In example `permitted`, the basic no-lookahead learning without exploration works very well, and both lookahead and exploration tend to be counterproductive. This is not too surprising observing that a lookahead or exploration pattern here would only blur the fact that a good choice is immediately interpretable as such, depending on the failure or success of the action. In example `schedule`, the lookahead is crucial for learning, and the exploration is again either counterproductive, or at least not advantageous (depending on the lookahead). In example `cases`, a long lookahead is again not efficient, and the exploration is not necessary. In example `choice-scc`, a very long lookahead is beneficial, which is to be expected in this example since a good choice at the beginning of the execution can be identified as such only after the three first steps. Seeing several successful steps afterwards to counter the effect of the failures at the beginning. Even in the case of a long lookahead, exploration with the high probability of 0.5, improves dramatically the results, where a long lookahead is insufficient to reach an almost optimal behavior. This shows the importance of exploration in this kind of situations where better strongly connected components are only reachable through worse paths that the system tends to avoid in the case of pure exploitation.

Note that the training was performed on sequences of length at most 50, but the behavior of the controller is verified on sequences of length 200, showing that a training on short sequences allow the controller to generalize its behavior on longer sequences. This gives evidence that a finite training is effective to learn an optimal behavior on very (possibly arbitrary) long sequences. Of course, without having a good estimate on the number of states of the environment, a"combination locks" in it can hide behaviors that deviate from the learned control.

Results using the naive loss appear as shaded lines in Table 1, for comparison with our actual loss. We will use as point of comparison the values of the parameters where the use of one loss or the other raises results that are almost optimal. In examples `schedule` and `cases`, we can see that both losses perform similarly: the situations where the training is optimal are the same for both losses. In examples `permitted` and `choice-scc`, we see that the naive loss performs very badly in comparison with the actual loss. In both cases the naive loss never manages to reach an optimal behavior for the system, while the actual loss performs very well for good choices of parameters.

Additional Experiments. Several other experiments were made using direct variations of our training scheme. We tested two standard techniques from deep learning: diminishing the value of the exploration/exploitation ratio ϵ along the training, and using two "dual" networks. One of which is updated at every step as usual, and the other is trained only at the end of a training sequence but is used to generate these sequences. Depending on the examples we tested these variants on, the results were either slightly better or similar to our results without these.

Another kind of experiments that we did was using combinations of pairs of our examples from the training suite. We devised examples mixing the behaviors of `permitted` and `schedule`, and mixing the behavior of `permitted` and `choice-scc`. Both of these combined examples were built using examples for which the optimal values of the parameters were very different. Surprisingly, we found that we still were able to learn these examples, using the same training pattern but alternating variables l and ϵ from those that achieved the optimal values for the two original examples. On the other hand, the length and number of training sequences had to be chosen using some additional heuristics, because the original values for these were not efficient for training. We detail our results in the following table. P is the number of training passes; a training pass involves running the usual training scheme with the first values of (l, ϵ) with N sequences of length L, then again with the second values of (l, ϵ). Every experiment was repeated 20 times, and the lowest, highest, and average failure rates are in the shaded columns (Table 2).

Table 2. Parameters and results for combined examples

	Values of (l, ϵ)	L	N	P	lowest	highest	average
permitted and schedule	$(5,0)$ and $(0,0)$	8	1000	2	0.0	98.0	5.0
permitted and choice-scc	$(50, 0.5)$ and $(0,0)$	50	10	8	1.5	66	33.5

5 Conclusions and Discussion

We presented a methodology for constructing control for a system that interacts with a black-box environment: it is not restricted to a specific objective, and it can be applied to various types of systems and environments. Instead of training the control for a specific system, we suggested the use of small, well designed, examples, which feature various potential challenges for training. We demonstrated our approach on training a set of examples using the DyNet tool.

Compared with the impressive use cases of deep learning, such as image recognition, translating natural languages, autonomous driving or playing games, the learning-based control synthesis problem that we considered here seems much simpler. However, it allows studying the principles and effect of different learning techniques.

Our use of recurrent deep learning, based on RNNs or LSTMs, has several benefits. First, the method is independent of knowing the states of the environment. The states of the constructed controller are kept implicitly in the hidden layer(s) of the neural network. We are oblivious of whether two internal representations are isomorphic w.r.t. the strategy, nor do we have to care.

Some works on deep reinforcement learning use recurrent deep learning, e.g., [9,10,17]. This was done for interactive Atari games, where the single current observed screen frame does not provide a complete current state. Since the control objective is the standard one, these methods apply a standard loss function that is based on the square of the difference between the current and the previous objective value.

Our long term goal is to expand this approach for constructing distributed schedulers for systems with concurrent processes that will lower the number of failed interactions between the participating processes. This can then be compared with an alternative approach for constructing schedulers that is based on distributed knowledge [2,3].

References

1. Angluin, D.: Learning regular sets from queries and counterexamples. Inf. Comput. **75**(2), 87–106 (1987)
2. Basu, A., Bensalem, S., Peled, D.A., Sifakis, J.: Priority scheduling of distributed systems based on model checking. Formal Methods Syst. Des. **39**(3), 229–245 (2011)
3. Bensalem, S., Bozga, M., Graf, S., Peled, D., Quinton, S.: Methods for knowledge based controlling of distributed systems. In: Bouajjani, A., Chin, W.-N. (eds.) ATVA 2010. LNCS, vol. 6252, pp. 52–66. Springer, Heidelberg (2010). https://doi.org/10.1007/978-3-642-15643-4_6
4. Silver, D., et al.: Mastering the game of go with deep neural networks and tree search. Nature **529**(7587), 484–489 (2016)
5. Silver, D., et al.: Mastering chess and shogi by self-play with a general reinforcement learning algorithm. CoRR, abs/1712.01815 (2017)
6. Neubig, G., et al.: DyNet: the dynamic neural network toolkit. CoRR, abs/1701.03980 (2017)
7. Gerth, R., Peled, D.A., Vardi, M.Y., Wolper, P.: Simple on-the-fly automatic verification of linear temporal logic. In: Dembinski, P., Sredniawa, M., (eds.) Protocol Specification, Testing and Verification XV, Proceedings of the Fifteenth IFIP WG6.1 International Symposium on Protocol Specification, Testing and Verification, Warsaw, Poland, June 1995. IFIP Conference Proceedings, vol. 38, pp. 3–18. Chapman & Hall (1995)
8. Goodfellow, I.J., Bengio, Y., Courville, A.C.: Deep learning. In: Adaptive Computation and Machine Learning. MIT Press (2016)
9. Hausknecht, M.J., Stone, P.: Deep recurrent Q-learning for partially observable mdps. CoRR, abs/1507.06527 (2015)
10. Heess, N., Hunt, J.J., Lillicrap, T.P., Silver, D.: Memory-based control with recurrent neural networks. CoRR, abs/1512.04455 (2015)
11. Peled, D., Iosti, S., Bensalem, S.: Control synthesis through deep learning. In: Bartocci, E., Cleaveland, R., Grosu, R., Sokolsky, O. (eds.) From Reactive Systems to Cyber-Physical Systems - Essays Dedicated to Scott A. Smolka on the Occasion of His 65th Birthday, pp. 242–255. Springer, Cham (2019). https://doi.org/10.1007/978-3-030-31514-6_14
12. Pnueli, A., Rosner, R.: On the synthesis of a reactive module. In: Conference Record of the Sixteenth Annual ACM Symposium on Principles of Programming Languages, Austin, Texas, USA, 11–13 January 1989, pp. 179–190 (1989)

13. Pnueli, A., Rosner, R.: Distributed reactive systems are hard to synthesize. In: 31st Annual Symposium on Foundations of Computer Science, St. Louis, Missouri, USA, 22–24 October 1990, vol. II, pp. 746–757 (1990)
14. Safra, S.: On the complexity of omega-automata. In: 29th Annual Symposium on Foundations of Computer Science, White Plains, New York, USA, 24–26 October 1988, pp. 319–327. IEEE Computer Society (1988)
15. Sutton, R.S., Barto, A.G.: Reinforcement Learning - An Introduction. Adaptive Computation and Machine Learning, 2nd edn. MIT Press (2018)
16. Wonham, W.M., Ramadge, P.J.: Modular supervisory control of discrete-event systems. MCSS **1**(1), 13–30 (1988)
17. Zhu, P., Li, X., Poupart, P.: On improving deep reinforcement learning for pomdps. CoRR, abs/1704.07978 (2017)
18. Zielonka, W.: Infinite games on finitely coloured graphs with applications to automata on infinite trees. Theor. Comput. Sci. **200**(1–2), 135–183 (1998)

A Formal Model for Reasoning About the Ideal Fitness in Evolutionary Processes

Thomas Gabor$^{(\boxtimes)}$ and Claudia Linnhoff-Popien

LMU Munich, Munich, Germany
`thomas.gabor@ifi.lmu.de`

Abstract. We introduce and discuss a formal model of evolutionary processes that summarizes various kinds of evolutionary algorithms and other optimization techniques. Based on that framework, we present assumptions called "random agnosticism" and "based optimism" that allow for new kinds of proofs about evolution. We apply them by providing all a proof design that the recently introduced notion of final productive fitness is the ideal target fitness function for any evolutionary process, opening up a new perspective on the fitness in evolution.

Keywords: Evolution · Evolutionary algorithms · Fitness

1 Introduction

Evolution in its broadest sense describes a process that finds solutions to complex problems via the application of comparatively simple local operators. Mostly, this process can be described as a search that starts quite uninformed and uses the knowledge gained through trial and error to guide the further search process. Note that usually this happens without central control and mostly without even any central viewpoint that would allow to overlook all parts of the evolution. However, evolution is often implemented deliberately (using evolutionary algorithms in software, e.g.) in order to search or optimize for a specific result according to an externally given target.

While this target is often provided directly to the evolutionary process so that intermediate results may be evaluated, many studies empirically show better results when using slightly different goal than going directly for the external target metric. Our recent study [8] has brought up empirical evidence that one such "indirect" metric (called *final productive fitness*) might be theoretically optimal (even when or perhaps because it is extremely costly to compute). However, little formal framework exists to reason about evolutionary processes (specifically goals in evolutionary processes) at such a broad level in order to formally prove a claim of optimality.

The aim of this paper is to show what kind of formal framework *would be sufficient* to produce a formal proof of final productive's fitness optimality. To this end, we first introduce two bold but crucial assumptions hat allow us to strip

© Springer Nature Switzerland AG 2020
T. Margaria and B. Steffen (Eds.): ISoLA 2020, LNCS 12477, pp. 473–490, 2020.
https://doi.org/10.1007/978-3-030-61470-6_28

away much of the complexity of reasoning about evolution. Then we construct the desired proof from them to show how they work. We hope that the novel tools (i.e., mainly Assumptions 1 and 2) designed here can be used for other high-level arguments about evolution.

All necessary definitions involving evolutionary processes are given in a consistent way in Sect. 2. Section 3 then discusses the issue of the ideal fitness function and introduces the tools to reason about it. We give a short glance at related work in Sect. 4 and conclude with Sect. 5.

2   Definitions

We follow the formal framework sketched in [8] to a vast extent but substantially expand it in generality. We provide an example in Sect. 2.3.

2.1   Evolutionary Processes

For all definitions, we aim to give them in such a basic form that they can span over various disciplines, from biology to formal methods. We use $\mathfrak{P}$ to denote the power set.

Definition 1 (Evolution). *Let $\mathcal{X}$ be an arbitrary set called* search space. *Let $g \in \mathbb{N}$ be called the* generation count. *Let $X_i \subseteq \mathcal{X}$ for any $i \in \mathbb{N}, 0 \leq i \leq g$ be a subset of $\mathcal{X}$ called* population. *Let $E : \mathfrak{P}(\mathcal{X}) \to \mathfrak{P}(\mathfrak{P}(\mathcal{X}))$ be a function called* evolutionary function.

A tuple $(\langle X_i \rangle_{0 \leq i \leq g}, E)$ is called an evolution *over $\mathcal{X}$ iff $X_i \in E(X_{i-1})$ for all $i \in \mathbb{N}, 1 \leq i \leq g$.*

Any element of the search space $x \in \mathcal{X}$ is called solution candidate (or sometimes just solution for short). Members of a given population $x \in X$ are obviously always solution candidates, but are often also called individuals. Every i within the generation count $1 \leq i \leq g$ is called a generation number with X_i being the respective generation's population. If no confusion is possible, both i and X_i will also be called a generation. X_0 is called the initial population.

Note that an evolution can be generated given a configuration consisting of a search space $\mathcal{X}$, an initial population X_0 and an evolution function E. However, many possible evolutions can follow from the same configuration. Often, the initial population X_0 is not given as a set but instead generated (semi-)randomly. We write that as an initialization function $I : \mathfrak{R} \to \mathfrak{P}(\mathcal{X})$ where $\mathfrak{R}$ stands for random inputs.[1] Notation-wise, we omit random inputs and write $X_0 \sim I()$ (or simply $X_0 = I()$ if no confusion is possible) for the initial population generated by such a function.

Definition 2 (Target). *Let $\mathcal{X}$ be a search space. A function $t : \mathcal{X} \to [0; 1]$ that assigns all elements in the search space a scalar value is called a* target function.

---

[1] In computers, these are often provided by a seed value and a hash function.

A target function assigns a value to each point in the search space, i.e., to any given solution candidate.[2] We assume that target values are bounded, so w.l.o.g. we can assume the target value space to be restricted to $[0; 1]$ in Definition 2. Again this can be generalized but is rarely useful in praxis. Also note that target functions themselves are unconstrained: They can always be applied to the whole search space. Hard constraints must be implemented by altering the search space or "softening" them by representing them with different target values.

Furthermore, w.l.o.g. we assign every goal function a minimization semantic: For two solution candidates $x_1, x_2 \in \mathcal{X}$ we say that x_1 fulfills a goal t better iff $t(x_1) < t(x_2)$. Any solution candidate $x \in \mathcal{X}$ so that $t(x) \leq t(x') \ \forall x' \in \mathcal{X}$ is called a global optimum. An algorithm searching for increasingly better solutions candidates is called an optimization algorithm. A configuration, a target function and an evolution form an evolutionary process:

Definition 3 (Evolutionary Process). *Let $\mathcal{X}$ be a search space. Let $E : \mathfrak{P}(\mathcal{X}) \rightarrow \mathfrak{P}(\mathfrak{P}(\mathcal{X}))$ be an evolutionary function. Let $t : \mathcal{X} \rightarrow [0; 1]$ be a target function. Let X_i be a population for any $i \in \mathbb{N}, 0 \leq i \leq g$.*

A tuple $\mathcal{E} = (\mathcal{X}, E, t, \langle X_i \rangle_{i \leq g})$ is an evolutionary process iff $(\langle X_i \rangle_{i \leq g}, E)$ is an evolution.

Effectively, an evolutionary process consists of a history of past populations (X_i) and the means to generate new population (E). We often implement the evolutionary function by giving an *evolutionary step function* $e : \mathfrak{P}(\mathcal{X}) \times \mathfrak{R} \rightarrow \mathfrak{P}(\mathcal{X})$ and write $X_{i+1} \sim e(X_i)$ (or simply $X_{i+1} = e(X_i)$ if no confusion is possible) for any population X_{i+1} that evolved from X_i by applying the evolutionary step function alongside with some (omitted) random input.

An evolutionary process also carries a target function t. An evolutionary process $\mathcal{E}$ is *optimizing* iff $\min_{x \in X_0} t(x) \geq \min_{x' \in X_g} t(x')$. For many mechanisms in stochastic search as well as for more natural phenomena like biological evolution or human software development processes, optimization is a rather strong property. However, if we have sufficient space within a population and access to the target function, we can turn all evolutionary processes into optimizing ones by just saving the currently best individual alongside the evolution, i.e., ensuring that $\arg\min_{x \in X_i} t(x) \in X_{i+1}$.

Definition 4 (Elitism). *An evolutionary process $\mathcal{E} = (\mathcal{X}, E, t, \langle X_i \rangle_{i \leq g})$ is called elitist iff for all $i \in \mathbb{N}, 1 \leq i \leq g$, it holds that $\min_{x \in X_{i-1}} t(x) \geq \min_{x' \in X_i} t(x')$.*

All elitist processes are optimizing. If not noted differently, we from now on assume every evolutionary process to be elitist by default.

---

[2] Note that by giving a function only parametrized on the individual itself, we assume that the target function is static. Dynamic optimization is an entire field of research that we heavily use in this paper. However, we leave dynamic target functions in our formalism to future work.

2.2   Evolutionary Algorithms

An evolutionary algorithm is special case of evolutionary process that uses an evolutionary function made up of a number of standard components called *evolutionary operators*. We now introduce standard definitions for these components that most instances of evolutionary algorithms can be mapped to. However, the field of evolutionary algorithms is vast and there are variants that alter many smaller details of how they work. It is interesting to note how robust the general concept of evolution is to such variations.

Nearly all evolutionary algorithms that use set-based populations introduce a fixed population size $n \in \mathbb{N}$ for all generations. This allows to keep memory resources easily manageable as the overall memory consumption will not increase over time. We also use this opportunity to introduce the concept of fitness functions. Note that $\mathfrak{E}$ is the space of all evolutionary processes.

Definition 5 (Fitness). *Let $\mathcal{X}$ be a search space. A function $f : \mathcal{X} \times \mathfrak{E} \times \mathfrak{R} \to [0; 1]$ is called a* fitness function. *This function takes an individual, its evolutionary process up until now, and random input and returns a scalar value.*

The fitness function can be regarded as generalization of the concept of a target function (cf. Definition 2). It represents the goal definition that the evolutionary process can call upon and actively follows, which may or may not coincide with the target function. In addition to the solution candidate itself, it is able to process additional information about the context. Various approaches may allow nearly arbitrary information here. For a rather general approach, we just pass on a snapshot of the evolutionary process that generated the individual until now. This includes:

- The current population that the evaluated individual is a part of allows to define the fitness of an individual relative to its peers.
- The history of all populations until now allows to observe relative changes over time as well as trace the ancestry of individuals throughout evolution.
- The number of the current generation allows the fitness function to change over time and implement, e.g., a cool-down schedule.

Note that the random input that is also passed along allows fitness functions to also vary fitness values stochastically. However, most fitness functions will not make use of all this information. In these cases we allow to trim down the fitness function's signature and simply write $f(x)$ for an individual $x \in \mathcal{X}$ if all other parameters are ignored.

In many practical instances, developers will choose the target function as a fitness function, i.e., $f(x) = t(x)$ for all $x \in \mathcal{X}$, and for most target functions, evolution will end up achieving passable target values this way. It is the main point of this paper, however, to prove that the optimal choice in general is a different function derived from the target function.

Alongside the fitness function f an evolutionary algorithm also uses various selection functions. In general, a selection function returns a subset of the population for a specific purpose.

Definition 6 (Selection). *A function* $s : \mathfrak{P}(\mathcal{X}) \times \mathfrak{E} \times \mathfrak{R} \to \mathfrak{P}(\mathcal{X})$ *is called a selection function iff* $s(X, \mathcal{E}, r) \subseteq X$ *for all* $X, \mathcal{E}, r$. *This function takes a population, its evolutionary process, and random input and returns a subset of the given population.*

Again note that we allow for a multitude of information that will rarely be used directly in any selection function and that will be omitted if not necessary. Most importantly, however, any selection function is able to call any fitness function since all its inputs can be provided.

As seemingly limitless variations of selection functions exist we use this opportunity to provide a few examples and at the same time define all families of selection functions that we use for the remainder of this paper. (Note that the current population X is always provided with an evolutionary process $\mathcal{E}$.)

Random Selection. This function $\varrho^m(X, \mathcal{E}, r) = \{x \sim X\} \cup \varrho^{m-1}(X, \mathcal{E}, r)$ selects m individuals of the population at random. Note that $x \sim X$ is one element $x \in X$ sampled uniformly at random. We define $\varrho^0(X, \mathcal{E}, r) = \emptyset$.

Cutoff Selection. This function $\sigma^m(X, \mathcal{E}, r) = \{\arg\min_{x \in X} f(x, \mathcal{E}, r)\} \cup \sigma^{m-1}(X, \mathcal{E}, r)$ selects the m best individuals according to the fitness function f. We define $\sigma^0(X, \mathcal{E}, r) = \emptyset$.

We can now move on to define the evolution function E. For all variants of evolutionary algorithms there exist certain building blocks, called *evolutionary operators*, that most evolutionary functions have in common. They take as arguments some individuals and return some (possibly new) individuals. During the execution of an evolutionary operator its input individuals are referred to as *parents* and its output individuals are referred to as *children*.

Mutation. This operator $mut : \mathcal{X} \times \mathfrak{R} \to \mathcal{X}$ generates a randomly slightly altered individual from a parent.

Recombination. This operator $rec : \mathcal{X} \times \mathcal{X} \times \mathfrak{R} \to \mathcal{X}$ takes two individuals to combine them into a new individual.

Migration. This operator $mig : \mathfrak{R} \to \mathcal{X}$ generates a random new individual.

Again, countless variants and implementations exist, most importantly among them there is non-random mutation and recombination with various amounts of parents and children. For brevity, we omit everything we do not use in this paper's study. Please note that all of these operators return entirely new individuals and leave their parents unchanged. In practical applications, it is equally common to apply (some of) these operators *in-place*, which means that the generated children replace their parents immediately. We, however, opt to just add the children to the population (and possibly eliminate the parents later) so that parents and their children can exist side by side within the same generation. Our main aim in doing this is that it makes elitism much easier to achieve.

As these operators work on single individuals, we define a shortcut to apply them to sets of individuals:

Definition 7 (Application of Operators). *Let $X \subseteq \mathcal{X}$ be a set of individuals in search space $\mathcal{X}$. Let s be a selection function. We write $X \downharpoonright_{mut} s = \{mut(x) \mid x \in s(X)\}$ and $X \downharpoonright_{rec} s = \{rec(x_1, x_2) \mid x_1 \in s(X), x_2 \sim X\}$ for the sets of children when applying the respective operators. For consistency, we also write $X \downharpoonright_{mig} s = \{mig() \mid x \in s(X)\}$ to create $|s(X)|$ many new random individuals, even though their values do not depend on the individuals in X.*

We are now ready to define a scheme for the evolution function E in evolutionary algorithms. We do so by providing an evolutionary step function e as discussed above with parameters $A_1, A_2, A_3 \in \mathbb{N}$:

$$e(X) = \sigma^{|X|}(X \cup (X \downharpoonright_{rec} \sigma^{A_1}) \cup (X \downharpoonright_{mut} \varrho^{A_2}) \cup (X \downharpoonright_{mig} \varrho^{A_3})) \tag{1}$$

Note again that in this evolutionary step we place all generated children alongside their parents into one population and then cutoff-select the best from this population.[3] As it is common, we use random selection to select mutation parents. The selection function for the recombination parents is also called *parent selection*. We use cutoff selection on one parent with a randomly selected partner here. This gives some selective pressure (i.e., better individuals have a better chance of becoming recombination parents) without overcentralizing too much. Although many approaches to parent selection exist, we choose this one as it is both effective in practical implementations and mathematically very clean to define. The final selection function that is called upon the combined population of potential parents and new children is called *survivor selection*. We simply use cutoff selection here for ease of reasoning. Many evolutionary algorithms use more advanced survivor selection functions like roulette wheel selection where better individuals merely have a higher chance of being picked. We choose a hard cutoff for this kind of selection, mainly because it is simpler to define and understand, and its transparent to elitism. Since the cutoff point varies with the population's fitness structure that is subjected to random effects, the practical difference between both approaches for our examples is negligible. Note that we can emulate a lot of different selection schemes by choosing an appropriate fitness function: As the fitness function can vary at random, we can for example make the cutoff more fuzzy by simply adding noise to each fitness evaluation instead of changing the selection function. Also note that adding all the children non-destructively and using cutoff-selection makes the algorithm elitist if $f = t$.

We parametrize the evolutionary step function with the amount of recombination children A_1, amount of mutation children A_2 and amount of migration children A_3. These are also often given as rates relative to the population size.

Definition 8 (Evolutionary Algorithm). *An evolutionary algorithm is an evolutionary process $\mathbb{E} = (\mathcal{X}, E, t, \langle X_i \rangle_{i \leq g})$ where the evolutionary function is given via an evolutionary step function of the form described in Eq. 1, where a fitness function f is used for all selection functions and evolutionary operators and the target function t is only accessible insofar it is part of f.*

---

[3] In the field of evolutionary computing, this is called a $\mu + \lambda$ selection scheme.

Note that for the ease of use in later notation, we will often denote two evolutionary processes that differ solely in their fitness function (ϕ vs. ψ, e.g.) by denoting that fitness function as a subscript ($\mathcal{E}_\phi$ vs. $\mathcal{E}_\psi$). Independently of that we denote the best individual of the final generation of $\mathcal{E}_\phi$ according to some fitness or target function ψ with

$$|\mathcal{E}_\phi|_\psi = \arg\min_{x \in X_g} \psi(x) \tag{2}$$

and the best of all generations with

$$||\mathcal{E}_\phi||_\psi = \arg\min_{\substack{x \in X_i \\ i \in \mathbb{N} \\ 0 \leq i \leq g}} \psi(x). \tag{3}$$

It is clear that if $\mathcal{E}_\phi$ is elitist with respect to ψ, then $|\mathcal{E}_\phi|_\psi = ||\mathcal{E}_\phi||_\psi$. Note that when we use a fitness function $f \neq t$ then we usually obtain the overall result of the evolutionary algorithm by computing $||\mathcal{E}_f||_t$ or $|\mathcal{E}_f|_t$ if we are confident about the elitism at least to the extent that we do not worry about substantial results getting lost along the way. In most cases we will assume that if f is close enough to t at least in the final generations, elitism with respect to f grants us quasi-elitism with respect t, i.e., if $f \approx t$ and $\mathcal{E}_f$ is elitist with respect to f, we assume that $||\mathcal{E}_f||_t \approx ||\mathcal{E}_f||_f$.

2.3   Example

We provide a running example accompanying these definitions.[4] For a target function, we choose two common benchmark functions from literature as they are implemented in the DEAP framework [2,12]. The first problem is based on the two-dimensional Schwefel function although we adjusted the target value space to fit comfortably within $[0;1]$ (cf. Fig. 1a). We chose only two dimensions for ease of visualization. Higher-dimensional Schwefel is also covered in [8]. The Schwefel function is characterized by many valleys and hills of varying depth. The global optimum is at $X = Y \approx 420$. By contrast, our second example is the H1 function [14] that features one very distinct global optimum at $X = 8.6998, Y = 6.7665$. However, it feature very many little (hard to see) local optima throughout the whole surface. We took the classical H1 function, which is defined as a maximization problem and turned it upside down to produce a minimization problem (cf. Fig. 1b). For both target functions $t \in \{t_{Schwefel}, t_{H1}\}$ we construct the same evolutionary algorithm.

The search space is given as $\mathcal{X}_{Schwefel} = [-500; 500] \subseteq \mathbb{R}^2$ and $\mathcal{X}_{H1} = [-100; 100] \subseteq \mathbb{R}^2$ respectively. We initialize the search by generating X_0 from 25 random samples within the search space in both cases. The size of this population remains constant with application of the evolutionary step function e, which is constructed according to Eq. 1 with $A_1 = 0.3 \cdot |X|, A_2 = 0.1 \cdot |X|, A_3 = 0.1 \cdot |X|$.

---

[4] The code for all examples can be found at github.com/thomasgabor/isola-evolib.

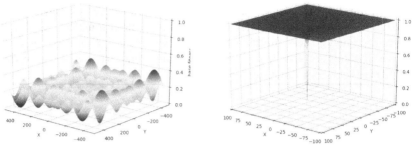

(a) Normalized two-dimensional Schwefel   (b) Inverse normalized H1

Fig. 1. Benchmark target functions used for the running example.

Let w be the range of a single dimensional value in the search space (i.e., $w_{Schwefel} = 1000, w_{H1} = 200$), then the mutation operator returns

$$mut((X,Y)) \in \{(X \oplus \delta, Y), (X, Y \oplus \delta) \mid \delta \in [-0.1w; 0.1w]\} \tag{4}$$

chosen random uniform where $\oplus$ only adds or subtracts as much of its second argument so that the resulting value remains within the search space. We further define the recombination operator so that its result is at random uniform picked from

$$rec((X,Y),(X',Y')) \in \{(X,Y),(X,Y'),(X',Y),(X',Y')\}. \tag{5}$$

Note that both operators include random cases where the operator does not do anything at, which does not harm the overall search and can be further counter-acted by increasing the respective amount of selected individuals for that operator. The migration operator just samples random uniform from the search space, returning $mig() \in \mathcal{X}$.

To illustrate the behavior of evolution, we ran independently initialized evolutionary processes for each problem 500 times each for 50 generations. Figure 2 shows all solution candidates found within a specific generation among *all* evolutionary processes. We can clearly trace how the search start random uniform and then focuses towards the global optima, sometimes getting stuck in local optima in the target value landscape (compare Fig. 1).

3   Approach

We apply the framework to give the definition of productive fitness. To present the full proof design we introduce and discuss Assumptions 1 and 2. We continue our example in Sect. 3.3.

3.1   The Ideal Fitness

So far, we discussed some example definitions using the target function as fitness, $f = t$, and noted that it works (but not optimally). Obviously, having f correlate

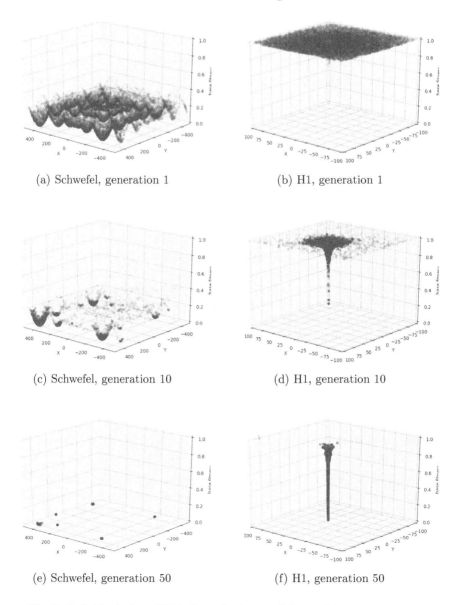

(a) Schwefel, generation 1

(b) H1, generation 1

(c) Schwefel, generation 10

(d) H1, generation 10

(e) Schwefel, generation 50

(f) H1, generation 50

Fig. 2. Individuals from 500 independent runs of the evolutionary processes.

to some extend with t is a good thing if in the end we value our results with respect to t. However, it has long been known that augmenting the fitness with additional (meta-)information can greatly aid the optimization process in some cases. This fact is extensively discussed in literature [1,15] including previous works by the authors [7,8]. We sum the results up in the following observation:

Observation 1. *There exist evolutionary processes $\mathcal{E}_\phi = (\mathcal{X}, E_\phi, t, \langle X_i \rangle_{i \leq g})$ and $\mathcal{E}_t = (\mathcal{X}, E_t, t, \langle X_i' \rangle_{i \leq g})$ whose configurations only differ in the fitness function and there exist fitness functions $\phi \neq t$ so that $\|\mathcal{E}_\phi\|_t < \|\mathcal{E}_t\|_t$.*

Observation 1 states that an evolutionary process can yield better results *with respect to t* by *not using t* directly but a somewhat approximate version of t given via ϕ, which includes additional information but likewise "waters down" the pure information of our original target. It is somewhat surprising that a deviation from the original target can yield an improvement. Commonly this phenomenon is explained by the *exploration/exploitation trade-off*: In an unknown solution landscape made up by t, we gain knowledge through evaluating solution candidates. When we have evaluated all solution candidates $x \in \mathcal{X}$, we simply need to compute $\arg\min_{x \in \mathcal{X}} t(x)$, which of course is infeasible for most practical search spaces. Giving limited time resources, we need to decide if we put additional effort into exploring more and new parts of the search space in hope of finding valuable solution candidates there or if we exploit the knowledge we have already gathered to further improve the solution candidates we already evaluated. This can be seen of a trade-off between large-scale search for exploration and small-scale search for exploitation.

Dealing with the exploration/exploitation trade-off certainly is one of the central tasks when implementing metaheuristic search and has been covered extensively in literature. Many of these approaches have been discovered bottom-up, often by analogy to biological or physical processes. Even though many similarities between approaches have been discovered, there does not exist a general framework for how to construct the right fitness function for a specific target function and evolutionary process.

Problem 1. *Given a target function t, what is the theoretically best fitness function ϕ^* for an evolutionary process $\mathcal{E}_{\phi^*}$ to optimize for t, i.e., optimize $\|\mathcal{E}_{\phi^*}\|_t$?*

We gave an answer to that question for the special case of standard evolutionary algorithms in [8]: We defined a measurement called *final productive fitness* and have sketched a proof that it represents the ideal fitness function for evolutionary algorithms. However, it is important to note that computing it a priori is infeasible. We approximated final productive fitness for an evolution a posteriori and provided empirical evidence that evolutionary algorithms are working better the better their fitness approximates final productive fitness.

In this paper, we formally introduce the necessary tools to provide the full proof of the ideal fitness for evolutionary algorithms. First, we need to re-iterate a few definitions of [8] in order to formally define final productive fitness.

Definition 9 (Descendants [8]). *Given an individual x in the population of generation i, $x \in X_i$, of an evolutionary process $\mathcal{E}$. All individuals $x' \in X_{i+1}$ so that x' resulted from x via a mutation operator, i.e., $x' = mut(x, r)$ for some $r \in \mathfrak{R}$, or a recombination operator with any other parent, i.e., there exists $y \in X_i$ so that $x' = rec(x, y, r)$ for some $r \in \mathfrak{R}$, are called* direct descendants *of x. Further given a series of populations $(X_i)_{0 < i < g}$ we define the set of all descendants D_x as the transitive hull on all direct descendants of x.*

The main idea behind productive fitness is to measure an individual's effect on the optimization process. If the optimization process is stopping right now, i.e., if we are in the final generation g, then we can equate any individual's effect with its target function value. However, for any previous generations an individual's effect on the optimization corresponds to the best target function values that its descendants have achieved within the evolution.

Definition 10 (Productive Fitness [8]). *Given an individual x in the population of generation i, $x \in X_i$, of an evolutionary process $\mathcal{E}$. Let $D_x \subseteq \mathcal{X}$ be the set of all descendants from x. The productive fitness after n generations or optimistic n-productive fitness ϕ_n^+ is the average achieved target value of x's descendants n generations later, written*

$$\phi_n^+(x) = \begin{cases} \text{avg}_{x' \in D_x \cap X_{i+n}} \, t(x') & \text{if } D_x \cap X_{i+n} \neq \emptyset \\ 1 & \text{otherwise.} \end{cases} \tag{6}$$

Note that in case the individual x has no descendants in n generations, we set its productive fitness $\phi_n^+(x)$ to a worst case value of 1.

From [8] we repeat two major arguments against this definition:

- The use of avg as an aggregator over target values might be a bit pessimistic. By doing so, we penalize an individual's fitness if that individual bloats up the optimization with many low-value individuals. However, if it thereby also delivers at least one superior descendant, we should actually be fine with that when we only care about the end result. If such effects actually occur in practical scenarios is up to future work to discover. Empirical evidence discovered in [8] strongly argues in favor of using the average, which is why we repeat it in this definition. In the proof we will later derive a min-version from one of our assumptions.
- Assigning the value 1 in case the given individual has no further descendants in generation $i + n$ is a design choice. We might leave the productive fitness in this case undefined or at least assign a value outside the common range of target function values. We suggest that even without living descendants there might still be inherent value to having explored certain solution candidates (and having them clearly discarded for the ongoing process). Still, determining this incentive is up to future research.

Of course, productive fitness ϕ_n^+ only measures the effect locally after a fixed amount of generations. For the effect for the whole evolution we can now easily define the notion of final productive fitness.

Definition 11 (Final Productive Fitness). *Given an individual x in the population of generation i, $x \in X_i$, of an evolutionary process $\mathcal{E}$ with g generations in total. The final productive fitness of x is the fitness of its descendants in the final generation, i.e.,*

$$\phi^\dagger(x) = \phi_{g-i}^+(x). \tag{7}$$

Described shortly, the final productive fitness of an individual x can be seen as an answer to the question: "How much did x contribute to the fitness of the individuals of the final population?" We claim that optimizing for that measurement results in the optimal evolutionary process (as considered in Problem 1).

Practically, of course, optimizing for that measurement is rather difficult (which in fact may be the entire reason it is the optimal fitness function): To make the completely right decision in generation $i = 1$, we would have to evaluate all possible future generations for each single individual being involved in any selection or altered in any way by evolutionary operators. Within a single generation, these are exponentially many possibilities, which of course grow exponentially with each generation. Still, in [8] we designed some approximation of final productive fitness that can at least be computed a posteriori for an already run evolution, giving some insight into the algorithm's workings. In this paper, we now provide the full design for a proof of final productive fitness's optimality, although there are still many risky new tools involved.

3.2 Proof Design

We hope that the notion of final productive fitness is intuitive enough so that it seems plausible how $\phi^\dagger$ might be the ideal fitness function ϕ^* for any evolutionary algorithm. However, evolutionary processes are highly stochastic entities and little framework exists to reason about their performance. We now first provide such a framework, although we resort to making some strong assumptions along the way.

Assumption 1 (Random Agnosticism). *Random effects residing in selection functions and evolutionary operators exert the same general effects on the evolutionary function E regardless of the used fitness function.*

The main intention behind Assumption 1 is, of course, to exclude any concept of randomness from the proof design. We effectively assume that the distribution of outcomes (i.e., selected individuals or generated children) depending on random inputs does not depend on the fitness function. At first, this is a certainly outlandish and strong assumption, especially as it allows us to deduce quite strong properties. We just give a few reasons why it might be viable:

- Wherever random effects are used, they are usually designed to break clear fitness borders (for example when using a fuzzy cutoff vs. a discrete cutoff). In these cases, random effects overpower the effect of the fitness function so that (in the extreme case, consider random selection) the used fitness function has little impact on the outcome. If we flip the perspective around, different fitness functions then also have little difference for the outcome.
- Within the evolutionary function E, typically lots of random effects come together. Even if some of their distributions are altered by using a different fitness function, as long as they are not altered towards a specific result, the effect may still cancel out on the larger scale. Basically, we expect the outcome distribution of the whole evolutionary function E to approach the normal distribution irregardless of (un-systematic) mix-ups.

– From practical perspective, the shape of outcome distributions is rarely considered directly when constructing an evolutionary algorithm. That should usually indicate that not much effect can be observed there in most cases.

Eventually, all these reasons are flawed, of course. Otherwise, we would not have kept Assumption 1. Still, we feel that proofs built on Assumption 1 might have practical relevance for the time being.

It would be natural to follow up the effective elimination of randomness (coming from Assumption 1) by replacing all possibly random outcomes with the expected value of the distribution and treating all function as non-stochastic. However, the expected value is still computed from the distribution, so this would not make things much easier. Instead, we opt of the ideal outcome, which can be derived much easier, but might shift effects drastically: A recombination operator that performs so bad on average that it brings down the whole evolutionary process might now look like it gives rise to a very effective evolutionary process just because it has a very small chance of getting a really good result.

Assumption 2 (Based Optimism). *For an evolutionary function E with a limited amount of possible outcomes, the best possible outcome is representative for its expected average result.*

We recognize that "limited" is not fully defined here. We suggest that future work looks into enumerability or local boundedness. For practical purposes, however, it is clear which of the classic operators are affected: Random initialization and migration can generate individuals across the whole search space. If we minimize over their possible outcomes, the whole algorithm reaches the global optimum in a single step. Mutation and recombination (with any kind of selection) on the other side are limited operators: Given certain individuals as input parameters, they will only navigate a limited range of options related to those individuals. Again the main argument for the plausibility of Assumption 2 is that the results usually approach normal distribution anyway and there is no real reason why they should act any differently given exactly the two fitness functions we are about to compare. However, given that we completely alter the rules of evolutionary algorithms with this one, it is definitely a bold assumption. Further note how we interpret the qualification "best" in Assumption 2: For a given evolutionary function E, its notion of "best" corresponds to its fitness function. So if we choose the best of two evolutionary processes with different fitness functions, we might actually choose two different points in the outcome distribution (depending on the fitness), which again is an immensely powerful tool based on a big assumption.

What Assumption 2 then provides is means to simplify Definition 10: Productive fitness is defined as the average fitness of all descendants. We can now use the *best* fitness of the descendants to compute the fitness measurement which we will call *optimistic productive fitness*.[5] Note that implementing these assumptions has a great effect on the behavior of the evolutionary process. However, we do not claim that they leave the evolutionary process intact, we just claim that a clearly better fitness function remains the better fitness function even in the altered setting.

The tools provided by Assumptions 1 and 2 are rather novel and very powerful, so we are aware that any results based on them should be taken with a great amount of caution. However, in order to present these tools at work, we can use them to provide a proof that final productive fitness $\phi^{\dagger}$ is one answer for Problem 1.

Proof 1 (Problem 1). *Let $\mathcal{E}^{\dagger} = \langle \mathcal{X}, E^{\dagger}, t, (X_i^{\dagger})_{i<g} \rangle$ be an evolutionary process using optimistic final productive fitness $\phi^{\dagger}$. Let $\mathcal{E}^* = \langle \mathcal{X}, E^*, t, (X_i^*)_{i<g} \rangle$ be an evolutionary process using a different (possibly more ideal) fitness ϕ^*. According to the transformation discussed in Sect. 2.1, let both $\mathcal{E}^{\dagger}$ and $\mathcal{E}^*$ be elitist. Let $X_0^{\dagger} = X_0^*$. We assume that $t(||\mathcal{E}^{\dagger}||_t) > t(||\mathcal{E}^*||_t)$, i.e., because of elitism*

$$\min_{x \in X_g^{\dagger}} t(x) > \min_{x \in X_g^*} t(x). \tag{8}$$

From Eq. 8 it follows that there exists an individual $x \in X_g^*$ so that $x \notin X_g^{\dagger}$ and $t(x) < \min_{y \in X_g^{\dagger}} t(y)$. The better individual x could not have been introduced into the population of $\mathcal{E}^*$ by migration (or random initialization for that matter) as we could use Assumption 1 to just introduce x into $\mathcal{E}^{\dagger}$ then.

Then x needs to stem from an individual x' that is an ancestor of x, i.e., $x \in D_{x'}$, so that x' was selected for survival in $\mathcal{E}^*$ and not in $\mathcal{E}^{\dagger}$, which implies that $\phi^{\dagger}(x') > \phi^*(x')$. However, since x is a possible descendant for x', the computation of $\phi^{\dagger}(x')$ should have taken $t(x)$ into account,[6] meaning that x' should have survived in $\mathcal{E}^{\dagger}$ because of elitism after all, which contradicts the previous assumption (Eq. 8). □

3.3   Example

We now illustrate the notion of productive fitness for our running example. For each of the individuals generated in Sect. 2.3 we computed an a posteriori approximation for final productive fitness: Basically, we took the descendants that *have in fact been generated* during evolution as a representative subset of

---

[5] Note that the best possible choice for the average fitness of descendants is the minimum of the possible descendants' fitness values. When we are allowed to adjust the random choice for the best possible outcomes, worse-than-optimal children will not be born. This changes the game: Our ideal choice from the vast space of random possibilities now yields at most one (i.e. the best possible) descendant per individual per generation.

[6] Note that $t(x)$ cannot be compensated by other descendants of x' with possibly bad objective fitness since we assumed optimistic final productive fitness following Assumption 2.

the descendants that *could have been generated*. This allows us to compute a value for $\phi^\dagger$ for an already finished evolution.[7]

Note that the notion of final productive fitness is most powerful in the beginning of the evolutionary process, when it carries information about the whole evolution to come. Figures 3a and 3b provide a clear situation how final productive fitness is a better fitness function than the target function:

- The final productive fitness landscape has fewer valleys as its local optima correspond to individuals that remained in the final generation of some evolutionary process. This makes the landscape less deceptive and individuals are more clearly guided towards at least somewhat good results.
- The basins around the optima are wider, again making the local optimization towards the final result more clear.
- The differences between the global optimum and other local optima are more pronounced, giving an edge to the global optimum.

As discussed, if we could use final productive fitness during evolution, it would allow for better results. However, approximations of various quality may exist for specific problems or problem instances [8].

In Figs. 3c and 3d we can see how the final productive fitness landscapes deteriorates with the progressing evolution. As we can see from the red dots, evolution has focused on certain areas of the solution landscape, leaving wide areas without a meaningful final productive fitness to be computed. This effect is even more prominent in Figs. 3e and 3f, where individuals that are still randomly generated in certain areas die out rather quickly, leaving them with a productive fitness of 1. Note that productive fitness cannot meaningfully be computed for the last generation so we deliberately choose to show generation 49 last here.

Note how Fig. 3 also illustrates the usage of different evolutionary operators: For the Schwefel function, many individuals have a good final productive fitness when the evolution starts. That means they have direct descendants who manage to achieve nearly optimal target values. By contrast, H1 shows no individuals with good productive fitness in the beginning, meaning that the final results were mostly discovered via the migration operator *mig* as that is not traced by productive fitness.[8]

4   Related Work

We first introduced the gist of the formal framework for evolutionary processes as well as the notion of productive fitness in [8]. In this paper, we provide and discuss the full, substantially extended framework and introduce the assumptions and tools a proof design for productive fitness's validity can be built with.

Theoretical work on evolutionary algorithms has been traditionally focused on the complexity of the search process (on rather simple search problems) or

---

[7] For details on how this is done, please refer to [8].

[8] Migrants are generated randomly and are thus not ascribed to be any individual's descendant. How to include migrants in productive fitness is left for future work.

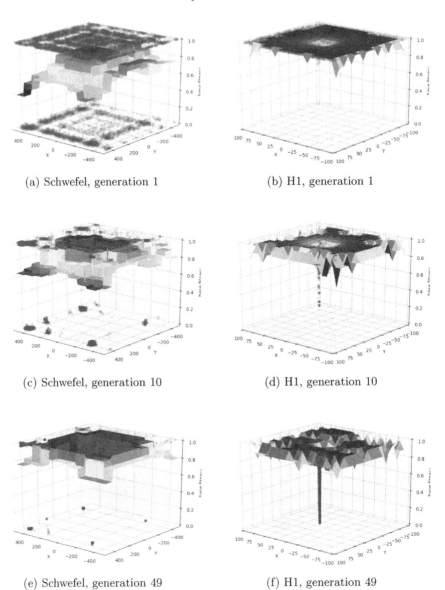

(a) Schwefel, generation 1

(b) H1, generation 1

(c) Schwefel, generation 10

(d) H1, generation 10

(e) Schwefel, generation 49

(f) H1, generation 49

Fig. 3. Individuals from 500 independent runs of the evolutionary processes plotted with their a posteriori approximated final productive fitness. The surface represents the same data set as the scatter points, where each tile has the Z value equal to the average Z value of all the points within it.

the performance of various types and variants of algorithms in general. We point to [4–6] for a few selective examples without any attempt at giving a full overview over this old and comprehensive field of research. By contrast, we fully work out the difference between a target function that is given from the outside world and a fitness function that (potentially) emerges implicitly throughout the process of evolution. As this concept in itself is rather novel, the constructs supporting it have been freshly developed as well (and are still in their infancy).

It should be pointed out that there probably exists a connection from the assumptions and approximations we make to a complexity-based analysis of evolution, as these tools allow us to rule out exponentially many options and thus bring the respective computation to a feasible level.[9]

Various meta-measurements of fitness in evolutionary algorithms have been designed. We would like to point out *effective fitness* [13], which describes the fitness threshold under which individuals can manage to increase their dominance in the population. This usually is a harsher border than *reproductive fitness* [11], which is the probability of an individual to successfully produce offspring. Both follow a similar line of thought of measuring what fitness an individual needs to have for certain effects to occur, but none suggest using the meta-measurement as a fitness value itself.

5   Conclusion

We have introduced and discussed a formal description of evolutionary processes that summarizes various kinds of evolutionary algorithms and other optimization techniques. Based on that framework, we defined the notion of productive fitness as it is defined in [8], where an argument was sketched why it might be the ideal fitness function. In this paper, we introduced the tools necessary to implement the proof, discussed their validity and thus gave the full proof design. We argue that while the approach is somewhat bold, the assumptions made could be useful for similar arguments about evolutionary processes and hope the perspective on fitness functions given here will open up new ways to reason about highly dynamic and uncertain processes, especially evolution.

We pointed out future work where we encountered open questions. We consider the connection suggested to traditional runtime analysis of evolutionary algorithms and subsequently to the No Free Lunch theorem [10] and how it related to the cases of having and using as well as finding and approximating the ideal fitness function to be especially promising. In addition, we suggest that it might be of particular relevance to also expand the scope of the framework beyond evolutionary algorithms; even the proof design might be adapted to not only work for fitness used by evolutionary operators but for example to deliver the ideal reward function for reinforcement learning [3,9].

---

[9] As no computational limit on biological evolution, e.g., has been recognized it could be an interesting endeavor to use the framework presented in this paper to translate arguments from runtime analysis of evolutionary algorithms back to a more general concept of evolution.

References

1. Brown, G., Wyatt, J., Harris, R., Yao, X.: Diversity creation methods: a survey and categorisation. Inf. Fusion **6**(1), 5–20 (2005)
2. DEAP Project: Benchmarks (2020). https://deap.readthedocs.io/en/master/api/benchmarks.html. Accessed June 1 2020
3. Dewey, D.: Reinforcement learning and the reward engineering principle. In: 2014 AAAI Spring Symposium Series (2014)
4. Doerr, B., Happ, E., Klein, C.: Crossover can provably be useful in evolutionary computation. Theoret. Comput. Sci. **425**, 17–33 (2012)
5. Droste, S., Jansen, T., Wegener, I.: On the analysis of the (1+1) evolutionary algorithm. Theoret. Comput. Sci. **276**(1–2), 51–81 (2002)
6. Friedrich, T., Oliveto, P.S., Sudholt, D., Witt, C.: Analysis of diversity-preserving mechanisms for global exploration. Evol. Comp. **17**(4), 455–476 (2009)
7. Gabor, T., Belzner, L., Linnhoff-Popien, C.: Inheritance-based diversity measures for explicit convergence control in evolutionary algorithms. In: Genetic and Evolutionary Computation Conference, pp. 841–848 (2018)
8. Gabor, T., Phan, T., Linnhoff-Popien, C.: Productive fitness in diversity-aware evolutionary algorithms (2021). (submitted)
9. Hadfield-Menell, D., Milli, S., Abbeel, P., Russell, S.J., Dragan, A.: Inverse reward design. In: Advances in Neural Information Processing Systems, pp. 6765–6774 (2017)
10. Ho, Y.C., Pepyne, D.L.: Simple explanation of the no free lunch theorem of optimization. In: 40th IEEE Conference on Decision and Control (Cat. No. 01CH37228), vol. 5, pp. 4409–4414. IEEE (2001)
11. Hu, T., Banzhaf, W.: Evolvability and speed of evolutionary algorithms in light of recent developments in biology. J. Artif. Evol. Appl. **2010**, 1 (2010)
12. Rainville, D., Fortin, F.A., Gardner, M.A., Parizeau, M., Gagné, C., et al.: Deap: a python framework for evolutionary algorithms. In: Conference Companion on Genetic and Evolutionary Computation, pp. 85–92. ACM (2012)
13. Stephens, C.R.: "Effective" fitness landscapes for evolutionary systems. In: 1999 Congress on Evolutionary Computation (CEC 1999), vol. 1, pp. 703–714. IEEE (1999)
14. Van Soest, A.K., Casius, L.R.: The merits of a parallel genetic algorithm in solving hard optimization problems. J. Biomech. Eng. **125**(1), 141–146 (2003)
15. Wineberg, M., Oppacher, F.: The underlying similarity of diversity measures used in evolutionary computation. In: Cantú-Paz, E., et al. (eds.) GECCO 2003. LNCS, vol. 2724, pp. 1493–1504. Springer, Heidelberg (2003). https://doi.org/10.1007/3-540-45110-2_21

A Case Study of Policy Synthesis for Swarm Robotics

Paul Piho[(✉)] and Jane Hillston

University of Edinburgh, Edinburgh, UK
paul.piho@ed.ac.uk

Abstract. Continuous time Markov chain models, derived from process algebraic descriptions of systems are a powerful method for studying the dynamics of collective adaptive systems. Here, we study a formal modelling framework, based on the CARMA process algebra, where information about the possible control actions of individual components in such systems can be incorporated in the process algebraic description. The formal semantics for such specifications are defined to give rise to continuous time Markov decision processes. Here we show how, together with a given specification of desired collective behaviour, such models can be readily treated as stochastic policy or control synthesis problems. This is demonstrated through an example scenario from swarm robotics.

1 Introduction

Computational modelling and simulation approaches provide a useful set of tools for studying complex dynamics of both man-made and natural collective systems. Various formal modelling approaches have been proposed to simplify the creation of such models. In particular stochastic process algebras with continuous time Markov chain (CTMC) semantics [3,14,18], have provided a powerful high-level framework for modelling collective systems, allowing compositional definitions of complex models and formal semantics for automation of model creation.

Process algebra-based models have been used to study a variety of phenomena in literature in order to better understand the processes involved or predict the real life performance of the system. Stochastic process algebras with underlying CTMC-based semantics lend themselves well to numerical or statistical analysis as well as various model-checking methods proposed over the years [15,16]. In the context of man-made or engineered systems the interesting questions often relate to policy or parameter synthesis problems. In particular, how the components in such systems should be designed so that a system level objective is achieved. The link between high-level process algebraic models and the related policy synthesis models is usually not made explicit. In this paper we present a swarm robotics-inspired case study where this connection is made explicit by incorporating the information about control actions or possible choice of parameters into the process algebraic description of the system.

© Springer Nature Switzerland AG 2020
T. Margaria and B. Steffen (Eds.): ISoLA 2020, LNCS 12477, pp. 491–506, 2020.
https://doi.org/10.1007/978-3-030-61470-6_29

We consider an existing stochastic process algebra CARMA [18] which has previously successfully been applied to a range of application domains like pedestrian movement [12], urban transportation services [25], availability of cloud services [20] and ambulance deployment [11]. The language features a set of communication primitives that, in conjunction with attribute-based filtering of communication partners, are capable of capturing a versatile set of communication behaviours. The set of communication primitives in CARMA correspond to broadcast and unicast, making it particularly suitable for open collectives where the participants of the communications cannot be known in advance.

The aim in this paper is to demonstrate through an example scenario from swarm robotics [7,19] that processes algebraic constructions in CARMA lend themselves well to stochastic policy or parameter synthesis problems. Swarm robots provide rich modelling examples in the context of collective systems, since the directly controllable behaviours and interactions are those of individual robots but the design goals for the systems are phrased in terms of the aggregate behaviour of the entire collective rather that of individual robots. To that end, CARMA can be equipped with continuous time Markov decision processes (CTMDPs) based semantics [22] providing a natural formalisation of policy synthesis problems and bridging the gap between the formal high-level modelling and policy synthesis problems for collectives such as robot swarms. The contribution of this paper is to illustrate these constructions with a case study and show how ideas from formal modelling and policy synthesis come together in a framework for stochastic control or parameter synthesis problems.

The paper is structured as follows. In Sect. 2, as background, we introduce the notions of CTMDPs and population CTMDPs. In Sect. 3 we give a brief overview of the CARMA-based modelling framework for policy synthesis through a simple example. In Sect. 4 we present the swarm robotics-inspired case study. Finally we end the paper with related work and conclusions in Sects. 5 and 6.

2   Background

The underlying mathematical model considered in this paper is a CTMDP. In particular, we consider a high-level formal modelling framework where the constructed models can be related to a CTMDP. To start let us give the definition of a CTMDP and introduce the related policy or parameter synthesis problems.

Definition 1. *A continuous-time Markov decision process (CTMDP) is defined by the tuple $\{\mathcal{S}, \mathcal{A}, q(i, j \mid a)\}$ where $\mathcal{S}$ is the countable set of states, $\mathcal{A}$ set of actions and $q(i, j \mid a)$ gives the transition rates $i \rightarrow j$ given the control action $a \in \mathcal{A}$. We use $\mathcal{A}(i)$ to denote the set of feasible actions in state i.*

The evolution of CTMDPs is described by the following: after the process reaches some state and an action is chosen, the process performs a transition to the next state depending only on the current state and the chosen action. The time it takes for state transitions to happen is governed by an exponential distribution with a rate given by the function q in Definition 1. The actions at every such step are chosen according to some policy as defined below.

Definition 2. *A policy is a measurable function $\psi : \mathbb{R}_{\geq 0} \times S \times A \to [0, 1]$ which for every time $t \in \mathbb{R}_{\geq 0}$, state $i \in S$ and action $a \in \mathcal{A}(i)$ assigns a probability $\psi(t, i, a)$ that the action a is chosen in i at time t. In other words, policy ψ defines a distribution over actions in any state of the CTMDP at time t. We call a policy where, for every $t \in \mathbb{R}_{\geq 0}$ and $i \in S$, we have that $\psi(t, i, a) \in \{0, 1\}$, a deterministic policy. A policy ψ independent of t is a stationary policy.*

Note that fixing a policy ψ resolves the non-determinism in the model and since the times that state transitions take are exponentially distributed the result is a continuous time Markov chain.

When we consider a system consisting of a large number of components with identical behaviours it is often convenient to consider a special case of CTMDPs.

Definition 3. *A population CTMDP (pCTMDP) is a tuple $(\mathbf{X}, \mathcal{T}, \mathcal{A}, \beta)$ where:*

- $\mathbf{X} = (X_1, \cdots, X_n) \in S = \mathbb{Z}_{\geq 0}^n$ *where each X_i takes values in a finite domain $\mathcal{D}_i \subset \mathbb{Z}_{\geq 0}$.*
- β *is a function such that $\beta(a, \mathbf{X})$ returns a boolean value indicating whether action $a \in \mathcal{A}$ is available from state $\mathbf{X}$.*
- $\mathcal{T}$ *is a set of transitions of the form $\tau = (a, \mathbf{v}_\tau, r_\tau(\mathbf{X}))$ such that $\beta(a, \mathbf{X}) = 1$, $\mathbf{v}_\tau$ is an update vector specifying that the state after execution of transition τ is $\mathbf{X} + \mathbf{v}_\tau$ and $r_\tau(\mathbf{X})$ is a rate function.*

In order to give semantics to the above definition of a population CTMDP we associate it with the equivalent CTMDP in the following way:

- the state and action space of the corresponding CTMDP is the same as for the population CTMDP.
- the set of feasible actions for state $\mathbf{i} \in S$, denoted $\mathcal{A}(\mathbf{i})$, is defined by

$$\mathcal{A}(\mathbf{i}) = \{a \in \mathcal{A} \mid \beta(a, \mathbf{i}) = 1\}.$$

- the rate function q is defined as

$$q(\mathbf{i}, \mathbf{j} \mid a) = \sum_{\tau \in \mathcal{T}, \tau = (a, \mathbf{v}_\tau, r_\tau(\mathbf{j})), \mathbf{i} = \mathbf{j} + \mathbf{v}_\tau} r_\tau(\mathbf{i}).$$

To form a policy synthesis problem for a given CTMDP we need a reward or a cost function which maps a chosen policy to a real value. A common approach for defining a reward function, for example, is as a function of the expected behaviour of the resulting CTMC.

3   CARMA-C for Policy Synthesis

CARMA [18] is a stochastic process algebra for quantitative modelling of collective adaptive systems. It supports the specification of complex stochastic behaviour, based on continuous time Markov chains, in a compositional way. In particular, each component in CARMA consists of a process definition P and a local store γ. CARMA models then consist of a collective N, composed of individual components or agents C, operating in an environment $\mathcal{E}$. This structure of CARMA models is illustrated in Fig. 1.

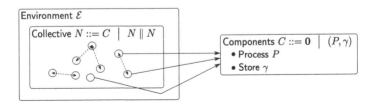

Fig. 1. Illustration of the structure of CARMA models.

The Function Labelled Transition Systems (FuTS) style operational semantics [10] of CARMA, as described in [18], give rise to a labelled transition system which can be simulated directly or translated into a CTMC for numerical analysis. The aim of this section is to introduce the extension CARMA-C [22] for specifying policy synthesis problems. The underlying CTMDP model allows us to specify non-deterministic behaviour, corresponding to different possible action choices, in a CARMA-C model. The approach is to incorporate the non-determinism into the store definitions. In CARMA each attribute in store refers to a single value that is used in the semantics, for example, to evaluate guards or filter communication partners. Instead, in CARMA-C we relax this construction and allow store attributes to refer to value domains which leads to non-determinism over a range of possible behaviours. Note that a parametric CTMC would be another reasonable choice for the underlying semantics that account for non-determinism. The semantics of the languages would not change much in that case as the construction of the parameter space of a CTMC from the high-level model description is analogous to the construction of the action space.

In the following we describe CARMA-C and as a running example present the model for the case study in Sect. 4.1. This example model is outlined below.

Example 1. The model considers a simple robot swarm where an exploration phase is modelled by a random walk on the graph structure in Fig. 2. The swarm attempts to discover and gather at the target location (x, y). This is modelled by an exploration followed by an aggregation phase. The switch between the two phases happens via broadcast communication. When any single robot detects the target at (x, y) it broadcasts this knowledge to the rest of the swarm.

Fig. 2. Spatial structure for the example.

3.1 Local Store

Let us start by considering the local stores of components. The local store is used to hold the attributes of an individual component. For example, a location attribute of a component can be used to implement communication within a given range. CARMA and CARMA-C differ in their treatment of the local store—in CARMA-C we use the store attributes to also specify the action space of the underlying CTMDP. By associating each attribute in a store with a value domain rather than a single value, we introduce the non-determinism required to establish an action space. Here, the local store of each of the robots can be defined to hold attributes for location, denoted loc, set of known target locations, denoted target. The robustness parameter, succp, taking values in the interval $[0, 1]$, models how reliably the robots move when navigating towards a target.

$$\gamma_l = \{\text{loc} \mapsto \{(0,0)\}, \text{target} \mapsto \{\emptyset\}, \text{succp} \mapsto [0, 1]\}$$

The location loc and target target are defined to have singleton value domains consisting of pair $(0,0)$ and the empty set respectively. The robustness parameter succp on the other hand takes values in the real interval $[0, 1]$.

In the semantics of CARMA-C the available control actions in the underlying CTMDP are associated with the possible ways we can refine the defined store to correspond to single values from the defined value domains. In particular, a control action f from a state of the CARMA-C system resolves all non-determinism in the descriptions. As an example, we can suppose that a given control action f applied to γ_l gives the following: $f(\gamma_l) = \{\text{loc} \mapsto (0,0), \text{target} \mapsto \emptyset, \text{succp} \mapsto 0.7\}$. This control action results in a local store of a component at location $(0,0)$ with no known targets. The parameter succp, when a target is known, captures the probability of the component successfully moving towards it.

3.2 Processes

Next let us consider the process definitions P. The processes are composed of action primitives corresponding to input and output actions for broadcast and unicast communication. Note that broadcast in CARMA is non-blocking—the output action is executed even if there is no component able to receive the message. Unicast on the other hand is blocking. Unicast output is denoted by $\alpha^* [\pi_s] \langle e \rangle \sigma$ while unicast input is denoted by $\alpha [\pi_s] \langle e \rangle \sigma$. Similarly broadcast output is denoted by $\alpha^* [\pi_s] \langle e \rangle \sigma$ while broadcast input is denoted by $\alpha^* [\pi_r] (\boldsymbol{x}) \sigma$.

The following notation is used

- α is an action type which is used to distinguish between different actions.
- π_s, π_r, π denote boolean predicates that have to be satisfied before the action can be executed. As mentioned previously, the communication in CARMA and CARMA-C is attribute-based—guards are used to filter out communication partners based on attributes such as location or communication range.
- e is an expression built using appropriate combinations of values, attributes and variables. In the semantics, the expressions are evaluated over the sending component's local store and passed on to the receiving component.
- x is a variable which takes on the values that were communicated to the receiving process by the sender.
- σ is a function from $\Gamma \rightarrow Dist(\Gamma)$ where $Dist(\Gamma)$ is the set of distributions over the set of possible stores Γ. The function σ thus denotes a store *update* and defines how the given store is changed as a result of an action.

The processes are composed via the standard constructs—action prefix (.), choice (+), and parallel composition ($\|$). The behaviour of processes can be further modified by setting guards on processes. As an example, we can consider the following processes that we use to model the scenario in Example 1.

$$Explore \stackrel{\text{def}}{=} [\pi_r]random^*[\circ]\langle\circ\rangle\{\textsf{loc} \mapsto R(\textsf{loc})\}.Explore$$
$$+ [\pi_d]directed^*[\circ]\langle\circ\rangle\{\textsf{loc} \mapsto D(\textsf{loc})\}.Explore$$
$$+ [\pi_r]sense^*[\circ]\langle\textsf{loc}\rangle\{\textsf{target} \mapsto \textsf{target} \cup \{\textsf{loc}\}\}.Explore$$
$$Listen \stackrel{\text{def}}{=} [\pi_r]sense^*[\circ](\{(x,y)\})\{\textsf{target} \mapsto \textsf{target} \cup \{(x,y)\}\}.Listen$$
$$Robot \stackrel{\text{def}}{=} Explore \parallel Listen$$

Our example can then be modelled by the processes illustrated in Fig. 3. The broadcast actions $random^*$ and $directed^*$ describe a random walk and a directed walk towards (x,y) respectively. Despite being defined as broadcast actions, neither of these actions have any effect on the other robots in the collective because the outgoing message is set to be empty. The guards π_r and π_d check whether the target location is known or not and make sure only one of the actions $random^*$ and $directed^*$ is enabled at a time. The guards are evaluated conditionally on a chosen control action f in the following way.

$$\pi_r = \begin{cases} true & \text{if } f(\gamma)(\textsf{target}) = \emptyset. \\ false & \text{otherwise.} \end{cases} \qquad \pi_d = \begin{cases} true & \text{if } f(\gamma)(\textsf{target}) = \{(x,y)\}. \\ false & \text{otherwise.} \end{cases}$$

The $sense^*$ action models the detection of the target location. In particular, the broadcast output action models the robot detecting and sending the target location to the rest of the swarm. The corresponding broadcast input action models the robot's ability to receive such a message.

The actions $random^*$ and $directed^*$ change the loc attribute of the robot component according to functions R and D respectively. The (random) function

Fig. 3. Behaviour of individual *Robot* components.

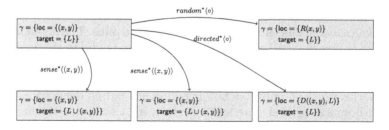

Fig. 4. Local component store changes induced by actions.

R corresponds to the next location being selected uniformly from the set of available next locations defined by the graph structure in Fig. 2. Similarly, D corresponds to the next location taking the robot closer to the target with some probability p, specified by the robustness attribute succp, and to one of the other directly connected locations with probability $1 - p$. This defines a distribution over the possible unresolved local stores the components can evolve to and models unreliable navigation. The *sense** action updates the set of target locations with the current location of the sending robot.

The functions R, D as well as the set operation $\cup$ are applied element-wise to all elements in the relevant value domains as illustrated in Fig. 4. For example, consider the update loc $\mapsto R(\text{loc})$. This means that the function R is applied to every element in the value domain for loc. The store update for a given initial store are illustrated in Fig. 4.

3.3 Environment

Finally we are going to address the environment. An environment is defined by a *global store* γ_g that models the overall state of the system and an *evolution rule* ρ. The global store is defined similarly to the local store. To continue the example, we define two global store variables—one corresponding to the rate at which the actions *random** and *directed** happen, denoted mover. We specify the value domain for this variable to be $[0, \infty)$. Similarly, we specify the value domain for the store attribute senser, corresponding to the rate of the action *sense**, to be $[0, \infty)$. Finally, we specify an attribute that keeps track of the location of the target. In particular,

$$\gamma_g = \{\text{mover} \mapsto [0, \infty), \text{senser} \mapsto [0, \infty), \text{tloc} \mapsto \{(1, 1)\}\}.$$

The evolution rule gives, depending on the *current time*, the global store and the current state of the collective, and a control action f, a tuple of functions $\varepsilon = \langle \mu_p, \mu_w, \mu_r, \mu_u \rangle$ called the *evaluation context*. The functions μ_p and μ_w depend on the activity type α and the stores of the sender (γ_s) and receiver (γ_r) and determine the probabilities for eligible receivers to receive a message corresponding to an output action α. In the case of μ_p, the function gives a probability of a broadcast message being received successfully. In contrast μ_w deals with the unicast communication and returns a weight value. The probability of a given receiver receiving the message is obtained by normalising the weight with respect to the sum of weights of all possible receivers. The functions μ_r and μ_u depend on the activity type and the sender store. The function μ_r determines the rate with which a given output action is performed and μ_u defines the updates on the environment (global store and collective) induced by the action.

In our example, suppose f denotes the action chosen at time t and let γ_s and γ_r denote the sender and receiver store respectively. Firstly, we define

$$\mu_p(f(\gamma_s), f(\gamma_r), sense^*) = 1 \qquad \text{for all stores } \gamma_s \text{ and } \gamma_r.$$

In particular, a broadcast message is received with probability 1 by all eligible receivers. There are no unicast actions in this model so the definition of μ_w is trivial. Supposing $f(\gamma_g)(\mathsf{mover}) = r_m$, $f(\gamma_g)(\mathsf{senser}) = r_s$ we can say that the rates of the actions are given as follows.

$$\mu_r(f(\gamma), random^*) = \mu_r(f(\gamma), directed^*) = r_m \qquad \text{for all local stores } \gamma$$

$$\mu_r(f(\gamma), sense^*) = \begin{cases} r_s & \text{for all local stores } \gamma \text{ such that } f(\gamma)(\mathsf{loc}) = f(\gamma_g)(\mathsf{tloc}) \\ 0 & \text{otherwise} \end{cases}$$

Thus, the *sense** action, in this case, is only possible from the location $(1,1)$. The global store definitions and the composition of the collective do not change so μ_u is again trivial. This completes the description of the CARMA-C model.

3.4   System

As mentioned, a CARMA-C system is composed of a collective of components operating in an environment. For the running example we define the robot components as a pair composed of process description and a store $(Robot, \gamma_l)$. Finally we consider a collective of N robots denoted $(Robot, \gamma_l)[N]$ in (γ_g, ρ).

Further details on the decision process semantics are omitted here due to space constraints and can be found in [22]. We simply note that the state of the pCTMDP corresponding to the described CARMA-C model are represented by one counting variable for each considered location. The set of feasible actions in each state corresponds to the choices of the mover, senser and succp attribute values from the sets $[0, \infty)$, $[0, \infty)$ and $[0, 1]$ respectively. The value domains of the remaining attributes are trivial to resolve being defined as singleton sets.

4 Case Study

4.1 Stationary Target

In the previous section we gave the CARMA-C model of the robot swarm example. In this section we explore this model further. To start we describe the CTMDP model that arises if appropriately chosen semantics are applied. As discussed in Sect. 2 it is often useful to consider the population structure of the model.

The process state of the robots does not change throughout the evolution. Thus, the only part of each component's state that changes is the location attribute. Let us denote the state space of the pCTMDP by the counting variables

$$\mathbf{X} = (X_{01}, X_{00}, X_{10}, X_{11}, X_{01}^{11}, X_{00}^{11}, X_{10}^{11}, X_{11}^{11})$$

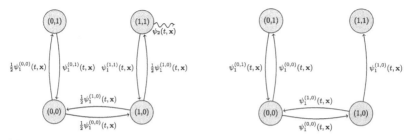

(a) Before broadcast – random walk   (b) After broadcast – directed walk

Fig. 5. Behaviour of individuals in the swarm model with 4 locations under some deterministic policy ψ.

where X_{ij} denotes the count of robots at location (i, j) that do not know the target location while X_{ij}^{11} denotes the count of robots at location (i, j) that know that the target location is $(1, 1)$.

The rates with which the actions are performed are linked to the global store variables mover and senser that are only specified through their value domains. This corresponds to the first part of the action space for the pCTMDP—at each state of the model we need to specify the particular values to be used for mover and senser. The second part of the action space corresponds to the local succp attribute. For each location we have to specify the value of succp from the interval $[0, 1]$. A policy, following the definition given in Sect. 2, is a function

$$\psi : \mathbb{R}_{\geq 0} \times \mathbb{Z}_{\geq 0}^8 \times \mathbb{R}_{\geq 0}^2 \times [0, 1]^8 \to [0, 1]$$

assigning a probability for each of the possible combinations of attributes mover, senser and succp for each time $t \in \mathbb{R}_{\geq 0}$ and state $\mathbf{x} \in \mathbb{Z}_{\geq 0}^8$. Remember, that the choice of succp has to be made for each location giving rise to four copies of $[0, 1]$ in the signature of the function. The above corresponds to the non-trivial parts of the policies ψ. To give a perfectly precise description according to the semantics the policy would also have to assign values for each of the loc and target attributes. However, as explained, the value domains for these remain singleton sets throughout the evolutions and thus the choice of policy with respect to those attributes is trivial. Denote the resulting space of probability distributions by Π. In the following we are going to consider deterministic policies such that

$$\psi : \mathbb{R}_{\geq 0} \times \mathbb{Z}_{\geq 0}^8 \times \mathbb{R}_{\geq 0}^2 \times [0,1]^8 \to \{0,1\}.$$

Application of a policy ψ to the pCTMDP corresponding to the model gives us behaviours of individual robots as given in Fig. 5. We have denoted by $\psi_1^{(i,j)}(t, \mathbf{x})$ the rate of robots moving out of location (i, j) at time t given the population state $\mathbf{x}$ under the deterministic policy ψ. Similarly, $\psi_2(t, \mathbf{x})$ denotes the rate of sensing and broadcasting the message about the target.

Policy Synthesis. In this section we are going to restrict the space of policies Ψ to those that are stationary, or in other words, not dependent on time. However, instead of having policies that map each state of the population to the same fixed value, we are going to model the situation where the movement rate of the robots decreases as the density in a given location increases. Congestion or interference is a common problem in swarm robotics that usually leads to degraded performance [17,21,24]. This happens especially in the cases where robots are moving towards a common target region and have to compete for available space. For this example we are considering one possible way to capture such effects on the swarm behaviour.

In order to model the congestion effects we are going to construct the policy ψ so that some maximum movement rate r_m, given by the global store attribute mover, of robots is multiplied by the exponential $e^{-a \times \frac{x}{N}}$ where x denotes the population density at the given location. In particular, the rate of movement out of location (i, j) under policy ψ becomes $\psi_1^{(i,j)}(t, \mathbf{x}) = r_m e^{-a \times \frac{x_{ij}}{N}}$, where x_{ij} is the population density at location (i, j). Such exponential degradation of the performance of individual robots in a swarm was reported, for example, in [17]. The constant a controls how fast the rate of movement decreases with the increase in number of robots in a given location. The higher values of a correspond to more severe effects of congestion. The meaning of this model would be that if the entire swarm is in the same location the congestion has the effect of approximately halving the rate of movement.[1]

In the context of the running example we consider the synthesis of the succp parameter. That is, how robust the behaviour of the robots should be for the collective to satisfy its goal. We consider the following objective: with probability greater than 0.9, 80% of the swarm reach the target location $(1, 1)$ in the finite time interval $[0, 10]$. We will refer to this as Obj_1.

---

[1] Note that the above construction could equivalently be done directly in the definition of the rates of *random*∗ and *directed*∗ actions.

4.2   Moving Target

In this section we are going to propose and study an extension to the model considered in Sect. 4.1. In particular, there we assumed that the target location remains the same throughout the evolution of the system. We extend the model by considering a target whose location will change over time. To achieve that we add an extra component, named *Target* to the system. Suppose the initial state of its local store is $\gamma^{targ} = \{\text{loc} \mapsto \{(1,1)\}\}$. For the movement we are going to define the following process

$$Move \stackrel{\text{def}}{=} [\pi_{mt}]move^*[\circ]\langle\circ\rangle\{\text{loc} \mapsto K(\text{loc})\}.Move$$

where K maps locations $(1,1) \mapsto (1,2)$. The guard π_{mt} is defined to stop the target after reaching location $(1,2)$. A simple way to model that after the target has moved to a different location the robots have to look for it again is to suppose that the robots also have a process that defines the broadcast input action corresponding to $move^*$.

$$ListenT \stackrel{\text{def}}{=} move^*[\circ](\circ)\{\text{target} \mapsto \{\emptyset\}\}.ListenT$$

$$Robot \stackrel{\text{def}}{=} (Explore \parallel Listen \parallel ListenT, \gamma)$$

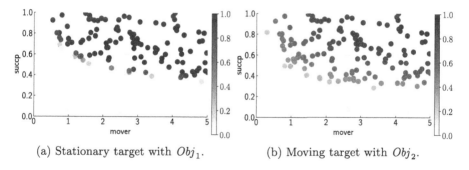

(a) Stationary target with Obj_1.   (b) Moving target with Obj_2.

Fig. 6. Probability of success with both mover and succp varying. Constant a fixed to 0.7.

In particular, when the target location changes the robots immediately know that their current set of target locations is no longer valid. To complete the extension we need to define the rate at which the target moves and the probability with which the broadcast resulting from $move^*$ is received. In our example we set the rate of $move^*$ to 0.05 and assume that all robots will be aware of when the target has left its current location. Finally, the global store update for action $move^*$ changes the value domain for the attribute tloc to correspond to the location of the target component. This ensures that after the target moves the sense actions will be available only from the new location of the target. The rest of the model remains the same. The objective, denoted Obj_2, for the new scenario is the following: with probability greater that 0.9, 80% of the swarm reach the target locations while the target is there, in the finite time interval $[0,30]$.

4.3   Simulation Results

In both of the described models we have left the exact values of succp and mover unspecified. The third parameter in the model descriptions is the congestion parameter a. This parameter would in general relate to the physical size of the considered location, size of the robots and their collision avoidance behaviour. For this simulation analysis we are going to simplify the situation by considering a range of 21 equally spaced values in the interval $[0.5, 0.9]$ and see how the results to the policy synthesis problems change with these values. Similarly, for each value of the congestion parameter we consider 10 classes of policies with each keeping the movement rate attribute mover constant in the interval $[0.0, 5.0]$.

For each class of policies where the constant a and rate attribute mover are kept constant we are going to vary the values of succp. We treat the policy synthesis problem as a logistic regression problem, aiming to separate the values succp based on whether the objectives would be satisfied or not. This is done by sampling values of succp and simulating the CTMC dynamics resulting from

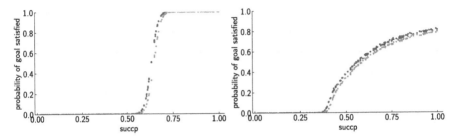

(a) Satisfying Obj_1 for the stationary target example.

(b) Satisfying Obj_2 for the moving target example.

Fig. 7. Probability of success with fixed mover $= 1.0$ and varying succp. Blue results correspond to congestion parameter set to 0.5 while red results correspond to congestion parameter 0.9. (Color figure online)

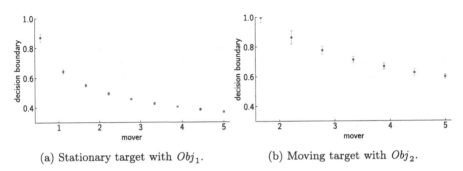

(a) Stationary target with Obj_1.

(b) Moving target with Obj_2.

Fig. 8. Changes in the decision boundary for logistic regression as mover changes. Points indicate the mean over the tested values of congestion constant a with error bars indicating the range of values acquired.

fixing a policy of the constructed models. This is akin to works on parameter synthesis which aim to find the regions of the parameter space where a given specification is satisfied [5,6,9].

The approach for this is standard: consider a linear function $y = w_0 + w_1 p$ of single explanatory variable (in this case value of succp, denoted p) and a logistic function $\sigma(r) = 1/(1 + e^{-w_0 - w_1 p})$ where $\sigma(p)$ is interpreted as the probability of success given succp value p. We are going to expect the goal to be satisfied if $\sigma(p) > 0.5$. The weights for the regression model are going to be fitted based on trajectories sampled using stochastic simulation for 200 random succp values. For each of the resulting 42000 parametrisations of the model we generated 5000 trajectories using Gillespie's algorithm. Based on these trajectories we estimated the satisfaction probability for the defined objectives. Currently, the tools for CARMA do not support the non-deterministic specifications described here. In this paper the structure of the models as well as the policies are relatively simple and for each choice of policy (or parametrisation) of the model we can readily construct a chemical reaction network model that captures the behaviour of the CARMA-C model. These models were constructed and simulated with the DifferentialEquations.jl [23] package for the Julia programming language which includes methods for specifying chemical reaction networks and implements stochastic simulation algorithms for simulating the underlying CTMC.

Figure 6 shows the empirical success probabilities for a fixed value of parameter $a = 0.7$. We can see that for the simpler model with stationary target there is a quicker transition from not satisfying the objective to satisfying the objective as either of the succp or mover parameters are increased. For the example with the moving target this transition is more gradual. This observation is confirmed by Fig. 7 where both the constant a and the rate of movement mover are kept constant while varying the attribute succp. In the case of the moving target example we see that setting the movement rate of the robots to 1.0 means the defined objective will not be satisfied. In both cases varying the parameter a within the rage $[0.5, 0.9]$ does not have a large effect on whether the objective can be satisfied. Finally, Fig. 8 presents the results of the logistic regression being performed on the simulation data. Unsurprisingly the effect of varying the congestion constant gives a more pronounced effect on the decision boundaries for the logistic regression. Similarly, the stationary target scenario is more robust to unreliable navigation by the robots. The decision boundary for the stationary target falls below 0.5 for faster robot components. This is due to robots not moving out of the target's location when the location is known.

Finally, we make a note about the computational difficulty of treating such problems. Even for the relatively simple problems presented here, the computation time becomes large. The multi-threaded (16 threads) sampling of trajectories for the fixed policies took 5.9 h in total for the stationary target example while the moving target simulations took about 11.4 h.

5   Related Works

There exists a large body of work on CTMDPs both from the model checking and optimisation perspectives. CTMDP models incorporate non-determinism in the model description which is usually interpreted as possible control actions that can be taken from a given state of the system. The model checking approaches seek to verify whether or not a CTMDP satisfies the requirements for a given class of policies. These commonly deal with time-bounded reachability [1,8]. The optimisation perspective is to find a policy which maximises some utility or minimises a cost function. In both cases the core issue is scalability; statistical or simulation-based approaches offer a set of tools feasible for complex systems of collective behaviour [2,4]. An alternative interpretation would be to consider the non-determinism as being uncertainty about parts of the system's behaviour. In the context of process algebras this idea has been considered in [13] to integrate data and uncertainty into formal quantitative models in a meaningful way.

6   Conclusion

In this paper we have presented a swarm robotics-inspired case study which presents a framework fitting together ideas from formal modelling and policy synthesis. In particular, we described a model expressed in the CARMA-C language equipped with CTMDP semantics and set up a simple policy synthesis problem where parameters can be changed or controlled. The semantics of the language presented does not discriminate against more complex cases like time-dependent or probabilistic policies. With an appropriate choice of policy space we could, for example, consider scenarios where the movement rate of the robots further degrades with time. This makes the considered framework a powerful modelling tool for stochastic control problems for collective systems. However, as seen, the statistical and simulation based approaches considered here, while in general more scalable than exact methods, are already becoming time-consuming for relatively simple problems. For the examples in this paper we may be able to decrease the number of evaluated policies for reasonable estimates but further work on approximate methods on policy synthesis for the models is of interest to reduce computational burden and allow dealing with complex policies.

References

1. Baier, C., Hermanns, H., Katoen, J., Haverkort, B.R.: Efficient computation of time-bounded reachability probabilities in uniform continuous-time Markov decision processes. Theor. Comput. Sci. **345**(1), 2–26 (2005)
2. Bartocci, E., Bortolussi, L., Brázdil, T., Milios, D., Sanguinetti, G.: Policy learning in continuous-time Markov decision processes using Gaussian processes. Perform. Eval. **116**, 84–100 (2017)
3. Bernardo, M., Gorrieri, R.: Extended Markovian process algebra. In: Montanari, U., Sassone, V. (eds.) CONCUR 1996. LNCS, vol. 1119, pp. 315–330. Springer, Heidelberg (1996). https://doi.org/10.1007/3-540-61604-7_63

4. Bortolussi, L., Milios, D., Sanguinetti, G.: Smoothed model checking for uncertain continuous-time Markov chains. Inf. Comput. **247**, 235–253 (2016)
5. Bortolussi, L., Policriti, A., Silvetti, S.: Logic-based multi-objective design of chemical reaction networks. In: Cinquemani, E., Donzé, A. (eds.) HSB 2016. LNCS, vol. 9957, pp. 164–178. Springer, Cham (2016). https://doi.org/10.1007/978-3-319-47151-8_11
6. Bortolussi, L., Silvetti, S.: Bayesian statistical parameter synthesis for linear temporal properties of stochastic models. In: Beyer, D., Huisman, M. (eds.) TACAS 2018. LNCS, vol. 10806, pp. 396–413. Springer, Cham (2018). https://doi.org/10.1007/978-3-319-89963-3_23
7. Brambilla, M., Brutschy, A., Dorigo, M., Birattari, M.: Property-driven design for robot swarms: a design method based on prescriptive modeling and model checking. ACM Trans. Auton. Adapt. Syst. **9**(4), 17:1–17:28 (2014)
8. Butkova, Y., Hatefi, H., Hermanns, H., Krčál, J.: Optimal continuous time Markov decisions. In: Finkbeiner, B., Pu, G., Zhang, L. (eds.) ATVA 2015. LNCS, vol. 9364, pp. 166–182. Springer, Cham (2015). https://doi.org/10.1007/978-3-319-24953-7_12
9. Češka, M., Dannenberg, F., Paoletti, N., Kwiatkowska, M., Brim, L.: Precise parameter synthesis for stochastic biochemical systems. Acta Informatica **54**(6), 589–623 (2016). https://doi.org/10.1007/s00236-016-0265-2
10. De Nicola, R., Latella, D., Loreti, M., Massink, M.: A uniform definition of stochastic process calculi. ACM Comput. Surv. **46**(1), 5:1–5:35 (2013)
11. Galpin, V.: Modelling ambulance deployment with CARMA. In: Lluch Lafuente, A., Proença, J. (eds.) COORDINATION 2016. LNCS, vol. 9686, pp. 121–137. Springer, Cham (2016). https://doi.org/10.1007/978-3-319-39519-7_8
12. Galpin, V., Zon, N., Wilsdorf, P., Gilmore, S.: Mesoscopic modelling of pedestrian movement using CARMA and its tools. ACM Trans. Model. Comput. Simul. **28**(2), 1–26 (2018)
13. Georgoulas, A., Hillston, J., Milios, D., Sanguinetti, G.: Probabilistic programming process algebra. In: Norman, G., Sanders, W. (eds.) QEST 2014. LNCS, vol. 8657, pp. 249–264. Springer, Cham (2014). https://doi.org/10.1007/978-3-319-10696-0_21
14. Hillston, J.: A Compositional Approach to Performance Modelling. Cambridge University Press, New York (1996)
15. Kwiatkowska, M., Norman, G., Parker, D.: PRISM: probabilistic symbolic model checker. In: Field, T., Harrison, P.G., Bradley, J., Harder, U. (eds.) TOOLS 2002. LNCS, vol. 2324, pp. 200–204. Springer, Heidelberg (2002). https://doi.org/10.1007/3-540-46029-2_13
16. Legay, A., Delahaye, B., Bensalem, S.: Statistical model checking: an overview. In: Barringer, H., et al. (eds.) RV 2010. LNCS, vol. 6418, pp. 122–135. Springer, Heidelberg (2010). https://doi.org/10.1007/978-3-642-16612-9_11
17. Lerman, K., Galstyan, A.: Mathematical model of foraging in a group of robots: effect of interference. Auton. Robots **13**(2), 127–141 (2002). https://doi.org/10.1023/A:1019633424543
18. Loreti, M., Hillston, J.: Modelling and analysis of collective adaptive systems with CARMA and its tools. In: Bernardo, M., De Nicola, R., Hillston, J. (eds.) SFM 2016. LNCS, vol. 9700, pp. 83–119. Springer, Cham (2016). https://doi.org/10.1007/978-3-319-34096-8_4
19. Luckcuck, M., Farrell, M., Dennis, L.A., Dixon, C., Fisher, M.: Formal specification and verification of autonomous robotic systems: a survey. ACM Comput. Surv. **52**(5), 1–14 (2019)

20. Lv, H., Hillston, J., Piho, P., Wang, H.: An attribute-based availability model for large scale IaaS clouds with CARMA. IEEE Trans. Parallel Distrib. Syst. **31**(3), 733–748 (2020)

21. Soriano Marcolino, L., Tavares dos Passos, Y., Fonseca de Souza, Á.A., dos Santos Rodrigues, A., Chaimowicz, L.: Avoiding target congestion on the navigation of robotic swarms. Auton. Robots **41**(6), 1297–1320 (2016). https://doi.org/10.1007/s10514-016-9577-x

22. Piho, P., Hillston, J.: Policy synthesis for collective dynamics. In: McIver, A., Horvath, A. (eds.) QEST 2018. LNCS, vol. 11024, pp. 356–372. Springer, Cham (2018). https://doi.org/10.1007/978-3-319-99154-2_22

23. Rackauckas, C., Nie, Q.: DifferentialEquations.jl – a performant and feature-rich ecosystem for solving differential equations in Julia. J. Open Res. Softw. **5**, 15 (2017)

24. Schroeder, A., Trease, B., Arsie, A.: Balancing robot swarm cost and interference effects by varying robot quantity and size. Swarm Intell. **13**(1), 1–19 (2018). https://doi.org/10.1007/s11721-018-0161-1

25. Zon, N., Gilmore, S.: Data-driven modelling and simulation of urban transportation systems using CARMA. In: Margaria, T., Steffen, B. (eds.) ISoLA 2018, Part III. LNCS, vol. 11246, pp. 274–287. Springer, Cham (2018). https://doi.org/10.1007/978-3-030-03424-5_18

Maple-Swarm: Programming Collective Behavior for Ensembles by Extending HTN-Planning

Oliver Kosak$^{(\boxtimes)}$, Lukas Huhn, Felix Bohn, Constantin Wanninger,
Alwin Hoffmann, and Wolfgang Reif

Institute for Software and Systems Engineering at the University of Augsburg,
Universitätsstraße 2, 86159 Augsburg, Germany
kosak@isse.de

Abstract. Programming goal-oriented behavior in collective adaptive
systems is complex, requires high effort, and is failure-prone. If the system's user wants to deploy it in a real-world environment, hurdles get
even higher: Programs urgently require to be situation-aware. With our
framework Maple, we previously presented an approach for easing the
act of programming such systems on the level of particular robot capabilities. In this paper, we extend our approach for ensemble programming
with the possibility to address virtual swarm capabilities encapsulating
collective behavior to whole groups of agents. By using the respective
concepts in an extended version of hierarchical task networks and by
adapting our self-organization mechanisms for executing plans resulting
thereof, we can achieve that all agents, any agent, any other set of agents,
or a swarm of agents execute (swarm) capabilities. Moreover, we extend
the possibilities of expressing situation awareness during planning by
introducing planning variables that can get modified at design-time or
run-time as needed. We illustrate the possibilities with examples each.
Further, we provide a graphical front-end offering the possibility to generate mission-specific problem domain descriptions for ensembles including
a light-weight simulation for validating plans.

Keywords: Task orchestration · HTN-Planning · Swarm behavior ·
Robot swarms · Multi-agent systems · Multipotent systems

1 Motivation

The range of versatile applications for collective adaptive systems and especially for multi-robot systems steadily increased during the last years due to the
potential benefits these applications can deliver for research, our daily life, or
society in general. We can find examples that already profit from this development everywhere, e.g., for research in space exploration [18] or meteorological
science [4,13,22], for autonomous search and rescue in major catastrophe scenarios [2,15], among many others. One crucial hurdle that every application needs to

---

Partially funded by DFG (German Research Foundation), grant number 402956354.

T. Margaria and B. Steffen (Eds.): ISoLA 2020, LNCS 12477, pp. 507–524, 2020.
https://doi.org/10.1007/978-3-030-61470-6_30

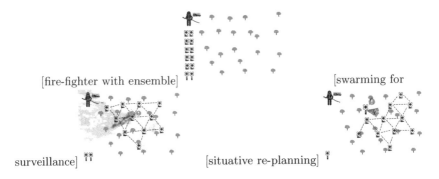

[fire-fighter with ensemble]

[swarming for

surveillance]

[situative re-planning]

Fig. 1. Fire-fighter orchestrating an ensemble to deal with a forest fire scenario.

take before a user can actually profit from it is that of proper task-orchestration for the collective. Unfortunately, the current trend is that instead of aiming for a generic solution for that problem, every single new application requires a new software approach for its realization [3,9]. Besides varying hardware require-ments [21], the often high complexity of performing specific goal-oriented task orchestration and planning for such ensembles hinders the reuse of previously successfully applied approaches for a broader set of applications. Achieving a general approach becomes even more complex as tasks show a high versatility or the user requires the ensemble to act in different problem domains. With our approach Maple [12], we already developed a task orchestration and execution framework for multipotent robot ensembles [15] having the potential to fill that gap. In multipotent systems, robot ensembles being homogeneous at design time can become heterogeneous concerning their capabilities at run-time by combin-ing physical reconfiguration on the hardware level with self-awareness [10].

In this paper, we demonstrate how we extend our approach to *Maple-Swarm* for supporting the operation of whole collectives by introducing the concepts of *agent groups* and virtual *swarm capabilities*. Swarm capabilities encapsulate collective behavior, where the local interaction of individuals provides useful emergent effects on the ensemble level, e.g., for distributing in an area with a potential field algorithm [20] or searching for the highest concentration of a parameter with an adapted particle swarm optimization algorithm [23]. We assume that we can alternate the specific swarm behavior with different param-eters for the swarm capability like we present in [11]. To integrate these new concepts, we adapt to how we perform the designing, task planning, and task allocation process of Maple. In Maple-Swarm, we further extend the concept of hierarchical task networks (HTN) [6] we use for defining partial plans for specific situations and for generating situation-aware plans with automated planning at run-time. With agent groups, addressing *all agents, any agent, a set of agents,* or a *swarm of agents*, we extend the flexibility the multipotent system has for executing tasks. We thereby further increase the autonomy of multipotent robot ensembles that can choose which concrete agents adopt the respective roles at run-time in a self-organized manner while still preserving the possibility for the user to keep control over actions of particular robots, when necessary.

The running example we use for illustration purposes assumes a fire-fighter requiring to handle a forest fire scenario (cf. Fig. 1). Within a defined area, fires may ignite spontaneously. The fire-fighter needs to instruct its available ensemble of mobile robots to move to that area, continuously observe it, identify new fires, and extinguish them as fast as possible. Because of the size of the area, the high amount of robots available, and other urgent tasks only a human can accomplish, it is not always a feasible option for the fire-fighter to manually define routes for all robots or to react ad-hoc to newly identified fires. Instead, the fire-fighter wants to specify how the ensemble should react in different situations on an abstract level and let the system act appropriately and as autonomously as possible. Then, the system should decide on what to do according to its current state and that of the environment, e.g., by applying useful collective behavior.

The remainder of the paper is structured as follows. In Sect. 5 we subsume approaches for solving the problem of task orchestration for ensembles. In Sect. 2, we briefly reflect on the current state of Maple and its integration in our reference architecture for multipotent systems and illustrate our objectives. In Sect. 3, we propose our solution Maple-Swarm. In Sect. 4 we demonstrate the functionality of our approach for the firefighter scenario as proof of concepts. In Sect. 6 we conclude our findings and point out possible future research challenges.

2   Current State and Objectives

In multipotent systems, we generally differentiate between the *user device* and the *multipotent ensemble* consisting of multiple agents implementing a layered software architecture (cf. Fig. 2). The user device offers the possibility for designing problem domain definitions and thereby acts as an interface to the multipotent ensemble. The different layers each agent in the multipotent ensemble implements encapsulate their own functionality and communication pattern.

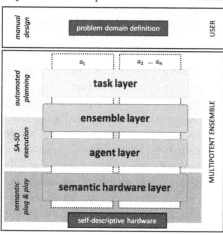

Fig. 2. Simplified multipotent systems reference architecture for ensembles from [10].

On the lowest layer, we enable hardware access to self-descriptive hardware with the *semantic hardware layer*. A self-awareness mechanism that detects changes in the respective agent's physical hardware configuration updates the set of capabilities the agent knows it can currently execute with that hardware autonomously [7]. On the superordinate *agent layer* and *ensemble layer*, we implement the necessary self-organization mechanisms to form ensembles with a market-based task allocation approach [14] and to autonomously execute tasks [13] introduced by the *task layer.* On task layer, we evaluate the user-specified problem domain definition against the current state of the world the system is currently aware of and generate plans for this situation with an automated planner. We integrated this automated planner in our approach for a multi-agent script programming language for multipotent ensembles (Maple) [12]. There, we extend the approach of hierarchical task network (HTN) planning [5] for defining a problem domain and generating plans. We prefer this approach of plan-space planning over that of state-space planning [8] because of its efficiency and a higher level of control in real-world applications [6]. Plans in HTN are not "invented" by the planner (as in state-space planners), but selected and combined from a set of predefined partial plans. This achieves more control over the system where it is urgently needed, e.g., our fire-fighter scenario from Sect. 1. We use partial plans to define how robots need to execute capabilities for successfully accomplishing the plan, i.e., define partial plans on the level of the particular robot's capabilities. According to the situation of the system that is defined by the world state, the automated *planning* in Maple then can generate plans that are relevant for the respective situation. The multipotent system itself then updates the world state by executing plans and thereby generates new situations. To make plans executable, Maple includes a mechanism to *transform* generated plans into executable tasks that include necessary coordination information. We provide the possibility to define sequential, concurrent, alternative, and repeated as well as parallel and synchronized capability *execution.* For the concrete execution of plans, we let the multipotent system autonomously form appropriate ensembles at run-time.

Challenges for Maple-Swarm: For integrating agent groups and swarm capabilities encapsulating collective behavior in Maple-Swarm, we obviously need to adjust the way we *design problem domains* and *generate plans* for ensembles. While in Maple, we can already design tasks for the ensemble by using a common knowledge base enlisting all possible robot capabilities including their parameters and return values, we need to adapt this knowledge base accordingly for swarm capabilities. For the valid application of the application of swarms we present in the following, we assume swarms of robots to be ensembles of potentially heterogeneously configured robots that nevertheless are capable of executing the capabilities necessary for the respective swarm behavior (e.g., move with a certain movement vector, communicate measurements with each other). While we do not want to investigate the concrete execution of swarm capabilities here (we focus on this in [11]), we nevertheless require to define an appropriate interface including possible parameters and return types of swarm capabilities. This is necessary for initializing the task designer interface that requires a fully described capability knowledge base as well as for using return values of swarm capabilities during plan design and planning. We thus need to integrate the results of swarm capabilities in our concept of planning variables and adapt our planning mechanism accordingly. Further, we require to integrate the concepts for the respective agent groups we want to enable the problem domain designer to make use of in partial plans.

Addressing a group of robots with agent groups in a swarm capability requires an *adaptation of the market based, self-awareness enabled task-allocation mechanism* [13] we currently use in Maple for executing plans. To achieve this adaptation, we need to address two related challenges: Our task-allocation mechanism relies on the *self-awareness* information describing whether a robot can provide all required robot capabilities a task requires, delivered by the semantic hardware layer (cf. Fig. 2). Each robot uses this information it has available locally for validating its fitness for participating in that task. In case of a task requiring a swarm capability, we need to derive necessary self-awareness information on whether the robot can execute the task according to the capability's parametrization at run-time. A specific robot might be able to provide a swarm capability implementing a dedicated collective behavior for *some* parametrization but not for *all*: In case the swarm capability encapsulates the collective behavior of an adapted particle swarm optimization (PSO) [23] algorithm like we present in [10], the search parameter can require a wide range of different robot capabilities for performing measurements, depending on the concrete parameter specified by the user. The robot does not necessarily have all of these capabilities available and thus is not capable of participating in all possible instances of the swarm capability. Thus, we need to extend our self-awareness mechanism to not only provide information on whether a capability is *available* but also if it is *executable*, i.e., if the particular agent has all capabilities available that the swarm capability addresses with its specific parameters.

We further need to enable the *task-allocation mechanism* to deal with agent groups. In Maple [12], we can transform generated plans into tasks that address specific agents at any time (e.g., directly after planning). Now, we need to perform this transformation with respect to the current situation at run-time before we allocate them to actual robots. While in Maple, capabilities included in partial plans directly address particular agents, this is no longer the case in Maple-Swarm. Partial plans can contain any combination of capabilities, either addressing particular agents or any type of agent group. Thus, we require to adapt the requirements for tasks included in plans concerning the set of necessary capabilities a robot must provide for being able to work on that task accordingly. We need to do this appropriately for all possible combinations of capabilities addressing *particular agents*, *any agent*, *all agents*, a *set of agents*, or a *swarm of agents*. Also when a plan includes these agent groups, we need to determine the tasks we actually require and generate them at run-time.

Assumptions: We assume that in the simplified multipotent system, we evaluate our task orchestration framework with and perform task allocation in to validate the functionality of Maple-Swarm, we already have an appropriately configured system to abstract from physical reconfiguration needed otherwise. If necessary, we can create such situations, e.g., with our self-organized resource allocation mechanism we already proposed in [7].

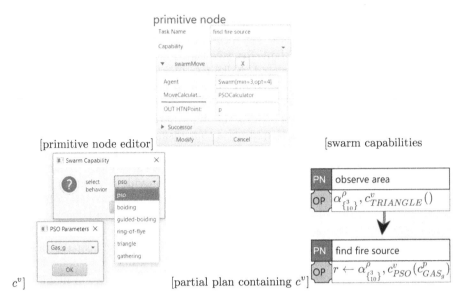

Fig. 3. The problem domain definition interface, here used for swarm capabilities.

3 Approach

In the following, we extend the possibilities available for defining the problem domain with the concepts of configurable, virtual swarm capabilities, and agent groups. Further, we describe how we extend our current graphical designer interface based on HTN, illustrate the necessary adaptations to our planning algorithm, and the transformation process for generating executable tasks from plans. Moreover, we describe how we adapt the self-awareness and self-organization approach for task allocation accordingly. We refer to the human creating a problem domain description in the form of Maple-Swarm hierarchical task networks $\mathcal{HTN}$ with our graphical tool as the *designer*. Further, we call our algorithm creating plans $\rho \in \mathcal{P}$ for the executing multipotent system as the planner $\mathbb{P}$. In our $\mathcal{HTN}$ and ρ resulting from executing $\mathbb{P}$ on the $\mathcal{HTN}$ and the world state ws (holding the current variable assignments), we use the concept of *planning* agents $\alpha^\rho \in \mathcal{A}^\rho$ to define roles of responsibility within a plan. To robots that adopt roles in ρ and that form an ensemble $\mathcal{E}$ for executing that plan at run-time, we refer to as *executing* agents $\alpha^e \in \mathcal{A}^e$ instead (Fig. 3).

3.1 Extending the Knowledge Base for Swarm Capabilities

In Maple, we already enlist possible (physical) robot capabilities $c^p \in \mathcal{C}^p$ including their necessary set of parameters and their return values as a triple $\langle c^p, \text{PAR}_{c^p}, \text{RET}_{c^p} \rangle$ in a capability knowledge base. $\mathcal{C}^p$ are such capabilities a robot can execute alone with physically available hardware, e.g., measure the concentration of a gas of type g with a GAS_g sensor. For a physical capability $c^p_{\text{MV-POS}}$,

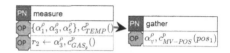

Fig. 4. Addressing $c_{\mathrm{PSO}}^{v} \in C^{v}$ to a swarm of $\mathrm{MIN} = 4$ and $\mathrm{MAX} = 8$ agents and $c_{\mathrm{STR}}^{p} \in C^{p}$ to any agent of this swarm.

Fig. 5. Parallely addressing $c_{\mathrm{TEMP}}^{p} \in C^{p}$ to an agent set $\{\alpha_1^{p}, \alpha_3^{p}, \alpha_5^{p}\}$ and $c_{\mathrm{GAS}_g}^{p} \in C^{p}$ to α_3^{p} and then $c_{\mathrm{MV\text{-}POS}}^{v} \in C^{p}$ to all agents

that moves a robot to a certain position, e.g., the designer can find an entry defining the respective parameter $\mathrm{PAR}_{c_{\mathrm{MV\text{-}POS}}^{p}} := \langle \mathrm{X,Y,Z} \rangle$ and the return value $\mathrm{RET}_{c_{\mathrm{MV\text{-}POS}}^{p}} := \langle \mathrm{X,Y,Z} \rangle$ within the knowledge base. The designer can use all entries in the capability knowledge base to include them in partial plans ρ^{PART} and address them to planning agents $\alpha^{p} \in \mathcal{A}^{p}$ within the problem domain description in the $\mathcal{HTN}$. For expressing this association between capabilities and $\alpha^{p} \in \mathcal{A}^{p}$, we use *operators* (OP in our figures). We now extend this knowledge base with virtual swarm capabilities $c^{v} \in C^{v} \subset C$, i.e., $c^{p} \in C^{p} \subset C$ and $C^{p} \cap C^{v} = \emptyset$ and $C^{p} \cup C^{v} = C$ by adding their respective information. This enables the designer to define ρ^{PART} addressing any capability, no matter whether it is physical or virtual (cf. Sect. 3.1, addressing a swarm-agent introduced in Sect. 3.2). Despite there is a great difference in executing a c^{v} instead of a c^{p} because all $c^{v} \in C^{v}$ can only be executed by whole collectives while all $c^{p} \in C^{p}$ also by particular robots alone, we enable the designer to abstract from the details when designing any ρ^{PART} for the problem domain. To include a virtual swarm capability, e.g., for executing PSO algorithm to determine the position of the highest concentration of a certain GAS_g (cf. Sect. 3.1), we thus include an entry for $c_{\mathrm{PSO}}^{v} \in C^{v}$ with the parameter $\mathrm{PAR}_{c_{\mathrm{PSO}}^{v}} := \mathrm{GAS}_g$ and the identified position $\mathrm{RET}_{c_{\mathrm{PSO}}^{v}} := \langle \mathrm{X,Y,Z} \rangle$ (cf. Sect. 3.1). This enables the designer to use virtual capabilities similar to physical capabilities.

3.2 Extending the Maple Domain Description Model

For creating a $\mathcal{HTN}$ and the partial plans ρ^{PART} it contains, the designer can use all elements of our extended HTN planning approach from [12], i.e., compound nodes (CN), primitive nodes (PN), world state modification nodes (WS), re-planning nodes (RP), as well as our concept for looped execution of nodes. A partial plan ρ^{PART} thus consists of nodes containing information the designer requires the system to execute, e.g., $\rho_1^{\mathrm{PART}} := [\mathrm{PN}_1, \mathrm{PN}_2, \mathrm{WS}, \mathrm{RP}] \in \mathcal{HTN}$. In contrast to CN (a commonly known element of HTN [6]) we use for structuring the $\mathcal{HTN}$ and for achieving situation awareness concerning the world-state during planning (cf. Sect. 3.3), all other nodes can occur in a plan ρ and thus contain instructions the multipotent system should execute. We now describe the new possibilities the designer has to define instructions in these other nodes.

Planning Agent Groups and Virtual Swarm Capabilities: In Maple, one specific plan ρ can contain one or more PN that can assign capabilities to different planning agents $\alpha^\rho \in \mathcal{A}^\rho$ in multiple *operators* (OP). Thereby, each ρ generates requirements for executing agents $\alpha^e \in \mathcal{A}^e$ to be met at run-time. We distinguish between multiple classes of planning agents. Particular planning agents $\alpha_i^\rho \in A_I^\rho \subset \mathcal{A}^\rho$ can be reused across the plan. To adopt the role of an α_i^ρ we consequently require α_i^e to provide all capabilities assigned to α_i^ρ within ρ in any node. While it was only possible to require the execution of a capability from such a specific α_i^ρ in Maple [12] (cf. Sect. 3.1), we now allow the designer to also specify that a *swarm of agents* $\alpha_{\{^{MIN}_{MAX}\}}^\rho$, *all agents* $\alpha_\forall^\rho$, *any agent* $\alpha_\exists^\rho$, or a set of particular agents $\{\alpha_1^\rho, ..., \alpha_n^\rho\}$ need to execute a specific capability in an operator. This becomes necessary for swarm capabilities $c^v \in \mathcal{C}^v$ encapsulating collective behavior (cf. Sect. 3.1). We can not or even do not want to determine precisely how many executing agents $\alpha^e \in \mathcal{A}^e$ in an ensemble should execute a swarm capability $c^v \in \mathcal{C}^v$ at run-time. An ensemble executing $c_{PSO}^v \in \mathcal{C}^v$ (cf. Sect. 3.1), e.g., can achieve the desired emergent effect with very different swarm sizes and thus we want to decide on the number of participating entities at run-time rather than at design-time concerning the current situation the system finds itself located in. Nevertheless, there may be minimum and maximum bounds for swarm behavior to emerge at all and stay efficient [1]. For enabling the designer to define such bounds, we introduce a *swarm-agent* $\alpha_{\{^{MIN}_{MAX}\}}^\rho \in A_S^\rho \subset \mathcal{A}^\rho$. This can become handy, e.g., if at least MIN and at most MAX agents should execute c_{PSO}^v (cf. primitive node *search* in Fig. 4). An execution agent can take the role of up to one α_i^ρ and additionally adopt any number of swarms-agent roles. Thus, we can also express the concept of *any-agent* $\alpha_\exists^\rho = \alpha_{\{1\}}^\rho$ as a specific swarm-agent. With an operator addressing a capability in ρ to the *all-agent* with $\alpha_\forall^\rho \in A_\forall^\rho \subset \mathcal{A}^\rho$, the designer can achieve that all i agents in an ensemble $\mathcal{E} = \{\alpha_1^e, ..., \alpha_i^e\}$ created at run-time need to execute the associated capability (A_I^ρ, A_S^ρ, and $A_\forall^\rho$ are pairwise disjunct sets). This can be useful, e.g., when all agents should gather at a dedicated position pos_1 by executing c_{MV-POS}^p after measuring parameters of interest at different locations (cf. PN *gather* in Fig. 5). Similarly, by associating a capability with an *agent-set* $\{\alpha_1^\rho, ..., \alpha_n^\rho\} \subseteq A_I^\rho$, the designer can require that a concretely specified set of particular agents $\{\alpha_1^e, ..., \alpha_n^e\} \subseteq \mathcal{E}$ executes the associated capability (cf. measuring temperature with c_{TEMP}^p in PN *measure* in Fig. 5). Like with associating a capability to a particular planning agent α_i^ρ in an operator, the designer can reference to a single planning agent with the any-agent $\alpha_\exists^\rho$. Both α_i^ρ and $\alpha_\exists^\rho$, require that one $\alpha^e \in \mathcal{E}$ executes the capability at run-time. But instead of determining a particular role α_i^ρ at design-time that needs to execute all capabilities in ρ assigned to α_i^ρ, using $\alpha_\exists^\rho$ allows for any α^e to take the role of $\alpha_\exists^\rho$ in addition to any role it already took. This means that any one of $\{\alpha_1^e, \alpha_2^e, \alpha_3^e\}$ adopting the roles $\{\alpha_1^\rho, \alpha_2^\rho, \alpha_3^\rho\}$ later on can also execute the capabilities assigned to $\alpha_\exists^\rho$. This can also be useful when using $\alpha_{\{^{MIN}_{MAX}\}}^\rho$ in plans, e.g., if after determining a point of interest with c_{PSO}^v, anyone of the agents that executed c_{PSO}^v should stream a video from that point of interest with c_{STR}^v (cf. PN *observe* in Fig. 4). While we introduce the swarm-, all-, set-,

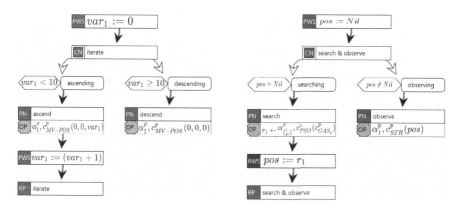

Fig. 6. Modify var_1 at planning time PWS   **Fig. 7.** Modify pos at run-time RWS

and any-agent having virtual swarm capabilities in mind, a designer can also make use of them for addressing physical capabilities $\mathcal{C}^p$. To indicate to the designer, that for executing a virtual swarm capability we require a collective and not a particular planning agent, we restrict the possibilities the designer has for addressing any $c^v \in \mathcal{C}^v$ to the respective planning agents.

Planning Variables: We further extend the concept of variables we use for expressing situations of the world state in our problem domain description, aiming for more flexibility and expressiveness. The designer now can require that values of variables update dynamically in partial plans not only during planning time but also at run-time. Moreover, we extend the way how updated variable values can be used within parameters of capabilities and in conditions, we evaluate during execution or planning. During planning time, we can update variable values only by explicitly using *planning time world-state modification nodes* (PWS) in partial plans [12]. A PWS node can contain one or multiple assignments to variables where the left side is a variable and the right side is an expression containing variables or constants, e.g., $\{var_1 := 1\}$, $\{var_2 := 2 \cdot var_1\}$, or $\{var_1 := 1, var_2 := 2\}$. This can be useful, e.g., if we want to create plans containing iterative behavior. We can achieve such by using a variable in a capability's parameter and in a condition the planner $\mathbb{P}$ evaluates during planning at the same time. If, e.g., we require an ensemble to repeat a primitive node containing $c^p_{\text{MV-POS}}$ with $par_{c^p_{\text{MV-POS}}} := \langle 0, 0, var_1 \rangle$ for 10 iterations, where var_1 is a variable we update during planning, we can achieve this by explicitly updating the value of var_1 in a PWS node (cf. Fig. 6).

We further extend our problem domain description in a way that we can also use the results of capability executions to update variable values during run-time. If we want to use variables updated that way, we need to differentiate between two cases concerning the way we want to use them in partial plans. **A)** When we use variables in primitive nodes that are updated by the executing ensemble during run-time within the same partial plan, there is no need for

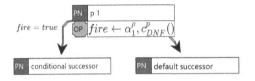

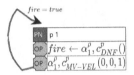

Fig. 8. IF/ELSE block evaluating the result of c^p_{DNF} that can detect fires.

Fig. 9. WHILE block, terminated if a fire is detected.

making these updates explicit within world state modification nodes. Because the ensemble executing the plan produces the new variable value itself by executing the respective capability, it is aware of that update and thus can use it in a following PN. In the partial plan in Fig. 4, e.g., we can use the result r_1 from executing c^v_{PSO} in the PN *search* as a parameter for c^p_{STR} in the PN *observe* after storing the result r_1 with a RWS node in the variable *pos* which we can use in a subsequent RP node. **B)** When we use the results of any capability's execution contained in one specific partial plan ρ^{PART}_1 in another partial plan ρ^{PART}_2, we require to make the update to that variable explicit within a *run-time world state modification node* (RWS). We can use this if we do not necessarily want the ensemble executing ρ^{PART}_1 to be the same than that executing ρ^{PART}_2. If, e.g., in contrast to the example in Fig. 4 we want to explicitly let another ensemble consisting of α^ρ_1 execute c^v_{STR} instead of the ensemble executing c^v_{PSO}, we can store the result of c^v_{PSO} in an additional variable (POS) in a RWS node. Now, we can still access POS after finishing the value-producing plan during a subsequent re-planning that is aware of the update in PN *observe* (cf. Fig. 7). We further can use RWS to generate even more situation awareness, e.g., decide on the next PN according to the result of a capability's execution with conditional successor nodes (cf. Figs. 8 and 9). Each PN in a $\rho^{PART} \in \mathcal{HTN}$ can have any number of conditional successors assigned with variables in addition to a default successor (cf. planning variables in Sect. 3.2), evaluated by the ensemble at run-time.

3.3   Extending the Maple Planner

Executing the automated planner $\mathbb{P}$ on an $\mathcal{HTN}$ and its accompanying world state ws (that holds the current values of relevant variables), i.e., applying $\mathbb{P}$ ($\mathcal{HTN}$, ws), results in a plan ρ and a modified version of ws. Depending on the current situation represented in an up-to-date world state (updated by previous capability executions or world state modifications, cf. planning variables in Sect. 3.2), this ρ then connects partial plans (using $\oplus$) from $\mathcal{HTN}$ whose execution the designer intended to be necessary for that situation (cf. Fig. 10).

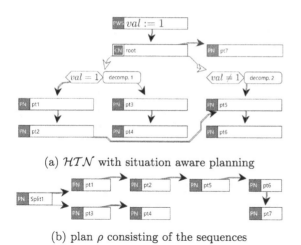

(a) $\mathcal{HTN}$ with situation aware planning

(b) plan ρ consisting of the sequences
$[pt_1, pt_2, pt_5, pt_6] \oplus [pt_7]$ and $[pt_3, pt_4]$

Fig. 10. Because $val = 1$ in the world state, $\mathbb{P}\,(\mathcal{HTN}, ws)$ results in the plan $\rho = [split1] \oplus (\rho_1^{\text{PART}} \oplus \rho_4^{\text{PART}} \mid \rho_2^{\text{PART}})$, consisting of two concurrent sequences.

By evaluating conditions on variables in the world state, $\mathbb{P}$ decomposes a compound node CN into a $\mathcal{HTN}'$, which is a subcomponent of the original $\mathcal{HTN}$. Each $\mathcal{HTN}'$ then includes the associated partial plans, i.e., when decomposing CN $root$ in Fig. 10a with the variable $val = 1$, the resulting $\mathcal{HTN}'$ consists of the subordinated partial plans $\rho_1^{\text{PART}} := [pt_1, pt_2, pt_5, pt_6]$, $\rho_2^{\text{PART}} := [pt_3, pt_4]$, and a successor $\rho_4^{\text{PART}} := [pt_7]$ ($\rho_3^{\text{PART}} := [pt_5, pt_6]$ is not included). If the designer intends to have multiple concurrent plans, the designer can add multiple concurrent successors to a decomposition node. If a decomposition node with concurrent successors is encountered when running $\mathbb{P}\,(\mathcal{HTN}, ws)$, then a *split node*(e.g., *split1* in Fig. 10) connects the concurrent partial plans resulting in the plan $\rho = [split1] \oplus (\rho_1^{\text{PART}} \mid \rho_2^{\text{PART}})$, where the $\mid$ operator indicates that those partial plans can be executed concurrently. Using split nodes results in a plan consisting not only of one but multiple sequences as the output executing $\mathbb{P}$, each consisting of concatenated partial plans (cf. Fig. 10b). To make explicit how these concurrent sequences of partial plans are concatenated, a split node specifies which sequence continues the original plan (cf. double lined arrow in Fig. 10b) and which are concurrent sequences. If the CN is decomposed and has a default successor (e.g., ρ_4^{PART}), then this successor gets concatenated with the previous original plan, i.e., $\rho = [split1] \oplus (\rho_1^{\text{PART}} \oplus \rho_4^{\text{PART}} \mid \rho_2^{\text{PART}})$ in Fig. 10. The operation $\rho_1^{\text{PART}} \oplus \rho_4^{\text{PART}}$ sets the starting node of ρ_4^{PART} as the default successor of each node in ρ_1^{PART} which has no default successor yet. In contrast to CN and PWS, the other nodes PN, RWS, and RP are effectively included in a plan ρ if they occur in a partial plan ρ^{PART} that $\mathbb{P}$ selects during planning. By using a RP, the designer can enforce the generation of new plans at run-time. RP nodes hold a reference to another node of the $\mathcal{HTN}$ indicating where to start a subsequent execution of $\mathbb{P}$ at run-time with updated variables in the world state (cf. planning variables in Sect. 3.2).

3.4   Extending the Self-awareness and Market-Based Task-Allocation

We extend our local self-awareness mechanism to maintain the functionality of our market-based task-allocation mechanism introduced in [14]. While we redefine the task allocation problem in this section, we do not modify the task allocation process itself and still fall back to our constraint satisfaction and optimization-based solution from [13] and [7]. Referring to our multipotent systems reference architecture (cf. Fig. 2), each $\alpha^e \in \mathcal{A}^e$ can only provide a (physical) capability c^p and participate in a specific plan ρ requiring that capability, i.e., adopt the role of the associated α^ρ included in ρ, if all necessary hardware for c^p is connected. Thus, α^e can execute, e.g., the capability $c^p_{\text{GAS}_g}$ for measuring the concentration of GAS_g when it has a respective GAS_g connected. If this is the case, we add this capability to the set of available capabilities $C_{a^e} \subset C$ of α^e.

In contrast to physical capabilities, virtual swarm capabilities $c^v \in \mathcal{C}^v$ do not require any hardware. Instead, the *parametrization* PAR_{c^v} of a specific swarm capability referencing other capabilities $c^p \in \text{PAR}_{c^v}$ determines whether the agent can execute c^v or not and thus, if the virtual capability is available to the executing agent or not. A virtual swarm capability c^v_{PSO}, e.g., parametrized to find the source of a GAS_g (e.g., a fire) requires the physical capabilities $c^p_{\text{GAS}_g}$ and $c^p_{\text{MV-VEL}}$ (for moving with a given velocity) to be executable. Thus, a $c^v \in \mathcal{C}^v$ is only available to a α^e, if all capabilities included in the virtual capability's parameters are also available to the agent, i.e., $c^v \in C_{a^e} \Leftrightarrow \forall c^p \in \text{PAR}_{c^v} \mid c^p \in C_{a^e}$.

To form an ensemble $\mathcal{E}$ consisting of executing agents that are collectively able to execute a certain plan ρ, we formulate a task allocation problem. We define a task $t_{\alpha_i^\rho}$ for each different role of an identified planning agent $\alpha_i^\rho \in \mathcal{A}_I^\rho$ that is included in a plan ρ first. Thereby, we generate a set $T_I^\rho := \{t_{\alpha_i^\rho} \mid \alpha_i^\rho \in \rho\}$ of tasks we need to assign to executing agents for finally executing ρ at runtime. Besides information on how to execute ρ cooperatively within $\mathcal{E}$, which we do not further focus on here[1], we include a set C_t of required capabilities in each task's description. An executing agent α^e can adopt the role of a α_i^ρ if it has all necessary capabilities available for the respective task, i.e., we require $C_t \subseteq C_{a^e}$ for the respective role's task to achieve a valid adoption. If this is the case, an executing agent α^e can participate in the market-based task allocation mechanism by generating a proposal $\text{PRO}_{\alpha^e}(t)$ for that task $t \in T_I^\rho$, cf. Eq. (1). All $\alpha^e \in \mathcal{A}^e$ then send their proposals to the plan's coordinator. This coordinator then can select one proposal for every task $t \in T_I^\rho$ generated from the planning agent roles α_i^ρ contained in the current plan ρ to achieve a valid task assignment. The coordinator can perform a valid task allocation TA for ρ if there exists an injective function f mapping each task $t_{\alpha_i^\rho}$ generated from ρ to a distinct executing agent $\alpha^e \in \mathcal{A}^e$, cf. Eq. (2). This executing agent then adopts the role of the planning agent the task was generated for.

---

[1] We describe how we coordinate plans containing only physical capabilities $c^p \in \mathcal{C}^p$ in [12] and how we extend that process for virtual swarm capabilities $c^v \in \mathcal{C}^v$ in [11].

$$\forall t \in T_\rho^I : \quad \text{PRO}_{\alpha^e}(t) \Leftrightarrow \mathcal{C}_t \subseteq \mathcal{C}_{\alpha^e} \tag{1}$$

$$\text{TA}(T_\rho^I) \Leftrightarrow \exists_{f:T_\rho^I \to \mathcal{A}^e} \forall_{t_j \neq k \in T_\rho^I} : f(t_j) \neq f(t_k) \wedge \text{PRO}_{f(t_j)}(t_j) \wedge \text{PRO}_{f(t_k)}(t_k) \tag{2}$$

While this adaptation of the self-awareness of executing agents in the market-based task allocation mechanism can handle virtual swam capabilities, we need to perform a second adaptation to also support the agent groups introduced in Sect. 3.2. For realizing the $\alpha_\forall^\rho$, $\alpha_\exists^\rho$, and $\alpha_{\{\substack{\text{MIN}\\\text{MAX}}\}}^\rho$, we need to extend the original requirements concerning the necessary capabilities for tasks $t \in T_I^\rho$ before we start the task allocation TA. If the designer addresses capabilities with $\alpha_\forall^\rho$ in the plan ρ which we can collect in the set of capabilities $\mathcal{C}_\forall$, for creating a proposal an α^e needs to provide all these capabilities in addition to the capabilitites each task $t \in T_I^\rho$ already requires, i.e., $\text{PRO}_{\alpha^e}(t) \Leftrightarrow (\mathcal{C}_t \cup \mathcal{C}_\forall) \subseteq \mathcal{C}_{\alpha^e}$ (cf. Eq. (1)).

Concerning adaptations of the task allocation, we fortunately can handle $\alpha_\exists^\rho$ and $\alpha_{\{\substack{\text{MIN}\\\text{MAX}}\}}^\rho$ equally as we can express $\alpha_\exists^\rho$ as $c_{\{1\}}^\rho$. For every occurrence of $\alpha_\exists^\rho$ or $\alpha_{\{\substack{\text{MIN}\\\text{MAX}}\}}^\rho$, we create a *swarm task* t_{SW} which we collect in a set T_{SW}^ρ. Similar to tasks $t \in T_I^\rho$ we request proposals from executing agents for all $t_{\text{SW}} \in T_{\text{SW}}^\rho$. Further, we extend the requirements for a valid task allocation to $\text{TA}(T_I^\rho) \wedge \text{TA}(T_{\text{SW}}^\rho)$, where $\text{TA}(T_{\text{SW}}^\rho)$ is valid if we have at last MIN proposals from distinct executing agents for every task $t_{\text{SW}} \in T_{\text{SW}}^\rho$ (cf. Eq. (2)). To select a range of MIN and MAX agents for every $t_{\text{SW}} \in T_{\text{SW}}^\rho$, we can optionally accept any further proposal for the respective task from a distinct agent until we reach the respective limit of MAX.

4   Proof of Concepts

We demonstrate the new possibilities of Maple-Swarm within an exemplary $\mathcal{HTN}$ consisting of partial plans $\rho_1^{\text{PART}}, \ldots, \rho_4^{\text{PART}}$ and the plans resulting in different situations for our motivating example in Fig. 11.

In a first partial plan $\rho_1^{\text{PART}} := [\text{PWS}_1, \text{PN}_1]$ we include in $\mathcal{HTN}$ during the designing process, we initialize the relevant variables in the world state (PWS_1 sets variables f_{WS} to Nil, initializes the area of interest A where $\langle 0, 0, 40, 40 \rangle$ defines x and y coordinates as well as length and width, and F to $\{\}$) and direct the whole ensemble to the center of the forest at $\langle 20, 20 \rangle$ which we want to survey in an altitude of 50 m. We achieve this by using the physical capability $c_{\text{MV-POS}}^p$ with the parameter $\langle 20, 20, 50 \rangle$ and addressing the agent group $\alpha_\forall^\rho$ (commanded in the respective operator included in PN_1). If we do not know any fires located in the forest (i.e., $p_{fire} = Nil$), we design another partial plan $\rho_2^{\text{PART}} := [\text{PN}_2, \text{RWS}_2, \text{RP}_2]$ to let a swarm of agents $\alpha_{\{\substack{10\\50}\}}^\rho$ consisting of a minimum of 10 and a maximum of 50 agents execute a virtual swarm capability to equally distribute in the area of interest (A) with the potential field algorithm

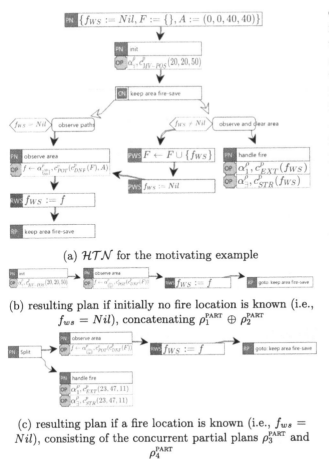

(a) $\mathcal{HTN}$ for the motivating example

(b) resulting plan if initially no fire location is known (i.e., $f_{ws} = Nil$), concatenating $\rho_1^{\text{PART}} \oplus \rho_2^{\text{PART}}$

(c) resulting plan if a fire location is known (i.e., $f_{ws} = Nil$), consisting of the concurrent partial plans ρ_3^{PART} and ρ_4^{PART}

Fig. 11. An example $\mathcal{HTN}$ consisting of situation-aware partial plans for handling the fire-fighter scenario from Sect. 1 including possible plans resulting from executing $\mathbb{P}\,(\mathcal{HTN})$.

encapsulated in c_{POT}^v in PN$_2$. We assume, that the swarm can autonomously adapt the altitude for gaining surveillance quality according to the amount of swarm members like it is proposed to be achievable in [20]. We can achieve such behavior with an appropriate implementation of the respective swarm capability c_{POT}^v (we explain how we can achieve this in the accompanying publication concerning the execution of swarm capabilities [11]). In that partial plan, we use the capability c_{DNF}^p for detecting new fires (i.e., such not already included in F) on the ground as the parameter of c_{POT}^v to return the position of a fire $f := \langle f_x, f_y, 0 \rangle$ as soon as one member of the swarm detects a fire. Detecting a fire then causes an

update of the world state in RWS$_2$ that sets the variable f_{ws} to the result of c_{POT}^v, i.e., $f_{ws} := f$, followed RP$_2$ referencing the only CN in the $\mathcal{HTN}$ (keep ara fire-save). If the ensemble is aware of a fire, i.e., the world state holds a respective entry and $f_{ws} \neq$ NIL and contains the location of the fire (cf. Fig. 11a), we design two concurrent partial plans and $\rho_3^{\text{PART}} := [\text{PN}_3]$ and $\rho_4^{\text{PART}} := [\text{PWS}_{4\text{-A}},$ PWS$_{4\text{-B}}$, PWS$_1$, PN$_1$] we want the ensemble to execute in that situation. In ρ_3^{PART}, we address α_1^ρ to execute a physical capability c_{EXT}^p for extinguishing the fire at the identified location and α_3^ρ to should stream a video from that execution to the user by executing a respective capability c_{STR}^p, PAR$_{c_{\text{STR}}^p} := f_{ws}$ which we include in an respective operator in PN$_3$. We can thus let the system decide with respect to the current availability of capabilities in the ensemble whether one executing agent α^e is sufficient for executing that plan (i.e., $\alpha_1^\rho = \alpha^\exists$) or two agents are used instead. As parameter for both, c_{STR}^p and c_{EXT}^p, the planning process generates a copy of the concrete position of the fire, e.g., if $f_{ws} := \langle 23, 47, 11 \rangle$, we use the parameter $\text{PAR}_{c_{\text{EXT}}^p} := \langle 23, 47, 11 \rangle$ and $\text{PAR}_{c_{\text{STR}}^p} := \langle 23, 47, 11 \rangle$. We need that copy because in the concurrent partial plan ρ_4^{PART}, we add the identified location of the fire f_{ws} to a set of known fires F in $\text{PWS}_{4\text{-A}}$ and then reset f_{ws} to Nil in $\text{PWS}_{4\text{-B}}$ before an other ensemble again executes *observe area* in the concatenated partial plan ρ_2^{PART}. Given this problem domain description, executing $\mathbb{P}$ on $\mathcal{HTN}$ and ws thus results in a plan consisting of $\rho_1^{\text{PART}} \oplus \rho_2^{\text{PART}}$ if $f_{ws} = Nil$ (cf. Fig. 11b) and in a plan consisting of ρ_3^{PART} concurrent to ρ_4^{PART} if $f_{ws} \neq Nil$ (cf. Fig. 11c). Besides this exemplary $\mathcal{HTN}$, we demonstrate the functionality of our approach with video materials and provide our application including source files for the presented examples from previous sections on GitHub[2].

5   Related Work

Some research already exists focusing on the problem of task orchestration for collectives, ensembles, aggregates, or swarms. A framework providing a scripting language for multi-vehicle networks is Dolphin [17]. With Dolphin, a human operator is able to define tasks for particular robots and teams of robots without explicit knowledge of the concrete implementation of these tasks' execution. While a user can define tasks for pre-formed robot teams with Dolphin, it does not support a possibility for exploiting emergent effects of collective behavior like, e.g., swarm algorithms can deliver. Further, Dolphin does not include the possibility for online and situation-aware re-planning that can generate new tasks at run-time as we support in Maple-Swarm. PaROS [3] is another multi-robot tasks orchestration framework. It introduces primitives for collectives the user can define tasks with and let them distribute within a swarm of UAV. Unfortunately, only homogeneously equipped UAV are in the focus of PaROS and there is no support for multi-robot systems in general. While PaROS does support some promising abstractions for encapsulating certain swarm behavior in tasks for groups of UAVs, it does not aim at interconnecting those tasks in complex programs with parallel, concurrent, alternating, or iterated execution of different swarm algorithms we aim for in Maple-Swarm. Further, there is no feature providing situation-awareness and run-time task generation. With TeCola [16], users can program missions for heterogeneous teams of robots on an abstract level. By abstracting the robots and capabilities of robots as services available to the user, TeCola reduces complexity for coordinating ensembles. TeCola eases the programming of robot teams with primitives for abstracting robots in teams and missions but still requires fine-grained management of those during task specification. Neither collective behavior achieved by swarm algorithms nor situation-aware task generation is supported by TeCola. Voltron [19] provides a task orchestration framework for robot teams. While the authors can achieve

---

[2] Materials on https://github.com/isse-augsburg/isola2020-maple-swarm.git.

the abstraction of particular robot actions including parallel task execution, scaling, and concurrent execution, by introducing so-called team-level programming, they lose the ability for controlling and specifying tasks for particular robots. Up to now, with Voltron a user can not specify collective behavior in the form of swarm algorithms. While Voltron does include a mechanism to compensate for failures at run-time, e.g., to maintain the execution of once-defined tasks, it does not support other situation-aware modifications of missions. There is no possibility for an autonomous generation of tasks at run-time like we provide with re-planning in Maple-Swarm. Recapitulating the findings in the literature, we can see that up to now there exists no task orchestration framework supporting all features we integrate into Maple-Swarm. While all presented approaches deliver benefits for programming collectives, each lacks some aspects that are of great relevance in our opinion.

6   Conclusion

Performing task orchestration for multi-robot systems is complicated, especially for domain-only experts. In this paper, we propose our approach for easing this by extending the task definition layer of our multi-agent script programming language for multipotent ensembles with virtual swarm capabilities encapsulating collective behavior. We, therefore, extended our current approach Maple concerning the graphical task designer interface, the automated planner, and the market-based task allocation mechanism including the local self-awareness functionality for every robot to Maple-Swarm. Users are now able to address tasks not only to particular robots but whole ensembles. Thereby, users can make use of collective adaptive behavior, e.g., of swarm behavior and useful emergent effects arising thereof. We demonstrated the new possibilities in examples as well as in the proof of concepts for a fire-fighter case study we provide online. Our next steps include the integration with our reference implementation for a multipotent system that can execute swarm capabilities with mobile robots.

Acknowledgement. The authors would like to thank all reviewers for their valuable suggestions.

References

1. Barca, J., Sekercioglu, Y.: Swarm robotics reviewed. Robotica **31**, 345–359 (2013)
2. Daniel, K., Dusza, B., Lewandowski, A., Wietfelds, C.: Airshield: a system-of-systems MUAV remote sensing architecture for disaster response. In: Proceedings of 3rd Annual IEEE Systems Conference (SysCon) (2009)
3. Dedousis, D., Kalogeraki, V.: A framework for programming a swarm of UAVs. In: Proceedings of the 11th Pervasive Technologies Related to Assistive Environments Conference, pp. 5–12 (2018)
4. Duarte, M., Costa, V., Gomes, J., et al.: Evolution of collective behaviors for a real swarm of aquatic surface robots. PLoS ONE **11**(3), 1–25 (2016)

5. Erol, K., Hendler, J., Nau, D.S.: HTN planning: complexity and expressivity. AAAI **94**, 1123–1128 (1994)
6. Georgievski, I., Aiello, M.: An overview of hierarchical task network planning (2014). CoRR abs/1403.7426, http://arxiv.org/abs/1403.7426
7. Hanke, J., Kosak, O., Schiendorfer, A., Reif, W.: Self-organized resource allocation for reconfigurable robot ensembles. In: 2018 IEEE 12th International Conference on Self-Adaptive and Self-Organizing Systems (SASO), pp. 110–119 (2018)
8. Koenig, S.: Agent-centered search. AI Mag. **22**(4), 109 (2001)
9. Kosak, O.: Facilitating planning by using self-organization. In: IEEE 2nd International Workshops on Foundations and Applications of Self* Systems (FAS*W), pp. 371–374 (2017)
10. Kosak, O.: Multipotent systems: a new paradigm for multi-robot applications. Org. Comp. Doc. Dis. Coll. **10**, 53 (2018). Kassel university press GmbH
11. Kosak, O., Bohn, F., Eing, L., et al.: Swarm and collective capabilities for multipotent robot ensembles. In: 9th International Symposium on Leveraging Applications of Formal Methods, Verification and Validation (2020)
12. Kosak, O., Bohn, F., Keller, F., Ponsar, H., Reif, W.: Ensemble programming for multipotent systems. In: 2019 IEEE 4th International Workshops on Foundations and Applications of Self* Systems (FAS*W), pp. 104–109 (2019)
13. Kosak, O., Wanninger, C., Angerer, A., et al.: Decentralized coordination of heterogeneous ensembles using jadex. In: IEEE 1st International Workshops on Foundations and Appl. of Self* Systems (FAS*W), pp. 271–272 (2016). https://doi.org/10.1109/FAS-W.2016.65
14. Kosak, O., Wanninger, C., Angerer, A., et al.: Towards self-organizing swarms of reconfigurable self-aware robots. In: IEEE International Workshops on Foundations and Applications of Self* Systems, pp. 204–209. IEEE (2016)
15. Kosak, O., Wanninger, C., Hoffmann, A., Ponsar, H., Reif, W.: Multipotentsystems: combining planning, self-organization, and reconfiguration inmodular robot ensembles. Sensors **19**(1), 17 (2018)
16. Koutsoubelias, M., Lalis, S.: Tecola: a programming framework for dynamic and heterogeneous robotic teams. In: Proceedings of the 13th International Conference on Mobile and Ubiquitous Systems: Computing, Networking and Services, pp. 115–124 (2016)
17. Lima, K., Marques, E.R., Pinto, J., Sousa, J.B.: Dolphin: a task orchestration language for autonomous vehicle networks. In: IEEE/RSJ International Conference on Intelligent Robots and Systems (IROS), pp. 603–610. IEEE (2018)
18. Lorenz, R.D., Turtle, E.P., Barnes, J.W., et al.: Dragonfly: a rotorcraft lander concept for scientific exploration at titan. Johns Hopkins APL Tec. Dig. **34**, 374–387 (2018)
19. Mottola, L., Moretta, M., Whitehouse, K., Ghezzi, C.: Team-level programming of drone sensor networks. In: Proceedings of the 12th ACM Conference on Embedded Network Sensor Systems, pp. 177–190 (2014)
20. Villa, T.F., Gonzalez, F., Miljievic, B., Ristovski, Z.D., Morawska, L.: An overview of small unmanned aerial vehicles for air quality measurements: present applications and future prospectives. Sensors (Basel, Switzerland) **16**(7), 1072 (2016)
21. Wanninger, C., Eymüller, C., Hoffmann, A., Kosak, O., Reif, W.: Synthesizing capabilities for collective adaptive systems from self-descriptive hardware devices bridging the reality gap. In: Margaria, T., Steffen, B. (eds.) ISoLA 2018. LNCS, vol. 11246, pp. 94–108. Springer, Cham (2018). https://doi.org/10.1007/978-3-030-03424-5_7

22. Wolf, B., Chwala, C., Fersch, B., et al.: The scalex campaign: scale-crossing land surface and boundary layer processes in the tereno-prealpine observatory. Bull. Am. Meteorol. Soc. **98**(6), 1217–1234 (2017)
23. Zhang, Y., Wang, S., Ji, G.: A comprehensive survey on particle swarmoptimization algorithm and its applications. Math. Prob. Eng. (2015)

Swarm and Collective Capabilities for Multipotent Robot Ensembles

Oliver Kosak$^{(\boxtimes)}$ ⓘ, Felix Bohn, Lennart Eing, Dennis Rall,
Constantin Wanninger ⓘ, Alwin Hoffmann ⓘ, and Wolfgang Reif

Institute for Software and Systems Engineering at the University of Augsburg,
Universitätsstraße 2, 86159 Augsburg, Germany
kosak@isse.de

Abstract. Swarm behavior can be very beneficial for real-world robot applications. While analyzing the current state of research, we identified that many studied swarm algorithms foremost aim at modifying the movement vector of the executing robot. In this paper, we demonstrate how we encapsulate this behavior in a general pattern that robots can execute with adjusted parameters for realizing different beneficial swarm algorithms. We integrate the pattern as a virtual swarm capability in our reference architecture for multipotent, reconfigurable multi-robot ensembles and demonstrate its application in proof of concepts. We further illustrate how we can lift the concept of virtual capabilities to also integrate other known approaches for collective system programming as virtual collective capabilities. As an example, we do so by integrating the execution platform for the Protelis aggregate programming language.

Keywords: Swarm behavior · Multi-agent systems · Robot swarms · Multipotent systems · Collective adaptive systems · Ensembles

1 Motivation

The use of ensembles or swarms of autonomous robots, especially unmanned aerial vehicles (UAV), is very beneficial in many situations in our daily life. This statement is validated by the multitude of different applications for ensembles that emerged during the past decade making use of the benefits collective behavior can deliver, e.g., with emergent effects achieved by swarm behavior. Unfortunately, the current trend is that every single new application also requires a new software approach for its realization [3,8]. While these specialized approaches show beneficial results for their dedicated applications, e.g., using collective swarm behavior for searching [27], or distributed surveillance [15,16] among many others, users can find it hard to adapt them and profit from previous developments in (even only slightly) different use cases.

To come by this issue, we propose to make use of a *common pattern* instead that can express the collective swarm behavior of a certain class in general. Developers of multi-robot systems can implement such pattern once at design time

Partially funded by DFG (German Research Foundation), grant number 402956354.

T. Margaria and B. Steffen (Eds.): ISoLA 2020, LNCS 12477, pp. 525–540, 2020.
https://doi.org/10.1007/978-3-030-61470-6_31

and parametrize it differently at run-time to achieve specific emergent effects. We identified such a common pattern researchers frequently use for implementing *movement-vector based swarm behavior* of different types in swarm robotic systems. While producing a different emergent effect each, we can see that swarm algorithms like the particle swarm optimization algorithm [27], the commonly known flocking behavior originally analyzed in [21], shaping and formation algorithms [22], and distribution algorithms [15,16] make use of the same set of local actions: measuring one or multiple specific parameters, communicating with neighbors in the swarm, and modifying the movement vector of the robot.

For this paper, we implement such a common pattern in our reference architecture for multipotent multi-robot ensembles [9,14]. Therefore, we introduce the concept of *configurable, virtual, collective capabilities* that encapsulate complex behavior of individual robots by composing other capabilities, i.e., services a robot already provides, and produce collective behavior when executed cooperatively in an ensemble. For example, to realize flocking behavior following [21], each individual robot requires to execute certain capabilities in an appropriate combination, perform position and velocity measurements, needs to exchange resulting values with swarm members and adapt its movement vector accordingly, which then results in the collective emergent effect of the individuals forming a flock as an ensemble. By executing such a virtual capability collectively in a multi-robot system, we can realize swarm behavior and achieve useful emergent effects. We further validate the concept of virtual collective capabilities by demonstrating how other approaches for programming collective behavior can be integrated into our multipotent systems reference architecture by the example of Protelis [19] as a further example of a virtual collective capability. The contributions of this paper thus are: *1)* The identification and demonstration of a common pattern for realizing swarm behavior for collective adaptive systems, *2)* the extension of our current reference architecture for multipotent systems with the concept of virtual capabilities, *3)* the integration and evaluation of virtual capabilities realizing collective behavior for multipotent systems with our common swarm pattern and the external approach Protelis [19].

The remainder of the paper is structured as follows. In Sect. 2 we illustrate our objectives and highlight the challenges we need to tackle and then propose our solution in Sect. 3. In Sect. 4 we demonstrate the functionality of our approach for our case study in a simulation environment and deliver proof of concepts supported by expressive video materials. In Sect. 5 we subsume approaches for programming collectives and analyze current implementations of swarm behavior for swarm robotic systems. In Sect. 6 we conclude our findings and point out possible future research challenges.

2   Challenges Resulting for Multipotent Systems

Extending our multipotent systems reference architecture [9] with virtual swarm capabilities for exploiting useful emergent effects and to easily program collective systems poses some challenges. In multipotent systems, robot ensembles being homogeneous at design time can become heterogeneous concerning their capabilities at run-time by combining physical reconfiguration on the hardware level with self-awareness. We aim at exploiting this property for enabling robots to implement the reference architecture to also adapt at run-time for participating in swarm algorithms. While we already provide the possibility of extending the range of domain-specific capabilities in multipotent systems when it is necessary, we want to reduce the effort a system designer needs to invest when integrating virtual capabilities. In our multipotent systems reference architecture (cf. Fig. 1), we integrate capabilities within the *semantic hardware layer* which is an interface to self-descriptive hardware [25]. The semantic hardware layer recognizes new hardware connected to the robot and updates the available capabilities respectively in a self-aware manner. It provides these capabilities to its superordinate *agent layer* that can make use of them when involved in an ensemble (coordinated on *ensemble layer*) that currently executes a task introduced on *task layer*.

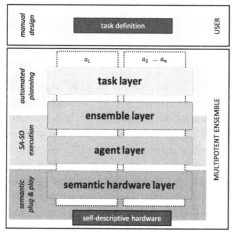

Fig. 1. The multipotent systems reference architecture for multi-robot ensembles, simplified version adapted from [14].

We generate tasks by automated planning on the task definition the system's user introduces through an interface on *task layer*. Agents $\alpha_{1..n} \in \mathcal{A}$ in the multipotent ensemble then allocate these tasks cooperatively to agents capable of solving the task. These agents then form an ensemble coordinated by one specific agent through its ensemble layer, e.g., α_1 (cf. Fig. 1). The ensemble then executes the respective task by the appropriate interplay of the coordinator's ensemble layer and the other ensemble members' agent layer. To enable the system to make use of such new capabilities that are coupled with physical hardware, an expert first needs to make changes to this core element of the system. Necessary adaptions include, e.g., extending the domain model of the ensemble appropriately, implementing the hardware access (drivers) accordingly, or integrating the new hardware physically into the system (hardware adapters, wiring). While adaptations of the domain model are necessarily required when a user introduces new hardware modules that offer new capabilities, e.g., an GAS_x sensor module offering the previously unknown capability of *measuring*-GAS_x, we aim at avoiding this for virtual capabilities. If a capability is not directly associated with and not only available through the presence of dedicated physical hardware, e.g., for participating in swarm algorithm A instead of algorithm B or for executing a Protelis program C instead of program D, we aim at avoiding such modifications to the core system for certain classes of capabilities. Our challenge here is to identify such classes where it is possible to separate a fixed part from a variable part. Then, we can implement that fixed part into the system *once* at design-time as a *virtual capability*, and integrate the variable part dynamically at run-time as the virtual capability's *parameters*. Further, we also require to adapt our current mechanism for task execution accordingly. For realizing virtual capabilities aiming at collective behavior, we need to introduce the possibility of direct communication between instances of the same type of virtual capabilities which was only possible through agent layer up to now. Without the direct exchange of relevant information between participating entities many external programming approaches for ensembles can not function because they rely on some form of directly accessible messaging interfaces [19,20].

3   Approach

To be available to an agent $\alpha \in \mathcal{A}$ in the multipotent systems reference architecture [14], a capability requires a set of physical hardware modules, i.e., sensors and/or actuators (S/A). While the set of S/A does not need to be the same for every instantiation of a capability, we require the set of S/A to have the necessary user-specified functionality [5,25], e.g., determine the *presence* of an object. For their execution, capabilities do require a set of parameters, e.g., a direction vector for a *move* capability. In this paper, we refine this capability concept (cf. light-grey part of Fig. 2) by differentiating between virtual and physical capabilities (darker part of Fig. 2). Therefore, we demonstrate how we can combine already existing physical capabilities $\mathcal{C}^p$ for achieving collective behavior that we can parametrize in *virtual capabilities for collectives* $\mathcal{C}^v$. We apply this concept in a virtual capability for movement-vector based swarm behavior (cf. *Movement-Vector Based Swarm Capability* in Fig. 2) realizing the general pattern for individual agent participation in respective swarm algorithms. We further introduce a second virtual capability offering an interface between agents and their capabilities in our reference architecture and other collective programming approaches (cf. *External Collective Programming Capability* Fig. 2).

We assume that every agent can communicate with any other agent in the ensemble $\mathcal{E}$ it currently participates in. This is necessary to realize certain types of swarm behavior (e.g., particle swarm optimization PSO [27]) because we can not assume local sensors for all spatially distributed relevant values (e.g., measurements of other agents). Moreover, we can not assume to have perfect local sensors for every robot enabling it to externally determine the state of other robots precisely enough in a real-world setting. We achieve this by exploiting the communication middleware of the multi-agent framework Jadex [1]. With this framework, we can ease the conceptualization and implementation of our distributed multipotent systems through the use of Jadex Active Components, which are autonomously acting entities. Implementing each instance of $\mathcal{C}^p$, $\mathcal{C}^v$, and $\mathcal{A}$ as such active components and encapsulating their functionality in services each enables their direct interaction where this is necessary. We further assume that no outages (e.g., communication, sensor failures, broken robots) occur.

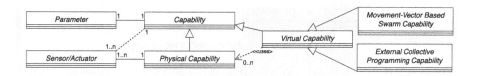

Fig. 2. General concept model for virtual capabilities. Instead of direct access to S/A, we provide access indirectly through associated physical capabilities.

3.1   Static and Dynamic Model of Virtual Capabilities

We differentiate between virtual capabilities $\mathcal{C}^v$ and physical capabilities $\mathcal{C}^p$ which both refine the previous concept of a capability, i.e., a service a robot provides for execution. In comparison to physical capabilities, virtual capabilities are not directly associated with S/A. Instead, for executing a virtual capability we require it to invoke associated other (physical) capabilities. Thus, virtual capabilities do only have indirect access to hardware but can be used to construct more complex behavior. Consequently, the set of parameters for a virtual capability needs to include additional information, e.g., the set of other capabilities it needs for its execution. This has also consequences for our currently established self-awareness [13], and self-organization mechanisms [12] we use to execute plans in multipotent systems. Because the execution of a virtual capability might require the cooperation within the ensemble $\mathcal{E} \subseteq \mathcal{A}$ executing it, we allow for every α_i executing a specific $c^v \in \mathcal{C}^v$ to directly exchange information with other $\alpha_{j \neq i}$ within the same ensemble that are executing the same instance of c^v. Further, communication is an urgent requirement for collective programming approaches we want to enable as external capabilities. We therefore separate each $c^v \in \mathcal{C}^v$ in an active part $c^{v:\mathrm{ACT}}$ and a passive part $c^{v:\mathrm{PAS}}$. While the active part differs for all $c^v \in \mathcal{C}^v$, we can define the passive part as a procedure RECEIVE($c^v, \mathcal{V}_{\alpha_i}$) used for receiving relevant data $\mathcal{V}_{\alpha_i}$ from another agent α_i executing the same virtual capability c^v in general for all $c^v \in \mathcal{C}^v$. RECEIVE updates the values for these other agents stored in a shared map $\mathrm{M}^{\mathcal{E}} := \langle \alpha \in \mathcal{E} \rangle, \langle M^\alpha \rangle$ holding the most recent values M^α received from all $\alpha \in \mathcal{E}$. To enable the exchange of data, the active and passive part of each $c^v \in \mathcal{C}^v$ share this map. This means, when receiving $\mathcal{V}_{\alpha_{i \neq j}}$ in $c^{v:\mathrm{PAS}}$, an agent α_j can update the entries referenced in $\mathcal{V}_{\alpha_i}$ concerning α_i in $\mathrm{M}^{\mathcal{E}}$ and subsequently access the data in $c^{v:\mathrm{ACT}}$. In our code snippets, we indicate that α_j executing c^v sends $\mathcal{V}_{\alpha_j}$ to a specific other agent α_i executing the same instance of c^v with $\alpha_i.\mathrm{SEND}(c^v, \mathcal{V}_{\alpha_j})$. Besides shared data and data received from other agents, in our algorithms we indicate local input with NAME := $\langle \mathrm{INPUT}_1, ..., \mathrm{INPUT}_n \rangle$.

3.2   Termination and Results of Virtual Capability Executions

Like for physical capabilities, we can define different termination types for virtual capabilities. Physical capabilities can terminate internally on their own or require external events for termination. A robot executing, e.g., its physical capability for moving to a certain position $c^p_{\mathrm{MV\_POS}}$ can rely on the automatic

---

Algorithm 1. $c^{v:\text{FIN-COORD}} := \langle \text{F:AGGR}_{c^v}, \text{F:TERM}_{c^v} \rangle$

1: $\text{R}_{\text{AGGR}} \leftarrow \text{F:AGGR}_{c^v}(\text{M}^{\mathcal{E}})$ # *aggregates the ensemble's current measurements*
2: $\text{TERM} \leftarrow \text{F:TERM}_{c^v}(\text{R}_{\text{AGGR}})$ # *decide for termination using the aggregated result*
3: **if** TERM **then**
4:     $\text{STORE}(\text{R}_{\text{AGGR}})$ # *if terminating, store the result for external evaluation*
5:     **for** $\alpha_i \in \mathcal{E}$ **do**
6:         $\alpha_i.\text{SEND}(c^v, \text{TERM})$ # *broadcast the termination decision in the ensemble*

---

termination of $c^p_{\text{MV\_POS}}$ when it reaches the position defined in the parameters. Instead, a physical capability $c^p_{\text{MV\_VEC}}$ that moves a robot in a direction using a speed vector does not terminate itself as the movement does not have a natural end and thus needs to be terminated externally. Likewise, virtual capabilities can terminate their execution internally or require external termination. This is especially relevant for all virtual capabilities that implement collective behavior. We can define termination criteria with appropriate parameters for some swarm behavior, e.g., executing a virtual capability implementing a PSO can terminate itself when all agents in the swarm gather within a certain distance [27]. For other swarm behavior, e.g., achieving the equal distribution of robots in a given area with the triangle algorithm [15], we do not want to define such criteria (e.g., for achieving the continuous surveillance of that area) or even can not do it at all (e.g., for steering a swarm in one direction with guided flocking [2]) and thus rely on an external event for termination. Besides defining when to terminate a c^v implementing swarm behavior or other collective behavior, we also require to quantify the emergent effect of executing c^v and store it for up-following evaluation like we do with the results originating from physical capability executions. For PSO, e.g., we finally want to determine the position the highest concentration of a parameter an ensemble was searching for was measured. In this case, we can calculate the position of relevance by calculating the ensemble's center of gravity when the geometrical diameter of the swarm, i.e., the euclidean distance between the $\alpha_i, \alpha_j \in \mathcal{E}$ having the greatest distance between each other, gets lower than a user-defined threshold. For such calculations and to determine termination for virtual capabilities therewith, we extend the role of the ensemble coordinator that is responsible to coordinate a plan's execution [10]. Concerning the results of (physical) capability executions, the coordinator only acts as a pass-through station for results originating from any capability execution in the ensemble. The coordinator stores each result in a distributed storage and evaluates data when necessary, e.g., for deciding on the current plan's progress or during replanning on the task layer (cf. Fig. 1). To determine the termination of a virtual capabilities execution, we now enable the coordinator to also aggregate, analyze and post-process the intermediate results from virtual capabilities before storing them by using capability specific procedure $c^{v:\text{FIN-COORD}}$ (cf. Algorithm 1). Because we guarantee with an additional constraint in our constraint-based task allocation mechanism [6] that the agent adopting the coordinator role always also participates in the execution of the collective behavior, i.e., executes the

Algorithm 2. $c_{\text{SW}}^{v:\text{ACT}} := \langle C_{\text{SW}}^{p}, \text{CALC}_{\text{SW}}, \mathcal{E}_{\text{SW}} \rangle$

1: **repeat**
2:   **for each** $c_i \in C_{\text{SW}}^{p}$ **parallel do**
3:     $\text{M}^{\text{SELF}}[c_i] \leftarrow \text{EXEC}(c_i)$ # execute all relevant capabilities and store the results
4:     $\text{M}^{\mathcal{E}}[\text{SELF}] \leftarrow \text{M}^{\text{SELF}}$ # store local results in the map for all ensemble results
5:   **for each** $\alpha_i \in \mathcal{E}_{\text{SW}}$ **parallel do**
6:     $\alpha_i.\text{SEND}(c_{\text{SW}}^{v}, \text{M}^{\text{SELF}})$ # distribute stored results in the ensemble
7:     $\text{PAR}_{c_{\text{MV\_VEC}}^{p}} \leftarrow \text{CALC}_{\text{SW}}(\text{M}^{\mathcal{E}})$ # calculate the new movement vector
8:     $\text{EXEC}(c_{\text{MV\_VEC}}^{p})$ # update the current movement vector
9: **until** TERM   # decide on termination using the received value

---

respective $c^{v:\text{ACT}}$, it can also receive values other ensemble members send and thus has access to $\text{M}^{\mathcal{E}}$. By using an aggregation function F:AGGR_{c^v} taking $\text{M}^{\mathcal{E}}$ as input parameter that is specific for each c^v, we can quantify the emergent effect every time the entries in $\text{M}^{\mathcal{E}}$ change (L. 1 in Algorithm 1). If the termination criteria (F:TERM_{c^v} in Algorithm 1) holds for the current result (L. 2 in Algorithm 1), the coordinator can store that result in the distributed storage (L. 4 in Algorithm 1) and distribute the current termination state TERM within the ensemble (L. 6 in Algorithm 1). Each agent can receive this signal with a respective service $c^{v:\text{FIN-PART}}$ to receive the coordinator's termination signal TERM with $\text{RECEIVE}(c^v, \text{TERM})$. The service $c^{v:\text{FIN-PART}}$ shares TERM with the active part $c^{v:\text{ACT}}$ of c^v in $\text{TERM}^{\mathcal{E}}$, which we use to stop the execution of c^v. For $c^v \in \mathcal{C}^v$ that can terminate externally only, we can thus enable the user to also have the possibility to terminate the execution of c^v.

3.3 A Capability for Movement-Vector Based Swarm Algorithms

For achieving emergent effects generated by movement-vector based swarm behavior, we introduce a *Movement-Vector Based Swarm Capability* c_{SW}^{v} with its according parameters $\text{PAR}_{c_{\text{SW}}^{v}}$ (cf. Fig. 2). This virtual capability realizes swarm behavior from the class of movement-vector-based swarm algorithms such as the PSO [7,27], flocking [21], or the triangle formation [18] among others, that can be of use for multipotent systems. We illustrate the respective active part $c_{\text{SW}}^{v:\text{ACT}}$ of c_{SW}^{v} in Algorithm 2 that executes a general pattern capable of producing the mentioned swarm behaviors. In a first step, each agent executing c_{SW}^{v} measures and remembers relevant values according to the set of physical parameters C_{SW}^{p} included in $\text{PAR}_{c_{\text{SW}}^{v}}$ in parallel (cf. L. 3 in Algorithm 2). After finishing the execution of all capabilities in case of self-terminating capabilities or after starting to execute non-self-terminating capabilities respectively, agents executing c_{SW}^{v} in parallel exchange these local measurements M^{SELF} with all agents in the current ensemble $\mathcal{E}_{\text{SW}}$ that execute the same instance of c_{SW}^{v} (cf. L. 6 in Algorithm 2). Each agent $\alpha \in \mathcal{E}_{\text{SW}}$ remembers these measurements in the virtual capability's locally shared map $\text{M}^{\mathcal{E}}$ that holds the most recent values for all neighbors including itself (cf. L. 4 in Algorithm 2). By using this aggregated measurements $\text{M}^{\mathcal{E}}$, each agent then is able to determine the necessary adaption to its current move-

Algorithm 3. $c^v_{\text{EXT}} := \langle \text{PROG}_{\text{EXT}}, \text{PC}_{\text{EXT}}, \mathcal{E}_{\text{EXT}} \rangle$

1: **repeat**
2:    $\text{M}^{\mathcal{E}}_{\text{SNAP}} \leftarrow \text{M}^{\mathcal{E}}$ # *create a snapshot of the current ensemble values*
3:    $\langle C^p_{\text{EXT}}, \text{TERM}_{\text{EXT}}, \text{PC}_{\text{EXT}}, \mathcal{V}_{\text{EXT}} \rangle \leftarrow \text{PROG}(\text{PC}_{\text{EXT}}, \text{M}^{\mathcal{E}}_{\text{SNAP}})$ #*execute the program*
4:    **for each** $c_i \in C^p_{\text{EXT}}$ **parallel do**
5:       $\text{M}^{\text{SELF}}[c_i] \leftarrow \text{EXEC}(c_i)$ #*execute capabilities required by the program*
6:    $\text{M}^{\mathcal{E}}[\text{SELF}] \leftarrow \text{M}^{\text{SELF}}$ #*store results for next iteration of the program*
7:    **for each** $\alpha_i \in \mathcal{E}_{\text{EXT}}$ **parallel do**
8:       $\alpha_i.\text{SEND}(c^v_{\text{EXT}}, \mathcal{V}_{\text{EXT}})$ #*distribute relevant data of the program*
9: **until** $\text{TERM}_{\text{EXT}} \vee \text{TERM}$ #*check termination set by the program or coordinator*

---

ment vector (cf. L. 8 in Algorithm 2) for achieving the intended specific swarm behavior encapsulated in CALC$_{\text{SW}}$ (cf. L. 7 in Algorithm 2). As all agents in $\mathcal{E}_{\text{SW}}$ repeatedly execute this behavior until a specific termination criteria TERM holds (passed over to the passive part $c^{v:\text{PAS}}$ of c^v_{SW} from the coordinator, cf. Sect. 3.2), they achieve the specific swarm algorithm's emergent effect collectively (cf. L. 9 in Algorithm 2). By adjusting CALC$_{\text{SW}}$ in particular, we can exploit this generally implemented form of a virtual capability to execute different swarm algorithms that would require an individual implementation each otherwise.

3.4   An Interface for External Collective Programming Languages

During the design of multipotent systems, we can not foresee all necessary functionality in specific use cases a user of the system might have in mind. Therefore, we offer the possibility of external programming to the system's user. We do this by introducing virtual capabilities $c^v_{\text{EXT}} \in \mathcal{C}^v$ for external collective programming approaches which become a fixed part of the multipotent system and represent an interface to the run-time environment of a specific programming language each. In contrast to c^v_{SW}, where we need to define the actual calculation CALC$_{\text{SW}}$ within the host system and its respective programming language (i.e., that the multipotent system reference architecture from Sect. 2 is implemented with), we are not restricted to that when using a specific c^v_{EXT}. Instead, we encapsulate necessary information in a program written in the respective external programming language and only need to define the interface for the communication of that programming language's execution environment and the multipotent system's implementation. These external programs then define, how values we generate within the multipotent system are used and transformed into instructions for the multipotent system. Like for any $c^v \in \mathcal{C}^v$, we enable each c^v_{EXT} to execute other already existing capabilities $c^p \in \mathcal{C}^p$ of the multipotent system, i.e., choose respective parameters and read results from those capabilities' execution that we store in $M^{\mathcal{E}}$ through the defined interface (L. 5 in Algorithm 3). This way, a user can program new complex behavior PROG$_{\text{EXT}}$ in the external programming language while also using already available functionality provided by $\mathcal{C}^p$ within our system. The programmer only needs to know the interface to relevant $c^p \in \mathcal{C}^p$ and does not require further knowledge of the underlying multipotent system, e.g., if the PROG$_{\text{EXT}}$ requires the change the current movement vector of the executing robot. For its execution, the respective c_{EXT}^v then uses $\mathrm{PROG_{EXT}}$ as an additional parameter (cf. Algorithm 3). This way, and to allow for changing the behavior of c_{EXT}^v, the programmer can dynamically exchange the external program at runtime. With the start of the capability execution within the active part of each $c_{\mathrm{EXT}}^{v:\mathrm{ACT}}$, we run $\mathrm{PROG_{EXT}}$ from its entry point by handing over a program pointer $\mathrm{PC_{EXT}}$ and a snapshot of the current state of $\mathrm{M}^{\mathcal{E}}$ (initially empty, L. 2 and 3 in Algorithm 3). When the execution of $\mathrm{PROG_{EXT}}$ stops, we require it to return a data vector $\langle C_{\mathrm{EXT}}^p, \mathrm{TERM_{EXT}}, \mathrm{PC_{EXT}}, \mathcal{V}_{\mathrm{EXT}} \rangle$ encapsulating instructions from the external program to the multipotent system. The first entry indicates whether the external program's control flow requires that physical capabilities C_{EXT}^p get executed in the following (L. 4 and 5 in Algorithm 3). The second entry determines, whether $\mathrm{PROG_{EXT}}$ already reached its termination criteria $\mathrm{TERM_{EXT}}$ and the execution of c_{EXT}^v can be finished internally (L. 9 in Algorithm 3). The third entry determines, what the next program counter $\mathrm{PC_{EXT}}$ is if $\mathrm{TERM_{EXT}}$ does not hold. Because information on which values need to be within the ensemble $\mathcal{E}_{\mathrm{EXT}}$ is encapsulated in $\mathrm{PROG_{EXT}}$ but the distribution itself is performed by the multipotent system's agent communication interface, in a fourth entry $\mathcal{V}_{\mathrm{EXT}}$ determines those values (L. 7 and 8 in Algorithm 3). While $\mathrm{TERM_{EXT}}$ does not hold and no termination signal is received from the coordinator of $\mathcal{E}_{\mathrm{EXT}}$ in $c^{v:\mathrm{FIN\text{-}PART}}$ (cf. Sect. 3.2), the execution of c_{EXT}^v continues to execute $\mathrm{PROG_{EXT}}$ with the current $\mathrm{PC_{EXT}}$ in the following iteration. Thereby, it uses an updated version of $\mathrm{M}^{\mathcal{E}}$ (L. 2 in Algorithm 3) containing latest local values (L. 6 in Algorithm 3) as well as such received in $c_{\mathrm{EXT}}^{v:pas}$ meanwhile (Sect. 3.1). Each $\mathrm{PROG_{EXT}}$ adhering to this convention thus can access the set of locally available physical capabilities and use the communication middleware of our multipotent system in the current ensemble. This creates a high degree of flexibility in the way of programming with our approach.

4 Proof of Concepts

To demonstrate the flexibility of our approach we give proof of concepts in the following. We, therefore, implemented a virtual capability for movement-vector based swarm algorithms c_{sw}^v and evaluated it with different parameters to achieve different emergent effects. We demonstrate the concept of a virtual capability for the movement-vector based swarm behavior with video materials[1] isolated in a NetLogo simulation[2] and integrated with our multipotent systems reference implementation. Further, we demonstrate the feasibility of integrating an external programming language for collectives as a virtual capability by example.

4.1 Executing Movement-Vector Based Swarm Algorithms

We validate the concept of the virtual capability for movement-vector based swarm algorithms c_{sw}^v we introduced in Sect. 3.3 using different parameters for

---

[1] https://github.com/isse-augsburg/isola2020-swarm-capabilities.git.
[2] NetLogo download on https://ccl.northwestern.edu/netlogo/download.shtml.

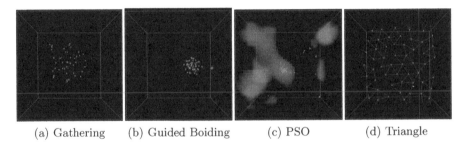

(a) Gathering   (b) Guided Boiding   (c) PSO   (d) Triangle

Fig. 3. Screen shots of a simulation environment showing the use of a swarm capability for different parameters resulting in respective emergent effects (top down perspective). See footnotes 1, 2 for video material and a respective NetLogo simulation source file.

realizing different emergent effects. In a simplified major catastrophe scenario, a firefighter might want to a) gather its ensemble of mobile robots, b) move them collectively to the area where, e.g., a gas accident happened, c) search for the source of the gas leak, and d) survey the area close to the leak (video materials on our GitHub). We can instruct our system, e.g., with our task-orchestration approach for ensembles Maple-Swarm [11]. To handle this scenario we can use the c_{sw}^v with different sets of parameters in steps a)-d) each (cf. Figs. 3a to 3d), illustrating the flexibility of our concept of c_{sw}^v including its termination functionality. For all instances of c_{sw}^v we execute to realizing the desired emergent effect for achieving a)-d), we assume the following: A sufficiently equipped ensemble $\mathcal{E}_{sw}$ is available concerning the set of physical capabilities C_{sw}^p necessary for that concrete instantiation which we can achieve, e.g., with our self-aware and market-based task allocation mechanism [13] in combination with our self-organized resource allocation mechanism [6]. For each result of CALC, we normalize (NORM) the resulting distance (DIST) vector originating from the robots current position POS_α and scale it with the robots maximum velocity with ν. We assume a working collision avoidance system provided by the robotics controller.

a) For *gathering* the ensemble, we can execute c_{sw}^v with $C_{sw}^p := \{c_{POS}^p\}$, where c_{POS}^p measures the executing robot's current position (cf. Fig. 3a). Each robot can terminate the execution of c_{sw}^v locally when the diameter DIAM() of the swarm is below a user-defined threshold x, calculated with the measurements available in $M^\mathcal{E}$, i.e., $TERM_{sw} := DIAM(M^\mathcal{E}[*][c_{POS}^p]) \leq x$. We calculate the desired moving vector using the ensemble's center of gravity GRAV(), i.e., $CALC() := \nu \cdot NORM(DIST(POS_\alpha, GRAV(M^\mathcal{E}[*][c_{POS}^p])))$. Both, DIAM() and GRAV() only require information concerning the position of each robot in $\mathcal{E}_{sw}$, thus results from executing c_{POS}^p stored in $M^\mathcal{E}$ are sufficient therefore.

b) For *controlling the ensemble to a goal location* with an adapted flocking approach following the idea of boiding in [21], we execute c_{sw}^v with $C_{sw}^p := \{c_{POS}^p, c_{VEL}^p\}$, where c_{POS}^p measures the executing robot's current position and c_{VEL}^p its current velocity (cf. Fig. 3b). We can calculate the desired moving vector by appropriately weighting the three urges for the cohesion COH of the ensemble, the separation SEP from the closest neighbor in the ensembles, and the alignment ALI of the individual robot's moving direction with that of the ensemble known from [21]: $\text{CALC} := \omega_1 \cdot \text{SEP}(M^{\mathcal{E}}[*][c_{\text{POS}}^p]) + \omega_2 \cdot \text{COH}(M^{\mathcal{E}}[*][c_{\text{POS}}^p]) + \omega_3 \cdot \text{ALI}(M^{\mathcal{E}}[*][c_{\text{VEL}}^p])$. To guide the ensemble to the goal location we exploit how ensemble members evaluate $M^{\mathcal{E}}$ for adapting their movement vector (L. 7 in Algorithm 2) by adding an additional entry for a non-ensemble member (i.e., a dedicated leader robot or any other position-aware device) that also measurements of C_{SW}^p frequently. Because all ensemble members use the complete map $M^{\mathcal{E}}$, the emergent effect is what we aim for: guiding the collective to a goal location the non-ensemble robot is moving to. Robots can not terminate the execution of c_{SW}^v locally in this case because they have no information on the goal location and thus rely on an external termination signal TERM from their coordinator (who possibly requires to receive it from the user itself).

c) For *searching for the highest concentration* of a certain parameter, we execute c_{SW}^v with an adapted version of the particle swarm optimization algorithm (PSO) [27] (cf. Fig. 3c). Obviously, we require to contain the respective capability for measuring the parameter of interest c_{PAR}^p in C_{SW}^p, in addition to c_{POS}^p and c_{VEL}^p, i.e., $C_{\text{SW}}^p := \{c_{\text{PAR}}^p, c_{\text{POS}}^p, c_{\text{VEL}}^p\}$. To determine the movement vector of robot α, we define $\text{CALC} := \omega_1 \cdot \text{DIST}(\text{POS}_\alpha, \text{MAX}(\text{MAX}(M^{\mathcal{E}}[\text{SELF}][c_{\text{PAR}}^p], \text{MAX}^{\text{SELF}}))) + \omega_2 \cdot \text{DIST}(\text{POS}_\alpha, \text{MAX}(\text{MAX}(M^{\mathcal{E}}[*][c_{\text{PAR}}^p], \text{MAX}^{\mathcal{E}})) + \omega_3 \cdot \text{DIST}(\text{POS}_\alpha, \text{RAND}(x, y, z))$ as the weighted sum of distance vectors pointing from the robot α's current position α_{POS} to the position with the iteratively updated highest measurement of the parameter of interest from the robot itself MAX^{SELF}, the whole ensemble $\text{MAX}^{\mathcal{E}}$, and a random direction $\text{RAND}(x, y, z)$ included for exploration. Similar to the execution of c_{SW}^v for gathering in a), we can let the agents in the ensemble decide on the termination on c_{SW}^v by determining whether the diameter of the ensemble is below a threshold x, i.e., $\text{TERM}_{\text{SW}} := \text{DIAM}(M^{\mathcal{E}}[*][c_{\text{POS}}^p]) \leq x$.

d) For realizing the *distributed surveillance* of an area of interests, we adapted the triangle formation algorithm from [15] to also work within a 3D-environment (cf. Fig. 3d). With this algorithm, we can exploit the emergent effect of a swarm distributing in an area holding a predefined distance s to each other at a given height h. To produce the desired emergent effect, a robot α requires position measurements of its two closest neighbors only, i.e., $C_{\text{SW}}^p := \{c_{\text{POS}}^p\}$. To determine the required movement vector, we first need to determine the two closest neighbors $\alpha_{1,2}$ of α in the ensemble, i.e., $\neg\exists\alpha_i \in \mathcal{E} : \text{DIST}(\alpha, \alpha_i) < \text{DIST}(\alpha, \alpha_1) \wedge \neg\exists\alpha_i \in \mathcal{E} \setminus \alpha_1 : \text{DIST}(\alpha, \alpha_i) < \text{DIST}(\alpha, \alpha_2)$. We then calculate the center of gravity $\text{GRAV}(\alpha_1, \alpha_2)$ between α_1 and α_2 and determine the distance vector pointing from α to the closest intersection point of the plane at height h (defined parallel to ground level) and the circle around the center of gravity with radius $\sqrt{3} \cdot \frac{s}{2}$ (being perpendicular to the straight defined by α_1 and α_2) as the goal position of α. While we can define a condition for termination of the execution of c_{SW}^v, e.g., in case that all distances between closest neighbors only vary marginally for all robots in the ensemble, we do not want to specify such in the case of continuous surveillance. Like in b), we require an external termination TERM signal from the user or another external entity.

```
1 module count_neighbors
2 let num_of_neighbors = sumHood(nbr(1))
3 num_of_neighbors
```

```
1 module term_after_iterations
2 def iterations () = rep(x <- 0) { x + 1 }
3 def term_after(x) =
4     if ( iterations () > x) { self .term() }
5     else { iterations () }
6 terminate_after(10)
```

```
 1 module measure_temp
 2 import ParamFactory.get;
 3 def measure_temp() {
 4     let cap_type = self.getType("temp")
 5     let measurement_param = get(cap_type)
 6     let param = measurement_param.get()
 7     param.set("measureOnce", true)
 8     let temp = self.request(param, cap_type)
 9     temp
10 }
11 measure_temp()
```

Fig. 4. Minimal Protelis programs demonstrating the feasibility of the integration: Communication between agents (top left), enforcing the self-termination from the host system (bottom right), and accessing to capabilities of the host system (right).

4.2   Protelis as an Example for an External Virtual Capability

We demonstrate the feasibility of integrating an external programming language into the multipotent systems reference architecture by example. Therefore, we instantiate the concept of an external collective programming capability with c_{PROT}^v providing an interface for the Protelis Aggregate Programming approach [19]. To validate the concepts we introduced in Sect. 3.4, we give a proof of concepts concerning the relevant parts executing an external capability. These concepts are the *communication* between participating agents, commanding the *execution* and making use of the *results* of capabilities running on the host system, and ensuring *self-termination* of the external capability, if necessary. According to [19], for communication between entities, Protelis requires a network manager. With c_{PROT}^v we implement such (L. 7 in Algorithm 3). We can validate its functionality with the minimal example of a Protelis program we give in Fig. 4 (top left) that counts all members of the ensemble using the nbr construct in L. 2 in Fig. 4 (top left). The example showcases the ability of communication between agents executing c_{PROT}^v. In the Protelis program in Fig. 4 (right), we demonstrate how external capabilities can define required access to physical capabilities of the multipotent system host system (implemented in JAVA) using the self construct of Protelis for measuring temperature (L. 11 in Fig. 4 - right). In L. 4–7 of Fig. 4 (right), we access the knowledge base of our architecture by importing the ParamFactory (L. 2 in Fig. 4 - right). We use this knowledge base for loading the correct format of the necessary parameters for the measure temperature capability. For achieving this, we make use of the JAVA Reflection API. With self.request (L. 8 in Fig. 4 - right), we define the request the external capability has concerning the execution of physical capabilities (L. 3 in Algorithm 3) whose result we return in L. 9 in Fig. 4 (right) when it is available. To avoid the blocking of the Protelis program's execution when it requests a capability execution, we implement the data interface to our multipotent system as a reload cache. To validate the correct program flow and validate correct self-termination of c_{PROT}^v, in the Protelis program we give in Fig. 4 (top left) we let each member of the ensemble iterate a counter (L. 6 in Fig. 4 - bottom left). Because there is no access to physical capabilities included in the program, the execution of each instance terminates after 10 iterations and accordingly notifies the encapsulating external capability c^v_{PROT} with TERM_{EXT} evaluating true when it finally reaches self.terminate() in L. 4 in Fig. 4 (bottom left). Thus, we demonstrate the feasibility of integrating an interface between Protelis and our multipotent systems reference architecture with a specific virtual capability as a proof of concepts for our concept of from Sect. 3.4. We provide video material for demonstration purposes on GitHub. The integration of c^v_{PROT} currently is limited to only execute one Protelis program per agent in parallel and relies on capabilities provided by the host system to terminate on their own (cf. Sect. 3.2).

5 Related Work

The literature on swarm behavior, swarm algorithms, or swarm intelligence is manifold. When swarm behavior should be exploited in a real-world application, there are two common directions researchers currently follow. The first direction is that of focusing on one specific behavior found in nature that gets analyzed and migrated to technical systems. Examples for that direction are manifold, thus we only can give an excerpt of research relevant for this paper. To achieve a collective transport of an object, the authors in [4,17] developed a specialized controller by using an evolutionary algorithm for mobile ground robots. While they achieve the desired effect, suffer from the evolutionary algorithms inherent properties of high specialization and the lack of generality: The generated controller can not be used in any other use case. To achieve a close-to equal distribution of swarm entities in a given area, e.g., for distributed surveillance, the authors in [16] adapt a potential-field based deployment algorithm. Unfortunately, the algorithm thus can only be used for exactly that use case. While the authors of [15] propose that they can adapt their swarm approach for distributed surveillance to also achieve flocking and obstacle avoidance they, unfortunately, do not further investigate in this direction. In our opinion, this is a step in the right direction to generate a general pattern for achieving swarm behavior which we try to make with our approach. In [23] the authors adapt the particle swarm optimization algorithm (PSO) [27] for the use of UAV in disaster scenarios to explore an area and detect victims. While the authors can adapt parameters to achieve different goals, the approach is still limited to that narrowly defined area and can not easily be extended. With an adapted flocking algorithm based on the approach of [21], the authors in [24] demonstrate how UAVs can achieve swarm behavior that is very close to that of natural swarms. Unfortunately, the implementation is very specific and can solely achieve this specific swarm behavior.

The second direction researchers follow is that of abstracting from specific applications and use cases and developing a general framework for collective behavior that can be programmed or parametrized in different ways. There already exist interesting approaches for programming collective behavior addressed in the ASCENS project [26]. Protelis [19] is one approach we also categorize in this direction. The authors center it around the idea of abstracting entities in a collective system as a point in a high dimensional vector field. Programming of the collective happens by performing operations on that field. By using implicit communication between entities, the programmer can achieve that changes performed in these fields are distributed within the collective. While a user can exploit this behavior to implement complex collective on an abstract level, it is not easy to achieve swarm behavior for complex mobile robot tasks solely with Protelis. Its lack of general hardware integration and a general task concept necessary for goal-oriented robot collaboration requires Protelis to be integrated into a further framework as we perform it in this paper. Another programming language aiming at collective systems is Buzz [20]. In comparison to Protelis, the authors of Buzz directly aim at integrating their programming language within robot operating systems. They provide swarm primitives for achieving a certain desired collective behavior each. Unfortunately, Buzz also lacks a concept for goal-oriented task orchestration. Further and like for using Protelis, a user of Buzz currently requires a system specifically designed for the respective programming language. With our approach, we can overcome this by providing the possibility to use programs written with any of the two languages in an integrated task orchestration framework. Further, we also try to find some general abstraction from specific applications and use cases in our approach. Moreover, we can use it to analyze and implement specific swarm behavior. Thus, we try to close the gap between the two methods currently existing in the literature.

6   Conclusion

The research community already exploits the positive properties of swarm behavior like robustness and scalability within many different approaches for controlling the behavior of collective adaptive systems. In this paper, we demonstrated how we can subsume many of these approaches by extracting their general swarm behavior in a virtual capability for movement-vector based swarm algorithms. We integrated this virtual capability into our reference architecture for multi-potent systems. We further demonstrate how we can use instances of virtual capabilities to provide adapters to other programming approaches for collective systems on the example of Protelis [19]. Thus, virtual capabilities, in general, can compose existent capabilities of robots, i.e., complexly integrate already provided robot services, which we can exploit to create collective behavior in ensembles. In future work, we will elaborate on if and how we can drop our current assumption of having a steady communication link between ensemble members. This will help us to better deal with failures or complete break down of robots.

References

1. Braubach, L., Pokahr, A.: Developing distributed systems with active components and jadex. Scalable Comput. Pract. Experience **13**(2), 100–120 (2012)

2. Celikkanat, H., Turgut, A.E., Sahin, E.: Guiding a robot flock via informed robots. In: Asama, H., Kurokawa, H., Ota, J., Sekiyama, K. (eds.) Distributed Autonomous Robotic Systems, pp. 215–225. Springer, Heidelberg (2009). https://doi.org/10.1007/978-3-642-00644-9_19

3. Dedousis, D., Kalogeraki, V.: A framework for programming a swarm of UAVs. In: Proceedings of the 11th Pervasive Technologies Related to Assistive Environment Conference, pp. 5–12 (2018)

4. Dorigo, M., et al.: The SWARM-BOTS project. In: Şahin, E., Spears, W.M. (eds.) SR 2004. LNCS, vol. 3342, pp. 31–44. Springer, Heidelberg (2005). https://doi.org/10.1007/978-3-540-30552-1_4

5. Eymüller, C., Wanninger, C., Hoffmann, A., Reif, W.: Semantic plug and play - self-descriptive modular hardware for robotic applications. Int. J. Semant. Comput. (IJSC) **12**(04), 559–577 (2018)

6. Hanke, J., Kosak, O., Schiendorfer, A., Reif, W.: Self-organized resource allocation for reconfigurable robot ensembles. In: 2018 IEEE 12th International Conference on Self-Adaptive and Self-Organizing Systems (SASO), pp. 110–119 (2018)

7. Kennedy, J., Eberhart, R.: Particle swarm optimization. In: Proceedings of ICNN'95-International Conference on Neural Networks, vol. 4, pp. 1942–1948. IEEE (1995)

8. Kosak, O.: Facilitating planning by using self-organization. In: 2017 IEEE 2nd International Workshops on Foundations and Applictions of Self* Systems (FAS*W), pp. 371–374 (2017)

9. Kosak, O.: Multipotent systems: a new paradigm for multi-robot applications. In: Organic Computing: Doctoral Dissertation Colloquium, vol. 10, p. 53. kassel University Press GmbH (2018)

10. Kosak, O., Bohn, F., Keller, F., Ponsar, H., Reif, W.: Ensemble programming for multipotent systems. In: 2019 IEEE 4th International Workshops on Foundations and Applications of Self* Systems (FAS*W), pp. 104–109 (2019)

11. Kosak, O., Huhn, L., Bohn, F., et al.: Maple-swarm: programming collective behavior for ensembles by extending HTN-planning. In: 9th International Symposium on Leveraging Application of Formal Methods, Verification and Validation (2020)

12. Kosak, O., Wanninger, C., Angerer, A., et al.: Decentralized coordination of heterogeneous ensembles using jadex. In: IEEE 1st International Workshops on Foundations and Application of Self* Systems (FAS*W), pp. 271–272 (2016)

13. Kosak, O., Wanninger, C., Angerer, A., et al.: Towards self-organizing swarms of reconfigurable self-aware robots. In: IEEE International Workshops on Foundations and Applications of Self* Systems, pp. 204–209. IEEE (2016)

14. Kosak, O., Wanninger, C., Hoffmann, A., Ponsar, H., Reif, W.: Multipotent systems: combining planning, self-organization, and reconfiguration in modular robot ensembles. Sensors **19**(1), 17 (2018)

15. Li, X., Ercan, M.F., Fung, Y.F.: A triangular formation strategy for collective behaviors of robot swarm. In: Gervasi, O., Taniar, D., Murgante, B., Laganà, A., Mun, Y., Gavrilova, M.L. (eds.) ICCSA 2009. LNCS, vol. 5592, pp. 897–911. Springer, Heidelberg (2009). https://doi.org/10.1007/978-3-642-02454-2_70

16. Ma, M., Yang, Y.: Adaptive triangular deployment algorithm for unattended mobile sensor networks. IEEE Trans. Comput. **56**(7), 847–946 (2007)

17. Mondada, F., Gambardella, L.M., Floreano, D., et al.: The cooperation of swarm-bots: physical interactions in collective robotics. IEEE Rob. Autom. Mag. **12**(2), 21–28 (2005)

18. Nishimura, Y., Lee, G., Chong, N.: Adaptive lattice deployment of robot swarms based on local triangular interactions. In: 2012 9th International Conference on Ubiquitous Robots and Ambient Intelligence, pp. 279–284 (2012)
19. Pianini, D., Viroli, M., Beal, J.: Protelis: practical aggregate programming. In: Proceedings of the 30th Annual ACM Symposium on Applied Computing, pp. 1846–1853. ACM (2015)
20. Pinciroli, C., Beltrame, G.: Buzz: an extensible programming language for heterogeneous swarm robotics. In: 2016 IEEE/RSJ International Conference on Intelligent Robots and Systems (IROS), pp. 3794–3800 (2016)
21. Reynolds, C.W.: Flocks, herds and schools: a distributed behavioral model. ACM SIGGRAPH Comput. Graph. **21**(4), 25–34 (1987)
22. Rubenstein, M., Cornejo, A., Nagpal, R.: Programmable self-assembly in a thousand-robot swarm. Science **345**(6198), 795–799 (2014)
23. Sánchez-García, J., Reina, D., Toral, S.: A distributed PSO-based exploration algorithm for a UAV network assisting a disaster scenario. Fut. Gener. Comput. Syst. **90**, 129–148 (2019)
24. Vásárhelyi, G., Virágh, C., Somorjai, G., et al.: Outdoor flocking and formation flight with autonomous aerial robots. In: 2014 IEEE/RSJ International Conference on Intelligent Robots and Systems, pp. 3866–3873 (2014)
25. Wanninger, C., Eymüller, C., Hoffmann, A., Kosak, O., Reif, W.: Synthesizing capabilities for collective adaptive systems from self-descriptive hardware devices bridging the reality gap. In: Margaria, T., Steffen, B. (eds.) ISoLA 2018. LNCS, vol. 11246, pp. 94–108. Springer, Cham (2018). https://doi.org/10.1007/978-3-030-03424-5_7
26. Wirsing, M., Hölzl, M., Koch, N., Mayer, P. (eds.): Software Engineering for Collective Autonomic Systems. LNCS, vol. 8998. Springer, Cham (2015). https://doi.org/10.1007/978-3-319-16310-9
27. Zhang, Y., Wang, S., Ji, G.: A comprehensive survey on particle swarm optimization algorithm and its applications. Math. Prob. Eng. **2015** (2015)

Author Index

Abdi, Mehrdad II-9
Aharon, Khen II-457
Aho, Pekka I-543
Ahrendt, Wolfgang III-9
Aichernig, Bernhard K. I-426
Alt, Leonardo III-178
Amendola, Arturo III-240
Ashok, Pranav I-331
Audrito, Giorgio II-344

Bacci, Giorgio I-275
Bacci, Giovanni I-275
Bacher, Isabelle II-55
Baier, Christel I-240
Baranov, Eduard I-404
Barbanera, Franco I-39
Bartoletti, Massimo III-25
Basile, Davide I-368, III-467
Becchi, Anna III-240
Beckert, Bernhard I-60, III-43
Bensalem, Saddek II-457
Bernardo, Bruno III-60
Bettini, Lorenzo II-361
Beyer, Dirk I-143, I-168, I-449
Blasco, Ernesto Calás I-543
Bloem, Roderick I-290
Bohn, Felix II-507, II-525
Boigues, Ismael Torres I-543
Bon, Philippe III-404
Borgarelli, Andrea I-558
Bourr, Khalid II-361
Braithwaite, Sean I-471
Brünjes, Lars III-73
Bubel, Richard III-9
Buchman, Ethan I-471
Bureš, Tomáš II-295, II-440

Casadei, Roberto II-344
Caselli, Ashley II-205
Castiglioni, Valentina II-380
Cauderlier, Raphaël III-60
Cavada, Roberto III-240
Chakravarty, Manuel M. T. III-89, III-112

Chapman, James III-89, III-112
Ciatto, Giovanni II-205
Cimatti, Alessandro III-240
Claret, Guillaume III-60
Cleophas, Loek I-211
Collart-Dutilleul, Simon III-404
Comptier, Mathieu III-393
Coto, Alex I-22

Daca, Przemysław I-331
Damiani, Ferruccio I-81, I-558, II-344
De Nicola, Rocco II-161, II-261
Demeyer, Serge II-3, II-9
Di Giandomenico, Felicita I-368
Di MarzoSerugendo, Giovanna II-205
Donetti, Simone I-558
Drechsler, Rolf III-326
Dubslaff, Clemens I-240
Duong, Tan II-261

Eing, Lennart II-525
Ellul, Joshua III-131
Enoiu, Eduard I-350
Eugster, Patrick III-178

Fahrenberg, Uli I-262
Fantechi, Alessandro I-368, III-389, III-467
Faqeh, Rasha II-416
Ferrari, Alessio III-467
Fetzer, Christof II-416
Filliâtre, Jean-Christophe I-122
Fränzle, Martin III-255
Friedberger, Karlheinz I-449

Gabbay, Murdoch J. III-73
Gabor, Thomas II-473
Gashier, Eamonn III-195
Geisler, Signe III-449
Gerostathopoulos, Ilias II-440
Gheyi, Rohit II-138
Given-Wilson, Thomas I-404
Glesner, Sabine III-307

Gnesi, Stefania   I-368, III-389, III-467
Goes, Christopher   III-146
Goldberg, Yoav   II-457
Göttmann, Hendrik   II-55
Griggio, Alberto   III-240
Große, Daniel   III-326
Gu, Rong   I-350
Guanciale, Roberto   I-22
Gurov, Dilian   I-3, III-235, III-348

Hähnle, Reiner   I-3, II-3, II-117
Hamers, Ruben   I-489
Hansen, René Rydhof   II-280
Haxthausen, Anne E.   III-389, III-415,
    III-449
Heinrich, Robert   II-295
Hennicker, Rolf   II-224
Herber, Paula   III-235, III-307
Herdt, Vladimir   III-326
Hermanns, Holger   I-240, II-416
Heydari Tabar, Asmae   II-117
Hillston, Jane   II-491
Hnětynka, Petr   II-295, II-440
Hoffmann, Alwin   II-507, II-525
Hoffmann, Jörg   II-416
Huhn, Lukas   II-507
Huisman, Marieke   I-421, III-273
Hungar, Hardi   III-293
Hyvärinen, Antti E. J.   III-178

Incerto, Emilio   I-307
Inverso, Omar   II-243, II-261
Iosti, Simon   II-457

Jacobs, Bart   I-509
Jaeger, Manfred   I-275
Jähnichen, Stefan   II-161
Jakobs, Marie-Christine   II-72
Jakobsson, Arvid   III-60
Jansen, Nils   I-290
Jensen, Peter G.   I-385
Jensen, Peter Gjøl   I-275
Johnsen, Einar Broch   I-103, I-558
Jongmans, Sung-Shik   I-489
Jørgensen, Kenneth Y.   I-385

Kamburjan, Eduard   I-3
Kanav, Sudeep   I-168

Kirsten, Michael   I-60
Klamroth, Jonas   I-60
Klauck, Michaela   I-240, II-416
Kleinekathöfer, Jan   III-326
Klüppelholz, Sascha   I-240
Knüppel, Alexander   I-187
Köhl, Maximilian A.   I-240, II-416
Könighofer, Bettina   I-290
Konnov, Igor   I-471
Kosak, Oliver   II-507, II-525
Kosmatov, Nikolai   I-525
Křetínský, Jan   I-331
Kröger, Paul   III-255

Lamela Seijas, Pablo   III-161
Lande, Stefano   III-25
Lanese, Ivan   I-39
Larsen, Kim G.   I-325, I-385
Larsen, Kim Guldstrand   I-275
Laursen, Per Lange   III-415
Lecomte, Thierry   III-393
Legay, Axel   I-211, I-262, I-325, I-404
Lentzsch, Daniel   II-25
Liebrenz, Timm   III-307
Lienhardt, Michael   I-81
Linnhoff-Popien, Claudia   II-473
Lochau, Malte   II-55
Longuet, Delphine   I-525
Lorber, Florian   I-290
Loreti, Michele   II-380
Lundqvist, Kristina   I-350
Luthmann, Lars   II-55

MacKenzie, Kenneth   III-89, III-112
Maderbacher, Benedikt   I-426
Maffei, Matteo   III-212
Mantel, Heiko   II-3, II-72
Marescotti, Matteo   III-178
Mariani, Stefano   II-189
Martínez, Héctor Martínez   I-543
Masullo, Laura   III-467
Mazaheri, Arya   II-117
Mazzanti, Franco   III-467
McIver, Annabelle   I-216
Melkonian, Orestis   III-89, III-112
Meywerk, Tim   III-326
Mikučionis, Marius   I-385
Milosevic, Zarko   I-471

Molinero, Julien   III-393
Monti, Raúl E.   III-273
Morgan, Carroll   I-216
Müller, Jann   III-89, III-112
Muñiz, Marco   I-385

Napolitano, Annalisa   I-307
Naumann, David A.   II-93
Nielson, Flemming   II-280
Nielson, Hanne Riis   II-280
Norouzi, Mohammad   II-117
Nyberg, Mattias   III-348

Omicini, Andrea   II-205
Orlov, Dmitry   II-44
Otoni, Rodrigo   III-178

Pace, Gordon J.   III-3
Pacovský, Jan   II-440
Paolini, Luca   I-81
Parsai, Ali   II-9
Paskevich, Andrei   I-122
Peled, Doron   II-457
Peleska, Jan   III-434
Pesin, Basile   III-60
Petrov, Tatjana   II-397
Peyton Jones, Michael   III-89, III-112
Piattino, Andrea   III-467
Piho, Paul   II-491
Poulsen, Danny B.   I-385
Pugliese, Rosario   II-361
Pun, Violet Ka I   II-138

Rall, Dennis   II-525
Reif, Wolfgang   II-507, II-525
Reisig, Wolfgang   II-171
Ricós, Fernando Pastor   I-543
Rius, Alfonso D. D. M.   III-195
Runge, Tobias   I-187

Sabatier, Denis   III-393
Sánchez, César   III-3
Scaglione, Giuseppe   III-240
Schaefer, Ina   I-187, I-211, III-235
Scherer, Markus   III-212
Schiffl, Jonas   III-43
Schlingloff, Bernd-Holger   III-366
Schneider, Gerardo   III-3
Schneidewind, Clara   III-212
Schürmann, Jonas   II-311

Seceleanu, Cristina   I-350, I-421
Seifermann, Stephan   II-295
Sharygina, Natasha   III-178
Smith, David   III-161
Soulat, Romain   I-525
Spagnolo, Giorgio O.   I-368
Steffen, Bernhard   II-311
Steffen, Martin   I-103
Steinhöfel, Dominic   II-117
Steinmetz, Marcel   II-416
Stoilkovska, Ilina   I-471
Stolz, Volker   II-138
Stumpf, Johanna Beate   I-103
Sürmeli, Jan   II-329
Susi, Angelo   III-240

Tacchella, Alberto   III-240
Tapia Tarifa, Silvia Lizeth   I-558
Tegeler, Tim   II-311
ter Beek, Maurice H.   I-211, I-368, III-467
Tessi, Matteo   III-240
Tesson, Julien   III-60
Thompson, Simon   III-161
Tiezzi, Francesco   II-361
Tini, Simone   II-380
Tognazzi, Stefano   II-397
Trentini, Daniele   III-467
Tribastone, Mirco   I-307
Trinh, Van Anh Thi   III-415
Trubiani, Catia   II-243
Tuosto, Emilio   I-22, I-39, II-243
Turin, Gianluca   I-558

Ulbrich, Mattias   I-60, II-25

van Bladel, Brent   II-9
Vercammen, Sten   II-9
Vinogradova, Polina   III-89, III-112
Viroli, Mirko   II-344
Vos, Tanja   I-543

Wadler, Philip   III-89, III-112
Walter, Marcel   III-326
Walter, Maximilian   II-295
Wanninger, Constantin   II-507, II-525
Watson, Bruce W.   I-211
Wehrheim, Heike   I-143
Weidenbach, Christoph   II-416
Weigl, Alexander   II-25
Weininger, Maximilian   I-331

Westman, Jonas   III-348
Widder, Josef   I-471
Wirsing, Martin   II-161, II-224
Wolf, Felix   II-117

Zahnentferner, Joachim   III-112
Zambonelli, Franco   II-189
Zamfir, Anca   I-471
Zunino, Roberto   III-25

Printed in the United States
By Bookmasters